The Naked Man

By the same author

STRUCTURAL ANTHROPOLOGY

TOTEMISM

THE SAVAGE MIND

THE SCOPE OF ANTHROPOLOGY

THE ELEMENTARY STRUCTURES OF KINSHIP

TRISTES TROPIQUES

Introduction to a Science of Mythology (*Mythologiques*)

1. THE RAW AND THE COOKED

2. FROM HONEY TO ASHES

3. THE ORIGIN OF TABLE MANNERS

4. THE NAKED MAN

Claude Lévi-Strauss

THE NAKED MAN

Introduction to a
Science of Mythology: 4

TRANSLATED FROM THE FRENCH BY
JOHN AND DOREEN WEIGHTMAN

HARPER & ROW, PUBLISHERS, New York
Cambridge, Hagerstown, Philadelphia, San Francisco,
London, Mexico City, São Paulo, Sydney
1817

Contents

6 CONTENTS

Illustrations

FIGURES

PLATES

Table of Symbols

$\triangle$, $\bigcirc$	man, woman
$\triangle = \bigcirc$	husband, wife
$\triangle \quad \bigcirc$	children; brother, sister
$\Rightarrow$	transformation
$\rightarrow$	is transformed into, is followed by
$:$	is to . . .
$: :$	as . . .
$/$	opposition
$\equiv$	congruence
$=$	identity, or equality (according to the context)
$\neq$	difference, or inequality (according to the context)
$\cup$	union, reunion, conjunction
$\cap$	intersection
$//$	disjunction
$>$	larger than . . .
$<$	smaller than . . .
f	function
$x^{(-1)}$	x inverted
$\simeq$	isomorphism
$+$, $-$	these signs are used with various connotations, depending on the context: plus, minus; presence, absence; first or second term of a pair of opposites.

To my mother, in her eighty-fifth year,
and in memory of my father

Prologue

οὐδ' ὅσον ἐν μαλάχῃ τε καὶ ἀσφοδέλῳ μέγ' ὄνειαρ.

Hesiod, *Works and Days*, V, 14

From the Rocky Mountains to the Pacific Ocean, between the 40th and 50th parallels approximately, lies an area consisting mainly of tertiary and quaternary basaltic lava, deposited in horizontal or folded layers, and through which older rock formations protrude here and there. The Cascade Mountains, lying about two hundred or so kilometres back from the sea coast along a south-west–north-east axis, represent the most notable folded range of volcanic rocks. Their western slope slants towards the sea, and on that side the surface is for the most part irregular, with marine deposits, chiefly of tertiary origin, overlapping volcanic formations of the same period, as well as the older metamorphic mass of the Olympic Mountains, and those of the coast range and the Klamath Mountains, where, as in the Sierra Nevada to the south, intrusive Jurassic rocks are to be found, alongside others dating from the Carboniferous period.

On the other side, as far as the foothills of the Rockies, stretches the plateau of the Columbia River, varying between two hundred and more than five hundred metres above sea level, and cut by deep gorges through which flow the Columbia itself and its chief tributaries, the Snake and the Spokane. Throughout this area, the lava was subjected to extensive folding during the Pliocene, thus forming the anticline of the Cascade Range and a series of synclines, the present lowlands. These tectonic deformations caused a partial displacement of the Columbia River bed towards the east, but the gorges carved out by the river and its tributaries as they cut through the anticlines obstructing their courses prove that the hydrographic network was already in existence when the anticlines appeared (Hunt, pp. 348–53; Mendenhall). Between the Columbia and Snake Rivers there are basalt outcrops, caused perhaps by some great flood which washed away the top soil and swept it towards the estuary, or, according to other specialists

(Bretz–Smith–Neff), by more complex factors such as intense humidity following arid conditions and responsible for the formation of a hydrographic network liable to frequent and prolonged flooding, due to the melting of glaciers and the overflowing of rivers, and also probably of a large lake, into valleys which were still ice-bound.

The Cascade Range, the highest peak of which, Mount Rainier, is more than 4,000 metres above sea level, acts as a barrier against the moist winds coming from the sea, thus causing a difference in climate between the western and eastern regions. The western area, through the entire length of which runs a trough-shaped depression, occupied to the south by the valley of the Willamette and to the north by Puget Sound, enjoys a mild climate with abundant rainfall, especially in winter; it is covered for the most part by conifers of various species. To the east of the Cascades, the Columbia plateau has a semi-arid climate with considerable differences in the mean temperatures between winter and summer. There are forests only on the mountains, while the rest of the country consists of dry sage-brush savannah or grassy prairie-land, both devoid of trees and shrubs, except in the valleys, where there are aspens and willows.

To the south, the Columbia plateau gradually merges into the Great Basin, while at the same time the altitude rises. Klamath country, in the southern part of Oregon, illustrates the transition. From the physiographical point of view it closely resembles the Great Basin, but whereas lakes fed by run-off and with no natural outlets slowly dried up through evaporation after the end of the rainy era, those which lie along the faults are fed by permanent springs and streams, and the River Klamath provides them with an outlet to the sea. So, until recent times, their level has remained relatively constant, and it is precisely this stability which has prompted archaeologists to search in the vicinity for evidence of continuous occupation since very early times (Cressman 1, pp. 377–82).

Generally speaking, the whole area just defined seems to be one of the oldest and most regularly inhabited sites in North America. Since the populating of the continent occurred entirely, or to a very large extent, as a result of migratory movements from Asia through the Bering Strait in the era when America was emerging as a land mass (cf. below, pp. 607–609) – or, according to some theorists, by way of the sea some 35,000 to 40,000 years ago when optimum climatic conditions prevailed (Pocklington) – it is worth noting that, without going so far back in time, archaeologists have recently produced evidence of human settlements in the Yukon basin in northern Alaska which may be more than 20,000 years old; it takes the form of bone tools found along with the bones of mammoths, edentata and extinct species of the horse and camel (Old Crow River). More firmly established, perhaps, is the dating of the Onion Portage deposit on Kobuk River in north-western Alaska, as being 13,000 years old (Anderson).

The routes by which the immigrants reached America still remain conjectural. The north-west coast is so sheer and so deeply indented by fjords that the possibility of their having followed the shore-line on foot would seem to be excluded. Small bands of hunters, after entering America without even realizing that they were crossing quite a different continent, so wide was the land bridge joining Asia and America at certain periods in prehistory, must have penetrated a fair distance into the interior by following routes temporarily freed by the glaciers. But as yet no trace has been found of these population movements either inland or along the coast. It is true that the sea level has varied so considerably during the whole period with which we are concerned that the former coastline may today be either submerged or so high up on the mountain slopes as to have remained undiscovered.

Be that as it may, dates of comparable antiquity have been supplied by numerous sites in British Columbia and in the states of Washington and Oregon: continuous occupation for at least 12,000 years, on the terraces of the Fraser River near Yale; chipped stone projectiles, 13,000 years old, at Fort Rock Cave in the east of Oregon; and in the eastern part of the state of Washington, on the River Palouse, the bones of the so-called 'Marmes man', which have been estimated to be between 11,000 and 13,000 years old; this last mentioned site was inhabited without interruption from the ninth millennium B.C. up to the historic period (Borden; Bryan; Kirk; Grosso), and its oldest levels seem to be contemporaneous with other deposits in southern Idaho, such as Wilson Butte and Jaguar Cave, where bone tools have been found, associated with the remains of extinct fauna belonging to the Felidae, Edentata, Equidae and Camelidae families. This first period possibly lasted from the thirteenth millennium B.C. to about the ninth. It would appear to have been followed by a second period, which continued until the sixth millennium, and of which Lind Coulee offers one of the most characteristic sites. As early as this period, the first traces of the 'old Cordillera culture', which extended from Alaska to California, were beginning to be noticeable in the form of broad-tipped projectile points. At the same time, tools other than those associated with hunting and used for the grinding or pounding of seeds and wild roots began to make their appearance. The same development can be traced at the Dalles, along the middle reaches of the Columbia River, at the entrance to the gorges of the Cascade Mountains, where there is also evidence of the first attempts to evolve an economy based on fish, which was later to become a typical feature of the Plateau cultures (Cressman 2; Sanger; Crabtree; Osborne; Browman-Munsell).

A third period, from the sixth to the fifth millennium, would seem to correspond to the full flowering of the 'old Cordillera culture', evidence of which can be found on both sides of the Cascade Range, in the Puget Sound area as well as on the Plateau. A variety of stone and bone tools, remnants of basketwork and weaving, and perhaps the use of the spear-thrower would suggest an economy which combined hunting and fishing with the gathering of wild plants. It might well be that the following periods, from the fifth to the second millennium, during which fishing and gathering seem to have taken precedence over hunting, are to be explained by the disappearance of big game, owing to climatic changes leading to more arid conditions.

About 4650 B.C., the formidable eruption which destroyed Mount Mazama – the site of which is now occupied by Crater Lake – projected volcanic ash a long way from the point where the explosion occurred, thus making it possible to establish a date limit for the sites beneath the ash. This period also saw the appearance of a microlithic industry, indicative of northern influences. About 1500 B.C., there are numerous indications of the use of wood for mallets, adzes, wedges and gouges, and of the use of stone, deer antlers or rodents' teeth, while semi-subterranean houses became more widespread. As early as the beginning of the Christian era, all the known historical characteristics of the Plateau cultures were already present and seem to have hardly varied during the next eighteen centuries, until the introduction of the horse around 1750. But commercial exchange, which occupied such an important place in the lives of the various communities, goes back very much further, since the sea shells found during excavations date at least from the sixth or seventh millennium (Browman-Munsell).

Let us turn our attention now to the southern region of the Plateau, to the borders of Oregon and California where my enquiry begins. A similar overall picture would seem to emerge in this area too. Various sites in Klamath country appear to have been inhabited for at least 6,500 years, since the ash projected by the eruption of Mount Mazama covers the lower layers. That these layers may be much older still is clear from various indications: a sandal made from vegetable fibres found at Fort Rock and at least 9,000 years old, according to radio-carbon dating; stone tools associated with the bones of Equidae, Camelidae, and perhaps also mammoths. Broadly speaking, an archaic economy based mainly on hunting seems to have gradually given way, as a result of Great Basin influences, to an economy associated with the use of wild products; then fishing, which was difficult for the Basin communities because of the absence of fish in lakes with no outlets, would seem to have become the chief activity in a region where, as we have seen, (see above, p. 14), lakes linked to the hydrographic network and provided with an outlet to the sea, contained an abundant supply of trout, salmon and other species. Villages of the historically recorded type appeared about the beginning of the seventh century A.D. (Cressman 1).

From the geographical point of view, the region inhabited by the Klamath has features connected both with the Great Basin and the Cascade Range, but differs from them through containing considerable lacustrian deposits dating from the Pliocene, which occupy part of its area and through which isolated volcanic cones protrude in places. Rainfall is slight but enough to ensure the growth of pine forests, interspersed on arid ground with vast stretches of sage-brush savannah, or along rivers and near lakes with grassland and aspens.

As in all other regions west of the Rockies, both agriculture and pottery were absent. Or rather, it would be more accurate to say that they were disregarded, since the natural environment afforded a rich supply of vegetable food sources in forms which, although often not immediately edible, could be made so thanks to the extreme technological ingeniousness of the natives. In Klamath and to a lesser degree in Modoc territory, swamps provided a supply of pond or water lilies (*Nufar polysepalum*). Natural beds of these plants covered several thousand hectares of the Klamath Marshes, where the fallen seeds formed a floating viscous mass, which could be harvested by canoe. The importance of these seeds, known as *wocas*, in the diet of the Klamath, can be judged from the fact that these Indians referred to them by no fewer than five different names, according to their degree of ripeness and the fresh or rotten state of their outer casing. In order to remove their gummy secretion, the kernels had either to be left to ferment in water, or precooked in steam, after which they were shaken up with an abrasive mixture of pounded wood, charcoal and ash. They were then baked in a basket filled with red-hot cinders; lastly they were ground with a special type of grinding stone which was shaped so as to have two handles to facilitate manipulation.

In addition to the lily seeds, the Klamath and Modoc made use of all kinds of roots, bulbs, tubers and rhizomes, the chief of which belonged to the liliaceae (*Camassia quamash, esculenta*) and the umbelliferae, the false caraway (*Carum oregonum*). They gathered berries, seeds, wild fruits and edible lichens, and extracted sweet resin from certain conifers. In April and May they removed and ate the soft cambium underneath tree bark. From the lakes and marshes they took rushes, bulrushes, reeds and cats'-tail grass for the weaving of mats, caps and baskets.

The gathering of bulbs and roots kept the women busy during the months of July and August; then in August and September came the harvesting of the lily seeds. During the entire summer period, when the men hunted or occasionally fished, the winter villages with their large semi-underground dwellings, each one of which housed several families, were abandoned, and the inhabitants scattered to live in huts made from a framework of branches covered with rush matting. This semi-nomadic existence came to an end in October and November, which were the months for gathering seeds and berries. The village houses were then rebuilt with the beams which had been dismantled and kept in storage, and the Indians shut themselves up for the winter months, which were devoted to ritual celebrations. In May came the thaw and the melting of the snow. This marked the beginning of the great fishing season, which lasted until June. The fish, which were caught either with nets or in traps, were dried in the sun but not smoked, and stored away for the winter.

The Indians called the Klamath, a name of unknown origin, referred to themselves as *ma'klaks*, 'the men'. Together with their southerly neighbours, the Modoc of northern California, they constituted a linguistic group formerly referred to by the name Lutuami, and whose degree of affinity with the Sahaptin family is still uncertain (Voegelin, Aoki). The Klamath and Modoc cultures were similar in many respects, such as intensive reliance on bulbs, roots and seeds of wild plants, the use of fibres or beaten bark for most clothing, before the introduction of leather garments under the Plains influence, the custom of cremating corpses together with the material possessions of the deceased and offerings, and initiation rites during which novices built cairns with rocks and stones. However, with the Modoc, fishing occupied a less important place than hunting. Not only were they more influenced by Californian cultures, they were also more war-like in temperament and kept their prisoners of war as slaves, whereas the Klamath, among whom social distinctions were less marked, usually preferred to sell their prisoners of war at the great Columbian intertribal fairs. In Modoc society, only the shamans were allowed to have guardian spirits and to call upon them; among the Klamath, on the other hand, anyone could claim this privilege, provided he possessed the appropriate gifts.

Among the Klamath and the Modoc, marriages were concluded by means of reciprocal visits and the interchange of presents between the families; there had to be no known kinship ties between bride and bridegroom, although they could belong to the same territory or even the same village. Polygamy was allowed, and sororal polygamy frequent. With the Klamath, residence was patrilocal (except when the husband was poor or had no parents), while among the Modoc it was patrilocal temporarily, then more permanently matrilocal until such time as the couple might opt for independent residence. The kinship structure included a series of ordinal terms corresponding to the various age groups and matrimonial statuses. The sex of the connecting relative was used as a means of differentiating between ascendants and their collaterals, the sex of the speaker (*Ego*) to differentiate between siblings and their descendants. Reciprocal terms were used between individuals separated by two generations, and also between a husband's sister and the child of the wife's brother. Five terms were used to define brothers and sisters according to their relative age and their sex. Beyond the immediate family, the brother–sister terminology was extended by the speaker to his cousins, while the terms designating uncles and aunts were applied to all his parents' cousins. A single term was used for all the more distant degrees of kinship. The terminology relating to affines, reduced to its simplest expression, consisted of two reciprocal terms designating respectively the husbands of two sisters and the wives of two brothers.

Births took place outside the family dwelling. The woman in labour was ritually 'cooked' on a bed of hot stones, kept to a very strict diet, and subject to various obligations, such as scratching her head with a special instrument, a practice also imposed on women secluded because of menstruation or in mourning. Boys and girls had to undergo initiation ordeals; the former were sent to some remote spot where they had to pile stones into cairns, dive into the icy water of lakes and rivers, climb mountain peaks, and run and fast in order to provoke visions in which their guardian spirit would be revealed to them; the girls had to dance without stopping or falling for five consecutive nights, and during the day were secluded in a hut in the bush and had to respect certain taboos, such as not touching their heads, combing their hair or washing, or eating meat or fish.

As has already been said, the Klamath and the Modoc cremated corpses on funeral pyres, which were erected in certain sacred places. The Modoc used occasionally to kill a slave or horses to put on the pyre, unless some onlooker redeemed them with an offering of equal value. The deceased's next of kin subjected themselves to steam baths in special bath-houses which were said to have been constructed by the demiurge, and undertook a mystic quest in order to recover the spiritual powers their ordeal had taken from them by plunging them into a state of dereliction, evidenced by their renunciation of the produce of their hunting, fishing and gathering expeditions, as well as of their winnings from gambling and games. Both the Klamath and the Modoc were keen gamblers and games-players, and their champions enjoyed a considerable reputation which spread far beyond the tribal frontiers. I shall come back to this aspect of native culture when I discuss certain myths in which gambling and games-playing are given prominence (cf. below, pp. 32–3, 350–52).

Like most Plateau communities, the Klamath had no political organization. They were subdivided into four or five local and autonomous groups, whose common language and culture gave them a vague feeling of solidarity, which manifested itself on occasions in hostility towards strangers and acted as a substitute for tribal unity. The territories occupied by the local groups were separated by unclaimed areas a few kilometres wide, and occasionally there would be fighting between groups. The aim would be to destroy the enemy group's villages and possessions, and to capture women and children in order to sell them as slaves to communities outside the area. These local groups varied greatly in size, and might consist of anything between one village or thirty. The largest group, which comprised half the total population, claimed to have been created first; it believed itself to be superior to the other groups and declared its chief to be preeminent.

The Klamath waged war from time to time against their Shasta, Takelma, Paiute, Kalapuya and Achomawi neighbours, mainly for commercial reasons. They were keen traders and took slaves and other plunder to the intertribal fairs at the Dalles in order to exchange them for horses. On the other hand, they were on peaceful terms with the Modoc, the Molala, the Tenino, the Wishram and the Wasco. The more resolutely warlike Modoc had, in addition to their civil chief, a war chief who was appointed for life, but their tribal conscience did not permit the kind of internal conflicts frequent among the Klamath; these could arise from an act of revenge committed by a man against his parents-in-law while he was living with them, although himself a member of a different local group; or by a similar act on the part of one village against another following a murder and the demand that the culprit should be handed over or some material compensation granted. In all cases warlike mimes and shamanistic rites were performed before the expeditions, and afterwards there were dances during which the newly captured prisoners were beaten and the severed members of dead enemies were displayed as trophies, and the women brandished scalps on the ends of sticks. The Modoc were satisfied with one scalp, which they burnt.

They also shared out power between the war chief, the shaman and the civil and political chief. The main function of the latter, who had no powers of coercion, was to prove himself to be above all a persuasive orator in the communal meetings attended by adults of both sexes. It would seem that the chieftainship function appeared much later among the Klamath, whose social life was governed mainly by a kind of traditional duality between the shamans and the rich. A single word, *lagi*, was used both for the chief and for a rich man who possessed several wives, horses, armour made of leather or wooden slats, well-filled quivers and precious furs. In addition to owning these material assets, the chief had to win military victories, possess exceptional spiritual powers and display a gift for oratory. Although, strictly speaking, the chieftainship was not hereditary, it probably stayed within the same family.

The religious beliefs of the Klamath and the Modoc were organized somewhat loosely around two poles: on the one hand the person of the demiurge, the creator of mankind and edible plants, the founder of shamanism and sweat rites, and on the other, a network of localities haunted by spirits capable of adopting many forms, and various communities of giants, dwarfs, and baby spirits. The ghosts of the dead, who were often reluctant to pass into the beyond – an inverted world situated far to the east – were thought to haunt the earth, looking for living souls to capture. The seat of the soul was in the heart, and it departed when the last remnants of flesh surrounding that organ were consumed on the funeral pyre. Natural phenomena, such as clouds, thunder, lightning, the sun, the moon, the stars and the winds, were also personified.

Among the Klamath, any individual of either sex gifted with more than ordinary powers could become a shaman and effect medical cures, during which he or she was possessed by guardian spirits. Shamans lived in large houses decorated with paintings and stuffed animals representing these spirits. The roof was surmounted by a carved wooden statue, decorated with feathers, also representing a spirit. As distinctive ornaments, the shamans wore diadems or necklaces made from the feathers of the red-headed woodpecker, plumed head-dresses or necklaces made from the feathers of the golden woodpecker, caps made from mink or badger's fur decorated with feathers, and necklaces of bear's claws; in addition, they blackened their faces.

A period lasting from December to January was known as the 'nameless' period. The severe winter cold had already set in by then, but there was still an abundant supply of food, and this was the time for the celebration of the rites under the guidance of the shamans. A large audience was summoned for the occasion. The shaman's herald interpreted the words which his master was uttering too quickly for intelligibility, or distorting by covering his mouth with his hand. During the ceremony, which lasted five days and five nights, the shaman would dance and perform conjuring tricks, such as swallowing fire or a string with arrowheads fixed to it, causing various objects to appear or disappear, ingurgitating and degurgitating them at will, together with great quantities of water, and making stuffed animals show signs of life or fish, seeds or blood appear by magic in a waterproof basket filled with water. In addition to caring for the sick, the Klamath shamans controlled the weather, found lost objects and practised other forms of divination.

Modoc shamanism had rather different features. Only the shamans could acquire guardian spirits, as the outcome of a quest, as in the Plains, or through dreams, as in California. For men, the most favourable period for the acquisition of these powers lasted from marriage until the onset of old age, but for women, it occurred after the menopause, because the spirits had a horror of menstrual blood. The initiation procedure was much longer and more complex than with the Klamath; the final entry into the body of shamans took place in winter at the request of the candidate, who organized the ceremony, officiated at it, and fed and paid the participants. The new shaman had to celebrate the winter rites for five years in succession (Miller; Gatschet 1; Bancroft; Curtis, Vol. 13; Spier 2; Barrett 3; Ray 3; Th. Stern 2).

The perfunctory nature of this account is not entirely due to the fact that it is essentially a summary. The truth is that almost all the data we have on the Klamath and the Modoc were supplied by elderly informants, already living on reservations, and who were describing from memory their former way of life, which was already extinct by about 1870. The Columbia plateau was probably frequented as early as the eighteenth century by Canadian trappers, then by employees of the Hudson's Bay Company and later by the North-West Fur Company. Little remains of the very earliest observations; the Plains Indians make their first appearance in published accounts with Lewis and Clark, after the latters' journey across the continent in 1805–6, and in the writings of subsequent travellers. Even then, the evidence at our disposal is no more than fragmentary notes and occasional references concerning a society already in a state of collapse as a result of the smallpox epidemics which, from 1830 onwards, decimated the native populations, who were to suffer even more seriously from the Gold

Rush which began in 1848 and led to bloody battles with the Whites. The Klamath and the Modoc ceded their territories to the American Government, which acquired California in 1846 and Oregon two years later, but the Modoc rebelled against the living conditions in the reservation and were only finally conquered and subdued in 1873. By the time Gatschet and Curtis undertook to record their customs and traditions, their culture was no longer a living one. Spier's admirable monograph, which was written in 1925–6, is to an even greater extent a reconstitution of the past. It is fortunate that, in addition to these inventories of a vanished world, we have collections of myths which have continued to be part of the oral tradition and preserve something of the spirit and inner vitality of a culture wiped out more than a century ago.

So the stage has now been set for the first act of this book and the scene laid for action. But before the curtain goes up, I should point out that the following pages contain a condensed form of the substance of my lectures at the Collège de France during the years 1965–6, 1967–8, 1969–70 and 1970–71. My 1966–7 lectures have already found a more relevant place in *The Origin of Table Manners* (Part VI). Those of the 1968–9 session were entirely devoted to solving a difficulty I had encountered in connection with Salish mythology: as if, through the effect of a double refraction, a mythic series common to the Klamath-Modoc group and to the Sahaptin is projected further north in the form of two parallel, and partly overlapping, series, one concerned with fire and water, the other with fog and wind. The mechanics of the phenomenon had to be elucidated, and it had also to be determined how so many features of French folklore, transmitted orally to the Indians by Canadian trappers, came to occupy a privileged place alongside the second series. Once the problem had been defined and, let us hope, solved, the comparative analysis could proceed, but to avoid swelling still further a volume already much longer than the previous ones, I have left out this incidental discussion, although I shall frequently have occasion to refer to it.

In addition to these major difficulties, the composition of this book, which could in any case only advance slowly since the fourth volume is not merely a continuation of the others, but must tie into place all the loose threads left hanging in the course of the argument, was twice interrupted by further obstacles: firstly, the events of May 1968, which created during the subsequent months an atmosphere hardly conducive to intellectual concentration and then, during the winter of 1968–9, a period of ill-health. Lastly, the gaps and uncertainties in the source material constituted a series of handicaps, many of which would never have been overcome but for the help of colleagues to whom I take this opportunity of expressing my gratitude. Mlle S. Débarbat, of the Paris Observatory, Professor D. H. Hymes of Pennsylvania University, Professor B. J. Rigsby of the University of New Mexico, Professor Th. Stern of Oregon University, the late Professor J. Rousseau of Montreal University, Professors P. and E. Maranda of the University of British Columbia, and Professors E. Wolff and P. Gourou of the Collège de France have kindly supplied me with valuable information relating to astronomy, linguistics, geography, zoology and botany, as well as with hitherto unpublished documents. René Leibowitz, although he in no way shares responsibility for the ideas on the subject of music I put forward in the finale, graciously agreed to read and discuss this section of the text, and thus helped me to clarify my ideas and my terminology. I am obliged to John Hess of the Paris office of the *New York Times*, to the New York office of the same paper and to the *Seattle Times* for the photograph of Pillar Rock (Plate 1), which forms an appropriate counterpart to the first plate in *The Raw and the Cooked*. M. Yvan Simonis of Laval University supplied me with the material of Plate 4, taken from the original edition of Père Dablon's *Relation*, which is apparently easier to consult in Montreal than in Paris, since the copy belonging to the Bibliothèque Nationale seemed to have disappeared at the time when I was preparing this volume for the press. Dr Audrey Hawthorn, Curator of the Museum of Anthropology of the University of British Columbia, supplied the photograph used for Plate 3, and gave me permission to reproduce it.

Mlle Nicole Belmont helped me to assemble the documentation, Mme Jacqueline Duvernay translated the German sources, Mme Evelyne Guedj typed the manuscript, M. J.-M. Chavy drew the maps and diagrams. To all of them, and also to my wife who read the proofs, I express my thanks.

PART ONE FAMILY SECRETS

Incest is fine, as long as it's kept in the family.

Quoted by *Playboy*, October 1965, p. 43

1 The Hidden Child

ὄν ποτ᾽ ἔχουσ᾽ ἐν ὠδίνων
λοχίαις ἀνάγκαισι
πταμένας Διὸς βροντᾶς
νηδύος ἔκθλον μάτηρ
ἔτεκεν, λιποῦσ᾽ αἰῶ-
να κεραυνίῳ πλαγᾷ
λοχίοις δ᾽ αὐτίκα νιν δέ-
ξατο θαλάμαις Κρονίδας Ζεύς·
κατὰ μηρῷ δὲ καλύψας
χρυσέαισιν συνερείδει
περόναις κρυπτὸν ἀφ᾽ Ἥρας.

Euripides, *The Bacchae*, v. 88–98

In the course of the previous volume (*OTM*, pp. 200, 252, 305), it became evident that the South American myth concerning the bird-nester and the North American one featuring the wives of the sun and moon belong to one and the same transformation group. This was moreover apparent from the fact, already established in *The Raw and the Cooked*, that the South American myths dealing with the origin of fire or water are accompanied by a parallel series in which the heroine is a star, the wife of a mortal (M_{87-92}); as it happens, this series, which deals with the origin of cultivated plants, is an inversion — in respect of the sexes — of the North American star-husband series, of which the story featuring the wives of the sun and moon is a part.

In the present volume, we shall have to enquire more deeply into the structure of this enormous mythic group, which covers virtually the whole of the New World. But, having already demonstrated the presence and the role of the same myths in both the south and the north in forms which, in some cases, have undergone transfiguration, I cannot omit quoting those instances in which the reference myth (M_1, M_{7-12}) appears in North America in a literal form: its occurrence is all the more remarkable in that it

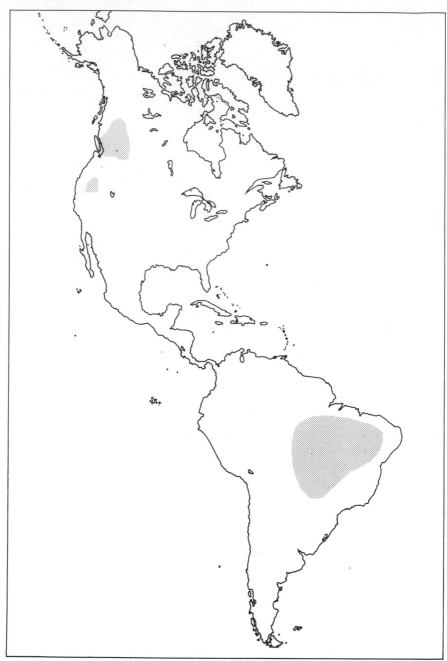

Figure 1. Major areas of distribution of the reference myth in both North and South America

falls within a territory bounded approximately by the Klamath River basin to the south and by the Fraser River basin to the north — in other words, a very limited area in relation to the scale of the continent as a whole, and moreover in the north-western part of North America, that is, a long way away from the tropical regions of South America, where the homologous versions also occupy a relatively restricted and continuous stretch of territory (Figure 1).

For the purposes of this enquiry, which is complicated by the threefold difficulty of the distance between the two areas, the abundance of the available versions and the linguistic and cultural diversity of the groups from which they originate, I propose to adopt a hybrid method, partly systematic and partly geographical. Moving upwards from south to north, I shall first of all single out a small group of variants which would seem to have a continuous, although small, area of distribution along the borders of northern California and the southern part of the present state of Oregon, in spite of the heterogeneous nature of the tribes concerned, half of whom are members of the Klamath-Modoc linguistic family which occupies an isolated position within the vast Penutian group, while the other half — including the Shasta, the Atsugewi, the Achomawi and the Yana — belong to the Hokan family. Next, I shall study versions belonging to the northern Sahaptin and their neighbours, the Chinook; thirdly and lastly, versions belonging to tribes of the Salishan linguistic family, which extends far into Canadian territory. For reasons which may eventually be elucidated by new discoveries in the fields of archaeology and historical linguistics, this method of arranging the material makes it possible to carry the analysis a step further at each stage (Figure 2).

It is for a similar reason that I propose to deal first with the Klamath-Modoc group, whose archaeological and ethnographical position I outlined in the Prologue, and to analyse a series of old documents, collected by Albert S. Gatschet in 1877 or thereabouts. They belong to the chronicle of the culture hero Aishísh, which, as Gatschet observes, 'forms a portion of a long cyclus of related myths' (Gatschet 1, Part I, p. lxxxv, n.; cf Barker 1, p. 22).

M₅₂₉. *Klamath-Modoc. 'The birth of the hero'*

Once a young woman called Letkakáwash, who was carrying her baby on her back like all Indian women, piled up wood in order to cremate the body of an old sorceress. Actually she was proposing to leap into the fire herself with her son. The demiurge, Kmúkamch, perceived that she was ready to leap into the burning pile, but he managed to save only the

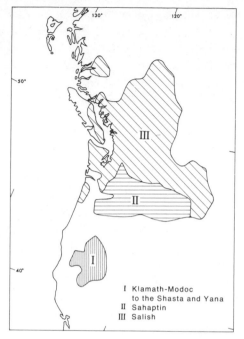

Figure 2. The chief communities studied in the present volume

baby. Being uncertain where to place it, he put it in his knee, went home and complained to his daughter that he had an ulcer which pained him excruciatingly. His daughter tried to squeeze the ulcer open. To her great surprise a baby emerged from the wound.

The babe cried and cried until the 'father', in order to soothe it, proposed to give it a name. He mentioned several but the child cried on and on. Then he proposed to call it Aishílamnash, which means 'the one secreted in the body', which stopped its cries somewhat but not entirely. It became restful and quiet when he proposed the name of Aishísh. The boy accepted the name and lived in the company of Kmúkamch, his foster-father; he became an expert in the making of elegant clothes (shirts) and a keen gambler who won all the stakes, even from his father, who became jealous on account of his superiority (Gatschet 1, Part I, pp. lxxxv–vi).

The identity of the sorceress and the reason for the young woman's suicide will be explained later. The name of the heroine, Letkakáwash, is that of the red-headed tangara (*Pyranga ludoviciana*), a small bird of the passeriae family; the males are brilliantly coloured during the breeding season. The name of the demiurge which Barker transcribes as *gmokamč*, can be split up into *gmoč* 'to be old' and the augmentative suffix *?mč*, that is, 'the great old man'. Aishísh (Barker: *?aysis*) comes from the verb *?aysi* 'to hide, keep', and therefore means 'the hidden one' or 'the concealed one'. The following myths describe the characters in greater detail and recount their quarrels:

M$_{530a}$. *Klamath. 'The bird-nester'* (1)

There is a story that at the beginning of time, Kmúkamch, the demiurge, who lived with his son Aishísh, began to create things and beings, and in particular, all kinds of fish. He made a dam so that the Indians could scoop up the fish every time the south wind blew and left the bottom of the rivers dry.

But Kmúkamch fell in love with one of his son's wives and tried to get rid of him. He claimed that the young birds nesting on a Kenáwat stalk were eagles. He commanded his son to capture them, after taking off his shirt, his belt and his hair-ribbon. Aishísh, now naked, climbed up but found only little birds of a very common species. Meanwhile the stalk grew as he climbed and Aishísh was unable to get down; he went back to the nest and waited.

Kmúkamch took all Aishísh's clothes away, dressed himself in them and took on his son's physical appearance. Only the daughter-in-law whom he coveted did not suspect his duplicity; the others refused to consort with him, since they were convinced he was not their husband.

Aishísh, marooned at the top of the tree and with no food to eat, became nothing but skin and bones. Then two butterfly-females saw him in the nest. They brought him water and food, combed his hair, poured oil on his emaciated body and carried him down in their basket.

Aishísh set off to look for his wives. He found Tchika (chaffinch) and Klétish (sandhill crane) busy digging roots. Tchika's child recognized him first. The two wives, then a third called Tühúsh (mud hen, *Fulica americana*), rejoiced to see their husband whom they had believed dead. To all three he gave neck-wear made from quills of porcupines he had killed.

On hearing that his son was still alive, Kmúkamch prepared to greet him. Aishísh enjoined his young son to jerk his grandfather's pipe off into the fire. When the pipe was completely burnt, Kmúkamch died. He came to life again later and tried to take his revenge on his son, by daubing pitch all over the sky and setting it on fire. The pitch turned into a lake which covered the whole world: only Aishísh's home remained untouched. His third wife, Tûhûsh, tried to put her head out and a drop of pitch landed on her forehead. Ever since, this mark has remained on the mud hen (Gatschet 1, Part I, pp. 94–7).

M530b. *Klamath. 'The bird-nester' (2)*

Aishísh was a past master in games of skill and chance. When they went gambling, he and his companions built fires. Aishísh's fire burned with a clear, bright, purplish blue flame, the Silver Fox's fire was yellow, while Kmúkamch's fire made only a thick smoke. As a marksman, Aishísh excelled all his companions; when they commenced gambling and betting games, he pocketed all the stakes.

Aishísh had five wives: Mud Hen, Long-tail Squirrel, Sandhill Crane, Mallard and Chaffinch. Kmúkamch, who coveted Long-tail Squirrel, plotted secretly to kill his son. He pretended to remember a place where his dead father used to trap eagles. He took Aishísh there and pointed out to him which pine tree he should climb (kápka). The tree grew so high that the hero could no longer get down from it, and moreover, there were only birds of a very common species in the nest.

Kmúkamch dressed himself in his son's clothes and took on his appearance. He slept with Long-tail Squirrel with whom he was in love, but both this wife and the others were suspicious and did not really believe he was their husband. Those who were in the habit of gambling with Aishísh also suspected it was really Kmúkamch, for instead of the flames going straight up into the sky, the fire lit by the usurper produced only a smoke which curled up, and his arrows missed the mark. Aishísh's companions missed him so much that they quit gambling.

The women for their part wept constantly, with the exception of Mallard, who did not mourn for Aishísh. Sandhill Crane wept so much that Aishísh heard her from where he was marooned, and he too wept. Far away, up in the sky, Aishísh was moribund for he was nothing but skin and bones.

Two butterfly-girls saw him. They told their father about him and he ordered them to go and help the hero. They gave him food and water and he told them what had happened. They took him back down to the ground in a willow basket lined with a wild cat's skin. Aishísh lay sick a long time. At last he recovered (Gatschet 1, Part I, pp. 99–101).

The games of chance mentioned in the myths played an important part in Klamath and Modoc society (Spier 2, pp. 76–80: Angulo-d'Harcourt, pp. 204–205; Ray 3, pp. 122–30). In certain games only teams from neighbouring tribes – national teams, as it were – could play as two opposing sides. The captains of each team directed the game, while their companions encouraged them with chants and cheers, and tried to put the opposing team at a disadvantage by all sorts of cheating devices. Each man contributed as much as he could to the stakes. In this way, very considerable quantities of valuable goods changed hands. Charms and talismans, such as obsidian blades and the dead bodies of small animals found by chance, were thought to bring or preserve good luck. On their way to the game the players lit fires. Good or bad omens were deduced from the colour of the flames and the direction of the smoke.

There were several types of gambling games, all based more or less on the same principle. Each player had a pile of differently marked pieces that he arranged in a certain order, then kept hidden under a basketwork mat. His opponent had to offer a guess as to the arrangement and indicate it by a formal signal. But, before pronouncing his final decision, which was preceded by a clap of the hands, he was permitted to make preliminary guesses in order to confuse his opponent and induce him to shift the position of the pieces. During these preliminary confrontations, the opponents studied each other closely, the one whose turn it was to guess hoping that his opponent would give the game away by some obvious sign or by some hasty rearrangement of the pieces. Gambling games involved not only acquired expertise, but also psychology, insight and a capacity for bluffing. This explains why the players were not all equally talented and why recognized champions enjoyed tremendous prestige extending far beyond the confines of their tribe.

The identity of the hero's wives sometimes remains uncertain. Barker (2, p. 395) and Stern (3 MS) translate the name of the second wife $st'ok'wa$ as 'half-grown mud hen' and not 'squirrel', the rendering given by Gatschet and Curtin. And yet, Barker, in his version of $M_{530a, b}$ (see below, M_{538}) keeps the meaning given by his predecessors. One of Gatschet's informants translated the same word as 'fish'. Similarly, in the version given by Curtis (M_{531a}, XIII, pp. 210–12), the wives are listed as: coot (a water hen), a kind of crane or heron, a small fish ($stókoa$), a small bird, a duck and a tick. It will be seen that Barker gives a different list of wives, as also does Curtin (see below, M_{541}) and even Gatschet for a Modoc version in which figure: mole, badger, porcupine, bitch, crane, mallard (*Anas boschas*), wren and other birds, butterfly, and a host of other wives who are not even named (Gatschet 1, Part I, p. lxxxvii).

I shall return to this problem when I deal with the northern versions (see below, p. 347). Similarly, Gatschet translates the word *wan* as 'silver fox', whereas Barker (2, p. 459) translates it as the red fox. The difference is not as great as it seems, since Gatschet (1, Part II, p. 474) mentions that he calls the red fox 'silver' when its coat becomes lighter coloured in winter.

On the other hand, it is clear that when M_{530} and M_{531} describe the magic plant which grows and causes the hero to be marooned, they are referring to different botanical species. *Kenáwat* would seem to be an edible prairie plant with a sweet-smelling flower (Gatschet 1, Part I, p. 146), probably a kind of sorrel (horse-sorrel), which reaches a height of one or two feet, but which has a much more rapid rate of growth in climates warmer than that prevailing in the Klamath highlands, where the cold causes stunted growth (Gatschet 1, Part II, p. 127). As for *kápka*, it is a species of low pine, *Pinus contorta*, according to Gatschet (*ibid.*, p. 118) and Barker (2, p. 148 under *gapga*), the fibre-bark of which is peeled off and eaten by the natives when the sap rises in the spring. So one version mentions a plant, the other a tree, but both have in common their edibility, and the fact that they are smaller than plants and trees of the same species either for some contingent reason, such as the coldness of the climate, or in comparison with other representatives of the same family. On each occasion, the myth changes the vegetable species from an edible food eaten by man into a metaphoric 'cannibal', and a deceitful one into the bargain, since it harbours very ordinary birds instead of the eagles the hero expected to find.

These birds (*skûle*) could be meadowlarks (cf. Barker 2, p. 390; *sqol'e*, '*meadowlark*'), the semantic function of which was discussed in the previous volume (*OTM*, pp. 231–9) and which, since they nest on the ground and fly low, are diametrically opposed to eagles, the masters of the sky, a fact which gives an additional emphasis to the contrast between the high and the low, already indicated by the vegetable species.

As regards the fur-skin with which the butterfly-girls line their basket, we can recall the following reproach noted by Gatschet (1, Part I, pp. 186, 189): 'You say you are rich and you don't even spread a wild cat's skin!' made by a disappointed, newly married wife to her husband, on finding herself deprived of even the most rudimentary comfort – a small tanned fur-skin to sit on as a protection against damp. The function of the episode relating to the porcupine necklaces will be explained during the discussion of Barker's more recent version (see below, p. 55 *et seq.*).

At this point, it is more appropriate to stress the already obvious symmetry between the North American and South American versions of the bird-nester story. The hero of M_1, a supposedly pre-pubescent boy, rapes his mother. The hero of $M_{530-531}$ has no mother, and not only is he adult and married, he is the husband of many wives; in some versions he is credited with a score or more. At the beginning of M_1, the hero has not yet been given the penis sheath, the only item of clothing ever worn by the Bororo; the North American hero is presented as possessing the most ornate garments, and his father has to force him to strip completely so as to don his attire and assume his physical appearance. If my interpretation of M_1 was correct, the raping of the mother expressed the boy's refusal to move into the men's house and to leave the female-dominated world of childhood. Aishísh, on the contrary, is so strongly on the male side that he is carried by his father for a second period of gestation[1].

In support of this theory, in *The Raw and the Cooked* (pp. 48, 55, 59, 63, 76) I stressed the fact that the hero of M_1 is a transformation of heroes in related myths whose surname — *baitogogo* in Bororo — means 'the secluded man', and who, like him, have names suggestive of their vestimentary elegance and physical beauty. At that stage in the argument, the suggestion could appear far-fetched. It is now confirmed by the North American version in which a character, whose adventures correspond exactly to those of the South American hero, is called 'the concealed man' or 'the secreted man', and his physical beauty is constantly extolled, so much so, in fact, that in Klamath there is a word meaning personal beauty *aishíshtchi*, 'Aishísh-like', derived from the hero's name (Gatschet 1, Part I, pp. lxxxv–xxxvii; Part II, p. 18). And, as we have just seen, in the North American myths his name is given a meaning which is symmetrical with the one I suggested in connection with South American examples.

This symmetrical relationship is characteristic of all aspects of the myth. For instance, incest with the father's wife, which is the starting point of M_1, is reversed in $M_{530-531}$ to become incest with one of the son's wives. Through a desire for vengeance in the first case, and for nefarious reasons in the second, the father sends his son to the top of a tree or rocky cliff, ostensibly to look, in the one instance for macaws, the prototype of fruit-eating birds, and in the other for eagles, the prototype of birds of prey. The stranded hero endures hunger and thirst and his body becomes emaciated, either through an external act of aggression (M_1) or through internal decay ($M_{530-531}$), until he is taken back down to earth by male, cannibalistic vultures, as in M_1, or by harmless butterfly-women, as in $M_{530-531}$.

When he returns to his own people, the hero of M_1 plans his revenge with

---

[1]According to Gatschet (1, Part I, p. lxxxviii), the Klamath word for 'father' *p'tíshap*, in Modoc *t'shíshap*, has the meaning of the 'the feeder', being a derivative of *t'shín*, 'to grow'. Barker (2) gives *tsin* without comment 'to grow (said only of a person)' and *tis* or *ptisap* 'father'.

the help of his younger brother; the hero of $M_{530-531}$ does likewise, but with the help of his young son. The guilty father is burnt to death in the one instance, and drowned in the other.[2]

This last opposition is of particular interest, because of the transformational relationship established in *The Raw and the Cooked* between the reference myth (M_1) and the Ge versions (M_{7-12}), which deal in the one instance with the origin of (celestial) water, and in the other with (terrestrial) fire. This transformational relationship reappears between myths, which, as we have just seen, are systematically inverted along a different axis. It is a striking fact that $M_{530-531}$ contains features which lead to a comparison both with M_1 and M_{7-12}. As in this last group, it is a tree, and not a rocky cliff face, which causes the hero to be disjoined from his own people. In both contexts, his search ends in disappointment, either because he finds common birds instead of rare ones, or because the nest contains nothing but eggs. In all the myths, the marooned hero's sufferings are described in the same way; he is starving, parched and covered with excrement. In M_{7-12}, the hero is rescued by the jaguar, a ferocious animal which passes by the foot of the tree: he is therefore saved from below. The hero of $M_{530-531}$, who is brought back to earth in a basket by butterfly-women, harmless creatures which have flown up to him, is saved from above. In all cases, the helpful animals feed the hero, give him water to drink, clean him and, while he is enjoying their hospitality, there occurs an event decisive for mankind: in M_{7-12}, this is the discovery of cooking fire, which is replaced in $M_{530-531}$ by a different discovery; the point will be established later (see below, pp. 45–6).

The conclusion to the Klamath myths also links up with the Bororo one. It will be remembered that, in order to punish his people for their wicked behaviour towards him, the hero of M_1 creates torrential rain which puts out all the fires in the village except the one in his grandmother's house, where he has taken refuge. He therefore reveals himself as being simultaneously master of (celestial) water, which he can unleash, and master of terrestrial fire, which he alone is able to preserve. Symmetrically, in order to punish his son for his wicked behaviour towards himself, the father of the

---

[2]It would be tempting to carry the comparison still further, since in $M_{530-531}$ the guilty father dies as a result of being disjoined from his pipe, that is, a *perforated stem*, whereas in M_1 he is conjoined with a *perforating* stem, the deer antler by which he is pierced. However, I prefer to leave the pipe episode aside for two reasons: firstly, it is not present in all versions; in those given by Curtis (M_{531a}) and Barker (M_{538}), the pipe is replaced by one or several external hearts 'which the old man wore like a bag round his neck'; a version given by Stern refers to a pendant attached to a necklace), and secondly, in order to establish a paradigm, it would be necessary to engage in a discussion involving an enormous and complex group of myths covering practically the whole of California.

hero in $M_{530-531}$ causes a rain of fire to fall from the sky; only the hero can protect himself from it, and he changes it into a lake which spreads over the whole earth but not into his own home, where he is safe with his faithful wives: 'Long after, Kmúkamch revived and tried to take his revenge on his son by daubing pitch all over the sky and setting it on fire. But Aishísh held out a tray (above him), and although his wives were very afraid, he said "Not me he may kill ever". The pitch turned into a lake which covered the whole world. Only Aishísh's house remained dry.' (Gatschet 1, part 1, p. 96.)

So, rain water which puts out all the fires but one (M_1) is changed, in the North American myth, into a rain of fire which swallows up all the houses but one. And whereas the water in M_1 acts as anti-fire, the fire im $M_{530-531}$ acts as water. I observed, in connection with M_1, that a more complex story (in comparison with M_{7-12}) made it possible to leave the etiological aspect of the myth in a latent state; and we shall see later that the same is true of the group to which $M_{530-531}$ belong.

The reader may now say: agreed, a group of myths belonging to tropical America reappears unchanged in North America. But what does that prove, apart from the fact that America was populated by successive waves of immigrants from Asia, who brought with them myths, some of which still remain recognizable in several of their North American and South American versions? This has been known for a long time and there is no lack of myths with parallel versions in the North and the South. It is hardly a matter of interest that one more should be added to an already long list.

To pose the problem in this way would be completely to misunderstand the significance of my enquiry. I am not trying to discover why these resemblances occur, but how. The peculiar feature of the myths I am comparing is not their similarity; in fact, they are often dissimilar. The aim of my analysis is rather to bring out certain characteristics they have in common, in spite of differences sometimes so great that myths I include in the same group were formerly considered as being completely separate entities.

Consequently, those instances in which similarity is strikingly obvious are no more than extreme cases. No doubt they are of great interest, in that they carry their own conviction and do not depend on structural analysis and on acceptance of the complex interplay of transformations. But the observation of certain resemblances at the empirical level does not in itself constitute proof. It is well known, and amply borne out by the errors of comparative mythology, that such resemblances can be extremely deceptive. This is why comparative studies based on the single criterion of resemblance quickly degenerated into intensely wearisome verbiage. If, as Leach has said, I have been able to restore comparative studies to some respectability, this has been through the realization that resemblance has no reality in itself; it is only a particular instance of difference, that in which difference tends towards zero. But difference is never completely absent. It follows that critical analysis must take over from the making of empirical inventories to face the basic problem of those conditions in which a resemblance can have a wealth of meaning far surpassing what might be implied by a random coincidence, an effect of convergence or a common origin.

Once this is accepted, resemblances no longer belong to the domain of pure observation. Instead of being apprehended as empirical data, they are comprehended as rational entities. They cease to be merely observable, and become demonstrable since they can be distinguished in degree, not in nature, from differences which can never be reduced without a demonstration. The need for demonstrable proof is thus extended to the whole field.

So, far from claiming to establish, between the myths, kinship or filiation links which are reinforced by surface similarities, I start from the principle that a myth can never be reduced to its appearance. However diverse appearances may be, they conceal structures which, although probably less numerous, are also more real. They present themselves as absolute objects, from which nothing can be subtracted and to which nothing can be added: they are matrices which, by means of successive deformations, engender types which can be arranged in series and should enable us to determine the most minute shades of meaning in each myth, considered as a concrete, individual entity.

This method does not always need to appeal to history, but neither does it completely disregard history. Since it brings out unsuspected links between the myths and classifies the variants in an order which at least indicates the necessary sequence of certain transformations, it raises historical problems suggesting hypotheses that history, left to itself, might otherwise not have thought of and, in so doing, provides more effective help than could be given by any prosaic inventory of the already available findings of history.

It is therefore as much a concern for possible historical implications as a desire to increase the plausibility of a comparison based on formal resemblances which prompts me at this point to draw attention to a series of features common to the two semantic fields forming the background to the bird-nester myth both in north-western and in tropical America. I mentioned a number of these features earlier, at the beginning, and in the subsequent course of the present work, in order to give preliminary notice, as it were, of the point at which we have now arrived (cf. *RC*, pp. 48, 55–6, 152, n. 7, 289, n. 2, 299, n. 11; *HA*, pp. 112, 189–90, 197–200, 217, n. 12, 309, n. 19, 371, n. 5, 456, n. 30, 460–61). Without recapitulating all the examples, I propose to concentrate now on some outstanding instances of parallelism which relate to the myths discussed above.

The Mataco of the Chaco, who have been linked in recent linguistic classifications with the Panoan family, have, like the Klamath-Modoc and the Bororo, a character to whom they give the name *tawkxwax* or *tacjuaj*, which could mean 'the invisible one' or 'the hidden one'. Like the Ge, they say that cooking fire was obtained from the jaguar, and they share other myths with tribes acquainted with the bird-nester theme, for instance, those concerned with the origin of women or with the snake's mistress (cf. Campana, pp. 309, 314–17 and *RC*, *HA*, *Index of Myths* under 'Mataco'). The story goes that since Tawkxwax, the trickster demiurge, had no wife (M_{532}, Métraux 3, pp. 39–40), he plunged his penis into his arm, and conceived a boy. The boy was brought up by an old woman, and became a miraculous fisherman. At that time, all the water and all the fish in the world were contained in the trunk of a huge tree, where fishing could take place at all seasons. But, through an intemperate action, the hero split the trunk and created a flood which covered the whole earth, except for one tree at the top of which he had taken refuge. Finally, this tree too was submerged and the hero was swept away to his death. His father, the demiurge, succeeded in causing the flood to subside and channelled the waters into 'the bed of the river which today flows near Buenos Aires'. We have already seen that the Klamath-Modoc myths associate the hidden child with the origin of fishing, which was changed into a seasonal activity by the Mataco hero, and with the origin of the hydrographic network, for which that same hero bears posthumous responsibility. These features are to be found in an even more strongly marked form in the Nez Percé myths, and it is worth noting at this juncture, that they include the story of the trickster demiurge (M_{533}, Spinden 1, pp. 19–21) who fertilizes his own elbow by pricking it with his penis and then gives birth to a son. Even more significant is the fact that this child helps his father to recover his eyes, which he had lost through the foolish belief that he could remove them with impunity and then put them back in their sockets. It has already been established (*RC*, pp. 190–93) that this motif, which is also present in South America, is based on an opposition between eyes and excrement, representing respectively parts of the body which are naturally irremovable or intended to be removed.

The child, who is irremovable for nine months and then is ejected, with no possibility of return, from the body of which it formed an integral part, may therefore play the part of mediatory term between eyes and excrement. This is why the demiurge succeeds in rectifying the mistake of *exteriorizing his eyes* by *interiorizing his child* through self-impregnation. It is true that the South American myths stress the opposition *eyes/excrement*, whereas the myth just quoted shifts it to *eyes/child*. But it so happens that the father, who sometimes carries the child in his hip, in that case gives birth to his children through the anus (M_{542a}; Phinney, p. 52, n. 2). They are therefore excrement children, and innumerable myths belonging to the same area – such as those in which Coyote has his own private council, consisting of excrement sisters which he ejects from his body whenever he needs advice, and reabsorbs immediately afterwards, cf. below, pp. 264, 310–11 – attest the operative value of a tripartite schema:

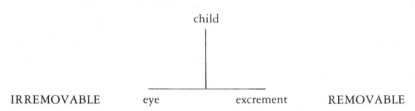

In the North American group too, Coyote is the bird-nester's father and is responsible, in the course of his peregrinations, for the creation of order in the universe, a task which includes, among other things, the institution of seasonal periodicity to which the reproductive cycle is linked.

The pregnant man motif has a wide area of distribution in North America, extending from the Paiute and the Pawnee in the south and east, to the Eskimo in the north, by way of Athapaskan such as the Kaska, and some Salish tribes such as the Tillamook (L.–S. 5, Ch. XII; Rink, pp. 443–4; Lowie 4, *passim*; Teit 8, p. 472; E. D. Jacobs, pp. 141–3). It is also found among the Kalapuya, the Coos, and as far away as Siberia (Frachtenberg 1, pp. 5, 49; Jacobs 6, p. 239; 4, pp. 375–6; Jochelson, p. 365). The motif would seem to be even more widely distributed in South America, since it covers two enormous areas to the north-west and south-east of the bird-nester region, one of them stretching from Panama and the West Indies to the north-west of the Amazonian basin and Peru, and the other from Central Brazil to Bolivia and the Argentine Chaco. The first group includes the West Indian Carib (Rouse, p. 564), the Cuna of Panama and the Choco (Holmer-Wassén, pp. 24–5; Wassén 1, pp. 133–4; 5, pp. 70–71), the Surara and the Waika (Becher 1, p. 104; Zerries 4, p. 273), the

Catio (M_{254b}; *HA*, p. 204; Rochereau-Rivet, p. 100), the Uitoto (Preuss 1, pp. 51, 304–14), the Tukuna (Nim. 13, p. 122), the Omagua (Métraux 15, p. 702) and in a weaker form, the Aguaruna (Guallart, pp. 92–3). The second group includes the Ofaié (Nim. 1, p. 377; Ribeiro 2, pp. 114–15), the Umutina (Oberg, p. 108; Schultz 2, pp. 172, 227) and the Yuracaré (Kelm, in Zerries, *loc. cit.*, p. 273). Zerries (*loc. cit.*) has made an inventory of the motif which coincides more or less with mine.

The hidden child, silent by definition, is sometimes changed after birth into a whimpering baby (M_{529}). This also happens in a myth (M_{534}, DuBois Demetracopoulou, pp. 333–4) belonging to the Wintu of northern California, who are not far distant from the Klamath and the Modoc: a child, after being at first hidden by his sisters, escapes and utters such dreadful howls that he puts the entire community to flight. His cries only cease at the sight of his sister's menstrual blood, which fills him with such terror that he runs away and vanishes into water.

Slight though this detail may seem, it nevertheless suggests that the hidden child, being closely conjoined to his father's body, or to his family as a whole, when they keep him in seclusion, has a certain correlational and oppositional relationship with the whimpering child who disjoins all his kinsfolk from himself. The whimpering child in the Californian myth cannot stand the sight of menstrual blood, whereas the hidden child in the South American myths sprinkles himself with it and sometimes even absorbs it as nourishment (Wassén 1, p. 116; Rochereau-Rivet, p. 100).

If we accept this suggestion, the pregnant man motif must be considered as a particular instance of the more general motif concerning a family which conceals one of its children from the community, shuts it away in a hiding place and washes and feeds it in secret. It will be seen that this motif has an important place in those North American myths which most directly concern my demonstration, and the hero of which sometimes has a name similar to that of Aishísh whom his adoptive father first concealed in his knee; e.g. *weämauna*, 'the hidden one', in Yana (Curtin 3, pp. 121, 339, 421). For the time being, it is enough to point out that the same affinity is to be found between the two themes in South American myths and rites. In fact, I showed this to be so in discussing the name of the hero of several Bororo myths, Baitogogo or 'the secluded man', which could only be interpreted correctly by reference to Ge and Caraja customs regarding the seclusion of adolescent boys or an adolescent girl of noble birth. Korumtau, the hero of a Mundurucu myth (M_{16}), is a hidden child in both senses of the term, since his father gave birth to him without the intermediary agency of a woman and then tried to conceal him from the community (*RC*, pp. 55–8).

It should now be noted that, in the north-east of North America and in a vast region of South America, a similar transformation enables us to move from the hidden child motif to that of the hidden wife. The transition can be made by means of the Sanpoil, for like other Salish tribes both inland and along the coast they 'subjected their daughters to a rigid programme of supervision and concealment so that they would be more respected and made more desirable as wives' (Ray 1, pp. 136–7). Although the Athapaskan-speaking Navajo today live in the south, they originally came from the north, so it is perhaps permissible to mention the mythic origin of their *ethkay-nahashi* masks, which represent a boy and a girl walking one behind the other; it was in this form that two young girls[3], kept in seclusion and in darkness by their parents, were resuscitated after committing a mortal sin (Haile-Wheelwright, pp. 24, 31, 107; cf. below M_{792}, p. 558). The Salish-speaking Lilloet who live along the borders of Athapaskan territory have a story about incest between close relatives, in spite of the father taking the precaution of shutting his daughter up in a box near his bed so that no one can come near her (M_{535}, Teit 2, p. 340). The hidden child is not the only instance of a human being concealed in some receptacle or other, such as a basket, a box, a flute, a cocoon, an underground pit, or a roof thatch; the same happens to the miniature wife whom a man tries to

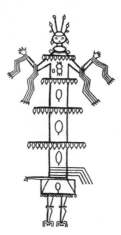

Figure 3. Navajo drawing representing one of the hidden girls. (From Haile-Wheelwright, p. 25)

[3] This transformation is the reverse of the one in M_{538}, where a male child splits into a boy and girl who subsequently commit incest. I respect the form of the tribal name decided upon by the Council of the Navajo nation which, on April 15th, 1969, adopted the spelling Navajo instead of Navaho, the form traditionally used by anthropologists.

protect from his brother's advances. The myths of both North and South America recount this story in such similar terms that I need do no more than juxtapose two examples selected from the many versions available:

M_{660a}. *Klikitat. 'The hidden wife'* (an extract; cf. below, p. 339)

There was an eagle, and there was his younger brother, Skunk. Eagle used to spend all his time hunting. A woman came along and Skunk hid her. His elder brother would arrive back in the evening, drop meat into the house and sleep in the house over night. In the dark, Skunk talked with his wife, and as day dawned his elder brother would wake up and wonder why his younger brother happened to be laughing and talking in the dark. The latter would reply: 'I laugh because a mouse comes here to me and runs over my face (or bites my rectum)' (Jacobs 3, p. 207; 1, 202–203).

Here now is a South American version:

M_{95}. *Tucuna. 'The girl of the umari fruit'* (RC, p. 171)

Unknown to his brother Epi, Dyai took as his wife a young girl who had miraculously appeared to him. He rolled her between the palms of his hands, thus reducing her size until he was able to conceal her inside his bone flute.

For four days, he went nightly to bring the girl from the flute and take her into his hammock, where he played with her in silence. On the fifth night, she laughed and the little snail-shell bells on her armbands tinkled. Epi immediately asked, 'My brother, with whom are you laughing?' 'No one,' answered Dyai, 'the broom laughed because I tickled it' (Nim. 13, p. 127).

The similarity is all the more impressive in that the married brother in the North American version is a skunk while in the other version the unmarried brother has, as I have shown, a certain affinity with the opossum (RC, pp. 171, 179–80), and both of these are animals which the myths of both North and South America place independently in a correlational and oppositional relationship while at the same time reversing their respective functions (RC, p. 249, n. 22; HA, pp. 80, 81).

But there is more to it than that. The two heroes of the Tucuna myth, both hidden children, are born from their father's swollen knees, whereas the heroes of the Klikitat myth have as their counterparts in Klamath mythology Marten and Weasel (members, like the skunk, of the mustelidae family). In the myths, these animal characters act as doublets of Kmúkamch and Aishísh, respectively the pregnant man and his hidden child. The equivalence between Marten and Kmúkamch and between Weasel and Aishísh, which was postulated by Gatschet (1, Part I, pp. 107–108), is not contested by Barker (1, p. 389), who sees it as the result of the confusion of two characters who were originally distinct. However, in a story recorded by Barker three-quarters of a century after Gatschet, Marten and Kmúkamch are still considered as being one and the same (Barker 1, p. 73). Besides, there is another argument in support of Gatschet's theory.

In the majority of South American myths containing the hidden wife motif, the wife is a star (RC, pp. 164–70). The Klamath have a myth about the marriage of Marten and Weasel, which is an inversion of the myth about the marriage between Eagle and Skunk, which in turn is similar as we have seen to the South American myths featuring the star-wife of a mortal, except that it does not specify the wife's origins. In the Klamath myth ($M_{536a, b}$; Gatschet 1, Part I, pp. 107–18; Barker 1, pp. 71–7), Marten, far from coveting the pretty wife found by his brother, dissuades the latter from marrying her, denounces her as having murderous intentions and sings the praises of the one-eyed women who, he claims, are more industrious. The fact that the one-eyed women are the sun and the moon, as Gatschet clearly realized (1, Part I, p. lxxxiii), is borne out not only by the Eskimo comparisons he quotes, but by many others too: one-eyed stars in Kodiak mythology (Golder, pp. 24–6, 30), 'One-eye' as the Sanpoil name for the sun (Ray 2, pp. 135–7) and many references elsewhere to the sun as being squint-eyed (Adamson, *passim*); to which must be added the vast amount of similar data from South as well as North America, which I examined briefly in another context (OTM, p. 157 *et passim*).

It would be wrong, then, to dismiss all Gatschet's interpretations in principle, even when he shows himself to be obsessed by the solar mythology which was fashionable during the last century. I have already expressed my views on this point (RC, p. 290). Max Müller and his school must be given great credit for having discovered, and to some extent deciphered, the astronomical code so often used by the myths. Their mistake, like that of all mythologists of the period and more recent ones too, was to try to understand the myths by means of a single and exclusive code, when in fact several codes are always in operation simultaneously. It is impossible to reduce the myth to any one code, nor can it be explained as the sum of several codes. It would be truer to say that a group of myths constitutes in itself a code, the power of which is superior to each individual code it uses to decipher manifold messages. It is tantamount to an 'intercode' – if I may be pardoned the neologism – which makes possible the reciprocal conversion of the messages in accordance with rules, the range of which remains immanent in the different systems which, through its operation, allow the emergence of an overall significance distinct from their particular meanings. [4]

While, then, it is possible to accept the view first put forward by Gatschet that the Klamath and Modoc demiurges have an astronomical connotation, I do not believe, as he does, that this solves the problem. It is only the first stage in the discussion, and it needs to be followed by many others before the real analysis can begin. Even in their familiar form as Marten and Weasel, the two demiurges have a cosmological function ($M_{536a, c}$; Gatschet I, Part I, pp. 109–18; Curtin I, pp. 288–309); they decapitate the winds and exterminate the thunders. As far as Kmúkamch and Aishísh proper are concerned, there would seem to be no reason to question the authenticity of certain comments recorded by Gatschet, even though he sometimes adds embellishments which make it impossible to tell who is speaking, the investigator or the native informant: 'When the sun is environed by lamb-clouds, this is figuratively expressed by "Kmúkamch has taken the beaded costumes of Aishísh and dressed himself in them". A peculiar red smoke or haze appearing in the north-western or western sky announces his arrival; he is also recognizable by his bulky posterior . . . by this they evidently refer to the heavy, white, mountain-shaped summer clouds' (Gatschet I, Part I, p. lxxxiv). One myth (M_{537}; *ibid.*, p. lxxxi) explains how, after visiting the underworld, 'Kmúkamch travels in the path of the sun till he reaches the zenith, builds his lodge and lives there with his daughter'. Gatschet concludes from this, although it is not easy to see why, that the daughter represents the clouded or mottled evening sky. However, his identification, also unsupported by argument, of the fox, Kmúkamch's constant companion, with the sun-halo (I, p. lxxxii) is not without interest: it fits in with the affinity between the opossum and the rainbow I have already detected in South America, an affinity which, among certain Plains tribes of North America, is transposed to the skunk; the two animals form then a semantic pair (*RC*, p. 249) with, as we have seen, the skunk playing the part of companion or younger brother in more

---

[4] Here I am harking back to Plutarch, a precursor of the structural analysis of myths: '. . . it seems to me that it would not be irrelevant to say that in each individual case there is not one of these interpretations which is completely perfect, but that taken all together they make their meaning absolutely plain, for it is not drought alone, nor the wind, the sea, nor darkness, but everything which is harmful and is likely to lead in part to loss or decay that is called Typhon' (p. 68). Similarly, Benveniste writes (p. 60): 'It is a term with a general meaning which happens to be applied to a specific reality and becomes the means of designating it, instead of the opposite being the case.'

northerly areas, whereas Klamath and Modoc mythology assign this role to the fox.

Curtin (1, pp. xxix, 48–9), another devotee of solar mythology, perceives a scarcely contestable astronomical symbolism in the episode devoted to the death and resurrection of the demiurge Kumush, the Modoc name for Kmúkamch: after he was hurled into the flames (cf. above, M_{530}), 'nothing was left of him but his skull and disk in the ashes. At last, after a very long time the morning star saw them and called out "What's the matter, old man? Why do you sleep so long? Get up!" Kumush sprang up and began right away to track (his brother) Wanaga' (cf. below, M_{541}). Curtin comments on the episode in the following terms: 'Each day the sun dies physically and is consumed, leaving only his body reduced to ashes. But he had in his body an indestructible golden disk which prevents him from disappearing for ever . . . The morning star must rouse him. At its summons, the golden disk rises from the pile of ashes, the sun is renewed completely and goes forth to run his course till consumed again.' It should be noted, in connection with the indestructible disc to which I shall refer again presently, that the Modoc shamans 'used small disks formed of tule with a pair of feathers on either side, symbolizing the spirits of the shaman and vaguely associated with the frog' (Ray 3, pp. 37–8).

Further north, the Kathlamet, the Tillamook, the Chinook and the Bella Coola believed that the life force is located in a disc, a ball or an egg, which are sometimes said to be situated at the nape of the neck (Boas 5, p. 192), and even the Klamath seemed to attribute supernatural properties to eggs (Spier 2, p. 102). As for the Modoc name for the demiurge's brother, it is identical with the Klamath *wanaka*, which Gatschet (1, Part II, p. 474) translates as 'young of red fox or silver fox, sun-halo', this time quoting a native expression in his rendering. Finally, we can attribute the same importance as Gatschet does (1, Part I, p. lxxx) to the fact that the Klamath and the Modoc, who are fond of naming their various localities by reference to the peregrinations of the demiurges, call a crescent-shaped rock on Lower Klamath Lake *shapashkéni* because it is believed that 'Sun and Moon once lived there'.

But if Kmúkamch connotes the sun and his son Aishísh the moon, a further parallel between the North and South American versions of the bird-nester story comes to light and finds expression in various ways. As I believe I proved in *The Raw and the Cooked*, the Bororo hero is an incarnation of the constellation Corvus and, less directly, the character of his father is linked with the Pleiades (*RC*, pp. 226–37, 242–5). Consequently, these two characters also denote celestial objects. But there is more to it than that:

we know that the Bororo myth is a transformation, by means of an etiological inversion, of Ge myths in which the hero is also a bird-nester sent to his death not by his father but by his brother-in-law. In Serenté mythology at least, each of the characters relates to the sun or the moon, through the intermediary agency of the luminary associated with his particular sociological moiety, since the moieties are dedicated respectively to the sun and moon. So we are back again to Kmúkamch and Aishísh, though the roles played by the two characters are now reversed. The Serenté associate the bird-nester with the solar, southern moiety, and his persecutor with the northern, lunar moiety (*RC*, pp. 75–6). In the preceding volume (M$_{495}$, *OTM*, pp. 427–8), I had already noted the persistence of astronomical connotations in those North American myths which are transformations of the bird-nester story and we now have further confirmation of the fact, but this time in myths which remain faithful to the prototype. The special problem posed by the inversion of the solar and lunar affinities of the two heroes will be dealt with later (see below, pp. 71–2).

Lastly, it should be noted that, in Ge as in Klamath and Modoc mythology, the sun and the moon figure predominantly in two complementary mythic series: the bird-nester series, as I have just recalled, and another one in which the sun and moon, who are respectively an elder and younger brother, instead of belonging to different generations, become involved in a series of sometimes farcical adventures in which the younger brother perishes through foolhardiness while his wiser elder brother is entrusted with the task of bringing him back to life. In this respect, we need only compare the misadventures of Sun and Moon in numerous Ge versions (cf. M$_{163}$, *RC*, pp. 292–3) and of Marten (or Mink) and Weasel in the Klamath and Modoc myths to which I have briefly referred to be convinced that the mythological structures of North and South America are closely related.

2 Foolish Women and Wise Virgins

Mir schaudert das Herz,
es schwindelt mein Hirn:
bräutlich umfing
die Schwester der Bruder!
Wann ward es erlebt,
dass leiblich Geschwister sich liebten?

R. Wagner, *Die Walküre*, Act II,
Scene 1

No doubt the analysis of the Klamath myths would not have proceeded beyond this point, but for one of those happy accidents with which anthropologists are sometimes favoured; about 1955, there appeared, having been miraculously preserved in the memory of an old Indian woman, a more complete and coherent version of the Aishísh chronicle of which Gatschet, Curtis and Stern had recorded only fragments ($M_{529-531}$); even in it there are certainly many gaps, since she remembered that in former times it took several days to tell the whole myth.

What makes this version so valuable is that it begins with a detailed account of the events preceding the enigmatic opening episode of Gatschet's story, in which the heroine builds a pyre in order to burn a sorceress's body and then throws herself and her baby into the flames, without it being explained who the sorceress is, or why the heroine wants to commit suicide.

The fuller versions given by Curtis (M_{531a}) and Stern (M_{531b}, unpublished; cf. below, p. 165) certainly suggest a reason for this episode, but they do no more than explain that the sorceress had killed an incestuous brother, who, like his sister, suddenly appears at the beginning of the story, and whose origins are specified only in Barker's more recent version. Barker himself (1, p. 22) confesses that he was surprised at his informant linking this first story with the Gmokamch (= Kmúkamch) myth, 'never having seen the Gmokamch story beginning in this fashion anywhere else'. However, as I have just recalled, the narratives given by Gatschet, Curtis and Stern already hinted at the existence of an initial sequence by leaving a gap where it could have been inserted. Consequently, the re-emergence of the Barker version in Klamath mythology at a time when it seemed probable that little or nothing remained of their ancient traditions is more than surprising; it was quite unhoped for. The reader will appreciate, then, why, at the risk of wearying him with lengthy extracts, I should treat Barker's text and his commentary with particular care and attention.

M 538. *Klamath. 'The story of Aishish'*

Once, they say, there lived a woman who had many children: one only was a girl with long red hair who got married to someone from the Gowasdi area [an area to the north-west of Upper Klamath Lake (Spier 2, p. 16; Barker 1, p. 158; 2, p. 158)]. However, she kept coming back home for she was in love with her youngest brother and she always insisted that he should take her home.

Once they had to camp for the night and the girl crawled into bed beside her brother. Then he woke up and was shocked to find her next to him. 'What a fool she is! Whatever will she do to me being a wife to her own brother!' He crawled slowly out and found a big tree-limb and pillowed his sister's head on it. Then he returned home. When he told his mother what had happened she feared that something very bad would come upon them.

The sun had long been up when the woman awoke. In her fury at being abandoned, she started a huge fire, burning up everything, her brothers and their wives. But she spared her mother. While searching around in the ashes, the old woman found the corpse of Meadow Lark, one of her daughters-in-law, who, being pregnant, had buried her stomach under a mortar. From her burned-through back the mother-in-law picked up two children, a boy and a girl. She was very much afraid that the girl would be just like her aunt, so she stuck the children together with pitch, making a single male creature with two heads. Then she advised the little boy never to bend down to look at his shadow and never to shoot an arrow into the sky.

The child grew up and began to suspect something mysterious was going on. A shrill-voiced bird, the killdeer plover (*Charadrius vociferus*) persuaded him to shoot his arrow into the air. The arrow came straight down and split the children in two. The boy, who had never seen the other head, was surprised to find a little girl beside him. Then she told him she was his sister. When they went home the grandmother realized she knew all the time what would happen.

The little girl always went hunting with her brother and kept asking him questions. 'Who are we? Why are we without a father and a mother? Why does our grandmother always cry? Why do we live this way? Let us go over there and ask the sun and we will shoot him if he does not tell us.'

When the sun rose, they questioned him, but as he paid no attention to them, the little girl shot an arrow into the sun's cheek, leaving a black mark which is still there. The wounded sun begged them to pull the arrow out quickly and agreed to tell them. He explained that the woman who had orphaned them lived in the water and he showed them exactly at which spot.

When winter came, the sister planned to go to this spot, on the pretext that she was going torch-hunting. Night after night, they brought back many, many fish and waterfowl. At last they heard the murderess's cry 'gochgochgochgodjip!' The grandmother too heard it and she was afraid she would find her daughter's head in with the fish. This in fact was what happened, but she was very sad and frightened because she loved her daughter, even though the latter had killed her own kin.

Fearing the old woman's anger, the young people decided to escape through the hearth ashes, advising all the domestic utensils not to say where they had gone, and shut the hole behind them with a piece of coal. But they forgot Awl, who showed the old woman how they had escaped. She at once followed them.

But the children had had several days' start. [Curtis's version begins here.] On one occasion the boy shot an arrow up into a tree and was unable to get it back down. He asked his sister to get it for him. She refused to do so unless he told her how he was related to her. 'You are my sister?' 'No.' 'Aunt?' 'No.' 'How is it – mother?' 'No.' Then he named every relation one after the other, but the little girl rejected them all until the brother said, 'Then you're my wife!' So, at the little girl's suggestion, they lived together as husband and wife, although they were brother and sister.

Knowing they would do this, the grandmother was still pursuing them. While inspecting the ashes of their sleeping-places, the grandmother saw the impression of the little girl's stomach and realized the latter was pregnant. She also found the skin of a bear which her grandson, having now become a man, had killed. She crawled into the fur.

Meanwhile, the young couple had a child and, in accordance with custom, the young man went off into the brush in order to pray, fast and obtain the protection of the spirits. The old woman changed into a bear, caught up with him, killed and ate him.

Then she returned to her grand-daughter's house and asked for water. While she was drinking, the little girl threw red-hot stones into her anus. Then, on the pretext of making her vomit up the excess water she had drunk, she stepped on the old bear's stomach so that the hot stones would bring the water to the boil and cook her. Then that bear (ogress) died.

I would like to interrupt the narrative for a moment to point out that it is here that Gatschet's version begins (M_{529}). From now on, the two stories will continue along parallel lines, although Barker's version is different on several very important points, and contains more detail than Gatschet's. I shall therefore keep closely to Barker.

Then the little girl built a big pyre, set fire to it and with the baby on her back got ready to jump into the fire. Kmúkamch [for the sake of simplicity I will keep to transcriptions of proper names which are closest to Gatschet's] viewed the scene, sitting upon the mountainside and he admired the baby. As the mother was jumping into the fire, he struck the child's foot with a mallet and the baby fell far away. Then he picked it up and tried unsuccessfully to put it on his forehead, on his neck . . . finally, he put it under his knee.

He limped home and complained to his daughter that his leg had swelled up a great deal. She diagnosed an abscess, punctured it, and saw hair. The child emerged and cried and cried. Father and daughter gave him every sort of name they could think of, but he got worse. He only became quiet when they named him Aishísh. Then he grew big, became a man and had many wives: Mudhen, Green Heron, Snowbird, Squirrel, Mallard . . . Kmúkamch had his eye on Squirrel as she picked her fleas. He wondered why his son loved her more than his other wives. Mallard was jealous and thinking similar thoughts. Then Kmúkamch fell in love with his pretty daughter-in-law, and he put on the fire wood which always sparked. He wanted the sparks to fly on to Squirrel's clothes and force her, since she was naked under her blanket, to reveal her charms by pulling up her garments in order to protect them from the sparks.

Now Kmúkamch planned to kill Aishísh – for a long time he plotted how to set about it. Then one day he found a plant, perhaps a reed, in which meadowlarks were nesting. He told Aishísh he had found an eagle's nest, but that it was so high he felt too old to climb up there. He told his son to climb up, having first of all obliged him to take off all his clothes. Then the reed started to grow very high: when Aishísh arrived at the nest, in which he found only little birds which he threw out, he could no longer get down. Marooned at the summit and without food, he became very thin. Kmúkamch made little Squirrel his wife.

The butterfly-sisters who were flying around the tree caught a hair floating in the air and wondered where it had come from. They found Aishísh but he was just bones, and almost dead from hunger and thirst. Then they took him down and looked after him. He always lay by the hearth, although this did not prevent him having many wives: the butterfly-sisters, Grasshopper, Ant and several more.

Every day porcupines came and danced on his body and covered Aishísh with dust and taunted him thus: 'Wish someone would cut our wrists!' They took advantage of the fact that he was sick, but as soon as he was better he killed them and cut off their wrists and feet and made beads for his wives with their quills. This is why Grasshopper wears a necklace round her neck. Then he made mocassins for them, and perhaps earrings too. They were very proud of these adornments and so they dug up edible roots – all except Grasshopper, who was very lazy and who just sang and wore out her mocassins very quickly by rubbing her legs together.

Aishísh wanted to go home, and bade farewell to his wives. 'Now you have everything you need,' he told them, for he had fixed everything nice for them before he left. At home, in his own country, his first wives were still inconsolable, all except Mallard, who didn't care whether he was dead or what had happened to him, and Squirrel who slept with Kmúkamch, even though she knew perfectly well he had cuckolded his son. Snowbird had a son, and the baby recognized Aishísh and said, 'Daddy, daddy'. Aishísh (or so the informant thought) got his wives back again.

The hero ordered his little son to throw Kmúkamch's hearts (the informant believed he had several) into the fire. They popped up (out) and dripped like pitch all over the earth. Aishísh put his family into a cave, but Mudhen wanted to look out and see what was happening and brown spots dripped on to her nose. The narrator does not remember what happened next: 'Maybe I went to sleep while they were telling the myths' (Barker 1, pp. 25–49).

Instead of complaining about the gaps in her extraordinary memory, let us rather, pending the appearance of as yet unpublished documents,[1] make the most of the new details and episodes scattered throughout her narrative, and which will provide the starting point for an analysis.

[1] Barker 1, p. 1, refers to manuscripts by Spier. For more recent documents collected by Stern (1, 3), cf. below, p. 165.

As has already been indicated (p. 34), Barker's version throws light, in the first place, on the porcupine episode, which was already present although with fewer details in Curtis's version. Through their taunting in the songs, to which reference is also made in Stern's version (M_{531b}), these rodents to their detriment provide the hero with the means of making adornments: necklaces, mocassins and earrings, embroidered or woven with quills; and he leaves his insect-wives only after providing for them. It will be remembered that, in the myths, Aishísh is always depicted as the master of fine clothes. The fact that this power dates from his stay with the helpful animals brings us even closer to the South American versions of the bird-nester story. The Bororo hero invented the bow and arrows in order to drive off the lizards which, as they decomposed, were covering him with filth, whereas Aishísh invents adornments and jewellery when persecuting porcupines are covering him with dust. In the first instance, the filth is moist; in the second, it is dry, since the native terms *boq* and *nkililk* used in the myth refer respectively to a whitish dust (the verbal form has the double meaning of 'to be dusty' and 'to be white-haired') and a light dust that is easily blown about (Barker 2, pp. 66, 266). I shall return later to this opposition, which is no more fortuitous than the others (below, p. 114).

It is at the helpful jaguar's expense that the hero in the corresponding Ge myths obtains other cultural advantages: cooking fire, and, in certain versions, bows and arrows and yarn, the chief use of which, for these virtually naked Indians of Central Brazil, was the making of plaited or woven adornments. I showed in *The Raw and the Cooked* and mentioned again in a condensed form in *From Honey to Ashes* (pp. 20–32) that the South American bird-nester cycle belongs to a vast transformational group which makes possible the transition from the invention of cooking fire to that of meat on the one hand, and of ornaments and jewellery on the other. It is thus confirmed that geographical distance performs a function comparable to that of semantic distance. The Bororo myth about the origin of adornments (M_{20}) is a transformation, along several axes, of those concerned with the origin of meat (M_{21}) and cooking fire (M_1, which in turn is a transformation of M_{7-12}). Yet, if we leap over the thousands of kilometres separating Central Brazil from the north-west of the United States, we find a myth about the origin of adornments, the armature of which exactly reproduces that adopted by the South American Indians to explain the origin of cooking fire. On the other hand, this myth is itself a transformation of other myths, the geographical source of which is very close to its own; however, it reproduces their message only at the cost of inverting the code. In Klamath mythology, Aishísh, who is a man, gives jewellery made from porcupine quills to his wives, who are personifications of insects. Conversely, North American communities living on the east side of the Rockies believe quill embroidery to be the work of insects: ants, who take a woman's place so that she can give the garments they have embroidered to her husband (M_{480}; *OTM*, pp. 363–5, 382–5).

Considered in itself and taken as a whole, M_{538} displays a periodic structure: the episodes are repeated from one sequence to the next. There are three successive cases of incest: the first, in which the incest is thwarted, involves a married woman living at a distance and her brother who has remained at home; the second, in which the incest is consummated, involves a brother and sister who have grown up joined together; and the third involves a father-in-law and the wife of a son who, in a sense, had been born joined to him. Two family groups die by fire, either together or one after the other: firstly, brothers with their wives, then a mother and later her daughter. The meadowlark comes in twice: as a human character, she saves her own children by burying them underground; as a bird, she drops her accomplice's child while trying to carry him up into the sky. Pairs of close relatives undergo conjunctions and disjunctions alternately: a brother and sister are conjoined by the arrow which splits them apart; a mother and son are conjoined by fire (when they are about to perish together) and disjoined by the demiurge's mallet; a father and son are conjoined when the father makes himself pregnant with the son, and disjoined when, on the contrary, he tries to get rid of him in order to enjoy his wives. The disjunctive arrow fulfils the reverse function to that of the pitch: it separates the twins by falling from high to low. But when it is shot from low to high, it plays the same part with regard to the sun as is played by the pitch when it spreads from high to low and drops on to Mudhen, since, in either instance, the victim is left with a permanent black mark on his or her face. In the case of the mudhen, the mark is evidence of the fact that, for a moment, sky and earth were joined together by pitch. In the sun's case, it provides evidence of the fact that a brother and sister become separated from each other, in spite of the pitch which welded them into a single being. When I have constructed the transformation group of which M_{538} illustrates only one aspect (see below, pp. 216–22), all these instances of parallelism, interchange and opposition will take on their full significance.

It is appropriate, however, to emphasize straight away the firm construction of the first part of the myth, the part which is lacking in the older versions recorded by Gatschet and Curtis and in Stern's contemporary versions. Leaving aside for the moment the heroine's baby who grows up to be Aishísh and is the chief protagonist in the second part, the story revolves around characters belonging to three successive generations: firstly, the old mother; next, her daughter, her sons and their wives; and lastly, her two grandchildren. The myth gives a specific description of only three characters belonging to the middle generation: a young unmarried boy, who has, on the one hand, an incestuous sister married, we are told, to a geographically remote husband, and, on the other, a sister-in-law called Meadowlark, like the bird denoting the junction between the sky and the earth (*OTM*, p. 237). The system is therefore bounded at both ends by doubly contrasted semantic functions: *union/disjunction*, and *vertical axis/horizontal axis*. Within this system, and as the action unfolds, the mother replaces the dead daughter in the role of ogress (which is figurative and sexual in the one case and literal and alimentary in the other); simultaneously, this same daughter, as if she had been driven by her mother from the position she occupied, takes the place of her niece, who is also an incestuous sister; at the same time, the brother who resists the advances of the first changes into a nephew who allows himself to be seduced by the second.

Although these commutations follow on from each other in the course of the narrative, their respective logical bases display a remarkable comparative symmetry. The two older women, in spite of the criminal actions performed by the second, are deeply attached to each other: the daughter spares the mother and the mother is filled with anguish as the hour of retribution approaches for her murderous daughter, and afterwards her one thought is to avenge her death by pursuing and killing her grandchildren. The relationship between the two women therefore is one of contiguity. The niece on the other hand, feels sufficiently removed from her aunt to be able to kill her with her own hands; and yet, as her grandmother constantly proclaims during the story, she is like her, since both are incestuous, although one fails to consummate the incest, whereas the other succeeds. Thus, the mother, who is contiguous with her daughter, becomes a real ogress and transposes on the literal plane the function which remained figurative in the case of her daughter. Symmetrically, the niece, who resembles her aunt, actually commits incest, thus transposing on to the literal level the act which the aunt had only managed to achieve figuratively by lying down beside her brother.

The reader need only look at the relationships shown in Figure 4 to see that the family structure described in the myth is, as it were, folded back upon itself along three axes: the mother is superimposed on the daughter; the potentially incestuous uncle and aunt are superimposed on the actually incestuous nephew and niece; the sister-in-law who conjoins the high and

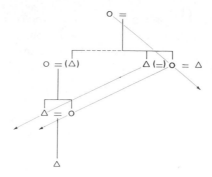

Figure 4. The genealogical pattern of myth M_{538}

the low is superimposed on the brother-in-law, who disjoins the near and the far; with the result that the set of relationships forms a perfectly closed system from which nothing can now emerge except Aishísh, whose adventures provide the sequel of the story.

Who, then, is the incestuous sister? In Barker's version she is described, periphrastically, as 'the red-headed woman from Sprague River', that is, we are told about her physical appearance and where she lives with her husband, to the north-east of Upper Klamath Lake. The place called Gowasdi is located above the northern end of the lake, approximately at the junction of Sprague River and Williamson River, the combined waters of which enter the lake a little farther south (Figure 5). The myth does not give the name of the aquatic animal with the strange cry that she turns into after committing her crimes.

A very old Modoc version, obtained by Curtin from an Indian woman who had been deported to Oklahoma in 1873, enables us to solve these puzzles, while at the same time presenting us with another. This version, which is just as complex as Barker's, links the story of the incestuous sister with the exploits of two celestial brothers, who are probably the same as the two children stuck together, but it seems at first sight to have no connection either with the story of Aishísh or with that of the bird-nester:

M_{539}. *Modoc. 'The star brothers'*

At the time when animals and humans were indistinguishable from each other, five brothers lived on the south side of Klamath Lake. They were bad men. The eldest was married to Meadow Lark but the other four brothers were without wives. The youngest was called Tûtats. His sister Tekewas, now married to Otter who lived not far away, had been very fond of Tûtats ever since she was a little girl. But although she always tried to prolong her visits every time she came to see the family, she never saw her beloved brother because her mother kept him hidden underground in a big bark basket and only brought him out when no one was there.

One day, when he had been taken to the river to swim, Tûtats lost a hair (from his head). On her next visit, Tekewas found it and asked her mother about it. 'Why do you come so often and bother your brothers?' replied the mother. 'You are Otter's wife and you should stay with him.' The next time she came back laden with presents and promised to give beads to whichever brother would take her back to her husband's house. Tekewas refused each one in turn and said she wanted Tûtats to go with her. At the same time she told the sun to go quickly so that it would be dark soon.

Since what her brothers feared most was that she would stay all night, they decided to get Tûtats out. They combed his long hair which reached down to his feet and handed him over to his sister, without paying any attention to his tears, for he did not want to go with his sister.

He walked behind her crying. Tekewas scolded the sun so severely that he was scared and disappeared below the horizon. They had to camp. Brother and sister lay down and, as soon as he was asleep, she went over to lie by him, which woke him up. Taking advantage of the fact that the sister was asleep, he put a log by her side and hurried home to warn his brothers of the danger threatening them. For he thought his sister would come and kill them all.

The brothers asked Spider to put them in her basket and take them up into the sky. Tekewas came along and was so mad at having been left behind that she set the house on fire. Although Spider had told the brothers not to look down until she had reached the sky, one brother looked down over the edge (of the basket). That minute the web broke and the five brothers fell out into the fire.

Meanwhile, the mother and daughter were fighting, each armed with a wooden paddle. Tekewas knocked her mother's paddle into the fire, and pushed her brothers one at a time into the flames with her own paddle. The two women were now fighting, the mother on the south side of the fire and Tekewas on the north side. The mother managed to pull Tûtats' heart out of the fire and changed him into Mount Shasta; then she retrieved the other four hearts and each heart became a mountain, but less high than Mount Shasta.[2]

[2] The Klamath and Modoc, who used to cremate their dead, still remembered in 1925–6 that the heart was the part of the body most difficult to burn (Spier 2, p. 72).

When Tekewas thought she had killed her brothers, she went home to her husband's house. The mother hunted for Meadow Lark; she was dead too but had given birth to twins. The old woman pressed them together and they became one child, whom she called Wéahjukéwas. She made a hole in the ground and hid him.

Before long, Tekewas came back to the house to bother her mother; on seeing a little blanket the grandmother had forgotten, Tekewas realized that Meadow Lark's child was still alive. The old woman denied this but helped her grandson to grow up quickly by magical means, and warned him to remain hidden in the long grass. The child began to trap birds and he learned their language. One day he noticed his shadow was double. He shot an arrow up into the sky; the arrow came back and split off one half of him. He changed his brother into a baby and reared him secretly, pretending he had lost all his things in order to wheedle extra food, clothes and arrows from his grandmother. The latter finally noticed that he had only one head; he had to tell her his secret. The old woman looked after both children and hid them more carefully than before.

Tekewas continued to harass her mother. 'Go off,' cried her mother, but to no purpose. 'You have killed your brothers. My spirit is old. You can kill me if you want to, but don't torment me. Go away and let me alone.' But Tekewas had spotted the children's tracks. One day, the children wounded a white-necked duck who promised to talk to them if they took the arrow out of his wound. When this was done, the bird told them the story of their parents and warned them that their aunt was trying to kill them. She now lived in a lake in the form of a duck: when she assumed human form she had long red hair. They could kill her if they wanted to, but without telling their grandmother of their intentions. She would certainly not allow this, for she could have killed her daughter and saved their father, had she wanted to.

The boys went duck shooting and obtained from their grandmother a canoe, strong arrows and a sharp knife. One day they saw long red hair floating in the water and their aunt's ugly head. The woman taunted and threatened them. She also put her breast against the side of the canoe and tried to tip it over. The grandmother heard their loud screams but they reassured her, saying, 'We belong to the earth; she won't hurt us.' The next time Tekewas tried to tip the canoe over they cut off her head. The blood made the water black and to this day it still is black around that place. They pushed the body down into a deep hole among the rocks in the water and told her: 'You will never be great again. You will be small and weak and people will say that you are too nasty to eat.' The spirit at once left the body and flew around the lake in the form of an ugly bird.

Then the boys shot a large quantity of ducks, and while the grandmother prepared to bring them in, they asked everything inside the house to help them — the fire, the water, the wood, the bows and arrows, the pounder, the basket and the digging tools, but they forgot Awl. When the old woman screamed with rage at finding her daughter's severed head under the pile of ducks, Awl revealed that the two boys had fled through a hole near the fire.

The boys travelled towards the east because they wanted to be servants of the sun. The first house they visited on the south side of Tula Lake was their aunt's. She was Duck, the wife of Bull Snake, and they taught her and all the other animals not to carry their young in their forehead. They killed their uncle and changed the pieces of his body into rocks and snakes.

Still travelling eastwards, they experienced a series of adventures, during which several localities were given the names they have today. On the way they talked about which one they would rather serve, the sun or the moon. The elder said he would rather serve the sun; the younger preferred the moon, so that people couldn't see him. 'But,' replied the other brother, 'people will always look at us. They will watch for us and be glad when they see us.'

They arrived at the home of the ogre Yaukùl, who had two servants, Crow and Louse. The elder brother killed the ogre in a fight and changed him into a predatory bird which caught dead fish. He changed his two servants into the creatures whose names they bore. In spite of their aunt Duck's warning, they crossed the mountains because they wanted to go on travelling eastwards, and there they met Yahyáhaäs, the one-legged giant. Five times running they attacked him and got the better of him, either by breaking his pipe while theirs remained impervious to all the giant's attempts to break or pound it, or in a wrestling contest. Finally they forced the giant to wander eternally around on the mountains, and to appear in dreams to doctors (shamans) who had become his servants. In return, the giant condemned them to become no longer persons but stars 'and between summer and winter, people will fight over you'. The brothers changed into stars which are visible early in the morning towards the end of winter and which are the heralds of spring (Curtin 1, pp. 95–117).

I have replaced all proper nouns by their semantic equivalents, wherever

Curtin provides a translation. Several are not translated, but sometimes these gaps can be filled. For instance, Yaukùl certainly means 'bald eagle', as is clear both from the description of the animal into which he is changed by the Dioscuri, and from the Klamath homophone, *yawá¡l*, which has that meaning (Barker 2, p. 466). Similarly, the fate to which Yahyáhaäs is condemned by his victors must obviously be linked with the Klamath word *yayaya-as* (Barker 2, p. 467, *yay'ahy?as*) 'a bewitching power which inspires the magician when he casts his formidable spells, known to the natives as shaman's poison' (Gatschet 1, Part II, p. 100). We cannot be so specific about the interpretation of Tekewas, the name of the incestuous sister, and Tûtats, that of her brother. Perhaps Tekewas comes from the Klamath root *tak* meaning red.[3] It will be remembered that in the Klamath version this character is called the 'red-headed woman', and in the Modoc version too the colour red is stressed: when seen from a distance the woman appears to be red all over (*loc. cit.*, pp. 96, 99). As for the name Tûtats, there might be a link with the Klamath word *túta*, 'to remove, seize, snatch' (Gatschet 1, Part II, p. 423), because the hero is brought out from an underground hiding place, and also because there is, in Wintu mythology, a disinterred hero called Tulchucherris, whose name means a 'person or a thing taken from the ground' (Curtis 3, p. 121; cf. also Xaxōwilwal, the 'disinterred man', the name of the same hero in Hupa mythology, Goddard 1, pp. 135–49, or Wanátcaláiyawēk in Wiyot, Reichard 1, pp. 162–5).

On the other hand, there is nothing ambiguous about the first part of the myth. It corresponds in all respects to a famous myth known as 'Loon Woman', the fifteen or so versions of which, all of north Californian origin, were catalogued and analysed by Demetracopoulou. We must now add the Klamath version from southern Oregon which could not have been known to Demetracopoulou, as well as certain Chinook variants which are probably confined to the story of the split twin; but it will become clear from the Klamath version that this episode plays a fundamental part in the story. Wherever it occurs, we can assume that the Loon Woman myth is also present, either directly or in a modified form. Demetracopoulou's study is useful on so many points that it would be wrong to criticize her for the inadequacies of her method, which was based on the historical approach, no other method being in fact available at the time. I have already refuted the principles of the historical school (*OTM*, pp. 227–33). On the one hand, the

---

[3] I would also like to mention in passing, but without insisting on it since it is possibly only superficial, the resemblance between Tekewas and the name of the Modoc heroine, Letkakawash or Látkakáwas, a character who, in M_{529}, M_{541}, is an inversion of the incestuous sister figure in M_{539} (cf. pp. 45, 78–9).

historical method involves defining the myth arbitrarily, without for one moment envisaging the possibility that it might not be an isolated story, adequately definable in terms of its empirical form, but rather a local or temporary state of a transformation which may give rise to several others, all governed by the same necessity; it follows that the real object on which the analysis should centre is the group as a whole, not any one of its particular features. On the other hand, the myth, after being detached, in accordance with subjective criteria, from the group of which it nevertheless forms a component part, and whose existence has not even been suspected, is then split up into a medley of unrelated episodes, elements or themes which are unfolded at random according to whatever whim or lapse of memory it is convenient to impute to the story-tellers: absent from one version and present in another, they are found outside the myths in different contexts, 'there being nothing intrinsic in the incidents themselves which would cause them to adhere to one another in a set pattern and thus initiate a myth' (Demetracopoulou, p. 120). In these conditions, if the myth under consideration presents a certain unity, this unity can only be supplied by a central theme which, in order to assume a tangible form, must choose from an albeit amorphous tradition those images and incidents best suited to serve its purpose. According to Demetracopoulou, the motif in this case may be described as catastrophic incest, which brings destruction to the community as a whole, and the victims of which try to seek revenge. However, apart from the fact that this simplistic formulation leaves out all the concrete substance of the myth — although, as we shall see, every detail is, as it happens, strictly motivated — it makes no attempt to explain the denominators common to several versions, in particular the one which has given its name to the myth, since it has generally appeared to be the most constant and the most important, namely, the transformation of the incestuous sister into a loon. But, what is even more serious, this wrong approach leads at the same time to the introduction into the myth of such gratuitous suppositions as that '. . . the welfare of the family and the community depends on the successful concealment of a beautiful child' (loc. cit., p. 122). I shall demonstrate that the solution of the problem of the hidden child is much simpler, provided we look for it in the actual material of the myth, and not in the mind of a mythographer keen to suggest an interpretation: a boy, much loved by his parents and concealed by them in an underground pit inside the family house, stands in a symmetrical relationship to the boy hated by his affine and abandoned by him at the top of a tree in the brush: the hidden child is therefore an inversion of the bird-nester.

Before we reach the point at which this equivalence can be proved, much ground will have to be covered in order to link up the various stages of the transformation. I shall begin by explaining the organization and distribution of the Loon myth, with the help of the syncretic version worked out by Demetracopoulou (pp. 107–108).

The parents of an exceptionally handsome boy hide him away, in particular from the attentions of the opposite sex. A woman, often the hero's sister, picks up a (long) hair and decides to marry the man to whom it belongs. She discovers who he is, forces him to accompany her, and asks the sun to disappear in order to hasten the coming of darkness, so that she can share the adolescent's bed. The latter is either reluctant to yield to the woman's advances or unable to succumb to them, for before he left something had been done to him by his parents to prevent intercourse. He escapes, leaving a log in his place.

Fearing the woman's anger, the whole family decides to escape to the sky, with or without the help of the spider. One member of the family makes the mistake of looking down during the ascent, the cord breaks and he and his companions fall into a fire, which has either been lit by the woman or by the escaping group themselves (M_{545a}). The fire usually starts a world conflagration. All the victims are burnt up, except for their hearts, which the woman makes into a necklace. Or else one bursting heart flies out of the flames and falls a long way away. Two sisters discover it, reconstitute the body from this one organ, resuscitate it and marry the boy.

According to other versions (including those of the Klamath and the Modoc), one of the victims of the fire gives birth posthumously to two children, whom their grandmother forms into a single being but who later revert to being separate individuals. These children, or the child or children of the resuscitated hero (M_{545a}), are told the story of their birth by a bird whose life they have spared. They kill the culprit who changes into a diver (loon), rescue the hearts and bring their parents back to life.

In this basic form the myth is found over a relatively limited area, which includes adjacent tribes in northern California and also, as we have seen, in southern Oregon. From south to north, these are, in order, the Yana, the Wintu, the Atsugewi, the Achomawi, the Shasta, the Karok and the Modoc (Demetracopoulou, pp. 102–103), to whom must now be added the Klamath. The area of distribution is hardly more than three hundred kilometres in length, and there seems to be no doubt that all the versions have a common origin. Demetracopoulou (pp. 103–107) quotes a Wintu version as an example (M_{545a}). It includes a lamentation in the original dialect on which the author offers no comment, but containing the names

Anana and Omanut, corresponding to Aniduidui and Ommanutc, the chief characters in the Shasta versions (Dixon 1, p. 14) or Ane'diwi'dowit and O'manuts (Frachtenberg 2, p. 212).[4] This point is not without significance, since we shall see (see below, pp. 116, 117) that the Yana versions, although southern in origin, look northwards, as it were. Consequently, I do not think I am misrepresenting the facts in keeping the Klamath and Modoc versions at the centre of the discussion.

It so happens that in 1884 Curtin recorded a shorter Modoc version containing original elements. These make it possible to effect a transition to another Modoc myth which, by completing an initial phase of my argument, brings me back to the story of the birth of Aishísh, the point from which I started (M_{529}), but which was completely left out of the first Curtin version of the Loon Woman myth.

M_{540}. *Modoc. 'The Loon Woman'*

Five wildcat brothers and their two sisters lived together. All the brothers were married except the youngest. So great was his beauty that his father and mother kept him in a basket under the ground. Every night they brought him out, washed his face, combed his hair and fed him, and put him back before his brothers and sisters were awake.

However, the eldest sister had had such tender feelings towards him ever since the time when he was a baby, that she would marry no one else. To the great indignation of her elder brother, she would lie every night on the ground near the hole where his basket was. When the Chief's son asked her to marry him, the girl was angry: 'If you want him in the house,' she told her mother who was trying to persuade her, 'you can marry him yourself.' She wanted to make everyone do as she liked.

One day, the hidden boy told his parents that his sister uncovered his basket and talked to him. He begged them to take him to a little island out in the ocean.[5] The eldest of the brothers and his youngest sister fed him in secret.

---

[4] On the other hand, the name of the Wintu hero, Talimleluheres, meaning perhaps 'the one who was made (or who became) beautiful' (DuBois-Demetracopoulou, p. 335) is to be considered in the light of my remarks on p. 35.

[5] The term thus translated by Curtin cannot refer to the sea, but, as is explained later in the myth, means a very large lake. All the known evidence points to the fact that, in ancient times, the Klamath and the Modoc were unacquainted with either salt or the sea. The Klamath referred to the sea by means of a compound word derived from the Chinook dialect: *solcoq* literally 'salt' and 'water' (Barker 2, pp. 79, 384).

The elder sister hunted everywhere for her beloved, over the mountains and out on the flats. At last she discovered the island where her
younger sister was mounting guard. However, the latter had managed to
escape with her brother in a magic canoe made from a hollowed out spear
of tula grass. The elder sister was mad; then she sat up on her knees and
began to travel fast and as she travelled a terrible fire roared and blazed.
The village where her parents lived caught fire. Some inhabitants became
animals, the others were burnt up, including the family of the girl who
had started the fire. Only the little sister escaped, for she too was a
powerful sorceress.

The elder sister took her victims' hearts and made herself a necklace
from them. Then she swam back to live on the island. The little sister felt
lonesome. For a long time she watched her sister. While she was asleep
she took the hearts, then cut off her sister's head, which went back on to
the body uttering a mournful noise: 'Cry all you want to,' said the
younger sister picking up a handful of ashes and throwing them over her,
'You can never burn people up again. Henceforth you will always live in
the water. When people taste you they will say that your flesh doesn't
taste good and they will spit it out.' Right away the wicked sister
changed into a large sea-bird and flew away from the lake.

The girl rebuilt the houses by magical means. She gathered together
all the bones she could find and put them in a basket of boiling water. She
rolled herself up tight in a mat and hid her face.

At sunset, all the dead revived and went back to their houses, where
they lived very happily (Curtin 1, pp. 268–71).

This version corresponds still more closely to the Loon Woman myth
than the first part of M_{538} and M_{539}. However, at the same time, certain
significant changes can be noted in relation to previous versions. The
incestuous sister, instead of entering into an exogamous marriage, is
determined to remain a spinster. She rejects a good match and refuses to
leave the family home because she does not want to move away from her
beloved brother. Her counterpart in $M_{538-539}$ merely returns to visit her
family more frequently than custom demands. Consequently, in M_{540}, the
portrait of the incestuous sister is more vigorously drawn and she is more
sharply defined. One the other hand, the interchangeability between
mother and daughter, which in the previous myths provided a means of
keeping the action going, is no more than hinted at in this myth, when the
daughter suggests ironically that the mother should marry the husband
intended for herself. The truth is that there is no need to keep the action

going in M_{540}, since the story leads directly to the collective resuscitation with which the Loon Woman myth usually ends.

Not only is the heroine of M_{540} changed from a married into an unmarried woman, she also splits up into two diametrically opposed sisters. I am using the verb here in the figurative sense, although not forgetting that the other myths describe what must be interpreted as a literal instance of splitting, since it concerns a character who is in fact two children who have been stuck together.

The younger sister in M_{540}, who decapitates her elder sister and brings about her transformation into a water bird, plays the same part as the niece in M_{538}: the latter also kills her incestuous aunt and changes her into a bird; and yet she is like her, since she has the same feelings towards her own brother as the other woman has towards hers. Consequently, in the one instance the myth presents us with an aunt and her niece who are in opposition to each other, yet alike; in the other, with two sisters, also from different age groups, who are opposed to each other because they are not alike. It will be remembered that, in M_{539}, the niece and nephew of M_{538} are changed into twins of the same sex, but that in the course of the story a pretended age difference is introduced between them. They are siblings like the two women in M_{540}, but belong to the opposite sex and yet are so alike mentally that together they carry out the same decapitation which, in the other myths, is entrusted to only one of the two characters, who then proceeds to decapitate the other.

Let us leave aside for the moment this last stage of the permutation and reflect on the one illustrated by M_{540}. It initiates an inversion of $M_{538-539}$, which must now be examined since it clearly belongs to the same group as the preceding transformations; however, being radical in nature, it allows a clearer definition of the semantic field covered by all the myths.

M_{511}. Modoc. 'The story of Aishish'

Once upon a time there was a young Indian woman who lived with her five brothers on the south side of Klamath Lake. She was called Lát-kakáwas. Every day the brothers went fishing in a canoe near an island in the middle of the lake. Látkakáwas prepared food for her brothers and only left home to gather wild seeds. When she was at work she looked like a common old woman, but 'when she shook herself and went out of the house, she was young, blue and beautiful'.

Kmúkamch, the Old Man [Kumush in Modoc, but I shall continue to use the Klamath name], lived on the eastern side of the lake. The people living on the western side used to admire Látkakáwas's beauty when she changed from looking like an old hunch-backed woman. Each young man from the village tried in turn to steal up to her before she could make herself old and ugly: they were disappointed and made fun of her.

All day the heroine's brothers went to catch and dry salmon; they returned as soon as it was dark. One night she complained to her eldest brother that men were coming to visit and pester her. He promised her that as soon as she had finished gathering enough seeds, he would take her to the island where no one would bother her.

On the west side of the lake lived a young man so beautiful that his father kept him in a basket. When all the village youths had failed to get near to Látkakáwas, the young man was taken out of his underground hiding place and dressed in beautiful clothes; he was 'blue, golden and green like the clouds in the sky', and he was beautiful beyond anything in the world. He was given magic powers so that by travelling underground he could surprise the heroine at daybreak. Látkakáwas knew he was there, he pleased her, so she did not turn old. They did not exchange a word and Látkakáwas related the incident to her brothers.

The latter decided to move to the island the very next day. Just about sundown they had caught two big salmon. They would go at dawn and dress them and then come back for their sister who would meanwhile pack up her belongings. But as soon as they left, the visitor from the west appeared, and he shone with so bright a light that the young girl was dazzled.

Early in the forenoon, the five brothers arrived and began to pull down the house. At midday they spread mats from the house to the canoe for Látkakáwas to walk on. When she got into the boat she forgot all about the visitor and even forgot that she had fallen in love with him. But the young man was holding on to the canoe, although they did not see him. The brothers worked in vain until the middle of the afternoon; they were exhausted. Then the young man freed the canoe.

However, he swam behind them in the form of a salmon, because he wanted to see the girl he loved. She sat in the middle of the canoe with one of her brothers. Two brothers sat in the front of the canoe and two at the end.

As they paddled along, one of the brothers saw a beautiful salmon, all blue, gold and green. He speared it and pulled it into the canoe, and at that moment the fish changed into a young man; but he died at once.

Látkakáwas cried and blamed her brothers. The brothers felt badly; they burned the young man's body along with offerings of beads and mats. They took from the ashes a disk as bright as the sun in the heavens: it was the crown of the young man's head. 'Take it to Kmúkamch,' said the brother who had killed the salmon to his sister. 'He is at Nihlaski in his sweat-house. He can bring a man to life with only one hair from his head.'

Látkakáwas put the disk in her bosom, gave each of her brothers a bundle of head-scratchers (in connection with the mourning ritual, cf. *OTM*, p. 504) and said she would never return again if the demiurge did not bring her husband back to life. She travelled all day and when night came camped at Koaskisé and at dawn gave birth to a wonderfully beautiful boy. According to native custom, she strapped the baby on to a board, put the board on her back and went off to the demiurge's sweat-house.

She made her request. Kmúkamch boiled the disk in a basket of water, into which he put heated stones, and told Látkakáwas not to look. After a little while the disk came to life again, but when Kmúkamch saw how beautiful the young man was, he became jealous and at once resolved to kill him so that he could get the disk and at the same time acquire the young man's beauty.

When Látkakáwas unwrapped herself, she saw that her husband was dead and she cried all the time the demiurge was preparing the funeral pyre. She asked him to put more wood on the fire and when the body was half-consumed, she got up, put the baby on her back and leapt into the flames. The demiurge just had time to snatch the child from the fire.

The baby cried and cried until it heard the name it wanted to hear [Isis in Curtin's transcription: I shall continue to use the form Aishísh]. The demiurge found the disk among the ashes and tried to put it on his knee, under his arm, on his breast, his forehead and his shoulders. But it would not stay anywhere. Finally he managed to fit it into the small of his back. Right away he became young and beautiful. Since 'the father of Aishísh' disk had become part of him, he himself became the child's father.

Then Kmúkamch travelled towards the north and hid the baby in his knee. Two old women, in whose house he spent the night, delivered it. To those who asked where the child had come from, he replied, 'The earth has given me this baby son' (cf. M$_{539}$ 'We belong to the earth', p. 58). Then he went to live on the south-east side of Tula Lake and reared the child. When Aishísh was old enough to marry, the Mowatwas ['people from the south', tribes from the Pit River area, cf. Barker 2, under *mowat*] brought him a hardworking woman called Mole. Crow turned everyone to stone, including the demiurge and his son. But they at once became men again and went off to live in Leklis [a locality to the north of Tula Lake, cf. Ray 3, p. 209; *liklis*].

At this point, there occur several similarly constructed episodes which I propose to group under the heading of 'initiatory sequence'. The demiurge sends his son into desolate places, which are the haunts of spirits. In order to win their protection, he has to plunge into icy mountain lakes, carry and pile up stones until he becomes exhausted, pray and dream. The hero overcomes all these ordeals and returns endowed with magic powers. Now he could be a great chief, but his father dissuades him: 'We will go away where you can keep all the strength the mountains and swimming places have given you, and where you won't get bad and dirty from the earth and people.' As can be seen, the demiurge is no advocate of social commitment! He and his son prepare to build themselves a fine dwelling at the top of a mountain. Kmúkamch occupies the northern half of it and Aishísh the southern half. The door opened towards the east. The myth continues as follows:

On that mountain, which they thought uninhabited, lived two women, Tree Toad and Nada, a bird (cf. Gatschet 1, Part II, p. 230: Klamath *na'ta*, 'a species of small black duck'; Barker 2, p. 275: *n'a.t'a*, 'common or Wilson snipe'). They both fell in love with Aishísh and wanted him to be their husband. The demiurge said he would accept the one who could bring water first from the lake. Tree Toad came back first because she had found some water in a pool, but the hero chose the fresh water Nada brought. The demiurge tore Toad to pieces. The pieces became rocks, which are in the lake now.

Still enamoured of solitude, the heroes travelled towards the northeast and eventually came to Lost River which the demiurge filled with salmon and histis fish (cf. Barker 2, p. 187: Klamath *hist'y*, 'mullet sp.'). After further wanderings, father and son took leave of each other. Aishísh took up his abode on a mountain on the eastern side of Tula Lake, and Kmúkamch started off for the west.

Aishísh had many wives in his new abode: Mole, Badger, Ducks and other birds, Butterfly . . . The one called Wren (?Gatschet 1, Part II, p. 437: Klamath *tcika*, 'a little grey or dark-coloured bird building its nest in the grass', or a chaffinch; cf. Barker 2, p. 88, *c'ikay*, 'snow-bird, chaffinch') soon had a son. But she was uneasy about Kmúkamch's absence.

However, Kmúkamch returned, bringing with him bundles of seeds which he threw in different directions. That is the origin of wild plants. And since he had fallen in love with his son's wives, he began to think how to get rid of Aishísh.

Using as a pretext the fact that he had no feathers for his arrows, he sent Aishísh to find some young eagles at the top of a tree. Aishísh took off his clothes and climbed up to the nest, then threw the eagles to the ground. As he threw the last one, he saw that the tree, at Kmúkamch's word, had grown so tall that it almost touched the sky. The demiurge picked up Aishísh's clothes and put them on.

When he came back, the women thought at first that he was their husband. Kmúkamch hurried the sun down and right away it was dark. Only Butterfly, Badger, Wren and Mole suspected the truth. The next morning they refused to go with him, along with the other wives, to Pitcowa, a broad flat north-east of Tula Lake, a place where a gambling contest was to take place. As he travelled, Kmúkamch set fire to the grass. As the smoke did not go straight up into the sky, his companions became suspicious.

Meanwhile, Butterfly and Badger were tracking their husband. They found him half-dead at the top of a tree, which Badger tried to uproot but could not. Butterfly managed to reach the top. She fed Aishísh and rubbed him with bear fat; he was almost a skeleton. Then she brought him down in a basket.

The two women looked after Aishísh and gave him clothes. They also told him about the other wives' misbehaviour. After the gambling was over, the people began to play ball at Pitcowa. When Kmúkamch stooped to pick up the ball, a doctor (shaman) made the south wind blow. This raised his blanket, and everyone saw the disk on his back, which looked like a great scar. Then they knew it was Kmúkamch and they whooped and laughed.

When Aishísh was restored to health, he set off, with his two faithful wives. As he travelled, he set fire to the grass; the smoke went straight up into the sky, showing that Aishísh was coming. Kmúkamch was scared and started to tremble. The first person to see Aishísh was his little boy. The mother was almost out of her mind; she had been camping with the child and feeding him on roots. 'Yes,' the hero said to her, 'the two wives I didn't care for saved me.'

The demiurge tried in vain to placate his son. But Aishísh had a big fire built, called to his wives who were with Kmúkamch and burnt their feet. Then he changed them into ducks and water birds for future people to eat. Then he threw Kmúkamch into the fire and burnt him to ashes. But in the ashes was the disk.

The next morning at dawn the morning star, Kmúkamch's magic charm (medicine), called out to the disk: 'Why do you sleep so long? Get up, old man!' That minute Kmúkamch came alive. Henceforth, he was to live as long as the disk and the morning star.

Aishísh now knew that his father was immortal. He wandered for a long time in the mountains and, as he travelled, he sang a beautiful song that no one else could sing. Kmúkamch followed Aishísh everywhere for years and at last overtook him. He wanted to be reconciled with his son, but Aishísh refused: 'Go wherever you want to in the world and I will go wherever I want to. I feel you are not my father. I hope that when the people who are to come into the world hereafter arrive, no father will ever treat his son as you have treated me.' Kmúkamch went to Tula Lake to live. Aishísh turned one of his faithful wives into a butterfly, another into a badger and a third into a wren. Then he went to live alone on the top of Mount Tcutgosi (Curtin 1, pp. 1–16).

I would like to begin my analysis of this long myth by drawing attention to the frequent references made in it to real-life customs, such as the catching and drying of salmon, the dismantling of the winter house, the cremation of corpses with offerings, sweat-baths and initiation rites – the latter being described in such minute detail that this part of the myth reads like a course in religious instruction – and contests involving games of skill or chance. At the same time, the initiatory sequence is in several ways a reversal of the one at the end of M_{539}.

To begin with, it is not situated at the same point in the myth, since in M_{541} it occurs earlier in the story. Secondly, M_{541} describes the initiation from the male standpoint: it enumerates the ordeals, indicates the localities concerned and gives an account of the novice's emotions, while leaving undefined the supernatural beings revealed by dreams or hallucinations. Running counter to this empirical approach, M_{539} adopts the viewpoint of the spirits themselves, and makes them the protagonists of the story. The heroes measure their strength against them in the course of ordeals which bear no direct resemblance to those the Indians have to face in their quest for supernatural protection.

However, the initiation is not the same in both cases. Among the Klamath, shamanism was not an exclusive privilege reserved for the few; all individuals whose supernatural powers were above average could claim the status of shaman (Spier 2, p. 107); however, ordinary revelations had to be actively sought by the novices, whereas in Modoc society the intiative rested with the spirits who determined shamanistic vocations (Ray 3, p. 31). So the former revelations originated, as it were, in front of the looking-glass, the latter behind it. It is clear that M_{541} is concerned with the quest for power which was obligatory for all adolescent boys and even supplies its origin by presenting the hero as the first initiate. On the contrary, in the corresponding sequence of M_{539}, we are given an account of the origin of shamanistic initiation: after encountering several exceptionally formidable spirits, the heroes confront the giant Yahyáhaäs (see above, p. 59), whom they vanquish and force to become the special patron of shamans. The myths also formulate the opposition in another way: they refer implicitly to the characteristic dualism of Klamath society, which made a clear distinction between the power of a chief or of a man richly endowed with material possessions — in Klamath one word served for both — (Spier 2, p. 38; Barker 2, p. 212) and the powers of a shaman. Once his initiation is completed, Aishísh could become a great chief, but he chooses not to, whereas no sooner have the dioscuri in M_{539} instituted the magic power of shamans than they are denied the right to use it, since this same power has arranged a different destiny for them. What exactly does this mean? Aishísh has no wish to dirty his hands by becoming involved in politics; he therefore deprives men of his wisdom and abandons them to the vagaries of fate. Aishísh's non-participation in human affairs becomes negative participation in the other myth, which describes only the maleficent aspect of shamanism, the 'poison' used by shamans to cast spells on their fellow-Indians.[6] So, in the one instance a 'non-chief', in the other 'non-shamans', bear the responsibility for human wretchedness: the former because he deprived men of the good chief he might have been; the latter through having given mankind bad shamans.

It will be remembered that at the end of M_{539} the dioscuri become stars. So the parallel which has just been established with the other version strengthens the hypothesis that Kmúkamch and Aishísh also have an astronomical connotation. No doubt Curtin's narratives have to be treated with a certain caution since, like Gatschet, he was so obsessed with solar mythology that one sometimes wonders if his passion did not lead him in all innocence to embellish the text with appropriate details. But even if we make adequate allowance for this bias, it seems certain — unless we reject the text en bloc — that Aishísh's real father, and Kmúkamch his adoptive father, are on the sun's side, and Aishísh and his mother on the side of the moon.

[6] This does not mean that, in other areas, the deadly power of the shamans cannot be put to beneficent use, as is explained in different myths (Curtin 1, pp. 148–58).

Aishísh's father lives eternally in a shining disc, which the demiurge incorporates into his own body and thanks to which, although he is reduced to ashes every evening, he is recalled to life at daybreak by the morning star. Aishísh's mother appears alternately either as a ravishing young girl or as an old hunch-backed woman, two characters one is tempted to interpret as being the full moon and the crescent moon.

In support of this astronomical dualism, I have already mentioned that present in the corresponding Ge myths (see above, pp. 46–7), at the same time noting, however, that the astronomical functions of the protagonists are inverted as between North and South America. M_{541} makes it possible to overcome this difficulty, thanks to the episode in which the two heroes decide to leave the earth and go and live in an almost celestial abode: on the inaccessible summit of a mountain, where they build a splendid red house of which the demiurge occupies the northern part and his son the southern part (cf. also M_{539}, above, p. 57). Consequently, and in spite of the fact that the bird-nester and his persecutor are alternatively sun or moon according to whether the myths originate in Brazil or in the northern hemisphere, their position remains constant in respect of the cardinal points: in Modoc as in Serenté mythology, the persecutor belongs to the northern moiety, the victim to the southern moiety. In the movement from one hemisphere to the other, only the sun and the moon change sides.

Another episode still further strengthens the hypothesis of an astronomical connotation, although it relates to much less remote myths. In the incident featuring the two women – one a toad, the other a bird – who claim the hero as their husband, and whom the former's father puts to the test by sending them to fetch water, it is not difficult to recognize the myth featuring the wives of the sun and moon which was discussed at length in the previous volume (*OTM*, Parts IV and V). No doubt, what we find in M_{541} is no more than an allusion, but it is one which is also present, as will be seen later, in the mythology of the Nez Percé ($M_{661a, b}$). But, in both North and South America, the opposition is between a hardworking woman and a frog, two beings whose relative qualities are to be decided through a contest organized by two ascendants. In both these cases, the frog proves to be lazy, and also dirty, either because she emits black saliva or because she brings back water from a stagnant pool. In the myth featuring the wives of the sun and moon, the two women climb up into the sky in order to marry the brothers, Sun and Moon. In the Modoc myth, they climb a high mountain in order to live with a man and his father, who have an undoubted affinity with the same celestial bodies.

I have said that many details in the Modoc myth are a reflection of anthropological reality. The myth is no less observant of geographical truth, since all the localities named actually exist. In the course of their wanderings, the heroes stop at places which can often be located on the available maps. They modify the original landscape, leaving their mark as they travel by creating sources of food or surface irregularities, such as fish, vegetation and rocks, which are still in existence in each locality.

At the beginning of the myth, we are on the south side of Lake Klamath. But which Lake Klamath? There are (or rather, there used to be, the area having since dried up) two lakes of this name, about thirty kilometres apart, the upper lake in Klamath country and the lower one in Modoc country. It is therefore tempting to opt for the lower lake, but two reasons rule it out. Nihlaksi, the demiurge's abode to which the heroine journeys so that her husband can be brought back to life, is a 'bold headland culminating in an elevation reaching about 6,680 feet bordering on Upper Klamath Lake' (see the map in: Gatschet 1, Part I, *nilakshi*, 'day-break', *ibid.*, p. xx); she stops on the way at Koaskisé, a locality the name of which is reminiscent of the Kohasti in Gatschet's transcription (*loc. cit.*), and is none other than the Gowasdi named in M$_{539}$, a village at the northern tip of the upper lake (cf. also Spier 5, p. 16: *kowa'cdi*; Barker 1, p. 196: *gowasdi*).

After his encounter with the heroine, the demiurge first heads northwards. Then, travelling possibly in the opposite direction (although no mention is made of this in the myth), he takes up his abode to the south-west of Tule Lake, then at Leklis (Ray 3, p. 209: *liklis*), which is in the north. This series of cross-country journeys brings the hero to Lâniswi (Ray 3, p. 208: *lani'shwi*) in the extreme south of Modoc country, then to Sla'kkosi, which it is difficult to identify (Ray 3, p. 210, *chalklo'ki* is a good way to the east). On the other hand, there is no doubt about the next stage in the initiatory peregrination: 'Gewa'sni, a pond deep down among the rocks on the summit of Giwa'syaina' (Curtin 1, p. 8); *yaina* (Gatschet 1, Part II, p. 100; Barker 2, p. 472: *y'ayn'a*) means 'mountain' or 'eminence' in Klamath, and *gewash*, *giwash* (Gatschet 1, Part I, p. xxx; Barker 2, p. 145: *gi. was*) refers to Crater Lake in the extreme north-west of Klamath country. Ada'wa, the next stage, remains uncertain, unless it is the same as Aga'wesh, the Klamath name for the lower lake (Gatschet 1, Part II, p. 16) or Agá (Ray 3, p. 208), a locality to the south-west of the same lake. Then the hero goes to Ka'impeos (cf. Ray 3, pp. 25–6: *ka'umpwis*), to the south of Clear Lake, along the southern border of Modoc country. This last journey completes the sequence.

The inaccessible mountain on which the heroes then take up their abode has no name, but it can be seen from the shores of Tule Lake, which the

Modoc (Ray 3, p. 18) believe to be the centre of the world. From there, the heroes head north-east (Curtin 1, p. 11), explore Lost River and halt for a while at Nusâltgaga (Ray 3, p. 210: *nushaltka'ga*), a place on the bend of the river where it curves northwards. As for the subsequent stages, Bla'ielka, 'Blaiaga, the mountain where Kmúkamch and Aishísh lived' (M_{543}; Curtin 1, p. 37) corresponds perhaps to the outskirts of the town of Bligh or Bly, in the upper valley of the Sprague River bordering on Paiute country (cf. Barker 3, p. 211, *blay*, 'above, high'; Gatschet 1, Part II, p. 215, *m'lai*, 'steep', an element in the names of several mountains). The identity of Mount Kta'ilawetes (from *qday*, 'rock'?) is uncertain. In the myth, Mount Du'ilast, where the heroes take leave of each other, is situated to the east of Tula Lake. M_{543} (Curtin 1, p. 32) refers to Little Shasta by the same name. If this is the mountain so named on the maps, it is several kilometres away in the opposite direction. Despite the distance, it is more probably Mount Lassen, which is about 150 kilometres south-west of Tule Lake and is called Little Shasta by the Yana (Sapir-Swadesh 1, p. 172; Kroeber 1, p. 338). Mount Tcutgosi, the last place mentioned, remains problematical.

However, even after making allowances for any remaining uncertainties and for errors and confusions that may have crept into my account, it is clear from this summary that the leading characters in the myth travel the length and breadth of Modoc territory, and even venture into Klamath country, where the story begins, and which Aishísh has to cross in order to visit the mountains near Crater Lake. This gives an inter-tribal value to the territory in which the myth takes place, a value which is further emphasized by the fact that the heroes, while staying to the south-east of Tule Lake, that is, in the very heart of Modoc country, are visited by the Mo'watwas, 'people from the south' (a name given by the Modoc to the tribes from Pit River and more especially the Achomawi, their traditional enemies), who in the myth, come, however, to offer one of their daughters in marriage. The area covered by the myth thus takes on the character of an indivisible heritage. This explains why a great many of the place names can be found on the map (Figure 5), and why at the same time certain correspondences can be established in the various versions – according to whether they belong to Klamath or Modoc mythology – between northern and southern parts of the country which can be considered as being approximately the counterparts of each other. I have given several reasons for supposing that the Modoc version, like the Klamath one, begins on the shores of upper Klamath Lake, which is in Klamath territory. However, since the heroes set off shortly afterwards in the direction of Tule Lake, which is close to lower Klamath Lake, it is in fact as if they were setting off from the latter.

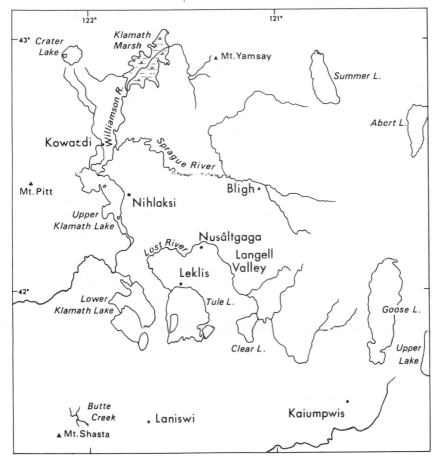

Figure 5. The territory of the Klamath and the Modoc

It is equally worthy of note that an important sequence of the Modoc myth should take place to the north-east of Tule Lake, in the valley of Lost River. Topographically, this region is similar to that lying fifty kilometres or so to the north and comprising upper Klamath Lake, the mouth of Williamson River and its tributary Sprague River, which is the scene of the action in the Klamath version.

In this connection, the name of the locality where the gambling contest is held is particularly significant. According to Curtin, Pitcowa is situated to the north-east of Tule Lake. Gatschet (1, Part I, pp. xx, xxxi; Part II, p. 268) refers by the same name (Pitsua) to an area which is also to the north-east, but of upper Klamath Lake.[7] We may say, then, that whichever special perspective we adopt, that of the Klamath or that of the Modoc, the two geographical patterns play the part of combinatory variants and are interchangeable in topographical contexts which are simply displaced.

When we move from the geographical to the semantic plane, we are no longer dealing with simple instances involving homothetic spaces which, in a sense, can be adjusted so as to be superimposed one upon the other, but with inverted functions. In both the Klamath and Modoc versions of the Loon Woman myth (M_{538}, M_{539}), the main opposition is between a hidden child who is closely guarded by his parents in the family house and a sister obsessed by incestuous desires, although her exogamous marriage has removed her physically as well as mentally from her own kin. Consequently, the initial situation shows the brother as being *inside*, his sister *outside*.

In M_{541}, this pattern is radically reversed. The heroine refuses marriage so as not to leave her brothers, and even wants them to turn her into a secreted girl. However, the real hidden child is an adolescent boy from another village. He visits the heroine in the hope of inducing her to enter into an *exogamous* marriage, and of thus taking her off to the *west*, since his own village is situated west of the lake, while the heroine's is to the south. This union is then a double inversion of the one hoped for by the incestuous sister when, with a view to *endogamous* union, she takes her brother off to her husband's village, which lies to the *east* of their native village. So it is clear that, contrary to the situation in M_{538} and M_{539}, the sister in M_{541} is *inside* and the hidden child *outside*. The latter is no longer a brother whom she would like to turn into a sacrilegious husband, but a stranger, in other words, a non-brother. Furthermore, the match is a particularly desirable one, since the young couple fall in love at first sight.

But, although she is charmed by the beautiful stranger's appearance, the heroine of M_{541} never for a moment considers leaving her brothers. All she asks of them is that they keep her under even closer guard. It is as if she had one overriding passion – to take care of her brothers, to gather edible plants

---

[7] Curtin states precisely that Pitcowa is in the southern part of Langell Valley. In Curtis's version of the Klamath myth (M_{531a}), Aishísh, after being set free by the butterflies, lands at Pitswa, 'a depression in Landsley Valley'. In spite of the able assistance of my eminent colleague, M. Pierre Gourou, it has been impossible to find any valley of this name even on very detailed maps of Oregon. As a last resource, I wrote to Professor Th. Stern of Oregon University, a leading specialist on contemporary Klamath society, and he was kind enough to confirm that no valley in the area has ever been called by this name, and that Curtis's memory probably played him false. In one of the versions recorded by Stern himself (1, 3; M_{531b}), the butterfly-sisters land the hero 'to the east of Mount Shasta'.

and cook for them. In this respect too she is opposed as an *actual mother/ provider* to the *potential mistress* embodied by the sister in the other versions. However, in all cases, the story features a sister who is too concerned about a brother or brothers, since the normal behaviour for a girl is to leave her own family and take a husband, to share his bed and look after his house. So the heroines of M_{538}, M_{541} are all equally guilty of excess, although in different ways. They all misuse the sibling relationship either on the domestic and alimentary level or on the sexual and conjugal level. Each is incestuous in her own way, literally in one case, figuratively in the other.

The Modoc variant, M_{540}, acts as a point of juncture between $M_{538-539}$ and M_{541}. The heroine, like the girl in M_{541}, refuses to get married but is prompted in this by the same unchaste motive which leads the heroine in $M_{538-539}$ to return to her people, although she is married and living away from home. The young hero of M_{540} who, to begin with, is hidden underground in the family house begs to be taken to an island to live under the protection of a young, virtuous sister. The latter is a prefiguration of the heroine in M_{541}, who has to be exiled to an island in order to escape from the amorous intentions of a young hero. He, in turn, echoes the one in M_{540}, with the difference that he is exogenous rather than endogenous.

But there is more to it than that. The incestuous and almost cannibalistic sister in $M_{538-540}$ is disjoined once and for all both from mankind and from her own family when a member of this family kills her and changes her corpse into a loon. The prospective husband in M_{541} changes into a salmon, in an attempt to remain conjoined to those whom he would like to have as his affines, and who, in killing him, restore him to his original human form. The loon is a bird, the salmon a fish; both are connected with water and migrate along an east-west axis (which, as has been noted, plays an important part in the myths). Salmon swim up the rivers from west to east in the spring and autumn (Spier 2, p. 148) and loons, which spend summer on the inland lakes, ponds and rivers, settle near the coast or on the sea-shore when winter comes (Thomson, p. 212; Brasher, Vol. I, p. 3; Godfrey, pp. 11–12).

The relevance of the *loon/salmon* opposition is also brought out clearly by the way in which the myths define the two species by the use of contrasting attributes. Two features of the loon ('huart' in French Canadian: *Gavia immer*) are stressed in particular: its summer plumage, characterized by a black band flecked with white around the neck (Figure 6) of which the heart-necklace motif is reminiscent, and its flesh which is said to be inedible, so that the bird is a form of anti-game. M_{541}, on the other hand, stresses the two reverse features of the salmon: its gleaming iridescent

Figure 6. Great Northern Diver. (Redrawn from Snyder, p. 25)

scales, 'all blue, gold and green' (Curtin 1, p. 4), and its excellence as food, since the brothers, as is explicitly stated in the myth, spend all their time catching and drying salmon. Indeed, they kill the hero, in salmon form, in order to eat him, whereas in the other myths the male or female avenger kills the guilty heroine because, as they explain, once turned into a loon, she is not even edible.

I will try to give a formal definition of this complex system, which consists of no less than five oppositional pairs:

a) [^{2} depraved ^{1}heroine, ^{3}unlawful ^{1}wife of a ^{4}brother] $\Rightarrow$ [^{5}loon];

b) [^{5}salmon] $\Rightarrow$ [^{1}hero, ^{3}lawful ^{1}husband of a ^{2}virtuous ^{4}non-sister];

c) [^{5}loon] = [^{5}salmon $^{(-1)}$].

In transformations a) and b), the inversion of the two members can be explained by the fact that the hero of b) only becomes a lawful husband in the eyes of the woman and her brothers after he has been changed from a living salmon into a dead man. On the contrary, the heroine of a) is punished for having wanted to be an unlawful wife by being changed from a dead woman into a living loon. The redundant double opposition: *hero husband/heroine wife* can be reduced simply to a masculine/feminine opposition. On the other hand, although the heroine of b) is a sister to her brothers, she is the reverse of a sister once she is defined in terms of the matrimonial alliance, and the asymmetrical relationship *brother/non-sister* thereby becomes relevant.

The formula c) means that the hero-salmon of M_{541} is an inversion of the heroine-loon in $M_{539-540}$. But M_{541}, in addition, refers to the latter by her opposite, in the person of the heroine whose morbid attachment to her brothers is prompted by virtue, not vice. This heroine is called Látkakáwas. She has the same name in the first myth we studied (M_{529}), which coincides point by point with the second part of M_{541}, from the episode of the young woman's suicide right to the end.

It will be remembered that Látkakáwas is the name of a bird,[8] the red-headed or scarlet tanager (see above, pp. 30–31), and therefore appropriate (although the brilliant plumage is characteristic only of the male bird, a detail disregarded by native ornithology) to immortalize the memory of a heroine who was burnt to death. The brilliant colouring of the tanager makes it the opposite of the loon, which has white markings on black. Furthermore, the tanager builds its nest in trees and at the tips of branches, whereas the loon nests on the ground near water. Lastly, the two species do not migrate along the same axis. In winter, the loon remains roughly in the same latitude, at least in the area with which I am dealing, and moves in an east-west direction. The tanager flies to the far south. It is, then, as if the myths were using what I would like to call 'zoemes', reducible, like the phonemes of the linguists, to clusters of differential elements combined in a variety of ways. Oppositions taken from real life suggest others of a symbolic nature. Tanager Woman is chaste but fertile, Loon Woman is lascivious but sterile; one sacrifices herself on a pyre which the other uses to destroy her own people. The picture becomes more complex with the appearance of the meadowlark (represented in the west by the species *Sturnella neglecta*) in M_{538} and M_{539}. This bird is yellow like the tanager, although less vivid in colouring, and it nests on the ground. So it is in opposition to the tanager in respect of the high and the low. But it is also in opposition to the loon on three counts — chromatism, weakly contrasted plumage, and land instead of water.

	Loon	*Tanager*	*Meadowlark*
chromatic/achromatic	−	+	+
marked/non-marked	+	+	−
high/low	−	+	−
land/water	−	o	+
N–S/E–W	−	+	+

Meadowlark Woman is neither chaste like Tanager Woman, nor lascivious like Loon Woman. She is as fertile as Tanager Woman, and, unlike Loon Woman, she is a faithful wife. Above all, she is a good mother, a quality which can hardly be ascribed to Tanager Woman, who deliberately leaps on to a fire with the intention of killing her child as well as herself. Meadowlark Woman, the victim of a fire (lit by Loon Woman) manages to save her unborn children:

[8] Barker (2) gives a similar form in Klamath, *kakkakla.w'as*, meaning yellow-headed blackbird, which would therefore be *Xanthocephalus xanthocephalus*.

	Loon	Tanager	Meadowlark
virtuous/depraved	−	+	+
fertile/sterile	−	+	+
agent/sufferer	+	+	−
victim of fire/causer of fire	−	+	+
saviour/destroyer	−	o	+

The fact that, in some myths, the meadowlark is featured as a pregnant woman on the point of giving birth suggests that the action takes place in summer. The other myths in the group, which include the story of the bird-nester, would also seem to confirm this, since the nest contains either meadowlarks (M_{530}, M_{531}, M_{538}, M_{560}) or newly hatched young eagles (M_{541}). Whether we are dealing with the young of the golden eagle or the bald eagle, the fact is that they cannot look after themselves and do not leave the nest for good before midsummer or early autumn (Bent, *Birds of Prey*, Vol. I, pp. 300–302, 340). On the other hand, the hero who is marooned at the top of the tree is rescued by butterflies, which the myths of neighbouring tribes classify as migratory insects.

M_{542a}. Nez Percé. 'The Butterfly Woman'

Coyote, the demiurge, was taking a walk. A Butterfly Woman saw him and proposed he should have sexual intercourse with her. As she was pretty and wore a fine dress, Coyote agreed. But she clasped him to her and crushed him to death. Then she threw the corpse into the water. It floated downstream and finally landed on the shore. Coyote was revived by a magpie pecking at his fat. Coyote struck his hip and out scrambled his children (cf. above, pp. 39–40), who immediately started to battle with each other. So he made them run back inside, but not before he had asked the advice of the youngest, who explained to him how to avenge himself on the butterfly woman by prying her apart: 'You will kill no more,' said Coyote to the murderess as she breathed her last. 'The human race will soon appear on the earth and men will say, "Here Butterfly flies about, it is the new season".' (Phinney, pp. 51–9; M_{542a}, Boas 4, pp. 153–4).

The Butterfly Woman who, in the myths of the inland Sahaptin is a transformation of the Skate Woman featured in the mythology of the Yurok and other coastal tribes of California (M_{292d}; *HA*, p. 309, n. 19), is also a transformation of the butterfly-sisters in the Klamath and Modoc myths, since the latter prove to be helpful and then become good wives to the hero they have saved. However, as is explained in M_{542}, the difference lies in the fact that, in this myth, Butterfly Woman makes her appearance out of season in the form of a monster, confirming *a contrario* that, when entrusted with the reverse role, the butterfly appears at the right season. As regards the butterfly-sisters' transformation into two wives, one a butterfly, the other a badger, thus forming a dioscuric pair entrusted with the same mission as the previous couple, it should be noted that, in M_{541}, it occurs after another distortion of the same type: Bird Woman and Frog Woman, the two females who want to marry Aishísh, provide a more strongly marked oppositional relationship than the wives of the sun and moon, who are respectively autochthonous and foreign, or human and animal (frog), in the North American myths to which their reappearance here provides an echo (see above, pp. 67–8). No doubt a correlation should be established between these amplified oppositions and the opposition between the demiurges indicated in M_{541}: they are, respectively, father and son and are associated with the sun and the moon, whereas M_{539} establishes the opposition more modestly between two brothers who at the end change into twin stars. I shall deal later (in Part Three, 3) with these problems relating to the transformations of the astronomical code.

For the time being, attention should be concentrated on a different type of phenomenon, and one which directly concerns the ethno-zoological code which I am still deciphering. There is, as it happens, a Modoc myth containing a detailed description of one of Aishísh's many marriages and in which 'snow-birds' carry out the function which the other myths in the group assign to butterflies:

M_{543}. *Modoc. 'One of Aishísh's marriages'*
When Aishísh built a house at the top of Mount Tcutgosi (here: Teutgosi; cf. M_{541} *in fine*), he first of all went deer hunting. On the south side of the mountain lived old Yaulilik with her son and two daughters. The family was very poor. The mother knew Aishísh's reputation (as a good hunter) and urged her daughters to marry him, as he would provide them with meat. But they should not be fooled by Kmúkamch (Kumush), who often tried to pass himself off as his son.

Even so, when they arrived at the village, Kmúkamch succeeded in fooling them. But Aishísh soon came back laden with freshly killed meat, and the girls realized they had been tricked. They hurled themselves at Kmúkamch and scratched him with their bone head-scratchers. There was nothing left of old Kmúkamch but his bones and the disk (cf. M_{541}, above, p. 67). Then the girls left.

Aishísh felt lonesome without his father. He split a mountain apart with an arrow and through the opening came a river so deep the girls could not cross it. Aishísh came and sat down near them and cut off their heads. Then he went to Mount Shasta, lay down at the top and cried.

The mother of the girls and her young son discovered the heads, then the bodies which had got caught in their fishing nets. The old woman succeeded in bringing her daughters back to life, and started for the village in order to find out who had killed her daughters.

Hardly had the girls recovered when they decided to gather edible seeds on Mount Shasta. They camped there for several days. As they climbed to the summit in search of water, the youngest heard a weak voice saying: 'You are drinking my tears!' She picked up a bright red hair and knew that it belonged to the man who had killed her and her sister. In the middle of a smooth and level place she saw a skeleton in which only the eyes were living. The bones were those of Aishísh, and thousands of deer had stamped on them to take their revenge on the man who had killed so many of their people.

The elder sister was frightened of the skeleton, but the younger wanted to bring it back to life, in spite of the fact that it smelt badly. When they returned to the camp she rubbed and fed the skeleton with deer fat. Gradually flesh returned to the bones and at last Aishísh came to life.

He drank water and slept. While he was sleeping, porcupines danced round him and sang a taunting song. When he had recovered, he killed them, cut off their hands and feet and pulled out their quills to give to his wives and mother-in-law.

Soon the elder sister had a son, then the younger. They all went back to Yaulilik's house. Aishísh killed ten deer or more with his young brother-in-law and put them in his belt as if they were just rabbits.

One day, while he was looking for a spring from which to drink, he remembered it was near the place where Kmúkamch had sent him up the tree to fetch eaglets (cf. $M_{530, 531, 538, 541}$). This made him feel lonesome. His wives had plenty of meat and lacked nothing; he decided to go away.

The elder sister wanted to go with him, and the younger, although afraid that something might happen to her in a strange country, finally decided to go along with them. On the fourth day, the elder sister was careless and caused her child's accidental death. Aishísh, overcome with grief, said: 'I did not think my wives would cause me greater grief than my father, but you have! I thought my children would live and that they would go to the swimming places, talk to the earth and mountains, and that they would be wise and able to do things. Since my son is dead, I no longer want to live in this world.' He asked for the other boy to be brought to him, placed his lips on the top of his head and took the breath out of the child. He placed the two corpses side by side and told the women that he had taken the children's breath into himself, but that their bodies were half his and half theirs. He said that this was the last time he would have a wife. He changed his wives into snow-birds; his brother-in-law became Kengkong'kongis, a supernatural spirit, who appears in dreams to shamans. Then he went far away towards the north (Curtin 1, pp. 27–38).

This myth, which I have given in a severely abridged version, is important on several counts. It represents a kind of cross-section of all those examined up until now (for this kind of patterning see *HA*, pp. 353–8). It is reminiscent of the bird-nester story; it concerns foolish virgins who, like the Loon Woman, are guilty of an incestuous union (with the father of the man who ought to have been their husband) and who are also murderesses, since they kill a relative (in actual fact, an affine instead of brothers, and whom they skin alive instead of burning him to death, but with the same result — the continued existence of the disk — as when the same victim perished on a pyre, cf. M_{541}). Next, the myth subjects the two women to decapitation, a form of death reserved in the other myths for Loon Woman; lastly, in its own way, that is posthumously, it reduplicates children who die too young, before they can become the heroic, dioscuric pair imagined by their father: it divides the children into two parts, the souls, of which Aishísh takes possession, and the bodies, which he hands over to the mothers, saying to them, 'These children are half mine and half yours.' The conclusion is an even more overt repetition of the myth featuring the celestial brothers (M_{539}), since in both instances the question at issue is the origin of shamanistic powers.

If it is legitimate to interpret the Modoc name *kengkong'kongis* (the name given to these powers in M_{543}) by a comparison with the Klamath word *ken*, 'snow', plus the verbal form *qẃanqkanga*, 'who walks with a limp', the approximate meaning is, 'the lame snowman'. This interpretation is all the more acceptable in that the Klamath describe the homologous spirit in M_{539} as a 'lame man who turns his shorter leg to good account by chasing his victims across the mountainside, for this was his way of taking advantage of the slope' (Barker 2, p. 467, and cf. pp. 185, 336; cf. Gatschet 1, Part I, pp. ci, 180, where Yayayá-ash is a one-legged man). So we might well be dealing with the same family of spirits which in M_{543} is defined in respect of the double consideration of snow and altitude. Old Yaulilik unleashes snowstorms as she moves from place to place, and her daughters become snow-birds. 'Men would make sport of them and find them under the bushes, and they would die from the cold and snow of which they themselves were the cause.' In this way, then, the myth's connotation with winter is firmly established, and is echoed by the transformation of the helpful sisters from butterflies into snow-birds.

Unfortunately, it would seem to be difficult to establish with any certainty to which species these *yaulilikumwas* birds belong. The popular term 'snow-bird' is used as a translation not only of *yaulilikumwas* but of at least two other words which have almost identical forms in Klamath and in Modoc: *tchika*, also a generic term for 'bird' (cf. Barker 1, pp. 38–9; 2, p. 88), and *ma'idikdak* (Gatschet 1, Part II, p. 206,'black-headed snow-bird, *Junco oregonus*'; Curtin 1, p. 125). As for the form Yaulilik, it would seem to be related phonetically to *yaukùl* (Curtin's transcription), which denotes the bald eagle (cf. above, p. 59); as regards the word ending, all we find in Barker (2, p. 232) is *l'il'i.ks*, 'a masculine proper noun impossible to analyse', and (3, p. 192) *či.l'il'ig*, 'baby birds'.

It is made clear that the three native terms denote similar if not identical species by another Modoc myth (M$_{544}$; Curtin 1, pp. 125–8), in which two Ma'dikdak sisters have adventures very similar to those of the Yaulilik sisters. After setting out to marry the sons of chiefs, they take the wrong trail and find themselves in the house of Wus, the fox, who tries to pass himself off as one of the future bridegrooms. But he does not deceive the girls, because he 'does not smell good' (cf. M$_{103}$, *HA*, p. 117). So he changes them into toothless, hunch-backed old women, clad only in rags. However, the young men welcome them, and during the night they change back into beautiful girls, who make sport of their father-in-law who had mistaken them for hags. Then, after being changed into green-headed ducks by Wus, they float off homewards. Their mother, however, gives them back their female form. Laden with presents, such as clothes, beads and porcupine quills, the youngest brother goes to the girls' house and becomes their husband.

One overall impression emerges from these various incidents: the 'snow-birds' have no real distinguishing feature and are often referred to by the general term for 'bird'; they are of no interest to humans, who consider them to be inedible and ridicule them for not even having the sense to shelter from the cold and the snow. The Tillamook, an isolated Salish group living along the north-west coast of Klamath country, had the same attitude to snow-birds: 'they are worthless, good for nothing. No one will use them for any purpose' (E. D. Jacobs, p. 69).

The fact is that in North America several species or varieties of the *Junco* genus are covered by the general appellation of snow-bird. Like meadow-larks, these birds build their nests on or near the ground, but they differ from them, as from the tanagers and butterflies, in that they rarely, if ever, migrate and in winter sometimes do no more than look for a place in the vicinity, where the temperature is a little milder than in the mountains, their summer habitat (Brasher, Vol. IV, pp. 152–3; Godfrey, pp. 460–62; Jewett *et al.*, pp. 638, 641). In this respect, these birds are both similar to and different from loons: like loons, they remain at the same latitude but move down an almost vertical axis towards a lower altitude, instead of along a horizontal axis linking the inland lakes and rivers to the coastal region.

Juncos have rather nondescript plumage, which is a blend of black, grey and fawn. So, in respect of colour, they are achromatic like loons, but unlike loons which, 'once they become adult acquire a strongly contrasted pattern of black and white markings' (Thomson, p. 212), their combination of drab, blended shades makes their absence of chromatism an unmarked feature.[9] Similarly, in the chromatic register, meadowlarks with bright but not strongly marked plumage are in opposition to tanagers. Lastly, juncos are in contrast to loons because of their small size, and because they live on land and not on water.

In order to justify the relevance of the two connected oppositions: *chromatic/achromatic* and *marked/unmarked*, it is worth recalling that, in Modoc society, the category of colour was of exceptional importance. Bancroft (Vol. I, p. 330) draws attention to the fact that they used the plumage of brightly coloured birds to decorate their clothes. And Curtin's inflated lyrical style, which is devoid of true poetry, would never of its own accord have produced such bold expressions as 'she was young, blue and beautiful', which constantly occur in his narratives. It is true to say that the prose of the Modoc myths is as brilliantly colourful as the pearly lustre of the haliotis or ear-shell. It is shot through with vivid glints of red, violet, blue, green and gold.

Red denotes power and cruelty, blue physical beauty and youth, whether the adjective refers to the hair or to the designs tattooed on the women's chins and which, according to an early traveller, gave a 'blue, darkly, deeply, beautifully blue tint to the skin' (Bancroft, *loc. cit.*, pp. 332–3).

It can, then, be easily understood how such a colour-conscious culture should have constructed its mythic zoemes by means of differential gaps in

---

[9] Within the system under consideration. We shall see later, however, that in a different system a species known as the 'red-backed' junco appears, on the contrary, as strongly marked (cf. below, p. 491).

which the modes of colour play a no less important part than social manners and customs. Leaving aside for the moment the nomenclature of the hero's village wives because of its unstable nature, in which there will nevertheless appear a hint of a single underlying opposition when we come to study the more northerly versions of the bird-nester story (see below, pp. 347–9), it has to be noted that the loon acts as a point of juncture between pairs of terms which are simultaneously in contrast to it and to each other. The loon, meadowlark and tanager zoemes are compatible, since a slight simplification of the data, without creating any contradiction between the myths, makes Loon appear as Meadowlark's sister-in-law, while Meadowlark can be considered as Tanager's mother. But the loon zoeme also belongs to another triad, in which all the relationships are incompatible: Loon Woman is in opposition to the butterfly-sisters, since she is a killer and the sisters are helpful. The butterfly-sisters and snow-birds are similar in their helpfulness, the butterflies by their opposition to the sky (from which they bring down the hero), the birds by their opposition to the earth (from which they extract the buried hero). Although, unlike Loon Woman, the snow-bird sisters are helpful, they suffer a fate similar to hers: they are decapitated. A last and most important point is that the butterfly and snow-bird sisters play the part of combinatory variants: they fulfil the same functions in mutually exclusive contexts. The butterfly-sisters appear in a series which is symmetrical with those featuring the birds; this is no doubt still the story of Aishísh, but in one instance it is an inversion, in the other a reproduction of the Loon Woman myth.

PART TWO ECHO EFFECTS

Rêve, dans un long solo, que nous amusions
La beauté d'alentour par des confusions
Fausses entre elle-même et notre chant crédule.

It dreams in a long solo of how, for diversion
Of the beauty all around, it devised a confusion
Between their living selves and our credulous song.

Mallarmé, *L'Après-midi d'un faune*
Translation from *Poison and Vision* by
David Paul, Vintage Books, Random House,
New York, 1974

The porcupine episode, which is also included in the Modoc myth M_{543}, is in a sense anticipated in this myth by another episode not found elsewhere. Before the rodents dance on the hero's body and challenge him as he lies sick and helpless in the camp where the two sisters live, he, the hero, has already suffered a similar and even more cruel fate: thousands of vengeful deer have trampled on him and mangled his body, promptly reducing it to a skeleton and transforming the surrounding area into a flat and barren waste.

I linked the porcupine episode (see above, p. 53) with the origin of adornments and ornaments, and M_{543} confirms this hypothesis. But how are we to explain the deer episode of which the porcupine sequence would seem to be merely a doublet?

Not only does M_{543} replace the butterfly-sisters by snow-birds, it also breaks new ground in another way. It depicts Aishísh not as the master of games of skill and chance, but as the master of hunting. The myth even gives prominence to this attribute, which is either absent from other versions or present there only in a very weakened form. According to M_{543}, Aishísh possessed so much deer meat that 'if all the people in the world came to eat it, he would still have nearly as much left'. The bird-girls' family, on the other hand, has no meat; their old mother has to go and beg for some in order to feed them, and the reason why she urges her daughters to marry Aishísh is that she has heard he is a good hunter and hopes that there will be plenty to eat in his house. Consequently, in the initial situation, Aishísh has all the meat and the other protagonists have none at all. When the sisters visit him, the first thing he does is to offer them cutlets. He is no sooner married than he goes hunting and provides his in-laws with a vast store of dried meat.

It can then be supposed that, in the two similar episodes, the myth is referring on the one hand to the origin of meat (of which, at the beginning, the hero is the sole master) and on the other to the origin of adornments and ornaments. This hypothesis is of paramount importance, since I established in the first part that the bird-nester myth exists in South and North

America in almost identical forms, and since, in the two previous volumes of the series (*RC*, *HA*), I think I provided convincing proof that this myth, which related to the origin of water or fire, is transformed independently into a myth explaining the origin of meat and another explaining the origin of adornments; we now find these two motifs associated in a single myth which is careful to point out (since it alludes to the fact quite explicitly) that its hero was initially the bird-nester.

We have seen that this myth is situated half-way between the straight version, which is the one featuring the bird-nester (here transformed into: trampled upon by the deer),and its inverted form, illustrated by the Loon Woman myth. This last myth is also concerned with the origin of two things: what might be called anti-adornments, in the form of the necklace made of hearts wrested by a woman from her closest relatives,[1] and anti-meat, in the form of the loon whose flesh men will spit out because it is inedible.

I would like at this point to introduce a new aspect of M_{543}. Not only does it contain a description of a period of Aishísh's life not found in other versions of the hero's exploits, but it sets the action of the story in a different place: on the slopes of Mount Shasta, which the women climb, and at the summit of Duilas, Little Shasta, where their brother takes up his position in order to observe the women's ascent from a distance. We are, then, at the extreme western edge of Modoc country, that is, almost in foreign territory; and farther away still, but in a southerly direction, if Little Shasta refers not to the nearby mountain known by this name but, as among the Yana, to Mount Lassen (see above, p. 74).

But it is also in regions inhabited by tribes culturally and linguistically different from the Klamath and the Modoc that we find versions of the Loon Woman myth, in which the buried hero, who is more dead than alive, is given an important place. This hero is the sole survivor of the fire started by the homicidal woman. His heart flies out of the fire and falls a long way away in a lonely spot, where it is either trampled on by deer or buried deep in the ground by its own impetus. Two kindly women discover the vital organ, look after it and feed it, and the man is brought back to life. Thus, in one of the Wintu versions (M_{545a}; DuBois-Demetracopoulou, pp. 355–60, cf. above, p. 67; see below, p. 138), the heart, which the heroine hears singing in the distance and towards which she directs her steps, says to her: 'Woman! have no fear of me! Come!' And the woman replies: 'Yes!' Many animals had passed that way and there was a great deal of dust (compare the

---

[1] Whereas, in order to commit incest, she mentions an offer of real adornments: the beads which, she claims, her husband intends for her brothers and which one of them must come and fetch.

description of the porcupine episode in M_{538}, above, p. 52). Both to the east and the west, the tracks of innumerable deer were visible . . .

I propose to devote even more attention to the versions found among the Yana, who, although separated from the Modoc by the Achomawi and the Atsugewi tribes living along Pit River, place the deer episode on Mount Shasta in the same way as M_{543} does. In order to facilitate the reading of the proper names, I have taken the liberty of simplifying Curtin's transcriptions, while at the same time, wherever possible, quoting in brackets their phonetic equivalents as recorded in Sapir's versions.

M_{546}. *Yana. 'The Loon Woman'*

At some distance east of Jigulmatu (*djīga'lmadu*: Round Mountain, Sapir 3, p. 188, n. 293) lived old Juka (*dju'ga*) 'Silkworm', with his many sons and daughters. The eldest was called Tsorédjowa (*ts. !orê'djuwa*) 'Eagle'; the younger Hakalasi (*'ak!ā'lisi*) 'Loon'. It so happened that Hakalasi fell in love with her brother Hitchinna (*'itc!i'nna*) 'Wildcat'. She even dreamed once that he was her husband. A man called Metsi (*me'ts. !i*) 'Coyote', who was no relative, lived as a guest in the great house.

The day Hakalasi had her dream, all the men happened to be out hunting. They came back at night and the next morning went out to swim. Tsorédjowa made food ready for them. Hakalasi went up on top of the sweat-house and began to sing and call for her husband. Nobody understood what she meant, for all knew she had no husband. With the exception of Hitchinna, who was lying in a corner wrapped up in the skin of a wildcat, the brothers came out of the house in turn and went to the young girl to ask her for an explanation. She sent them all away, and the old father realized it was Hitchinna she wanted. Hitchinna rose, washed and dressed himself nicely. The sun was high in the sky: they went off together.

After walking a long distance, they camped and lay down together. But Hitchinna was frightened and, as soon as his sister was asleep, he got up and ran away quickly, leaving a piece of rotten wood in his place. At daybreak he arrived back at the sweat-house.

Chuhna (*tc'u'nā*) the 'Spider', Juka's sister who lived with him, was the greatest person in the world for spinning threads and twisting ropes. She had a willow basket as big as a house, fastened by a rope to the sky. She had a presentiment that her niece would want to seek revenge, so she made all her family get into the basket so that she could take them up into the sky. Coyote got in first and settled down in the bottom of the basket. All the inhabitants of the sweat-house followed him.

Hakalasi woke up with a block of rotten wood in her arms. She was angry and rushed back to the village: it was empty. She ran round in every direction looking for tracks. Then she looked towards the sky and saw the basket rising up towards the sun. She then set fire to the house which was soon ablaze.

When they were almost at the sky, Coyote, wondering where they were, made a little hole in the bottom of the basket to look down. That instant the basket burst open and all the occupants fell into the burning sweat-house, all except Tsorédjowa who had been the last to climb in and who was outside on the top of the basket. She was able to catch on to the sun and so was saved.

Hakalasi watched her brothers burn. Their bodies burst open one after the other and their hearts flew out. Hakalasi caught them in a net fixed to the end of a pole. She caught them all except two, her father's and her eldest brother's. Juka's heart came down on an island in the middle of a river near Klamath Lake. There it turned into Juka himself. He was buried up to his chin in the ground – only his head was sticking out.

The eldest son's heart flew as far as the foot of Wahkalu (wa'gal ū: Mount Shasta; Sapir 3, p. 161, n. 260), where the son also became himself again. But he fell so deep into the earth that only his face was sticking out above the surface.

Hakalasi put all the hearts she had caught on a string and wore them round her neck. She tried first of all to live in a lake east of Jigulmatu, but could not find a place deep enough. So she went to Crater Lake to the north-west of Klamath Lake. Two Tsanunewa brothers – Tsanunewa is the name of a fisher-bird – lived not far from there with their old grandmother. While they were out catching ducks, they heard and saw Hakalasi spring out of the water.

Meanwhile, Tsorédjowa had come down from the sky and had found only a heap of bones and ashes where the sweat-house had once stood. She went round in mourning apparel and started looking for her sister. She went everywhere and arrived at Klamath Lake and finally reached the Tsanunewa brothers, to whom she told her story. They fed her on ducks, and asked her what kind of person her sister was. They recognized the lady of the lake and offered to go and catch her. Tsorédjowa promised to give them (otter) skins and beads and even said she would marry them. However, all they wanted from her were red and green deer bones to make arrowheads. Tsorédjowa went off to the mountain to fetch the bones. The elder took the red bones and the younger the green. (The fat on the leg bones, according to an explanatory note, turns some red and others green.)

The brothers reached the lake at daybreak. They made themselves small by magical means and climbed into tiny canoes made from the stems of tule grass. When Hakalasi appeared, neither was able, as both had feared, to hit her heart. However, they struck her in the neck and in the armpit; after a time she rose to the surface and died. They dragged her corpse to the shore and left her near their house: after they had all dined on fish, they casually suggested to Tsorédjowa that she should go out and see what they had caught. She recognized her sister, took off her skirt and wrapped the body in it. Then she counted the hearts, but her father's and her eldest brother's hearts were not there.

The two Tsanunewas told her that they often heard someone crying far away towards the north. Tsorédjowa rushed off in this direction. Soon she recognized her father's voice. She looked right and left, then she saw her dear father's head. Feverishly she dug the earth with a sharp stake until at last she released the body. Juka was all bones. Tsorédjowa wrapped him in a deerskin and carried him back to the house from which she had started, in order to pick up her sister's body. She carried them both home to her old village to the east of Jugalmatu. She hid the bodies away and set off to look for her brother.

At the foot of Mount Shasta lived a certain Jamuka (*zaamuk'u*) 'Acorn Worm', with his wife and two daughters. One day, while the sisters were gathering wood, they heard someone singing without knowing where the voice came from. They went back again to the place and the younger sister discovered a human head sticking out of the ground and covered with tears: it was dirty and ugly. The sisters dug for two days and finally drew out the whole body. It was nothing but bones. They wrapped it in their skirts and went to get wildcat skins. When they told their father what they had found, he suspected the body might be a survivor of the massacre, news of which had just reached him. So he told his daughters to take good care of him. When they came back with the skins, they saw that a great stream of water was running from his eyes. Deer came down from the neighbouring hills to drink of that water.

For days the sisters fed their protégé and every night they slept at his side. The man began to look better, but he cried all the time and deer came to drink the water that spurted from his eyes. When he began to talk, he asked for a bow and arrows and told the women to go home. Within the space of one night, he killed in succession four bucks which came to drink of his tears, and the following night he killed even more.

The girls were frightened, but their father was glad. He cut up the venison for drying. The hero was completely well now and he went to live with his new family. He cried no more, but a salt spring was formed in the place where he had shed so many tears. The spring is still in that place to this day and deer go in herds to drink from it. Hunters watch near the spring and kill much game, as Juka's son had done.

Tsorédjowa went from house to house enquiring about her brother, and at last she came to Jamuka's house where she found him. Satisfied that he was happy with his two wives, she hurried back to her village. In one night Tsorédjowa made a great sweat-house, prepared a big water-tight basket and filled it with water. On the second night she put in all the hearts, including her sister's which she had taken out of the corpse, and then dropped hot stones in the water. When the water started to boil, she covered the basket and placed it on top of the sweat-house. Then she went in and slept.

At daybreak the basket overturned and the people crowded round the sweat-house, shivering with cold and demanding to be allowed in. Tsorédjowa opened the door and asked all the people into the sweat-house. She recognized her brothers, then her sister. There was nothing bad now in the sister's heart — it had become pure (clean). Tsorédjowa explained what had happened to the absent brother, and the men went back to their usual tasks.

One day, Jamuka advised his son-in-law to go and introduce his wives to his parents. As soon as he saw his son coming, old Juka took a big blanket, caught him in it and hid him. Two other brothers took his wives to be their wives. They never saw their first husband again, for old Juka kept him secreted and made him a Weänmauna, that is, a hidden one.

When the women went to visit their father taking him (nice things of all kinds) gifts, they explained the situation to him, 'I think that is well enough,' he said. 'His father has put him away. His brothers are as good for you as he was.' The sisters agreed with their father, and after that went back and lived in Juka's house (Curtin 3, pp. 407–21).

The analysis of this myth must be carried out in stages. It presents a particularly difficult task in that we have little or no anthropological information about the Yana. They were a tiny community, who, like their northern neighbours the Atsugewi, the Achomawi and the Shasta, belonged linguistically to the Hokan family. They lived between Pit River and Sacramento River, in a hilly region dominated by Mount Lassen. In spite of being fully integrated into the life of the American settlers, by whom they were paid a regular wage, the Yana were shamefully massacred in August 1864, in circumstances of which Curtin gives a moving account (3, pp. 517–20). Fewer than fifty survived. We will never know if our rudimentary picture of their culture is to be explained by their former primitivism (Kroeber 1, p. 340) or by the fact that only scraps of information have come down to us.

Let us first of all go through the names given to the characters in the myth. We are already familiar with the Loon Woman in the role she also has in Yana mythology. Her brother is called Wildcat, a name he shares with the rest of his family in a Modoc version of the same myth (M₅₄₀). He is old Juka's son (Sapir 3, pp. 55, 68, n. 106; Sapir-Swadesh 1, p. 207). Juka is the name of a variety of parasitic silkworm found on poisonous sumacs, known in America as poison oak, or poison ivy (*Rhus diversiloba*). Coyote, who, in a great many communities in California and elsewhere, plays the part of demiurge and trickster, is here given only a secondary role. Chuhna, the spider, retains the role assigned to her in a Modoc version (M₅₃₉) but, being an aunt on the father's side, she loses the maleness normally attributed to this character in Yana tales (Sapir 3, p. 29, n. 45). Later it will become clear why, and also why the heroine, who brings her own family back to life and thus redeems her guilty sister, is given the name Eagle.

All Curtin says about the Tsanunewa brothers is that they are fisher-birds, a fact which is confirmed in an Achomawi version (M₅₅₂; Angulo-Freeland, p. 126): *tsànúnné.wa*, the mythic name of the killdeer *Charadrius vociferus*, which we have already encountered (see above, p. 49); but the popular Yana term is *dutdu-* (Sapir-Swadesh 1, p. 79). The name Jamuka denotes a kind of worm, the identity of which will be discussed later (see below, p. 114). The Yana applied the word *weänmauna* to 'children, mostly girls, whom high-ranking families used to keep in seclusion, sometimes until the age of thirty' (Sapir-Swadesh 1, p. 172). These secluded children either married very late or never at all (Sapir-Spier 1, p. 274). If they are married, the myths quickly re-establish their celibate status (Curtin 3, pp. 349, 421).

As told by the Yana, the deer episode is presented in a somewhat different form from the one given it in the Modoc (M₅₄₃) and Wintu (M₅₄₅ₐ) versions, where we first encountered it. The hero is not only crying his eyes out ('you are drinking nothing but tears'), as is stated in M₅₄₃: his tears form a salt stream at which deer come to drink. Thus, he attracts them and his pathetic condition does not result from his being attacked and trampled on by them, but from previous and quite different circumstances. So the Yana myth combines the two themes, tears and deer, and in so doing explains, not of course the origin of hunting since the brothers were hunters from the start, but how this occupation became easier after the appearance of salt licks, where herds of deer come to drink and near which hunters can lie in wait and kill quantities of game. It is a fact that Yana territory contained salt: 'Near the central village of Wichuman'a, some miles east of Millville, there was a saline swamp. The dark coloured mud was taken up and dried for use as salt. The Achomawi, the Atsugewi and the Wintu all resorted to this place to collect stocks of salt, a fact which illustrates more or less continuous friendliness. This explains why the Achomawi referred to the Yana as Ti'saichi, "salt people"' (Kroeber 1, pp. 339–40; Sapir 3, p. 54, n. 78; Sapir-Spier 1, p. 245). The locality in question is probably not the same as the one in the myth. Furthermore, Mount Shasta, where several episodes take place, is a very long way away from Yana territory. However, it was visible from several places (Sapir-Spier 1, p. 247) and it has already been noted (see above, p. 90) that these Indians referred to Mount Lassen, which is situated on their south-eastern border, by a name which means literally 'Little Mount Shasta' (Kroeber 1, p. 338; Sapir-Swadesh 1, p. 172). As has been observed in connection with Modoc myths, it would seem that the Yana too established a kind of ideal connection between their home localities and those in a more northerly region to which they had no hesitation in dispatching their heroes, since those in M_{546} visit places as far removed from their homeland as Klamath Lake and Crater Lake.

The routes followed by the heroes can be worked out in part (Figure 7). At the beginning of the myth, we are somewhere to the east of Round Mountain: 'I'da'lmadu, Bone-Place, between Montgomery Creek and Round Mountain . . . the rocks and stones are supposed at one time to have been bones, hence the name' (Sapir-Spier 1, p. 245). After committing all her crimes, Loon Woman heads first of all in a more easterly direction, then turns northwards, stops for a while at Klamath Lake and settles to the north-west of this lake, in the waters of Crater Lake, where her sister, who is also travelling by way of Klamath Lake, joins her.[2]

After the death of her elder sister, the younger one returned to the Klamath Lake area. Carrying the remains of her father and sister, she arrives back at her native village; then, after much wandering, she reaches the foot

---

[2] This itinerary seems to be clearly indicated by the context. Curtin (3, p. 411) states explicitly: 'She went north-west of Klamath Lake to Crater Lake.' Nevertheless, it should be noted that there is also a Crater Lake in Achomawi country in the northern part of Fall River basin (cf. Kniffen, caption under Plate 55b, p. 324). But even if this were the Crater Lake in question, the myth still takes the heroine into foreign territory, and it is this point I am anxious to establish rather than the specific course of a journey. I am trying to show that all the myths in this group have a cosmopolitan, and even in a sense an international, character.

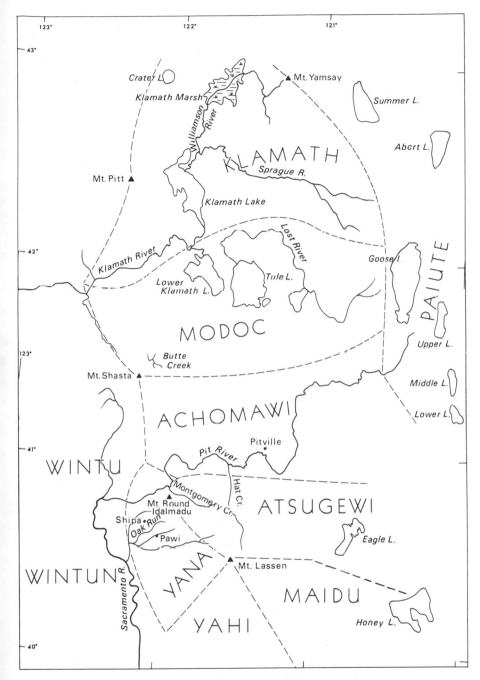

Figure 7. Geographical area of Loon Woman myth

of Mount Shasta, and finally returns to the village and brings her relatives back to life.

The most complete version published by Sapir (3, pp. 228–32; M_{547}) was recorded by Dixon about 1900; it contains additional details and differs from Curtin's version on several points. I shall discuss it later, noting merely that in it the massacre is said to take place at Ship'a (*ci'p!a*), and that Loon Woman, who in this instance is an unmarried woman from a different tribe, comes from a lake situated much farther to the east, near Hat Creek ('Ākā'l'imadu, cf. *ak'ā'lisi*, "diver"; or *àkā'lili*, "lake", -*madu*, "place": Hat Creek in Atsugewi territory', Sapir-Spier 1, p. 247), that is, the very region to which the incestuous sister in M_{546} travels after committing her crimes. Consequently, as in the Klamath and Modoc versions, it is possible to plot the respective positions of Loon Woman and her relatives along an east-west axis. When she was a married woman, she lived to the east of her native village (M_{538}). An unmarried and virtuous woman, she lived also to the east of the village inhabited by her potential husband (M_{541}). Having again become an incestuous sister in M_{546}, she goes off in an easterly direction after killing her own kin. And, in M_{547}, in which she becomes a lascivious stranger with murderous intentions, she travels westwards in order to execute her twofold purpose.

It is clear from these considerations that all the myths are describing a spatial structure of the same type. They either try to find it locally, or they refer directly, without transposing them, to areas outside the tribal territory, but which would seem to have the same value and the same meaning for several communities. Through the agency of the myths, each tribe thus asserts a mystic right of ownership over a vast territorial entity, of which it occupies only a part.

I shall come back to this point, since there is still much to be said about the salt marshes and springs which led me to embark on this discussion. The fact is that another, different impression emerges from the Yana version: it is as if the appearance of the salt springs provided a solution to the problem of hunting, which would otherwise be fraught with ecological difficulties. As the myth explains, but for the salt springs which lure the herds into the bottom-lands, hunters would have to make dangerous expeditions into the mountains. Indeed, when the Tsanunewa brothers, who are fishers, needed deer bones to make arrowheads, they had no means of procuring them themselves and had to ask for the help of a heroine called Eagle who, being able to fly as high as the sun, could reach the mountain tops, where the deer live and die and where their bones can be collected. It will also be remembered that, in the Modoc version of the same episode, the hero is attacked by deer when he ventures near the summit of Mount Shasta.

Viewed from the etiological angle, the Yana myth fulfils, then, a dual function. It describes the origin of the salt springs which facilitate hunting, and then the origins of ornaments and adornments made from porcupine quills. Strangely enough, the Modoc version (M_{543}) keeps to the same construction, although these Indians and their neighbours the Klamath did not use salt, to which they referred by a word borrowed from Chinook jargon (see above, p. 63). However, they were not unfamiliar with salt, even in its terrestrial aspect, as is clear from the fact that, in their version, salt still plays a part, while being at the same time reduced to its simplest expression: tears, a mode of salt familiar to all men by virtue of their physiological constitution. Reduced to this common denominator, salt figures quite clearly in the Modoc version, in which its appearance also precedes that of quill ornaments.

This being so, an observation of fundamental importance must now be made: we are becoming aware of the gradual emergence of a mythic configuration, analogous in part to the one I defined in *The Raw and the Cooked* and at the beginning of *From Honey to Ashes* (p. 32). Let me recall its essential features. Myths dealing with the origin of cooking fire (M_{7-12}) which, in an inverted form, become a myth explaining the origin of rain, celestial water which puts out domestic fires (M_1), are transformed in the first place into myths about the origin of ornaments and adornments, and then into myths about the origin of honey. The proof that this last transformation is a genuine one is provided by the fact that honey, the means of the origin of adornments, becomes an end in itself in myths which can be independently established as having a transformational relationship with the preceding ones. Their existence therefore constitutes an *a priori* condition of the existence of the others and, on examination, they are found to possess all the empirical properties postulated in the light of the initial hypothesis.

Barring two differences, this structure reappears in the North American myths just discussed. In the first place, they replace the category of the sweet by that of the salty. In order to combine the two systems into one, we need do no more than subsume these two categories under the more general one of condiment. And do not ornaments provide a condiment for the human body, just as flavours added to food constitute its ornamentation?

Secondly, the internal connections in the North American system form a more complex pattern than the one peculiar to South America, which I illustrated in a simplified form in my diagram (*HA*, p. 32). The same links exist in North America, but are duplicated. In M_{543}, as in M_{546}, the condiment operates on two levels: as the *means* of meat, and as the *antecedent* of adornments. These myths are, therefore, in opposition to others studied previously (M_{530}, M_{538}), in which adornments are featured as an *end*, without any reference being made either to food or to condiments.

The question then arises: are we dealing with a chance resemblance between the myths of North and South America and one which, precisely because of the differences just noted, should not be used as proof of their common structure? There are two possible answers.

First of all, we can try to determine whether the North American myths concerned with the origin of salt and adornments do not result from the same transformation which, in South America, leads from myths about the origin of terrestrial fire or celestial water to those concerned with the origin of adornments and honey. It will be confirmed not only that this is what actually happens but also that the armatures which give rise to the transformation display, in both cases, properties which are strictly in correspondence with each other. However, we have not yet reached the appropriate point at which I produce what I consider to be the final and definitive proof (see below, p. 143 *et seq*.).

Let us begin with the other possibility, which would seem more suited to the present stage of the argument. If we respect the conventions of the diagram already published in Volume Two, and which is reproduced here for the convenience of the reader (Figure 8), it may be said – disregarding for the moment system S_1 and its inversion S_{-1}, both relating to the origin of cooking viewed from a positive angle (the cooking of food) or a negative angle (the water which extinguishes domestic fires) – that until now we have discussed only the left-hand section containing myths about the origin of adornments and honey. Provided we read salt for honey and quills for shell beads (the porcupine being unknown in tropical climates),[3] we can now recognize the same local structure in the North American myths.

What happens, then, on the other side, that is, the right side of the diagram? Provided we discover that here too the North American myths exhibit the same traits as those of the South, we shall be well on the way to confirming the hypothesis that the myths of both hemispheres featuring a bird-nester hero have a common structure.

---

[3] However, it should be noted that these tiny black and white beads which, threaded in alternate order on to a soft thread or sometimes a stiff fibre, are in such common use in South America – especially among the Bororo, who have a myth (M_{20}) giving the required reference and dealing precisely with the technique of threading on to stiff fibres – are very similar to porcupine quills, since the quills are comparable in diameter and show a similar alternation of light and dark areas. As for the *honey* $\Rightarrow$ *salt* transformation, it is also found in South America among the Machiguenga (*HA*, p. 284, n. 4) and the Ayoré (Muñoz-Bernand: *Mythologie*, pp. xxx–xxxv).

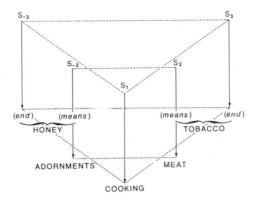

Figure 8. The armature of the system including the reference myth

The right side of the diagram shows a transformation which is symmetrical with the other one, since it gives rise, again in two stages, to myths about the origin of meat and tobacco. Tobacco, the means of obtaining meat in the first stage, becomes an end in the second. Do the North American myths contain a transformation of this type, that is, linking meat and tobacco?

Merely to pose the question is to answer it. One of the Modoc myths already discussed (M_{539}) contains a long episode which would remain totally unintelligible unless interpreted in this way. Since I had not yet formulated my hypothesis, this episode seemed so superfluous that I merely mentioned it in passing, without trying to incorporate it into my analysis.

It is the episode in which the two heroes, who are walking towards the rising sun, twice pit their strength against that of Yahyáhaäs, the one-legged ogre.

The first trial of strength involves breaking the opponent's pipe, either by puffing too hard on it or by hurling it against a rock. The second is a wrestling match, the loser of which is doomed to death by fire. It follows that Gatschet's version of the Aishísh saga is simply fusing the two trials of strength into a single contest, when it relates how the demiurge Kmúkamch perished in a fire because he had lost his pipe.

With regard to the corresponding episode in M_{539}, two points need to be stressed. Firstly, the hero or heroes begin by claiming that they have neither pipe nor tobacco. One of them even explains that he has been travelling so long that, in two summers, 'all his tobacco was gone' (Curtin 1, p. 115). Secondly, the ogre Yahyáhaäs is presented as being a selfish master of hunting since, although he always has one or two freshly killed beasts hanging from his belt, he does not offer meat to his visitors. At the same time, his house is covered not with bark but with deerskins, and vast quantities of meat are lying around to dry (*ibid.*, pp. 114–15).

Curtin's collection (1, pp. 148–68; $M_{549a, b, c}$) contains three other myths featuring this same ogre, which can be used to elucidate these points. To avoid making the argument too laborious, I do not propose to analyse them in detail; it will be enough to indicate their general trend. These myths feature great hunters, men or women, whom Yahyáhaäs prevents from engaging in their favourite pursuit by presenting them with two alternatives: either they must make their peace with him by means of tobacco smoke or he will beat them in a wrestling contest and kill them. The heroes forget their fire-drill and have no tobacco. The ogre forces them to wrestle with him and he throws them over a cliff into a lake, where they drown or where their bodies are broken on the rocks.

In an inverted variant (M_{549c}), unmarried sisters are in the habit of making a ring of fires round the mountains to drive the deer to the top, where they are easier to kill. The men from the neighbouring village dare not marry them or compete with them since they kill those who dare to approach them as if they were game. Yahyáhaäs comes along and claims them as his wives, and is so demanding that they can no longer go hunting. The sisters attack the ogre with magic streaks of fire, and then challenge him to make a fire like them with his own power, without the help of any implement. Then they wrestle with him and win and burn him on a great pile of wood. They transform his remains into a spirit, which will roam around on high mountains. However, they have lost their gift as hunters, and so are resigned to the idea of marrying the men from the village and letting them hunt in their stead, but as the sisters neither look nor smell good, the young men run off and hide. After many adventures they nevertheless achieve their aim, and almost instantly they and their husbands turn into spirits who haunt mountains.

There are several instances, then, in which the characters in the myths lose the power to hunt or are deprived of meat, either because they have no tobacco or have forgotten their fire-drill, two indispensable requisites for the smoker, which no one, as is clearly stated in the myths, should be without, especially while travelling. It is a remarkable fact that the myths in this group make no allusion to cooking fire, and that they envisage fire in three other and quite separate modalities: a funeral pyre, a brush fire for surrounding game and fire produced by means of a drill to light a pipe for smoking. These three modalities correspond to actual, everyday uses: the Klamath and the Modoc, as well as the Yana and several other Californian tribes, including the Carrier in the far north, used to cremate their corpses; the firing of the brush was used as a supplementary device in large game hunting (Ray 3, p. 187)[4] and, as is indicated in the myths, they smoked wild tobacco, *Nicotiana attenuata* or *bigelovii*, which was perhaps also cultivated by some Klamath groups (Spier 2, p. 87). Logically considered, the three technical devices form a system: the funeral pyre is destructive, the fire lit by the drill is constructive, and the brush fire combines both aspects, since it destroys vegetation but provides men with game. However, only the fire lit by means of the drill occupies a marked position in the myths: without this fire, which is doubly cultural, in origin as well as in purpose, men lose the goodwill of the spirits and turn them into enemies.

So, as in South America (*HA*, p. 260), a condition of dynamic imbalance is visible at the centre of the group of transformations. In the case of both salt and honey, the myths envisage the possibility of man's return to a natural state; for salt, too, in its three forms — mud extracted from swamps and ready for consumption once it has been dried, salt springs where the animals come to drink, and tears secreted by the human body — illustrates the paradox of a form of raw 'cooking', the only kind capable of allowing food to attain perfection, but through the operation of natural processes. In contrast, at the other end of the group, tobacco, which forms a counterpart to honey or salt, appears both as an aspect of culture (since a pipe and a fire-drill are necessary in order to smoke it) and as the supreme means of communicating with the supernatural world.

To ensure such communication was, indeed, the function of tobacco among the Klamath and the Modoc, for whom no doubt smoking was an everyday pleasure but who also assigned a special place to tobacco in their shamanistic rites. Spier's assertion (2, p. 87) that the shamans smoked only as a relaxation, is hardly in keeping with his previous references to the special pipes with distinctive shapes (very long stems encased in rattlesnake skin) reserved for them, and to the mixture of tobacco and poisonous roots that only the shamans smoked. The ritual use of tobacco also seems to be confirmed by an invocation quoted in Gatschet (1, Part I, p. 167) and in which the shaman refers to his pipe by the same term as he uses to designate his shamanistic equipment in general.

The information collected by Ray (3, pp. 55, 59–70) among the Modoc confirms that which emerges from myths, unless — as is hardly likely — the shamanistic practice differed radically in the two tribes. Before beginning a

---

[4] In Atsugewi, *'yunasïi*, ring of fire round a mountain . . . they burnt five or six mountains a year' (Garth 2, p. 132). Both in the daytime and at night, the Klamath and the Modoc used to light rings of fire round the mountains in order to hunt deer (E. W. Voegelin 2, p. 169).

course of treatment, the Modoc shaman smoked in a manner which had been dictated by his spirits. Each shaman had his own particular style of blowing the smoke on to the hands or body of the sick person. Informants record that a certain shaman had the largest pipe ever seen and that it used to light up automatically. A fellow-Indian (Klamath) wanted to trade for the pipe; the owner agreed, for he knew that the pipe, which was inhabited by his tutelary spirit, would return to him of its own accord. Once the pipe fell into the water; the others tried to find it, but failed; yet that very evening the shaman found it in its usual place in the lodge, and, what is more, already lighted. Another shaman infected an Indian who had insulted him with a fatal disease by blowing smoke from his pipe towards him.

Pipes and smoke constitute, then, mediatory agents which have the power to influence a certain category of spirits. These spirits roam over the mountain and, in normal circumstances, only the shamans have dealings with them. But it is possible for ordinary mortals to encounter them; for instance, travellers who are crossing the mountains — and who must therefore take with them their pipes, fire-drills and tobacco — and also hunters. This brings us to the crux of the hunting problem for these Indians; large game was only to be found in the mountains where, for practical as much as for mystical reasons, they were loath to venture.[5]

This anthropological paradox is confirmed by further indications, in addition to those provided by the myths, or which emerge from my analysis. Spier (2, p. 155) notes that, in spite of the abundance of game in their territory, the Klamath were poor hunters: 'We know very little about hunting deer,' one of his informants admits. Their inefficiency can be explained not only by the fact that a good hunter had to enjoy the special protection of the spirits, but also by the circumstance that only solitary individuals in search of some supernatural revelation would venture into the heavily wooded mountains.

Unlike the Klamath, the Modoc attached more importance to hunting than to fishing. Hunting activities started towards the end of September 'when camps were moved to higher elevations'. The men hunted deer while the women gathered huckleberries, which ripened in late September (Ray

[5] The English word 'deer' which is used in the myths (or at least in the available transcriptions), normally refers to the small species of the animal. But judging from several remarks made by a man who lived with the Modoc shortly after 1850, it would appear to mean larger animals and particularly the North American elk: 'It seems odd to say that elk should go further up into the mountain as winter approaches instead of down to the foothills and plains below as do the deer; but it is true . . . There are warm springs up the mountain . . . where a kind of watercress grows, and wild swamp berries in warm marshes or on the edges, and here the elk survive.' And a little further on: 'About mid-winter, the chief led his men on a great hunt towards the highest spurs of the mountain' (Miller, pp. 213, 271).

3, p. 182). The hunting period lasted until December, although they had to go back to the winter village in early October to rebuild and refurbish the houses, the framework of which had been dismantled in the spring. While the women were engaged on this work, the men continued to hunt in the mountains, and even later in the year, if food supplies were short. This eventuality was one they particularly dreaded, because the 'nature of the Modoc habitat and way of life precluded productive hunting of large game during the winter' (ibid., p. 185).

This being so, hunting takes on a paradoxical character, for two reasons: to avoid a food shortage the hunting season has to be at its peak at the very time when the Indians are forced to leave the mountain haunts of big game in order to build their winter villages. Also, hunting can become an urgent necessity at the period in the year when it is most difficult to practise. An activity which should be carried out normally to ensure survival compels the person practising it to behave in a manner which is abnormal on two counts: spatially, since he has to hunt in the mountains where he is exposed to an unequal struggle with the spirits, unless he can pacify them with offerings of special tobacco, as the shamans do, and temporally, since the hunter runs the greatest risks at a time when he could settle into his cosy half-underground house with its covering of rush matting and clumps of turf, and being thus protected from the full severity of winter, live there safe and sound by drawing on his stocks of food.

This contradictory aspect of everyday existence also comes out in another way. In order to hunt, the Klamath sometimes had to move outside their territory, on to the western slopes of the Cascade Range (Spier 2, p. 155). The Modoc myths also bear witness to the fact that, for these Indians, hunting was not merely an atypical occupation, but even an exotic one. In the south-east of the Modoc territory, according to M_{549a}, two brothers, Weasel and Marten (incarnations of Aishísh and Kmúkamch, cf. above, p. 44), live at the top of a high mountain. As a reward for having burned the ogre Yahyáhaäs to death in a huge fire, Weasel marries the daughter of that country's chief. But, unlike Marten's wife, who was a Shasta, she cannot settle down in her new home and so she goes off. This means that the daughter of traditional enemies can adapt better than a fellow-tribeswoman to the cultural heroes' way of life, in circumstances in which the latter rescue the humans from the cannibalistic giant, who, according to $M_{549b, c}$, is preventing them from realizing their possibilities as hunters. For, at that time (M_{549a}), the people lived solely on seeds and roots (Curtin 1, p. 148).

It will be remembered (cf. above, p. 83) that, in Klamath and Modoc mythology, the ogre is either one-legged or a cripple. In the second volume of this series (*HA*, pp. 459–64), I discussed the semantic function of limping and suggested that, in America at least, it symbolized a lack of periodicity. Yahyáhaäs, however, turns this disability to his own advantage: the fact that one of his legs is shorter than the other enables him to run across the mountain slopes as fast as a normal individual would over flat ground. This is tantamount to saying that in the conditions peculiar to his haunts, his *victims, and not himself, become the true cripples*. Since he travels about on legs of unequal length in a world of sloping surfaces, the two anomalies cancel each other out. Only, then, for the master of the mountains does hunting satisfy the demands of a well-ordered periodicity. On the other hand, as has already been shown, hunting proves arhythmic for humans, who must struggle up mountainsides for which their legs are unsuited, and run counter to the ideal course of their existence by exposing themselves to the full severity of winter, whereas culturally things were so arranged that they might have enjoyed shelter in a comfortable house.

Yahyáhaä's limping not only confirms my interpretation of the paradoxical nature of hunting among the tribes along the borders of California and Oregon, it also provides striking confirmation of the relationship I was trying to establish between the myths of North and South America, in which the origin of hunting is presented as being a function of that of tobacco. It is true that we know of no Klamath or Modoc myths which can be related unmistakably to the origin of tobacco. However, the fact that the armature of the corresponding South American myths is present implicitly in the myths I have just been discussing is immediately obvious if we compare them with a Chaco myth, which explains the origin of tobacco, while introducing the same dialectical relationship between the absence and presence of periodicity. In the Chaco myth (M_{24}; *RC*, pp. 100–107; *HA*, *passim*), an ogress poisons her husband with her menstrual blood, thereby turning him into a cripple. So, like her homologue in the Modoc myths, she succeeds in making her victim aperiodic by turning to advantage her own periodicity which, as in the other case too, is pathological in nature. She next devours the birds taken from the nest by her husband, and then tries to devour him as well; he escapes from her, flings her to her death in a pit-fall and burns her body on a pyre, the ashes of which yield the first tobacco.[6] So, an open conflict between an ogress and a cripple, which ends with the ogress being flung into a pit-fall and then burnt on a pyre, leads to

---

[6] The comparison between the myths of North and South America acquires even greater significance from the fact that the Indians in this particular area of North America cultivated their tobacco (or the plants they used as tobacco) on beds of ashes (cf: Sapir-Spier 2, p. 269; Sapir 8, p. 259; Goddard 4, p. 37). This was their only form of agriculture.

the presence of tobacco. We have only to reverse the formula to obtain a concentrated expression of the Modoc myths featuring Yahyáhaäs. In Modoc mythology an overt conflict between male characters (or female in M_{549c}) and a one-legged or crippled ogre, resulting from the absence of tobacco, causes the ogre to be either hurled to his death over a cliff or burnt on a pyre.

At the same time, we can confirm that the duplication of the armature, observable on the left of the diagram as we move from the myths of the southern to those of the northern hemisphere, is repeated at the other end of the field. On the one side, the presence of salt, a free gift from nature to culture, constitutes the means of hunting, the antecedent of adornments. On the other side, the absence of tobacco (or, to be more precise, of the smoker's equipment, his pipe and fire-drill, which, as manufactured objects, correspond more closely to adornments) constitutes the antecedent of hunting, for the same reasons which make these objects the means whereby harmonious relationships can be maintained with the supernatural world. In the last resort, these reasons refer to the techno-economic sub-structure, which is what we must always look to first if we are to try to understand the differential gaps between ideologies.

What I have just demonstrated is a kind of mirror-effect, as a result of which two mythic systems, situated at a considerable distance from each other, are reflected in one another, while at the same time undergoing distortions which can be ascribed to the structure of the reflecting surface, which is different in either case. On the other hand, it should not be forgotten that it was the analysis of a particular episode in a Yana myth (M_{546}) that led me to this result. This particular myth both reproduces and transforms, in a still more systematic fashion, myths which are situated quite close to it in space. As this myth sends the protagonists wandering through Modoc territory and even makes them venture as far as the northern frontiers of Klamath country, it must be supposed that the Yana had some knowledge of foreign territories.[7] Actually, the previously noted references to Klamath Lake and Crater Lake are accompanied by information relating to both localities and myths which are known to be situated in the same region.

In order to prove this, I shall have to embark on a very detailed

---

[7] There is perhaps some justification for extending to all the tribes in the region the remark made by a former observer, who shared their life at a time when they were still free to go wherever they chose: 'These Indians have a great thirst for knowledge, particularly of the location and extent of countries. They are great travellers . . . Geography is taught by drawing maps in sand or ashes with a stick . . . they heap the sand or ashes in ridges or spurs to show the ranges of mountains' (Miller, p. 240).

comparison of several myths. Since the reader will constantly have to refer back to ground already covered, there is a danger that he may lose the thread if I do not begin by indicating, in broad outline, the interpretation I am proposing. In the first part of this book, I was able to make use of myths, the hero of which is a bird-nester. In the second part, I introduced the Loon Woman myth, which is, in several ways, a transformation of the first. In various respects, these transformations are tantamount to inversions: the hero is trampled down instead of being raised up; the origin of anti-adornments (collars made from human hearts), snatched by a woman from her brothers, replaces the origin of adornments (porcupine quills) lavished by a man on his wives, etc.

So, at this stage, we have at our disposal two mythic series corresponding to each other, but one, as it were, has a rotatory power to the right while the other has a rotatory power to the left. Developing what may appear to be a bold analogy, I propose to establish that the originality of the Yana myth can be explained by a form referred to in chemistry as racemic. It welds the two types into a single body and neutralizes their opposition. However, as will also be seen, it can do this only by inverting both of them along an axis different from the one on which the original opposition was situated. This phenomenon results from the fact that, in order to build up its story by placing end to end segments of narrative borrowed alternately from both series, the Yana myth has to recast them quite considerably.

The myth begins with a description of a family consisting of a father, his numerous sons and his two daughters. The composition of the family is a reversal, on two counts, of the one presented by the corresponding Klamath myth (M_{538}): a mother (*father*), her numerous sons, her daughter and a daughter-in-law (*pregnant wife/young virgin*).[8] Since the brothers do not occupy a marked position in either myth, it can be said that the daughter, the future Loon Woman, constitutes the invariant term, the central figure around which the family configuration rotates in the two myths.

Regarding the *pregnant daughter-in-law/virgin daughter* opposition, it will be noted that the former is called Meadowlark in M_{538}, the latter Eagle in M_{546}. Both are life-savers, although one acts passively and in terms of the low (she dies in a fire, but after lying face downwards to protect the children in her womb), the other actively, in the terms of the high (she hangs on to the sun, a celestial fire, so as to be able eventually to save her relatives). We know from M_{531}, M_{538}, and M_{560} that the eagle and the meadowlark are in a correlational and oppositional relationship to each other. In this case a true

---

[8] The Modoc, who live between the Klamath, the Achomawi and the Shasta, in one version (M_{540}) mention a father and mother.

'Eagle' (for that is her name) brings her own people back to life, whereas in M_{531} etc. false eagles, who are really meadowlarks, provide a father with a pretext for sending his son to what he believes will be his death.

In another Yana version to which I have already referred (M_{547}; Sapir 3, pp. 228–32) and in which the life-saving sister does not appear and her name is taken over by a brother, a single character called Meadowlark, fulfils an intermediary function between that of her homonym in M_{538} and that of the Eagle in M_{546}. This character is an old woman, who lives alone to the east of the village. It follows that the Loon Woman, in this myth a stranger who has come from the east, has to pass Meadowlark's house before reaching her destination. She stops at the house and claims to be the old woman's niece. The old woman, however, is suspicious and even contemplates killing her visitor. Being of a somewhat changeable nature, she abandons this idea and, instead, offers sensible advice which the other woman will not follow. She could have been a life-saver like Eagle, but like Meadowlark in M_{538}, resigns herself to her fate.

The incestuous sister in M_{538} is married, and lives somewhere to the east of her native village. The Yana versions separate out these attributes and present either an incestuous, but unmarried, sister (M_{546}), or a lascivious killer and a stranger like the other one whose position in relation to the family makes her however non-incestuous, and who lives in the east (M_{547}). It will be remembered that the Modoc — the northern edge of whose territory borders on the area occupied by the Klamath and the Achomawi, southerly neighbours of the Yana — also adopt intermediary solutions in their myths: like the Klamath, they marry the sister to a man outside the tribe, but add the detail that she continues to hang around the parental house (M_{539}); or else they present her as being unmarried (M_{540}) as in one of the Yana versions, but without ever adopting the extreme formula of the other version.

From this point onwards, the analysis becomes more involved since, in addition to the versions already quoted, the counterpoint of the myths brings in by implication the Modoc myth (M_{541}) which links up the bird-nester story to an inversion of the Loon Woman myth (see above, p. 70 *et seq*.). The first scene of M_{541} reflects the economic life of the community: the heroine's brothers are fishermen; in M_{546}, they are hunters. In the continuation of M_{546}, there are an increasing number of indirect references to M_{541}.

Let us consider, for instance, the setting of the story: a large communal house or sweat-lodge which, for the sake of the mythic purpose, the text of M_{546} sets in opposition to a family home. This is not in keeping with what

Kroeber says about the Yana, but he is led astray by the deeply rooted conviction of the American school that myths always reflect anthropological reality, and so he fails to take into account the dialectical relations existing between the myths and which often lead them to run counter to reality. I shall come back to this point which seems to me to be of prime importance (see below, p. 103). For the moment, let me simply single out two details in M_{546} which show that, unlike M_{541} and other myths in the set, the Yana myth explodes the family group in order to replace it by a unit which is at once broader and more limited: human society, as symbolized by the sweat-house. In the first place, the list of characters includes Coyote, who is not a member of the family, but who lives there as a guest. In the second place, the Sapir version of the myth we are dealing with, in which strangers are also featured (the Loon Woman herself, as well as several visitors from outside the tribe), tells how the stranger tried to persuade the village girls to join her in spying on the men in the sweat-lodge. 'No,' one replies, 'we never look inside when the men are taking their sweat baths.' Whatever the ethnographical reality may have been, it is quite clear from the text that the sweat-house, in this case, is fulfilling the function of a men's house and is in opposition to the *family home*, the setting of the story in the other versions. Even considering the matter from the strictly ethnographical standpoint, Sapir and Spier (1, p. 257) admit the possibility that, in Yana society, some among the earth-lodges were built as sweat-lodges, 'that is, primarily as men's gathering places and dormitories'. In Shasta society the sweat-houses actually were men's houses (Holt, p. 306).

In the family home, the young hero, the object of his sister's lust, is kept permanently hidden at the bottom of a pit specially prepared for this purpose. In the men's house in M_{596}, he is lying all by himself in a corner for temporary reasons. So in the two cases seclusion presents opposite characteristics, being institutional in the first and occasional in the other. And, when the incestuous daughter climbs on to the roof of the sweat-house in which her brother is resting and loudly proclaims her love, she is clearly in opposition to the virtuous sister in M_{541}, who, after climbing on to the roof of the family house, from which vantage point she can catch a glimpse of her suitor, manages not to betray her feelings.

Whereas the stranger in M_{547}, like the heroine in the northern versions, hastens the arrival of nightfall, the incestuous sister in M_{546} appears to be less impatient, although the myth makes it clear that the sun is still high in the sky when the desired brother is handed over to her. On the contrary, she makes the most of the daylight to spin out this stage of their journey. The inversion would seem to be called for by the requirements of a plot which presents the other sister as being in league with the sun; the reason for this will soon be made clear.

In neither case is the marriage consummated; either the young man escapes from his sister's incestuous embrace (M_{546}) or, when the incest motif is absent through the heroine belonging to another tribe (M_{547}), an acorn cup is fitted over the hero's penis as a means of preventing copulation.

The spider, who is a man in M_{547} and other myths, becomes a woman in M_{546}, and, what is more, a kinswoman: the father's life-saving sister, an inversion of the father's destructive sister, the Loon Woman's role in respect of her nephews in the other versions (M_{538}, M_{539}).

According to these same versions, the passengers in the basket constitute a biological family. The Yana myths present them as a village community, headed by Coyote, who is no more than a guest; 'everyone in the sweat-house followed him' (Curtin 3, p. 409). According to M_{539}, one brother makes the mistake of looking down during the ascent. In M_{546} and M_{547}, on the other hand, Coyote is the culprit, and the myth is careful to stress that he is a guest, but not a member, of one of the village families: he thus fulfils the semantic function of non-brother.

In M_{546}, only the eldest sister escapes disaster, a privilege which one of the Modoc myths (M_{540}) — again one which is half-way towards the Yana myths, since it also features two contrasting sisters — reserves for the youngest. In this version, all the inhabitants of the village, except the family which had remained on the ground, escape by changing into birds; the youngest sister, who remains on the ground, also escapes the fire. In the Yana myth (M_{546}), we find a strict inversion of this sequence: although they manage to rise up into the sky, all the inhabitants of the village perish, except the eldest sister who succeeds in reaching an even greater height than the others, being already endowed, as her name Eagle indicates, with the nature of a bird.

All these reversals preserve an operational significance, down to the tiniest details. The fire-raiser in M_{546} captures her victims' hearts with a kind of butterfly net, the construction of which is painstakingly described in the myth. This *net* used for *capturing* is an inversion of the *paddle* which is used by the homologous heroine in M_{539}, not to remove hearts from the fire, but to push them into it. And the two instruments have an obvious correlational relationship with others: for instance, the heavy club used by Loon Woman in the other Yana version (M_{547}) to *push back* the *eyes*, not the *hearts*, of her victims into the fire; and also the *mallet* or stick used by the demiurge in M_{531} and M_{538} to thrust the heroine's baby out of the pyre (cf. Barker 1, p. 36, n. 26). This last link is made all the more definite by the fact that M$_{538}$ tells the story of the birth and adventures of a *boy victimized by his incestuous father*, whereas M$_{546}$, which differs on this point from all the other versions of the Loon Woman myth (but we are also beginning to guess why), duplicates the character of the survivor, turning him into an elder brother and a *father*, both of them *victims of an incestuous daughter*. After being thrown high into the air by the blaze, their two hearts come down, one on to an island in a river near Klamath Lake, the other at the foot of Mount Shasta. This gives a twofold opposition in relationship to the other versions: *island/mountain*, and *mountain foot/summit*.

We come now to a transformation of prime importance. Why does M$_{546}$ state that the hearts, almost as soon as they touch the ground, reconstitute the bodies of which they were part? The explanation is given in the continuation of the story: it is to allow the bodies to be buried, one up to its neck, and the other up to its face. In other words, we have here a situation which is both a repetition and an inversion of the bird-nester story along two axes. Father and son, who, in the bird-nester story, were in opposition to each other as persecutor and persecuted, appear together, in M$_{546}$, as being jointly persecuted. And far from one of them being sent by the other to the top of a tree or a rocky cliff, they are both buried in the ground, hurled downwards, instead of the son alone being raised upwards. As I foretold, we now have confirmation that the Loon Woman myth is an inversion of the bird-nester story. Furthermore, the hero of the Yana version M$_{546}$, like his Modoc homologue in M$_{540}$, is called Wildcat. It would perhaps be unwise to make too much of this detail of the myth since, in the other Yana version (M$_{547}$), he is called Eagle. However, even if the detail is a pure accident, it would be wrong, I think, not to emphasize that the Klamath hero is brought down from the tree where he had been stranded in a basket lined with a wildcat skin, a symbol of luxury for the Indians (see above, p. 34; Sapir 3, p. 36, n. 55), and that South American bird-nesters have similar names, or names which have the same connotation. The bird-nester in Kayapo-Gorotire mythology is called Botoque, the name of an adornment, and, in Bororo mythology, the hero's name, Gueriguiguiatugo, can be broken down into two words, the second of which, meaning 'the painted one', refers periphrastically and in aesthetic terms to the jaguar (cf. *RC*, pp. 92, 160, n. 12), whose pelt is greatly prized.

But, if the bird-nester character is symmetrical with that of the buried hero, it would seem normal that his rescuer, who is endowed, in South America, with either a terrestrial (jaguar) or a celestial nature (vulture), according to whether we are thinking of the straight or the inverted versions – and, for the same reason, in North America, with a celestial (butterfly-sisters) or a terrestrial nature (snow-birds) — should acquire the even more exalted celestial nature of the eagle, when the position of the victim, the counterpart of his own, is itself inverted from the high to the low.

Let us look at the episode featuring the Tsanunewa brothers. It will be remembered that, according to Curtin, the name refers to fishers, which are consequently carnivorous like the eagle, but — if the bird in question is a killdeer (plover), as is suggested in another source (see above, p. 95) — on a much more modest scale. I have two observations to make on this subject. Firstly, in the Sapir version (M_{547}), where the life-saving heroine does not appear and the name Eagle is transferred to the persecuted hero, the role of avengers is also assigned to two water birds: the diver, 'a small duck which lives in muddy water', and the heron. Together they tackle Loon Woman, although in fact the heron leaves the task mainly to his companion. Here, the most strongly marked opposition is, then, between a diver — probably a grebe — and the loon. I shall deal with it again in Section 2 of Part Three.

Secondly, the Tsanunewa brothers replace the two Dioscuri who, in the other versions of the myth, have, like them, the task of killing the culprit: they are brothers too in M_{539}, and are informed by a 'white-necked duck', whereas here it is a woman called Eagle who acquaints them with the facts.[9] Whereupon, they pierce Loon Woman's body with arrows and bring back the corpse whole, a point which is in glaring contrast to other myths in the group, in which the Dioscuri decapitate her with a knife and bring back only the severed head.

There are reasons for this divergence, as for the others. The Dioscuri in the Klamath and Modoc versions appear, as it were, as specialists in duality: as twins they are joined in their mother's womb, and become separate beings the moment their grandmother removes them from it; but she immediately sticks them together again to form a single being, who later manages to break apart into two individuals. When they behead their aunt, a close relative, they are also, in a sense, cutting into the quick of their own family, and once again reveal their paradoxical nature, the analysis of which must be left until later. For the moment, it is sufficient to note that their nature differs in all respects from that of the Tsanunewa brothers: they are close relatives of the other characters in the story, instead of being total strangers; they are twins, not brothers of different ages; they are born and grow to manhood during the course of the myth, whereas the Tsanunewa brothers, when they first appear, are able to hunt and even to marry (since

[9] But if the word *tsanunewa* refers to the killdeer, as it does in the Achomawi language, there is an additional torsion to be noted in relationship to M_{538}, where the shrill-voiced bird itself plays the part of informant.

Eagle offers herself to them). So the Klamath and Modoc versions approach the Dioscuri from the inside, whereas the Yana version describes them from the outside. Supplementary in the one case (since they originate from a duplicated body), the Dioscuri become complementary in the other, as is stressed by the respective preferences of the Tsanunewa brothers for red or green bones, and by their choice of a different part of their victim's body into which each shoots his arrow.

If, as I have supposed, the buried hero forms a counterpart to the elevated bird-nester, it follows that, in turn, the sisters who save the eldest brother are a counterpart of the butterfly-sisters who, in the straight versions (M_{530}, $_{531}$, $_{538}$), fulfil the same function in respect of the man marooned at the top of the tree. The word *jamuka* (Sapir-Swadesh, *zaamuk'u*) means, in Yana, the acorn worm. So it is possible that the mythic transformation is using a real-life metamorphosis for its own purposes: in nature, too, caterpillars turn into butterflies. The larval sisters in M_{546}, as well as those who in M_{530}, $_{531}$, $_{538}$ have reached adulthood, release the hero from his terrestrial or celestial prison, look after him and tend his wounds; in all these myths, he also becomes their husband.

On the other hand, the two old men in M_{546} who are called after caterpillars obviously form a contrasted pair. They are respectively the hero's father and father-in-law, and one takes from him the wives the other has given him. They are personifications of two species of larvae character-ized by diametrically opposed habits, since one, unlike human beings, feeds on *poisonous leaves*, whereas the other, like human beings, feeds on *edible seeds*.

In the Yana version (M_{546}), the inversion of the porcupine episode by means of the deer episode which replaces it is even more obvious than in the Modoc version which, as always, occupies a middle position in the sense that it combines the two motifs. In this instance, the hunter is not the victim of his game: on the contrary, he lures the deer with the salt water he exudes and the animals thus become easy prey. A humidified hero, the provider of a salt spring, and a source of gustatory delight for beasts heavy with meat, is thus opposed to a hero covered with powdery ash (see above, p. 53) and bothered by ornament-bearing beasts. By the same token, the etiological function of M_{546} becomes clear: it explains the origin of salt springs, that is, doubly beneficial terrestrial water; it provides areas from which salt can be extracted and it acts as a natural attraction for big game (whereas porcupine quills have a cultural attraction for humans), thus facilitating the process of hunting.

In the Klamath and Modoc versions, the bird-nester, once he is restored to health, recovers the wives who had been taken from him by his father. In the Yana myth, the buried hero's sister finds him staying at the house of women who are being encouraged by their father to marry him. However, it is as if the story, on approaching its conclusion, was compressing its motifs, as a fugue does in the stretto: between one group of myths and the other, the alternating passages seem to accelerate and to become shorter. Immediately after this inverted allusion to the bird-nester myth, we come back again to the Loon Woman story, also in an inverted form: instead of a younger sister (M_{540}) bringing her own people back to life after cursing her sister whom she turns into a bird, in M_{546} an elder sister repeats the same miracle, but this time to the advantage of the younger sister, who is both morally redeemed and physically brought back to life by the elder. Lastly, the final episode brings together the subject and the answer of the fugal composition in a series of subtle chords. Instead of a hero who gets the better of his father once and for all, and regains possession of the wives taken from him by the father, we have a father who gets the better of his son once and for all and changes him from a temporarily secluded child into a permanently hidden one; he also appropriates the wives, who become his or those of the older brothers. The myth ends, then, in the same way as the bird-nester myth, except that the content of the story is reversed. As it happens, the inverted story reproduces an episode of the Loon Woman myth, but puts it at the end not at the beginning. In respect of the myths it is recasting, the Yana version operates two reversals, one affecting the content of the two plots, the other the order of events in one of the stories. There is no denying the self-evident fact that, since it concludes with the transformation of the hero into a hidden child, the Yana version of the Loon Woman myth, although it tells the same story, gives the events in reverse order and finishes exactly at the starting point of the Modoc versions.

If it is the case, as I said at the beginning, that the Yana myth reflects the more northerly versions, it does so not in the manner of a single mirror but of several, the reflective properties of which create different types of symmetry. Although they lived on either side of a common frontier, the Klamath-Modoc and the Hokan-speaking groups to which the Yana belonged spoke different languages, had different interests and looked upon each other as mortal enemies. But at the same time, a certain use of symmetry could provide them with a means of overcoming the opposition resulting from their geographical proximity and their political or economic rivalry. In a different context (L.-S. 19), I have emphasized the functional role of symmetry, which can so mould the rites and myths of neighbouring communities that they present inverted images of each other: this creates the relationship best suited for the reconciling of the resemblances brought about by geographical or historical circumstances, and which are not easily discarded, with the differences each community cultivates in order to emphasize its original character.

In the case of the myths we have just been discussing, this normal situation is complicated by a factor which is less so. Not only do these myths effect a transformation of one story along several axes, they locate it in one particular stretch of territory, the nature of which they cannot change, since it has an objective reality; the most they can do, occasionally, but not systematically, is to shift the same, simple topographical pattern a few kilometres this way or that on the map to fit it over another similar one, to which the same function can thus be assigned. But some localities – Crater Lake, upper Klamath Lake and Mount Shasta – would seem to be so firmly engraved on the imagination of various tribes that, even when these places are not within their territory, they cannot bring themselves to change the names.

In order to overcome this new type of difficulty, mythic thought has to bring into operation an additional kind of symmetry. And we can now see that the symmetry we have detected in the myths corresponds exactly to the inversion of perspective which occurs when the same stretch of territory is looked at from opposite ends. This is precisely the situation of the Klamath and the Yana. The Klamath look south from upper Klamath Lake in the direction of Mount Shasta; the Yana look north from Mount Lassen and Mount Shasta towards Klamath Lake and Crater Lake. It follows that their respective views of myths closely linked with this common territory are inverted; what the Klamath consider as the beginning, the Yana think of as the end.

On a smaller scale, we have already noted a hint of the same phenomenon in the Modoc myths. Owing to the fact that the first part of M_{539} is an inversion of M_{541}, while at the same time occupying the same place (that is, the story of the wise virgin is substituted for that of the mad woman), the initiatory sequence common to the two myths undergoes a perceptible shift: it comes before the bird-nester story forming the second part of M_{541}, and concludes the celestial brothers' story which replaces it in M_{539}. But it is when we compare myths deriving from very different communities that these transformations take on their full significance. Since the bird-nester myth and the one featuring the Loon Woman are widely present together throughout the groups of tribes acquainted with them, they are reflections of each other; and should it happen, as in Yana mythology, that they are welded into a single mythic body, racemic in form and thus neutralizing their opposition, this mythic body itself must be a reflection of another – even if it is only a potential one – of which it presents an enantiomorphous image, like the images produced in the minds of people living on either side of the same frontier, by the same stretch of territory looked at from opposite angles.

In order to bring out more sharply the points at issue, I have contrasted the Klamath-Modoc and the Yana versions, since they originate from tribes situated well to the north and south of the area of distribution of the Loon Woman myth. In so doing, I have neglected some intermediary or marginal versions, which must now be examined.

The Atsugewi and the Achomawi, who are Hokan-speaking like the Yana, used to live between the Yana and the Modoc in the Pit River basin, so called because of the many blind pits dug in the ground as deer traps, or perhaps as defences along the tracks leading to the villages (Miller, p. 373; Garth 2, p. 132). To the west, Achomawi territory bordered on that of the Shasta, who were also Hokan-speaking and with whom they had an ambiguous relationship (Miller, p. 33; Kniffen, p. 301). To the south, the Atsugewi inhabited the valleys of several tributaries of Pit River; their southern neighbours were the Yana and the Maidu, a mountain-dwelling tribe belonging to the Penutian linguistic family (Figures 7, 9). These are the five groups, whose myths I am about to examine; I start with an Atsugewi version which can serve as reference myth, first because of the wealth of detail contained in it, and secondly because of the geographical position occupied by the Atsugewi at the centre of the intermediary zone we are now dealing with.

M_{550}. Atsugewi. 'The Loon Woman'

At one time, people had no flint for their arrow points; they made them from bark and this did not work well. Ground-Squirrel [*Eutamias townsendi?*] went to Flint Man and said he was hungry; he was given pounded flint to eat. He ate much of it; he shammed sickness and defecated blood. Flint Man thought he would die, so he left him and went out. Squirrel made up a large bundle of flints, dug a hole under the ground and managed to get away.

When he got back to his house, he hid his treasure, apart from one flint – a knife which, to the amazement of everybody, he used to cut up his meat. He shared the flints among his fellows: 'With these,' he explained, 'you can kill deer better and can cut up the meat.' All the people in the village sat there chipping their flints; the next day they killed great quantities of deer.

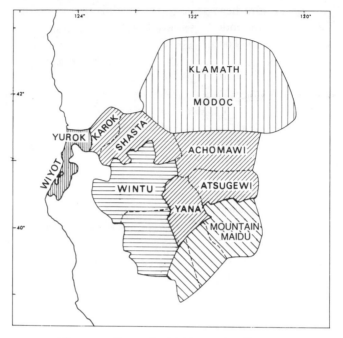

Figure 9. From the Maidu to the Klamath

After this, one day Dog travelled far to the west to steal fire from a woman who owned all the fire. From the roof of the house he looked down into the smoke-hole and caught a few sparks in his ear, put in a little dry tinder, then ran off home. At the request of the Fire Woman, Blue Jay the trickster caused rain to fall, but Dog ran so fast that he reached the village at sunset. The next morning he gave the fire to the village people. Henceforth, in addition to hunting, they could roast their game.

That night, an Indian called Wildcat had a bad dream. He left the big house and went to the little house near by, where his two sisters Eagle and Loon were sleeping. Fearing that there might be further visits, Loon smeared her body with pitch. The next night, encouraged by his first attempt, Wildcat had connection with Loon and some of his fur was left sticking to the pitch. Now that Loon had discovered who the visitor was, she became very angry and set the sweat-house ablaze. The people grew afraid, accused Wildcat, and agreed to let him go off with his sister. However, Butterfly had removed Wildcat's membrum and put a pathetically small one in its place. Loon went off with her lover, and being anxious to make him her husband, she made night come on quickly. But, in spite of all his endeavours, Wildcat could not satisfy Loon. Early in the morning, while Loon was asleep, he put a log of wood in his place and ran away.

Meanwhile, spider had begun to make a net, and as soon as Lynx returned, everyone got into it. Coyote, the father of the two sisters, got in first. Eagle flew off. The net was already high in the sky when the outraged Loon reached the village and set fire to it. In vain she begged her brothers to wait for her. Coyote, being anxious to have one last look at his daughter, made a tiny hole in the net. It immediately burst and all in it fell into the blazing house. Loon quickly made a seed-beater—a kind of woven racquet used by the women to beat the bushes and make the seeds fall into their basket (cf. Kroeber 1, plate 29 and p. 814; Garth 2, pp. 139, 151); when the bodies of her victims exploded (popped) and their hearts shot into the air, she used the seed-beater to catch them as they fell. She let her father's heart go, and missed three others. Wood-worm's heart fell far over towards Shasta. Butterfly's fell far to the east. Blue Stone's heart disappeared.[10] Eagle was not burned, for she was flying about weeping and making the mountains, for up until this time the world had been uniformly flat.

Loon strung the hearts and put them about her neck as a necklace, and went to one lake after another until she finally came to one at the head of Butte Creek, and there she stayed. Meanwhile, Eagle was looking for the hearts that had escaped and making mountains. She discovered Wood-worm at last in a country towards the north, where two sisters called Beads had dug out the heart which was buried in a deer-lick, formed by Woodworm's tears. When Eagle discovered that her brother had become a person again and was happily married to the Bead girls, his saviours, she returned to near the head of Butte Creek. Here lived two brothers named after small brown water birds, who revealed to her Loon's where-abouts: 'She had a necklace about her neck and looked at herself all the time in the water.' They agreed to kill Loon on condition Eagle would give them arrow points of deer bone: one wanted bone from deer at a time when their hair was turning red, the other at a time when they dropped their antlers.

The boys argued about who should shoot first, but finally agreed that both should shoot at once. They took Loon's body back to her sister Eagle, who skinned and stuffed it, saying that from then on 'loons must

[10] The blue paint came from a kind of rock found in Achomawi territory (Garth 2, p. 147); also, the Chilula called the stones used for boiling water 'blue stones'.

cry and laugh in the springtime'. Eagle found the other two missing hearts and added them to those on the necklace.

Eagle went back to her native village, which was near Pitville, and rebuilt the sweat-house. She laid the hearts in the water in the river near by, then went into the house and slept. In the early dawn, all the hearts came to life again and all the people trooped back into the house, and went on living as before (Dixon 4, pp. 174–7).

There are several known Achomawi versions of this myth; all differ from each other, and from the Atsugewi version. According to one (M$_{551}$; Dixon 4, pp. 165–7), the Loon Woman arranged to go off with Wildcat 'whom no one ever touched or saw, since he was kept like a treasure in a sack which was hung up inside the house'. They both set off westwards, and made camp together, but the young boy fled at dawn and returned to his hiding-place.

In this myth, Loon Woman starts a fire by screaming and rolling about on the ground: as she does so, the ground bursts open to reveal gorges and canyons. In the village, the people take fright: one person called Cocoon Man makes a speech, and Mice brothers weave a cord from spliced rye-grass, which they shoot into the sky by means of a skilfully aimed arrow. Everyone climbs up it, but Coyote, Loon's father, turns round to have a last look at his daughter. The cord breaks, the climbers fall into the fire, and Loon catches the hearts in a net: she keeps most of them in order to make herself a necklace, and gives the rest to Silver Fox (the Achomawi demiurge; cf. Kroeber 1, p. 315; Garth 2, p. 195).

Loon then travels all over the world, while her sister Eagle, who is looking for her in order to take the hearts from her, 'kicks up the earth and makes mountains'. She finally secures the hearts, rebuilds the sweat-house and lays the hearts in the river near by. Loon's victims come back to life at dawn. Then Silver Fox gives them each a name, and tells them to go off and spread all over the world; he tells each one where to live, gives him his cry and paints him with his colours. Then they go off, some in one direction, some in another.

A version recorded by Curtis (Vol. 13, pp. 209–10; M$_{552}$) takes the form of the terminal episode of the myth about the creation of the world. The two demiurges Qan (Fox) and Jemul (Coyote), after creating the world and human beings, introduced war in order to limit the growth of population, and natural death to ensure the effectiveness of the check. They thus made it impossible for their two sons to return to life. Qan was very angry about the consequence of their action, for which he held Jemul responsible, and tried in vain to kill him. The demiurges were reconciled; one created the lake and river network and the other all the varieties of fish.

It was about this time that Jemul's daughter fell in love with her cousin called 'Fighting Man', son of the old chief Apóna (cf. Angulo 2, p. 125, *a-pónáhá*, 'Cocoon'). She took him off in a westerly direction, but at night he crept away and hid in the sweat-house. The young girl returned to the village, but on failing to get the boy back, she hurled flames at the building. 'Well,' said Qan, 'let her burn it up and we will go up into the sky.' On his orders, Yuninu (Mouse) shot a straw into the heavens, where it remained fixed and became a ladder. Qan and Jemul climbed up it and disappeared for ever.

Another version (M_{553}; Angulo-Freeland 2, pp. 126–32) begins by contrasting Coyote's two daughters, who are called Eagle and Loon. Eagle is well behaved and hard working; Loon is always flirting and, worst of all, does not take the usual precautions when she has her monthly periods, a fact which brings the hunters bad luck. The other village chief, called Cocoon, remembers that 'her mother made trouble that way long ago'. Cocoon is the father of a secreted son, whom he keeps rolled in a buckskin at the back of the sweat-house. The other sons Wolf, Weasel, Marten and Wildcat live there too. Coyote's two daughters used to sleep in a camp apart from the others, and arrive early to cook the hunters' breakfast.

As in M_{550}, the story continues with an account of Wildcat's incestuous visits. Although he is a cousin rather than a brother, Loon is equally furious and attacks the house by shooting her lightning through the smoke-hole; in other words, there is a difference from M_{550} in that she produces fire which is celestial in origin. And when she is offered Wildcat as her husband, she refuses him. The fact of being raped by Wildcat has given her a psychological shock and made her aware of the strong feeling she has for Woodworm, the hidden son of Cocoon, the old chief. This is the husband she now claims. The old father thinks it better to let her have her way, although he fears that Woodworm will not be able to satisfy her because of his tiny penis, and that in her disappointment at his inadequacy, Loon will resume her attacks. So they all decide to give Woodworm an enormous penis, which is so cumbersome he has to haul it along the ground. Coyote fears that it may disembowel his daughter, so, without the others knowing, he wrenches it off and throws it into the fire. Loon goes off, followed by her bashful lover; on the pretext that a storm is about to break, she sets up camp and prepares a comfortable bed, where, however, Woodworm lies flat on his belly, offering passive resistance to Loon, who tries unsuccessfully to turn him over. When she falls asleep from exhaustion, Woodworm gets up, finds a tree stump with a protruding branch and uses it to give his partner the illusion that he has satisfied her. Then he escapes and arrives breathless at the village, unable to speak.

The inhabitants are terrified when they see the approach of the fire started by Loon Woman in her fury of disappointment. The Spider brothers join forces and weave a long rope. Giant Lizard, also called The One-Without-Children, ties it to the end of an arrow which he plants in the sky. Eagle is the first to climb up, followed by the old chief Cocoon, then by Woodworm and the other brothers, Giant Lizard and lastly Coyote. His daughter Loon sees him and calls out to him; he turns round, the cord breaks and everybody falls into the fire which has set the whole village ablaze, except Eagle, Cocoon, Woodworm and another brother who have already succeeded in reaching the sky.

Loon collects the hearts in a winnowing basket. She keeps her father's and notices that four hearts are missing, in addition to Giant Lizard's, which is the last to fall and has shot right through the basket and landed on top of Mount Shasta. Being convinced that Lizard will cause her ruin, she tells her father that from now on they will assume the appearance of the animals whose names they bear. She will go and live in Tule Lake, Honey Lake, Goose Lake and Upper Lake (cf. map, Figure 7). She will recognize her father by his cry, and will answer him with her own.

Not far from there live Bluejay and his wife Tsanunéwa, whose name means Snipe or Killdeer or some other small marsh bird (Angulo-Freeland 2, p. 130; see above, pp. 49, 95). Bluejay is worried about having had no luck in hunting for a long time, and suspects the presence of Loon, whose mother has already caused similar trouble. Guided by a very beautiful song which seems to come from Mount Shasta, he discovers Lizard's heart half buried in the ground. He digs it out and takes it back to his wife. She puts it in a waterproof basket filled with warm water, and the heart comes back to life in the form of a baby. The child grows up very quickly and becomes a boy with a large protruding forehead. His adoptive mother encourages him to shoot arrows straight into the sky. One day, one falls back down on him and knocks the bump off his forehead, and it turns into another child.

Killdeer Woman's relatives, who live along the edge of the lake, reveal Loon's whereabouts to the young hero. This version of the myth, however, mentions two women by the name of Loon: one lives in the water, wearing a necklace made of hearts, and the other is her old mother, who has her house among the reeds. On Bluejay's orders, the two boys visit the old woman and borrow her boat, promising to give her half their catch. They watch the young Loon Woman go into her mother's house; the mother combs her long hair, and they admire her beauty. The next morning, the younger of the two boys shoots her with an arrow and hides the body in the boat under a pile of ducks, which he has also killed. When the old woman finds her daughter's body, she starts off after the killer, releasing lightning as she goes and setting the brush on fire. But Bluejay raises a strong wind which drives back the fire, and the elder of the boys, Lizard-Without-Children, shoots the sorceress dead. So both the Loon women die.

There is so much to be said about these myths that I must proceed in stages. First, a few remarks about the characters: we are already familiar with Eagle and her sister Loon, and their brother or cousin Wildcat, as well as with Coyote who retains his role as trickster but who, after being first a guest in the Yana version, here becomes the father of the two heroines, as well as a kinsman and a colleague of the old chief Cocoon, the owner of the sweat-house.

The name cocoon refers to the caterpillar of a large butterfly with brightly coloured wings (*Attacus*? Cf. p. 130), which spins its cocoon in the bushes. The Californian Indians used to gather these cocoons and make them into ritual objects, and perhaps the Yana too (Sapir-Spier 1, p. 259) made use of the cocoons of the caterpillar, whose name in their myths is given to the hero's father. It will be remembered that this species of caterpillar feeds off the poisonous leaves of *Rhus diversiloba*. In certain groups, at least, the pods of this plant could take the place of the cocoons (Goldschmidt, p. 426).

The character called Cocoon in the myth is a wise, gentle old man. He has a son called Woodworm, a large grub which lives under the bark on conifers, especially the sugar pine (*Pinus lambertiana*), on the resin of which it feeds. Perhaps its vernacular name *ámòq* (Angulo-Freeland 2, p. 125) can be compared with that of another larval character in the Yana version: Jamuka.

Not a great deal is known about Giant Lizard, except that he often appears as a surly, quarrelsome character, presumably because he is in mourning for his children.[11] The killdeer plover, *tsanunewa*, who is represented by two brothers in the Yana version, becomes the adoptive mother of a child who, like the child in the Klamath–Modoc versions, turns into two, but whose connection with the Tsanunewa brothers in M_{546} is established by the fact that, like them, these twins insist on arrow points made from deer bone, which are distinguishable in the one instance by their colour and in the other by the period of the year at which they are gathered.

[11] For mourning names, cf. Garth 2.

At the same time as Butterfly becomes male and takes his place among Loon Woman's victims, he cedes his helpful animal role (cf. $M_{530, 531, 538, 560}$) to two Bead sisters. The beads were probably sea shells, used both as ornaments and as currency, and which Pit River tribes obtained from the coastal communities in exchange for furs. This trade took place along an east-west axis: the furs travelled downstream and the shell beads upstream (Kroeber 1, pp. 309–11; Garth 2, p. 147). This is an important point, since in M_{550}, the Bead sisters live near Mount Shasta, that is, to the north-west of Atsugewi territory; and, in an Achomawi version, M_{551}, the direction of the incestuous journey is inverted, in relation to the Klamath-Modoc and Yana versions. M_{551} states explicitly that Loon Woman and Wildcat head westwards (cf. above, p. 120). Consequently, the fur-carrying hero sets out from the east, and the Bead sisters come from the west, that is, they follow the same direction as the trade exchanges, whereas Loon Woman, who creates anti-adornments in the form of the necklace made of hearts, travels in the opposite direction from the one followed by the real adornments.

These remarks lead to a consideration of the geographical aspect of the myths. In M_{550}, the action takes place between Pitville in the south, along the upper reaches of Pit River, Mount Shasta to the west, an indeterminate locality situated a long way to the east (where Butterfly's heart falls), and finally Butte Creek and its lake, which is difficult to identify since there are several streams with this name; however, the reference is to a northerly limit, which could correspond to a lake and a river, Butte Lake and Creek, both of which are situated along the border of Modoc country (cf. Kroeber 1, p. 318; Ray 3, p. 208; map, Figure 7).

If this is indeed the case, we have to accept the fact that, as I have noted in the case of most versions, the Atsugewi myth takes place almost entirely outside tribal territory. Hence, the apparent paradox that, in the Yana versions, Loon Woman comes from Hat Creek (or travels there) in Atsugewi country, whereas the Atsugewi themselves move the action further north, as if to keep it outside their tribal limits. M_{553}, however, covers an even vaster stretch of territory, since it ranges from Mount Shasta in the north-west to Honey Lake, which forms the south-eastern border between the Achomawi, on the one hand, and the Maidu, the Paiute and the Washo, on the other (Kroeber 1, p. 391; Heizer 2, see maps); the territory also includes Tule Lake in Modoc country, Goose Lake on its western border and Upper Lake, even further to the east (see above, p. 121).

As I observed in connection with the Yana version (M_{546}), this geographical syncretism gives rise to phenomena of reduplication, which affect the content of the myths. Compared to the Klamath and Modoc versions, the Achomawi and Atsugewi myths appear as diploid forms, which duplicate all the functions.[12] This is evident to varying degrees in all the four versions, but the procedure is probably applied most systematically in M_{553}. It features two fathers, Coyote and Cocoon, with contrasted characters; two incestuous brothers, Wildcat and Woodworm, one active and the other passive: the pitch 'eats' Wildcat in the figurative sense, since the hair from his coat remains stuck to it, while Woodworm actually feeds on it; two ways of preventing incest: an over-large penis or a pathetically small one; and two ways also of foiling the attempt at incest: the impotence of the male partner or the substitution of a tree branch better able to fulfil his function (in contrast to the inert log mentioned in the other versions). The escape from the fire-raiser involves co-operation between two characters: Lizard, who shoots the arrow, and Spider, who in turn splits up into the small and the large spider who have to join forces in order to spin a long enough rope. If we take into account the fact that Loon spares her father's heart, and fails to catch four and then a fifth, six hearts in all are missing from her necklace (that is, three times as many as in the Yana version, which was already doubling the number given in other versions). This incomplete anti-adornment is contrasted, in the adverse function, with two Bead sisters embodying true adornments. Loon chooses to live in four different lakes. In order to carry out his mission as avenger, Lizard has first of all to change into a dioscuric pair, whose victim too is duplicated, since M_{553} features both an old and a young Loon Woman. The other Achomawi version (M_{551}), although short, contains at least two indications which prove the same point. It accentuates the contrast between the two sisters; and by attributing the creation of gorges and canyons to one sister, and the creation of mountains to the other, it divides the surface of the earth into two aspects, negative and positive respectively. M_{552} emphasizes the dual nature of the demiurges.

It is worth noting that M_{553}, in which the scene of the action is extended as far as the border of Klamath country, is also the myth which most closely preserves several aspects of M_{538}, a myth originating from this area. Both myths feature a 'split' child (but in one he has a bump on his forehead instead of two heads); both split the Loon Woman into mother and daughter, an inference I was able to draw on the basis of the Klamath version, but which is demonstrated much more directly in the Achomawi version. In a sense, the Klamath myth hinted at several of these splittings I

---

[12] This procedure appears a particularly interesting subject of study, since other examples are to be found in California (cf. Angulo-Freeland 3, p. 252).

have just described, but suggested a diachronic interpretation of them: the child is split in two because he was originally formed from two individuals who had been stuck together; the mother recreates her daughter because she has gradually become aware of her sentimental attachment towards her. The Achomawi myth, on the contrary, sets out all its pairs, as it were, in the present moment. Or, when it has recourse to an historical justification (in explaining the daughter's present behaviour by her mother's past behaviour, see above, pp. 120–21, 122–3) it gives an inversion of the meaning of the corresponding element in the Klamath myth: in the one case, the daughter's behaviour is the final cause of the mother's; in the other case, the mother's behaviour is the efficient cause of the daughter's.

Still more striking is the contrast between the ways in which the Yana (M_{546}) and Achomawi (M_{553}) myths proceed in order to generate various forms of symmetry. It will be remembered that the Yana version succeeds in welding two stories into one, but only by observing a twofold condition: it has to invert the content of one story and to incorporate the other into it by reversing the narrative sequence. The internal symmetry of this version is, then, partly achieved by diachronic means; however, if we transpose it into synchronic terms, we must imagine it as being deployed along a vertical axis: on either side of the symmetrical plane, two series of images succeed each other and reconstitute a single myth, rather like the entity formed by a real-life person and his image as reflected in a mirror held slightly at an angle above him. The head would be tangent to its own reflection and the other parts of the body would be reproduced at various points in the same order, with the feet at the two extremities. I showed (see above, p. 116) that this type of symmetry also corresponds to the way in which images of one and the same landscape would fit together from end to end, when formed by observers looking at it from opposite points of view. Such was indeed the case with the Klamath and the Yana, living as they did at opposite extremities of a stretch of territory, with the whole area of which the myths, whether Yana or Klamath, claim to be concerned. However, one part of this territory appears to enjoy a privileged status: the part corresponding to Klamath country, the features of which are transposed by the other tribes into terms of their local topography, although they still continue to refer to the original localities. The symmetry of the Yana myth reflects this ambiguous attitude: it is as if the Yana, through the formal organization of the story, were expressing their claim to be looking at Klamath territory simultaneously from two different angles: one, the real one, having a south to north orientation, and the other, an imaginary one – since it would imply that they themselves were Klamath – with a north to south orientation. In the final analysis, the reason why the internal symmetry of the Yana version is concerned first and foremost with the axis of narrative succession rather than with that of simultaneity is that the Yana lived along the border, or even beyond the pale of the myth's chosen territory, but in order to incorporate that territory into their mythic heritage they had to behave as if they lived within its confines.

Compared to their external position, that occupied by the Atsugewi and the Achomawi can be seen to be median: these tribes live at the centre of the area of distribution and not along the edge. So, instead of having to follow through a series in one direction, then repeat the same movement in the other direction – which, as we have seen, is the oscillation corresponding to the construction peculiar to the Yana version – they have to solve a different problem: that posed by the presence of a myth, which is also part of their own mythology, along both their northern and their southern borders. In order to cope with this duality, they have recourse to a device which is the reverse of that employed by the Yana: they systematically reduplicate all the terms at each stage in the story, that is, carry out a series of operations which, at each point, creates a pair instead of two consecutive series of single operations. The diagrams in Figure 10 illustrate these different constructions, which in short are an expression of the fact, consistent with the geographical situation of the tribes, that one is outside and looking in while the other is on the inside and looking out.

It is worth noting that these narrative constructions correspond closely to similar patterns in the plastic arts, widely known as 'split representation' (L.-S. 5, Ch. XIII). There exist two styles of splitting, one in relation to the horizontal plane, the other in relation to the vertical plane. The art of New Caledonia provides the classic example of the first type, with its roof spires representing a person seen from chest to head, and extended by means of the back parts, which would normally be invisible, arranged in reverse order: thus, above the forehead can be seen the two front sides of the head, then the hair or head-dress, then the sides of the head at the back, and, crowning the whole, the nape of the neck in the form of a flat disc, which forms a counterpart to the one representing the chest or belly at the base of the structure (Figure 11; cf. Leenhardt, pp. 98–100; Guiart, pp. 13–15). This perpendicular structure can be recognized as being identical in form with the construction found in the Yana myth. On the other hand, the splitting observable in the north-west coast art of North America centres on a symmetrical vertical plane, on either side of which, as in the Achomawi myth, the two halves of the body are unfolded to the right and the left, while at the same time the relative distance of each part from the median

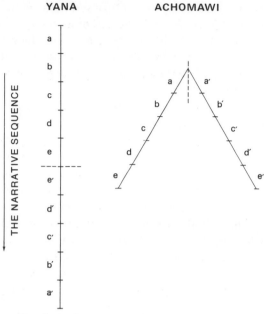

Figure 10. The diploid structure of the Yana and Achomawi myths

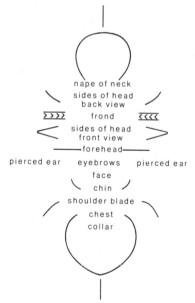

Figure 11. The pattern of stylization of a classic roof spire, New Caledonia. (Copied from Guiart, p. 15)

plane is respected. We might even venture to say that these two types of plastic figuration also correspond to different viewpoints, the same object – in this instance, the body of a human or an animal – being looked at respectively either from the outside or the inside (Figure 12).

The New Caledonian approach corresponds to the view that might be obtained from a distance or by means of an aerial survey; the north-west coast approach implies that the model is imagined as being split lengthwise and opening into two halves which, at least in the case of hinged masks, fold back and present their inner sides to view.

This being the case, we should now move on, from the northern, southern and central parts of the area of distribution of the Loon Woman myth to see what happens along the transverse axis, that is, from east to west.

The mountain-dwelling Maidu were neighbours of the Achomawi and Yana to the south-east. According to their version of the myth, the action

Figure 12. Vertical splitting and horizontal splitting. (Copied from Guiart, p. 14 and Boas 26, Fig. 232)

takes place 'a long way to the north'. These Indians are referring, then, by implication to the same stretch of privileged territory as the other tribes: in geographical terms, they do the same as the Wintu, who, although they live in the extreme south-west of the myth's area of distribution, acknowledge its northern affinities by retaining the Shasta names of the characters (see above, p. 63).

M_{554}. Maidu. 'The Loon Woman'

Eagle and Loon were the only two women in a sweat-house on the edge of a lake, where they lived with their brothers and cousins. There was one man in the sweat-house who took a bath every two days instead of every one day. Intrigued at finding an extremely long hair in the water, Loon discovered that it belonged to the brother she had been in love with for a long time. Next day she waited for them all to go in bathing. Coyote was among them; he stayed behind and took possession of her. Probably the young girl had been awakened by this incident, for immediately after-wards she confessed her love for her brother Wood Bug, and when the chief of the village, Sokotim maidü (cf. Shipley 1, *sokot*, '*Attacus cocoon*'), proposed other husbands, starting with Coyote, she began to hurl flames of fire, and announced that, at her order, the sun would soon burn down the house. Finally, her beloved brother was sent out to her, but not before he was given a penis sheath in the form of an acorn cup to prevent him having any connection with the woman.

The sun was already sinking when they left; but the woman looked at it and made it go down at once, so that night fell. But in vain did she proclaim that people from now on would imitate her example and go crazy; she could get no response from her lover. At dawn, the latter put a log into the woman's arms in his place and fled.

Everybody climbed into a net Spider had made, and which she started to draw up into the sky. When Loon woke up, she ran to the village with fire darting out [before her]. Lizard, who was at the bottom of the net, wanted to look at his sister; he made an opening, but the net tore. As the bodies fell into the fire, their hearts began to burst and to fly out through the air. Loon caught them with a scoop-shaped utensil made from plaited straw (cf. Dixon 6, Figure 47$_{a-b}$, p. 188) or with a seed-beater. Lizard's was first, but she 'missed the hearts of all the best ones'. She strung the hearts she had on a string for a necklace. Then she went away still further north, and lived in a lake. Meanwhile, Eagle was circling about in the sky overhead and swore that she would find the hearts wherever they had dropped, on mountains or in valleys. She found all but two, those of the best men of all. She went farther to the north, where she at last learned from the Water-Ousels and their grandmother that her sister was living in the lake near by. She went back to the village to get her brothers' bows and arrows. She gave them to the Water-Ousels, who killed the wicked sister while she was looking at herself in the water. 'You will never be able to harm people again,' proclaimed Eagle, 'for now you will be a bird that can be killed.'

Eagle returned to the village and threw the hearts into the lake. Next morning all the people had come to life. Then Eagle left for the north again to find the hearts that were still missing. There was a woman living there with two daughters. They heard something singing beautifully and followed the sound, and one day discovered the missing hearts buried in a piece of ground made salty by their tears and where the deer came to lick. The girls dug up the hearts and took care of them. These hearts belonged to Wood Bug and Fisher [or Pekan; fisher (*Mustela pennanti*), in Maidu *inbukim*, cf. Shipley 1, p. 201 *?inbuk*, 'fisher, animal'], who came back to life again and married the two sisters.

When she met her brothers, Eagle announced that human beings could avoid death by being immersed in water, unless she and her people were beaten in their attempt to obtain long life. She repeated the same words to her parents when she went back to the village. 'If we get beaten, the sweat-house will turn into a mountain and we will scatter.' And they all waited there to see what would happen . . . (Dixon 2, pp. 71–6).

In several respects, this Maidu version inverts the Achomawi and Atsugewi myths. The women live in the big house ('sweat-house' in the text; cf. above, p. 110) and not outside it, and the kinship links are particularly close, since the house is occupied by a single family. As a result of this, one character disappears; this is Wildcat, although he plays the main part in the versions distributed along the north-south axis from the Modoc to the Yana. There is a consequent redistribution of the roles: one of the village chiefs, Cocoon, remains unchanged, but the other chief, Coyote, plays the part of incestuous brother left vacant by Wildcat, and Lizard takes Coyote's place, and so changes from being an avenger, as in the Achomawi version (M_{553}), to being a trickster. The two commutations are equivalent, then, to an inversion. At the same time, his heart, which was the last to be missed, becomes the first to be caught. The Maidu version, like the Atsugewi one (M_{550}), repeats, but does not unduly emphasize, the motif of the salt-lick frequented by deer, which in the other myths occupies such a marked position. The absence of this motif from Achomawi mythology can probably be explained by the scarcity of salt in their territory; it would even seem that over-indulgence in respect of salt was viewed with disfavour (Kroeber 1, p. 310; Garth 2, p. 139). It will also be noted that the arrows used to kill Loon are not made specially with a particular type of head, but come from the store of weapons normally used by the absent brothers.

Most important of all, however, the Maidu version replaces the kind of synchronic splittings which occur so frequently in M_{553} by bringing into play a form of periodicity which is unmistakably diachronic in character. This transformation seems all the more significant in that each version also contains a preliminary hint of the other form. In M_{553}, the metamorphosis of the criminal heroine into a loon heralds the appearance of seasonal periodicity: henceforth the bird's cry will be heard in the spring. M_{554}, for its part, refers on two occasions to the kind of dualism so frequent in the Achomawi version, although always hypothetically: for instance, by mentioning two different utensils which could be used to catch the hearts, but without specifying which one the heroine actually employed, and by preserving the distinction, which is so clear in M_{551}, between the two geographical aspects of the terrain, but in the form of a vague allusion to the mountain tops and the valley bottoms, where the lost hearts might possibly fall.

M_{554}, on the other hand, is careful to locate several essential aspects of the plot in time: instead of being hidden in space, the Maidu hero is, in a sense, hidden in time: he goes out less often than his brothers. And although the Atsugewi version (M_{550}) is in opposition to the Achomawi one (M_{551}), in the sense that one ends by stating that 'people went on living as before', and the other by stating that 'the victims who came back to life became animals of different species and spread all over the world', they are both in opposition to the Maidu version which links the dispersal of humans (not animals) to man's short life-span. M_{551} concludes with the diversity of species, which constitutes a kind of spatial equivalent of seasonal variations (RC, p. 305), whereas the conclusion of M_{550} that 'people went on living as before' evades the notion of temporal periodicity, immediately after the myth has referred to it by ascribing to the loon the function of heralding seasonal change. M_{554}, on the other hand, allows temporal periodicity to play its major role, which is to limit the span of human life.

Nevertheless, the etiological aspect of all these myths is so important that I prefer to discuss it separately (see below, pp. 134-8). I shall go straight on to the Shasta versions. The Shasta were Hokan-speaking, like the Achomawi, the Atsugewi and the Yana, and occupied to the west of the Achomawi on the other side of Mount Shasta a position roughly symmetrical to the one occupied by the Maidu on the eastern slopes of Mount Lassen.

The two available versions are rather short. I propose to summarize them together and to indicate the differences as I go along.

$M_{555a, b}$. *Shasta. 'The Loon Woman'*

A woman and her ten sons were living together with her only daughter (M_{555b}: ten children of whom the eldest was a girl). The girl fell in love with her youngest brother and the mother had to hide him from her (M_{555b}), or he hid himself of his own accord, while another brother committed incest (M_{555a}). However, the heroine succeeded in having the boy she loved entrusted to her keeping. According to M_{555a}, it would appear that incest again took place, but in both versions the hero escaped fairly promptly and tried to climb up to the sky with his own people. The sister saw her family half-way up in the sky, having been informed (of their escape) by Ashes, whose complicity the fugitives had omitted to obtain (M_{555b}), or by automatically watching the sparks fly up from the fire she was stoking (M_{555a}). She called out; her mother (M_{555b}) or one of her brothers (M_{555a}) made the mistake of looking back: the cord broke and everybody died in the fire.

As it exploded, the beloved brother's heart flew off and came down near a river (M_{555a}), or on the ocean shore (M_{555b}). Only M_{555a} supplies the additional detail that the heroine gathered up the charred bones and used them as a hair ornament. Two duck girls (M_{555a}) or seagull girls (M_{555b}) found the heart, resuscitated its owner as a whole person again and married him. The women gave birth to boys (M_{555a}), or to a boy and a girl (M_{555b}). Acting on their own initiative, or at their father's instigation, the children found the murderous aunt's house. They took her arrows and reinforced them with flint tips, but she vigorously repulsed their attacks (M_{555a}). Or alternatively, the father himself started fighting his sister, but failed to kill her (M_{555b}). Finally, Meadowlark told them that the ogress's heart − 'bright and shining' (M_{555b}) or 'like fire' (M_{555a}) − was hidden in her heel. When an arrow hit her in that vulnerable spot, she fell with such a crash that it was heard throughout the whole world. She was buried, after her house had been burned down (M_{555a}) (Dixon 1, pp. 14−15; Frachtenberg 2, pp. 212−14).

There is an unpublished Karok version, the text of which I have been unable to obtain. Judging by Th. Kroeber's use of it to construct a syncretic narrative and by her comments (pp. 41−65, 171), it would seem to be very like the Shasta version, and Demetracopoulou (*loc. cit.*), who had also seen it, has nothing particular to say about it. The Karok were members of the same linguistic family as the Shasta, and were also their immediate neighbours to the west. I shall come back later (p. 138, *et seq.*) to the Wintu versions.

None of these first western versions contains the episode of the resuscitated hearts, except in respect of the hero. The other members of the family die without any hope of resurrection, as is indicated very forcefully in M_{555a}, a variant which does more than simply omit the episode; it inverts it by replacing the unburnable hearts by charred bones which the heroine uses as a head-dress, and not as a necklace. But the two Shasta versions carry out an even more radical inversion by transforming the heart itself, an initial means of resurrection in other contexts, into a means of extermination: the heroine's body is invulnerable, apart from the heart which is hidden in her heel. Instead of the hearts, which she has made external, being used as a means of resuscitating relatives she has killed, she herself is killed by being pierced through her heart, which had been external from the outset, and which is taken as a target by murderous relatives.

It is beginning to be apparent that, in the west, the Shasta myths, like the versions on the other side, invert the central myths, but along different axes. They are diploidal, like the Achomawi and Atsugewi versions; but, by raising the number of children to ten (instead of the five listed in M_{553}, Wolf, Weasel, Marten, Wildcat and Woodworm), they are mechanically totalizing functions which the central myths reduplicate organically in order to create complementary relationships. The children in question live with a mother, not with one, or two, fathers. The role of helpful informants, which in the other versions devolves on creatures associated with water, such as the killdeer or the water-ousel, in the Shasta versions becomes the role of baleful informants ascribed to beings associated with fire, such as ashes or sparks who either actively or passively inform the female killer. At the same time, the opposition, which is so clear in the Atsugewi myth, between two types of fire, one constructive, the other destructive, is replaced by an opposition between two destructive fires: one lit by the murderess, in which her own people die, and the other which burns in her heel and will eventually bring about her own death. The list of transformations could be extended further, but those I have mentioned are enough to illustrate the economy of the Shasta versions.

Two myths in the group have a particularly clear etiological character. The Atsugewi version (M_{550}) starts with an explanation of the origin of flint arrowheads which make hunting possible, of knives for carving meat, and fire for cooking it. So, from a culinary viewpoint with which we have been familiar since the first volume of this study, we are dealing here too with the origin of culture. The fact that these events immediately precede the first case of incest and the burning of the village by the lascivious sister would be incomprehensible and might suggest that the mythic narrative is arbitrary, had I not already, in *The Raw and the Cooked*, established the homology between the union of the sexes and the threatened conjunction between the sun and mankind: 'Conjunction between a man and a woman,' I wrote, 'represents in miniature and on a different plane an event which to some extent resembles, symbolically speaking, the much dreaded union between the sky and the earth' (*RC*, p. 328). In order to obtain cooking fire, humans have to decide to enter into a closer relationship with an otherwise destructive element, and to expose themselves to the danger of a conflagration. This is what happens in the Atsugewi myth, first of all with the appearance of incest, a social symbol of cosmic conjunction, then with the appearance of destructive fire, an actual consequence of this same conjunction: in her frantic desire for union with the brother who should have remained furthest removed from her, the heroine, according to the particular version, hurls flames (M_{550}) or lightning (M_{553}), or brings the sun dangerously close to the earth (M_{554}).

For the dead to be resuscitated and disorder to cease, the mythic protagonists have to submit three times to the demands of cosmic periodicity: first of all, by creating mountains, that is, modulated space; then by arming the primitive arrows with heads defined in relationship to the calendar, since they must be made of bone ($\neq$ stone) and be taken from animals killed at different periods of the year; finally, by allowing the loon to exercise the positive function of heralding the change of season. Only then can 'people go on living as before'.

One of the Achomawi versions (M_{551}) fulfils the same etiological function, but expresses it in an inverted form. From the formal point of view, first of all, since the significant episode occurs at the end instead of at the beginning. It then deals with the origin of species, their diversity and their dispersal. One myth, then, begins by describing the origin of culture, while the other ends by describing the origin of the natural order as it emerges from primitive chaos. The difference between them affects the content, and is particularly brought out by the fact that M_{551} lays more stress than M_{550} on the specific nature of the forms of geographical relief, since it makes a distinction between hills and valleys (Eagle 'kicks up the earth and makes mountains'). But because the characters in the myth, who at the beginning are members of a human family all living under the same roof, finally turn into animals of different species who disperse in all directions, they will probably be safe henceforth from incestuous unions and the risks consequent on the abuses of proximity; however, the result is that for them, contrary to what is proclaimed at the end of M_{550}, life will never go on as before.

Consequently, the two etiological versions we have here can be seen to be counterparts of each other, although one is written, as it were, in the key of culture, the other in the key of nature, and although the two forms that periodicity is likely to assume — the spatial and the temporal — are not present in them in the same proportions: envisaged from this angle, M_{551} would appear to be totally spatial (diversity in relief characterizied by mountains and valleys, and diversity of species linked to their dispersal), whereas M_{550} maintains an even balance between the spatial and the temporal orders (geographical relief and seasonal periodicity). Faithfully following its practice of systematic reduplication (see above, p. 124), M_{553} juxtaposes the natural and the cultural aspects, and entrusts their personification to different characters. One hard-working sister is the embodiment of culture: from this we can judge how justified a reliable investigator (Garth 4) was in considering industriousness to be the chief criterion of culture among the Pit River tribes. The myth accuses the other sister of contaminating the hunters through being careless about her monthly periods: she is, then, entirely defined in terms of a natural function which she refuses to bring into line with the demands of culture. As for the spatial and temporal aspects of periodicity, they are also present, but in a weakened form, and, in the case of the first, characteristically reduced to the duality of two species: the coyote and the loon, the only ones to assume their animal nature singly and jointly. M_{553}, on the other hand, which omits the resurrection of the dead motif at the end of the story, replaces it in the middle with the motif of their rebirth, that is, their resurrection modulated, in a sense, by periodicity (since the dead man, having reverted to babyhood, has to grow and develop before he can resume his former physical appearance); the rebirth involves reduplication, which might appear arbitrary, were it not clear that the particular position of the myth within a certain transformation group compels it to obey logical constraints affecting the narrative content.

The same observation can be made with regard to the relationship of inversion existing between the Achomawi versions. M_{550} and M_{551} are both in opposition to M_{552}, in the sense that M_{552} expressed the transition from mythic to historic time by systematically negative formulae: the dead can no longer be resuscitated, the demiurges disappear for good, and the old chief Cocoon (described in other contexts as a calm and wise old man) is here given a son called Fighting-Man; and all this happens in a story in which war has just been presented as a solution to the population problem: war, the decimation of a single species, as opposed to the diversification of the animal world into clearly defined species prior to their dispersal throughout the world.

I have already noted (see above, p. 132) that the Maidu version (M_{554}) concludes with the speculative suggestion that, in future, humans will no longer be able to resuscitate their dead, and that consequently their life-span will be limited. In this sense, M_{554} is a synthesis of the other versions: like M_{551}, it links periodicity with dispersal but, like M_{550} and M_{552}, it emphasizes the temporal rather than the spatial aspect. M_{554} even gives the temporal aspect of periodicity the most powerful expression it can possibly have from the human point of view, since the point at issue is the duration of their existence and not that of the seasons. Seasons and human generations succeed each other but the seasons return whereas human generations do not.

Consequently, the conclusion of the Maidu myth combines those of the Achomawi and Atsugewi myths, while at the same time standing in opposition to each of them: life starts up again as before since the family is resuscitated and reunited and will not change into animals. However, life will no longer be the same, since the possibility of resurrection will disappear (in M_{552} it has already done so): consequently, the living will also be transformed, if not into the animals, at any rate into dead people. And geographical relief which was pre-existent to zoological diversity, according to M_{551}, and to seasonal periodicity, according to M_{550}, becomes, in M_{554}, the consequence of the periodicity of human life. M_{550} moved from culture to nature, whereas M_{554} follows the reverse movement: because of the appearance of death, the earth-covered village house loses its inhabitants; it reverts, then, to the state of nature and makes possible the appearance of geographical relief in mountain form: lately a human dwelling, now a product of culture abandoned by its occupants.

The Maidu version also reveals its synthetic character in another way: in a sense, it deduces a philosophy from the events it recounts and shifts the explanation from the physical to the moral level: instead of accounting for zoological or telluric diversity, it claims to explain the origin of moral disorder: 'Because of my behaviour,' the incestuous and murderous sister repeats, as if the statement were a *leitmotif*, 'human beings will in future imitate my example and go crazy.'

So, she institutes a certain kind of behaviour, instead of following, as in M_{553}, the lamentably famous example of a previous member of her family.

In this version, too, human beings disperse without turning into different animal species; it is clear, then, that for her the diversity of the patterns of moral behaviour within human society constitutes, in respect of moral norms, an equivalent of the diversity of human beings on the level of reality.

Whereas the Maidu version, originating from the extreme south-eastern tip of the area of distribution, appears the most philosophical version of all, the Shasta versions, which come from the other side, are exactly the reverse. Here we find no trace of any etiological function, since the relevant episode of the resuscitated hearts is absent. The Shasta versions impoverish the story and reduce it to schematic form, and their specific originality makes itself felt only through inversions unrelated to the message, which they serve, incidentally, to obscure; these inversions are kept strictly to the lexical level (see above, p. 134).

This being so, it is interesting to turn to the Wintu versions to which I have so far referred only briefly (pp. 62, 90), since the Wintu, also members of the Penutian linguistic family, occupy, along the western edge of the myth's area of distribution, a position comparable to that of the Maidu on the other side of the block formed by the Hokan-speaking tribes. The Wintu versions adopt, in relation to those originating from the central area, an attitude which is the exact opposite of that illustrated by the Maidu version: they make no attempt at synthesis, but simply juxtapose. There are two known Wintu versions of the Loon Woman myth, and it is probably not entirely fortuitous that these two versions, which are contradictory in relation to each other, are each independently in a correlational and oppositional relationship either with the Shasta versions or with the Achomawi-Atsugewi versions. This point deserves closer examination.

A first version, which has already been partly summarized (M_{545a}, see above, pp. 62, 90) adopts the Shasta viewpoint so determinedly that, as I have already observed (pp. 62, 130), it borrows the Shasta names of the leading characters. This does not, however, prevent it from asserting its originality by lexical transformations. Instead of a *mother living alone* (an inversion of the one *father* or *two* fathers featured in the more easterly versions), it mentions two parents, respectively the *father* and *mother* of ten children, as in the Shasta version. But here it is the eldest, not the youngest of the ten children who plays the part of the secreted boy taken off westwards by his sister (whereas in the Shasta version, M_{555b}, the boy's heart eludes his murderous sister by flying off in the same direction). Instead of climbing up a rope towards the sky to escape the fire lit by the heroine, the Wintu family light the fire themselves and try to reach the sky by means of the elevating power of the smoke. Their attempt fails because of imprudence on Coyote's part; they fall down into the flames, and the heroine gathers up their hearts, with the exception of that of the beloved brother, which falls a long way off. Consequently, the Wintu version comes back to the heart necklace motif, which is absent from one of the Shasta versions (M_{555b}) and transformed in the other (M_{555a}) into a head-dress made of bones which, like the hearts in the Wintu version, but unlike those in all the other versions, are retrieved from the cold ashes, not caught in the air before the burning is completed.

Two human women, transformations of the Duck girls or Seagull sisters in the Shasta versions, find the heart in a salt-lick frequented by deer – a motif not found in the Shasta and Achomawi versions, but which reappears in this one – bring the owner of the heart back to life, marry him and bear him two sons who are informed by a wounded bird of their aunt's where-abouts (cf. the meadowlark who acts as informant in the Shasta versions). On the birds' advice, they shoot her with blunt arrows. Their father recovers the heart necklace and immerses it in water. The next day the whole family comes back to life.

After going through a number of versions, we come back here then, to what might be called the canonical text, from which the Shasta variants deviated so emphatically. And since to do so, they had to transform the central versions, it is not surprising that the additional torsion imposed by the Wintu story brings us back, several times in succession, to the central versions: in respect of Coyote's role, the heart necklace motif and the resurrection motif. But it also happens, in certain cases, that the pos-sibilities of the combinatory system that have been left unused by the myths generate fresh models: for instance, the ascent *on* smoke, instead of *up* a rope or *in* a bag or net, which implies that the fire changes from being destruc-tive to helpful and so is lit by the escaping family and not by their persecutor (for an analogous transformation in South America, cf. *RC*, pp. 199–200). Still following the same line of argument, we may note that, in the course of the story, M_{550} replaces the flaked stone-tipped 'cultural' arrows by 'natural' arrows with deer-bone tips (see above, p. 119). No mention is made of the former in the Shasta versions, and one of them (M_{555a}) reconverts the latter into flaked stone-tipped arrows, which in turn the Wintu versions, without reverting to the original reading, change into untipped arrows, the shafts of which have, however, to be sharpened (M_{545b}: DuBois-Demetracopoulou, p. 362).

Were our anthropological information less sketchy, this arrow triad would no doubt prove instructive in other ways too. The north Californian Indians believed that the stone arrowheads which were usually made of obsidian carried a natural poison, and that each particular variety of stone or colour of stone was appropriate for the hunting of a certain species of game (Garth 2, p. 154; DuBois 1, p. 125; Sapir-Spier 1, p. 268; Curtin 3, pp. 469–70; E. W. Voegelin 2, p. 191; Goldschmidt, p. 149). So, on the cultural level, the specificity of chipped stone arrowheads echoed that of the natural species, whereas the myths tend to associate bone tips with the anatomical peculiarities (M_{546}) or physiological characteristics (M_{550}) of a single species (*internal/external diversity*). In this respect, arrows without tips occupy an unmarked position.

The other Wintu version would appear, at first glance, to be out of line (M_{545b}; DuBois-Demetracopoulou, pp. 360–62), since it identifies Loon Woman with a mythological figure well known throughout both North and South America: the rolling head which begins by devouring first its own kinsfolk, then the whole of the community (cf. *HA*, pp. 317, n. 20, 388; *OTM*, pp. 91–113 *et passim*). However, just as the preceding version referred implicitly to the Shasta versions, while at the same time inverting them on the lexical level, it is clear that M_{545b} refers us back to the Achomawi-Atsugewi versions, the form of which it respects, while simply reversing their message. From the formal point of view, the Wintu myth, rejecting the static group of ten children, opts for a double series of functional couples: four children divided into pairs, a pair of brothers and a pair of sisters with contrasting characters. And, as in M_{553}, the sister with the negative valency fails to behave with the modesty required of menstruating maidens.

Having been sent by her elder sister to look for bark to make a front-apron, the incestuous sister accidentally cuts herself. She licks the blood and the taste makes her so ravenous that she devours her whole body and becomes a rolling head, which goes all round the world devouring people.

Her family are terrified and climb up into the sky. The head is informed of this by some ancient faeces, and she grabs hold of the escaping family and, full of sexual excitement, succeeds in removing the brother from them by gripping him between her thighs (*sic*). As he will have nothing to do with her, she devours him, sparing only the heart, which she hangs round her neck. She then heads for the northern rivers and alights on a big lake, from which she emerges only at sunset to take the air on the south bank.

The family, who have escaped, make a good (watertight) cooking basket filled with water and red-hot stones. Armed with this basket, the elder sister takes up her position to the south-east of the lake. Humming-Bird does likewise to the north, carrying an untipped arrow with a sharpened end. He fatally wounds the culprit, who comes to die on the shore. Her sister takes the necklace and the heart, puts the latter into the boiling water, and the hero comes to life. 'But although he was a person, he did not look right and did not live very long.'

Consequently, like the Maidu version, this one ends by admitting that the dead cannot really be restored to life, and it frames its message with the help of devices reminiscent not only of the Maidu version but also of the Achomawi and Atsugewi ones. In each case, the heroine's fury is aroused by an initial experience: in $M_{550-554}$ it is incest, which leads her to burn her whole family; in the Wintu version it is the exquisite flavour of her own blood, that is, an alimentary form of incest, which fills her with the burning desire to commit true incest; and this frustrated desire is retransformed into an alimentary appetite, also inspired by the body of the unwilling brother.

The fact that, between M_{555b} and M_{545b}, the role of informant is transferred from ashes to faeces is quite in keeping with this interpretation; it is a question of a conflagration in the one case and of cannibalism — that is, a form of alimentary consumption — in the other, therefore ashes are to the former as faeces are to the latter. Lastly, it will be noted that the second Wintu version makes no mention of the destructive fire motif which is introduced by M_{550} as a consequence of the acquisition of cooking fire. However, the reason for this divergence is clear; it results from the fact that M_{545b} reverses the message of the other myth. M_{550} relates to the origin of culture formulated in culinary terms and which, as a necessary counterpart, involves the emergence of incest on the social level and destructive fire on the cosmic level. M_{545b} deals with the origin of cannibalism, the reverse of domestic cooking and which therefore excludes constructive fire (except metaphorically, cf. below, pp. 149–50), but itself constitutes the equivalent, on the alimentary level, of cosmic, destructive fire and of marriage between partners who are socially too close.

These remarks allow us to formulate several conclusions. First of all, from the point of view of formal analysis, they illustrate the number and diversity of the types of symmetry brought into operation by mythic thought when it imposes on a series of variants a succession of distortions which preserve the unity of the group, while at the same time allowing each variant to retain its original and specific character. The Klamath and Modoc versions, which I used as my starting-point, were already inversions of each other along several axes. And their paradigm, distorted by the ideology of the adjacent tribes, projects on to this screen a corresponding number of images, the global structure of which relates always to the same transformational group.

If we imagine these neighbouring communities as being laid out in a linear series (Figure 13), with the Hokan linguistic family in the centre, flanked on either side by the two representatives of the Penutian family – an arrangement which does little or no violence to the geographical reality – we see, on the same level and in what I would like to call their natural relationship, a variety of formulae, whose mutual generation, through a twofold process of imitation and distortion, has been demonstrated and explained by my analysis. Starting with the Yana, who would seem to have the most direct mythic links with the Klamath-Modoc – since they fuse two of their myths into one by the device of vertical splitting – we move on to the Achomawi-Atsugewi, who employ the same device but swing the whole system round to the horizontal level, then to the Maidu, who effect a synthesis of the two 'split' types; on the left, we come first to the Shasta, who restrict themselves to lexical inversions, then to the Wintu. The latter have recourse to a procedure which is in a symmetrical and oppositional relationship to the one used by the Maidu at the other extreme point of the diagram; instead of effecting a synthesis of opposites within a single story, they juxtapose them in the form of separate myths.

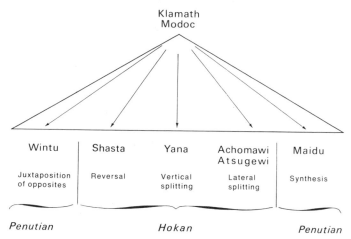

Figure 13. The transformational system of the Loon Woman myth

It is clear that the two Wintu versions represent discordant readings of the same myth: in one instance (M_{545a}), the surviving hero brings his relatives back to life, in the other (M_{545b}), it is the kinsfolk who survive and who fail to bring the hero back to life for any length of time. As all the other versions divide up into two groups, according to whether they resuscitate the hearts by plunging them either into a receptacle full of boiling water or into the cold waters of a lake or river, it is tempting to look for the same duality in the Wintu versions. M_{545b} states quite clearly that the heart was either exposed to the steam from boiling water or plunged into the boiling water itself, while M_{545a} talks vaguely about immersion in water and submersion under stones. These myths are available only in English transcription, but it may be significant that the operation is described in one text as 'soaking', and in the other as 'steaming' by means of red-hot stones plunged into water.

But the main thing is that we are now in a position to conclude the demonstration begun on p. 99. I postulated a complete homology between the mythic configuration expounded in respect of South America in *The Raw and the Cooked* and *From Honey to Ashes*, and the North American one I am now elucidating. In the first phase of the argument, I noted – on the left-hand side of the configuration, the central character of which, it must not be forgotten, is a bird-nester – myths relating to the origin of adornments and to the origin of honey, the latter substance being merely inverted as salt in the myths of this particular area of North America, which is too northerly for native American bees to survive there. Also, in each instance, the sweet or savoury condiment functions as an antecedent of, or as a means of obtaining, adornments in the myths relating to their origin, and it serves as an end in other myths connected with the first by a simple transformational relationship.

In the second place (p. 101 *et seq.*), I noted, along the right-hand side of the mythic configuration, in North as well as in South America, myths symmetrical with those of the left side by associating the origin of hunting with that of tobacco. However, the Modoc myth (M_{539}), the only one available at the time to provide evidence of the connection, did not do so completely, since it gave no explanation of the origin of tobacco. As it happens, myths which satisfy this condition are to be found farther north, but it would not have been right to use them in the argument as long as I have no means of linking them, logically and ethnographically, with the others. The Wintu version M_{545b} fills the gap, so I propose to take up the discussion again where I left off and to introduce a myth from one of the Chinook-speaking tribes. These tribes lived along the lower reaches of the Columbia River, much farther north than the Klamath and the Modoc, but the latter were well acquainted with them through attending their trade fairs:

M_{556a}. *Wasco. 'The origin of tobacco'*

On the right bank of Columbia River, about three miles below the

Dalles, lived a stonecutter who specialized in the making of arrow-points. One day, while he was working, he cut his finger; he licked off the blood and liked the taste of it so much that he ate his finger off, then the rest of his body, so that all remained was his skeleton with only a little bit of flesh left below his shoulders where he could not reach it, and his heart which was left hanging between his ribs (in his body). Having become an ogre he went to the next village and ate all the people. As nothing could penetrate his bones, no one could kill him.

His wife escaped southwards with their little son, being careful to travel right on top of the blades of grass so that she left no tracks. But the husband rushed off in pursuit and had almost gained on her when she took refuge in a house at the foot of a blue mountain. A very old man sat on one side making bows and arrows and his daughter sat on the other side making tobacco sacks.

The skeleton came in with a frightful wind. The old man hid the woman who had begged for his protection behind his back, then he seized a long arrow-point and thrust it into the skeleton's heart, while the latter was busy stamping the old man's arrows which broke into tiny bits. That instant the skeleton fell to the ground a bag of bones, and the wind stopped blowing when it fell. The old man told the wife to throw the bones out of doors.

The hill overlooking the house had plenty of wild tobacco growing on it. The old man spent all his time making arrowheads, and when his quiver was full he would start out to climb the mountain. He would return with the quiver empty but with handfuls of tobacco. The old man and his daughter lived on nothing but smoke (neither ate anything). The smoke they lived on came from the kind of pipe that is made straight. The man was really a hunter, but the only game he shot were the tobacco people.

The woman and her son lived with the old man and his daughter for a long time. When the boy was old enough, he hunted squirrels for his mother. One day he followed the old man out and saw him shoot at tobacco up on a bluff of high rocks. He did likewise, and at once five bunches of tobacco came down. The old man danced for joy for he had never shot so much on a whole day. He offered his daughter in marriage to the young man. 'This is why the people of the future will be willing to give their daughters to good hunters.' Although the old man was very satisfied with the abundance of tobacco, he saw it as a sign of his approaching death. However, the young man continued to hunt and the house was filled with tobacco. He decided then to go back to Columbia

River with his wife and mother. But when they reached his native village, they found only the bones of his father's victims. Thanks to his magic powers, he succeeded in making them as they had been before.

His mother was getting old and had food given her every day by her daughter-in-law. The hero decreed that in future it would be the duty of a daughter-in-law to care for her mother-in-law. Finally, the old woman decided she would go south with 'her daughter' (daughter-in-law?), where they would become guardian spirits to medicine women and give them the authority to smoke. The son for his part chose to be the guardian spirit of good hunters (in the north?) (Sapir 1, pp. 246–8).

The Chinook living along the lower reaches and in the estuary of the Columbia River were familiar with tobacco, which they cultivated on ash beds made from burnt logs (Sapir-Spier 2, p. 269; Ray 4, p. 97); they may, however, have obtained the first seed from employees of the Hudson's Bay Company. Before this contact with the Whites, the Indians used to go east to gather another plant, which grew on rocks in the mountains and was probably the kinikinnick (*Arctostaphylos uva-ursi*); they gathered other plants too, all reputedly much stronger than tobacco proper, and even capable of producing prolonged unconsciousness. The eastern origin of the plants formerly used for smoking is in keeping with the use of the straight tubular pipe, mentioned in the myth, since the Chinook used elbow-type pipes; the other type of pipe came from upstream, most likely from the Sahaptin (Sapir-Spier 2, p. 270).

Formerly, in Chinook society, only shamans and chiefs had the right to smoke. Ordinary people were given to believe that they risked death by consumption if they smoked. But the shamans always smoked before beginning a cure; they took five puffs at their pipe and inhaled the smoke. By this means, their tutelary spirit became more active and vigorous, and this gave additional assurance that the cure would prove effective.

Sapir (1, p. 246, n. 1) believes that 'this tale is evidently a composite of two distinct stories. The first part of the tale as here given is a variant of the widespread Rolling-Skull myth of which Curtin gives a Yana parallel (3, pp. 325–35). The second part of the tale, the hunting of the tobacco people as game, is only loosely joined on to the first.'

The comparison with the Wintu version M_{545b} allows us to reject this rather facile interpretation. In the Wintu myth, it was clear that the heroine's transformation into a rolling head is linked to the origin of auto-cannibalism which, on the alimentary level, is the equivalent of the sexual incest in the other version. M_{556a} is concerned with the origin of shamanistic powers as well as that of tobacco and, according to evidence supplied precisely by Sapir-Spier (2, p. 242), in Wishram and Wasco society shamanistic séances were tantamount to accepted forms of auto-cannibalism: 'When a man or woman heard his own song being sung, he or she became "like a fire inside, wild", and called on someone to cut off a bit of flesh so that they could eat it . . . he also wiped away his own blood with his hand and licked it.'

The coherence of the myth can also be demonstrated in another way. It begins by placing auto-cannibalism, then cannibalism in the ordinary sense, in a period when the only means of hunting was with arrow-points, i.e., the material means, since the rest of the myth describes a spiritual quest: the quest for the guardian spirits associated with tobacco, because tobacco provides the means of this quest. It was probably not only in Atsugewi society that 'during a hunt shamans smoke and call each mountain by name. They say to each one – don't hide your children, the deer; give my boys good luck; give them your children' (E. W. Voegelin 2, p. 172). For hunting to exist as a civilized art, men need more than arrow-points; they also need tobacco.

I have already mentioned that the Indians in this area believed that the stone arrow-points contained a kind of mineral poison which was certain to kill the game. In this respect, an additional correlation emerges between arrow-points and tobacco, since in Chinook society tobacco was a poison for people of lowly condition, and indeed once a poison for all smokers, according to more northerly myths explaining its origin. These are myths belonging to the northern Salish, the Thompson and the Shuswap, and their neighbours, the Chilcotin, who are an Athapaskan tribe (M_{556b-e}; Teit 5, pp. 304–30; 1, p. 646; Boas 13, p. 3; Farrand 2, p. 12). As they are all very short, I will present them in syncretic form.

During the course of their wanderings, the demiurges found the tobacco tree, a heavy branch of which swung with a pendulum-like movement, killing all who passed by; or the tobacco tree was poisonous, which produced the same result. The demiurges, or one of them, felled the tree – with a tool used for sharpening arrowheads, according to one version – and decreed that in future tobacco would no longer be poisonous, and could be smoked with impunity (Shuswap). In the Chilcotin version, the tool is replaced by a stick fixed at an angle so as to ward off the tree about to fall on the demiurge's body. According to the Thompson, the shadow cast by the tree was lethal; Coyote made himself a stone pipe, gathered the leaves and smoked them, and they were henceforth changed into tobacco.

So, whereas, in the present, stone arrowheads are poisonous for game (but beneficial from the angle of the hunter), in the old days, tobacco was poisonous for humans. It is the tool used for resharpening arrowheads which provides the means of removing its toxicity, thus turning it, in the same way as arrows, although in a complementary register, into a powerful aid for the hunting of the same game. The northern myths about the origin of tobacco thus provide complete confirmation of the link between meat and tobacco, which I had inferred from the interpretation of a less explicit Modoc myth (M_{539}).

Being now satisfied beyond doubt that the mythic configurations common to both North and South America are homologous on their right wing (Figure 8), I can return to the central part, which I had temporarily abandoned, in order to incorporate certain additional versions into the system (see above, pp. 107–43). The means had not yet been found whereby the presence of the same homology could be established at the centre of the configuration, that is, at the point where, in its South American modality, we find the myths about the origin of the cooking of food.

The problem has now been solved, since the Atsugewi version directly, and the others indirectly under cover of transformations which can be reduced to the same etiological motif, interpret the Loon Woman story (which has been shown to be an inversion of the bird-nester story) as being subordinate to the discovery of the civilized arts, in the triple form of flaked stone-tipped arrows for hunting, carving knives for the cutting up of meat, and domestic fire on which to cook it. So, it is true that in two areas of the New World, geographically remote from each other, a group of myths about the origin of cooking gives rise on the one hand to myths relating to the origin of adornments and condiments, and on the other to myths relating to the origin of meat and tobacco.

But there is more to it than that. The analysis of this mythic system, which was begun in *The Raw and the Cooked* on the basis of South American examples, led to the discovery of two further systems, symmetrical with each other and at the same time each linked independently to the first by transformational relationships: on the one hand, a group of myths dealing with the origin of man's short life-span (M_{70-118}), and on the other, a group relating to the diversity of animal species and the origin of the coloured plumage of birds ($M_{171-186}$). We have just seen these two motifs emerging, in a still allusive form, in the North American configuration, where they occur in the guise of conclusions, one to the Maidu version (M_{554}), and the other to one of the Achomawi versions (M_{551}).

The argument can be carried a stage further still, since, in dealing with the South American myths, I established a link between those explaining the origin of bird plumage and those explaining the origin of fish poison (RC, pp. 300–301); in North America, the same link appears, in an inverted form, between the origin of bird plumage (M_{551}) and that of flint arrowheads which are a hunting poison, a phenomenon also belonging to the state of nature, according to the tribes of the northerly part of the continent. Lastly, I shall be able to confirm, in the next section of this volume, that the origin of man's short life-span occupies a more important place in the North American configuration than would appear, and that the internal economy of the myths relating to this motif is absolutely identical with that of the South American myths. As for the establishing of order in nature through the institution of specific differences, I shall return to that issue in Part Four.

Dixon (5, p. 609) was therefore right in his presentiment that the Loon Woman myth, far from constituting an isolated formation, as Demetra-copoulou believed (see above, pp. 60–62), is part of a cosmogony. Sapir, for his part, was struck by the fact that one episode of the Loon Woman myth reappeared in the Yana one about the origin of fire:

M_{548}. Yana. 'The origin of cooking fire'

In former times, people only had a mediocre fire which was not hot. They used to hunt, fish and gather wild plants, but the food was not cooked and they ate it virtually raw. The elders held council and decided they needed real fire. They looked round in all directions and finally saw a light in the south.

Five good runners set off: Coyote insisted on going with them, although this made them angry. They arrived together at the village where fire was, and while the inhabitants were sleeping, they stole a few burning logs and ran off with them. Coyote insisted on taking his turn, but the fire burnt his hand and he threw it away. The whole world caught fire, rocks burst, the water evaporated and the inhabitants died.

Soon the fire reached Cipla (cf. above, M_{547}, pp. 98, 205–206), the village where the Eagle was chief, and everybody was pulled up into the sky by Spider. But Coyote, who was at the bottom of the basket, made a rent in order to look down. The basket burst and the occupants all fell into the fire one after the other, watched by Fire-Drill Woman. Black Bear's eyes popped in all four directions (sic). All the others were burned up completely, except Spider who remained in the sky (Sapir 3, pp. 23–5; cf. Curtin 3, pp. 365–70).

As in the Atsugewi version, the bringing nearer of the cooking fire or constructive fire, coveted by mankind, leads to a general conflagration; like one of the Achomawi versions, the Yana myth concludes, if not with the diversity of animal species, at least with the dispersal of one species, since, according to the myth, the bear's eyes episode explains why black bears are to be found in every direction (Sapir 3, p. 35, n. 53). On the other hand, we cannot fail to be struck by the analogy between the story of M_{548} and the one used by all the Ge-speaking communities of Central Brazil to explain the origin of destructive fire (M_{163}; *RC*, pp. 200–201). The two main characters are the brothers Sun and Moon who, in the Ge, Bororo and Bakairi narratives, play, respectively, the parts of demiurge and trickster, the roles of the leading characters in the Yana myth just summarized: Fox obtains the fire and Coyote lets it drop (see above, p. 148). In North America as in South America, this horizontal dioscuric pair is swung round to the vertical axis and is represented by characters who, instead of being brothers or companions, belong to different generations and are father and son. By taking account of this fact, I was able to confirm (see above, pp. 46–7) that the bird-nester myths were, in respect also of their astronomical connotation, identical in the Bororo-Ge set of myths and in the Klamath-Modoc set. It is significant, then, that the same formula should reappear to the south of the Atsugewi among the mountain-dwelling Maidu who describe the kinship links between the sun and the moon in three ways: sister and brother, wife and husband, or father and son (Loeb, p. 157, n. 40, p. 230; on the subject of the uncertainty about the sex of the sun and the moon, cf. L.-S. 18). In other words, and within a very restricted geographical area on each occasion, we observe the same transformations of the two heavenly bodies, from father and son into a dioscuric pair, and from a dioscuric pair into an incestuous couple.

We come back, then, to incest, the main theme of the Loon Woman myth. Sapir's informant (3, p. 35, n. 52) claims that Fire-Drill Woman, who plays the part of spectator in M_{548}, is none other than Loon Woman, who has both names. The other version in which she is featured as the chief heroine describes her as having 'a fire-drill in her hand. She broke the fire-drill, threw one half to the east and the other to the south (that is, exactly the reverse of what happens in real life: the sticks are kept whole and brought together). Fire blazed up where she threw the sticks and everything burned. Loon Woman had a big club and stood watching the fire' (M_{547}; Sapir 3, p. 232).

Consequently, the Yana versions too associate destructive fire with incest and consider both as being a function derived from constructive fire, to which the versions refer, either directly or indirectly through mentioning the instrument used to produce it. As the reader will know, a fire-drill is a stick which is held vertically between the palms of the hands and rotated alternately to left and right until the lower end, through rubbing against the sides of the hollow it is drilling in another stick or in a board, generates enough heat to ignite the straw or bark which has been placed beside it as tinder: the fire-drill is, then, an eminently 'incestuous' instrument, since combustion is caused by intimate contact between two closely related pieces, the reciprocal action of which is reminiscent of coitus (cf. *HA*, p. 246).

The Yana myth refers to the instrument in the inverted form of a female being who, because of the inadequacy of her male partner, creates destructive fire, whereas in the real life fire-drill, only the male element is active, and it kindles a creative domestic fire. This reverse functioning, which transposes the fire-drill on to the imaginary plane,[13] is in striking contrast to its occasional absence from certain previously discussed Modoc myths ($M_{549a, b, c}$; see above, pp. 102–103), an absence resulting, if not in the opposite of cooking fire in the form of a conflagration at least in the practical ineffectualness of cooking fire: without tobacco and a fire-drill, the smoke offerings demanded by the spirit of the mountains cannot be made, hunting becomes impossible and there is nothing to cook. If the situation is to be reversed, the spirit has to be conquered and then destroyed in a fire of cosmic proportions. The conjuring up of destructive fire (but for the purpose of killing a cannibalistic ogre) thus becomes the means and condition of a return to a form of culturized nutrition. It can be seen, then, that the group is also brought to a close by way of this route.

In conclusion, I would like to draw attention to another aspect of the myths we have been studying, and to solve the last problem raised by their comparison. When, towards the end of *The Raw and the Cooked*, I looked back over the general enterprise on which I had embarked, I illustrated it by means of a myth belonging to the Shipaia Indians (M_{178}), in which an incestuous brother and sister, knowing they have been discovered, take refuge in the sky. But on arriving there, they quarrel and the man pushes the woman, who falls back down to earth with a great crash. She changes into a tapir, while the brother who remains in the sky becomes the moon. Warriors summoned by another brother try to kill the culprit by shooting arrows at him: his multicoloured blood spurts out, causing the appearance

---

[13] Illustrated metaphorically by M_{545b}, which substitutes for the scene of the fire a different one, in which the incestuous sister lies on her back with her legs wide apart and waits for her male partner to fall from the sky, thus giving a true representation of the fire-drill in a myth in which as it happens the fire motif is not mentioned.

of female monthly periods and bestowing their distinctive plumage on birds.

As I said on that occasion, 'there exists at least one Brazilian tribe that, in the space of a single myth, follows the complicated course we have followed by putting several myths end to end in order to move from noise-making to eclipses, from eclipses to incest and from incest to unruliness and from unruliness to the coloured plumage of birds' (*RC*, p. 312). This myth is at once a repetition and an inversion of the Loon Woman myth: the brother, not the sister, takes the initiative; the brother's face is stained black by his partner, whereas in the other myth the sister is made white with the fur from her partner which sticks to the pitch she has smeared on her own body; the culprits escape to the sky to avoid their parents' vengeance after the incest has been consummated (the sister is pregnant), whereas, in the other context, the parents and relatives escape to the sky to avoid the vengeance of the culprit, furious at having failed to commit incest; the sister changes into a water bird, the poorest kind of game, or into a land mammal, the largest form of game — both, moreover, wearing anti-adornments: in South America, the ticks, which are 'the tapir's beads' (M_{145}; *RC*, p. 261), in North America, the necklace made of hearts; the brother either changes into the moon, a periodic luminary subject to eclipses, or is resuscitated for a brief period (M_{545b}) in the course of an operation determining the periodicity of human life (M_{554}); incest causes the appearance of monthly periods in all other women (M_{178}), or follows on from their appearance in the heroine herself (M_{545b}, M_{553}); all of which leads in the south (M_{178}) as in the north (M_{551}) to the origin of the coloured plumage of birds. Even the noise motif, which I linked up with charivari intended to combat eclipses and stigmatize prohibited marriages (*RC*, pp. 285–99), is found expressed in almost identical terms in South America and North America: in M_{178}, 'The woman fell *like a meteor* and landed on the earth very noisily.' And, in M_{555a}, after being shot in the heel where the hidden heart glinted and shone 'like fire', 'she fell and died. Everywhere, throughout the whole world, people heard her fall' (Dixon 1, p. 15).

In order to define the line of argument I have been pursuing since the beginning of this volume, I can, then, legitimately repeat what I said in *The Raw and the Cooked* in connection with the myths belonging to the other hemisphere: 'Looking back over the ground we have covered, we might say that we began with myths whose hero was a bird-nester and that, for the time being at least, we have arrived at myths that are concerned with the coloured plumage of birds . . . a problem that, from the formal point of view, is the same kind of problem as that posed by the advent of what might be termed alimentary order' (*RC*, p. 312). And indeed, the creation of a zoological order is half way between that of a cosmic order and that of a cultural order; the problems raised for all three kinds of creation are isomorphic (*RC*, pp. 315–16).

But I must reiterate here an observation I made before in connection with the homologous myths of South America: they never deal with the three problems simultaneously, since the level or levels they choose involve constraints which, from one myth to another, are expressed by various types of inversions and transformations. This point emerges again clearly from the analysis of the North American myths: the Atsugewi myth, M_{550}, stresses problems relating to the advent of the cultural order, and has an oppositional as well as a correlational relationship with the Achomawi myth (M_{551}) and the Maidu myth (M_{554}), which deal with the advent of a natural order, envisaged in the one instance from a spatial angle, and in the other from a temporal angle. We can say the same about the myths concerned with the establishment of a cosmological order: seasonal periodicity (M_{550}) and the creation of geographical relief (M_{550}, M_{551}).

However, these forms imposed on time and space illustrate somewhat modest aspects of the cosmic order. To ensure definitive validation of the homology I am trying to establish between the mythic configurations of South and North America, I must find further and better arguments in the group of North American myths. But let us first ask: what is the nature of the cosmological order instituted by the corresponding myths of Brazil? As myths concerned with the origin of cooking fire, they guard mankind from the twofold danger of the total absence of fire or its excessive, over-close presence: the domestic hearth, interposed between men and the sun, links them together and at the same time keeps them at a reasonable distance from each other. We have, it is true, encountered this aspect in the North American myths, but it is expressed there in a negative fashion which endangers the order or the world instead of consolidating it, since – executing a regressive movement – they make hot fire, which has replaced lukewarm fire (M_{548}), the sign and means of a conflagration. The exceptionally tragic tone of the Loon Woman myth, which gives it a sombre grandeur that cannot be easily paralleled, arises from the conversion it effects by regressing from an empirical order, which the other myths, on the contrary, are trying to explain and justify, towards an imaginary chaos which is the reverse of a cosmogony.

We should, then, have to make do with a lopsided and ambiguous solution, did we not recall that, in South America, myths concerned with the origin of cooking fire or terrestrial fire (M_{7-12}) are transformations of

M_1, the starting point of which is a case of incest, and which is concerned with the origin of celestial water in its maleficent form: storms and rain. In North America, on the contrary, it is the myth about the origin of terrestrial fire (M_{550}) which contains the incest motif. But what about the other forms which, in North America too, must have a connection with water?

I must pause here to emphasize that we are about to enter upon a decisive stage in the argument, a stage which will influence not only the rest of my demonstration but also the theoretical considerations on which it is based. If the structural analysis of myths is preparing the way for a scientific anthropology, such a science, like any other, should be able to set up experiments for the purpose of verifying its hypotheses and deducing, on the basis of certain guiding principles, hitherto unknown properties of the real world, in other words; to predict what will necessarily occur in certain given experimental conditions. I now feel ready to accept this twofold challenge. Knowing that in South America a myth about the origin of water is inverted into a myth about the origin of fire, and having now at my disposal a North American myth about the origin of fire which, as I have shown in several ways, is homologous with its South American counterpart, I must postulate that, if an inverted form of it exists somewhere, independently, within the same cultural and geographical area, this inversion will deal with the origin of rain and storms.

We need not look very far to find such a myth. Bordering directly to the west of the distribution area of the Loon Woman myth, the small coastal tribes of the Yurok and Wiyot (Figure 9) fulfil all the conditions required by my hypothesis. As the Loon Woman story is absent from their mythology, they cannot relate the origin of fire to it. On the other hand, they are familiar with the bird-nester story.

M_{557a}. Yurok. 'The bird-nester'

The Widower-Across-the-Ocean, the demiurge, wanted two girls badly, but they resisted his advances. Having tried various ruses, he managed to make one pregnant with magical means by assuming the appearance of a little boy. At that time, in order to give birth, women had to be cut open and killed with a knife (cf. Kroeber 1, p. 73; and 1, pp. 96–7, for the same belief among the Wiyot). They called the demiurge, and since they knew he was responsible for the pregnancy, they called upon him to discover a more satisfactory method. He made it possible for the child to be born naturally and kept him.

The boy grew up, married and had a little boy. The demiurge desired his daughter-in-law and persuaded his son to climb a tree to get young birds (perhaps birds of prey of the *Accipiter* genus) as pets for the boy. When he reached the top, his father caused a great wind to blow which broke all the limbs of the tree. He could not get down and was in great danger of being hurled to the ground, so he used the string from his hair to tie himself up the tree. It began to snow and he had to stay up in the tree for five days.

Convinced that his son was dead, the demiurge raped his daughter-in-law in spite of her tears and her son's tears. In order to rid himself of such an embarrassing witness, he contaminated him (with his sperm, according to several versions) and the boy's eyes became sore and he almost lost his sight.

Finally, the hero managed to climb down. On the way to the village he saw his small boy walking about shooting arrows blindly and making a clicking noise by pressing his tongue against his cheek; every time he did this, a bird (or a shell of the *Dentalium* species) dropped into his hand. The boy told his father all that had happened since his disappearance.

The hero caused a thick fog to descend, so that no one could see him; he collected his things and went off down the river with his little boy. In vain the demiurge tried to effect a reconciliation; the young man would not hear of it. He also decided to take leave of his son, and so all three set off in different directions (Jean Sapir, pp. 253–4).

I do not propose to dwell, at this point, on the episode of the blind child, which occupies a very important place in the mythology of more northerly tribes. It constitutes the final state of a transformation, the starting point of which is supplied by myths discussed elsewhere (*OTM*, pp. 233–8): a young hunter, unknown to himself an exile from birth, one day fails to shoot a bird which reveals to him who he is, and he thus succeeds in finding his own people. The Loon Woman myth gives an initial transformation of this theme in those versions ($M_{555a, b}$) in which the wounded bird reveals the whereabouts of their aunt to the children, but in order that they may kill her and so rid themselves of her for good. The Yurok myth effects an additional twist: it presents the child as blind, so that being no longer in a position to aim at birds — and consequently to miss them — he is certain of killing them by his magic power, a circumstance which, by definition, prevents them from 'enlightening' him.

It is a stated fact that the child can no longer be reunited with his father. Their reunion remains as precarious as the hero's resurrection in M_{545b}, and, like M_{551} and M_{554}, this myth ends with a dispersal in different directions.

The Erikson version, already indexed in *From Honey to Ashes* as M_{292d} (p. 309, n. 19), is even more explicit on this subject, and relates how the hero sent his son off into exile in the celestial world, the land of children and deer; it moves straight on to another episode (also found among the Wiyot, the Tolowa and the Hupa, M_{292c}; Kroeber 7, pp. 85–107; $M_{292f,g}$; Goddard 1, pp. 116–32) during which the demiurge succumbs to the advances of a certain Skate Woman who holds him fast between her thighs during copulation, captures him and sends him back to his native land across the ocean; so he too is separated from the world of humans. Moreover, the beginning of M_{557} already indicates that we are still at the centre of the same group of myths. According to M_{550}, the acquisition of cooking fire, that is, culture, leads to the appearance of incest, which is presented as one of its implied consequences. In this case, the incest only becomes possible on condition that its anatomical, and consequently natural, means has first been instituted: before women had vaginas it would not have been possible for a father-in-law to rape his son's wife; and although the demiurge fertilizes his first conquest, he does so by means which have nothing to do with copulation: after failing to gain his ends in the form of a handsome young man, he fertilizes the woman from a distance, after changing himself into a little boy.

One version of the same myth, which was recorded and summarized by Kroeber (1, p. 73; M_{557b}), is definite about two important points. Firstly, the demiurge's son owns all the dentalia in the world ('his things', as M_{557a} says) and, in order to take revenge on his father, he carries them away with him; but, according to this version, the demiurge overtakes him and recovers enough dentalia to supply men's future needs. The shells of the *Dentalium* species are used throughout the area for making the most highly prized adornments and serve as a much valued currency among the communities concerned. But the characteristics of the hero of M_{557} – who is brought into the world by a man, is the master of adornments, and the victim of the jealousy and cupidity of a father who deliberately leaves him to die on a high tree in order to marry his wife – correspond to those ascribed by the Klamath and the Modoc to their hero Aishísh. We are back, then, to our starting-point.

But we also meet up again with something even more important, which will take us further back still. The Kroeber version calls this hero Kapuloyo, the name of a divinity invoked by the Yurok 'when the wind threatens to destroy a house, or when it thunders. At such times, they look northwards stretching out their hands in that direction, and they pray: Kapuloyo, I am your son, help me!' (Spott-Kroeber, p. 233).

According to Kroeber (1, p. 119), the Yurok did not see much connection between the demiurge, Widower-Across-the-Ocean, and the principal divinity known as Above-Old-Man, who was worshipped by their neighbours, the Wiyot. However, his quarrels with his son are remarkably similar to those described in the previous myths. The bird-nester episode may be absent, but all the other details are just as reminiscent – if not more so – of the Klamath and Modoc myths from which we started (cf. M_{539}). The Wiyot, like the Yurok, regard the hero, who is victimized by his father, as the master of bad weather.

M_{558a}. *Wiyot. 'The master of rain'*

Above-Old-Man's wife bore him one son, whom he trained to be an expert hunter and gambler. But the pupil was so successful that his father became jealous of him: he herded all the game into an enclosure so that the son returned from hunting empty-handed, and he made sure that he was beaten at gambling. Having lost all his valuables, he resolved to find work and asked his father's advice. He recommended him to Thunder, who agreed to employ him. Since then, 'when it is a very bad storm, it means the boy is working. He had nothing, he was no good for anything. When there is a bad storm, it is the work of the Above-Old-Man's son' (Reichard 1, pp. 151–3; cf. *ibid*., pp. 156–61: M_{557d}).

There can be no doubt that we have met up again here with the hero of the Bororo myth (M_1), which acted as reference myth for the first volume of this study: the Bororo hero, too, was the victim of his father's jealousy, because he had committed incest with his mother: in M_{557}, however, where he is also sent off by himself, ostensibly to fetch young birds, the father commits incest with his son's wife. In both cases, the hero becomes the master of rain and storms.

This is not mere coincidence, illustrated only by this one very special instance found among the Yurok and the Wiyot, distant cousins of the Algonquin linguistic family (Haas 2, 3), who found their way to the Pacific coast. An extremely fragmentary version of the Yurok myth (M_{557c}: Curtis, Vol. 13) ends with the demiurge's son's decision to leave his mother, now that he has reached adulthood. He travels down the Klamath River by canoe. The woman, who is busy crushing acorns, runs after him, her stone pestle in her hand. When she reaches the coast, the canoe has already put out to sea and she hurls her pestle after it; but the pestle falls into the ocean and turns into a huge rock outside the mouth of the river.

By means of a geographical transposition, of which I have given other examples (see above, pp. 72–6, 96–8, 114–16, 124–5), this version connects the Yurok myth with the following story told by the Makah of Cape Flattery, who live six or seven hundred kilometres farther north and are the only representatives of the Nootka linguistic family on the mainland. This striking northern variation of the Bororo myth even contains a musical score.

M₅₅₈b,c. *Makah. 'The bird-nester'*

At the north-western extremity of Cape Flattery, a little south of the passage between Tatoosh Island and the mainland, there is a rock standing detached from the cliff which the Indians call Tsa-tsa-dak and which is commonly known to the Whites as Pillar Rock (Plates 1, 2). A young Indian used to climb to the summit in search of gulls which make it a resort during the breeding season. But one day he could not get down again, because, according to one version, the gulls beat their wings against the rock and, as an act of vengeance, made it grow hot and the heat caused the rock to grow higher. The hero's father, the village chief, organized a relief party, but the threads they had fastened to the gulls' feet in the hope that they would fly over the rock, could not reach the prisoner, neither could their arrows, which could not ascend sufficiently high. After a time the man grew weak and suffered from thirst. They shouted to him to pray for rain: he sang the following song and people still believe the singing of this song will bring rain:

'Rain, please come down and fill the depressions in the rock.'

When there was no more water in the little depressions of the rock, the hero sang again:

'You will always find me by the beating of my drum.'

Then he leapt into the air to his death. Other versions say that he dies on top of the rock on the seventh day. His spirit still lives on the rock and warns Indians when a storm is coming which will make it unsafe for them to go out to sea to hunt [whales] or fish (Swan 2, pp. 86–7; Densmore 3, pp. 197–9).

After this the reader will perhaps agree that it was no mere whim which led me to entitle the first chapter of the first volume of this work (*RC*, p. 35) 'The Bird-nester's Aria'! For, provided we allow for a triple inversion (*helpful/persecuting* father; *devoured/devouring* birds, and *ineffectual/effectual* life-savers) it is clear that we are dealing with the same story, which, in both North and South America, establishes the origin of bad weather. In addition, the episode of the vengeful gulls forcing the hero up into the sky stands in a symmetrical relationship to the one in which vengeful deer trample on him and bury him in the ground; this latter episode is found in several variants of the Loon Woman myth, which, as we must remember, is an inversion of the bird-nester story.

Let me add an additional proof. It will be remembered that the Bororo myth is an inversion of the Ge myths, the hero of which, also a bird-nester, becomes the master of cooking fire, which is stolen from the jaguar, who must henceforth eat meat raw. The system as a whole is based on three major oppositions: between terrestrial fire and celestial water, humans and the jaguar, and the cooked and the raw; the Bororo and Ge forms are therefore mutually exclusive and the Yurok and the Wiyot having adopted the Bororo form, we cannot expect them to show acquaintance with the Ge form. Like their Hupa neighbours, the Wiyot are even unaware of the belief, prevalent throughout the area (cf. M_{550}), that the first humans acquired fire through theft (Kroeber 7, p. 92). However, the absent myth throws light on the Wiyot one which replaces it, as if the Wiyot myth could only acquire its shape through being beamed, as it were, from this postulated source:

M $_{559}$. Wiyot. 'The origin of fire'

The panther asked the dog where he got fire. The dog said first of all that he had no fire, and the two companions got very angry, but the dog would not tell the panther anything. So when the panther killed game (deer) he ate it raw. The dog had two sticks, one of which had holes. He made fire spurt out by gyration. Even though there was wind and rain, he obtained fire by this method (Kroeber 7, p. 102).

The myth has the same armature as the Ge myths: between culture and nature, and mankind and the animals (represented in each area by the largest feline), a third character plays the part of mediatory agent, but, according to the particular case, he may be shifted in opposite directions: towards mankind, if he is a young male novice, and towards the beasts, if he is a domestic animal. The mediatory agent in the Ge myths seizes fire and carries it from one pole to the other; the one in the Wiyot myth is in possession of fire from the start. The reason for this difference is clear: the Ge myths introduce the first fire in the form of a burning log, that is, an object belonging to the natural world. The Wiyot myth, on the other hand, sees it as dependent on the fire-drill, a manufactured object belonging to the cultural order.

As it happens, this same transformation is to be found in South America and precisely in Bororo mythology, where the invention of the fire-drill is attributed to the monkey and this mediatory animal is contrasted with the largest feline, in this context the jaguar. I have show that the Bororo myth about the *invention* of *cultural* fire is a transformation of the Ge myths about the *obtaining* or the *theft* of *natural* fire (M_{55}; *RC*, pp. 126–32). On the other hand, the monkey is close to man, naturally, through physical resemblance, just as the dog is close to man, culturally, through social contiguity. The two tribes whose myths we are comparing are no doubt widely apart, but to justify the link up, it should be pointed out that the intervening distance can be bridged by examples taken from Guyana (*RC*, p. 127, n. 10), Arizona in the south-west of the United States, where they are to be found among the Yana and the Pima (Harrington 2, pp. 338–9; Russel 1, p. 216, n. *a*), and southern California among the Luiseño (C. G. DuBois, pp. 134, 146). The taxonomical principle based on the presence or absence of a tail, which was introduced in *RC*, pp. 130–31, for the purposes of the discussion of the Bororo myth M_{55}, seems to be also valid for Chinook mythology, in the north-west of North America (Boas 5, p. 191).

Like other myths that have already been analysed (see above, pp. 102–103, 148–50), the Wiyot story replaces fire by the instrument used to produce it. It also justifies this metonymical procedure: the drill is more clearly opposed to storms and rain than fire itself, since it allows men to seek shelter in order to make fire, whereas a blazing hearth out in the open would be in danger of being extinguished by storm and weather. This is perhaps why the Yurok believed that there was a relationship of incompatibility between the dog, who is master of the fire-drill, and water: they never took their dogs with them in their boats. It will be remembered that, in the Bororo myth (M_{55}), the monkey invents the fire-drill after risking death by travelling in a boat.

Consequently, in the myths of both North and South America, fire is opposed to water, either celestial or terrestrial; and, as I have already postulated, again both in the North and the South, myths which, in respect of their formal structure, are inversions of those relating to one element inevitably relate to the other element. At the centre of its area of distribution, the Loon Woman story appears as a myth about the origin of fire. It follows that the bird-nester story, which is symmetrical to it, appears on the periphery of the area as a myth about the origin of water. The fact that this remarkable transformation, which occurs in two places, hundreds of miles apart on the Pacific coast, is best illustrated in the mythology of the Yurok and the Wiyot, remote offshoots of the Algonquin family, opens up perspectives from which other conclusions will be drawn later (Part Three, 2).

PART THREE SCENES FROM PRIVATE LIFE

A lack of harmony between husband and wife, whatever its cause, leads to terrible unhappiness; sooner or later we are punished for having failed to obey the laws of society.

H. de Balzac, 'Une Double Famille', *La Comédie Humaine*, Editions de la Pléiade, 1, p. 991

1 *The Lewd Grandmother*

Sic dentata sibi videtur Aegle emptis ossibus Indicoque cornu.

Martial, *Epigrams*, I, 72

Have we, then, rediscovered in its entirety in North America the myth (M_1) which I used as the starting point for this study and have commented on persistently throughout all four volumes? The claim cannot yet be definitively substantiated because, in Bororo mythology, the bird-nester story is not only coded in sociological and meteorological terms, but also has an astronomical connotation. In order to establish the presence of this latter connotation in the North American variants in which I have so far found only certain plausible indications of it (see above, pp. 46–7, 71, 81), I must now go back to the beginning of this volume and cover the same ground again by a different route.

The bird-nester story was first encountered in Klamath and Modoc mythology. But it never appears there in an initial position or in isolation. Thanks to a late version (M_{500}), which recounts episodes already alluded to in previous versions, I was able to see the story as part of a whole, which links it to a sequence of earlier events; these events thus constitute a kind of 'overture' in which it was possible to recognize all the themes which, further south, went to make up the Loon Woman story. This is also the case in Modoc mythology, with, however, two observable differences. When it acts as an overture to the bird-nester story, the Loon Woman story is inverted: the foolish woman becomes a wise virgin; the married sister living away from home but constantly returning to the family house to be near her brother with whom she is in love is replaced by a home-loving sister who rejects marriage and assiduously keeps house for her brothers; that is, the sexual incest is changed into a kind of domestic intimacy, resembling it on the alimentary and economic level (M_{541}).

Symmetrically, and also in Modoc mythology, the Loon Woman story can also exist in its 'straight' form. But, when used as an overture, it leads into a different type of story: the saga of the celestial brothers (M_{539}), which has no obvious relationship with the bird-nester myth. At this point, then, we have at our disposal three mythic formulae, with three distinct corresponding messages:

$$M_{538} = (LW) + (\text{Bird-nester})$$
$$M_{539} = (LW) + (\text{Celestial brothers})$$
$$M_{541} = (LW^{-1}) + (\text{Bird-nester})$$

An initial conclusion can be deduced from these formulae. If M_{539} establishes compatibility between (LW) and (Celestial brothers), and M_{541} between (LW^{-1}) and (Bird-nester), it ought to follow that, in some way or other, there must be a correspondence between (Celestial brothers) and (Bird-nester^{-1}).

Thanks to Yana mythology, we were quickly able to introduce a fourth formula, since in the Yana narratives the straight form of the Loon Woman story acts as an overture to the inverted form of the bird-nester story (*hero guilty of incest* $\Rightarrow$ *victim of incest*; and *elevated hero* $\Rightarrow$ *buried hero*). In other words:

$$M_{546} = (LW) + (\text{Bird-nester}^{-1})$$

But there is still more to be said. In Part Two I was able to detect, between the bird-nester story and the Loon Woman story, not only an external link resulting from the fact that they are juxtaposed in the same myths, but also an internal, even organic, relationship. It is not enough to say that each story, taken separately, generates its converse. Together they form a system which clearly demonstrates their symmetry:

$$a)\ (\text{Bird-nester}) \equiv \left(\frac{1}{LW}\right)$$

$$b)\ (\text{Bird-nester}^{-1}) \equiv \left(-\frac{1}{LW}\right)$$

We shall see later that this transformation makes it possible both to arrive at the astronomical code and to elucidate the puzzling relationship between the bird-nester story and the one featuring the celestial brothers, with which M_{539} unexpectedly replaces it. The celestial brothers story uses an astronomical code to invert a message identical with the one in the bird-nester story, while at the same time using lexical terms which are transformations of all those in the Loon Woman story. Before reaching that point, we must complete the list of what I have called 'the overtures' to the bird-nester story. It includes more than the Loon Woman myth (M_{538}) and its inverted form (M_{541}). There are at least two others, and it is important to define the relations between them and the 'overtures' previously studied.

Here, first of all, is a version of which only a summary has been published. However, Professor Theodore Stern of Oregon University has kindly sent me the unpublished text, as well as others he recorded in 1951. I would like to express my gratitude for his assistance, which has proved invaluable on both this and other occasions.

M_{560}. *Klamath. 'The lewd grandmother'*

A boy and his sister lived with their grandmother. One day the grandmother asked them to take food to an old neighbour. He told them a story which the grandmother, on hearing the children's account of it, interpreted as a disguised improper suggestion. She pretended to be angry and marched over to the neighbour's house, but she herself took the initiative and had intercourse with him. When she got back home, and in order to account for her dishevelled appearance, she claimed she had been wounded. After several repetitions, the children discovered her immoral behaviour, which deeply offended them; they decided to run away, telling all but the awl not to reveal their trail. Awl, to begin with, upbraided the grandmother, but finally revealed the secret. The old woman rushed after them and realized from various signs that they had become incestuous. In fact, as they fled they had matured and had married; they had a child to whom they became exemplary parents.

The grandmother became an avenging bear and overtook her grandson while he was on a vision quest during his ritual isolation; she slew him. The young widow avenged her dead husband by slaying the grandmother. She then prepared to commit suicide and kill the child, but Gmukamps (Kmúkamch) managed to rescue the boy, whom he kept and called Aiisis (Aishísh) (Stern I, p. 31; 3).

The tale continues with the bird-nester story, in terms which are virtually identical with those in M_{530}. Although it begins differently, this version very soon adopts the same pattern as M_{531} and M_{538}, in which the grandmother, angered by her daughter's murder, of which her grandchildren are guilty, rushes after them in the form of a bear when told the facts by the awl (see above, p. 50). So, it is clear that only the overtures are different, and consist, in the one instance, of the lewd grandmother episode and, in the other, of the Loon Woman story.

The lewd grandmother story, in an independent form or linked to other narratives, occupies an important place in the mythology of the western and northern tribes: the Coos, the Tillamook (a small isolated Salish-speaking tribe living to the south of the main area occupied by this family), the Chinook, the Coast and Interior Salish.[1] As we shall see (below, p. 190; cf. *OTM*, M₃₈₄, p. 76), its area of distribution also extends eastwards and southwards. An exhaustive analysis of all the available versions would therefore be a considerable undertaking. I shall confine myself to distinguishing between the three forms that the same story assumes according to the particular area. In the interests of clarity, I propose to give a conventional title to each type: 1) *the provocative neighbour*; 2) *the grizzly's penis*; 3) *the incestuous grandmother*.

We already have an example of the first type in the version just quoted. Here is another, a much more detailed one, from a north-west Sahaptin group, whose habitat was hardly more than three hundred kilometres from Klamath country.

M₅₆₁. *Klikitat. 'The lewd grandmother'*

Young Wildcat lived with his grandmother. One day she sent him to an old neighbour to ask when it would be springtime. 'Tell her,' replied the old man, 'that the month is called lie-by-one-another (copulation) month.' The boy felt badly about such a rude reply and fled in tears; he gave his grandmother the message. The old woman, feigning anger, put all her valuables about her neck and marched away, announcing her intention to reprimand the neighbour.

Hardly had she arrived, when the old man, without paying attention to what she was saying, told her to straddle him (sit upon his penis), which she did. She had warned her grandson that he would hear all kinds of noises while she was punishing the ill-mannered old man. But there was such a din coming from the house that he rushed there, and found his grandmother with her legs in the air.

The young hero, revolted by this indecent spectacle, placed pitch all over the house and set fire to it. When he heard his grandmother's bladder burst in the heat, he went away.

As he went along, he found and ate a lovely piece of cooked meat. Then he wanted to drink from a neighbouring stream. To his great

---

[1] M₅₆₂ₐ (Cowlitz), Adamson, pp. 220–21; M₅₆₂ᵦ, c (Chehalis), *ibid.*, pp. 33–40; M₅₆₂ᵤ (Cowlitz), *ibid.*, pp. 185–8; M₅₆₂ₑ, f (Snuqualmi-Puyallup), Ballard 1, p. 137; M₅₆₃ₐ (Sahaptin), Jacobs 1, pp. 179–83; M₅₆₃ᵦ (Lilloet), Teit 2, pp. 323–5; M₅₆₃c, d (Thompson), Teit 4, pp. 66–7; 5, pp. 247–8; M₅₆₃ₑ (Shuswap), Teit 1, pp. 678–9. Cf. below, p. 478.

surprise, all his teeth came dropping out and fell into the water. He retrieved them and wrapped them up, then went on his way.

His steps led him to the home of a Grizzly Woman, who called him her husband and asked for his teeth in exchange for hers. These were very large, but the boy agreed to insert them in his gums. The next day, he arrived at another (woman) bear's place: she also suggested marriage. But before they could lie down together, Grizzly Woman came running to give the boy his teeth back. The second Bear Woman at once wanted to have them, and obtained them in exchange for her own. The same incident was repeated in Cougar Woman's house, with Bear again rushing in to give back the teeth she had borrowed the evening before, and in an Otter Woman's house, where Cougar Woman arrived to return what she had borrowed.

Lastly, the hero encountered five Mice sisters. They were nice and white, and he married them. Along came Otter Woman and threw the teeth to the boy, asking for her own back; but the teeth he gave her were actually the first ones he had received, that is, Grizzly Woman's. Fearing the anger of the offended ogress, the Mice started to dig a tunnel so that they could escape with their husband. Meanwhile, Grizzly Woman was attacking all the other animal wives. She could not find Bear Woman, who had become suspicious and gone off to bathe in the river, but she killed all the wives after Bear. Next she sought everywhere for the Mice, overtook them all and killed them too. Before dying, each mouse handed the hero over to the sister ahead of her in the tunnel. The youngest, who was in front, managed to escape with her husband.

Grizzly was hot, dry and exhausted. She waded into the water: she thought her two victims were underneath the water and that she could see their reflection. But in fact they were high above and laughing at her. They very rashly allowed Grizzly to join them and there, while they were ostensibly looking for each other's headlice, she killed them and threw their corpses down into the lake (Jacobs 1, pp. 24–7).

An effective analysis of this myth would require a preliminary study of the other types. I shall restrict myself to pointing out that the burst bladder incident, an inversion of the projected hearts in the Loon Woman cycle (for reasons which will transpire later), can be clarified from the syntagmatic point of view by means of a Coast Salish version, that is, a version originating from tribes living near the Klikitat on the western slope of the Cascade Range. In the Sahaptin version, the hero is called Raccoon and, like the one in M_{561}, loses his teeth because he has picked up and eaten a piece of cooked meat. This turns out to be his grandmother's vulva which burst into pieces and was sent flying by the heat of the fire (M_{562a}, Adamson, pp. 220–21). The vulva and bladder would seem, then, to be two combinatory variants of one and the same mytheme, the relevant function of which transposes, on to the alimentary register, an incestuous connection which, as we shall see, the other versions of the myth situate in the sexual register.

M_{563a}. *Cowlitz River Sahaptin. 'The lewd grandmother'*

Raccoon was told by his grandmother to fetch acorns, but he dropped the bucket, out they spilled and he ate them. When he got back, he was whipped from head to foot, which left him bruised and unconscious. When he came to, he went off all by himself to fish for crabs in a large stream, and ate them.

From the other bank, a Grizzly hailed him and asked him where the ford was: 'Where your anus opens to break wind,' replied the hero. Grizzly was angry and swam across the stream, hurled himself on the insolent young hero and gulped him down. The hero, however, who had a flint knife, plunged it into the ogre's heart and escaped through the anus. The grizzly gulped his opponent down several times in succession with the same result: finally, he fell dead.

Raccoon went back to his grandmother, boasting of what he had done to Grizzly. Together they chopped the monster all to pieces, but when it came to what to pack, the grandmother refused all the pieces in turn except the piece with the corpse's penis. Yet she loitered on the way, and the hero retraced his steps in order to help her. He came upon her unawares in an empty sweat-house, where she was masturbating with her part of the corpse. The grandson whipped her into unconsciousness.

The old woman called to her brother's children, who were five ducks living across the river, to come for her in their canoe. But instead of getting into it, she changed several times into a small, rough volcanic rock. Out of exasperation, her nephews took a stick and poked it into the rock, which made the old woman sneeze. Finally she agreed to get into the boat, but hardly had she arrived when she accused her grandson of having whipped her.

They looked for the culprit, who was very busy drying a great quantity of meat over a fire, and they demanded an explanation of why he had ill-treated his grandmother. He informed them of what his grandmother had done, and shared the meat with his uncles. Thus restored, the latter approved of what he had done (Jacobs 1, pp. 179–83).

The Chinook and the Coast Salish, who are neighbours of the Sahaptin, are also familiar with this myth; however, they occasionally replace the gathering of acorns by that of grasshoppers, of which the grandmother is similarly cheated by the hero (Adamson, p. 43), or they make the search for food begin with an encounter with a monster, sometimes a grizzly bear and sometimes a deer, whom the hero – in this case called Wren, the name of a very small insect-eating bird – kills by passing through his body from the mouth to the anus, instead of moving in the reverse direction (M_{564}, Jacobs 2, Part I, pp. 199–207). All these connotations would no doubt be worth studying, but the task would take too long for me to embark on it at this point. Thus, it is clear that the rude reply made by the hero of M_{563a} to the Grizzly, when the latter asks 'Where did you cross the stream?' is a transposition, in spatial terms, of the answer given by the old man in M_{561} to the hero enquiring about the time of year and the coming of spring, the season which is easiest to get through or 'cross'. In one case, the provocative reply cloaks an appetite for food, in the other sexual desire; one refers to the anus opening to emit wind, the other to the vagina opening to receive the penis. In M_{563a}, through an inversion of the same type, the sneezing stone is a prefiguration of the incest which, in other versions that we are about to study, this same grandmother commits with her grandson.

Similarly, the subterranean passage along which the hero of M_{561} is led by the mice, and which fails to save him from the homicidal bear, is a counterpart to the passage he opens up when he kills the same ogre by travelling through his body along the digestive tract, which is a different kind of tunnel. The fact that the myths constantly play on the ambiguity of the concept of consumption/consummation[2] understood sometimes in the literal and alimentary sense, sometimes in the figurative, sexual sense, emerges very clearly from the admonishment addressed by the hero to his grandmother in a Salish version (M_{562d}; Adamson, p. 186), after catching her in culpable congress with the only piece of meat she had agreed to carry: 'This is something to eat, not something to marry!' to which the old woman replies, 'I had to do it, since you won't sleep with me.' Whereupon the hero retorts: 'Grandmother, I'm hungry!' suggesting an appetite of a sexual nature, which is an inversion of the alimentary consumption of the grandmother's vulva in M_{562a}. This reply brings us to the third form of the story: *the incestuous grandmother*.

M_{564}. *Clackamas (Chinook). 'The lewd grandmother'*

Wren and his father's mother were starving. The old woman sent her

2 TRANSLATORS' NOTE: In French, the one word *consommation* has both meanings.

grandson hunting. By magic calls the boy caused bigger and bigger animals to appear. When the horned elk appeared, he killed it by traversing its body several times from the anus to the mouth, then from the mouth to the anus, and by cutting away every time a piece of heart fat. When it came to transporting the meat, the grandmother would only agree to carry the hind-quarters and, as soon as she was alone, she started masturbating with the elk's organ.

Wren caught her unawares and threw her off it; they returned together, ate and lay down, one at each side of the fire. The boy started to talk in his dreams: 'Oh, how I wish that a Klamath woman would come from somewhere and copulate here with me!' 'But my body is half Klamath,' declared the grandmother; and she sat on him to copulate with him.

Soon, they heard the noise of the paddling of canoes. They reluctantly separated, and the boy went out to see what news the travellers brought. 'Oh,' said the latter, 'people are telling one another that Wren and his father's mother are doing it to each other . . .' Humiliated and angry at knowing he had been discovered, the boy went back into the house, wrapped his grandmother in the elk's hide and threw her into the river.

A long way downstream, the corpse was fished out and recognized. Three shamans tried to bring it back to life; only the third one succeeded. He even managed to take off the old woman's wrinkled skin at the same time as the elk hide cover, since the two were stuck together, but he was unable to fix her teeth. As long as she kept her mouth shut she looked like a pretty young woman. She was offered in marriage to Wren; he saw her, liked her and married her.

He had been warned to take the elk hide everywhere he went with his wife, and the latter was careful never to reveal her toothless gums. One day, however, Wren tickled her so much she could not help laughing, whereupon she opened her mouth wide. The elk hide at once came back on to her, and completely covered her like a wrinkled skin. The boy recognized his grandmother: 'I've been deceived,' he said and hurled her into the water again.

But the second attempt to resuscitate her failed (Jacobs 2, Part I, pp. 199–207; cf. M_{566d}, Boas 10, pp. 119–22).

In discussing this third form of the myth, in which the grandmother's lewd behaviour is carried to the point of incest, it would also be worth while drawing up a detailed list of the commutations. Sometimes the grandmother is a mouse ($M_{562e, f}$; Ballard 1, p. 137) or a seasonal animal: a small blue-bird, the harbinger of rain (Adamson, p. 31, n. 2, p. 188), or a snow-bird (*spi'tsxu*, cf. M_{752}, see below, p. 491), who needs very little food in order to survive and who makes her grandson very ill-tempered when she tries to give him the same amount as herself (M_{562a}, Adamson, p. 220). On the other hand, according to a Chehalis River version, the grandmother is a glutton whose insatiable appetite deprives her grandson (M_{562b}; Adamson, p. 35) of food.

It also happens that the lack of food which forms one of the invariant features of the group, becomes the consequence, and not the cause, of the events described in the myths. Thus, in the Salish versions ($M_{562c, d}$; Adamson, pp. 36–40, 187–8), the jeering on the part of the canoists leads to fighting, during which the grandmother inadvertently pushes her grandson into the fire instead of her opponent; the boy is burnt to death. She brings him back to life by sticking the half charred bones together with pitch. But he rashly goes out into the sun, and the heat causes him to melt. 'If he had not got burnt, he would have been a big bird, and perhaps hunters would kill game in the same way as he killed the giant elk. But his ashes turned into a wren — a little one.' This is, then, and attempt to explain why and how hunting became difficult.

I noted (p. 167) in connection with $M_{561-562}$ that the episode of the burst bladder or the vulva hurled through the air was a transformation of the one involving the exploding hearts in the Loon Woman cycle. Other signs of an affinity between the two groups can be observed. For instance, Meadowlark Woman (whose eponym is opposed to the snow-bird, a form sometimes taken by the lecherous grandmother: see above), Loon Woman's sister-in-law, lies flat on her stomach in order to protect her unborn children from the fire in which she is about to perish. She thus protects her precious burden in the hollow formed in the ashes by her pregnant belly. Symmetrically, in order to enjoy her grandson's embrace in greater comfort, the lewd grandmother, who is deformed, insists on her partner digging a place to fit her hunched back ($M_{562c, d}$; Adamson, pp. 38–9, 187).

The Tillamook versions (M_{565a}, Boas 14, pp. 34–8; M_{565b-g}; E. D. Jacobs, pp. 54–72) establish a particularly significant connection between the two groups of myths, since this tiny community — a Salish-speaking one, like those in whose mythology the lewd grandmother story occupies such an important place — lived in an isolated position towards the south, half way towards the area of distribution of the Loon Woman myth. These detailed and complex versions deserve special study. I shall merely point out here that they fuse into a single narrative the lewd grandmother story, the Loon Woman story and the one about the child rescued from the fire who is conceived and delivered by his adoptive father (in other words, the hero, who plays the part of bird-nester in the Klamath–Modoc mythology). In this instance, however, a tender-hearted ogress, called Wild Woman, succeeds with some difficulty in stealing two children, whom she brings up. She condemns them to incest as a punishment for having discovered her clandestine relationship with an aged husband, from whom she is reputedly separated. She thus changes her grand-daughter (the younger of the two children, although the one who always takes the initiative) into a functional equivalent of Loon Woman; after which she kills her grandson. The tearful young widow of the man, who was 'a brother in respect of the high, a husband in respect of the low', tries to commit suicide, and throws herself and her baby into a fire. A supernatural character called Bald Eagle saves the child, hides him under his testicles and hands him over to his wife, who simulates delivery. In another version (M_{565e}, *loc. cit.*, pp. 65–7), Wild Woman herself commits incest with her brother. We have therefore a whole series of variants which could be put into an order illustrating the stages of the transformation leading from the Loon Woman cycle to that of the lewd grandmother; since the latter appears sometimes as an incestuous sister, sometimes as being responsible for another sister's incest – in this case her grand-daughter's – with a brother, who is none other than the grandson with whom she herself commits incest in the final stage of the transformation. The Tillamook, who live on the extreme edge of the myth's area of distribution, are probably not familiar with Loon Woman under this name. But, by inverting it, they retain a characteristic feature of her story: the incestuous sister is betrayed by the blobs of *black* pitch which stain her *white* throat (*loc. cit.*, p. 66); whereas, within the confines of the distribution area, the guilty woman is betrayed by the tufts of *white* fur from her brother's coat which have stuck to the *black* pitch which (in a manner more in keeping with zoological reality) serves as the background and not as the pattern on the background (cf. above, pp. 118, 151).[3] At the other end of the area of distribution, the Maidu version (M_{554}) explains the origin of incestuous relationships; like a final echo reverberating in the west, the Tillamook version (M_{565d}, *loc. cit.*, p. 62) explains why incest is forbidden: 'You see,' exclaims the grandmother on being found out, 'you can't hide anything . . . Hereafter, it will no longer be possible to make love in secret with a

---

[3] We know of other examples of a transformation inverting a positive into a negative image, in the manner of a photographic plate. For instance, the junco bird wears a collar of black beads, according to the Yokuts and the western Mono, but the Owens Valley Paiute, who are their immediate neighbours, give the bird a white deerskin tunic in the same myth (cf. Gayton-Newman, p. 47; Steward, p. 407).

close relative. Oh, my grandson, it is wrong to behave in this way; no one will do it again.'

It follows from the preceding observations that incest which might be termed 'vertical' — since it is between older and younger relatives of the direct line — is a transformation of the 'horizontal' type between relatives belonging to the same generation, which provides the theme for the Loon Woman story.

At the very beginning of this study, I noted exactly the same transformation between the reference myth (M_1) (itself transformable into the Loon Woman story, cf. above, pp. 111–13) and another Bororo myth (M_5), the central characters of which are also a grandson and grandmother, representing a kind of anti-natural couple. In the Bororo, as in the North American myth, the grandmother straddles her grandson in order to commit with him not, it is true, an incestuous act (which we recognized as being the contrary of a different kind of incest), but at least the contrary of incest: since she poisons him by emitting intestinal wind; this is a transformation of the incestuous relationships which the North American myths reintroduce by different means: they present the grandmother as copulating the wrong way round, instead of doing the opposite of copulating. She is given the active part to play, and — in several versions — is on top of her partner during copulation. Furthermore, the hero of M_{563a} answers the Grizzly Bear (into which M_{560} transforms a grandmother, who is cannibalistic instead of incestuous, or, more accurately, commits the incest, as it were, by proxy) with a rude retort: 'Where your anus opens to break wind!' in connection with which we have already established that it is part of a permutation in which (sexual) incest and (alimentary) gluttony also have a place.

It is therefore highly significant in this respect that the myths of tropical America and those of the northern hemisphere prove to have the same armature. In M_{560}, a grandmother changes her grand-daughter into an incestuous sister and herself into an ogress. In M_{562b}, she is first a glutton then incestuous. And M_5 itself consists of two successive sequences, the first featuring a grandmother who is incestuous in her particular way, and the second her grand-daughter who succeeds her and replaces her in the form of a glutton, almost an ogress (cf. RC, pp. 246–51). But there is still more to be said: the first sequence in M_5 is concerned with an old grandmother who breaks wind into her grandson's mouth, and whom the latter kills by plunging an arrow into her anus. Symmetrically, one of the Tillamook versions (M_{565g}, E. D. Jacobs, pp. 70–72; cf. also Wishram in: Sapir-Spier 2, p. 279) features a grandson who defecates on his grandmother's food and then kills her by plunging a sharp pointed stick into her wide open mouth.

According to M_5, armadillos, burrowing and carrion-eating animals, secretly bury the corpse in the family hut, under the very mat where the dead woman used to sleep. In M_{565g}, just as symmetrically, her homologue dies in the brush and the scattered fragments of her corpse become caught on trees where they give rise to funguses.

It will be remembered that M_5 is concerned with the origin of diseases, which are exuded by a woman with such an appetite for fish that she cannot evacuate waste matter in the natural way. The myth explains that, formerly, diseases were unknown; it was only to be expected that their appearance should shorten the human life-span. Here we have another point of similarity between the Bororo myth and the North American lewd grandmother cycle, since it will not have passed unnoticed that all the versions end either with the motif of premature aging or with the impossibility of resuscitating the dead. Moreover, it now becomes clear why the lewd grandmother cycle is a systematic inversion of the Loon Woman story: those symbols of resurrection, the *incombustible* hearts of relatives sacrificed by a sister guilty of sexual incest, can be transformed, very plausibly, into a bladder (M_{561}) or into the *well cooked* vulva (M_{562a}) of a kinswoman sacrificed by one of her descendants who, in eating the flesh, will become guilty of alimentary incest.

This comparison between myths belonging to both North and South presents another point of interest from the methodological angle. We shall see that it is possible, through the intermediary agency of the North American myths, to detect a link, which was not so obvious in the initial stage of our enquiry, between the Bororo myth (M_5), a transformation of M_1, and a group of Ge myths $\{M_{87-94}\}$, which are transformations of another group $\{M_{7-12}\}$, which in turn, as has been independently established, are themselves transformations of M_1. In the light of the North American group $\{M_{560}-M_{564}\}$, it would now appear that, like $\{M_{87}-M_{94}\}$, M_5 too is a myth concerned with the origin of man's short life-span. Moreover $\{M_{87}-M_{94}\}$, attribute the short life-span to the action of a *celestial* creature, who becomes the *wife* of a mortal and furthermore a *provider of food*, since it is she who tells men about *cultivated plants*. Symmetrically, M_5 attributes the origin of diseases, consequently also of man's short life-span, to a *terrestrial* (or aquatic) creature, the *sister* of a mortal and a *non-provider of food*, since she cheats men of their catch by devouring the *raw fish* herself. One is a *star* who changes into a *human wife* in response to her future husband's wish. The other is a *human sister* who is changed, at the wish of her brothers, into a *rainbow* (cf. *RC*, pp. 246–51).

When I discussed the theme of man's mortality in the South American myths, I showed that they developed it either in the form of the impossibility of rejuvenation or resurrection, or in the complementary form of premature aging (RC, pp. 161–3). The North American myths belonging to the lewd grandmother cycle retain this distinction, since, in the first type (the provocative neighbour), a very young hero suddenly loses all his teeth and so becomes a prematurely old man, whereas in the third (the incestuous grandmother), a very old heroine succeeds in getting rid of her wrinkles; but even the most famous shamans fail to give her back her teeth: the absence of teeth is responsible for a second death, and this time resuscitation is no longer possible (compare M_{561} and M_{564}; see above, pp. 166 and 169–70). It can be noted in passing that the Coast Salish believed in a similar opposition between death from sickness and death by decapitation: only the second was irrevocable (Ballard 1, pp. 137–8; Adamson, pp. 24, 167).

The fact that the falling out of the teeth is taken as evidence of premature aging or of the impossibility of resuscitation is in keeping with the general spirit of these myths (cf. RC, pp. 191–3, and see above, pp. 39–40; see below, p. 382) which, like those of tropical America, play on the opposition between the eyes, which are by nature irremovable and excrement which is destined to be removable. We cannot lose our eyes without injuring ourselves, whereas excrement has to be evacuated at regular intervals. The teeth occupy an intermediary position between the eyes (inseparable from the body) and excrement (separable): the aging process gradually separates man from his teeth, in spite of the fact that originally they seemed as much an integral part of him as his eyes. The teeth, being a negative expression of the periodicity governing human life, are also an inversion of the foetus, which, through its separability from the body, of which it seems to be a part, testifies to the same periodicity, but this time in a positive fashion, since it ensures the continuation of the species. From the collective point of view, the separation of the foetus in childbirth is therefore equivalent to the separation from the body of the incombustible heart which becomes, in spite of the destination of the corpse, a guarantee and a means of individual immortality. This explains the three-stage transformation I noted in the myths as giving rise to the mallet used by the demiurge to push a new-born baby away from the fire, and the paddle or basket used by the guilty sister to push the hearts of her kinsfolk back into the fire or to extract them from it (see above, p. 111). It will also be remembered that in certain versions of the Loon Woman myth, a heart is brought back to life in the form of a tiny child (M_{553}, p. 122). The heart's resistance to fire is a fact of experience, which must have been observable during the cremation of corpses (see above, p. 57, n. 2). As proof of the coherence of the system, we may also note that just beyond the fringe of the area where it was customary to cremate the dead, the Loon Woman myth transforms the hearts into eyes (M_{547}) and resurrects the dead by immersion in cold, instead of in boiling, water (M_{554}), thus preferring a modality of the raw to a modality of the cooked.

The Ge myths explaining the origin of man's mortality associate it with the introduction of cultivated plants, itself a positive function of the marriage between a star and a mortal, which takes place along the cosmological axis of the high and the low. The North American tribes who tell the story of the lewd grandmother do not cultivate the land. But their myths describe a union between a grandmother and her grandson, a union also situated, then, along a high/low axis – but an axis of a genealogical kind – and deduce from it consequences, of which they stress the privative aspects: the taboo on incest, marking the beginning of life in society; and the loss of miraculous hunting effected by natural means, leading to arduous hunting, the only kind that can be practised by men who have attained to the state of culture (cf. above, p. 171).

This is an appropriate point at which to recall that all the myths begin during a period of famine: the two main characters have nothing left to eat, either because of external circumstances, or as a result of gluttony or negligence on the part of one of them. According to certain Chinook versions (M_{566a}, Boas 7, pp. 142–53; M_{566b}, Sapir 1, pp. 153–65; M_{566c}, Jacobs 2, Part II, pp. 423–30; M_{566d}, Boas 10, pp. 119–22; M_{566e-f}, Ray 4, pp. 146–51), also found in Klamath mythology (M_{566g}; Stern 1, p. 39), Raccoon grows weary of gathering acorns in summer, because he is too hot; to speed the work, he does not bother to select the best, but picks up maggoty ones too.[4] When winter comes, he leaves only the maggoty ones for his grandmother, thus causing their first quarrel; the second quarrel occurs when, summer having come round again, he offers her berries which he has previously stuffed with thorns; thus turning her into a gallinacean, probably the *Bonasa* sp., a bird which, as will be shown later, symbolizes the appearance of man's mortality in the myths of this area. This motif is also found among the Bororo (cf. M_{21}, *RC*, pp. 94–5), since, in both cases, the animals into which one or several humans are changed after consuming fruit stuffed with thorns are creatures half way between men and animals (wild pigs) or between life and death (gallinaceae). The grandmother in the Kalapuya version (M_{567}; Jacobs 4, pp. 130–33) is also a gallinacean, who is

---

[4] It will be remembered that in the Loon Woman cycle, which is an inversion of that of the grandmother and the grandson, the acorn maggot has, on the contrary, a positive connotation (see above, p. 114).

deprived not of food but of drink by her grandson, Raccoon, too busy feasting on shrimps and shell-fish to draw the water she asks him for. She is changed into a stone in the Klamath version (M_{566g}); and in the Coos versions into a stone or a gallinacean (M_{568}; Jacobs 6, pp. 172–3, 181).

There are other points of similarity between the mortality myths of North and South America, which are of particular significance in that they do not relate simply to the message, but bring out certain common properties in the armatures. We must return to the episode in which the hero exchanges teeth with a succession of animal wives, and look at it in detail. However baroque it may seem, it presents an impeccably logical construction, the pattern of which is scrupulously respected both in the North and the South.

First of all we must go back to the beginning. In order to stay alive, the Bororo hero in the reference myth (M_1) has to overcome four ordeals. The first three, which are homologous with each other, concern certain musical instruments which have to be brought back noiselessly from the land of ghosts. The hero is successful, thanks to the help of three animals, the third of which almost fails. The fourth ordeal, which is of quite a different nature, exposes him to hunger and thirst at the top of a rocky cliff. He triumphs in the end, thanks to the material and moral support of his grandmother (she has given him her stick and told him what to do) but not without having been brought very close to death by his father. In depriving his son of all means of escape in the hope of destroying him, the father shows himself to be a metaphorical ogre. This aspect was not mentioned in *The Raw and the Cooked*, not because it would have been irrelevant to my demonstration, but simply because it had escaped my notice. Yet again, a comparison between myths originating in areas geographically very far removed from each other throws unexpected light on details which remained obscure, as long as the myths were being examined separately.

To establish the unity of the group formed by myths relating to the origin of the cooking of food and to man's mortality, it was enough to show how the first three ordeals described in M_1 could be transformed into those given equal prominence in other myths. Thus, according to M_9, to prevent mankind having to accept the affliction of mortality in exchange for the cooking fire conceded to them by the jaguar, the hero, on hearing three calls, has to reply only to the first two, which come from stone and hard wood, but not to the 'gentle call' of the rotten wood. Here again, then, we have three successive ordeals, all similar in kind and only distinguishable through their relative acoustic intensity. As in the reference myth, there is a fourth ordeal: the hero has to face an ogre who takes him by surprise through having assumed the appearance of his father and from whom he is able to escape by means of a trick. Consequently, between M_1 and M_9 not only are the first three ordeals repeated, in the sense that the hero must avoid either making or hearing a noise: the fourth ordeal is also the same, since it results from the appearance, in the story, either of a *father playing the part of an ogre* (M_1), or of an *ogre playing the part of a father* (M_9).

This additional affinity between two myths of Central Brazil would be much less obvious if a North American myth concerned, like M_9, with man's mortality, did not have exactly the same construction; the only difference being that what, in South American mythology, is the fourth and last ordeal becomes the first in the North American myth. Let us look at these two myths more closely (Figure 14).

Having lost all his teeth and become an old man about to die, the hero recovers his youth by obtaining another set of teeth: he exchanges his teeth, which have been carefully rescued from the bottom of the river into which they had fallen, for those of a Grizzly Woman whom he marries. We know who this woman is, or to be more specific, which semantic function she occupies in the group: she is the equivalent of the grandmother who, as her grandson's murderess, changes into a grizzly bear, or who — metonymy being replaced by a metaphor — behaves like a grizzly she-bear, since she copulates with the hindquarters of a male of the species. We can recognize the fourth ordeal in the South American myths simply by operating the following transformation:

M_1 (*father changed into ogre*) $\Rightarrow$ M_9 (*ogre changed into father*) $\Rightarrow$ M_{561} (*grandmother changed into ogress*).

Next follow three ordeals which are homologous with each other like the first three ordeals in M_1 and M_9, with the additional similarity that, in each case, the third ends in partial failure: in M_1 the helpful grasshopper returns half dead, thus connoting an intermediary condition between life and death, that the shortened human life-span illustrates in its own way (cf. *RC*, pp. 211–12); in M_9, the hero makes the mistake of replying to the call of the rotten wood, in spite of the jaguar's warnings, thus determining the appearance of man's mortality. Finally, in M_{561}, he almost succeeds in keeping the Grizzly Woman's teeth in place of his own, since, right from the beginning, he inserts them into his own gums, and so he has no difficulty in obtaining the teeth of the other animal wives in exchange for his own available ones, being able to pass the latter on to each new partner, as soon as the previous wife has handed them back. However, when it comes to the final transaction, he makes a fatal mistake: in exchange for his own

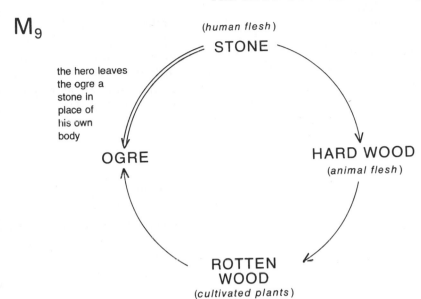

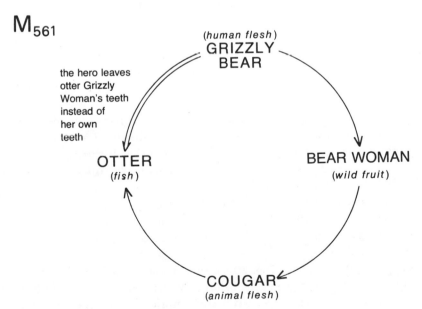

Figure 14. The common armature of myths M_9 and M_{561}

teeth, which Otter Woman is returning, he gives her Grizzly Woman's teeth. What does this signify?

The myth singles out one of the many differences between men and animals: men lose their teeth with age, animals do not. In other words, men grow old whereas animals remain young until they die. Having become prematurely old, the hero, in acquiring animal teeth in place of his own, is trying not only to recover his physical integrity but also to ensure that he will enjoy prolonged youth.

He fails in this undertaking for two reasons. Firstly, his successive transactions are with increasingly less impressive animals, whose diet also approximates more and more closely to that of humans. For instance, the otter appears at the end of the series, the reason being not only that it is a small, peaceable animal, but that it lives on fish, the main source of food for the tribes who owned or frequented the large fishing grounds along the Columbia River. Secondly, having inadvertently returned Grizzly Woman's teeth in exchange for his own, he is, in a sense, back to his starting-point: his hope of a long life has irrevocably vanished. We should note, incidentally, the symmetry between this symbolism and that of the South American mortality myths (M_{79-85}). According to the latter, man would have been spared his short life-span had he been able to imitate the animals − particularly reptiles and insects − which succeed in remaining young by sloughing off their old skins. In North America, on the other hand, the view is that prolonged youth, were it possible, would have resulted from man imitating animals who, unlike humans, do not lose their old teeth. We shall, however, have occasion to note that, in the area of North America with which we are concerned, the two symbolic formulae can exist side by side.

In *The Raw and the Cooked*, it was shown (pp. 152−3) that the three substances which call out to the hero − stone, hard wood and rotten wood − connote respectively human flesh, animal flesh and cultivated plants, in accordance with another group of Ge myths about the origin of man's mortality (M_{87-94}) which trace it back to the period when cultivated plants were introduced. The exchanges of teeth (instead of sounds) in M_{561} also have a connection with food. The grizzly bear − the largest and most dangerous animal in this part of the world, and one which could only be killed in a tussle between man and beast (Ray 3, p. 188; Jacobs 4, pp. 21−3) − was generally thought of as a man-eater (cannibal). This is why the Kalapuya (*loc. cit.*, p. 23) and the Salish of Puget Sound (Eells 3, p. 618; M. W. Smith 2, p. 246) forbade the consumption of its flesh. The same affinity between the grizzly bear's flesh and human flesh is also hinted at less overtly. These same Salish Indians, who hunted and killed grizzly bears but did not eat their flesh, used to burn the animal's body, although they were not in the habit of cremating their human dead (Elmendorf 1, pp. 116–17); their custom was, then, symmetrical with that of the more southerly Pomo, who believed that non-cremated human corpses turned into grizzly bears (Gatschet 1, Part 1, p. 86).

Certain myths, which will be discussed later (Part Four, 2, 3), establish an opposition between the grizzly she-bear (*Ursus arctos*) and the common she-bear (*Ursus americanus*) which feeds blamelessly on berries and other wild fruits: the myths which feature the cougar as hero regard him as a model hunter. Thus, the four animal wives in M_{561} illustrates a systematic series of diets, based respectively on human flesh (grizzly she-bear), wild fruits (common she-bear), animal flesh (cougar) and fish (otter).

So, as in South America, this cycle of myths about man's mortality is laid out on two parallel registers. In one, the gluttonous hero kills his grandmother and *burns* the corpse; as a result of which, he loses his teeth and *grows old prematurely*. In the other, a grandmother, greedy for either food or sex, or both, is *drowned* by the hero, but is brought back to life, albeit precariously, but does not succeed in recovering her teeth which she had lost through old age; in other words, in her case *youth cannot be recaptured*. From this point onwards, both the northern and the southern stories closely follow the same pattern, as can be seen from the diagrams in Figure 14. The hero has three successive encounters, involving ordeals from which he emerges more or less victorious. In M_9, the problem is an exchange of messages with stone, hard wood and rotten wood. M_{561} also involves an exchange – this time of teeth – with a grizzly bear, a common bear, and a cougar. In both series, the hero goes on to have a fourth encounter, in which he faces a danger which he *overcomes thanks to an element retained from the first encounter*. According to M_9, he meets *stone* first, and lastly the ogre, whom *he deceives* by leaving a *stone* in place of his own body, which this same ogre is preparing to devour. According to M_{561}, he encounters the *grizzly bear* first, the otter last; and he makes the mistake of leaving grizzly bear's teeth for otter, instead of otter's own teeth; consequently, the infuriated ogress prepares to kill him, but she cannot devour him, since she no longer has any teeth and her masticatory possibilities would seem to be limited to the destruction of toads, which she crushes between her gums in order to remove them from her head, that they infest like lice.

So, in the Ge myth, in place of his own body, the hero gives the ogre a stone, the metaphorical substance of the ogre's cannibalism. In the Sahaptin myth, the hero removes from the ogress the metonymic means of her cannibalism: her teeth. He is saved in the one instance, but at the price of mankind accepting a short life-span; in the other instance, he dies because he himself has been unable to avoid the limited life-span.

I would like to round off this discussion with a further observation. I gave the title of 'fugue' to the section in *The Raw and the Cooked* devoted to the South American myths about the origin of man's mortality, and this linking up (only one of several instances) of the structure of the myths with certain musical forms aroused a good deal of sceptical comment. Yet it was in no way arbitrary, and were additional proof needed, the analysis of the North American versions would confirm my argument that Western music discovered only at a late stage, and adapted for its own purposes through transposition into a different register, types of construction which had already been in use in mythology, in fully elaborated forms, for thousands of years. One has only to look at the diagram in Figure 15 to be convinced that M_{561}, like homologous myths in South America, is fugal in form. The exchange of teeth motif is developed in successive stages. Each voice is entrusted to a separate character, who replies to the preceding one; and runs after – literally, in this case – the following one. In each instance, too, the degrees and cadences vary, since the same motif is taken up successively by characters arranged in order of their decreasing size, and differentiated, qualitatively, in terms of their respective habits no less appreciably than voices and instruments are by their registers and timbres. In this particular myth, as in the one referred to on p. 115, even the stretto is present. It begins when Grizzly Woman, who had already appeared at the beginning, rushes forward to join in turn, and to reduce to silence, the successive interpreters of the theme. Then, with an accelerated rhythm, the plot recapitulates the stages of the hero's flight from death: a flight which is all the more poignant in that, instead of adopting, as at the beginning, the rhetorical symbols of eternal youth, it confirms the destruction of a creature of flesh and blood whom five wives, subsumed under the name of a single animal, pass on to each other in frantic haste from the eldest to the youngest, before they themselves perish one by one, and the hero, too, after them. The final majestic cadence fuses the beginning and the end, and concludes with a succession of alternately ascending or descending broken chords, accompanied by the axis of the high and the low acting as sustaining pedal. They unite – in the minor key, of course – sky and earth, air and water, life here below and the transcendent, and bring the failed transfiguration to its definitive conclusion: it is a fugue[5] indeed, an attempt to

---

[5] TRANSLATORS' NOTE: In French, the word *fugue* has the double meaning of musical fugue and flight, running away.

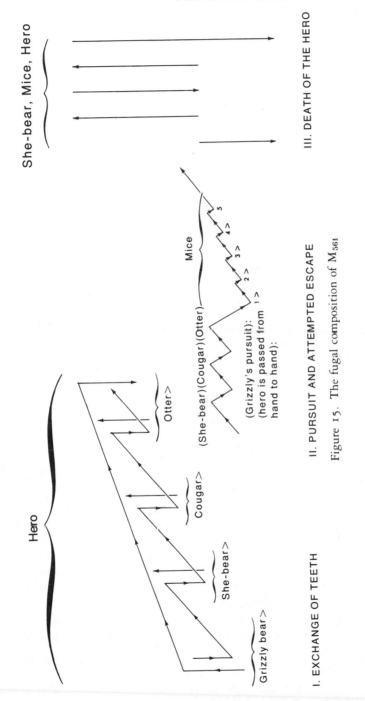

Figure 15. The fugal composition of M_{561}

escape the irreparable ravages of old age, but which leads only on to the horns of another dilemma (*RC*, p. 152): the choice between the decrepitude of age and violent death at the hands of an enemy.

In order to reassure any reader who might feel disquiet at my using as confirmation of each other myths originating from tribes which are not just separated by distance but dissimilar in all respects, I should mention the existence in the north-west of North America of versions concerned with man's mortality which resemble the South American forms even more closely than the ones I chose to examine in the first place, precisely because the apparent absence of any similarity at all strengthened my demonstration in obliging me to proceed deductively. This being so, we could not be dealing with myths which had simply been passed by borrowing from tribe to tribe or spread over vast areas during the peopling of America, but with separate formulations generated by the same underlying patterns. What is important for me is, then, generative patterns or schemas; I want first of all to prove their general validity and then to elucidate their mode of operation.

The Klamath and the Modoc, with whom the present investigation began, possess myths which are in a way perpendicular to the axes on which $\{M_1-M_5\}$ and $\{M_7-M_{12}\}$ are situated; they tell how men simultaneously acquired cooking fire and diseases

M_{471c}. Modoc. *'The origin of cooking fire'* (cf. *OTM*, p. 341)[6]

The first ancestors had no fire and ate their meat raw. For fire belonged to the ten Sickness brothers who lived in the east, and the ten Sun brothers who lived in the west.

Black Fox encouraged the ancestors to conquer fire for the people who were to come. He posted runners at regular intervals between his village and the one in which the Sickness brothers lived. There he stole fire from the striped squirrels who were guarding it, and the runners took it away in relays. The brothers pursued them, but failed to catch them. Since they could not get fire back, they decided to stay with men and persecute them. 'Till that time the Sickness brothers had never troubled people. But after fire was stolen they were everywhere in the world. People had fire but they had sickness too.'

Black Fox next decided to steal fire from the Sun brothers. He lay in wait for the brothers and succeeded in cutting off the heads of five

[6] In the index (pp. 535, 559) this myth is mistakenly attributed to the Klamath, who have a different version (M_{471b}).

brothers, with the help of their servant who betrayed them. The latter was called Káhkaas (Curtin translates this as stork, but the bird was probably the large blue heron, *Ardea herodias*, cf. Barker 2, p. 329: Klamath *q'ahq'ah?as*). Fox dared not attack the five remaining Suns, firstly because they were too powerful, and also for fear that if they were all killed perpetual night would prevail. Up to that time snow and storms had raged all through the year, but with the destruction of the five Suns alternation between summer and winter began. However, their respective duration had to be decided. Some wanted ten months of cold, others two only: 'for if there are ten months of cold people will starve to death; they cannot lay up roots and seeds enough.' They finally settled for three months of winter. Before turning into animals, the ancestors proclaimed that the people to come would be thankful: 'We have got fire for them; we have killed five of the Sun brothers; we have made winter short: they will be thankful' (Curtin 1, pp. 51–9).

The three coldest months probably correspond to the three Nordic brothers who are rashly attacked by the hero Rattlesnake in a variant from the same source (M_{569a}; Curtin 1, pp. 60–67); in this version, he breaks all but two of his teeth, which become poisonous ('bad medicine'); as an act of revenge, he creates and spreads abroad all kinds of sickness, which hereafter will curtail human life; only snakes, which slough off their skins, will be able to cure themselves of the diseases they have contracted.

A third version (M_{569b}; Curtin 1, pp. 68–72) features five wicked brothers who are hated by everybody, and on whom their sister inflicts sickness by failing to keep awake during the time of her maturity dance (cf. M_{81}). They are presumed dead, but they recover and kill all the people in the world, except a couple called Old Age whom they cannot kill. They are pursued in turn by these powerful spirits, and become old and die: 'This is how Old Age came into the world. If the five brothers had left the old man and his wife alone in their country there would have been no such thing.'

Consequently, these myths, which revive the problem of the groups of ten discussed in the previous volume (*OTM*, Part Six, 1), associate the shortened human life-span with the appearance of periodicity in its various aspects: physiological (M_{569b}), zoological (M_{569a}) or seasonal (M_{471c}). The Salish of Puget Sound (to whom we shall return in this connection, below, p. 541) and the Columbia River Chinook, both near neighbours of the Klikitat, whose myth, M_{561}, begins with the hero's attempt to find out when spring will come, celebrated this time of year as the season of resurrection:

M₃₅₂. Wasco. 'The origin of irrevocable death' (cf. HA, p. 396)

When Coyote's wife died, Eagle took his bereaved friend to look for her where the dead stay. They were taken by the ferryman to the isle of the dead in the middle of Columbia River, but no one appeared. They were told that the dead only appeared when it was pitch dark, their guardian, a frog, having swallowed the moon. Then the dead awake and have a good time.

Coyote saw that his dead wife was enjoying herself so much with a companion that he was jealous. Helped by Eagle, he killed the frog, stripped her of her skin and put it on himself; but he could neither jump like the frog nor swallow the moon, which stuck in his mouth a little. He spat it out, and just when day was about to dawn and the dead were about to withdraw, he captured them all in the box he had made specially for this purpose.

During the journey back, Coyote took hold of the box held by Eagle; curious to know the cause of the noise he heard coming from inside, he opened it a little way: at once the dead escaped and returned to their country. Coyote could only keep one crippled man, and he finally decided not to keep him either. 'If I had brought the box here and opened it properly,' explained Eagle, 'people would live again in the spring, just as the trees do' (Sapir-Spier 2, pp. 277–8. Wishram version in Sapir 1, pp. 107–17).

We thus find the problems again being formulated as they are in certain South American myths concerned with man's mortality and the impossibility of resurrecting the dead (M_{19}, M_{85}, M_{86}; RC, pp. 156–63). But there is more to it than that: certain myths belonging to the same area of North America interpret mortality in terms of an acoustic code, as do M_9, M_{70}, M_{81}, M_{85}. This is all the more significant in that, as Boas pointed out (15, pp. 486–91), myths about the origin of death are rather rare in North America and, in particular, are lacking in the whole of the eastern region:

M₅₇₀ₐ. Cowlitz River Sahaptin. 'The origin of mortality'

The chief Jesus (*sic*) sent Coyote to fashion the earth. He made streams, indicated place names, planted trees and edible plants. 'Men will burn this wood,' he said, 'and keep themselves good and warm and they will not be cold.'

Two humans appeared, a man and a woman, who had neither mouths nor eyes. 'I will come to you and I will complete you,' said the demiurge, 'but do not reply to any call, for a dangerous being may call out to you.' However, they disobeyed. Jesus arrived, realized the devil had beaten him, and decided to make life short (Jacobs 1, pp. 238–40).

This story, although adapted in accordance with the Old and the New Testaments by a native informant who was a member of the Shaker sect, is similar to others scattered throughout the entire geographical area. The Klamath tell it in almost the same terms, and also confuse it with what they know of Genesis (M_{570b}, Gatschet 1, pp. xciii–iv), although they use it to explain not man's mortality but the appearance of the arts of civilization. A less adulterated myth belonging to the Salish of Puget Sound associates the motif of the calls which it is fatal to answer with man's mortality: 'The generation of beings about to be brought on to the earth shall be mortal. Of each family some shall die (young) but not all; some shall be left' (M_{570c}: Ballard 1, pp. 114–17). The Nez Percé change the motif into terms expressing a tactile or visual code: the dead can be heard, but they can neither be looked at nor touched. The demiurge violates this interdiction and because of this, the dead can no longer be resuscitated (M_{570d}: Phinney, pp. 278–85). In a Kutenai myth (M_{570e}: Boas 9, pp. 113–17), the demiurge, together with his companion, risks death because he replies to the calls of the Thunder Birds. The latter take the pair prisoner, but they escape. Since then, thunder no longer kills people: it need only make a noise.

In the myths mentioned so far, the protagonists are receivers of noise; in other contexts, they turn into producers of noise, thus undergoing a transformation homologous with the one whereby, in the mutually symmetrical myths of South America – M_1 and M_9–M_{10} respectively – the hero is either a subject or an object of noise (cf. *RC*, p. 149). So, as might have been expected, we find that a Nez Percé version of the myth about the losing and exchanging of teeth is an inversion, in every detail, of the lewd grandmother story, since Coyote, the trickster, is the main character and his mistake consists in emitting noise instead of receiving it, as in the myths about the origin of man's mortality, which have the same trickster as their hero.

M_{571a-c}. Nez Percé. 'The origin of the seasons'

Having been struck several times on the face by a flying object which he took to be a duck, Coyote caught it, then cooked and ate it. He then discovered it was a vulva (cf. M_{561}–M_{562}). When he went to look for water to drink after his meal, all his teeth came out of his mouth and fell into the water.

He came to a place where five Geese brothers lived. They had gone hunting and he found their pretty sister alone in the camp. Coyote turned himself into a handsome man and entered the house. The young girl invited him to lunch, but since he had no teeth, he had to be satisfied with pounded meat. His beloved son saw that he had no teeth and gave him a set of mountain goat's teeth. Thereupon the brothers came back from hunting and willingly accepted Coyote as their brother-in-law.

He insisted on accompanying the brothers on their next hunting expedition, but in spite of being told to utter no sound, he could not resist screaming like a wild goose. The brothers were flying (across the river) and carrying Coyote. As soon as he screamed, they dropped him. For a while Coyote managed to remain at a reasonable height by changing alternately into a feather or a heavy branch, according to whether he thought he was too low or too high. Finally he made a mistake; he fell and was killed.

The woman accused her brothers of killing her husband. She shot arrows at them, taking care to put her own heart in her little finger for safety. The three eldest brothers died (cf. M_{471c}, M_{569a}), but the two youngest aimed at her little finger where her heart was hidden and killed their sister.

The surviving brothers set off and almost died of hunger, being reduced to eating pieces of sinew from their bows. Finally they arrived at a house where old man Winter and his daughters lived. They were eating large dishfuls of food and between them they ate all the food. The young men left and came to another tent, which belonged to old man Summer and his daughters; these new hosts prepared such a copious meal that their guests were unable to finish it. Then the girls disentangled the tousled hair of the two brothers and became their wives.

One day old man Winter sent his daughter to the summer people to find out what had happened to the visitors. When he saw the girl coming, old man Summer roasted a piece of meat and threw it at her private parts, for she wore no clothes. She left the house biting off a piece of the meat and when she returned home, she threw what was left of the meat at her father, who finished it.

Winter and his daughters decided to wage war on the summer people, armed with ice-arrows which old man Summer melted by shaking his blanket, or according to another version, viscera (deer's liver and lungs). Having been rendered powerless and having received all the meat they wanted from their generous opponents, the winter people went off and never came back (Boas 4, pp. 144–8; cf. Spinden 1, pp. 149–52; Phinney, pp. 330–38).

So instead of making seasonal periodicity, posited at the beginning as a categorical assumption, exclude the rejuvenation of old men, the myth develops along opposite lines. Coyote, even though he is endowed with long-lasting teeth which (unlike Raccoon in M_{561}) he does not lose, dies a violent death (as does Raccoon at the end of M_{561}), because he has made too much noise: this is the reverse of M_{352} and of the series M_{570a-e}, according to which noise must not be heard; hearing it would result, if not in violent death for oneself, at least in preventing the dead from coming back to life. As if to redress the balance, once death has been made inevitable, it brings with it the assurance that, in spite of the terrors of a long winter, the periodicity of human life will go hand in hand with seasonal periodicity. The fact that the weapons used by Summer to fight Winter include deer entrails raises a problem. Perhaps the viscera are brought in at this point only to create a major opposition with the ice arrows used by the other side. It is well known that throughout this area, and even beyond, the liver was reserved in the first place for old people who, even though lacking teeth, could manage to chew this tender, boneless part of the animal (cf. OTM, p. 403). The Klamath language classifies animal viscera among rounded objects (Barker 1, p. 7, n. 1) and the Modoc, in one of their myths (Curtin 1, p. 24), establish an opposition between deer bones on the one hand and the flesh and livers on the other, the stone mortar and the fire feeding respectively on the former and the latter. In this context, the entrails, in being opposed to the hearts, which are incombustible and therefore on the side of the cold, have an affinity with the hot. However plausible these interpretations suggested by the syntagmatic chain may be, they cannot lead us to overlook the fact that the South American myth (M_1) which corresponds most closely to M_{571} – in the sense that both myths adopt the transformation: *receptive subject* $\Rightarrow$ *emitter of sound* and establish the origin of seasonal periodicity in similar fashion – ends with an episode in which a (hero disguised as) deer causes the death of his opponent, of whom nothing is left but the entrails, which had to be seen as having an astronomical connotation (RC, pp. 243–7; OTM, pp. 38–9, 105–106). We now propose to investigate this astronomical paradigm.

2 In Death as in Life

> *Usant à l'envi leurs chaleurs dernières,*
> *Nos deux coeurs seront deux vastes flambeaux,*
> *Qui réfléchiront leurs doubles lumières*
> *Dans nos deux esprits . . .*[1]
> Ch. Baudelaire, 'La Mort des Amants', *Les Fleurs du*
> *Mal*, CXXI, Editions de la Pléiade, p. 119
>
> *Vying with each other in consuming their final ardours,*
> *Our two hearts will be two great torches,*
> *Reflecting their double gleams*
> *[In the twin mirrors] of our two minds.*[1]

The lewd grandmother cycle, besides enabling us to establish connections with the South American myths which, like it, lead into the theme of man's mortality, is interesting in a different and quite important way. From the historical and geographical point of view it sheds a revealing light on the Plains area in the first place and then around the Great Lakes; it also allows us to see the myths of both these areas as being an extension of those we are already examining.

As far as the Plains area is concerned, I shall confine myself to putting forward a suggestion. It is probable – although to produce complete proof would involve going too far back – that one episode of the grandmother/grandson cycle to which I have already drawn attention (*OTM*, pp. 261, 262) is commutable with the lewd grandmother cycle, as can be seen from the three following transformations:

a) [(*foetus removed from a female animal*) ⇒ (*penis left attached to a male animal*)]
b) [(. . . *cause of fear for a grandson*) ⇒ (*cause of pleasure for a grandmother* . . .)],
c) [(. . . *handed over to foreign lovers by her grandson*) ⇒ (*appropriated by the grandson to consummate an incestuous union*)].

[1] TRANSLATORS' NOTE: The end of the line is *'ces miroirs jumeaux'* and is used by the author as the title of the next section.

In the Plains myths in which it occurs, this episode relates to an astronomical circumstance of supreme importance in native thought, since it marks the period when the foetus takes on its definitive form inside the female buffalo, a few months after the rutting season.

The lewd grandmother cycle also poses a problem relating to the periodic renewal of the generations, but does so in negative terms: it deals not with the annual birth of animal young, but with the impossibility of rejuvenation for old people, and of resuscitation for the dead. On the other hand, the appearance of a biological periodicity, itself conditioning procreation, is given prominence by the Nez Percé, who are distant relatives of the Sahaptin living further inland and whose myths in this respect represent an inversion of those belonging to tribes of the same linguistic family (Klikitat), established at the opposite end of the continuous stretch of territory occupied by the Sahaptin between the Rockies and the Cascade Range.

$M_{572a, b}$. *Nez Percé. 'The grandmother wrongly accused of menstruating'*
One day, when Little Raccoon had eaten all the crayfish he could eat, he climbed up into a tree to doze. A grizzly she-bear went up the tree too, and asked Little Raccoon to remove the frogs with which her head was covered. On the pretext that he was digging out a beastie that had fallen into his visitor's ear, Raccoon borrowed a long bone needle from her and plunged it in so far that he killed the bear.

The young hero went in search of his grandmother to help him cut up the beast. The old woman scratched her leg. When Raccoon saw that she was bleeding, he declared she must be having her menses and should go home and be segregated. Otherwise, he would be contaminated and no longer able to hunt. She did as he asked, but she did not wish to go. Raccoon took all the meat and ate it, making a fine speech the while in order to make the old woman believe that he was entertaining many guests: she would not therefore be surprised if there was no meat left for her: all she got was the hide and she had to make do with that. Not liking the way she had been treated, she put on the hide, changed into a grizzly bear and killed her grandson (Boas 4, pp. 196–7; Phinney, pp. 259–67).

The fact that the Nez Percé myth is an inversion of the lewd grandmother story can be seen, in the first place, from the method used by the hero to kill the she-bear, who in this myth is a gentle creature and in no sense an ogress. Instead of working his way through the bear's body from the anus to the mouth (M_{563}), he plunges a long needle through her ear, while he himself remains on the outside. Contrary to what happens in M_{562b}, Raccoon also eats all the meat and deprives his grandmother of food. And whereas, in M_{564}, the hero kills his grandmother and wraps the corpse in an elk's hide, which becomes a wrinkled skin, a premonitory sign of death for an old person, in M_{572} the old grandmother wraps herself in a bear skin, with the intention of inflicting premature death on a young hero.

Embarking now on a survey which will take us far to the east, let me note, first of all, that the Paiute, who are familiar with the lewd grandmother story (attributing it to a mother), relate how Coyote accused a woman of having her monthly periods in order to appropriate all the meat for himself, since it was taboo for menstruating women (M_{573}: Lowie 4, pp. 136–7 and p. 126). In the previous volume (M_{501b}; OTM, pp. 416–18), the same motif was noted in Menomini mythology, in a form which makes it comparable to the lewd grandmother cycle on two counts, since here too the story is concerned with a grandmother who copulates with a bear — a live bear, instead of a dead one — and on to whose pubis her grandson throws a clot of blood from the animal, after killing it. In revenge, the grandmother institutes female monthly periods, but her grandson takes advantage of her menstrual condition, which is now a reality, to eat as much meat as he can, and to hoard the rest for his own use. The incident of the blood clot thrown at a naked woman's pubis immediately calls to mind M_{571} (see above, p. 187), in which old man Summer behaves in a similar way towards old man Winter's daughter, a circumstance which would lead one to suppose that female physiological periodicity appeared at the same time as seasonal periodicity, a phenomenon linked by all the other myths in the group to man's shortened life-span.

Confirmation of this is provided most convincingly by an Algonquin-speaking community living opposite the Menomini along the other shore of Lake Michigan. In this version of the myth, the Mascouten combine all the motifs that I have brought together by means of less direct links.

M 574. Mascouten. 'The origin of menstruation'

Wisakä, the demiurge, lived with his grandmother. One day, when they had plenty of food, he sprinkled blood on the spot where the old woman usually sat, and, alleging that she was having her menses, he forbade her to eat with him. Since then, women have had monthly periods and have had to be secluded in a separate wigwam. If they kept their condition secret and ate in the main house, they would shorten their husband's life.

Wisakä had told his grandmother in confidence of this danger. So she hastened to warn a neighbour, who organized a feast and announced the new custom. This made Wisakä extremely angry because, being malicious, he would have preferred human beings to remain ignorant of what precautions to take and to have their life-span curtailed (Skinner 10, Part III, pp. 338–9).

M_{574} is strikingly symmetrical with the western versions. Instead of famine caused by seasonal alternation leading to a shortened life-span, at the beginning of the Mascouten myth abundance reigns. The blood kept in reserve provides the hero with the means of creating a disjunction between himself and his grandmother, whereas, in the other case, the return of abundance (through the hero killing a large animal) provides them both with the opportunity, if not the means, of a conjunction. In the one instance, human life is shortened through the grandmother's sexual misbehaviour, which the myth expresses by means of alimentary symbols. In the other instance, the care taken by the grandmother not to commit an alimentary misdemeanour related to her sexual state ensures for mankind a much longer life-span than would otherwise have been the case.

It can, then, be taken as an established fact that myths which at first were thought to be isolated in one western sector of North America link up with eastern versions belonging to tribes of the Algonquin linguistic family to form a coherent whole. Later, I shall demonstrate the point precisely in connection with the bird-nester story (see below, p. 600 et seq.). For the time being, I shall be content with this initial result, since it is sufficient to warrant my next step, which might otherwise appear hazardous: I propose to interpret certain obscure aspects of the Loon Woman myth (and, consequently, of the bird-nester story, of which it is an inversion) on the basis of an eastern Algonquin transformation which is not immediately comprehensible.

First, a brief backward glance. In order to establish the inverted position occupied within the Loon Woman group by the Yana myth (M_{546}), I used as evidence the way in which it altered the scene of the action. Whereas the Loon Woman myth begins in a family home, in M_{546} the leading characters live in a common or sweat-house also occupied by non-relatives, and to which women are not admitted. Since it would seem that, in the Yana myths, all buildings are referred to as sweat-houses, Kroeber (1, p. 340) concludes that the term also covers dwellings (see above, p. 109). This may be so, but, from the point of view with which I am concerned, this is not where the real problem lies. Kroeber himself stresses the part played by sweat-houses in the Californian communities: 'The Californian sweat-house is an institution of daily, not occasional service. It is a habit, not a medical treatment . . . It is an assembly of the men and often their sleeping quarters . . . It fulfils many of the functions of a club . . . Warmth was produced directly by fire, never by steam generated on heated stones. Women were never admitted except here and there on special ceremonial occasions, when sweating was a subsidiary feature or wholly omitted' (*loc. cit.*, pp. 810–11). But although, in Yana society, all these buildings may have been put to several uses, it is clear that M_{546} defines the sweat-house *hic et nunc* with reference to the opposition, essential in Californian thought, between the men's house and the family dwelling. The scene of the action is, from the mythic standpoint, a men's house in the full acceptation of the term; from the very beginning, this feature establishes an opposition between the Yana myth and those which stress the family nature of the house inhabited by the same characters. On the other hand, all the myths agree in setting Loon Woman's incestuous approaches to her beloved brother in the brush.

This triad – family house, men's house and brush – was already present in the very first myths analysed at the beginning of this study. The (literally) hidden boy in M_5 and his figurative homologue in M_1 are both loath to leave the family house and to take up their abode in the men's house, the only dwelling suitable for adolescents. And although the real incest in M_1 and M_2 takes place in the brush, and the inverted incest in M_5 in the family house, M_{124} (an inversion of M_1) moves the real incest to the men's house. Symmetrically, in the Loon Woman myths, the real incest takes place in the brush, but according to the Klamath-Modoc versions the hidden boy is in the family house, and in the men's house according to the Yana version.

Let us concentrate our attention on the transformation which occurs between M_1 and M_{124}, and which, as has just been recalled, is characterized by the removal of the guilty son (or sons) from the family home – to which the hero of M_1 remains symbolically attached, thus revealing his predisposition towards incest – to the men's house into which the heroes of M_{124} lure their mother in order to rape her. This reversal, which is followed, moreover, by several others, allowed me to postulate in *The Raw and the Cooked* (pp. 199–239) a relationship of symmetry between M_1 and M_{124}, that a 'well tempered' use of the astronomical references peculiar to each myth then enabled me to verify. M_1 relates to the *Corvus* constellation, M_{124} to that of Orion and the Pleiades. Granted the twofold condition that the movement of these constellations lends itself to a seasonal coding, and granted too ethnographic confirmations of the fact that native thought uses them to establish such a coding, all those correlational, symmetrical and oppositional relationships which internal analysis had led me to postulate between these particular myths and those which are transformations of them, or of which they themselves are transformations, could be justified by external evidence. This, in fact, was the point I demonstrated.

However, if this is true of the South American myths, and if the North American ones with which I have compared them are at the same time transformations of them, my task will remain unfinished until I have produced the same demonstration in the case of the North American myths. Certain South American myths, which provide systematic transformations of each other, refer either to the *Corvus*, or to the Pleiades and Orion. Or, in more precise terms, the bird-nester, the hero of the Bororo myth M_1, is changed into the *Corvus* constellation and the master of the rainy season, whereas the heroes of the Serenté myth M_{124} are changed into the Pleiades or into one of the stars forming the Orion constellation, and into masters of the dry season. Supposing — as I am trying to establish by internal analysis — that the story of the bird-nester in South and North America constitutes a single myth, the consequence must follow that its message is reversed as between one hemisphere and the other, just as, within the same hemisphere, a myth symmetrical to it expresses its message in inverted terms. In the two hemispheres, winter and summer occupy opposite places: so, if they are to connote the same season in both North and South, the content of the myths must be reversed or, if the myths remain the same — as we have seen they do in the case of the bird-nester story — their seasonal connotation must be reversed. In other words, granted that, in the southern hemisphere, M_1 connotes the *Corvus*, and M_{124}, which can be expressed as $\dfrac{1}{M_1}$, Orion and the Pleiades, it should be confirmable that, in the north, myths similar to M_1 connote the latter two constellations, whose symbolism would thus correspond to their symbolic role in the Ancient World, a coincidence which would be in agreement with cosmographical data, since the area on which I am concentrating in this study lies between $40°$ and $50°$ latitude North, like the old Graeco-Roman world.

We already possess some evidence that such is indeed the case. From the very first versions quoted, the North American bird-nester appeared as a master of water, since in the Klamath myths (see above, p. 36), Aishish succeeds in extinguishing the fire started by his hostile father. The hero of the Yurok, Wiyot and Makah myths ($M_{557-558}$, see above, pp. 153–6), the creator or harbinger of rain and storms, is even more clearly reminiscent of *nimbosus Orion* which appears in the night sky in January, the period of heaviest rainfall in Oregon (Frachtenberg 2, p. 232, n. 1). However, not one of these myths refers to the hero as a constellation. In order to show that he at least plays the part of a constellation, I shall adopt an indirect approach. We know that the Loon Woman myth is a North American inversion of the bird-nester myth. If we can find a myth reversing the Loon Woman story and the hero or heroes of which are a constellation, we can conclude that such too is the role of the hero whose myth has a relationship of inversion, although along a different axis, with the Loon Woman story. The demonstration will at the same time elucidate certain details in previously studied myths which still remain obscure; while giving them an astronomical connotation, it will further strengthen its own validity.

On the strength of these assurances, the reader will forgive me for suddenly transporting him to the opposite end of North America, although we shall remain in the same latitude, as our investigation requires. The most easterly representatives of the Algonquin linguistic family along the Atlantic seaboard were the group known as Wabanaki, 'the people of the rising sun', which consisted of four main tribes: Penobscot and Passamaquoddy in Maine, the Micmac in Nova Scotia and the Saint Francis or Abenaki in what is now the frontier area between Canada and the United States. One of their recorded myths brings together the incest motif, the loon and the origin of a constellation.

M_{575a}. *Wabanaki. 'The origin of the Orion constellation'*

A brother and a sister who were in love with each other decided to run away together. Their kinsfolk ran after them in order to punish them. The culprits were about to be caught on a frozen lake they were crossing, when ice broke under their feet; brother and sister vanished. A short while later they were seen to emerge in the form of a loon uttering its weird cry. In this form, the lovers rose up into the sky, where they became the Orion constellation (Speck 5, p. 352).

The Penobscot variant (M_{575b}; Speck 3, p. 20; 10, p. 52) is thought by some people to refer to the Pleiades and by others to a neighbouring constellation; the existence of a different name for the Pleiades (*mnábasuwak*, 'grouped together') makes the second reading more plausible and it could be a reference to Orion: 'Some call it *meda' wilé*, "loon". The origin of this is given in a myth relating how a man fell in love with his cousin and married her against tribal custom. For punishment the girl's brothers pursued him and were about to kill him when he fell through the ice and then rose to the sky in the form of a loon and became a star.'

An Ojibwa version originating from a region west of Lake Superior, almost equidistant from the Atlantic and the Pacific (M_{576}; Josselin de Jong 1, p. 1), inverts the two extreme forms in which the myth is found in eastern and western areas: instead of being brother and sister, one is a Sioux, the other Peoria, that is, they belong to mutually hostile communities. They decide to escape together in a canoe, but the young man's tribe refuses to receive them. Having been rejected on both shores of the lake separating their tribes, they stay in the middle, a storm blows up and they are drowned: 'Before finally disappearing, they rose to the surface one last time and uttered their cry, which ever since can be heard on Lake Peoria.'

It is clear, then, that the Loon Woman myth and the one featuring the incestuous lovers correspond to each other at opposite ends of North America. One takes place in winter, since the lakes are frozen, the other in summer as is shown by the fact that the brother and sister begin by camping out and when the guilty woman eventually assumes the form of a water bird she settles on lakes, where she can be seen every day swimming and diving, so the surface of the water cannot be frozen. Besides, it is a known fact that, as soon as the lakes freeze, the loon migrates in the direction of the coast, where the water surfaces are not icebound. In one group of myths, two siblings are conjoined in an incestuous union, and become still more closely united in death, since they are transformed first into a single creature, then into a single constellation. In the other group, the transformation of the sister into the same creature and the brother's marriage in a distant country disjoins them, also in a doubly definitive way. Her guilty desires having been frustrated, the incestuous sister pursues her kinsfolk up the vertical axis along which they try to escape from her, and she destroys them by fire. Conversely, the brother and sister in the Wabanaki myth, once they have satisfied their guilty desires, flee from their kinsfolk along a horizontal axis on which the latter try to overtake them in order to kill them, and they die in the icy water. Only the conclusions are the same, but even so, they are opposed to each other in another way. The Wabanaki myth is accounting for an astronomical configuration in the form of a constellation: a cluster of stars standing out brightly against the night sky. The Loon Woman myth accounts for a zoological configuration: white markings forming a collar which shows up against the dark plumage of a water bird. The Orion constellation forms an adornment of luminous beads in the winter sky in the register of the high, whereas the Great Northern Diver (*Gavia immer*), the bird featured in the myth, acquires its characteristic plumage in summer: it therefore forms on the water, in the register of the low, an adornment which alternates with the other along a double spatial and seasonal axis.

This being so, it is still easier to recognize the Wabanaki Diver or Loon – 'a model of constancy according to both legend and reality', and whose cry the Indians compare to 'a plaintive lament for the death of a lover' (Speck 5, pp. 352–3) – as being the virtuous sister and inconsolable wife in the Modoc version (M$_{541}$), who is an inversion of the Loon Woman in her local aspect as an incestuous sister and a parricide. Because Aishísh, the Klamath bird-nester, is the son of incestuous siblings (M$_{531}$, M$_{538}$), he can be identified – as is confirmed in M$_{557-558}$ by the meteorological function of his homologue – if not with Orion, at least with part of the Orion constellation. To establish the integrity of the character of the sister as the pivot around which all these myths revolve, we need only effect the following transformation:

> M$_{575}$ (*sister, faithful unto death to her lover who is her brother*)
> $\Rightarrow$ M$_{546}$ etc. (*sister, killer of her brother who refuses to become her lover*)
> $\Rightarrow$ M$_{541}$ (*sister, faithful unto death to her lover who is not her brother*), etc.

The symmetry between the loon myths found on opposite sides of North America is accompanied by a radical inversion of the qualities attributed to the bird in the two areas. There are four kinds of loons, all referred to in Canadian French as *huard* or *huart*: the Great Northern Loon, or Ring-necked Loon (*Gavia immer*), the Yellow-beaked Loon (*Gavia adamsii*), the Black-throated or Arctic Loon (*Gavia arctica*), and the Red-throated Loon (*Gavia stellata*). Several details in the myths we are concerned with, especially the description of the plumage, clearly relate to the Great Northern Loon.

It will be remembered that in the western myths the guilty sister's transformation into a loon is presented as a punishment. The loon is said to be 'ugly' (M$_{539}$); its flesh is spat out as being uneatable (M$_{539}$, M$_{540}$). The eastern Algonquin take a diametrically opposite view of the loon: 'Among water birds it holds pride of place. Its name, which means "chosen or admired bird" in Penobscot and Malecit, shows in what high esteem it is held as a harbinger of weather changes and because of its splendid plumage and its poignant cry . . . To kill a loon would be to commit an act of sacrilege' (Speck 5, p. 352). A group of myths discussed in the previous volume (M$_{444}$, *OTM*, pp. 244–8) give the name Loon to a dazzlingly beautiful and superbly attired character. The Passamaquoddy and the Micmac regard loons as hunters and messengers in the service of the demiurge. They are prophetic and helpful birds, who remained among men after the demiurge had left. When they utter their characteristic cry, 'looning' as the Passamaquoddy call it, they are calling to him; and men who ask for the demiurge's protection through the loon have their prayers granted (Rand, pp. 288–9, 378–82; Leland, pp. 19, 26, 50–51, 68; Prince, pp. 26–7, 51). In the Ojibwa rites, a wand carved in the shape of a loon is used to hit the water-drum in order to call the spirits (Densmore 2,

Figure 16. An Eskimo head-dress from Kotzebue Sound, made from the skin and feathers of a loon. (From Nelson, p. 417)

p. 96). M. Saladin d'Anglure, an Eskimo specialist, has assured me that the Eskimo neighbours of the northern Algonquin living to the east of Hudson Bay esteem and respect the Great Loon. He was kind enough to corroborate his statement by presenting me with a case of sewing requisites, a highly prized article among the Eskimo, made from the bones and skin of a great northern loon still bearing all its feathers.

However, even among the Micmac and the Passamaquoddy, it would seem that the Loon character is subject to instability: when he is the unhappy husband of Weasel women, who for their part are in love with marine Ducks, he kills his rivals and then commits suicide; or, after being tricked by his nephews, loons of a different species, he takes his revenge by feigning suicide, only to come back to life immediately afterwards ($M_{577a, b}$; Leland, pp. 164–9). The same ambivalence is still more obvious among the Iroquois; on the one hand, according to the Onondaga version of the origin myth, the Loon gave the alarm and saved the celestial woman when, after being hurled down from the sky, she was about to drown in the primordial water, while on the other hand, in the Mohawk version, the same bird was guilty of a mistake: on seeing the reflection of the wretched woman, he assumed she was rising up through the water. So it was the Bittern, a kind of heron whose name in Iroquois means 'the one whose eyes are always looking upwards', who saw the real angle of approach and took the appropriate rescue measures. In other contexts, the Loon is said to have sheltered the hearts of dangerous cannibals under his right wing, although in the end he agreed to hand them over. The Iroquois considered that loon meat was witch's flesh and never ate it ($M_{578a, b}$; Hewitt 1, pp. 179, 285; Curtin-Hewitt, pp. 136–7; Waugh, p. 135). The opposition between Loon and Bittern would appear to be less clear among the Blackfoot, although they attribute a definite role to each bird. They consider the Bittern to be sacred, perhaps because its name means 'beak pointed towards the sun', and they call the Loon 'fine charger' because of the way the bird beats its wings as if executing a warlike movement (Schaeffer 2, p. 39). Their neighbours, the Kutenai, did not eat the loon (Turney-High 1, p. 42). According to evidence of the myths, the same taboo must have prevailed in the distribution area of the Loon Woman cycle, that is, in north-western California and southern Oregon, and it is also found farther north, among the Tanaina and the Ingalik, who are western Athapaskan: 'Very few loons are eaten, as the black meat is considered to have a "funny" taste' (Osgood 2, p. 36; 3, pp. 40, 44). The Chippewyan, on the other hand, who are eastern Athapaskan in contact with the Algonquin, did not have the same prejudice (Seton, pp. 172–3), and the Coast Salish also ate the loon (Eells 1, p. 214; 3, p. 619; Olson 2, p. 50).

Generally speaking, one cannot but be struck by the fact that, throughout the entire north-west zone, the positive or negative valencies of the loon are inverted from one group to another, while remaining strongly marked in all groups. For instance, the Lilloet and the Snohomish, who are Salish living respectively along the lower reaches of Fraser River and in Puget Sound, have myths which seem to be diametrically opposed to the Loon Woman myth, whose area of distribution is nevertheless a long way to the south. The Lilloet present the Loon as the seducer of a young woman: the Snohomish regard him as a chaste adolescent, who allows himself to be seduced and captured by an ogress (M_{579a-e}; Teit 2, pp. 334–5; Ballard 1, pp. 101–102; Haeberlin 1, pp. 435–7). Yet the Squamish and the Klallam, in a neighbouring area, regard the Loon as the accomplice of a wicked father-in-law who tries to drown his son-in-law on the high seas (M_{579f}; Hill-Tout 7, pp. 527–8; M_{579g}; Gunther 2, p. 137).

Through fear of having to bring the whole of Eskimo mythology into play, I shall refrain from making a detailed study of a set of myths which has been subject to preliminary investigation by Boas (2, pp. 825–9) and Savard (pp. 126–54), and originates from all the Eskimo groups between Alaska and Greenland and also from several Indian tribes of the north-west coast and the interior, as far as the Arapaho and the Osage. The Eskimo versions, which are the most detailed, are of particular interest, since it is clear that they retransform the lewd grandmother cycle, itself a transformation of the Loon Woman cycle, in order to reconstitute the latter cycle, while at the same time changing the polarity of the central character:

M_{580a}. *Eskimo (Point Barrow). 'The blind boy and the loon'*

An old woman, her grandson and grand-daughter were the sole survivors of an epidemic, and had to rely for food on what the boy brought back from hunting expeditions. But he came back so laden that the grand-mother complained she had too much work to do drying and preparing the meat. She made her grandson blind. After that, he could no longer go hunting. The supply of meat got less and less, until at last even the old rotten meat was being used up.

When spring returned, a bear came close to the wigwam and, guided by his grandmother, the grandson succeeded in killing it. However, she made him believe he had missed the bear. She kept the fresh meat for herself and her grand-daughter and went on giving only rotten meat to her grandson. She also gave him polluted (dirty) water to drink (cf. M_5).

One day, the blind boy got into conversation with a loon. The latter took pity on him, and immersed him several times in the waters of a lake. This restored his sight. Once cured, he drowned his grandmother during a beluga hunt. At his suggestion, his sister and he chose partners in the same village, and they all lived together and became rich and happy (Spencer-Carter, pp. 65–8).

Although the circumstances might have led to incest, since brother and sister had been left alone in the world, incest did not occur and each married independently. With the exception of certain versions which invert the conclusion (see below, p. 215) the myth is so anxious to stress this ending that in some eastern variants it is further strengthened by the sister being made to enter into a dangerous and exogamous marriage: sometimes she even perishes among strangers ($M_{580b, c}$; Boas 2, pp. 828–9; Kroeber 11, pp. 169–70). The transition from endogamy to exogamy fits in with the reversal of the polarity of the Loon, since from being maleficent, she becomes beneficent. The same happens in an Athapaskan myth:

M_{581}. *Chilcotin. 'The woman married to a bear'*

An Indian woman was imprudent enough to marry a stranger, who turned out to be a bear. He took her off to spend the winter in his den. One of the woman's brothers found them, killed the beast and freed his sister. But she soon changed into a she-bear and massacred all her own people, except her brother and her younger sister, who, being the sole survivors, became an incestuous couple. The she-bear caught up with them and killed the woman. The surviving brother managed to rid himself of the ogress with the help of the loon and another bird, the black diver, who took her away in their canoe and drowned her (Farrand 2, pp. 19–22; cf. Bella Coola, Boas 12, pp. 111–14, for a very similar story).

It would seem, then, that for these northern communities, the loon's role was not only to prevent incest and encourage exogamous marriages (in contrast with what happens in the Loon Woman cycle); the loon also intervenes in the reverse direction, that is, neutralizes the dangers of a marriage which is too distant, but nevertheless still within the bounds of possibility in a part of the world where a great many communities believe themselves to be descended from a marriage between a human being and a bear or a dog.

Like the Bororo grandmother in M_5, the old Eskimo woman in M_{580} is guilty of inverted incest on the person of her grandson; in the Bororo myth, she poisons him with toxic body gases; in the Eskimo myth, she blinds him by damaging his snow-goggles, so that they no longer protect his eyes; and in both stories she defiles him by giving him tainted food to eat, either in the form of rotten meat or intestinal gases.

There is still more to be said. It will be remembered that the transformation which allowed us to make the transition from M_2 to M_5 changed 'horizontal' incest into a form that was not only 'vertical' but also reversed (see above, p. 173), and that the transformation allowing the transition from the Loon Woman to the lewd grandmother also changed 'horizontal' incest, inspired by sexual greed, into 'vertical' incest resulting from alimentary greed. When we move from the lewd grandmother group to the one featuring the blind boy and the loon, the second formula is transformed into alimentary greed changed into its opposite (since the grandmother prefers famine to too much hard work) and which prompts her to commit the reverse of incest: by making her grandson blind, she 'blocks' him above, an opposite process from him piercing her below.[2] The irresponsible behaviour of the Eskimo grandmother is so paradoxical in a community constantly exposed to famine that we can confidently postulate a derivative relationship between the group featuring the blind boy and the loon and the lewd grandmother group.

[2] Savard (p. 105) points out an interesting equivalence in Eskimo thought and language between good eyesight and virility. In support of the above argument, it can also be noted that the lewd grandmother is deprived of meat by her grandson, who keeps it all for himself on the grounds that the old woman is having her monthly periods (= pierced below), whereas in the other cycle, the grandmother does the same to her blind grandson (= blocked above).

It would, incidentally, be easy to establish, thanks to versions belonging to the Loucheux and Hare Indians ($M_{580g, h}$; Petitot 1, pp. 84–8, 226–9), in which the blind person is an old man who recovers his youth at the same time as his sight, that *restored vision* forms an oppositional pair with *lost teeth*. The fact that the Indian versions, still more so than the Eskimo ones, make it possible to move back from one group of myths to the other, is an additional indication in support of the derivational direction I have suggested.

The blind grandson is blocked above; versions from Baffin Island and Greenland ($M_{580d, e}$; Boas 1, p. 625; 8, p. 168. M_{580f}; Holm, quoted in Boas 2, p. 829) tell the story of a marriage between the sister and a man who belongs to a community without anuses, that is, he is a character blocked below. It is perhaps no accident, then, that the Eskimo east of Hudson Bay turn the loon's skin into a pouch for their sewing requisites, such as thread and needles, since the latter are piercing objects which also, however, make it possible to fasten securely together pieces of material that were originally disjoined, as marriage joins two partners together, provided they are neither too close to each other nor too far separated. As a reward for this help, the hero of M_{580} sometimes gives the loon a sharply pointed beak, suitable for spearing all kinds of prey. As a punishment for her wicked behaviour, the grandmother, in several versions, is changed into a male narwhal fish, and thus endowed with a sharp single horn.

But most often, the bird's reward consists of a precious necklace of *dentalia* shells which all loons have worn ever since (Plate 3). The episode confirms that this myth is in truth an inversion of the Loon Woman story, in which the necklace made of the hearts of close relatives is symbolic of anti-adornment, and is moreover contrasted in the myth itself with the porcupine quill bracelets, which represent true adornments (see above, pp. 51–2, 89). I have already had occasion to point out that the myths of this area of North America often transform porcupine quills into *dentalia* (*OTM*, p. 271).

However, as regards the aesthetic appeal of the plumage, curious variations can be observed from one tribe to another. In the Loon Woman myth, everything suggests that the bird's plumage is unlovely and sometimes the fact is expressly stated in the text (M_{539}). However, the Klamath, who have a rather different form of the myth, in the sense that they make no mention of the name Loon, relate in another context (M_{582}; Gatschet 1, Part I, pp. 132–3) that the demiurge gave the Loon the task of destroying the dam by means of which the masters of salmon held all the fish prisoner, so that they gave only rotten fish to their neighbours (compare with the grandmother in M_{580a}). The Loon carried out this mission, and the demiurge rewarded him by spitting chalk on to his body, thus forming white spots on his head and back. It will be noted, however, that this description of the Loon's ornamentation makes no mention of the breast, which, in the Loon Woman myth, is the most important part of the bird's anatomy. To offset the criticism that I may be paying too much attention to the actual wording of a text, subject by its very nature to various possibilities of accuracy, I would like to quote justificatory evidence provided by the Hare: these Indians also attribute the white spots on the head to chalk, but it is thrown by the Raven with the intention of disfiguring, rather than beautifying, a rival (M_{583}; Petitot 1, pp. 223, 296–7). The Eskimo of Hudson Bay, for their part, are very careful to establish a contrast between the Loon and the Raven and, in the case of the first bird, between the breast markings and those on the back.

M_{584a}. *Eskimo (Ungava). 'The origin of the spots on Loon's back'*
A man had two children that he wished might resemble each other. He painted one with a white breast and gave him square spots on the back. The other saw how comical his brother was and laughed so much that the latter became ashamed and escaped to the water. Ever since, Loon always presents his white breast in order to hide the spots on his back, which caused so much ridicule. The Raven, who was the second son, eluded the attempt to be painted in like manner and remained black (Turner, pp. 262–3).

The polar Eskimo (M_{584b}; Holtved 2, p. 99) trace Loon's origin back to a little orphan boy wearing torn clothes; those of Baffin Island (M_{584c}; Boas 8, pp. 218–19, 343), to a grandmother with torn, bloodstained clothes. However, in this case, the bird in question could be the red-throated Diver, which has russet feathers on its breast.[3]

On the other hand, an Eskimo myth from the west coast of Hudson Bay, which associates the Loon with sewing cases (see above, p. 203), also, like M_{584a}, contrasts its pied plumage with that of the Raven.

M_{584d}. *Eskimo (Hudson Bay). 'The origin of the Loon's speckled plumage'*
Raven and Loon were excellent dressmakers, and one day they agreed to

---

[3] Unless the myth is referring to a hunting technique similar to one found among the Micmac (Rand, pp. 378–9) and which is based on the Loon's supposed natural liking for bright colours, particularly red. An additional uncertainty results from the fact that in Boas's translation of M_{584c}, the bird is referred to as the web-footed loon; all loons have four toes, three of which are webbed (Godfrey, p. 11).

exchange proofs of their skill by making each other a suit of clothes. They sewed the skins together with thread which they rubbed with soot (lampblack). Raven took the needle first and sewed the skin on to Loon's body, which explains why Loon's plumage is speckled. When Loon's turn came, she took the needle and commenced work on Raven. But the latter would not sit still while she fitted on the skin. At last Loon lost patience and poured all the soot over her companion, thus making her black all over. In revenge, Raven took a stone and broke Loon's legs, thus making them flat (Boas 8, p. 320).

The Gavidae certainly have flattened fronts (Thomson, p. 212), but it is less easy to understand why, on both sides of Hudson Bay, the same myth in which the Loon and the Raven are in opposition should invert the description of the former's pied plumage: white on a black background in M_{584a}, black on a white background in M_{584d}, a procedure of which we have already encountered other examples (see above, pp. 117, 151, 172). The inversion remains problematical in the present instance, but we should note that it is accompanied by another: between new clothes or fresh paint ($M_{584a, d}$) and worn clothes ($M_{584b, c}$).

On the other hand, most Salish-speaking and Athapaskan-speaking tribes would seem to agree in comparing Loon's breast with the noblest adornments. The Chilcotin say it was given a necklace as a reward for having restored a blind man's sight (M_{580i}; Farrand 2, p. 36), or for having caught a tomb robber stealing jewels left on the corpses (*ibid.*; p. 47). According to the Shuswap and the Thompson (M_{585a}; Teit 1, pp. 667–8), the Loon was once a dishonest gambler who, after staking all his ornaments and losing, made off with his *dentalia* necklaces. As a punishment, he was changed into a bird, which still wears them round its neck. The inlaid pattern on a Thompson shaman's pipe represents Loon's necklace, and is similar to the actual necklaces sometimes worn by shamans, the pendants of which were Loons' heads (Teit 10, p. 381).

These few brief indications, which could be greatly multiplied, show that from the east to the west, and also from the south (relatively speaking) to the far north, the value attributed to Loon fluctuates on three levels. Considered aesthetically and sartorially, the bird wears precious necklaces, soiled clothes, or human hearts (gruesome adornments). Here we are on the level of *culture*. Considered from the sexual point of view, which is also that of life in *society*, the Loon can play three distinct roles: incestuous sister, separated for life from her beloved in the Loon Woman myth, or united with him in death in what, from now on, I will call the 'Wabanaki transformation' (M_{575}), or again, a sexually unmarked supernatural spirit, the arbiter of endogamous unions and distant marriages. Lastly, on a third level, the alimentary one, which consequently relates to *nature*, the Loon's flesh can be pronounced uneatable, either because it is said to have a nasty taste or because the bird is held to be sacred. A short myth belonging to the Micmac, who believed in the sacredness of the bird (M_{585c}; Parsons 4, pp. 80–82), introduces an additional aspect. Like Eskimo mythology, it presents the Raven and the Loon as being in opposition to each other, but as regards food not clothes: the Woodpecker married his two daughters to the Loon and the Raven; fresh food was served at Loon's marriage feast, rotten food at Raven's. So these eastern Algonquin actively contrast the Loon and the Raven in respect of food, in the sense that the Raven eats tainted food, which is what humans would be doing — according to the tribes along the Pacific coast — if they ate the Loon.

It is tempting to link up the instability characteristic of the mytheme with the habits of the Loon, which vary from one locality to another, even over short distances. The Tanaina, who are north-western Athapaskan, describe the loon as a seasonal bird 'except in Kachemac Bay which enjoys the mildest climate' (Osgood 3, p. 40). The Gavidae nest as far north as the Arctic; they migrate southwards in winter, or, local conditions permitting, they remain at the same latitude and only move from the icebound rivers and lakes inland towards the sea coast.

All the myths we have discussed so far present the Loon as a seasonal creature, but in defining its role, they neither stress the same characteristics nor interpret them in the same way. The seasonal valency could already be discerned in certain myths of the Loon Woman cycle. The Yana myth M_{547} begins at Shipa (see above, p. 98): 'S.ī ́p ̉a, "the-place-where-people-come-to-drink" (?), on a flat hill about half a mile above the head of Oak Run; formerly there was a lake there and a favourite stopping place for geese and ducks on their way north in the spring' (Sapir-Spier 1, p. 245). In the Atsugewi version, the Loon's cry or 'laugh' is a sign that spring is near. The Micmac on the other side of the continent also refer to the Loon's 'laugh', which they interpret as a sign of wind, a belief shared by the Naskapi (Parsons 4, p. 84, n. 3; Speck 5, p. 126). The eastern Algonquin imagine Glooskap, their demiurge, as having a vast retinue of servants, including several loons (see above, p. 198) on an equal footing with a character called Kulpejotei, a personification of the movement of the sun and the seasons (Leland, pp. 22–3). The Algonquin of Lake Superior also associate the Loon with wind, which the bird requires, so they say, in order to rise into the air (Kohl, p. 185). It is a fact that, because of its physical make-up, the Loon is as clumsy in taking off as it is in walking on the ground (cf. M_{584d}); however, once under way, it flies strongly and steadily (Thomson, p. 212). The Sweet-Grass Cree maintain that the arrival of the Loon heralds the thaw (Bloomfield 1, p. 82). The Kutenai watch its behaviour for signs of storms (Turney-High 1, p. 42). 'When it storms,' according to the Salish of Puget Sound, 'the Loon, whose grandfather is Thunder, goes on the lakes where it is calm. In April he comes down to salt water. Loon is chief of the salt-water people' (Ballard 1, pp. 101–103). The Siciatl (Seechelt) call the month of May by the name of Loon, because this is when the bird builds its nest and lays its eggs (Hill-Tout 1, p. 34).

The Loon's relationship to Thunder, to which I have just referred, is a far cry from the belief, current among the Assiniboine, that the Loon quarrelled with Bald Eagle, who changed into Thunder and killed his opponent with a thunderbolt (M_{585b}; Lowie 2, pp. 202–203). Returning now to the Coast Salish, we can note that the Twana 'had a legend that the Loon hibernated all winter. When he'd come out of hibernation, and first alight (*sic*) on the lakes and holler, then people knew that it was the month of the spotted-back Loon, and corrected the calendar if they needed to' (Elmendorf 1, p. 27). The Thompson, who are inland Salish, believe that the loon cries loudly and often when rain threatens. 'To imitate or mock the cry of the loon may cause rain' (Teit 10, p. 374). An Eskimo myth from the west coast of Hudson Bay relates (M_{586}; Boas 8, p. 320) how some men once, for sport, pulled out all the feathers of a live loon. In revenge, it caused a great fall of snow, which was so thick that the people could not reach their stores of meat buried under stones. Everybody died of starvation.

As can be seen, the beliefs relating to the loon vary extremely from one group to another. Some think the bird hibernates, others that it emigrates, sometimes from east to west, sometimes from north to south. In different contexts, the mere fact of its appearance, or the way in which it cries or behaves, has a significant function, relating either to changes in the weather – the onset of rain or wind – or to the return of a particular season, which may be winter or summer. Despite these fluctuations, which deserve to be examined more closely (but by someone with a better knowledge than I have of the ethology of the four species of the *Gavia* genus, and of the meteorological conditions in each locality), one major opposition predominates: the one which, on either side of North America, leads to a radical inversion of the values and functions that the myths of each area – the Pacific seaboard and the Atlantic coast – attribute to the loon.

Were additional proof necessary, it could easily be found in the different ways in which the myths of east and west contrast the loon and another water bird, which in the eastern Algonquin versions is the horned grebe (*Podiceps auritus*). Unfortunately, its identity remains uncertain in the western myths, although it is clearly a diver. Perhaps the tribes concerned do not bother to differentiate, any more than the Blackfoot who have only one term to cover ducks of the genus *Mergus*, grebes and bitterns (Schaeffer 2, p. 40).[4]

In one of the Yana versions of the Loon Woman myth, the Loon is done to death by a diver, which has a strong antipathy to the other species (M_{547}; Sapir 2, p. 232). In the version recorded by Curtin (3, pp. 412–15: M_{546}), the role of avenger is attributed to fisher birds, probably killdeer plovers. The Algonquin myths concerning the wives of the Sun and Moon (which already contain an inversion of the Loon Woman character in the sense that the heroines, far from aspiring to an incestuous union, want to marry the sun and moon, that is, distant husbands) also feature a pair consisting of the loon and a more humble water bird, by whom the heroines, survivors of a celestial adventure, are seduced, since they mistake him for the Loon. At the same time, then, as the Loon changes sex:

$$a) \; (loon \; \bigcirc) \Rightarrow (loon \; \triangle),$$

the respective hierarchical positions of the two birds are also inverted:

$$b) \; (loon < diver) \Rightarrow (diver < loon);$$

which, however, does not prevent the more humble bird finally killing the other in both cases. It will be remembered that the Chilcotin and Bella Coola myths ($M_{581a, \; b}$; above, p. 201) illustrate a third state of the transformation:

$$c) \; (loon + diver) \Rightarrow (exogamous \; wife \; of \; a \; bear = Loon \; Woman^{-1}).$$

The first conclusion to be drawn from the preceding remarks is that the Loon Woman cycle has a much wider area of distribution than was supposed by those exponents of the so-called 'historical' method, such as Demetracopoulou, who try to evolve a mythological system exclusively on the basis of features which empirical analysis reveals as being common to several versions. A myth, or a group of myths, far from constituting an inert corpus subject to purely mechanical influences operating by means of the addition

---

[4] It would therefore be unwise to enquire further into the possibility of a correlation between the loon's plumage, with its summer contrast between black and white, and that of certain ducks, which is subject to a brief seasonal 'eclipse' when light feathers are almost completely replaced by dark. In the case of one category of birds, the contrast between white and black is synchronic; in the case of the other, diachronic.

or subtraction of discrete elements, must be defined, in a dynamic perspective, as one particular state of a transformational group, temporarily in equilibrium with other states, and whose apparent stability depends, on a superficial level, on the degree to which the tensions prevailing between two states cancel each other out. Should one of the tensions become too powerful at a given point, the whole system swings over to form a new equilibrium between modified states. Such crises must have occurred many times during the course of history, before the myths expired, along with their reciters uttering the final text, petrified for ever like the inhabitants of Pompeii, who were surprised by a different cataclysm and whose gestures, as Proust says, were made eternal in the moment of interruption.

Although we now know that, contrary to accepted ideas, the area of distribution of the Loon Woman cycle extends as far as the eastern Algonquin, this does not mean that the myths of the Cascade Range area and those of the Atlantic seaboard are similar: they are not at all alike, or rather they are alike in so far as they differ from each other in several ways, and the resemblance lies in the modes of difference (L.-S. 8, p. 111). To be convinced of this, we had first of all to agree that all the myths are *saying something*; and then to verify that the Wabanaki myths (M_{575}) are not just saying something other than the Loon Woman myths, as exemplified from the Klamath to the Maidu and the Wintu: they are *contradicting* them, and to this end they invert means of expression which, however, remain common to both areas. It follows from this, in the first place, that stories which no one had ever thought of comparing constitute in fact a single myth, and illustrate various states of the same transformation; and secondly, that these complementary states can clarify each other reciprocally. Supposing, for instance, that we began with the negative, and supposing certain aspects of it remained incomprehensible for that very reason, as soon as we have access to the positive, we should be able, by comparing the two pictures, to interpret any previously obscure or confused details. We shall now see the process at work.

Let us begin by defining the structure of the permutation. When I analysed the Loon Woman cycle in Part Two, we saw that *disjunctive incest* — in the sense that it disjoined for life a brother and a sister, he being happily married with a distant wife, and she having been transformed into a bird — allows the myth to pose the problem of the resurrection of the dead and of the periodicity of human life. At the opposite end of the area, the Wabanaki transformation uses the notion of *conjunctive incest* — conjoining in death of a brother and a sister who perish together in preference to being separated — in order to explain the existence of a constellation, the course of which accompanies that of the seasons. It is a fact that, throughout this region of America, Orion and the Pleiades are dominant features in the calendar. For the Iroquois (Fenton, p. 7), the New Year begins during January/February, when the Pleiades reach their highest point at dusk, followed closely by Orion. The Shasta, at the opposite end of the area, knew that 'the beginning of the fall was marked by the first appearance of the Pleiades, just over the hills at daylight; and that their disappearance marked the beginning of summer' (Holt, p. 341). Probably we have to take this as meaning: when they were visible on the western horizon at daybreak, since in these latitudes the Pleiades rise in the morning in the east towards the end of spring, and this is the reason why they are not visible in summer.

Although the Klamath, who are neighbours of the Shasta, give the name 'Loons' to the Great Bear, whose position in the sky is in contrast to that of Orion and the Pleiades, at the same time it is a remarkable fact that, in respect of the Twins, a constellation lying close to the other two, they have beliefs which are extraordinarily reminiscent of the Wabanaki myths about incestuous siblings who were drowned in the frozen waters of a lake before becoming the Pleiades or Orion: 'The Gemini are twins, a boy and a girl. When they barely appear on the eastern horizon in the evening, they look over the lake and it freezes (December); later in the year, when they stand higher, this indicates that spring is coming' (Spier 2, p. 221). It will be remembered that the brother and incestuous sister of M_{575a} are drowned in a frozen lake, consequently in winter; after being first changed into a loon, they rise up into the sky, reaching their highest point in the form of Orion, which occupies this position at dusk, shortly before the return of spring.

Certain myths of the north-west of North America deal with conjunctive incest in a manner entirely comparable to that of the myths of the eastern Algonquin. The best example is provided by the Sanpoil, who are inland Salish living far from the main distribution area of the Loon Woman myth, but close to where its transformation is prevalent, in the form illustrated by the lewd grandmother cycle:

$M_{587a, b}$. *Sanpoil. 'The origin of incest and death'*

Once upon a time, there was a brother and sister who fell in love with each other at a time when the young girl was living by herself in the puberty hut. The boy went to her there every night. The mother became suspicious and discovered on the boy's body traces of the paint which she used to smear on the segregated girl every day. She told her husband, who, anxious to avoid becoming the laughing-stock of the villages, of whom he was chief, decided, with his wife's consent, to kill their son.

While the latter was sleeping, he plunged a sharpened piece of bone through his heart, and had his son's death announced discreetly to the people. The next day the body was buried at the bottom of a cliff.

Unaware that her brother had died, the young girl wondered why he did not come to her as usual in the evenings. Her little sister brought her food and told her what had happened. Then, alleging that her period of seclusion was at an end, the girl asked for her best robes to be sent to her. Thus attired, she ran to the ravine where her brother's body lay. All the fastest runners tried in vain to hold her back by grabbing her robe, but she quickly unfastened it and jumped over. United in death, the two lovers were exultant: 'We said we'd get together and now we have, for good. In times to come, other brothers and sisters will do the same thing.'

The father began to feel remorse: he wanted to bring his children back to life again by decreeing that death would not be final. His counsellors objected and he abandoned his plan. But as he was a powerful doctor, he caused the children of those who had not agreed with him to die. They in turn pleaded in favour of resuscitation. 'No,' the chief answered, 'my children are already rotting. I can't have them back. There will have to be dead persons in times to come.' That was the beginning of evil doctoring (Ray 2, pp. 133–5; Boas 4, p. 106).

Consequently, as in the Wabanaki versions, conjunctive incest here appears as being linked to periodicity, viewed from an astronomical or biological angle. But the Sanpoil who, unlike the Wabanaki, link conjunctive incest with the second form, simply reverse the theme in order to explain the advent of the first form.

*M*588. *Sanpoil. 'The origin of the sun and moon'*
A brother and sister were living together alone and the boy used to fish for the two of them. But one day he got stingy; he didn't take the salmon home but cooked and ate it himself. He even hid the salmon's eggs in his gaiters so that his sister could not find them. She found the eggs while doing the housework. Angered by her brother's behaviour, she left her brother and went away, refusing to listen to his apologies and entreaties.

In order to stay alive, she picked up some pitch gum which she chewed. Then she made a tule cradle and put the gum into it. The pitch changed into a child and in a little while he grew up. Soon the boy was able to go fishing for his mother, but he couldn't walk; his mother had to carry him down to the stream each morning. One day she forgot to get him. When she remembered and went down, she only found a pile of pitch.

The woman decided to make another son. She started by making five tule basket cradles, and put them one inside the other. She put a big rock on the fire, thus causing it to crack; a hot chip flew out and fell into the first cradle. It burned through that cradle, then through the second and third. When it reached the fourth one, the chip had cooled enough not to burn through it. The woman quickly tipped it into the fifth and last cradle, where it changed into a baby boy with only one eye. 'That's good enough,' thought the woman, 'he can take care of me.'

The child proved to be a good fisherman and hunter, but felt lonesome and asked if he could have a brother. Never at a loss, his mother got some roots and cooked them under the ashes. The first one she uncovered was not properly cooked and a girl. She didn't want a girl and threw her away. The next one was a good-looking boy.

The boys always fished and hunted together. They heard one day that people were trying to make a sun and a moon, and they decided to help by offering to become the two luminaries themselves. They bade their mother goodbye. They told their mother that if they succeeded they would probably not be back home again, but that she could see one in the sky in the daytime and the other at night.

The brothers went to the place where the people had gathered to put up a sun. The boys were thought to be good-looking fellows. A toad woman who was camped a little way off from the rest wanted to see the young strangers. She went outside and urinated into the sky. It began to rain and it kept up until the ground was flooded and all the camp fires were put out. The brothers had no place to go. They saw smoke coming from the toad's lodge and went over. As a big fire was burning inside, they asked their 'auntie' if they could come in and warm themselves.

The toad, however, refused to be addressed in this way since she had no relatives. She jumped on to the cheek of the younger brother and put her arms round his neck: 'Call me wife,' she begged. They could not get her down: even when he held his head near the fire in order to burn her, the boy only succeeded in giving toad the blisters she now has on her back.

Meanwhile the people were putting many animals and birds to the test in order to make a sun and moon, but something was wrong with every one: either it was too cloudy, or too cold, or too hot. When they tried Woodpecker in the role of sun, it became so hot that the rocks broke open and people had to spend all day in the water. The crane (or the heron) produced an interminably long day. When, in his turn, Coyote was tried, he lost no time in telling everyone all that he saw from his position in the sky, and the general feeling was that people's private lives should not be exposed in this way.

Then the people turned to the two strangers. 'All right,' said the younger brother, 'I'll be the moon even though I have this toad on me. You, brother, you will be the sun and you will shine so brightly that no one will notice you only have one eye' (Ray 2, pp. 135–7; cf. M_{371}, *OTM*, p. 59 and the group of myths M_{375}, M_{382} with which the above myth has obvious connections).

The fact that M_{587} and M_{588} form a group can be deduced in the first place from the complementarity which can be observed between the culinary symbols they employ. In order to justify the finality of death, and the inescapable periodicity of human life, M_{587} invokes the phenomenon of putrefaction. There is no question of this in M_{588}, which is concerned exclusively with the other two points of the culinary triangle: the raw and the cooked, the properties of which it analyses methodically: just as, in M_{587}, the dead cannot revive because they belong to the category of the rotten, so a newly born child cannot live if, like the heroine's first son in M_{588}, he remains in the category of the raw: the edible pitch which the mother eats straight from the trees and to which, after a short-lived existence, he irrevocably returns. The next two children, on the other hand, result from a process of cooking. But in one form, it is too fierce and produces an incomplete result: the second son is one-eyed. And gentle cooking in ashes, too hastily terminated, yields an imperfect result: the girl whom the mother rejects. Only the exactly right degree of cooking yields a satisfactory result: a son whom the myth describes as a 'good-looking fellow'.

So, after the elimination of the rotten (M_{587}) and the raw (M_{588}) as symbols of a viable periodicity, the second myth has recourse initially to terrestrial or cooking fire, considered in its two modes: brisk or slow. In order to understand how the opposition is formulated in the myth, it is necessary to know that the Sanpoil applied the term 'fireless' to a way of cooking certain foodstuffs which were allowed to remain for two or three days in an earth oven, into which heated rocks had been placed (Ray 1, p. 106). They had, then, two distinct types of cooking, in opposition to each other in respect of fire; but they practised other forms too, which were in opposition to each other in respect of water, since their culinary methods included also both boiling or steaming and roasting and drying on hot ash, this second process being sometimes tantamount to grilling (*ibid.*). To complete the use of culinary symbols, it follows that the characters created by the two forms of cooking, one using fire the other 'fireless', have also to be mediatized by water.

Like domestic fire, water appears in two forms. Firstly, celestial water, created by the toad, which extinguishes all fires except her own, a source of warmth for the heroes who are in particular need of it since they themselves are the product of heat. Celestial water, then, plays a destructive part. The myth sets terrestrial and protective water in opposition to it, as can be seen in the following episode in which the woodpecker — the master of celestial and destructive fire (cf. *RC*, p. 292, for the pan-American character of this mytheme) — creates a conflagration which forces the community to take refuge in water. So four terms, forming a sort of Klein group (cf. *OTM*, pp. 356–8 and 403): terrestrial constructive fire, celestial destructive fire, terrestrial protective water, and celestial destructive water, must be organized into a system and hold each other in balance for empirical periodicity to be established. And this empirical periodicity is in opposition to a Utopian absence of periodicity, just as the Utopia of an incestuous marriage, which is only brought to an end by the death of both partners, stands in opposition to a reversal of incest on the alimentary level (since the hero in M_{588} loses all feeling for his sister to the point of no longer even agreeing to feed her), a reversal which, through a veritable re-creation using the metaphorical symbols of culture, eventually leads to a natural order governed by periodicity. Although it is impossible for the dead to be resuscitated, and at the same time shocking to think that even those who die in their prime cannot be restored to life, the regular alternation of the sun and the moon, together with the reasonable duration of human life it marks with its rhythm, provide a middle term between the two manifestations of fate.

It is now clear where the interest of the Sanpoil myths lie. Through the twofold homology they establish between the alimentary and the sexual levels on the one hand, and between biological periodicity and astronomical periodicity on the other, they link up with the adjacent lewd grandmother cycle. At the same time, however, they retransform it in two ways: one harks back to the Loon Woman cycle by restoring the incestuous relationship between brother and sister; the other makes biological periodicity a function of the advent of the civilized arts, of which cooking remains the symbol in both contexts. Finally, M_{589}, which is a transformation of M_{588} (or vice versa), and which borrows the mytheme of conjunctive incest (doubly inverted by M_{588}, in order to account for the origin of the sun and moon), links up both with the Loon Woman cycle where incest plays a disjunctive role and with the Wabanaki transformation which, using the first mytheme, accounts for nocturnal (instead of diurnal) periodicity with the advent of the Orion constellation. I have shown (see above, pp. 201–205) that the cycle featuring the blind boy and the loon also has its place in the system. This is confirmed by a detail in M_{588}, since the brother's ruse of hiding the salmon eggs in his gaiters in order to deprive his sister of them is an inversion of that of the sister in the Eskimo cycle of the blind boy and the loon who manages to provide supplies for her starving brother by pretending to eat food, which she in fact hides inside her under-garments and presses against her naked body. The text of the myth, which at this point uses the term *uuinik*, cognate with others relating to marriage, would seem to confirm that, with the best of intentions, she is committing a kind of incest (cf. Savard, p. 128).

We can see, then, that the whole northern part of North America is the scene of a vast permutation. Starting from the Wabanaki transformation in the extreme east, we move to the Loon Woman cycle in the extreme west; then, moving northwards, we come to the Lewd Grandmother cycle, leading to the twofold Sanpoil transformation about the origin of death and the origin of the sun and moon. Moving farther north still, we encounter the cycle featuring the blind boy and the loon, which extends from west to east and finally brings us back to the Wabanaki transformation. At this eastern extremity, however, an additional torsion makes the situation more complex. The Eskimo myths (cf. M_{165}, M_{168}; *RC*, pp. 296, 297) which trace the origin of the sun and moon to the suicide or flight of two incestuous siblings are, one might almost say, *in situ* inversions of the blind boy and the loon cycle (in which the brother and sister conclude exogamous marriages) and at the same time they are diametrically opposed to the Wabanaki transformation, in which the lovers, instead of being eternally in flight from each other, are united in death and give rise to a constellation. It follows, then, that, to the potential transformational relationship between the extreme states of the group brought out by our inventory of the intermediary states, we can add an actual transformational relationship in those areas where the extremes meet.

3 '... These Twin Mirrors'

EDWARD   *Dazzle mine eyes or do I see three suns?*
RICHARD *Three glorious suns, each one a perfect sun;*
              Nor separated with the racking clouds,
              But sever'd in a pale clear-shining sky.
              See, see! They join, embrace, and seem to
              kiss,
              As if they vow'd some league inviolable:
              Now are they but one lamp, one light, one
              sun.
              In this the heaven figures some event.

Shakespeare, *King Henry the Sixth*
Part Three, Act II, Scene 1

I am now in a position to embark on the second stage of the demonstration, and for this purpose we must again go back over previous ground. It will be remembered that the Klamath and Modoc myths featuring Loon Woman (M_{538}, M_{539}) tell a strange story about posthumous twins, first of all stuck together by their grandmother to form a single individual and then split apart of their own accord to become two children of the same sex, or of different sexes. The myths do not bother to suggest any reasons for these changes, and so the story seems gratuitous and incoherent, not to say self-contradictory: why weld two children into a single being if the existence of this bipartite character is bound to be provisional, since it is only too eager to return to duality? Before accusing the myths of being arbitrary, we must, however, ask ourselves what the situation would be if, in the light of what has been so often verified in other contexts, we supposed that the Klamath and Modoc myths were telling a story the wrong way round, when it only has a meaning the right way round. The second law of thermodynamics is not valid in the case of mythic operations: in this field, processes are reversible, and the information they convey is not lost; it is simply converted into a latent state. It remains recoverable, and the role of structural analysis is to look beyond the apparent disorder of phenomena and to restore the underlying order.

Let us take, then, as our starting-point the myth I have called the Wabanaki transformation. The story it tells is perfectly satisfactory from the logical point of view, if not in the light of experience. A brother and a sister, exotic equivalents of Tristan and Isolde, who have fallen in love with each other, are physically united in death, in spite of the efforts of their kinsfolk to keep them apart. Welded into a single being, they reappear first of all in the form of a loon, then as the Orion constellation. Supposing that, in order to invert the message of this group of myths, we had also to invert the narrative sequence, we would have to start off with a brother and a sister bound together as a single being at the wish of their kinsfolk, and who bring about their own separation. The loon, in the first instance, is the means of conjunctive incest and, in the second, the cause of disjunctive incest.

If this interpretation is correct, it should follow that versions such as M_{539}, in which the bipartite character is split into two brothers and not into a brother and sister, must be regarded as derivative and as constituting a subsidiary stage in the chain of transformations. I shall come back to this point (p. 233, *et seq.*); however, before deducing consequences from a hypothesis, we should establish its plausibility. In this particular instance, the proof depends entirely on two conditions: have the 'split' twins in the western versions, like the united siblings in the Wabanaki transformation, an astronomical connotation? If so, is this connotation in opposition to the other, in the same way as the two groups of myths are in opposition to each other?

Let us consider, first of all, the Klamath myth (M_{538}). Here, the twins who have been stuck together split up into a brother and a sister who are worried because they do not know where they came from. The sister plies her brother with questions, and since he has no answers, she decides to ask the sun. To force the sun to talk, she shoots an arrow which pierces his cheek, leaving a black mark which is still visible (see above, pp. 49, 54). The same incident occurs in an inverted form in a Tillamook version which, as has been shown, exemplifies an extreme state of the Loon Woman myth (M_{565a}; see above, p. 171). The orphaned son of an incestuous couple is taken in by a family, who keep him in ignorance of his origins. However, the daughter of the house dislikes him and makes all sorts of offensive insinuations; in exasperation, the boy throws his ball at her face. In trying to protect herself, the girl, as she snivels, rubs her nose and eyes. Her nose grows longer, her eyes become smaller, and her wrists adhere to her neck. Finally, she turns into a mole, while the boy obtains Thunder-Bird as his guardian spirit. The two children then combine their respective skills – in her case the ability to burrow underground, and in his the gift of flight – and succeed in killing the ogress responsible for the incestuous behaviour and subsequent death of the boy's parents (E. D. Jacobs, pp. 45–54). So, whereas in M_{538} a *female twin*, and future incestuous sister, *pierces* the sun's cheek *in order to obtain information from him*, in M_{565a} a little girl, *who is not even a sister*, and whom, however, he will not marry, has her cheek *bruised* by her false brother, *because she is giving him information*; and, as a result of this, she changes into a mole, a chthonian creature who is diametrically opposed not only to the adoptive brother who flies through the air, but also to the luminary which shines in the sky. The hero takes leave of her for good and goes up to the heavens, where he enters into a very distant marriage with Thunder's daughter.

M_{565a} provides, then, *a contrario* proof that the injured sun incident in M_{538} fulfils a relevant function, which can only be to explain the origin of solar spots, which are visible to the naked eye for such practised observers as the Indians, when a light mist dims the sun's face (cf. Reichard 3, p. 63, n. 1). Being a diurnal instead of a nocturnal phenomenon, and consisting of dark markings on a light background instead of light markings on a dark background, the sun spots are unmistakably an inversion of a constellation.

But, in the first respect at least, they are also an inversion of moon spots, which, like them, are dark against a light background and appear on the orb of a heavenly body, except that the latter is nocturnal instead of diurnal.

The following retransformation presents no difficulty:

$$M_{538}\ (origin\ of\ sun\ spots) \begin{bmatrix} \text{the sun, wounded in the cheek} \\ \text{by the } sister, \text{ informs the siblings} \\ \text{of their } isolated \text{ condition} \end{bmatrix}$$

$$\Rightarrow \quad M_{358,\ 392,}\ etc.\ (origin\ of\ moon\ spots) \begin{bmatrix} \text{the man, marked on his body} \\ \text{by his } sister, \text{ informs her of} \\ \text{their degree of } proximity \end{bmatrix}$$

The preceding observation reveals a fact of supreme importance. From the extreme north to the extreme south of the New World, there can be found a group of myths to which I have often referred (*RC*, p. 296; *HA*, p. 204; *OTM*, pp. 91, 389; and above, p. 215); their etiological function consists in giving a joint explanation of the origin of the sun and the moon and of moon spots. The latter are said to have been made by a young girl on the face of a nocturnal visitor whose identity is unknown to her and who is none other than her brother. Shocked, the girl escapes to the sky and becomes the sun; the brother changes into the moon and tries in vain to catch her up. We can now understand why this vast group, which bases the advent of an astronomical configuration on disjunctive incest, belongs to the same set as those which have been studied up until now. We might even say that it constitutes the most plausible initial state for the whole series of transformations, firstly because of its very wide area of distribution, and secondly because of its rigid armature which limits its plasticity.

Starting from this group of myths, one transformation is enough to generate the version I singled out in Wabanaki mythology. Incest which is disjunctive through the wish of one partner becomes conjunctive by their common consent; the result is either the origin of the sun and the moon with its spots, or that of Orion and the Pleiades. At the same time, we can see why the myths present Orion and the Pleiades as being diametrically opposed to the sun and the moon. The two constellations are visible: 1) only at night; 2) during one half of the year; 3) and then always together. The sun and moon, on the other hand, are visible: 1) one during the day, the other by night; 2) throughout the whole year (although intermittently because of clouds and moonless nights); and yet rarely together. From California to Oregon, there is no lack of myths explaining why a luminary, which at the beginning was a single body and which lit up the sky continuously, split up in order to create the sun and the moon, or was killed by two brothers who became the sun and the moon, ensuring henceforth alternation of day and night (Sapir 1, pp. 171–3, 307–11; Boas 5, p. 157; etc.). The Wintu version (M_{589}; Curtin 3, pp. 121–60) stresses the incompatibility between the sun and the moon: 'Now you may go east,' said the Supreme Being to the sun, 'and begin your task. You will travel all the time, day after day, without stopping. All living things will see you with your glowing staff. And you will see everything in the world, but you will always be alone. No one can ever keep you company or travel with you.' It is significant, then, that an Eskimo myth from Alaska (M_{590}; Spencer, p. 258), in order to explain how, very exceptionally, it is possible to see both sun and moon at the same time, should take the opposite view to the norm, and present the two luminaries as a man and wife who have fallen out with each other.

The Klamath myth M_{538} illustrates the third state of a transformation which, after starting from disjunctive incest to explain the existence and course of the sun and the moon *with its spots*, in accordance with observed data, began by reversing the initial proposition and explained the existence and course of the Pleiades and Orion by conjunctive incest. In the second state, these constellations manifested themselves in the form of the loon, a bird with white speckles on a dark background (in contradistinction to the moon). With M_{538}, a new torsion brings us back to disjunctive incest by means of this same loon, but in order to explain the origin of the spots on the other luminary – a problem which the first state of the group had left unsolved.

We thus dispose of a diagnostic device, in order to determine where each myth is situated within the total group of transformations; it consists in the manner in which each myth describes the spots either on the sun or the moon, or the markings on the brother or incestuous sister, or those on the bird's plumage. One argument has already been put forward as proof of the fact that the myth explaining the origin of the sun and the moon can be inverted into the Loon Woman myth: in both instances, the telltale marks indicating the guilty sibling are found on the persons of the brother or the sister, and in the first case they are black on a light background (homologous with the spots on the moon) and, in the second case, light on a dark background (homologous with the loon's, as they are described in the same myths). We may also note (cf. above, pp. 76, 98, 121, 123, 138) that several versions of the Loon Woman myth clearly state that the brother and sister were together as they travelled from east to west, but that they came back separately in the opposite direction. The sun and the moon also travel from east to west, but separately.

Consequently, one detail of the reference myth M_1 which might have seemed insignificant acquires great importance. After he commits incest, the hero is betrayed by the ornamental feathers sticking to his mother's dark-coloured bark belt (RC, p. 35). This would almost be enough to put the Bororo story in the same column as the Loon Woman myths, although at a different level because of the periodic character of the transformation. As in a Mendéléev table, the transformation operates along several axes, one of which denotes the place occupied by each myth within a continuous series, while the other inverts the coding – alternately astronomical and meteorological – of the consecutive states for each change of hemisphere, since the same astronomical circumstances connote opposite seasons in north and south.

In the two previous volumes (HA, p. 279; OTM, pp. 39–40), I referred to certain Guiana myths, which seem to turn Orion into a sort of nocturnal counterpart of the sun. The Kalina maintain that Orion 'calls and supports' the sun. It is personified by a 'perverted' character; it would be interesting to know whether, as in the Wabanaki myth, this means that he was incestuous. The Pleiades constellation has similar relationships with the moon: it is a combinatory variant of the moon's halo, according to the Tucuna (M$_{82}$; *RC*, p. 158); and it is in a negative correlation with the moon in respect of honey in Chaco mythology (*HA*, pp. 112–14). In North America, the Blackfoot (see below, M$_{591}$) establish a correlation between the moon and the Pleiades. The Thompson (M$_{400b}$) think of the Pleiades as the moon's 'intimate friends', but also hold them responsible for its spots, and consequently for its dimmer light. At first I was puzzled by these correspondences, but they can now be seen to be based on a transformation which makes it possible to generate a whole series of myths:

(diurnal sky)   *(nocturnal sky)*

$$[\text{sun} // \text{moon}] \Rightarrow \qquad [\text{Orion} \cup \text{Pleiades}]$$

It should, however, be noted that the formula is characterized by imbalance, since each of its terms can be analysed as follows:

    a) (Orion, *nocturnal*) $=$ (sun, *diurnal*)
    b) (Pleiades, *nocturnal*) $\equiv$ (moon, *nocturnal*)

giving three nocturnal terms and only one diurnal. It is perhaps in order to overcome this difficulty that the Tucuna associate the Pleiades with the moon's *halo* rather than with the moon itself. Within the series of transformations, we shall soon see emerging (p. 233, *et seq.*) a family of celestial phenomena more or less directly associated with the sun and the moon; they will enrich our analytical vocabulary with terms which transcend or intersect the over-simple categories of the diurnal and the nocturnal. But it is already comprehensible that the sun spots may constitute a nocturnal aspect of day, and the moon's halo a diurnal aspect of night.

To provide provisional validation of the foregoing propositions and to confirm that their field of application covers both hemispheres, I would like to establish the reality of a very simple transformation, which allows us to make the transition from the Wabanaki myths to those belonging to the Amazonian area examined in *From Honey to Ashes* (pp. 272–3). In the latter myths, a brother condemns his sister to virginity and celibacy and, to preserve her virtue, he exiles her to the sky where she becomes the Pleiades. Thus we have disjunctive non-incest leading to the sister's metamorphosis by her brother into the Pleiades (M$_{276}$), instead of conjunctive incest involving the metamorphosis of the sister and brother into the same constellation, or into the one close to Orion (M$_{575a, b}$). Each of the two versions is, moreover, an independent transformation of the group's generative myth, the presence of which can be verified in all areas: this is the myth which, starting from disjunctive incest between a brother and a sister,

causes the appearance of the moon and the sun, whose alternation, according to a rhythm of short diurnal and nocturnal periods, lies halfway between
seasonal periodicity and a simple absence of periodicity.

All that would be fine if M_{538} were content to put forward a single instance
in opposition to the one referred to in the Wabanaki transformation and
previously in the myths explaining the origin of the sun and moon.
However, M_{538} mentions not one case of incest but three. The first,
disjunctive although never actually committed, involves an enterprising
woman and her unwilling brother. It leads to a *terrestrial conflagration* and
the posthumous birth of two children, who are welded together by their
grandmother. The children first recover their physical identity and then, in
trying to recapture their mental identity as well, they cause the appearance
of solar spots, an astronomical phenomenon. These same siblings thereupon
enter into an incestuous union, to which the grandmother puts an end by
killing the husband; she later falls victim to a plot engineered by her
grand-daughter, who brings together *terrestrial water and terrestrial fire*,
after which, the young widow is united with her husband in death. So we can
say that the second case of incest differs from the first in having a conjunctive character, like the one in the Wabanaki transformation; especially
since, in this case, too, it leads indirectly to the fusion of two characters: not
the brother and the sister, since M_{538} has already made use of this motif by
inverting it, but the young woman's child and the demiurge who inserts the
baby into his own body. Their subsequent separation makes a third instance
of incest possible: real, like the second one, but in a weaker form (it
involves, instead of blood relations, a father-in-law and the wives of his
supposed son), and disjunctive, like the first, since it brings about the
'separation' of the guilty wives, who, in several versions, are changed into
wild birds. With the exception of the conjunctive incest to which the two
protagonists of the Wabanaki myths aspire, and which results in the
'incorporation' of the baby by the Klamath demiurge, the two pairs of
individuals just referred to are opposed to each other in every way: they are
related collaterally or in direct line; belong to opposite sexes or the same sex;
are partners or rivals . . . It is easy to understand why: the Wabanaki
transformation intends the two heroes to become the Orion constellation
and (or) that of the Pleiades; and we know (see above, pp. 46–7, 71, 81)
that in the Klamath myths the demiurge and his son are placed in correlation to the sun and the moon. But it is not a case of true equivalence; or
rather, the equivalence remains potential only, since M_{538} nowhere expresses these connotations specifically. It only requires the two characters to

act in accordance with their respective astronomical vocations: intentionally according to M_{530}, unintentionally according to M_{538}, the demiurge creates a *conflagration* of *celestial* origin, from which, through an action which puts him into a position of congruence with *water*, also of *celestial* origin, his son protects himself and his own people.

In thus having recourse successively to three distinct modalities of incest (two cases, one sterile, one fertile, between collaterals; and one case prejudicial to a descendant involving his sterile wives and leaving aside the fertile wife), M_{538} accomplishes three operations. The first generates the solar spots, which were unaccounted for by the first state of the group ($M_{165-168}$, M_{358}, etc. are mainly concerned with moon spots), and for which they represent, as the English phrase has it, 'a piece of unfinished business'. The next inverts the second state of the group ($M_{575a, b}$), relating to Orion and the Pleiades, by reinstating personifications of the sun and the moon while not explicitly stating their astronomical identity. Lastly, the third describes two anthropomorphic divinities, who replace the sun and moon in a purely meteorological respect, but one which is again only implied metaphorically.

Consequently, it is the third case of incest in M_{538}, supplying the plot with its final twist, which generates the series of transformations that, for the sake of simplicity, I will call primary transformations, so as to reserve a second category for others subordinate to them (see below, p. 233, *et seq.*). It is an easy transition from the terminal episode of M_{538} to the transformation illustrated by the Yurok, Wiyot and Makah myths ($M_{557-558}$), in which the demiurges previously congruent with the sun and the moon are inverted on the side of the nocturnal and winter constellations – Orion and the Pleiades – whose astronomical identity they do not, however, take over, although they exercise similar meteorological functions as harbingers of storms and rain.

But we can also make the transition to the Loon Woman myth (M_{546}–M_{555}), which is an inversion of the bird-nester story, and in certain variants of which (M_{550}) the seasonal rhythm derives from the sister's search for her brother (a metaphor of conjunctive incest, although prompted by pure sentiments), and from the killing – willed by this same sister – of the real incestuous woman, who changes into a bird, a harbinger of spring. Another primary transformation, this time involving a change of hemisphere, leads us to the Bororo reference myth M_1, in which the incestuous pattern is inverted, in relationship to the North American bird-nester: a son commits incest with the father's wife, instead of a father with a son's wife; at the same time as, for cosmographical reasons, the same meteorological signified – the rainy season – has the *Corvus* constellation and not Orion as its tacit signifier. In *The Raw and the Cooked* (pp. 199–239), I showed how, in South America, this transformation always follows on from the preceding one. The Serenté myth (M_{124}), which illustrates it, subjects the reference myth M_1 to a series of radical inversions, the aim of which is to explain the origin of Orion and the Pleiades as astronomical signifieds on the one hand, and as signifiers of the dry season on the other. This whole argument is summarized in the table on p. 225.

Independently of its schematic nature and its omissions, this table poses two problems. The pan-American distribution of the myth about the incestuous origin of the sun and moon would, in any case, allow us to consider the group as being closed. But perhaps the closure could be better demonstrated by moving back from M_{124} to certain North American myths. Secondly, there may be traces at least, in the northern hemisphere of a transformation generating the *Corvus* constellation, as does the South American reference myth. Let us examine these two points in turn.

There is an American myth which explains the origin of the Pleiades by the behaviour of a band of greedy or underfed children who, to spite their parents, decide to go up into the sky and to change into a constellation (*RC*, pp. 240–43). This group is clearly linked to M_{124}, which it subjects to a double transformation: from the sexual code to the alimentary code, and from repletion to frustration.

The pan-American nature of this myth, which was established in the previous volumes (*RC*, pp. 240–46; *HA*, pp. 114, 133; *OTM*, p. 50), proves that the group is also closed at M_{124}. It is even possible to show that, at this point in the cycle, the closure is real and not merely potential. The Blackfoot, who live in the foothills of the Rocky Mountains and are the most westerly representatives of the Algonquin linguistic family, have a myth featuring the Pleiades, that I have already drawn attention to (*RC*, p. 242, n. 15) and which is patently an intersection of the other two:

M_{591}. *Blackfoot. 'The origin of the Pleiades'*

In the spring the buffalo calves have skins the colour and softness of which is highly prized by the Indians, and much sought after by wealthy people who make children's robes from them. Now there were once six brothers who pestered their parents to give them these skins, but the latter were either too poor or too indifferent, or too taken up with other tasks to satisfy their children's demands.

After the spring hunting season had passed, the boys were furious and decided to go up into the sky. They soon found themselves in the house of

	ASTRONOMICAL CODE:	METEOROLOGICAL CODE:
NORTH AMERICA	1/ M_{165} etc. (*disjunctive incest*) → sun, moon and its spots	
	2/ $M_{575a, b}$ (*conjunctive incest*) → Orion, Pleiades	
	3/ $M_{538 (I)}$ (*disjunctive incest*) → sun's spots	
4/		$M_{538 (II)}$ (*conjunctive incest*) → [sun, moon] (*figurative sense*)
5/		$M_{538 (III)}$ (*disjunctive incest*) → [fire, celestial water] (*figurative sense*)
6/		$M_{538b, c}$ (*incest absent*, father and son allies) → [Orion], rainy season
7/		$M_{557–558a}$ (*disjunctive incest*) → [Orion], rainy season
8/		$M_{546–555}$ (*conjunctive incest*) (*figurative sense*: brother and sister allies) → summer season

SOUTH AMERICA	1/ $M_{253, 358}$, etc. (*disjunctive incest*) → sun, moon and its spots	
2/		M_1 (*disjunctive incest*) →[*Corvus*], rainy season
	3/ M_{124} (*disjunctive incest*) → Orion, Pleiades . . . . .dry season	

the sun and moon, and they explained what their complaints were. They asked the sun, who seemed to understand, to have all the water taken away from the people. The sun made no answer to this request, but Moon took pity on the poor boys and at last Sun promised to aid her.

Now the next day on earth was very hot and during the night the moonlight was so strong that it never became cool. The lakes and rivers started to boil: all the water in the world evaporated. The Indians owed their salvation to their dogs, domestic animals which dug holes in the dried-up river beds until water spurted out of the earth like a spring. This is the way springs were made, and the reason why humans have a great respect for their dogs. On the seventh day, the dogs began to howl and look up at the sky. They prayed to the moon to take pity on them, if not on their masters. The sun and moon agreed to give the people rain: the boys remained in the sky and became the Pleiades (Bunched Stars) (Wissler-Duvall, pp. 71–2).

We cannot but be struck by the fact that, in referring to a time when celestial water was absent, both M_{591} and M_{124} feel the need to introduce the motif of chthonian water, as being the only kind capable of making up for the lack of celestial water. In both cases, then, the brothers are guilty of an indiscretion: on the sexual level, in M_{124}, where they rape their mother, after luring her into the men's house on a pretext connected with clothing (allegedly to help them to put on their head-dresses and adornments); and in M_{591}, for a reason genuinely connected with clothing. In both cases, too, the etiological consequences are the same: the origin of terrestrial water on the one hand; and of the dry season — that is, withheld celestial water — on the other. This armature remains unaffected by the change in hemisphere, except in respect of the timing of the heroes' transformation into the Pleiades, which occurs either at the beginning or the end of a period of drought.

We cannot fail to notice the part played by dogs, as mediatory agents between mankind and the celestial powers, and also as masters of drinking water, since this dual role is both an echo and an inversion of the one assigned to them farther west, in the myths of small Algonquin groups living along the Pacific coast away from the main community; these myths (M_{559}), in which dogs are presented as the masters of cooking fire, are transformations of those explaining the origin of rain in opposition to domestic fire, whereas in this Blackfoot myth rain stands in a relationship of complementarity to spring water. Moreover, this is probably not the only instance in which the Blackfoot myths and those of their Siouan-speaking neighbours, the Assiniboine, show striking affinities with those of the

Cascades area. Also on the subject of the Pleiades and their origin, other Blackfoot versions (M_{591b}; McClintock, p. 49; cf. also $M_{591c, d}$, Uhlenbeck 1, pp. 112–13; Josselin de Jong 2, pp. 37–8) explain why the children were unable to obtain the skins they coveted: the buffalo calves only had such skins in the spring, when the Pleiades were not visible. Consequently, when the constellation is present in the night sky, the fine coat is absent, and when the coat is present, the constellation remains hidden. A relationship of incompatibility exists, then, between the spring coat on earth and the Pleiades in the sky.

The problem of the Pleiades is also dealt with in the myths of the Cascades area. The Shasta (M_{591e}; Dixon 1, pp. 35–6) trace the origin of the constellation to an incident which occurred between Coyote and Raccoon. The former inadvertently killed the latter and served him up to his children. But the youngest child was left out. In revenge, he informed the young raccoons of the fate that had befallen their father. They killed all Coyote's children, except their accomplice, whom they took up into the sky with them. They can still be seen today in the form of the Pleiades. In winter, when raccoons hibernate, these stars are always visible and shine very brightly. But when the raccoons emerge in summer, the Pleiades disappear. In this case, too, the etiological schema is based on the incompatibility between two sets of circumstances, one terrestrial and the other celestial.

As can be seen, the Blackfoot versions provide a bridge between two sets of myths geographically remote from each other, but between which I had already established a connection through a more direct comparison: these are the myths of the Cascades area and those of the tropical regions of South America. In this connection, I should draw attention to another transformation effected by Blackfoot mythology, since it allows us to establish a link between the others and a last group of myths dealing with the origin of Orion and the Pleiades, a group the place of which has not yet been indicated in the general pattern I am now evolving. I am referring to the Guiana myths (M_{28}, $M_{135-136}$, M_{362} etc.), in which the constellations are said to derive from a mutilated character. In a Blackfoot myth (M_{592}; Wissler-Duvall, pp. 72–3), an adulterous woman, who deserted her family to live with a lunar character, disguises herself in man's clothing in order to go back and see her children. The latter recognize her first, then their father does, and tries to kill the unfaithful woman; however, she escapes through the smoke-hole like a shooting star, and the man only manages to cut off one of her legs with his knife. The woman goes back to the moon and her lover. Her mutilated body can still be seen on the moon.

The Blackfoot myth is a transformation of the Guiana myths in two respects. The mytheme constituted by the character with the severed leg here connotes moon spots (dark on a light background) and not a constellation (light on a dark background). This reversal of the astronomical code is a function of another expressed in sociological terms, since, instead of incest between siblings, we have here adultery with a celestial, and therefore remote, character; and the adultery motif, which inverts or weakens incest according to whether the partner is a stranger or a relative, makes it possible to link up the Blackfoot myths with the Guiana versions, where we find either a woman who kills her husband and immediately takes his brother as her lover, or a man who kills his brother because he covets the brother's wife. In *From Honey to Ashes* (pp. 263–6, 275–6), I established that the lewd heroine in the Guiana myths is a transformation of the girl greedy for honey in the Chaco myths; it would seem legitimate, then, to look for a new closure, co-extensive with the whole continent, in a series of transformations which – more rapidly than might be thought possible – would bring us back from the South American girl mad about honey to Loon Woman mad about her delectable brother in the myths of the north-west of North America.

The second point I raised related to the *Corvus* constellation. Although it belongs to the southern sky, the *Corvus* constellation remains visible in theory during the summer months, albeit very low on the horizon, even in latitudes where it passes unnoticed much more because of the length of the Arctic days than through its position in the sky. It is a fact that *Corvus* does not seem to have any place in the myths and beliefs current in this part of America, a gap which is perhaps in keeping with Spier's observation (2, p. 221) that the Klamath, although they live farther south at approximately 43° latitude, only give a name to the winter constellations. The Navajo, however, who are Athapaskan from the north, and who may have brought with them very archaic motifs (see above, p. 42) in addition to the story of the 'split' twins (see below, p. 558), were perfectly familiar with the *Corvus* constellation, of which they give the following analysis: 'feet far apart' (the irregular quadrilateral); 'his feathers'; 'his body'; 'his stick'; 'his fire' (Franciscan Fathers, p. 43). It is true that their present habitat is situated still farther south, around 37° latitude.

Besides, even if north-west American Indians had been acquainted with the *Corvus* constellation and had given it a name, there is no reason why this name should have been the one that we have used since the time of the Greeks.[1]

---

[1]TRANSLATORS' NOTE: The author points out that *la constellation du Corbeau*, which is normally translated in English as 'the Crow constellation', really refers to the Raven (*Corvus*) not to the Crow (*Cornix*). The two terms need to be distinguished.

This being so, it is all the more curious to discover among them myths which, without connecting the bird with a constellation, tell a story about it which is almost identical with the one current among the Greeks to explain the origin of the *Corvus* constellation:

M_{593}. *Takelma*. *'The thirsty raven'*
There was no water in the village. The lakes and rivers were dry. Raven and Crow, two young girls who were having their first menstrual courses, were told to go and draw water from the ocean. Finding the journey too long, Raven decided just to urinate into her basket-bucket.[2] She deceived no one and was severely scolded. Crow returned much later but with drinking water.

As a punishment, Raven was condemned never to find water in the summer; only in winter would she find something to drink. For that reason the Raven never drinks during the hot months; she speaks with a raucous voice because of her dry throat (Sapir 5, p. 163).

There are striking analogies between the Greek myth (*RC*, p. 237) and the American myth. In both stories the raven is sent to look for water. Through greed or laziness, he (she) fails in his mission, which consists in making up for the lack of celestial water with the only kind of terrestrial water available — spring or sea water. In both cases, too, the raven is condemned to the same fate: he will be thirsty in summer, and, because of his parched throat, his voice will become hoarse. I showed in *The Raw and the Cooked* that the Greek myth, which concerned a summer constellation, coincided with a South American story explaining the origin of Orion and the Pleiades (M_{124}). These are summer constellations in South America because of the change in hemisphere, but they suggest the beginning rather than the end of the dry season. We saw that the Blackfoot have a myth (M_{591}) very like M_{124}, which explains the origin of the Pleiades, in this instance harbingers of the rainy season. This being so, it is not inconceivable that this myth, or others of the same type, through being inverted without passing from one hemisphere to the other, should have come to coincide more or less with a myth of the Ancient World which, in comparable latitudes, was used to explain the origin of a constellation associated with the dry season.

For this to be true, it still has to be shown that M_{593} can be given an astronomical connotation, in addition to the meteorological one already

[2] An inversion of Toad's behaviour in M_{588} (see above, p. 212), when she urinates in the direction of the sky in order to cause rain to fall.

obvious from the text. The story of the thirsty raven belongs to a vast mythological corpus present all along the Pacific coast from the Tlingit in the north to the Coos, and of which Boas (2, pp. 656–7) has drawn up a partial and provisional inventory. The Tlingit versions (M_{594a}, Swanton 2, pp. 9–10, 120–21, 418) recount how constant storms caused famine and floods. Raven, the demiurge and trickster, was able to escape from the rising waters by 'flying to the highest cloud in the sky, and hanging on there by his bill'. When the waters had half subsided, he came back down to earth and arrived at the house of an old woman who was mistress of the tides. She could not believe her eyes when she saw that he had sea-urchins to eat, because at that time the tide was always high and sea-produce could never be harvested since the waves never went back. Angered by his hostess's incredulity, Raven stuck the spikes left over from the sea-urchins into her body and commanded the sea to withdraw: 'Finally everything became dry – this was the lowest tide that ever was. All kinds of salmon, whales, seals and other creatures lay on the sand flats. People collected enough from that ebb tide to last them for a long, long time.' This is the origin of the tides. Swanton (2, p. 120, n. a; M_{594b}) refers to another version in which the selfish mistress of foodstuffs is obliged to hand them over through the intervention of a third person. Her husband, who had been keeping a jealous watch on her, took his revenge by raising a flood. Since his name was Loon, it would no doubt be possible to find a path through the north-west coast mythology which would bring us back to the more southerly cycle, already discussed at length, where it is a heroine and not a hero, an arsonist and not the agent of a flood, who is called Loon. But I propose to disregard this problem, and to dwell for the moment on the question of the origin of the tides.

The Tsimshian version (M_{595}, Boas 2, pp. 64–5) refers to the time when tides were monthly. The people were deprived of shell-fish and other produce and went hungry for long periods. The demiurge in the form of a raven joined battle with the mistress of the tides, and instituted their alternation. To be revenged, the old woman caused a widespread drought. Far inland, under the roots of an alder tree, the thirsty demiurge at last found water, the chthonian origin of which is thus doubly demonstrated. We are back, then, with the more southerly versions.

The Takelma version, in the first place, and also the Hoh and Quileute variants ($M_{596a, b}$; Reagan, pp. 48–50; Reagan-Walters, pp. 315–16) say that Raven ate the shell-fish (clams) belonging to a rival, sometimes identified as the south-west wind. The latter takes his revenge by forcing the thief to remain thirsty: the water moves out of reach just as he is about to drink, and everything around him dries up. Finally, he changes into a bird. The Tillamook (M_{597a}; Boas, 14, p. 140) tell how the crow, in order to catch crabs and fish, gives his voice to the Thunder-Bird in exchange for low tide. But this magic tide is too low; terrified by the spectacle of the monsters of the deep, Crow asks Thunder-Bird not to let the waters recede too far, and the latter agrees.

The Coos also relate (M_{597b-f}; Frachtenberg 1, pp. 14–19; 3, pp. 34–8; Jacobs 6, pp. 234–5, 241–2) how Raven exchanges his voice, which used to be very loud, for that of the Thunder-Bird, 'the father of food', and for one of the two daily tides. He then obtains the second tide in exchange for lightning, which he could produce by blinking his eyes. Thanks to Raven, men can provide against hunger by gathering sea food twice a day.

The Squamish (M_{597g}; Hill-Tout 7, pp. 544–5) transpose the spatial schema of the alternating tides into the temporal register, thus using the simple transformation *sea* $\Rightarrow$ *sky* to restore to the Raven the meteorological function it had in the Ancient World: in order to save his kinsfolk from continuous drought, Raven steals the son of the master of rain, and will only give him back in exchange for occasional periods of rainfall: 'That is why it rains on certain days and not others; now dry and wet periods occur alternately.'

Like this Salish myth, the Coos' stories show that, in native thought, the alternation of the tides is also conceived of as an alternation between dryness and wetness, plenty and famine.[3] So, by means of very short forms of periodicity, native thought is expressing more fundamental oppositions. Thunder, the father of food, has the moon as his servant. When there is nothing to eat, the birds attack the moon and cause an eclipse; then abundance again prevails (Jacobs 5, p. 68). The myth refers in this connection to the noise and din made by humans to support the birds in their fight; this makes it clear that I was fully justified, in *The Raw and the Cooked*, in criticizing the popular interpretation of charivari at the time of eclipses as a way of driving off the ogre devouring the moon. Here, as we see, the ogre *is* the moon, and the noise contributes to his defeat. This remarkable reversal is accompanied by another, relating to the lightning which symbolizes celestial fire with a positive quality: here the fire is not, as in so many instances, the cause of a conflagration, or of famine and devastation, but on the contrary, an object of exchange used for obtaining a second tide, in other words, even greater abundance. I pointed out (M_{337}; *HA*, p. 445) an inversion of a similar kind in South America, and the

---

[3] Barnett (1, p. 13) quotes a saying used by the Whites to describe Indian eating habits: 'When the tide goes down, the table is laid'.

analogy would merit further investigation. Even if the enquiry were limited to the myths explaining the origin of the tides, the connotations from one tribal group to another are so numerous that they would require special study.

Thus, according to the Tsimshian myth (M_{595}), in ancient times low tide and abundance of food returned with the new moon. The Coos, on the other hand, consider the moon to be responsible for famine. For our purposes, it need only be noted that myths linking the origin of the tides with the raven – made thirsty because he twice claims the status of master of drought: on the vertical axis, when he controls the flood and on the horizontal axis, when he dries up the sea-shores – refer insistently to lunar, that is, astronomical, situations. The Blackfoot myth (M_{591}), the starting-point of the present discussion, no doubt links the moon with the disappointed boys who are to become the Pleiades; however, from the meteorological point of view, it places them in opposition to each other: in avenging her young protégés, the moon collaborates with the sun in drying up the earth and causing suffering to mankind: only later do the sun and moon send rain, whereupon the heroes change into the Pleiades constellation. Consequently, in the first role the full moon has a place comparable to that assigned to the *Corvus* constellation in the myths of the Ancient World. Finally, the reader will have noticed that the Takelma myth, a transformation of those explaining the origin of the tides, reproduces an incident from a Modoc myth (M_{541}, see above, pp. 68, 72) – although the Modoc live a long way from the sea – in which two water-bearers, women badly in need of a husband, not virgins approaching the age of puberty, propose to marry Aishísh, the demiurge; and, as we have already seen, the latter has a lunar connotation.

Can such an unexpected coincidence between the myths of the Ancient World and the New World be explained without our having recourse to the roundabout route I suggested earlier (see above, p. 229)? Although it would be logically satisfactory, to adopt it would immediately involve running into a historical difficulty: the peopling of America was carried out in a north-south direction; it would seem more probable, then, that the myths of the southern hemisphere should be transformations of those of the northern hemisphere, rather than vice versa. It cannot, of course, be postulated – neither, on the other hand, can the possibility be ruled out – that certain myths about the origin of the constellations or subsequently associated with them, came into being during the late Paleolithic or even before; if they did, they could have been carried by waves of immigrants from Asia to America, just as different population shifts, spreading in the opposite direction, would explain why these same myths were disseminated westwards as far as the Mediterranean basin. Vestiges surviving in Europe and in America could be evidence of a common origin in the very remote past. But we could, equally well, be dealing with a simple phenomenon of convergence, attributable to what I have called elsewhere (*HA*, p. 38, n. 6; L.-S. 14) empirical deduction: the raven's croak would no doubt be a sufficient reason in itself for different human groups to assume that the bird was thirsty by nature and animal ethology might even confirm that the raven, as is stated in the myths of both the Ancient World and the New World, drinks little or nothing during summer. Wrongly or rightly, the Ancients believed that ravens were subject to a chronic disease in summer, especially during the two months preceding the autumn, before the figs ripened (Pliny, X, xii and XXIX, iii; Aesop, Fable 134: 'The Sick Raven'). Finally, in order to justify the North American configuration without calling upon Ancient Greece for confirmation, we need only note the fact that, in the myths, the Loon and the Raven are often diametrically opposed to each other ($M_{584a, d}$; see above, p. 204). And since the loon is associated with a constellation which heralds the rainy reason, the internal logic of American mythology would in itself be powerful enough to compel the raven to 'produce', as it were, a myth similar to the one which the Ancient World created independently in relation to the summer constellation, which, in the Old World as in the New, is in phasal opposition to the other constellation. The American myth, too, refers to periodic drought: not the dryness of summer, which is not a serious matter in a coastal region where the contrast between the dry and the rainy seasons is not strongly marked, but that different dryness — more important for coastal communities — which leaves the shore exposed twice in twenty-four hours, thus allowing them to gather the sea food forming their basic diet.

In the transformation generating astronomical objects or phenomena on the basis of one or several cases of incest, I assigned an appropriate place to two states of the group which, moreover, are very closely linked with each other (see above, p. 222). Let us start by looking at the first of the two.

The Modoc myth M_{539} featuring the Loon Woman both resembles and differs from its Klamath homologue M_{538}. The points of resemblance are: the attempted incest of a woman with her brother; the violence she perpetrates when her plans are baulked; and finally, the miraculous survival of posthumous twins whom their grandmother tries unsuccessfully to 'stick together to make one'. From that point onwards, and as I pointed out at the time (see above, pp. 65, 164), the two versions diverge; and the divergence springs essentially from the fact that, in M_{539}, the twins are of the same sex, whereas those in M_{538} belong to different sexes. Furthermore, unlike their fellows in M_{538}, those in M_{539} are not in the least curious about their origin. Instead of interrogating the sky, they proclaim that they belong to the earth. Far from defying and wounding the sun, they proclaim themselves his servants, and decide to go and live with him; it is true, as we shall see, that in doing so they will 'mark' the sun in a different way.

The fact that the twins are of the same sex means that, unlike the pair of which they are a transformation, *they cannot commit incest*; consequently, they will be spared the experience of becoming *disjoined* from each other, like the incestuous brother and sister in $M_{165-168}$ (the origin of the sun and the moon), but prevented from becoming *conjoined* to each other, like those in M_{575} (the origin of Orion and the Pleiades). So they will be together, but separate. On a purely deductive basis, we can argue straight away that this intermediary state calls for an astronomical signifier fulfilling three conditions: 1) if disjunctive incest connotes incompatibility between day and night, and conjunctive incest compatibility between two constellations in respect of night and not of day, the intermediary transformation must connote the intersection of night and day; 2) if the constellations connoted by conjunctive incest are winter ones, it must be posited categorically that the luminaries connoted by disjunctive incest have a summer connotation (although this is not specifically stated in the myths, but perhaps only because the moon and the sun are at their brightest in summer when the sky is clearer); from which it follows that the intermediary transformation will be situated at a pivotal point between the two seasons; 3) if disjunctive incest establishes the advent of single luminaries and conjunctive incest that of constellations, the intermediary transformation must suggest these two types of celestial objects simultaneously. Experience, that is, the mythic text, completely confirms the first two conditions. The twins in M_{539} do become stars: 1) visible just before dawn, and 2) 'between summer and winter', as is carefully explained in the myth. We shall see presently that another transformation makes it possible both to fulfil the third condition and to understand why M_{539} adds the detail that, on seeing the two stars into which the brothers have been changed, 'people will fight'.

It would be gratifying to be able to identify these celestial bodies. According to the Modoc myth, their appearance just before dawn heralds the arrival of spring. A detail already quoted from Spier (see above, p. 210) suggests that they might be the Twins: when they move higher in the sky, according to the Klamath it is a sign that spring is near. In these latitudes, the Twins constellation reaches its culmination about March-April at dusk.

The myth, however, mentions dawn, and at that time of day, the Twins rise in July, reach their highest point in October and set in January; even if we take into consideration possible discrepancies caused by mountains on the horizon, it is difficult to reconcile the two items of information. Perhaps the myth is referring to planets rather than to a constellation. This, in any case, is what is suggested by a remarkable transformation found in Chinook mythology, and which I am now about to examine.

The Chinook Indians used to live along the lower reaches and the tributaries of Columbia River; they also controlled the large markets and fishing grounds where all the neighbouring tribes periodically came together. Because of this, the Chinook myths often appear to be eclectic in character; each represents a kind of common denominator uniting various versions which, if taken separately, might appear difficult to harmonize. But, while they offer this advantage, their highly referential and synthetic nature makes them extremely difficult to analyse.[4] This is particularly true of one story, which exists in several versions not easily reconcilable with each other, and which re-uses virtually all the myths discussed so far to form a kind of pot-pourri or, if a more flattering expression is preferred, to give an impressive recital of North American mythology. Because of its complexity, this myth will reappear at intervals in my argument. I do not propose to analyse it exhaustively; I shall merely summarize it, and then draw attention to certain of its aspects:

M_{598a}. *Clackamas (chinook).* *'The sun's husband'*

A chief and his wife continued to live in the same village although they were separated. She had a small son and female slaves, who admonished her when one evening she announced her intention of attending a celebration, where she ran the risk of meeting her former husband. But the inducements offered by the dance were stronger than her respect for the proprieties. And although she had promised to return home early and not to take part in the dances, the crowd pushed her right to the place where the man who had been her husband sat.

During the night, the baby woke up and cried for his mother. The slave girls carried him around fruitlessly. In desperation, they all went in turn to tell their mistress what had happened, and to beseech her to return; but each time the crowd jostled them away to the other end of the

---

[4] This is why I have chosen to disregard a Chinook version of the bird-nester (Curtis, Vol. 8, pp. 132–5), in which Salmon, the hero, has four wives (Mouse and Finch, who are unfaithful; Turtledove and Locust, who are faithful) and plays the part of a master of rain. This version is also syncretic in character, and the system to which it belongs could only be elucidated by a special study of Chinook mythology in its relationships with the mythologies of the surrounding communities.

house. When none of the others returned, the only slave left in the house set off, leaving the baby behind. 'Your son is almost dead now (from crying)', she called out to the mother, reproaching her for having stayed out all night. At this harsh recall to her maternal duties, the woman rushed back home; but the cradle board stood there empty. Or rather there was nothing inside but a stick of rotten wood, left by the ogress who had stolen the child while there was a thick, heavy fog. She fed her captive on (mashed) snakes, bull-frogs and toads. Then wherever she went, she packed him on her back in her basket.

Not far away there lived a man called Crane (probably a heron). When the boy grew up, he wanted to visit him, although his adoptive mother had told him not to. The man conversed with him as loudly as he could – the only way, so he insisted, of not being overheard by her (the ogress) – and explained to his visitor that he used to be fed on non-human kinds of food; he taught the boy to eat grilled trout. From then on he refused to share the ogress's daily fare. The latter accused the neighbour, who denied having told the boy anything, except a coarse joke about her manner of giving birth to her so-called son. She was so pleased at Crane's sally that she expressed acceptance of Crane as if he were her brother.

The hero had told his protector that, while the ogress carried him on her back, he would often in fun catch hold of the branches of trees until the woman's elastic neck, as she strained to go on, became stretched and thin as a hair. Crane advised him to take advantage of this game to cut off her neck with a flint he gave him. He added that all the trees, who were related to the ogress, would topple on to him in order to avenge her. He would have to climb right to the top of a white fir [*Abies concolor*], which would be the only one not to react to the murder. Then he should join his arrows and bow together to make a chain which would reach the sky.

And so this is what he actually did. In the celestial world, the hero first encountered cannibalistic crawling creatures: greyback lice, black lice, nits and fleas; and he commanded them to behave with greater moderation towards human beings. Against the will of the Darkness One, he instituted the regular alternation of day and night. Then he met in turn two hunters looking for their quarry and he asked them both the way but was given contradictory information. He took the advice of the first hunter, but he had cause to rue it because he landed in the house of cannibals. There was no one in it, and he could not even find the bowl where the urine was kept. He wanted to clean his hair with it before rinsing it in water. But he failed to find it and had to make do with water. Then he looked for a comb in a hide bag hanging from a rafter. He found a young girl inside, and as soon as her father and sister returned, she was offered to him in marriage. He refused to eat their meal of human flesh but he accepted the girl; but it was no good, because she lacked excretory and sexual organs.

The disappointed hero decided to take the other trail. It led to a very well provided home; a urine bowl, and a copper comb were lent to him by a young girl whom he found in a pack basket. And, after an excellent dinner with the family, he had no hesitation in marrying her. She had all the right female attributes. Furious at having been spurned, the inhabitants of the first house arrived full of jealousy and anger. They mocked their hosts for being 'holed and split'. The latter drove the cannibals away by burning deer bones which made a thick, dark smoke.

Quite some time afterward, the wife gave birth to Siamese twin boys. Her father had told her never to allow her husband to be with his face against the ground when she was delousing him. One day, she forgot to take this precaution. The man automatically dug at the ground, pierced a hole in the celestial vault and saw his village and his little brother who had been born after he left and who, along with all his people, had become blind through having wept so much over the loss of their beloved kinsman. He was filled with melancholy and his father-in-law guessed why. Having extracted the truth from his daughter and son-in-law, the old man became resigned to their departure. The spiders let a basket down to earth by means of a rope.

The hero was reunited with his own people, whose sight his wife restored with miraculous water. The houses were thoroughly cleaned before the young people moved in. Normal life was resumed. Blue Jay, the trickster, lived in the village and he was irritated at the sight of the Siamese twins. He cut the connecting membrane, and inflicted a wound on each one through which their entrails escaped. The two children died.

Their mother explained that if they had been allowed to live and grow up, they would have become separate without surgery. But now there was nothing more to be done. She took the little corpses, one under each arm, and went up into the sky in the form of the visible sun. She announced that when people saw her children on either side of her at sunrise, it would be a sign that a headman or a very wealthy man was going to die. If only one child was visible, it would mean the death of a less well-to-do man. The villagers wept so much over the twins' death that they again became blind (Jacobs 2, Part II, pp. 388–409).

The remarkable thing about this myth is that it builds a coherent syntagmatic chain by linking together paradigms borrowed from all the myths previously studied, while at the same time systematically inverting them. The Loon Woman paradigm generates the initial situation, with the difference that a married but incestuous sister, who shows too keen an interest in her brother, is transformed into a divorced mother who is too negligent towards her child, and forgetful of the proprieties to the extent of appearing in public with her former husband, thus committing a kind of social incest. Consequently, instead of the sister taking her brother a long way away (horizontal axis) and the brother vainly trying to escape from her by going up into the sky (vertical axis), the child captured by a total stranger (horizontal axis) succeeds in escaping from her by also taking the vertical way, which will lead him to the sky.

The Basket ogress, a stranger and not a kinswoman, is a replica and a transformation of the lewd grandmother (who in turn is a transformation of Loon Woman): she is not an older relative, and her neighbour causes her delight instead of annoyance in making a doubtful joke concerning procreation, not copulation, but nevertheless connected with her genitalia. In consequence of which, she addresses him chastely as brother, instead of making him her lover.

After Loon Woman and the lewd grandmother, the myth now refers to a third character. The child who becomes the bird-nester, after being saved by a male demiurge from his mother, a tearful widow who wants her son to die with her, is incorporated into the body of his adoptive father, then is separated from him and born again by means of a delivery through the knee, which is neverthless a real birth. The other child, who is stolen from his mother, a gay divorcee who used to abandon him in order to live a fuller life, is first of all shut away in a female demon's basket, then frees himself by cutting off the extremely long neck of the woman carrying him: this neck is virtually an umbilical cord which makes the delivery metaphorical by transferring it from the real position in the lower part of the body to the upper part. The bird-nester nearly dies because he has climbed to the top of a tree. The hero of M_{598a} is saved by the same expedient,[5] but he has to use a chain of arrows to cover the additional distance separating him from the sky: we shall encounter this detail again at a much later stage (in Part Five) and I propose to postpone any interpretation of it until then.

I also propose to leave until later the next episode relating to the origin of body lice, although we may note in passing that it refers to an inevitable concession that must be made by culture to nature. Likewise, the episode

---

[5] But in this case the tree in question is the white fir, a species which is not highly thought of: 'not good for anything; too wet even to burn' (Adamson, p. 162).

which comes immediately after, and in which the alternation of light and darkness instituted by the hero explains and justifies the extent to which day must give way to night. The fact that daily periodicity is the shortest observable form once again provides a comparison between M_{598a} and the lewd grandmother cycle. This cycle, too, is concerned with periodicity, but in its longest forms, as measured by successive generations; whereas the Nez Percé myths (M_{571-c}) – the narrative structure of which M_{598a} then goes on to follow – relate to medium periodicity: the rhythm of the seasons.

Lastly, M_{598a} is in opposition to M_{571} in another way, which links the two groups to the blind boy and the Loon cycle. In this cycle, the hero's sister entered into a distant marriage in a cannibalistic community consisting of people without anuses or vaginas, as does the hero of M_{598a}, when he has his abortive conjugal experience. An incident in M_{571}, on which I have already commented (see above, p. 192), implies that the daughters of winter, the first people visited by the heroes (also looking for a comb to tidy their hair) had no vaginas. But if the interpretation I suggested is accurate, in this case the application of *raw bleeding meat* causes the occurrence of female periods, which required, so to speak only a monthly piercing to ensure their appearance. The piercing of the cannibal girls in M_{598a}, which is intended to allow conjugal relationships to take place, should then be made more frequently, or should even be permanent in its effect. However, the procedure, a reverse of the other one, which is used by the sun's people to drive off their enemies by means of *smoke from burnt bones*, does not involve any anatomical change. M_{598a}, therefore, counters the relatively slow periodicity instituted by M_{571} with the non-institution of a periodicity of the same type, but shorter, than the narrative sequence implied. In mocking the sun people for being 'holed and split', the cannibals are showing their determination to remain blocked.

The episode of the two wives found in a hide bag also has echoes of the Loon Woman cycle, at the beginning of which the hero is a hidden child. But in the Chinook myth, the part is assigned not to a boy but to girls; and the hero marries them, instead of being himself hidden so as to be kept from marrying. Secondly, the girls hanging like the basket or bag ($M_{555a, b}$) holding the hidden child, illustrate a reverse situation: they are not hidden in the sense that the bag containing them is the one in which a visitor, exhausted by a long journey, would look straight away for the toilet requisites he needed to tidy his appearance. It is not a matter of indifference that the essential requisite should be a comb, since Loon Woman discovers her brother through a long hair he lost after combing himself (for the meaning of this episode, see below, pp. 389–90).

As in the Tillamook myth M_{565a}, which also both combines and trans-forms paradigms borrowed from other myths (see above, p. 171), the hero finally marries a celestial creature, that is, enters into the most distant of all unions, which is the reverse of an incestuous relationship. This more than exogamous marriage produces twins, who are joined together at birth, thus forming a counterpart to those in $M_{538-539}$, who were joined together after birth as an indirect consequence of an incestuous union. But there is another point to be noted too: the terrestrial husband of a solar woman, who pierces the celestial vault and looks down on his own village, is a direct transforma-tion, by a simple reversal of sex, of the terrestrial wife of a luminary, who was discussed at some length in the previous volume. The significance of the loop, linking the luminary's wife to the bird-nester almost without any intermediary stages, will be made clear later (see below, pp. 592–8). After the episode in which the blind recover their sight, and which is again reminiscent of the Eskimo cycle on the same theme that we shall meet again (see below, Part Five, 2), the twins, who are 'split' by a malicious act which causes their death (whereas in M_{539} they split themselves voluntarily in order to fulfil their destiny), are nevertheless transformed in both contexts into morning stars, not harbingers of spring, according to M_{598a}, but of violent death and sometimes of war (Jacobs 2, Part I, p. 281, n. 128a); a possibility not excluded by M_{539} in which the twin stars also portend fighting (see above, p. 234).

The most important point of all is that the Chinook myth completes the Modoc story, in the sense that, taken together, their conclusions provide full confirmation of the three conditions which I posited deductively in order to justify the transformation, which they both effect, of an incestuous brother and sister subsequently disjoined or conjoined, into two brothers who, being of the same sex, cannot commit incest, and of whom it must therefore be postulated that, once they too are changed into stars, they will be neither conjoined nor disjoined. The fact that this intermediary condi-tion is reflected sometimes in the opposition between summer and winter and sometimes in the opposition between fellow-tribesmen and enemies, will cause little surprise in the light of the long discussion of this transfor-mation in *The Origin of Table Manners* (Part Six). But the Chinook myth states even more precisely than M_{539} that the twin stars are visible on either side of the sun; it describes them, then, at the time of their heliacal rising, which clearly illustrates the intersection of night and day. Finally, this astronomical situation which brings the sun, normally alone in the sky, into proximity with two stars, provides the equivalent of a constellation, thus meeting my third condition. But there is still more to be said: this final configuration, which we have arrived at after listing a whole series of states, which are transformations of each other and of which it in turn is a transformation (Figure 17), is antisymmetrical, along several axes, to the configuration illustrated by the group in its initial state. In that configuration, we were concerned with the moon and the sun, that is, with the incompatibility of night with day; here, we are dealing with an ill-defined dawn in which the faint light of the rising sun is not enough to obliterate the glow of the stars, and which therefore accepts a certain compatibility between light and darkness. On the other hand, the initial state gave greater prominence to moon spots, that is, *one black* mark inside a *light* circle, itself standing out against a *dark* background; the final configuration, on the other hand, consists of *two light* marks against a *dark* background, outside a circle which, in the terminal myth, has no black spot inside it. We can even say that the myth excludes such a mark by preterition, in the sense that the little brother, who is blind in the literal sense, serves to exteriorize the moral blindness with which the hero is afflicted in M_{538}, and which he tries to cure by forcing the sun to enlighten him, thus wounding the luminary and causing its spots.

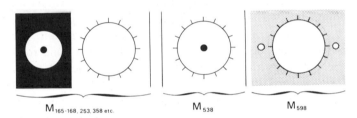

$M_{165-168,\,253,\,358\,etc.}$ $\qquad$ M_{538} $\qquad$ M_{598}

Figure 17. Celestial transformations

The stars in M_{539} herald the return of spring, but the absence of seasonal connotation in M_{598a}, which associates them with less regular occurrences, such as violent death or wars, suggests that the celestial bodies in question have a less strongly marked periodicity. It is tempting to identify them as planets, particularly since the Blackfoot (whose mythology we have shown to be closely related to that of more westerly areas) attached great importance to the conjunction, just before sunrise, of two planets, perhaps Venus and Jupiter. They identified them with two mythological characters, a star's son and the morning star respectively (McClintock, pp. 490, 523–4; cf. M_{482a-c}, *OTM*, p. 248). The conjunction of two planets at the moment of their heliacal rising is a recurrent phenomenon, but its much longer periodicity is less easy to observe than that of the constellations. Between

M_{539} and M_{578a}, we move, then, from empirical periodicity to another which is no less real, except that the Indians of North America, unlike the ancient Mexicans, were probably not familiar with it. Now, the other Chinook versions of the same myth mark a further step towards the absence of periodicity. After affecting the transformation of the stars into planets (if we assume that the celestial bodies in the Modoc myth, M_{539}, were not already planets), they transform planets into parhelia or other celestial phenomena of the same type.

This is the case with the Kathlamet versions ($M_{598b, c}$; Boas 5, pp. 192–193; 7, pp. 9–19) in which the father of the cannibals and of Moon is called Evening Star and the father of the Sun girl married by the hero Morning Star. As the girl goes up into the sky with her dead children, she transforms them into parhelia: according to whether one or two are visible, one or two chiefs will die.

Parhelia, also called mock suns or meteors, are brilliant spots of light, which are occasionally visible next to the sun when it is low on the horizon and its rays are reflected by clouds. Parhelia can be single, double, or multiple. The same phenomenon observed in the neighbourhood of the moon is called a paraselene. In addition to explaining the origin of parhelia, the Wishram and Wasco versions (M_{598d-g}, Sapir 1, pp. 171–3, 276–9, 303–307; Sapir-Spier 2, p. 277) purpose to explain why ants and wasps have slender waists: the inhabitants of the village had hung round their waists the rich gifts they had received from the celestial woman. On leaving, she wanted to have them back and pulled so hard that the possessors of the waists were almost cut in two. It will be remembered that, in M_{598a}, they became blind again. The dialectic of the group therefore generates, on the one hand, characters who are blocked below (with neither anuses nor vaginas) or above (blind); on the other, characters who are cut in two at neck level (ogress), lengthwise down the body (the twins), or at waist level (insects). These last have as their counterparts crawling creatures of celestial origin who will henceforth cause humans to be pierced. This point emerges *a contrario* from a Nootka myth, which will be discussed later (M_{600f}; see below, p. 403) and in which the first creatures the hero (who is an inversion of the one in M_{598a} because he is the only one of a group of brothers and sisters not stolen by the ogress and the one entrusted with the task of rescuing them) meets in the sky where he has gone to look for them, are not cannibalistic fleas and lice, but charming snail-girls, who have the misfortune to be blind, and whose sight he restores by piercing their eyes with the tip of his penis. On the contrary, in the corresponding Puget Sound Salish myths (M_{600i-m}; Ballard 1, pp. 106–12), the terrestrial ogresses who steal children are snail-women, moreover infested with vermin, the cause of unbearable itching.

Native lore includes among bad luck signs the conjunction of one or two stars with the moon. One star means that a woman is about to become a widow; two stars that she herself will die, as well as her two children. A rainbow near the moon at dusk signifies somebody will be murdered (Sapir 1, p. 193; Sapir-Spier 2, p. 277). The phenomenon in this case is probably a paraselene, the colours of which, like those of parhelia, sometimes resemble a rainbow.

All the tribes in this area who attribute a sinister nature to parhelia would seem to consider them as being in opposition to the rainbow, which connotes life. The same word *lakiyaa* is used for 'newly born child' and 'rainbow' in Yana (Sapir-Swadesh 1, p. 144). The Shasta are convinced that, in all seasons, rain always follows a confinement (Dixon 7, pp. 454–5). For the Coos, a rainbow is a sign that a birth, accompanied by rain, is about to occur in a high-ranking family (Jacobs 5, p. 101). According to the Wishram, a rainbow means that a woman is on the point of giving birth, and if the rainbow is a double one, that she will produce twins (Sapir 1, pp. 191, 193). So, for all these Indians, the rainbow is clearly in opposition to the conjunction of the moon with one or two stars (or planets), the conjunction being a sign of death *for* a woman, as we have already seen, and not the sign of a birth *by* her. Furthermore, lunar or solar conjunctions relate to the death of women or men respectively. We have here, then, the beginnings of a system:

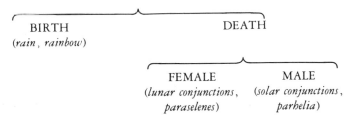

The Yana, in whose vocabulary the same word is used significantly for birth and rainbow, believe that parhelia are signs of approaching death (Sapir-Spier 1, p. 285). One of their myths illustrates the triadic system I have just outlined so exactly as to provide a kind of experimental proof of its validity (M_{599a}; Curtin 3, pp. 281–94; for a weak form of the same myth see M_{599b}, Sapir 3, pp. 233–5). In the times when night did not yet exist, the celestial people were divided into three camps: firstly, the two rainbows, father and son respectively, and their brother-in-law or maternal uncle, the master of rain and storms; then Moon and Cougar his wife, along with their daughters and Stars and the daughters' husbands; lastly, Sun and his wife Parhelion (*utjamhji*, Curtin, cf. Sapir-Spier 1: *utdja'm'djisi*, parhelion; Sapir-Swadesh 1: *udzamxzi-*, 'there is a parhelion') with Meteors, their three daughters. The young Rainbow wanted to marry one of the spinster daughters of Moon, the one called Morning Star (the only one, consequently, who is not incompatible with daylight). Moon, however, was in the habit of taking his daughters' suitors to the home of Sun, his brother, who would submit them to fatal ordeals. The hero survived these ordeals, thanks to the help of his uncle, the master of rain and storms. However, Moon would not admit defeat. He himself tried to destroy his son-in-law, but the latter got rid of him by sending him, together with his daughters the Stars into the night sky where, henceforth, he *will die and be reborn periodically* (Figure 18).

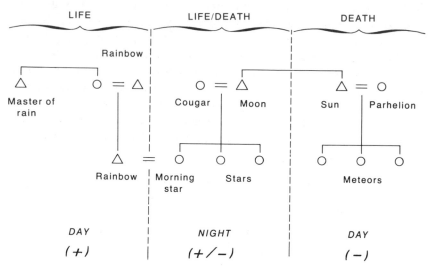

Figure 18. The triadic structure of the Yana myth M_{599}

Although parhelia are said to be caused by the formation of ice crystals in the atmosphere, they do not seem to be associated with any particular latitude. However, we cannot fail to be struck by the fact that the interest they arouse varies considerably in different parts of the world. In North America, in particular, all the references to the native beliefs about them relate to one northern, and practically continuous, area, stretching from the Pacific coast to the Atlantic seaboard — provided we agree to include the Wabanaki transformation in the same group as the myths of the Loon Woman cycle (Plate 4).

The reason for this northerly area of distribution is perhaps that, according to reliable witnesses, parhelia are particularly impressive in the vicinity of the Arctic Circle: 'Who would not feel the charm of those brief days when brilliant Sol receives a suite of two, four or even eight satellites, through the mysterious operations of the parhelia?' (Morice, I, p. 253). Yet the interest in parhelia stretches beyond the area occupied by the Eskimo and the Athapaskan. The Tlingit believe that parhelia accompanying the setting sun signify fine weather, but bad weather if the parhelia disappear first (Swanton 6, pp. 452–3). According to the Kwakiutl (Boas 20, p. 218), parhelia are a sign that a chief's soul has gone to the sun and it appears as a mother-of-pearl ear-ornament; a single parhelion foretells the death of a common man. Paraselenes have the same meaning. Double circles round the sun predict evil events, and meteors predict death.

The Bella Coola call the parhelion situated to the west of the solar disc 'our father's facial painting'; if it touches the earth it causes an epidemic (Boas 12, p. 36). The Lilloet believe that parhelia are the sun's children and forecast bad weather (Teit 11, p. 275). Similarly, the Thompson believe that when the sun grows tired of one kind of weather, 'he turns out his children'; the parhelia, his children, are thus a sure sign that the weather will change (Teit 10, p. 341). One of their myths (M_{598h}; Teit 4, pp. 54–5) accounts for the origin of parhelia in a way reminiscent of the explanation given by the Chinook. The Okanagon base their weather predictions on the number of parhelia which can be counted north and south of the sun (Cline, pp. 178–9). Their Sanpoil and Nespelem neighbours believe that parhelia foretell hot weather, and anthelia cold weather (Ray 1, p. 213).

On the other side of the Rockies, the Algonquin-speaking Blackfoot interpret parhelia at dusk as a sign of danger: 'When the sun paints his cheeks, in other words, when there are two large sun dogs (icksi, parhelia) in the Eastern sky, it is nature's sign of a big storm, accompanied by wind and a sudden drop in the temperature. And if the sun paints his forehead, his chin and both his cheeks (a quadruple parhelion), it foretells the imminent death of a chief' (McClintock, p. 56; Grinnell 3, p. 64). Travellers in former times noted the importance given to parhelia by the Great Lakes Algonquin: 'They also have various expressions for . . . a halo, double suns and other apparitions in the sky, which prove that they have paid considerable attention to the firmament' (Kohl, p. 119).

Sometimes, beliefs relating to parhelia spill over into the Central Plains, but only among tribes belonging to the Algonquin linguistic family, who are known to have come from the north, or among Siouan-speaking tribes adjacent to them. The myths of the Assiniboine, who are Siouan-speaking neighbours of the Blackfoot, echo the Loon Woman story: the incestuous sister kills all her people with lightning, and changes into a bird. Her brother brings his dead relatives back to life; they divide into two groups and go off in opposite directions (M_{609a}; Lowie 2, pp. 160–61; compare the Achomawi version, see above, p 120). According to these same Indians, the appearance of parhelia in winter is a sign of prolonged storms (*ibid.*, p. 56). The Arapaho, who are an Algonquin-speaking tribe from the north, believe that parhelia foretell very cold weather: 'The old Indians said the sun had camp fires on either side, and consequently they prepared for a very cold winter' (Hilger 2, p. 93). The Santee Dakota, immediate neighbours of the Ojibwa to the south-west of the Great Lakes, call parhelia and paraselenes *wi-a-cé-i-çi-ti*, from *a-cé-ti* meaning 'to light a fire' (Riggs 1, pp. 8, 25). According to the Oglala Dakota, a circle round the sun preceded the return of victorious warriors; it was also an inducement to celebrate the sun-dance, symbolic of a successful war expedition (Beckwith 2, pp. 404–405).

After this rapid survey, let us return to our starting-point. The Modoc refer to a green circle round the sun which forecasts a storm as *wänämsäkät-saliyis* (Curtin 1, p. 302). The Klamath expression for the solar halo, *wanam shakatchalish*, is a reference to *wan*, the fox, the faithful companion of Kmúkamch (Gatschet 1, Part II, p. 474); this link-up is a reminder of the one made in the Guiana languages between the opossum and the rainbow (see above, pp. 43, 45; *RC*, p. 249; *OTM*, p. 167). It is worthy of note that the Klamath attribute the same meaning to the loon's cry as the Modoc and Chinook give to the heliacal rising of the stars or planets, and the Chinook to parhelia: 'The call of the loon at early dawn is a sign that someone will kill another' (Spier 2, p. 138). If we move to the other end of the distribution area, and to the eastern Algonquin, where the Wabanaki transformation supplied the key enabling us to interpret a vast range of myths and to weld them into a whole, the idea of a parallelism between the loon's cry and parhelia emerges still more clearly. According to the Penobscot, the parhelia called *abas.éndan*, 'the middle' (probably to indicate the central origin of the sun's reflections), or 'the gate', are signs of a storm – rain in summer, snow in winter. 'The storm will come from the same sector as the one in which the ring surrounding the sun is broken.' These same Indians have the following to say of the loon: 'If it cries at night, the wind will blow the next day from the quarter opposite to that from which it is heard. If the cry comes from the opposite side of a lake, it will blow from thence, since loons seek a lee shore before the wind rises' (Speck 3, p. 33). The Shasta, who are immediate neighbours of the Klamath, would appear to use the same kind of reasoning in relation to parhelia: 'If seen near the sun at rising, they betoken war; and if one of the mock suns fades before the other, then the persistent one points in the direction of those who are to be beaten in the conflict' (Dixon 7, p. 471). So, from the Atlantic to the Pacific, we find the problem being treated in the same way and comparable use being made of the parhelia and the loon, sometimes on the meteorological level, sometimes on the social and political levels. It is therefore not surprising that a long series of transformations should have led us from the loon to Orion, then to sun spots; next to stars or planets which are in conjunction in relation to the sun; and lastly, to parhelia. Once again, the cycle of mythic transformations has come full circle: the parhelia bring us back to the loon.

Furthermore, the Salish-speaking Klallam and the Wakashan-speaking Nootka, who live opposite each other along the banks of the Juan de Fuca strait, have a common myth which retransforms parhelia, probably identified with paraselenes, into the moon spots with which our series of operations began. The Klallam versions (M_{600a-e}, Gunther 2, pp. 125–31) tell how a woman, whose children had all disappeared one by one, wept so much that she had to keep blowing her nose; the mucus from her nose, on falling to the ground, came to life and took the form of a baby who grew very fast and was named 'Mucus Boy' or 'Made of Mucus', in memory of his origin. When he reached adulthood, he set out to look for his brothers and sisters, whom an ogress had kidnapped and was holding prisoner after blinding them by sticking their eyelids together with pitch (Nootka, M_{600f}, Boas 13, p. 117; Sapir-Swadesh 2, pp. 89–101; cf. Chinook, M_{598a-g}). He set them free and killed the ogress. In the Klallam versions, the kidnapper is not an ogress but a wild beast (mountain lion?) who has married the hero's sister; this animal is the chthonian husband of a human female, who is unmistakably an inversion of a human male's celestial wife in the Chinook versions, since in both cases the woman gives birth to a double child: in the first instance, Siamese brothers and, in this myth, a child with two heads or two faces, who persists in insulting his uncle by calling him 'Mucus'. The latter, angry and humiliated, goes up into the sky where he becomes either the moon or the spots on the moon.[6] So, instead of the double child giving rise directly to combined planets or to parhelia, the characteristics of which can be summarized by means of a simplified formula:

a) 2 EXTERNAL light areas against *dark* / *SUN*,

[6] He is the sun's son and goes back to his father in the sky, in the Bella Coola version (M_{600h}; Boas 12, pp. 83–6). For the group as a whole, which extends from the Tlingit in the north to the Coos in the south, and only one state of which concerns us here, cf. Boas 2, pp. 734–5.

it gives rise indirectly to moon spots, the simplified formula of which is anti-symmetrical to the other:

b) 1 INTERNAL dark area against *light* / *MOON*.

   This being so, it is essential to note that the myth featuring Mucus Boy is, in several of its details, a repetition and an inversion of the Plains myth known as Stone Boy. The respective origins of the two heroes supply sufficient proof of the inversion, but they are also both the offspring of a woman whose children or brothers have all been carried off in turn by a wicked sorceress. In both cases, the miraculously born hero sets them free, but then has to become disjoined from them in order to avoid the malevolent intentions – or over-benevolent, i.e., incestuous, intentions, cf. M_{466} – of a close relative; unless, as in the Nootka version, he succeeds in marrying a very distant woman, who then becomes the visible sun. In the other two instances, he himself becomes either the moon or the moon spots, or a light-coloured stone on a hill top; as I have already shown (*OTM*, p. 389), this stone is the terrestrial counterpart of the moon, and was necessary in a mythic context which was already an inversion, in all respects, of the pan-American myth about the incestuous origin of the moon and its spots, and of the sun. The return to the stone, from which the celestial moon is eventually born, occurs incidentally *in situ* in the myths of the Coast Salish, where Moon the demiurge is the hero: after being conceived from a stone swallowed by his mother, he is stolen from his cradle and then freed by the action of his kinsfolk, instead of freeing them (M_{375a-o}, M_{382}; cf. Adamson, p. 380 *et passim*). A Salish version from Vancouver Island (M_{600g}: Hill-Tout 5, pp. 331–6) confirms this transformation. After resuscitating his ten brothers who had been killed by an ogre, and then freeing his sister who had been kidnapped, the hero returns to his village: but he is offended by an insulting allusion to his origins, and changes back into nose-mucus. The cycle *stone* $\Rightarrow$ *moon, moon* $\Rightarrow$ *mucus* is therefore completed by the commutation between stone and mucus, of which the same hero, in both cases, is the son. I shall return later (p. 332) to the transformation as a whole.

PART FOUR SCENES OF PROVINCIAL LIFE

Does not Society turn man, according to the settings in which he deploys his activity, into as many different men as there are varieties in zoology? The differences between a soldier, a workman, an administrator, a lawyer, an idler, a scholar, a statesman, a merchant, a sailor, a poet, a pauper and a priest, are just as great — although more difficult to grasp — as those between a wolf, a lion, a donkey, a raven, a shark, a sea-cow, a sheep, etc. There always have been, and there always will be, Social species as there are Zoological species.

H. de Balzac, Preface, *La Comédie humaine*,
Editions de la Pléiade, I, p. 4

TRANSLATORS' NOTE: Three of the titles of this part contain French literary references. *Poisson soluble* (in the singular) is a famous text by André Breton, an example of Surrealist automatic writing; *Scènes de la vie de province* was a title used by Balzac; *Du bon usage des excréments* echoes the titles of pious religious writings, e.g., *Du bon usage des maladies*.

1 Soluble Fishes

Insolubility is the property of a body incapable of being dissolved, or which amounts to the same thing, invincibly resistant to the action of menstruum.
See MENSTRUUM.

L'Encyclopédie (published by Diderot and d'Alembert)

To the north of Klamath territory, the Columbia River cuts across the plateau and through the Cascade Range; it would seem to have existed before the major geological upheavals, which determined the present character of the landscape but were powerless to obstruct its course. The Takelma and the Molala, small native groups which disappeared at an early date and about which little is known, once provided a buffer between the Klamath and the Kalapuya. The latter, whose language is related to that of the Takelma (Swadesh 6; Shipley 2), occupied the upper reaches of the Willamette. The lower reaches, and the confluence almost to the Columbia estuary, belonged to Chinook tribes who had settled along both sides of the water, as well as in the coastal zone, from the falls, at which point the river starts to burst through the Cascade Range, to the sea. The Chinook tribes — the Clatsop, the Kathlamet, the Clackamas, the Wishram, the Wasco, etc. — had as their eastern neighbours a body of Sahaptin-speaking communities which can be subdivided into several groups: the Columbia River Sahaptin, mainly represented by the Tenino; the northern Sahaptin, who included the Yakima, the Klikitat, the Cowlitz, the Walla, the Palouse, etc.; and lastly, the Nez Percé, who inhabited the foothills of the Rockies and marked the eastern boundaries of the Sahaptin linguistic family, since their speech had connections with its archaic forms. The Molala and the Cayuse, who used to be classed as Sahaptin, are now considered to be separate branches of the great Penutian phylum, to which the Sahaptin-Nez Percé group may also belong (Rigsby 1, 2; Voegelin).

In Part Three, I stressed the syncretic tendency of Chinook mythology, which is perhaps to be explained primarily by the geographical position of the tribes in that part of the Columbia estuary which serves as a common frontier for the Salish tribes to the north and the Sahaptin to the south and east, not to mention numerous other groups speaking isolated languages. But another factor was the political and economic role played by the Chinook, especially the Wishram and the Wasco, who were permanently settled on the major fishing grounds along the lower reaches of the Columbia and, because of this, organized the regular intertribal fairs attended by neighbouring communities, and even by Indians from farther afield.

Certain Chinook versions of the bird-nester myth are highly significant, for two reasons: they provide a continuous link with the more northerly versions which I propose to examine in Part Five, and they have already raised a theoretical problem to which I now propose to offer a solution very different from the one that has been suggested.

M_{601a}. *Wasco. 'The freeing of the salmon'*

There was once a great hunter called Eagle who lived with Coyote, his grandfather. On the pretext of looking for eagles which had nice feathers for arrows, Coyote told Eagle to climb to the top of a rock. He had previously forced him to take off his clothes so as not to spoil his garments, which were handsomely embroidered with shells and beads. Eagle carried out his mission, but when he tried to climb back down he realized that the rock was very high up and that the top reached nearly to the sky. What he had thought were eagle feathers were only coyote's entrails.

Coyote put on Eagle's clothes and made himself look like his grandson. In order to trick his daughters-in-law, he pretended to be worried by the old grandfather's absence and lay with Mouse and Woodpecker, Eagle's wives. He moved camp the next day and every day.

Eagle spent many days on the high rock; he was starving and grew thin. At last old Thunder came and split the rock; brush and sticks grew along the split. By means of these Eagle came to the ground and set off to look for his people. Two of his wives had remained faithful to him. When Coyote moved camp they followed the others from behind weeping. Finding the ashes warm in the abandoned camps, Eagle managed to overtake the two wives and they told him everything that had happened. That same evening, the hero entered the camp. Coyote began to whimper and cry and tried to give back the stolen garments. 'Keep my clothes,' said Eagle, 'and my two wives too.' Life went on as before.

One day, Eagle asked his grandfather to cut up two bucks he had

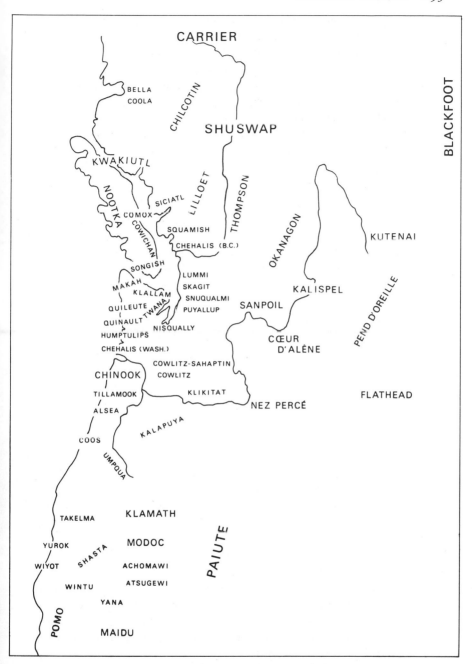

Figure 19. Tribal distribution in the west of North America

killed, and to bring back the meat. As the way back was long, Coyote camped for the night and lay down near the game. Rain started to fall and fell all night. Next morning the old man found the bucks were nothing but hanging bushes. 'This is my fault,' he thought, 'my grandson has paid me back.' On his way back to the camp, he had to pass several gulches full of deep, roaring water. He could not cross the fifth, lost his footing and was carried down to the great ocean.

There, he saw two women in a large canoe. They shone even more brightly than the sun, and were using very beautiful white wood paddles. The women's task was to keep the fish from leaving the sea and going into the river. To awaken their curiosity, Coyote turned himself into pieces of wood floating down the river. The eldest sister was tempted, but every time the youngest dissuaded her [from picking up the wood]. Finally, Coyote changed into a baby on a cradle-board, and the sisters had pity on him and took him into their boat.

As they had all kinds of fish, Coyote took advantage of their absences to help himself to copious meals. But when they came back he became a baby again, placidly sucking the eel's tail they had given him in place of a teat.

Coyote made himself a digging-stick from hard wood, with which he broke the sisters' dam. All the salmon escaped and crowded up the Columbia River, which henceforth would be at the disposal of mankind. Then Coyote took ashes and blew them on to the sisters, saying that henceforth they would be birds (a version recorded by Curtin in 1885, in: Sapir 1, pp. 264–7).

According to a more recent Wishram version (M_{601b}, Sapir 1, pp. 4–5), the birds could be terns or sea-swallows, which accompany the salmon as they swim upstream. From being originally *mistresses* of salmon in a stretch of *stagnant* water where they held them captive, the women consequently become *harbingers* of salmon as soon as the fish are free to swim in *running* river water. I shall come back to these two contrasting motifs. For the moment, I would like to draw attention to the comments with which Sapir accompanies his transcription. Let us say at once, in defence of the famous linguist, that he was extremely young when he worked with the Wishram, and that, had he been dealing with the myth at a later period, he would perhaps have been less closely bound by that narrow historicism which was one aspect of Boas's teaching; such historicism was, however, inevitable at the time, and also fruitful in that it limited each area of enquiry to encourage study in greater depth.

In relation to previously studied versions, the originality of M_{601a}

consists in combining the story of the bird-nester, in the form in which we have met it so far, with an episode which at first sight appears to be entirely new: the freeing of the salmon. Sapir could not fail to notice the synthetic composition of the myth, but he considers it to be accidental and arbitrary, asserting that 'two absolutely distinct myths have been welded into one'. He goes on to say that the bird-nester story exists as a separate entity, both in the myths of the Klamath to the south and in those of the Thompson and Shuswap to the north (the versions belonging to these Salish tribes will be studied in Part Five, as M_{667} *et seq.*). This proves, he adds, that 'this is distinctly a myth of the Plateau, presumably adapted — by the Wasco to the Eagle and Coyote cycle.' On the other hand, he considers the distribution area of the second myth, concerned with the freeing of the salmon, to be the Columbia River basin, since it is also present, as a separate entity, in the mythology of the Wishram and the Nez Percé (Sapir 1, p. 264, n. 2).

Sapir's second statement calls for qualification. Even the Nez Percé version to which he refers (M_{602a}, Spinden 1, pp. 15–16) contains an implicit reference to the bird-nester story: it begins with the hero's revenge, which would be unmotivated but for some previous conflict, which the myth does not mention, since it takes it for granted. The complete story, beginning with the bird-nester episode and ending with the freeing of the salmon, was to re-emerge twenty years later (M_{602b}, Phinney, pp. 376–81) in an account given by an old Indian woman who was said to have remained particularly faithful to the spirit of the ancient traditions (*ibid.*, p. vii). In the other Nez Percé versions published by Boas (4, pp. 135–44, M_{602c-h}), the two stories remain separate, but it is perhaps not an accident that they are given in sequence. A link which Sapir declares to be arbitrary is found, then, among communities very different from each other in speech, culture and way of life, although they were separated by no more than three or four hundred kilometres. This in itself would be sufficient reason for believing the myths to have an internal logic. But this logic can also be demonstrated more directly.

At first sight, the mythology of the Kalapuya, who are southerly neighbours of the Chinook, would appear to support Sapir's thesis: it contains the story of the freeing of the salmon but not, it seems, that of the bird-nester. However, the Kalapuya version of the first story takes a rather distinctive form, although one which is not exclusive to this tribe:

M_{603a}. *Kalapuya. 'The freeing of the salmon'*

In very ancient times, the frogs possessed all the drinking water. Every time anyone wanted a drink, they demanded an exorbitant price for each mouthful. One day, when Coyote was thirsty, he made some imitation money (money = *dentalia*) to pass himself off as a wealthy person, and protected his head with a helmet, which rendered him insensitive to the blows inflicted on him by the frogs. He drank slowly, taking his time, and surreptitiously tore open their reservoir. The water broke out, carrying with it salmon and other fish. 'Henceforth,' said Coyote, 'nobody will have to purchase drinking water. Everyone will drink freely, and frogs will live near river banks but never again will they keep all the water back' (Jacobs 4, pp. 135–6, 236–9. For similar stories, cf. Nez Percé: M_{603b}, Boas 4, pp. 187–8; Tillamook: M_{603c}, E. D. Jacobs, p. 147; Nootka: M_{603d}, Boas 2, pp. 892–4).

It is clear that this version stresses the release of *drinking water* rather than that of *edible fish*. And it is possible to suggest why by pointing out that M_{603a} is concerned with the *obtaining* of drinking *water* by the *demolition* of a dam, and that the Kalapuya have an exactly symmetrical myth explaining the *loss* of cooking *fire* resulting from the *erection* of another dam:

M_{604a}. *Kalapuya. 'The fire which was lost and found again'*

Panther (*Felis concolor*) and his brother Coyote lived together. One used to hunt while the other prepared firewood. One day, Whale's daughter came along with a view to marrying Panther. As the latter was away, Coyote received her and invited her to sit down on his brother's bed. Henceforth, each would have an allotted task: Panther would ensure their supply of food, Coyote would attend to the fire, and the woman would cook their meals for them.

One day, Panther decided to visit his parents-in-law, accompanied by his wife. Coyote would take care of the house during his brother's absence. The travellers set off; at dusk they came to a river. A ferryman, who had to be hallooed without a sound being uttered – otherwise he would not hear – crossed them over in his boat: he was a species of mudfish. The woman introduced her husband to her father. Panther went hunting for his parents-in-law, and then took leave of them, saying that they would all meet again some time soon.

A short while later, Panther asked his brother to take his wife along with him to visit her parents. On the way, she wanted to rest; as she sat down, she opened her legs. What Coyote saw filled him with desire. Feigning sickness he said that he had to return home. His sister-in-law

1. Pillar Rock. *On the right*, the coast of Cape Flattery; *in the background*, Tatoosh Island. (*Seattle Times* photograph)

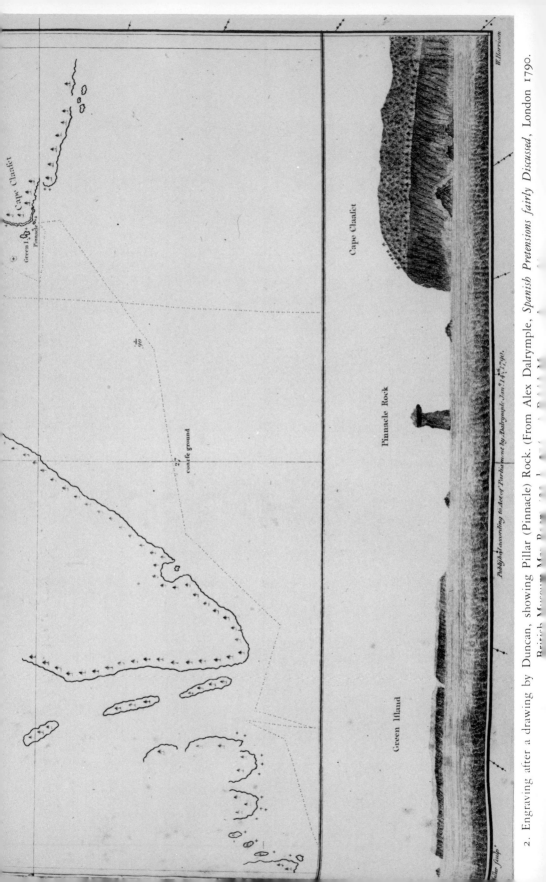

Cape Chaslet

Green I.

Pinnacle O.

conast ground

Cape Chaslet

Pinnacle Rock

Green Island

W.Harrison

Published according to Act of Parliament by A. Dalrymple Jan. 1st 1790.

2. Engraving after a drawing by Duncan, showing Pillar (Pinnacle) Rock. (From Alex Dalrymple, *Spanish Pretensions fairly Discussed*, London 1790.

would just have to wait for her husband, who would join her as soon as he had been informed of the situation.

Coyote, however, stopped near a small pond, into which he dived several times in succession until his faeces, which he had left lying on the bank, assured him that he looked exactly like a Panther. Then he went back to the woman, claiming to be her husband. Although convinced that this was not true, she allowed him to copulate with her. However, Coyote betrayed his true identity by making all sorts of blunders. Unlike his brother, he could not manage to make their packs roll along behind them; he insisted on hallooing to no purpose in order to hail the ferryman; and the only game he could kill for his parents-in-law was a large bullfrog.

That night, Panther dreamed that his brother had stolen his wife from him. He assembled his warriors and led them to the river bank. He demanded that 'Coyote's wife', formerly his own wife, and not Mudfish should act as his ferryman. She finally appeared, although she was pregnant and about to give birth. Father Whale, who could probably see into the future since he could forecast the course of events, ordered Mudfish to impale Coyote with a hard pointed pole while his false son-in-law was busy repairing the smoke-hole on the roof. Meanwhile, the canoe was coming close to the other bank. Panther jumped out, split open his wife's belly and took out the two children – his own and his brother's. He handed his own child over to the larger of two chicken-hawks (*Accipiter* sp.), who was to take it up into the sky, and threw his brother's child into the river. He also cut off the two braids of his wife's hair and gave them to the second bird.

The water started to rise. Running or swimming, or sometimes carried along by compassionate birds, the people sought safety at the top of the highest mountains. The copper-head snake was carrying fire along as he swam. The people hurled reproaches at Panther: 'The waters will not recede! What have you taken that you ought not to have taken?' 'Only my child and that woman's hair,' he replied. But it was precisely the hair that the water was pursuing. The chicken-hawk was ordered to drop it and the water went down.

The people noticed that fire was missing. The snake informed them that he was carrying it in his mouth, which has been burning ever since. Panther proposed that he should buy it. After bargaining with him, the snake agreed to hand it over to him in exchange for a covering of stiff-dry skin, the cause of the rustling noise snakes make to this day when they move along the ground. A huge fire was lit, but only the good, upper-class people could claim the right to enjoy it, while the poorer people shivered.

Urged on by Coyote, they thought up a ruse and proposed that they should devise an entertainment for the upper classes. However, instead of dance feathers, they decorated themselves with clippings of pitchwood, which went up in flames as soon as the dancers approached the fire. They were driven off and fled in all directions. Since then, even poor, lower-class people have been able to light a good fire (Jacobs 4, pp. 103–13; compare Nootka: M_{604c}, Boas 2, p. 894).

Another version (M_{604b}: *ibid*., pp. 215–21) states that Coyote had five premature babies instead of one, and adds the detail that he built a dam downstream in the hope of recovering his children, who were being swept along by the current. This created the flood which is also mentioned in M_{604a}, although its precise cause is not stated there.

I do not propose to dwell at this point on the chief characters in the myth. They form a pair of complementary animals, one a carrion-eater, the other a predator; and they transpose this duality on to the cultural plane by sharing roles: both keep the home provided, one with firewood, the other with game. Later, we shall meet a similar pair (M_{644} and its continuation, p. 297) and this will enable us to understand more clearly the reason for its first appearance in a myth which conjures up an era when even indispensable possessions like fire could be monopolized by a selfish minority, and enjoyment of them had to be negotiated. This feature would itself be adequate evidence of the symmetrical relationship between M_{603} and M_{604}, since M_{603} describes exactly the same situation with regard to drinking water as M_{604} with regard to domestic fire. But the symmetry is also obvious on other levels. In M_{603}, the trickster demiurge obtains drinking water for the people of the future; in M_{604}, he is initially the cause of men losing fire. For drinking water to be freely available, stagnant water (contained in a reservoir) has to become running water. Conversely, one individual is able to deprive the community of fire and to appropriate it, because a newly built dam prevents water from flowing, holds it back and creates a flood.

The episode in which the woman's plaits are cut off and handed to the chicken-hawk, who lets them drop into the river, is far from clear. Since it occurs in a myth about the origin of fire, I am tempted to compare it to a similar detail in the Salish myths dealing with the same motif (M_{650a}, see below, p. 316): the selfish mistress of fire keeps the latter in the braids of her hair, which are made from five burning and intertwined logs.[1] It will be noted that the heroine of M_{604a} is a whale, and what is more mistress of water, since she knows the secret of how to cross the river in the ferryman's boat and thus avoid getting wet. On the other hand, the mistress of fire in the Salish myth is unable to cross a river because she cannot bear her skirts to get wet. I shall leave the task of elucidating this transformation to others.

The chicken-hawk also forms an oppositional pair with the snake (Boas 10, p. 195) in Chinook myths; he is master of the deluge in Kutenai mythology (Boas 9, p. 41); and he undertakes the task of conquering fire in Tlingit myths (Swanton 2, pp. 11, 83). The fact that this last motif extends as far as Alaska is particularly significant, in that, as the myths indicate, the Kalapuya had a social structure based on a class system, which shows that, like other neighbouring tribes, they were indisputably linked to the north-west coastal communities, whose vast and complex mythology can only be studied through a process of sampling (cf. L.-S. 6). Their affinity with the northern tribes marks the Kalapuya and the Chinook as being different from their Salish neighbours. As will be seen later (cf. below, pp. 426–9), the latter trace the origin of cooking fire to a war waged by the terrestrial people against the celestial people. Consequently, unlike the Kalapuya, they believe that fire was conquered, not lost and then found again; and its presence today in human societies is the result of a cosmological transference from the sky to earth and not of a sociological distribution among unequal human groups.

A first point to be deduced from the preceding remarks is that the case of the Kalapuya illustrates the general reorganization of a system which must be recognized as existing, at least potentially and in schematic form, throughout the area under consideration. But there is more to be said. The reorganization results, in this instance, from the fact that one of the elements in the system, the bird-nester story, is absent or appears only in a barely recognizable form in Kalapuya mythology: Coyote transforms a gopher's entrails into a young girl; several animals try to marry her but she runs away. One of them takes his revenge by making her climb a tree, under pretext of gathering and eating astringent fruit which makes her choke; she dies and goes up into the sky to the land of the dead (M_{605}; Jacobs 4, pp. 199–201). Whether or not the *female fruit gatherer* is an inversion of the *bird-nester*, it is worthy of note that the latter does not appear in person in

---

[1] Compare the device employed by the animal hero, who undertakes to steal fire for the good of future generations, in most of the myths belonging to the same area. For instance, in Wishram mythology (Sapir 1, p. 295): 'He took two firebrands and tied them upright to his ears, so that the latter stood up like asses' ears . . .' It is tempting to see here the solution to the problem of the long-eared characters whose presence in the petroglyphs of several regions of America I have already mentioned (*OTM*, p. 70).

the collection of myths compiled by Jacobs, although it includes practically all the available material about the Kalapuya. Are we then to conclude, with Sapir, that if two myths A and B, which are merged into one story by the Wasco and the Nez Percé, can exist independently elsewhere and even be mutually exclusive, this proves that their merging was contingent? Certainly not.

In the first place, the mythology of the Kalapuya, like any other, has to be discussed in relationship to its infrastructure. The Kalapuya Indians, who live along the upper reaches of the Willamette, no doubt were aware of the existence of salmon, but could not catch them inside their tribal territory, because the fish were unable to travel upstream beyond the barrier of the falls (Farrand 3, Vol. I, p. 645). Consequently, for them the problem of the origin of salmon was an essentially theoretical matter, unrelated to their everyday existence. So we can understand why their myth on this subject should, in a sense, go off at a tangent. It makes only one brief mention of fish and concentrates on another dietetic aspect of rivers, as producers of drinking water, not food.

Two consequences follow from this. Firstly, the myth about the origin of salmon, through changing into a myth about the origin of (drinking) water, can be incorporated into a larger group, where it has as its symmetrical counterpart a myth, with the same armature, about the origin of fire. This, as we have seen, is exactly the relationship which can be established between M_{603} and M_{604}. Then, the mythic paradigm which joins and contrasts the origin of fire and that of water is precisely the one which enabled me to construct the bird-nester group in *The Raw and the Cooked*, although the bird-nester story itself does not appear in Kalapuya mythology.

Its absence should not surprise us, since, in the new system, the etiological function of the bird-nester is, as it were, made to serve other myths. If we call the bird-nester myth A and the myth about the freeing of the salmon (here changed into a myth about the origin of water) B, we can say that, in Kalapuya mythology, B excludes A, because B, while retaining its own code, uses it to transmit the same message that neighbouring communities (and the Bororo of South America) entrust to myth A.

We know, too, that the pan-American armature of A enables it to refer alternatively to the origin of water (M_1) or of fire (M_{7-12}). A being absent from Kalapuya mythology, the twofold etiological function is transferred to B, for reasons explained by the techno-economic infrastructure. By the same token, B is reduplicated in two forms, one straight, the other inverted. Thus, $\{A, A^{-1}\}$, $\{B, B^{-1}\}$, which fulfil identical functions, are not truly separate entities.

In fact, the problem raised by Sapir in connection with M_{601} is illusory. Myths cannot be compared to things, which have recognizable identities, whether they are encountered separately or in combination with each other. Neither does there exist any assortment of spare parts from which items could be selected and arranged in a mosaic, so as to form new myths assembled on an arbitrary basis. I take it as axiomatic that every myth, through the mere fact of its existence, constitutes a coherent statement. The elements it brings into play have no inherent value; their significance derives from the combinations of which they form part, and they have this significance only in relationship to the particular combinations. Consequently, a myth can be homogeneous from the semantic point of view, even when its component parts are to be found elsewhere as separate entities. Their association, in a given mythic text, may not be obligatory, but it cannot be arbitrary.

I wanted to begin Part Four by thus refuting an outmoded form of empiricism because, in Sahaptin mythology, the bird-nester myth has an even more complex construction than in the Chinook versions. If we had adopted Sapir's view and accepted the hypothesis that the Wasco version results from the running together of two separate myths, to develop a similar interpretation in respect of Sahaptin mythology, we should now be obliged to suggest the coalescence of three or four myths, instead of two. Superficial explanations of this kind drain mythology of all its complexity and reduce it to a mere conglomeration of discrete elements, all equally devoid of significance.

M_{606a}. *Klikitat. 'The freeing of the salmon'*

A man called Bow had two wives: Grizzly and Bear (who belonged to a different species from Grizzly – a black or brown bear, according to the different versions). One day, Grizzly announced that she was having her menses and would have to remain secluded until they ended. When she had recovered, she asked her two children to bring her her everyday clothes. The brother and sister were present while their mother was dressing, and noticed that she was gradually beginning to look like a Grizzly. They ran back and gave the alarm. In order to escape from the wild beast, Bear climbed high up into a tree, Buzzard changed into a loose door-flap, and Bow stayed hanging up, a mere bow in the house. Aided and abetted by their dog, the two children fled.

On arriving in the village, Grizzly destroyed all the things which had been persons. She did nothing at all to Coyote, who had transformed himself into the maggots on a log, for he was threatening to stuff her anus with maggots. Grizzly plied the dog with questions; finally, he told her which direction the two children had taken, and she ran after them.

They had already gone far, far away,* and the boy, who had become a big man, was living with his sister as her husband. One day, prompted by a sudden whim, he decided to explore a region where she had warned him never to go. There he encountered his mother, who suggested that they should have a mutual delousing session; she took advantage of this and killed him.

Grizzly next went to her daughter's camp. When she saw her mother coming, the daughter hid her baby and caused a spring to gush out. As it happened, Grizzly was thirsty but every time she tried to drink, the water became lower and lower. When she was finally reduced to crawling down into the spring, her daughter killed her by pushing her to the bottom of the dried-up gully. Coyote lost no time in making his appearance, for he wanted to get married and he had learnt that at this place was a woman with no husband. However, the young widow preferred to die rather than accept this offer of marriage. She lit a fire with all the food and meat, and threw herself into it. Coyote looked for her everywhere but in vain; he found only the baby on a cradle-board.

Uncertain what to do next, he had recourse to his usual informants: his two sisters whom he carried round in his intestines and excreted every time he needed to know the situation. But as soon as they had spoken, he pretended that the information they gave was useless and that he had known it all for a long time. [Sometimes, the excrement-sisters are called Pine-nut and Huckleberry; cf. Jacobs 1, p. 88, n. 5.]

To begin with, the sisters claimed that they were tired of answering questions, and Coyote had to threaten to send down rain as a result of which they would disintegrate. So they recounted in detail all that had happened; as always, Coyote retorted that he knew all about it. He told them to get back into his intestines and then he decided to adopt the little orphan.

The boy grew up fast, became a skilled hunter and married seven women: five were called Mice, one Cricket and the last Turtle-Dove. Coyote liked to lie on his back next to his daughters-in-law: he would light a fire, and when it crackled and popped he would wait to enjoy the spectacle of the women tucking up their skirts and revealing their privates, lest the sparks burnt their clothes. This is how he came to notice that Cricket and Turtle-Dove, of whom his son seemed to be more enamoured than the others, had black vulvas, whereas the five Mice had white vulvas. However, his son did not lust for this group of wives and Coyote resolved to appropriate them.

He went up to a rock cliff and on a ledge defecated two faeces, which he turned into two eaglets. Then he sent his son to capture them in order to obtain their feathers: he persuaded him that he needed them for his arrows. But first of all, he made him exchange his fine clothes for his own, which were in no danger of being spoilt. When the hero reached the eyrie, all he found was faeces. And the rock had grown so high that there was no way to descend.

Clad in the hero's garments, Coyote returned home in order to impersonate his son. The five white Mice welcomed him without much ado. But Cricket and Turtle-Dove treated him harshly and fed him on mere common things.

Meanwhile, the hero, who was called Eagle, was marooned at the top of the rock. The Spider let him down to the ground with a rope, in exchange for the promise, which later was scrupulously kept, that he would repay her with a vine rope. Eagle set out to look for his wives, for Coyote changed camp every day. He finally caught up with the two who were closest to him. Turtle-Dove's baby recognized him when he was a long way off, but the women refused to believe him and continued on their way. Finally, the hero managed to stop them by walking on the pack rope which was dragging along behind.

After the women had told him how they had been ill-treated, Eagle made himself small enough to be rolled up and carried along in their woven mat bundle. When they arrived at the camp, he assumed his normal appearance. Coyote gave him back his clothes and his unfaithful wives, and became an old man again.

One day, Eagle asked his father to help him to carry some game he had killed, but he gave him a rope made of deer intestines. It started to rain; the rivers swelled visibly. Other versions state that Coyote was slow in mooring his load and the fragile bonds broke. A great volume of water swept him downstream.

Coyote managed to build a makeshift canoe, but it broke up in the water. Next, he changed into a baby, then into a dead deer, in the hope that he would be given hospitality by an old woman and her grand-daughter who lived not far from there. However, the grandmother was not deceived by the carcass which proposed that she straddle it (cf. $M_{560-565}$). She tried to club Coyote on the head, but once more he floated away downstream.

He came to a region where five unmarried girls lived. They were water birds and, in order to arouse their pity, he assumed the appearance of a former tribesman who had come back to the place where he used to live long ago. These women kept salmon imprisoned in a lake. As they used to go every day to gather edible roots, he made them digging tools from elderberry wood, which is easily broken, but made strong sticks from oak for his own use. Thus equipped, and with his head protected by bone ladles piled on top of each other like helmets, he started to dig a trench out towards the river to release the water. The women had a premonition; they hastened to the scene and hit Coyote, but to no avail. The water flowed towards the river with all the fish.

Coyote walked a long time in a downstream direction. He was hungry, but didn't know how to set about catching fish. He defecated his sister who taught him how to club a fat salmon to death. Coyote put a stick through it, and roasted it over a fire. While he was waiting for it to be cooked through, he fell asleep. Some wolves came along, ate the fish and, as a derisory gesture, smeared the sleeping Coyote's mouth with fat. When Coyote awoke, he was surprised at feeling hungry, whereas the scraps which were scattered about and his greasy mouth pointed to the fact that he had already eaten. He started fishing again five times in succession, but always with the same result.

The faeces sisters, whom he summoned once more, denounced the wolves and urged Coyote to treat them in the same way, while the wild beasts slept, as they waited until the duck eggs they had gathered were cooked. For, the sisters added, one bad turn deserves another, and it is not right to sleep instead of eating. Coyote tricked the wolves in this way five times in succession. They, in turn, learned that everyone must stay awake and eat his own food.

Henceforth, Coyote was able to live on what he caught. As he travelled across the country, he created cascades, decided where there would be fishing sites and where the fish would be dried. He also fixed the places where the salmon would spawn and where their eggs would be gathered. Next, he created all the rivers and the different species of salmon: 'Here,' he decreed, 'there will be different salmon fishing places and people will speak different languages. The people at that place will catch salmon; they will exchange different kinds of food. They will trade things for salmon. And from that exchange, the people of the dry prairies will eat all sorts of things. In that way, there will be a good exchange and sharing of salmon at that place. Gladly and generously they will do this. The people who are coming are near now. When it becomes warm in the spring, the salmon will come up river as far as the river goes. Different kinds of salmon will be in the river. That is how it will be, according to my law' (Jacobs 1, pp. 79–91; cf. pp. 91–3, 103–107, 191–202).

We know of several variants of this long myth, but the elderly informants from whom they were obtained did not seem to know the exact zoological identity of the bird girls, who are the mistresses of fish. The Klikitat call them *wi'dwid* and translate this onomatopoeic term by 'snipe', 'swallow' or 'wild duck' (Jacobs 1, p. 86, n. 3; cf. p. 197). Perhaps it should be compared with the Klamath *čwi.did(ig)*, another onomatopoeic term (Barker 2, p. 99): 'Killdeer plover or snipe'. It will be remembered that, in the same context, the Chinook refer to terns as heralding the period when salmon run upstream. In each case, then, we are dealing with water birds, which have a relationship of contiguity, either spatial or temporal, with fish.

A similar kind of uncertainty can be observed between the different versions in respect of the zoological identity of the hero's wives. The Cowlitz River tribes ($M_{607a, b}$; Jacobs 1, pp. 103–107, 191–202) credit him with four wives, two with black vulvas – doves or turtle-doves – and two with white vulvas – the Mice sisters, who are occasionally replaced by a mouse and a cricket. In M_{607a}, the torrential rain brought about by the hero plays a dual role: it leads not only to Coyote's punishment, but also to that of the guilty wives who cannot cross a torrent and are changed from humans into mice (*loc. cit.*, p. 105). Coyote is saved by two species of resinous wood (Douglas fir and cedar), the boughs of which help him to hoist himself on to the bank, and on which, by way of thanks, he confers medicinal properties and uses as timber for manufacturing purposes (*ibid.*). We shall encounter this last aspect again in certain Chinook myths ($M_{618, 620}$; see below, p. 293), which begin in the same way as those we are now examining and will help us to interpret the initial sequence common to the whole group. According to M_{607a}, Coyote also changes into a baby in order to excite the pity of the five mistresses of Salmon. But the baby, who is an inversion of the Old Man returning to his native village in M_{606a}, makes improper advances to the women. For this reason, the youngest takes a dislike to him; the four others find him delightful, and each one in turn makes him sleep with her during the night. The meaning of this episode will become clear when we analyse the Inland Salish version (see below, p. 435). For the moment, I shall simply note the double dichotomy:

$$\text{Coyote} \begin{cases} \text{old man } (M_{606a}) \\ \\ \text{baby} \begin{cases} \text{lecherous } (M_{607a}) \\ \\ \text{well-behaved } (M_{601}) \end{cases} \end{cases}$$

Ballard (1, pp. 144–50; $M_{606b, c}$) recorded certain Coast Salish variants, which originated among their neighbours the Klikitat, and in which the hero is said to have two pairs of wives, who are respectively ring-doves and sawbill ducks, or sometimes mourning-doves and salmon milts. Coyote forces his son to remove his clothes before removing a so-called 'eagle' from its nest: 'Take off your mocassins,' he said to him, 'in order to succeed, take everything off from your feet up, even to your earrings' (loc. cit., p. 144). After being saved by the spider, whom he repays with a gift of strong rope, the hero goes back to the two wives who have remained faithful to him, and by walking on the long piece of plaited rope the young mother is trailing behind her, jerks them to a halt. When he returns to the camp he orders his father to give him back his clothes before they become completely dank and mouldy. He then causes torrential rain, which changes his unfaithful wives into ducks. Coyote is dragged along by the current and arrives at the home of the witsowit sisters (cf. above, p. 265), a name meaning sand-piper, the bird into which he changes them after freeing the fish. The wolves, over whom Coyote finally gains the upper hand, admit defeat and decide henceforth to live as wild beasts. Coyote continues on his way upstream and turns into a rock, a natural boundary indicating the point beyond which the salmon cannot go: this is a negative way (contrasting with the positive way in M_{606a}) of making commercial exchanges necessary, since those tribes without direct access to salmon had no other way of obtaining the fish. This interpretation, to which I shall return later, is confirmed by a more easterly version. The Flathead, a Salish tribe living in Idaho, believe (M_{608}; McDermott, p. 240) that Coyote created the Spokane Falls to prevent the salmon running up Columbia River as far as the territory of the Pend d'Oreilles (Kalispel), so as to punish the latter for refusing to give their daughters in marriage to strangers. However, before discussing the way in which this group of myths is brought to a close, we need to look carefully at the initial sequence of M_{606a}, which constitutes what might be called a 'fourth overture' to the North American bird-nester cycle.

Let us briefly remind ourselves of the sequence. A man called Bow has two wives, Bear and Grizzly. When the latter has her periods, she goes into seclusion and is transformed into the wild beast with the same name. In order to escape from her, the villagers change into household objects, and her children, after taking flight, live incestuously together. She pursues them and kills her son; her daughter causes her to die in a dried-up ravine, where Grizzly is trying to quench her thirst; the daughter then commits suicide by throwing herself on to a fire. Coyote saves her orphaned child and adopts him. The narrative then continues with the bird-nester story.

Because this mother, who changes into an ogress when she has her periods ('Overture IV') is commutable, in the initial position, with other characters, she is an obvious transformation of the incestuous sister in M_{538} ('Overture I'), of her chaste opposite in M_{541} ('Overture II'), and finally of the lewd grandmother in M_{560} and its continuation ('Overture III'). The same point can also be established by a different process of argument.

Firstly, the transformation of an older female relative into an ogress, and more particularly into a grizzly bear, does not occur simply in one group of variants as the distinguishing feature of that group. It is also to be found in myths in which the main heroine belongs primarily to the other types I have listed. This being so, the transformation has more than a merely hypothetical value: it is directly observable as an empirical attribute of a particular character. It will be rememberd that, in most versions of the Loon Woman myth, which in this respect belong to Overture I, the heroine's mother in the course of the story takes over the position previously held by her daughter (see above, p. 55). After the latter's death, she replaces her and assumes the appearance of a female grizzly in order to avenge her. The episode of her conflict with the incestuous couple, as it is told in myths belonging to this group, for instance M_{531} and M_{538}, exactly reproduces the corresponding episode in M_{606a}: the son or grandson is killed by the she-bear, then the thirsty she-bear is killed by her daughter or granddaughter; and finally, the latter commits suicide by burning. The same is true of M_{560}, which belongs to Overture III and in which the lewd grandmother character changes into an ogress who has assumed the appearance of a grizzly (see above, p. 165). The transformation seems to be absent as an internal operation from myth M_{541}, which belongs to Overture II, and of which, indeed, it is the only example. But this apparent omission can be explained by the fact that M_{541} inverts the Loon Woman story along several axes. The character of [1]/the older female relative, [2]/changed into a cannibalistic ogress/ the better to perpetrate [3]/the destruction of her son or grandson [4]/who has become his sister's incestuous husband/, only appears unrecognizable because it is expressed in the form of [1]/the male collateral (the heroine's brother), [2]/remaining the hardworking fisherman he has always been, [3]/although the salmon he kills for food [4]/is in fact his sister's exogamous husband/. In the latter instance, the persecutor retains his human nature in relationship to a victim who has assumed the appearance of an animal food good for humans to eat, whereas in the former instance the victim retains his human nature in relationship to a female persecuting animal which preys on humans. The identity of the character changes, but all the symmetrical relationships are preserved.

Secondly, certain peripheral myths, which can be recognized as border-line forms of the Loon Woman cycle, illustrate the inversion of the incestuous sister into a she-bear, or of the she-bear herself into the opposite of an incestuous sister. For instance, in a Chilcotin myth already quoted (M_{581a}, p. 177), an Indian woman married to a bear (i.e., an extremely exogamous wife) kills her own siblings, who had become an incestuous couple; and she is killed by a loon. Conversely, the Assiniboine, using almost the same terms as the Loon Woman myth, relate how incestuously inclined sisters are transformed into she-bears, which kill the entire popula-tion, blind their relatives and cause burns all over their bodies (M_{609b}; Lowie 2, pp. 161–2; cf. above, p. 245).

Not so far from the myth's main area of distribution, among the Wintu, we noted a version (M_{545b}; see above, p. 140) in which the guilty sister is also changed into a cannibalistic monster, so that the 'alimentary incest' of homophagy is added to sexual incest; in M_{606a}, it replaces it. In most of the southern versions of the Loon Woman cycle, the heroine's crime is made to appear even more heinous by the fact that she commits it during menstrua-tion, just as the heroine of M_{606a} is also menstruating when she is about to turn into an ogress. The myths thus postulate an implicit correlation between female periods, incestuous inclinations and cannibalistic appe-tites; this links up with the remarks made in the preceding volume (*OTM*, pp. 395–403) about the close relationship between head-hunting and the feminine sex. As Demetracopoulou (pp. 121–2) already realized, the myths also identify incestuous advances on the part of a sister with the violation of the taboos, very strict in California and further north, relating to pubescent girls and menstruating women. But Overture IV, as illustrated in M_{606a}, makes it possible to generalize the more limited paradigm used by Deme-tracopoulou. Because she is menstruating, a virgin is in danger of changing into an incestuous sister, and a mother into an ogress who eats her own people — which is what the sister herself does when her initial desires are frustrated. And the lewd grandmother in Overture III changes into either a cannibalistic ogress (M_{560}) or an incestuous relative (M_{564}) because she claims to be still sexually active, although — as we may presume, since this is the only relevant characteristic which distinguishes a grandmother both from a mother and a pubescent virgin — she can no longer menstruate.

The fact that the four overtures constitute a transformational group results in the last resort from the correspondence discernible between each of them and South American myths which, as was shown in *The Raw and the*

Cooked and has been frequently recalled in the present volume, themselves formed a transformational group. In the preceding sections, a relationship of homology was established between on the one hand the North American bird-nester cycle and that of Loon Woman, and on the other hand the South American bird-nester cycle and the cycle about the introduction of man's mortality. It was also shown that this general correspondence could be analysed in terms of more precise equivalences between north and south on the level of the homologous states of each transformation. Thus, the North American myths relating to Overture I, the theme of which is incest, refer back to M_1 and M_2 in South America. Continuing with the North American myths – Overture II is an inversion of the preceding one, and of Overture III, which is also an inversion of Overture I, but along a different axis, and which refers back, in South America, both to M_5 and to $\{M_{87} - M_{92}\}$; in other words, to a myth and a group of myths, each of which is an independent transformation of $\{M_1, M_2\}$ and $\{M_7-M_{12}\}$, which are transformations of each other. It is now clear that Overture IV refers back, in South America, to a group of myths $\{M_{22-24}\}$ which, as was shown in the previous volumes (*RC*, p. 104; *HA*, pp. 37, 436, *et passim*; *OTM*, p. 425), were also transformations of $\{M_1, M_2, M_7, M_{7-12}\}$. Provided the jaguar is substituted for the bear (an animal which does not live in the tropics), the myths of both North and South America introduce the bird-nester story after an episode in which a mother, who, amongst other things, has an ambiguous relationship with her children, appears first of all as a menstruating woman, changes into a cannibalistic wild beast and finally perishes – according to the North American myths, in a dried-up pit, or according to other versions, through being cooked internally – whereas, in the South American myth (M_{24}), the ogress dies *first* in a pit and *afterwards* is burnt on a fire.

The preceding arguments show that the four overtures of the North American bird-nester cycle stand in a transformational relationship to each other. However, a further question arises: what is the nature of this relationship, and how can it be analysed when viewed from the formal angle? According to what we have seen so far, we would appear to be dealing with a system involving four terms, each of which is definable by the semantic function of the chief character: an incestuous sister, a chaste sister, a lewd grandmother, and a mother who turns into an ogress during menstruation. But the mere listing of the four terms is enough to show that, from the logical point of view, they are far from being homogeneous.

A chaste sister (Overture II) may be the opposite of an incestuous sister (Overture I), but it is difficult to see how one could reduce the other two characters to such a clearly defined oppositional pair, and how one could discover any symmetry between this pair and the other one. Certain relationships no doubt exist between the four terms, but they must be more complex than would be allowed by a quadripartite structure, which would be reminiscent, even if only appoximately, of that of a Klein group (cf. *OTM*, pp. 356–8). It is of course possible to pass from one term to the other, which is what I have done in several ways in the preceding sections, but this diversity of approach is proof in itself that this cannot be achieved by a simple operation on each term. Except in the case of two sisters, the transition requires a sequence of operations.

The difficulty, when formulated in this way, is of interest from the point of view of methodology. As can always be observed in circumstances of this kind, it is not the myths which are at fault, but the incomplete analysis that has been made of them. The anomaly which is holding us up arises from a too hasty formalization. In defining the four overtures as I did, I bypassed two problems which require to be solved. First, following the apparent content of the myths too closely, I attempted to construct a *four*-term system with only three kinship relations, the reason being that, superficially at least, the myths illustrate four distinct uses of three kinship relations: grandmother, mother and sister. It followed from this that the first two were each used once, whereas the third had to be used twice: in order to define Overture II (incestuous sister), and Overture I (chaste sister). This procedure introduced an initial imbalance into the four-overture system.

Next, and more importantly, it should be realized that, according to which myths are being considered, sometimes only one of the three relations has a relevant function, sometimes several. For instance, the Klamath myth M_{538}, which was the starting-point of the analysis because it illustrated more clearly than the others what we have agreed to call Overture I, cannot be defined exclusively by reference to the incestuous sister, since it also features two other female characters: a grandmother who behaves like an ogress to her grandchildren, and a young married woman who is so protective towards the children she is carrying in her womb that she is ready to sacrifice her own life in order to save theirs. So far, this character, known as Meadowlark, had seemed to have no more than an anecdotal interest, and indeed she occupies only a modest place in the myths of the Loon Woman cycle. However, not only shall we presently see her reappearing in a parallel mythic series ($M_{612-642}$; see below, pp. 286–96) with a regularity which cannot be fortuitous, but also only by accepting that the *protective mother's* function in Overture I is as relevant as that of the cannibalistic grandmother and the incestuous sister, can we establish a correlational and oppositional relationship between this character and the character of the *mother turned ogress* (= destructive) in Overture IV. In both cases, the person in question is a mother, but in the one instance she is pregnant, in the other she is menstruating: two conditions to which a mother is equally prone, but which are mutually exclusive, like the loving and murderous attitudes that the myths associate respectively with the two conditions.

When approached from this angle, even the tiniest details in the myths throw light on each other. The mother in $M_{538-539}$ saves the children she is carrying in her womb from the fire by lying on her belly on the ground so that her body can protect them by acting as a shelter. Symmetrically, as long as the mother in M_{606a} is in the menstrual hut, the latter acts as a protection for other people (whom the woman is to massacre when she comes out); and when the myth states that her children came to visit her at the hut, it implicitly stresses the fact that the children were outside, not inside.

Superficial analysis was enough to break down the character of the sister into two symmetrical functions: an incestuous and cannibalistic sister on the one hand (Overture I), and a chaste and protective sister on the other (Overture II). We now discover that the character of the mother also covers two functions of the same type, thus giving a correlational and oppositional relationship between Overture I and Overture II. What, then, of the grandmother character, whose cannibalism is the only attribute mentioned in Overture I? The title I gave to Overture III provides an answer: the grandmother is sometimes lewd, i.e., exhibits a weak form of the incestuous tendencies she displays openly in a group of myths which, as I have shown (see above, pp. 163–89), also belong to Overture III. Consequently, in order to construct the four-term system, I now have at my disposal not three simple kinship relations, as I thought at the beginning (only, however, through taking the liberty of reduplicating the sister character – a procedure which was soon to appear unwarranted, since it could be applied only to this character), but three relations, each one of which masks a pair of oppositions. The sister can be incestuous or chaste, the mother cannibalistic or protective, the grandmother cannibalistic or incestuous. Lastly, the mythic combinatory process does not operate on terms, but on the differentials between pairs, each of which is taken from the initial group of six terms. We are now able, then, to structure the four overtures into a coherent system:

OVERTURES:	I	II	III	IV
SISTER	incestuous	protective		
GRAND- MOTHER	cannibalistic		incestuous	
MOTHER	protective			cannibalistic

Although satisfactory from the formal point of view, the system is deficient on semantic grounds. It explains how the myths are composed but tells us nothing about what they say. Let us try therefore to simplify the pattern, if only to learn yet again that every time we succeed in reducing a structure, there is no loss of meaning — contrary to what imperceptive critics too often assert; we acquire a conceptual tool which, when applied to the raw material of the myth, enables us to extract from it even more meaning than was first thought possible. But every simplification supposes that certain details of the myths, which we had thought we could safely disregard because they were devoid of meaning, have been given a significance and integrated within the framework of a general explanation.

The truth of this principle has been demonstrated in connection with the Meadowlark character. As a pregnant woman, she embodies the fertile mode of physiological youth, just as the menstruating mother character — who is correlative to her — also embodies youth (since she too is a mother) but in a temporarily sterile mode. So, in Overture IV, she has the same semantic function as devolves, in Overture I, on the incestuous sister, who is also menstruating, according to several versions, and sometimes married, but never a mother, since Overture I opposes Loon Woman and Meadowlark Woman, the latter assuming the maternal function as a pregnant woman who, correspondingly, cannot menstruate. It should not be supposed that I am crediting the Indians with physiological knowledge they probably did not possess. For the interpretation to be valid they had only to be acquainted with a fact of experience: a menstruating woman is not pregnant, and a pregnant woman does not menstruate.

Let us now try to interpret the grandmother character along the same lines. I have already put forward (p. 268) a reason of a formal kind for regarding her as a woman past the menopause, and the same conclusion can be deduced from myths belonging to Overture III, which seem, but only seem, to contradict the hypothesis. The hero of M_{501b}, and $M_{572-574}$ (see above, pp. 191–2) falsely accuses his grandmother of having her periods, but the episode occurs in that primordial, topsy-turvy world where even young women have not yet begun to menstruate. What we have here, then, is one instance among many of the trickster demiurge's comic imagination. By obliging the old woman to observe an alimentary taboo which no longer applies at her time of life, he is simply trying to appropriate all the meat, since the condition he is humorously attributing to his grandmother absolves him from giving her a share.

It is obvious that a woman beyond the menopause forms a system with a pregnant woman and a menstruating mother: like the former, she can no longer menstruate, and like the latter she cannot be pregnant. Far from defining her in terms of physiological youth, the myths in Overture III condemn her to a process of aging and are careful to stress its irreversible course (see above, pp. 175–84), thus creating an opposition with the other two eminently reversible conditions: as long as a woman can still have children she is alternately pregnant or not pregnant, available or menstruating.

To obtain a quadripartite system with an explanatory value it only remains now to deal with the heroine of Overture II, the chaste, protective sister, in the same connection. But no sooner does this logical necessity present itself than the myths themselves supply the required motif in the form of a detail which was previously overlooked either because it seemed to be of little interest, or, as was more probably the case in this instance, because it was given an incomplete explanation solely in terms of the syntagmatic chain, since, at the time, I did not have at my disposal the necessary paradigmatic set to bring out its significance in that differential light without which any attempt to grasp meanings is a pure illusion.

Let us go back, then, to the text of M_{541}. The heroine possesses the remarkable faculty of being able, at will, to assume the appearance either of a radiant young girl or of a bowed, emaciated old woman. In quoting and commenting on this feature (pp. 65 and 71), I was content to use it as an argument in favour of the lunar affinity of the demiurge's mother. But we can now see that it means very much more, *since it contrasts the chaste sister and the lewd grandmother in the same way as the pregnant woman is contrasted with the menstruating mother*. These last two women connote physiological youth, fertile and sterile. The first two women connote old age, reversible ($\equiv$ fertile) and irreversible ($\equiv$ sterile). But the lunar affinity is not thereby rendered invalid. On the contrary, it takes place in a more inclusive explanatory system, by allowing the establishment of additional links between the terms. The heroine, who can be alternatively young or old, has a metaphorical affinity with the moon and, if we take into consideration the fact that the North American Indians tended to overestimate rather than underestimate the connection between menstruation and the moon's phases (*OTM*, pp. 222–3), we can understand that there might be a metonymical affinity between a menstruating woman and the moon. So, in both North and South America we are dealing with a periodicity of short cycles, the serial nature of which I stressed in the previous volume (*OTM*, pp. 111–13), where I also established a correlational and oppositional relationship between it and a longer, structural type of periodicity, illustrated in the present context by the other two terms. These two terms are, precisely, in a relationship of complementarity to each other: a woman who dies while pregnant but in giving birth to posthumous children bears witness to the irreversible power of life, just as an old woman who has to be convinced that, in spite of her efforts to retain some kind of sexual activity, she has no hope of regaining her youth bears witness to the irreversible power of death. The older generations have to disappear, so that the young can take their place. The whole of the North American philosophy of death revolves around this theme: if the dead could be resuscitated or old people rejuvenated, the world would soon become overpopulated; there would no longer be room for everybody.

So, at the same time as we apprehend the latent mythic dialectic contrasting youth and age, fertility and sterility, short and slow periodicity, reversible and irreversible changes and life and death, we can grasp the pattern governing its development. In spite of, or because of, its simplicity, this pattern has a logical structure at the same time at it is semantically effective. It can be reduced to a quadripartite formula, in which the pregnant woman is opposed to the menstruating mother, just as the grandmother who cannot recapture her youth, in spite of her lewdness, is opposed to the sister, who counts on the reversibility of the aging process to ensure her virginity. In the last resort, the opposition between fertile youth and sterile youth, and the symmetrical opposition between reversible and irreversible old age, can be expressed in a form that we have already encountered on a previous occasion (cf. *OTM*, p. 403): $x, \ -x, \ \dfrac{1}{x} \ - \ \dfrac{1}{x}$.

2   The Market Place

I have just broadened my field of enquiry by including the Sahaptin versions
of the Bird-nester myth, and this has enabled me to effect a considerable
simplification of the model. In its new form, it combines the four different
ways in which the myth can begin, shows their logical relationships and
reveals their common meaning. However, as I mentioned on p. 261, these
Sahaptin versions pose further problems, since, in a sense, they complicate
the model by adding fresh episodes to the story, which thus seems to
become progressively longer. As we have already seen, the Chinook versions
produced an unexpected extension with the episode of the freeing of the
salmon, and this is why Sapir declared it to be a separate myth, arbitrarily
joined on to the first part of the narrative through some historical accident.
I have shown that this is not the case: the salmon-freeing episode, in its own
way, brings to light the latent content of a mythic pattern, which, in both
North and South America, is concerned with the origin of fire or water.
However, the Sahaptin versions do not simply retain this episode, while
leaving it in the same place as in the Chinook versions; they follow it up
with two additional episodes: the reciprocal theft of food, and the
demiurge's organization of the physical and social world (see above,
pp. 264–5).

It is as if the North American forms of the myth were composed of
building blocks like those used in children's construction sets. Once the
central piece corresponding to the bird-nester episode has been placed in

position (cf. $M_{529-531}$), each narrator seems to be free to add any number of blocks on either side. On one side, the episode of the mother, or the grandmother, who turns into a grizzly bear, or occasionally the incestuous sister episode; on the other side, and again according to the whim of the narrator, the episodes featuring the freeing of the salmon, the theft of food, and the ordering of the world. This gives a total of six elements, of which the Klamath and the Modoc use from one to three, according to the particular version: the central element followed, as the case may be, by the second and the first. The Chinook versions use only the third and fourth elements, the Kalapuya versions only the fourth (corresponding to a modified form of the freeing of the salmon); finally, the Sahaptin versions use from the second to the sixth, leaving out only the first, which corresponds to the Loon Woman cycle.

I showed, however, that the introduction of the fourth element into the Chinook version was not accidental, and I must now solve the same difficulty in connection with the last two elements, by enquiring whether they add anything new to the narrative. After stocking the rivers with fish and inventing fishing techniques, Coyote learns to his cost that he has not yet achieved a secure food supply, since the existence of food and of the practical means of obtaining it are not enough in themselves. A further requirement is that creatures as closely related as the wolf and the coyote must each agree to consume that portion of the natural resources to which they are entitled, instead of stealing from each other, and they must do so, even if the kinds of food intended for *terrestrial* and very similar quadrupeds differ from each other as widely as fish of *aquatic* origin and the eggs of birds of *celestial origin*. A microcosm defined in terms of different diets thus reflects the image of a still chaotic world. After experiencing all the disadvantages of such a world, Coyote brings it to an end by promulgating his law: not all fish will be caught anywhere; like the zoological species, human beings will be divided up into tribes on the earth's surface; they will speak different languages and will meet at fairs, where they will exchange foodstuffs, raw materials and manufactured goods. A well-ordered diversity will replace a chaotic medley of types; war and theft will disappear, to be replaced by markets.

The two new episodes introduced by the Sahaptin versions are linked, then, by a necessary relation, since together they fulfil one and the same complex etiological function. After the creation of salmon and fishing, they institute first of all the *spatial* diversity of species of fish and the *temporal* periodicity of their habits; then, the *cultural* diversity of peoples as it is shown by the multiplicity of languages; and lastly, the combined *economic* and *social* solution provided by intertribal exchanges covering both material possessions and women. Consequently, the same myth which, in South America, allows tribes at a low technical and economic level to institute the existence of a form of cooking reduced to its basic elements – fire, water and meat – plays a similar role in North America; however, the pattern changes and the myth has a different centre of gravity among communities who were fishermen rather than hunters, and who were able to create such elaborate institutions as the great international trade fairs held along the lower reaches of the Columbia River.

To enable the reader to appreciate the importance and complexity of these exchanges, I propose to quote, almost in full, the description recorded by Teit at the beginning of the century (13, pp. 121–2) and supplied by elderly informants. After explaining how the introduction of the horse gave a great impetus to native trade by allowing the Indians to transport to the markets baskets full of root-cakes and sun-dried berries, which in former times had been too heavy and cumbersome to be worth carrying, he states that in the past trading had been restricted chiefly to light, valuable articles.

The Inland communities sold pipes, tobacco, ornaments of certain kinds, Indian hemp [*Apocynum*], dressed skins, bows and some other things to the Coast tribes, in exchange for which they received chiefly shells of various kinds. Some horses were also sold to the Coast people. Trading at The Dalles was in skins, fur, fish, oil, roots, pemmican, feathers, robes, clothing, shells, slaves and horses. On the whole, products of the Lower Columbia, the Coast and the northern or Oregon country were exchanged for products of the interior east and north.

Many of the products obtained by the Columbia Salish at The Dalles and west of the Cascades were carried across country and sold to the Sanpoil, Okanagon, and others, at a profit. The Columbia also sold horses to these tribes and large quantities of shells and shell and bone beads. The beads and *dentalium* shells were on strings and sold by measurement. Freshwater shells were used as pendants, earrings, and the like, by all the tribes, but the larger, bright-coloured shells of two or three kinds procured from the coast were much more valued. It seems that the Sanpoil and Okanagon also obtained most of their copper and many stone implements, such as greenstone celts, adzes, war-clubs and the like, from the Columbia Salish, who also sold some coiled basketry and goatswool blankets to them. There was very little direct trading with the Thompson, the Okanagon doing most of this trade. Minor trading centres were near the mouth of the Snake and the Okanagon. The Columbia also did considerable trading with the Spokane. Products from as far south as the Modoc, Rogue River, and Shasta, reached The Dalles, also from a considerable distance north and south on the coast and from the Plains.

Revais {one of Teit's informants} said that the greatest intertribal trading place was at The Dalles. The people there lived entirely by fishing and trading. They bought almost anything brought to them, and resold it again. Grande Ronde, in eastern Oregon, was an important trading place. Other places were the mouth of the Cowlitz, near Scappoose; opposite the mouth of the Lewis; near Oregon City; the western Grande Ronde; the middle Nisqually, the upper Puyallup, near the mouth of the Okanagon; near Colville; and near the mouth of the Snake; but there were other minor trading places in the territories of most tribes. Considerable trade from the west and south-west of Oregon and from Klamath country (or river), passed through the Kalapuya to Oregon City and thence to The Dalles. There was also an old trade route from the coast by way of the Nehalem to near Scappoose, whence it branched north up the Cowlitz, and east up the Columbia. Nehalem, Cowlitz, Tlatskanai, Chinook and various tribes traded on the Columbia at this point. Things traded, say, at the Grande Ronde and Okanagon were re-traded at The Dalles. Products from the coasts of Washington and Oregon, Puget Sound, the plateaus of the interior to the north and east, the Plains, the interior of Oregon and northern California reached The Dalles.

Slaves were very numerous on the lower Columbia and at The Dalles long ago. They were boys and girls and some adults. All the Oregon tribes dealt more or less in slaves, and so did the Coast people. The Dalles people always bought slaves and resold them. Of the slaves who reached The Dalles, a few were Snake Indians, some were from the Coast, and others from California. Some were from Rogue River and the Shasta, by way of the Klamath and the Kalapuya, who bought them from other tribes or captured them in war. Practically nearly all were captives of war in the first place, but some were slaves' children and grandchildren. There were no interior Salish or Sahaptin people kept, or bought, as slaves, either at The Dalles or elsewhere.

Shells, beads, Hudson Bay blankets, robes, cloths, horses and fish were probably the principal things traded, also slaves, canoes, dressed skins, furs and the like. Furs sold by The Dalles people to the Hudson's Bay Company were all procured from other tribes. In later days they had few for sale, as the trapping tribes traded directly with various posts. Some people of the following tribes came to The Dalles in the trading season: Columbia, Spokane, Yakima, Klikitat, Tyighpam, Wallawalla, Umatilla, Cayuse and sometimes Palouse, Nez Percé, Klamath, Molala and Kalapuya. On the whole, the exchange of products at The Dalles was south and south-west *versus* north and north-east. The Wishram and Dalles people generally, and the Kalapuya, were always more or less hostile to the white traders. They resented the direct trade with neighbouring tribes, considering that they should by right act as middlemen.

How does such a system affect myths which we first encountered among communities of tropical America with a much more rudimentary economic structure? Basically in two ways. On the one hand, fish takes the place of meat as the main raw material of cooking; on the other, the transition from nature to culture is signified not so much by the elementary culinary process which changes the raw into the cooked, as by commercial transactions which allow the transition from a monotonous diet to a varied one, rather in the way we ourselves, through the improvement in living standards, think in terms of the items in what economists refer to as the 'housewife's shopping basket', unlike our forefathers who gave thanks for their 'daily bread'. In this system, in which the original relationships between each community and nature are, in a sense, complicated by the complementary relationships that the different communities gradually establish with one another, all the parts are coherent: there is an exchange of messages, thanks to the fact that some Indians spoke several languages, or used the Chinook lingua franca as a means of intertribal communication, long before the Whites adopted it in their dealings with the Indians and extended its use from the Californian coast to that of Alaska (Ray 4, p. 36, n. 9, p. 99; Jacobs 7); an exchange of goods: preserved foods, the chief of which was dried fish, either whole or in the form of flour, fish oil, furs, basketwork, sea-shells, horses and slaves; and thirdly, an exchange of women. In this last connection, evidence recorded among the Kalapuya, who were neighbours of the Chinook and the Sahaptin to the south of Columbia River, shows clearly that, in this area more than elsewhere, marriages were looked upon as being inseparable from commercial transactions, and indeed were part and parcel of them. 'Formerly,' according to one informant, 'when an Indian wanted a woman, he always had to buy her. He would not have been able just to choose one within the family circle; he had to obtain her from someone else in exchange for cash.' The husband of an adulterous woman demanded compensation in money from his rival; and if she had been raped, he demanded that the culprit should give him the equivalent of what he had paid for her, since 'nobody should have a woman for nothing'. Consequently, a father with several daughters could reckon on making a lot of money by marrying them off. There was a moment of dramatic excitement during the marriage ceremony when the young girl was carried to the place where the valuables for which she was to be exchanged were arranged in a heap. If her father considered the pile to be high enough he gave the order for her to be put down; if not, the man carrying her hoisted her still higher on to his shoulders. When there was agreement, the woman was handed over to the bridegroom's family and the money to the bride's family: 'money', i.e. valuables, consisted of sea-shells threaded on to pieces of string, the length of which could be readily measured by means of a guide mark tattooed on the forearm. When a man was described as being rich, this meant that he had plenty of money, belonged to the best society, would have no difficulty in obtaining a wife and owned many slaves (Jacobs 4, pp. 43–7). Similar attitudes are found throughout the area we have been studying. Among the Nez Percé, who were eastern relatives of the Sahaptin, the 'marriage visit', which the family and friends of the suitor used to make to those of the future bride, involved a solemn exchange of presents: dried meat, packed in leather bags, and new clothes were handed over in exchange for edible berries contained in plaited baskets and worn clothes. The husband's family also gave horses, implements and weapons; the wife's family expensive beads, ornaments and bead and quillwork (Phinney, p. 41, n. 1). The Modoc, on the opposite side of the area, compressed their philosophy of marriage into a pithy statement: the happy father of a young woman, who, once married, saw to it that her own family was kept supplied with food, exclaimed: 'That is what daughters are for, to feed us from whatever family they marry into' (Curtin 1, p. 264).

A Sahaptin myth, in which, as in the bird-nester myth, the chief characters are Eagle and Coyote — although here they are, respectively, an elder and younger brother, one a hunter and the other just a game-carrier — establishes an even more direct connection between fishing and the search for a wife. It tells (M_{610}; Jacobs 3, pp. 223–5) how Coyote met a pretty young woman who told him that she wanted to marry a person of noble rank. Coyote suggested Eagle, his brother; the woman was delighted and asked Coyote to sound him on this matter. Eagle, when asked, would have nothing to do with the plan, and Coyote thought that he himself would try his luck. But the woman preferred to change into a salmon. She knew that people would soon appear on the earth and that she would supply them with a superior form of food. Coyote made the first fish basket-trap, and decreed that this was how it would always be when the people arrived: 'Now,' he added, 'I am going as far as there is land, and as far as there are all sorts of different places. For in the future there will be in the same manner all kinds of different languages and peoples. And henceforth, no woman will on her own initiative marry a nobleman. In future men will seek women, and no woman will go about seeking men. That is how Coyote laid down the law for Salmon Woman, and this is the way it is to this very day; nowhere will a woman go forth to seek a nobleman in marriage.'

It will be noted that this transformation of a woman into a salmon to escape from an unwanted suitor links up with the one we have already met with in M_{541}, where a man changes into a salmon in order to follow the woman he loves (see above, pp. 66, 78). Like M_{541}, M_{610} is an inversion of the bird-nester myth, although in a different way and along different axes. In M_{610}, Eagle is older than Coyote; he rejects the only available woman, instead of possessing many wives. Far from trying to appropriate the woman for himself, Coyote even agrees to act as go-between with a view to persuading Eagle to marry her.

In M_{606a}, a Sahaptin version of the bird-nester, Coyote proposes marriage to a woman who, rather than accept, commits suicide in the hot embers of a cooking fire; consequently, the food disappears with her. Here, the opposite is the case: the woman whom Coyote would like to marry chooses to drown herself and, as a result, food appears. So, in M_{610}, salmon is created by a woman who is anxious to escape from Coyote, whereas, in M_{606a} and other myths ($M_{601-602}$, M_{607}), salmon are freed against the wish of women who welcomed Coyote as their adoptive descendant or ancestor, and without the latter putting himself forward as a potential husband.

We may now ask what these reversals correspond to. The two myths would seem to have the same etiological function, since M_{610} also explains the origin of salmon in the first place, then that of the diversity of peoples and languages, and lastly that of a well regulated social life. But the point is that the rules are not the same in both cases. M_{606a} deals with the establishment of fairs and commercial exchanges which, as we have seen, were associated with the buying of women (cf. above, M_{608}, and below, M_{614}, p. 282). All these transactions involved intertribal communication, since goods which a tribe could not produce itself had to be obtained from strangers, and since, as is so forcibly expressed by the Kalapuya when they make exogamy a function of wife-buying, it was necessary to marry non-relatives *as a consequence* of the rule which included women among the things that could be bought. M_{610}, however, is less concerned with external differences between groups than with internal differences within the group: differences between men and women who cannot observe the same rules of behaviour, and differences between nobles and ordinary people, or people of indefinite status, who cannot intermarry. These restrictive rules run counter to exchange: they stipulate an attitude of stand-offishness that the spirit of exchange suggests should be overcome. We can understand, then, why Coyote is so enthusiastic about the idea of his brother marrying the beautiful stranger, since the myths represent him as having a mania for exchange: 'Wherever he went, he found all sorts of things that were good: he would trade in order to obtain them, and they became his' (Jacobs 1, p. 100). Unfortunately for him, he does not always know when to stop. For instance, he exchanges his own penis for another which is able to fell trees, like an axe. Coyote, however, is rash enough to cross open ground; in the absence of trees, his penis turns against him and he has to return it hastily to its original owner: 'That is how Coyote was a trader' (M_{611a}; Jacobs 1, pp. 74–6; cf. Chinook, M_{611b}, see below, p. 438). Or, on another occasion, he cannot resist swapping eyes with a juggler, who can throw his up into the air and catch them again; when Coyote tries to do the same, the buzzard flies off with the eyes. Coyote makes himself a replacement pair with flowers, which wilt and so he becomes blind. Finally, he succeeds in exchanging eyes with a bird, which henceforth has to live close to the ground through short-sightedness, or with a snail, which has been blind ever since ($M_{612a, b, c}$; Jacobs 1, pp. 100–101, 109, 208–209; and M_{375b}, Adamson, pp. 173–4).

Coyote, the great 'trader', was also a keen appreciator of diversity. It was he who scattered the edible roots, fruit and seeds that a greedy child had stored away inside his belly ($M_{613a, b}$; Jacobs 1, pp. 62–4); the Nez Percé replace the child by a monster, whose body Coyote subsequently divided up and scattered in various parts of the country, by that act 'forenaming the various people' (M_{613c}; Phinney, pp. 26–9). The western Sahaptin, similarly, relate that 'he made all sorts of different things . . . peoples . . . languages. Since that time it is his law' (Jacobs 1, pp. 96–8). A series of myths from the same source or of Salish origin feature Coyote as hero and elder brother, with Fox as his younger brother ($M_{614a, b, c, d}$; Jacobs 1, pp. 96–8, 112–13, 169–71). The new transformation modifies the etiological function of the myths, which are now concerned with the origin of peoples who are not only strangers but enemies ('the Sioux', according to M_{614a}); with the origin of a competitive game, such as a running match, which takes the place of commercial exchanges; and with the origin of winter, whereas the fairs were held in summer. I shall return to this point later (see below, pp. 322–3). For the moment, it will suffice to note that the strangers visited by Coyote and Fox insist that they should run a race with their Chief's daughter. This Indian Atalanta will marry any competitor who outruns her, but losers are beheaded. Coyote fails and loses his head; Fox wins and brings his elder brother back to life. Whereupon, continues M_{614c}, the heroes kill everybody, except the people they hold to ransom and force to hand over all sorts of valuable objects. Coyote sings as he takes them away: 'This will be for procuring a wife, for the first gift exchange; this will be for brothers-in-law and sisters-in-law; this will be for nieces; this will be for a deceased wife's relatives. And this will be for illicit loves.' It is remarkable that we should again encounter here the concept of differentials being created within a decimated community, where the demiurge spares only the wealthiest members. We have already met it right at the beginning of the first volume of this series, in a Bororo myth (M_2, RC, pp. 49–50), the conclusion of which is worth recalling: 'He did not kill those who brought him many, but killed those who brought him few.' By a dialectical movement which was the reverse of the one I have just described in North America (p. 281), the South American myth dealt with the establishment of an *internal order*: one which makes it possible, within a social group, to create a distinction between superior and inferiors, nobles and common people. To institute the existence of *external order*, as it is expressed by the physical differences between neighbouring peoples, the Bororo use another myth based on the same pattern (M_3; RC, p. 51). The hero escapes death, which is cosmic in origin, because his progress is slowed down by a limp, whereas in the Sahaptin myths, the hero entrusted with the symmetrical mission begins by suffering a death which is human in origin, because he cannot run fast enough. It is clear that the mythic systems of both South and North America correspond to each other on this point too.

If the preceding analysis is correct, it follows that the same myths which the Brazilian Indians use to establish the origin of cooking are used by the Indians of the Columbia River basin to establish the origin of commercial exchanges. The South American myths about the origin of cooking are transformed, *in situ*, into myths explaining the origin of meat on the one hand, and cultivated plants on the other; that, at least, is what I was trying to establish in the first volume of this series. In a region of North America where fishing rather than hunting was the main source of food and there was no agriculture, myths about the origin of fish automatically changed into myths about the origin of exchanges, which enabled tribes to obtain fish when they had none, or if they had, to obtain berries, seeds and wild roots in exchange for fish. The existence of a market economy leads to a transformation on the level of the superstructures. Instead of the transition from nature to culture being expressed by means of a straightforward opposition between the categories of the *raw* and the *cooked*, it resorts to a more complex ideology which expresses the relevant opposition in terms of contrasting maxims: *every man for himself* and *give and take*.

All this can be established in another way, by introducing a group of myths also of Sahaptin origin, the initial sequence of which gives a literal repetition of Overture IV, the overture peculiar to the Sahaptin versions of the bird-nester story.

M_{615}. *Klikitat. 'The two she-bears'*

An Indian (called Bow as in M_{606a}, according to one version; Jacobs 1, p. 159) had married two sisters: the elder, called Grizzly and the mother of a little girl; the younger called Bear and childless. They would go everywhere to gather roots and wild fruits, but always in different directions. Grizzly forbade that it should be otherwise.

One day, Bear picked a quarrel with her niece and whipped her: the little girl was frightened and dared not complain. Her fear made Bear bolder; she went off to investigate the patches her sister had marked off for herself. There she found a great many huckleberries (this term designates various species, cf. Gunther 3, pp. 43–4). Ever since seeing her daughter in tears, Grizzly had been suspicious; she became furious when she recognized the sister's tracks. Bear, however, stole a march on her sister: she defecated wherever the berries were becoming ripe, returned home, killed her niece and took off her entire hide and dressed it on a stick, while she buried the little girl; then she fled, having resolved never to see her sister again.

When Grizzly reached home, she thought first of all that the child was standing at the water's edge, but she soon realized that she was dead. She followed Bear's tracks to the gathering grounds, where the faeces left by her sister called out to her from all directions. Grizzly became completely confused and ran right and left until she was tired out. Bear, however, had succeeded in obliterating her tracks and was never seen again (Jacobs 1, pp. 45–7; cf. pp. 159–63 and M_{654}, pp. 186–8).

Nearly all the myths belonging to this group emphasize a difference between the two women: one chooses only the ripe berries, the other gathers green berries, as well as leaves and twigs, which diminish the value of her harvest ($M_{618, 620, 630}$ etc.). At first, the women are careful not to encroach on each other's territory ($M_{615, 628}$); the situation deteriorates when, in the heat of their quarrel, they forget this rule of behaviour. In most versions, the consequence is a reciprocal massacre, after which the survivors part company for good. However, separation provides a lesson which the narrator of M_{615} expounds quite clearly: 'That is the Klikitat myth. Nowadays there are just bear and grizzly, and they are no longer persons. The myth does not say more. At the present time they never eat one another's food. And whenever they have found one or the other's eating place, they never go to that place. And that is how they have been ever since that time' (Jacobs 1, p. 47).

It is not important to know whether or not the etiology of the ursidae confirms the myth's conclusion. Like M_{606a}, M_{615} begins at a time when humans and animals were indistinguishable. A quarrel between mythic beings, who, in both cases, are a Bear Woman and a Grizzly Woman, leads in the one instance to the creation of mankind, through the setting up of fairs and markets, which allow humans to find their food *according to culture*, that is, by the exchange of their respective means of subsistence. In the other instance, the same conflict is resolved by the permanent transformation of the mythic beings into animals. Being now obliged to feed *according to nature*, each will henceforth find and eat his own food. Except in certain cases, which the myths also envisage, and for which they work out individual solutions, as we shall see presently (Part Four, 3), exchange has no place in nature, since nature offers no middle term between self-reliance and aggression against others.

Before broaching this last theoretical aspect of exchange, as it is presented in the myths, we need to look at one difficulty. As well as belonging to the group under discussion, M_{615} also forms part of another group which, ever since Dangel published his brief summary of it, has been referred to by American mythographers as 'fawns versus bears'. It is thickly distributed over a limited area, extending from the Kwakiutl of British Columbia in the north, to the Pomo and Miwok of central California in the south.[1] Let us

---

[1] This following inventory of the variants is not exhaustive: Clackamas: $M_{616-619}$; Jacobs 2, Part I, pp. 130–66; Kathlamet: M_{620}; Boas 7, p. 118; Thompson: $M_{621\,a-d}$; Boas 13, p. 16; Hill-Tout 4, p. 95; Teit 4, pp. 69–72; 5, pp. 218–24; Lilloet: M_{662}; Teit 2, pp. 321–3; Shuswap: M_{623}; Teit 1, pp. 681–4; Chehalis: M_{624}; Hill-Tout 2, pp. 360–62; Snohomish: M_{625}; Haeberlin 1, p. 422; Comox: M_{626}; Boas 13, p. 81; Kwakiutl: $M_{627\,a,\,b}$; Boas 13, p. 168, Boas-Hunt 1, p. 15; Kalapuya: M_{628}; Jacobs 4, p. 115; Coos: M_{629}, Jacobs 6, p. 152; Takelina: M_{630}; Sapir 5, p. 117; Klamath: $M_{631\,a-c}$; Gatschet 1, Part I, p. 118; Stern 1, p. 51; Barker 1, p. 7; Sinkyone: M_{632}; Kroeber 12, p. 349; Lassik: M_{633}; Goddard 5, p. 135; Kato: M_{634}; Goddard 6, p. 221; Yana: M_{635}; Sapir 3, pp. 203–208; Maidu: $M_{636\,a,\,b}$; Barrett 2, pp. 327–54; Miwok: $M_{641\,a-c}$; Gifford 2, pp. 286, 333; Kroeber 13, pp. 203–204; C. H. Merriam, p. 103; Shoshone: M_{642}; Lowie 12, p. 253; cf. also Klamath-Modoc: $M_{373\,a,\,b,\,c}$; Barker 1, pp. 50–57; Stern 1, pp. 39–40; Curtin 1, pp. 249–53. For a general discussion, see Boas 2, pp. 586–8.

pause to examine this point. Although the leading characters vary, these myths always describe a primitive state in which animals belonging to different species and standing in opposition to each other (sometimes the characters may be an animal and a plant) live in a state of proximity which is contrary to nature: at that time they were siblings, affines or friends. Before long cohabitation leads to disaster: the most ferocious creature kills the weakest, and the children take revenge by massacring their play-fellows. The killers flee, pursued by their victims' mother, and succeed in escaping from her.

The families who have turned into enemies consist of bears of different species (M_{615}, $M_{616-619}$, M_{621}, $M_{624-625}$, M_{628}, M_{629}, M_{630}), or bears and deer. The second form would seem to be peripheral in relationship to the first, since it can also be observed among the Kwakiutl in the north (M_{627}), as well as among the Klamath (M_{631}), the Athapaskan of California ($M_{632-634}$), the Yana (M_{635}), the Maidu (M_{636}), the Wappo (M_{637}), the Pomo ($M_{638-640}$) and the Miwok (M_{641}) in the south; and finally, to the east, among the Shoshone (M_{642}). But the motif can be traced even farther away from its main area of distribution, since we have already encountered it among the Assiniboine and the Ojibwa (M_{373a}, M_{374}, *OTM*, pp. 60–63). Since, in that context, the relevant opposition occurred between a human family and a family of frogs, for the transformation group to be transitive, there should exist an intermediary state contrasting deer and frogs. As it happens, this state is found among the Klamath and the Modoc ($M_{373b, c}$; *OTM*, p. 60). The cycle as a whole might therefore be expressed by the following formula: (*Grizzly : Bear*) :: (*Bear : Deer*) :: (*Deer : Frog*) :: (*Frog : Human*), but for one or two aberrant versions, which present difficulties. One, a Shuswap myth (M_{623}), establishes an opposition between bears and beavers, another belonging to the Kathlamet (M_{620}), between the American robin (*Turdus migratorius*) and Salmonberry Woman (salmonberry = *Rubus spectabilis*). Since I am not aiming at an exhaustive study of the group, I propose to leave aside these exceptions, which do not affect the unity of the system.

This unity is made clear by several coincidences which cannot be accidental, and which occur sometimes over quite considerable distances. First, a linguistic coincidence. Gatschet (1, Part I, p. 124) and Barker (1, p. 9, n. 5) were almost a century apart, and they both seem to have had difficulty in translating an expression, which they reproduced independently in their respective versions of the same myth. After the murder of their mother, the young 'antelopes' (or deer, cf. Stern 1, pp. 39–40) asphyxiate their little bear playmates. Throughout the operation, they chant *lepleputea* (Gatschet) or *leplep p'ot'e* (Barker). Gatschet believes this to be an archaic expression meaning roughly two pairs of opponents who are trying to asphyxiate each other with smoke. Barker gives a similar translation, but draws attention to certain philological difficulties raised by it. While it would be unthinkable to question the competence of either scholar, it is nevertheless a remarkable fact that, four hundred kilometres farther north, the Clackamas Chinook, who speak a different language, tell in one of their versions of the same myth (Jacobs 2, Part I, p. 148) how Grizzly Woman, thinking it is her enemy's children who are cooking in the stew and not her own, sings exultantly, and more than twelve times in succession, *'leplepleplepleplep'*, an expression which is left untranslated but seems to be phonetically identical with the one in the Klamath myth, and very similar to the one transcribed as *'WaLotEp helatep'*, etc. by Boas (7, pp. 124–5) in the Kathlamet version.

When I consulted him about the implications and significance of this coincidence, Professor Dell Hymes, a distinguished expert in the Chinook dialects, referred me to an exclamation uttered by Coyote in a Wasco myth: *'walxalaep walxalaep'* (Hymes 1). In his view, the Kathlamet expression is not analysable, although it appears to be similar to expressions denoting the action of breathing or calling for help. As for the Clackamas expression, Professor Hymes thinks it is the verb 'to boil', repeated several times in succession. To account for the occurrence in the same context of verbal forms phonetically similar in Klamath and Clackamas (although with different meanings) Hymes cautiously puts forward the hypothesis that the two languages may have preserved a very ancient phonetic symbolism since, in spite of their present remoteness from each other, both belong to the Penutian linguistic family.

But in any case these explanations would solve only part of the problem, since in a Thompson myth, that is, in one belonging to the Salish linguistic family, without any connection with the Penutian group, a grizzly bear tries to extinguish a fire with earth, while shouting *'lîpa, lîpa, lîpa'*, an expression which Teit (4, pp. 61, 113, n. 205) explains as follows: 'Bears make a noise somewhat similar to the sound of this word, which is likened to the Indian word LîpLîpt or LûpLûpt, meaning "dark".' So, the same phonetic group associated with the bear appears at different points hundreds of kilometres apart in three languages, one of which at least is completely different from the other two.

Let me now quote another coincidence which occurs over a distance at least as great if not greater than that separating the Klamath from the Thompson. One of the Clackamas variants (M_{616}; Jacobs 2, Part I, pp. 130–41) appears at first glance to be an inversion within the group, modifying on the one hand the sex of the leading characters (male bears run away with human wives) and on the other the narrative sequence (the episode of the mother who becomes a grizzly bear during menstruation occurs at the end of the myth instead of at the beginning). In this version, the grizzly bear puts out one of his wife's eyes, and the other bear blocks up his wife's anus.[2] Consequently, the two women become respectively blocked above or below, although the story throws no light on the motives behind the grizzly's behaviour, and the reversals I have mentioned change the plot so drastically that one might almost wonder if one was not dealing with a different myth. However, seven or eight hundred kilometres away, the Hokan-speaking Pomo have a quite regularly constructed version (M_{638a}; Barrett 2, pp. 327–34), which tells how the deer woman's children find their mother a very long way to the east, whereas they assumed she had been beaten to death by her sister-in-law, the bear. She had become the wife of the cannibalistic sun and had only one eye. One variant (M_{638b}; *ibid.*, pp. 334–44) even states that she has no head. The cannibalistic monster is, then, changed from a chthonian to a celestial character, and it is well known that in the myths belonging to this area of America celestial creatures are blind or one-eyed (*OTM*, pp. 151–3, and see above, p. 44). The solar ogre's servant is the bluebottle or 'bear-fly', who readily throws in his lot with his master's killers and with his widow; in the Kalapuya version (M_{628}; Jacobs 4, pp. 119–25), the blow-fly informs Grizzly that she is eating her own children, and not those of her victim. But in almost all the myths (Pomo, Clackamas, Thompson, Shuswap) it devolves on the meadowlark to give the same or a different warning to stimulate somewhat uncertain maternal feelings: she therefore fulfils a mission similar to the one assigned to the same character in the Loon Woman cycle, where she carries maternal solicitude to the point of self-sacrifice (cf. above, pp. 49, 54, 108, 271). An exhaustive study of the bears and fawns myth should therefore also take into account the role played by loons as male, helpful birds in one of the Pomo versions (M_{638a}; Barrett 2, p. 332).

It would seem from what has gone before that, in some cases, we are dealing with the same myth which has been borrowed by one tribe from another, rather than with variants evolved independently in different areas. This is true in the case of the Chinook, who were in a position to know the Klamath stories, since the Klamath frequented the banks of the Columbia River; this is borne out by the Chinook texts (Sapir 1, pp. 292–4). On the other hand, the recurrence of identical motifs in the Pomo and Chinook

---

[2] Consequently, she cannot defecate and in this aspect is an inversion of the grizzly she-bear in a Lilloet version (M_{622}; Teit 2, pp. 321–3), who is drowned by falling through a hole in the bottom of a canoe. The myth refers to the hole as 'the rectum of the canoe', thus likening the bear herself to faeces.

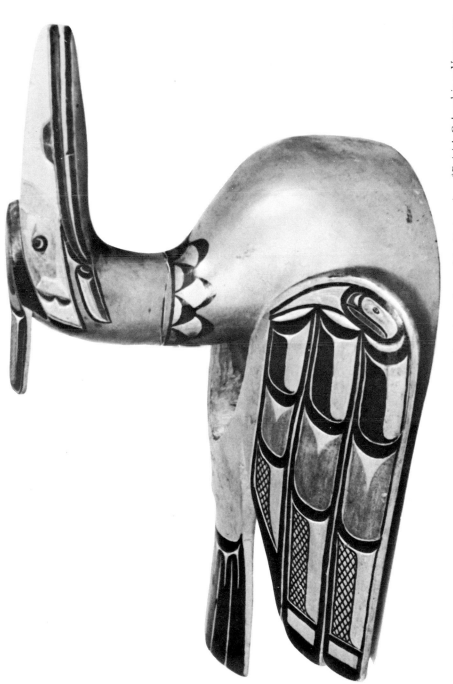

3. A Kwakiutl Indian head-dress in the form of a loon. (Museum of Anthropology of the University of British Columbia at Vancouver, A 6102; the Museum's photograph)

4. Engraving representing a parhelion. (P. C. Dablon, *Relation* etc. *en . . . 1670 et 1671*, Paris, 1672, p. 154)

versions is more easily explicable in terms of a latent pattern making itself felt throughout the distribution area of the myth. However, we have just noted that the influence of this pattern is not confined to the 'bears and fawns' cycle in the strict sense, since the myths belonging to this cycle constantly coincide with those belonging to the Loon Woman or bird-nester cycles. We may suspect, then, that these cycles, which cover approximately the same geographical area, constitute a series of parallel and superimposed mythological strata: when one layer is removed, another is exposed, and when that one has been lifted off, a third is revealed underneath . . . Although the materials which enter into the composition of the layers are different, the layers themselves have a common structure, which is a result of local pressures and of the nature of the mythological bed-rock.

Occasionally, the bed-rock surfaces at certain points where the strata, after being stretched and worn thin, have finally given way under the pressures exerted upon them. I have already quoted an example of this in the Clackamas version M_{616}, which distorts the two bears myth by subjecting it to several torsions, thus loosening up the fabric so that certain characteristic details of the bird-nester myth show through — e.g., the motif of the mother who changes into an ogress during menstruation, although the bird-nester myth belongs to a different stratum. Similarly, the Shuswap version (M_{623}; Teit 1, pp. 681–4) links up with M_{606a} through an episode which occurs in the last part of the myth instead of the first: the grizzly she-bear's corpse provides meat for the meal of which Coyote is robbed by the gatherers of bird's eggs (cf. also M_{671}; Teit 2, p. 306).

Generally speaking, the cohabitation of animal species with incompatible behaviour patterns is, in taxonomical terms, an anomaly as serious as the one expressed in the other mythological strata by incest between siblings. In the one instance, the more ferocious beast kills the one which acts as its companion, sister-in-law or co-wife, during a mutual delousing session; however, the victim had previously arranged for her children to be warned in the event of her death. These details are also found in myths belonging to the other strata: in similar circumstances, the woman who has changed into a wild animal kills her son or grandson, who also takes the precaution of ensuring that his wife and sister will be informed of his death.

The following transformation can be seen to occur, then, between one group and the other:

$$[Grizzly\ \bigcirc = \triangle = \bigcirc\ She\text{-}bear] \Rightarrow \begin{bmatrix} Grizzly\ \bigcirc = \\ \quad | \\ \bigcirc = \triangle \end{bmatrix}$$

Grizzly's son (grandson) takes the place of Bear Woman and — since the ogress is to be killed by her daughter or grand-daughter — the latter replaces the she-bear's sons who avenge their mother in the same way. Furthermore, the Sinkyone version (M_{632}; Kroeber 12, pp. 349–51) contains the incest motif, the incest being committed, as in the Loon Woman myth, at the time of the sister's first monthly periods. Her brother abandons her, but she joins up again with her fellow deer through scenting herself with myrtle, a fragrance the animals find irresistible. This is the origin of puberty rites. The Wappo version (M_{637}; Radin 5, pp. 47–9) links up with the bird-nester group through M_{24}: Bear Woman kills her husband who has climbed a tree to gather acorns, then devours his body and puts the head into a basket. Several other versions change the vertical disjunction peculiar to the bird-nester cycle, turning it into a means of saving rather than destroying life. The Shuswap (M_{623}) in the north, the Sinkyone (M_{632}) in the centre and the Maidu (M_{636}) and Miwok (M_{641}) in the south relate how the children, who are being pursued by the ogress, escape from her by climbing to the top of a rock. Some add the detail that the rock rises up and takes them off into the sky where, according to the Thompson of the Lower Fraser River (M_{621}; Boas 2, p. 615, 4, p. 16; Reichard 3, p. 184; Teit 5, pp. 218–24), they change into stars: they can still be seen chasing the ferocious grizzly bear in the constellation that we call the Great Bear.

So, like the bird-nester cycle, that of the bears and fawns includes an astronomical coding. When looked at in the light of their cosmological function — in the widest sense of the term cosmological — the two groups are even more closely linked. Just as the bird-nester myth refers to the origin of certain constellations — *Corvus* and the Pleiades — as well as to the origin of *water* or *fire*, the young heroes of the other group, who are sometimes changed into a constellation, end their adventures either in the chthonian world, where they are *burnt* to death (Wappo, M_{637}), or in the celestial world where they *drown* and, like the bird-nester in the mythology of the Bororo, the Wiyot, the Yurok and the Makah (see above, pp. 153–8), become the masters of rain and storms (M_{636}, Maidu; M_{641}, Miwok). The link with thunder is also brought out in one of the Pomo versions (M_{640}; Barrett 2, pp. 344–9). In the versions belonging to the Delta Thompson (M_{621}, Boas 13, p. 16; Teit 5, pp. 218–24), the heroes are involved in a long series of peregrinations before going up into the sky, and during their wanderings they impose order on the world exactly in the same way as Moon, the demiurge in the Salish myths (M_{375}). It will be remembered that the bird-nester in the Klamath and Modoc versions has lunar affinities, which contrast with the solar affinities of his persecutor, and that the same opposition exists in South America in Bororo mythology, and even more so in the Ge myths, where the leading characters belong to different moieties, associated respectively with the sun and the moon. It is appropriate, therefore, to draw attention at this point to the dualistic social structure of the Miwok, who attribute a cosmic significance to the conflict between bears and fawns. This structure is in keeping with a general bipartite division of beings and things, which extends the sociological formula of the moieties to the whole of creation, as is also the case among the Yokuts and the western Mono. In the Miwok system, the sun and the bear are on the side of the earth, the deer and the moon on the side of water (Kroeber 1, p. 455). Consequently, whether it is a question of the sun and the moon or characters representing them, of constellations in phasal opposition, of affines contrasted with each other through the giving or taking of a wife, or of animals belonging to antagonistic species, the pattern is the same and, in the first place, it brings together incompatible terms. Their juxtaposition gives rise to a crisis leading to an initial disjunction with a negative value. This is neutralized by a second conjunction which, whether completed or not, leaves the way open for a new disjunction, this time with a positive value. An exhaustive study of the bears and fawns group would have to take careful account of one fact: the second disjunction has as its intermediary agent the susceptible ferryman, who functions, one might say, as a semi-conductor: he carries some people across but intercepts others. This peculiar use of a motif which has been discussed at length in another context (*OTM*, Part VII, 1) would seem to be co-extensive with the group (cf. below, p. 318).

We thus gradually discern the outlines of a new itinerary which, following other stratigraphical layers, would take us again across the entire field of American mythology. I do not propose to shift my present enquiry to this level, since such a project would require as many volumes again. To conclude this discussion, which was inevitable through the convergence of two mythological cycles, one featuring the bird-nester and the other the fight between bears and fawns, it will be enough to sketch the overall structure of this last group of myths and to show that its variants have between them the same functions as were recognized as being characteristic of the first group.

I will begin by dividing the variants into two main categories, according to whether they concentrate on the adventures of the fleeing children or on those of the persecuting ogress. In the first case, the children who have been orphaned through their mother's death and who have taken their revenge by killing their playfellows, the wicked ogress's own children, either go off to

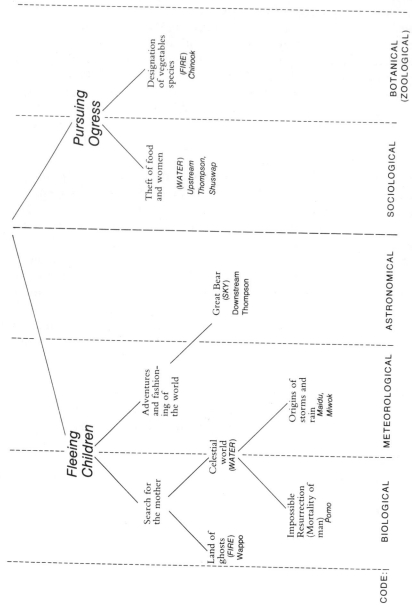

Figure 20. The structure of the bears and fawns group

look for their dead mother in the world beyond, or decide to embark on a life of adventure. If they take the first course, they arrive either in the land of ghosts where they are burnt to death (M_{637}), or in the sky, where they fail to bring their mother back to the land of the living (M_{638}); or alternatively, they are drowned and become the masters of storms and rain ($M_{636, 641}$). If they take the second course, they first of all organize life on earth, then ascend into the sky to become the stars forming the Great Bear (M_{621}; Teit 5, pp. 218–24; Boas 4, p. 16).

In the second category of variants, the fleeing children are forgotten as soon as they are out of danger, and attention focuses on the fate of the ogress. There are two possibilities: she dies or she survives. In the first instance, her corpse provides the meal which foxes, or other egg gatherers, take from Coyote by means of a trick (M_{621c}); in return, the demiurge's son rapes their women and appropriates their harvest (M_{623}; cf. also M_{671}). In the second instance, which is peculiar to the Chinook versions, the ogress is first weakened by diarrhoea and then drowned by the susceptible ferryman, but regains consciousness when the carrion crows start to eat her vulva. She smears her belly or face with the blood they have caused to flow, and asks all the trees what they think of her appearance. According to whether their reply is admiring or disparaging, she assigns different properties to each species, designating some to be used for firewood, others for manufacturing purposes. 'To every kind of tree that exists she gave a name and a function' ($M_{618, 620}$; cf. Tillamook in E. D. Jacobs, pp. 148–50).

This last episode constitutes a weak form of another which in those myths of the Coast Salish relating to the sun and the moon and the ordering of the universe (M_{375b}, M_{382}; Adamson, pp. 158–77) is given much greater importance. When Moon, the demiurge, whom the milt-girls steal after his birth to bring him up and marry him, decides to return to his own people, he first of all changes the children he has had by the eldest into trees, and those he has had by the youngest into fish. To each vegetable and animal species he gives a name and a function. We have here, then, an act of creation which lays stress on those elements of the animal and vegetable kingdoms that are of particular value for communities chiefly concerned with fishing, woodwork and basket making.

At this point, I would like to digress for a moment. The Salish myths describe the ordering of the universe in a way which may appear strange. The demiurge carries out a programme involving three stages: he changes his children into trees of different species and into all species of fish. After this, he embarks on a long journey during which he undertakes a medley of different tasks. These include the creation of quadrupeds, arts and crafts, social institutions and even children's games – apparently in no coherent order. Trees and fish are given pride of place, the former on land and the latter in water; in relation to these two major aspects of creation, all the others form a jumbled mass which the myths push into the background. This is understandable if we remember that fish provided the main source of food for these coastal and river communities, while the myths emphasize the importance of trees as providing firewood for the cooking and smoking of fish. Wood and fish, as combined culinary terms, were naturally of special significance for communities whose near neighbours (and some-times they themselves in their winter camps) were often short of wood and had to find other forms of fuel. Sometimes salmon was used as both food and fuel (Teit 13, p. 114; Strong, p. 76; Heizer 1, p. 188). Such expedients, which neutralized the opposition between food and the means of cooking it, may have been resorted to more frequently than one might suppose in areas such as the Columbian plateau which have very few trees and are almost desert-like in places, since the Cascades Range cuts off the moist sea winds. Certain Sahaptin myths describe the dreadful stench from a fire made of human bones (Jacobs 3, p. 237). Animal oils or fatty bones were widely used as fuel in the extreme north, from the Eskimo to the Chukchee; Herodotus mentions the same detail in connection with the Scythians (Hough, pp. 57, 188). However, for neighbouring tribes, and perhaps also for those directly concerned, this paradoxal form of cooking must have presented philosophical and logical problems similar to others we have already encountered (*RC*, pp. 149–52), and whose repercussions on the myths would be worth investigating more systematically than I am able to do here.

On the other hand, the tree episode reappears in an extremely weak form in a Sahaptin version of the bird-nester myth (M_{607a}, see above, p. 266), in which Coyote, who is being carried along by the current, owes his life to two trees he is able to grasp hold of, and which he rewards by bestowing medicinal properties on one and technical uses on the other. It is hardly necessary to point out that were there no fish in the water or trees on land mankind would be deprived of the raw materials necessary for making the preserved foods and manufactured objects exchanged in the markets. So the natural conditions for commercial transactions are created in this context, although their social conditions are absent in symmetrical versions: just as the tree episode is merely alluded to in $M_{606-607}$, the Thompson (M_{621c}) and Shuswap (M_{623}) myths, which borrow the episode relating to the theft of food from M_{606}, do not develop it. Not only do they fail to end social chaos by instituting exchanges, M_{623} even makes it worse by adding the theft of women to the theft of food.

The main point to be remembered is that the fawns and bears cycle is organized logically like a tree (Figure 20), the ramifications of which represent the complete series of transformations worked out in the previous volumes and by means of which I was able to construct the bird-nester group. On the left, three major branches relate to fire, water and the sky. The aquatic branch subdivides and diverges, on the one hand into the motif of the impossibility of resurrection, the origin of man's mortality (cf. M_{87-92}), involving, in the South American myths, a star who becomes a woman, and in this context a woman who changes into a star and who is responsible for or is a victim of man's shortened life-span; and on the other hand, into the origin of storms and rain, which in the corresponding South American myths is closely linked to the first theme (cf. $M_{91, 125}$; RC, 207–208), when they do not attribute rain directly to the influence of a constellation (cf. M_1). In these North American myths, the celestial branch leads to the origin of a constellation. We are therefore dealing with three modes of periodicity expressed in biological (mortality), meteorological (rainy season) or astronomical (Great Bear) terms.

On the right, a major branch divides into different forms of periodicity, expressed in sociological or botanical terms. We saw in *The Raw and the Cooked* that the institution of specific differences is a transposition of temporal diversity into the spatial mode. Some South American myths which deal with the problem in relation to the origin of the coloured plumage of birds are only slight transformations of those featuring the bird-nester (RC, pp. 313–18). It is significant, then, that North American myths about the specific differences between species of trees should be very similar to others concerned with the origin of the coloured plumage of birds (M_{621b}: Jacobs 1, p. 109; M_{643a-e}: Dixon 1, pp. 33–4; Goddard 1, p. 131; Jacobs 2, Part I, p. 92; Adamson, pp. 252, 254–5), and the argument of which is, in addition, identical with that of the Chaco myths (M_{175}; RC, pp. 305–306).

That is not all. The botanical taxonomy of the Chinook myths is mainly concerned with the respective properties of each species used as firewood, that is, amongst other things, for cooking. Consequently, the pattern of Figure 20 can be folded back on itself along its median axis: the constructive fire on the extreme right is then superimposed on the destructive fire on the extreme left (the Wappo and the Pomo cremated their dead). Similarly, the social disorder indicated in the Thompson, Shuswap and Lilloet myths, and which is doubly contrary to a natural order, occurs after Coyote has removed the grizzly's decomposing carcass from the water, thus producing a double inversion of the fresh salmon he is preparing to eat in the Chinook and

Sahaptin versions of the bird-nester. This detail, common to M_{623} and M_{671}, does not appear to be accidental, since, in M_{618}, Grizzly Woman has an attack of diarrhoea after eating the rotten fish deliberately placed along her path by the fleeing children, and at the other end of the myth's area of distribution, in Pomo mythology (M_{638b}; Barrett 2, pp. 334–5), Bear Woman's father is none other than the spirit of decay.

The she-bear in the Shoshone version (M_{642}; Lowie 12, pp. 253–4) falls into the water, remains there for a month and loses all her fur; and it will be remembered (see above, p. 288) that in the Lilloet myth (M_{622}) the same character is likened to excrement. So, it is clear that the Shuswap version, in which Coyote draws a putrid animal and not a fresh fish from the river, is referring to destructive or corrupting water; when the pattern is folded over, this version is superimposed on the ramification of the left branch which corresponds to water invested with a positive value. The operation thus brings together the *lack of a social order* (congruous with destructive water) signified by the theft of women and food (the latter being represented by the rotten carcass), and *the presence of a natural order* created by the heroes in the course of their wanderings. The tribes of the Fraser delta say that the black she-bear's children were the great organizers of creation (Boas 2, p. 586; cf. Teit 5, pp. 218–24, 295, 315–19; Hill-Tout 2, pp. 360–62). So the variants, taken all together, form a closed group.

3 The Noisy Scullion

MONSIEUR DIAFOIRUS: *He has no doubt prescribed plenty of roast meat?*
ARGAN: *No, only boiled meat.*
MONSIEUR DIAFOIRUS: *Ah! yes, roast or boiled, it's all the same. He has prescribed most prudently, and you could not be in better hands.*

Molière, *Le Malade Imaginaire*, Act II, Scene 9

The myths we have just discussed show how confusion of categories is replaced by an order which is at once social, economic and culinary. The order is made manifest by barter, as practised in fairs and markets and involving the exchange of foodstuffs, raw materials and manufactured objects: but slaves too can be bought and sold and even marriage is a commercial transaction. It is as if the market, like a convex mirror, reflected in microcosmic form all those operations which allow the social organism to function, and placed people and merchandise more or less on the same level. The myths imply that, through instituting the principle of exchange, the demiurge, once and for all, drew the line of demarcation between culture and nature, humanity and animality.

However, there are some things which cannot be exchanged since they are common property: for instance, drinking water and cooking fire ($M_{603-604}$); and there are other things which can be shared independently of any commercial transaction. Also, although the grizzly and the brown or black bear avoid encroaching on each other's feeding territory, in spite of the fact that they belong to similar species, other creatures are brought together by the search for food. Such is the case, for instance, of the carrion-eaters which live off the remnants of the meat that the predators seem to leave on purpose for them. Since, in native thought, exchange is a sort of test or touchstone of the transition from nature to culture, there is something disconcerting for the Indians in the economic relations between the differently sized members of the cat family. Should these animals be put on the side of nature, in spite of the fact that their sharing habits are in contrast to the guarded attitudes Grizzly and Bear maintain towards each other? Or should they be put on the side of culture, although the predator/carrion-eater relationship is one-sided, since, unlike partners who exchange food, the carrion-eater receives and does not give while the predator gives and does not receive? It is remarkable that the mythology of the Sahaptin and their neighbours, although recorded only in fragmentary form, should envisage all these different possibilities in turn; and even more remarkable that it should illustrate them each time by using a pair of animals. We have already encountered three such pairs. The one formed by Coyote and Wolf serves to establish the origin of exchanges, whereas the Bear/Grizzly pair has the opposite function. In Kalapuya mythology, a third pair, composed of Cougar and Coyote, deals with the particular case of elements, such as water and fire which belong to everyone and therefore must be neither sold nor monopolized. Finally, a last group of myths is concerned with the difficulty I drew attention to at the beginning: the difficulty of the confusions inherent in the natural order. Some animals, although they belong to different species, normally share their food. They are thus in opposition to the Bear/Grizzly pair; and since their sharing of an identical kind of food is not accompanied by theft, they are also in a double relationship of opposition to the Wolf/Coyote pair, whose foods, as described in the myth, are not identical (one eats birds' eggs, the other salmon) and who try to steal them from each other.

M$_{644a, b}$. *Klikitat. 'The wildcat and the cougar'*

Five brothers lived together. Going from the eldest to the youngest, they were called Cougar, Wolf, Fisher, Weasel and Wildcat. This last brother was still just a little boy. Cougar used to hunt for his brothers, and when he brought back the game he used to send Wildcat to peel off the bark of a tree with which to make a receptacle, in which they would boil the meat (by putting red-hot stones into the water), a pail for drawing water and – according to one of the two versions of which I am giving a joint summary – a third utensil: the dish on which to serve the cooked meat. However, added Cougar, Wildcat had to work in silence; for they were in the vicinity of a dangerous spirit and it would be wise not to attract his attention.

Wildcat set to work, but he found it difficult to remain silent. In order to do his work properly and remove a piece of bark without splitting it, he felt he had to sing; otherwise he became clumsy. He started to sing softly, then he got louder and louder. The ogre heard him and asked him why he was so glad. 'Because,' replied Wildcat, 'my brother shot an elk.' 'Good,' replied the ogre, 'I will eat it and you with it.' Feeling wretched and in despair, the boy went off.

The ogre, who looked like an old man, met with him near a creek where he had put his fish basket-trap. To Wildcat's great astonishment, this contained only sticks and no fish at all. But this did not prevent the ogre gulping down all the sticks. Wildcat was more terrified than ever; he ran to his house and gave the alarm. Cougar told his brothers to escape and to leave him to wait for the ogre alone with their youngest brother; the latter set about cooking enormous quantities of meat. The ogre came along, devoured this dinner in one gulp and fell asleep. He was a very strange person; when he was awake his eyes were shut, and when he slept they were open.

Wildcat took advantage of the fact that the ogre was sleeping to cut off his head with a stone knife. Thereupon, the two brothers fled in opposite directions, for they knew that pieces of the ogre's body would chase them. Wildcat ran downstream closely followed by the head; Cougar was pursued by the headless body and climbed to the top of a mountain where he was hidden by fog. The head fell into a waterfall and Wildcat was able to escape from it. Before taking leave of each other, the brothers had agreed that they would meet on the mountain, if they both arrived.

When Wildcat reached the place where they had agreed to meet, Cougar announced that he was tired of his rash behaviour and the dangers he was causing. They must never live together again. In vain the boy begged his elder brother to reconsider his decision: however would he manage to feed himself on his own? Cougar however was resolute. He agreed only to give his brother his spare weapons – a small arrow and a fish spear. With these, Wildcat would be able to procure for himself small game animals and fish. Cougar also promised that every time he killed a large animal (elk), he would ask Wildcat to share the feast: 'That is the way from that time on,' the myth concludes provisionally, 'the two brothers each go their own way. But, whenever Cougar shoots and kills game, he goes to fetch Wildcat so that he can come and eat at that place. When Wildcat has finished eating, once again he goes on, and whenever Cougar again shoots and kills an elk for him, he invariably searches for him. That is the way they are at the moment, these two brothers' (Jacobs 3, p. 194).

After Cougar left him, Wildcat resolved to behave, as we would say, 'like a grown-up person'. He hunted squirrels and hares, caught all kinds of fish and ate his fill. In the course of two successive encounters, he robbed Raccoon of his catch of fish and overcame Timber Rabbit in a scratching match. Since then, Timber Rabbit has become his favourite game. Meanwhile, Cougar had killed a deer and he set off to look for his brother in order to invite him. He found him seated at table, probably in front of the rabbit which he imagined to be a deer. In a Kathlamet version (M_{646d}; Boas 7, pp. 109–11), this episode is given a comic twist: Mink, who plays Wildcat's part, mistakes a mouse, a snail and a rabbit for an elk. Here, Cougar kindly allows his brother to finish his snack, then brings him to where the main meal is. 'That is the way from that time on the two brothers travel about. Wherever Cougar shoots and kills game, Wildcat eats at that place: Cougar invariably finds his brother so they can eat together' (Jacobs 3, pp. 192–6, 219–23).

The Cougar (*Felis concolor*), which is found in both North and South America, is the largest member of the cat family native to North America. The English transcriptions of the myths refer to it either as 'Cougar' or 'Panther' (cf. above, p. 256). Similarly, 'Wildcat' means the Lynx, although it is not always clear whether the animal is the *Lynx canadensis* or the *Lynx rufus*, which are both equally common in the area. The 'Weasel' and the 'Fisher' both belong to the Mustelidae family.

In assigning separate functions to the two characters before they assume their animal nature, M_{644} posits the following implicit equivalence:

$$\text{(culture)} \begin{bmatrix} \text{cook : hunter} \end{bmatrix} :: \text{(nature)} \begin{bmatrix} \text{carrion-eater : predator} \end{bmatrix}$$

each element of which subordinates the first activity to the second. We have already seen that tribes in this area consider the exchange of foodstuffs and not the cooking of food as marking the point of junction between culture and nature. Among the Sahaptin of the Columbia valley, cooking, which was considered as being simply another aspect of the search for food, was usually done by men (Garth 1, p. 52; cf. *OTM*, p. 484). However, it is not clear whether this unusual practice, which also existed among some northern Athapaskan living in very different social and economic conditions, is to be explained by the unmarked position that cooking occupied in the system, or whether the work was done by male slaves.[1] In the latter case,

---

[1] At the beginning of the nineteenth century, Lewis and Clark were surprised to see Chinook men doing the cooking; they may however have been slaves (Ray 4, p. 128). For the Inland Salish, we have

cooking would still be unmarked, but in respect of the agent rather than the activity.

However, the myth is not content to reduce an instance of natural compatibility, which raises a problem for the reasons I have indicated, to a form of cultural compatibility that native thought takes for granted, since it puts hunting, fishing and cooking on the same side, while reserving the other side for commercial transactions involving foodstuffs, most of which are dried or preserved and so have undergone a degree of culinary preparation. Other meanings are also present, but would be less easy to grasp, if we could not, as is always necessary, understand them in terms of differentials between versions which respect the argument of M_{644}, while at the same time inverting or reduplicating certain details or episodes in a way which, as we shall see, is far from arbitrary, but instead results from the inherent need of mythic thought, as soon as it elaborates a theme, to exploit the logical structure of that theme in order to build up the entire group of its transformations. These symmetrical variants of M_{644} belong to the Cowlitz River Sahaptin, the immediate neighbours of the Klikitat to the west and, to the south, of the Coast Salish, whose myths illustrate different states of the same transformation.

The Cowlitz variants ($M_{645a, b}$; Jacobs 1, pp. 113–21, 133–9) resemble M_{644}, except that the family of five brothers is reduced to Cougar and Wildcat, and in one myth (M_{645b}) the elder has a wife from whom he is separated by a considerable distance, and whom he is proposing to visit at the beginning of the myth. 'You must not leave me,' protests Wildcat, who insists on accompanying his brother. Cougar kills a large deer and, while he is cooking it, he sends Wildcat to look not, as in M_{644}, for bark, but for leaves to be used as a dish. The significance of this transformation, which might be thought to be of no consequence, will emerge later (pp. 306, 315).

Wildcat goes off singing about the copious meal which is being prepared, and throwing out imaginary invitations right and left. A wretched-looking old man hears him and accepts. Wildcat is at first touched, but

---

the following evidence, in myths belonging respectively to the Sanpoil, the Okanagon and the Thompson: 'You are a chief,' Fox said to Coyote as he planned to steal his fish, 'and your ancestors were all chiefs. You shouldn't cook. You go and lie down and I'll cook the salmon and call you when it is ready' (Ray 2, p. 174). In an attempt to conceal his lowly state, Skunk protests: 'You are making a mistake, I'm not the cook; I'm the chief' (Hill-Tout 8, p. 148). In another context, Coyote addresses a malevolent spirit in the following terms: 'Why, surely you are not cooking the meat! Chiefs never cook! Such work is only for women, slaves and the likes of me' (Teit 5, p. 312). It is said of the Lummi, who are Coast Salish, that 'they do not find it humiliating for men to assist in cooking, especially during ceremonial occasions' (B. Stern, p. 32).

changes his mind when he sees his guest devouring twigs and other odds and ends as if they were fish. He is even more dismayed when the ogre sits down at table with the two brothers and gulps down a whole deer, antlers, tablecloth and all.

The story continues, as in M_{644}, except that Cougar, not Wildcat, beheads the ogre, and is pursued by the head. He catches up with his young brother, who had been the first to make for the river, tucks him under his arm, and after further adventures of the same kind, creates a fog and heavy rain, which cause the head to lose trace of them. This happens none too soon, since Cougar is becoming exhausted. It will be noticed in connection with this episode that, in relation to M_{644}, the respective roles of the brothers are inverted, and that instead of one escaping downstream (but pursued by the head, an upper part) and the other upstream (but pursued by the body, a lower part), they both make for a river, i.e., move towards the low, and are pursued only by the upper part of the body, that is, the head. The slightly different text of M_{645b} does not invalidate this analysis, since although it says that the brothers go upstream, it does not contain the opposition between the valley and mountain, so strongly marked in M_{644}, and sends the brothers only along the valley. Lastly, in the Klikitat versions, Cougar takes advantage of the fog passively, whereas in the Cowlitz myth he conjures it up through his magic power and backs it up with torrential rain. The meaning of these transformations is not yet clear, but it is already obvious that they have a certain coherence on the formal level. From that point onwards, M_{644} and M_{645} diverge, or so it would seem.

M_{645a}. *Cowlitz. 'The continuation of the adventures of Cougar and Wildcat'*

The brothers stopped near a stream. Before he went hunting, Cougar lit a fire and told Wildcat to tend it carefully. The latter however started to play and forgot the fire, which went out.

Afraid of being beaten, he decided to go and steal some fire from the other side of the river, where some smoke was rising. He swam across and had no trouble in seizing one of the five burning logs, which belonged to an old woman. Then he came back. Wildcat's fur still bears the marks of the burns he suffered during this expedition. When the old woman saw that one log was missing, she tried to ford the river and run after the thief. The water soon came up to her knees and, fearing that her underclothes would get wet, she abandoned the idea.

Cougar had a feeling that something dreadful had happened; he stopped hunting and rushed back. Five naked giants, who had swum across the river, came in turn to avenge their grandmother. Each one had a different kind of game on his shoulder (in the following order: deer, brown bear, cougar, grizzly and human according to M_{645a}; grizzly, bear, deer, cougar and human according to M_{645b}; cf. below, p. 306). By resorting to a ruse, the brothers got the better of the first four of their opponents. While Cougar, who had defied them, was struggling with them, Wildcat cut their Achilles tendons. The last giant, however, who had not bothered to undress when crossing the river, was tougher. While wrestling, Cougar and he gradually rose up into the air and cut each other to shreds. Scraps of flesh fell to the ground, and Wildcat kept or discarded them, according to whether they were white or black; only the white pieces came from his brother, whom he would have to reconstitute at the end of the fight. However, he gave him the wrong liver (or viscera, M_{645b}). Cougar thought he would die. 'Oh, no,' Wildcat explained, 'it is better this way, for henceforth you will be a dangerous human being.' The other version is even more explicit: 'That doesn't matter,' said Wildcat, 'don't worry about those intestines. In future, if people kill and eat you, they will throw away your intestines and not eat them.' 'Very well,' concludes Cougar, 'I will keep the entrails of the dangerous being. With them, I will become a dangerous being too. Very well indeed' (Jacobs 1, pp. 117, 136).

Thereupon Cougar decided to leave his brother for good, and, as the latter was very upset, he gave him hunting weapons and promised that he would invite him to a meal every time he killed an elk. Wildcat did his best to hunt like his brother, but he was deluded about the size of the pathetic game he had caught. Cougar came along, enlightened him and offered him a more solid menu. Once again, the brothers parted.

Cougar met a young boy called Mink, who insisted on going with him. However, this caused him all sorts of problems. First of all, he had to drain a lake in order to remove Mink from the belly of a monster which had swallowed him during a duck hunt. Next, Mink insisted on knowing the name of a place where both had stopped to camp, although it was forbidden to pronounce the name. For the sake of peace and quiet, Cougar gave in and whispered: 'Tyigh' (*ta'ix*) and Mink started to shout out the forbidden word at the top of his voice, thus creating torrential rain, which soaked him to the skin. He was shivering with cold and Cougar had to shelter him in the case where he kept his fire-drill.

The next morning, Cougar told Mink to go 'to the house where his two wives' lived, in order to get something to eat. These wives were natural wells; they could only gurgle when they were spoken to, but they used to supply dishes of warm, ready-prepared food to anyone who waited, with closed eyes, after requesting nourishment. When the brothers had eaten and returned the dishes to their owners, Cougar decided to go on to look for another wife. He had in mind the daughter of an old man, who pretended to welcome him but who tried several times to kill him during his sleep. On each occasion, Mink warned his brother in time.

The old man put the blame on the young boy and sent him on dangerous missions, from which the other always managed to emerge unscathed. When informed by a meadowlark (cf. above, p. 288; below, p. 316) that his wife was a grizzly she-bear, Cougar killed the latter, roasted her breasts and served them up as a meal for his father-in-law. Then the two brothers ran off, but Cougar still had no wife . . . (Jacobs 1, pp. 113–21).

The other version (M_{645b}; *ibid.*, pp. 133–9) does not include the episode of the forbidden name; it identifies the food-providing wives with springs instead of natural wells, but this may be just a terminological variation, since the words 'well' and 'waterhole' can be applied to a spring when it produces a pond-like accumulation of water.[2] One Tillamook version refers to a 'lake' (E. D. Jacobs, pp. 135–6). More significantly, M_{645b} states that Grizzly Woman's father is Thunder, from whose deadly schemes the brothers have more difficulty in disentangling themselves. An inverted Clackamas variant (M_{646a}; Jacobs 2, Part I, pp. 256–67) explains how Thunder's human wife was granted the privilege of going out in the rain (celestial water) without getting wet, whereas in M_{645} an old woman (who therefore cannot be a wife), the mistress of a terrestrial fire (not celestial like thunder), shows herself to be incapable of fording a river (terrestrial water) without getting wet. I have already mentioned this group of transformations (see pp. 288–9), and I shall come back to them in connection with the Salish versions. The particular state I have just defined already suggests that the reason why the construction of M_{645} seems so complex is that it gives a linear presentation of homologous sequences which need to be superimposed for the correct interpretation to appear.

As regards the place with the forbidden name, the information available is contradictory. Jacobs (1, pp. 23, 118, n. 2), believes it to be the valley of the Tyigh, a tributary of the Deschutes River to the east of the Cascades Range in northern Oregon. Professor Rigsby, who has an expert knowledge of the area and the languages spoken there, has been good enough to

[2] TRANSLATORS' NOTE: The author is distinguishing between the French terms *source* (spring) and *puits* (well).

confirm in a letter that the Sahaptin village situated in the valley was known to its southern and northern neighbours as *tayx̣láma* or *táyxpam,* i.e., 'people of Tayx̣'. According to earlier evidence provided by Teit (13, pp. 100, 108), the Tenino were probably descended from these 'Tayx̣ people', who had settled in the valley of the same name, although Teit himself refers to it as 'bad country, full of canyons', or farther south. The name itself is supposed to date back to the time when the younger brother cried '*tai'x, tai'x*' several times as he rose up into the sky.

But what does the cry mean? Professor Rigsby can suggest no etymological source in Sahaptin and whether or not it once had a meaning, today it is just a place-name. In the correspondence referred to earlier (see above, p. 287), Professor Hymes assures me that the word has no meaning in Chinook either, although he quotes J. K. Gill's dictionary as giving a very common morpheme *ta,* perhaps derived from Sahaptin and connoting the idea of supernatural power.

When we turn to the Chinook, the situation becomes more complicated. The fact that the myth has the same etiological function with them as in the Sahaptin versions emerges clearly from a Lower Chinook variant (M_{646b}; Ray 4, pp. 151–6), in which Cougar promises Wildcat, his younger brother, that he will always leave him his share of the game as a reward for having rescued their sister, who had fallen into the clutches of a bear. The episode containing the place with the forbidden name, and the name itself, are to be found in another Chinook version belonging to the Kathlamet (M_{646d}; Boas 7, pp. 103–17), where it is clearly stated (p. 112, n. 1) that Tā'ix is the name of a mountain lake near the sources of the River Cowlitz. The name also appears in a Salish version (M_{650a}; Adamson, p. 206) originating from the lower reaches of the River Cowlitz.

It would seem, then, that there were two 'Taix', a few hundred kilometres from each other. Since all the myths in which the name occurs belong to tribes speaking different languages but which all lived in or near the Cowlitz valley, the siting suggested by Boas would seem to be the most plausible. In view of this, it is tempting to look for the origin of the name in the Salish languages, provided specialists in Salish phonology were to confirm the curious homophony which appears to exist between Taix, the place-name, which Mink was forbidden to pronounce, and his own name, which is Squaix in Lilloet and Qaix in the coastal dialects (Teit 2, p. 292 and n. 4).

Let us keep to the formal aspect of the myths which, in itself, raises quite enough problems. Three major differences divide the Klikitat versions

(M_{644}) from the Cowlitz (M_{645}). Firstly, in the one case Wildcat is asked to obtain bark from trees in order to make various cooking utensils, whereas in the other, he merely has to gather leaves for use as a serving dish. Next, in the Cowlitz versions, Wildcat has a second task: he has to watch over the fire and prevent it going out. Thirdly, also in the Cowlitz versions, Wildcat's two misadventures are echoed by the two suffered by Mink, the character who replaces Wildcat as Cougar's younger brother in the second part of the story.

The gathering of green leaves to be used as a makeshift dish demands far less ability and skill than the removing of whole unbroken pieces of bark to make three quite different kinds of utensil. Consequently, in the Cowlitz versions, Wildcat's contribution is played down and his lack of competence is still further demonstrated when he is shown to be incapable of looking after a fire, which is, after all, the prime duty of a cook. So, from one group to the other, Wildcat's professional status declines. But at the same time, that of Cougar, his brother, is reversed. The Klikitat versions define Cougar purely as a hunter and food-providing brother, whereas the others, in the episode about the exchange of the livers, describe how he became a dangerous being, and moreover partly inedible: this limits his nutritive ('food-providing') value, because of the taboo on the eating of Cougar's intestines, for which this episode provides an explanation.

The Wasco version of the same myth (M_{646e}; Sapir 1, pp. 294–8) goes even further, since it presents Wildcat as a more precocious hunter (and therefore less exclusively a cook). So, when the two brothers separate, they announce that Wildcat will become the patron of hunters and Cougar the patron of hunters and warriors. Consequently, each character is defined in terms of what might be called a professional vector, which unites cooking and hunting in the case of Wildcat, hunting and war in the case of Cougar, and the respective lengths of these vectors vary correlatively between several versions. Like most of the Chinook variants, M_{646e} identifies the masters of stolen fire with grizzly bears. The versions belonging to the River Cowlitz Sahaptin are less explicit, but it would seem that by not listing the game animals carried by the enemies of the two brothers in the same order, M_{645a} and M_{645b} tend to move the grizzly closer to or further away from the human.

M_{645a} : *deer, brown bear, cougar,* {*grizzly, human*}

M_{645b} : *grizzly*}, *bear, deer, cougar,* {*human*

The fatal conjunction, which is illustrated in M_{645a} in an anticipatory but still purely symbolical way, is, as it were, held in reserve in M_{645b}, since it is to receive special treatment in the last part of the story: this, as the reader will remember, is the episode where Cougar (who still had human characteristics in the mythic period before the categories became distinct) experiments with having a grizzly girl as his wife. So the Cougar's position in the two series is no less relevant than that of the humans and the grizzly, and the permutation of the remaining terms: *deer, bear/bear, deer*, would seem to be a consequence of the permutation of the other three.

According to the versions under consideration, Wildcat's first and only offence is to sing while carrying out his duties as scullion. Here, once again, we encounter the theme of noise as being antipathetic to cooking, a theme which has played a major part throughout this work, and which has assumed increasing importance since the point at which we first encountered it (*RC*, pp. 148–9; *HA, passim; OTM*, pp. 305–306, 322–3, 496–7). What is the consequence of the noise in the case we are concerned with here? It leads to an encounter between the heroes and an ogre, who gulps down all their provisions and is preparing to devour them too. This ogre keeps his eyes closed when awake and open when asleep, like the guardian spirits of darkness, as described by the Kalapuya in their version of the same myth (M_{647}; Jacobs 4, pp. 244–51). M_{644b}, on the other hand, explains that darkness was dispelled once the ogre disappeared (Jacobs 3, p. 222). We are dealing, then, with the same charivari as the one which accompanies eclipses in other myths, or, in a different context, is produced by instruments called, specifically, 'instruments of darkness'; and in both cases too, it signals or determines the regression of human beings to a pre-culinary stage, since people have to get rid of food and fast during the eclipse, and since the service known as 'Tenebrae' takes place at the most crucial point in Lent; and also since, in both instances, all fires have to be extinguished (*RC*, pp. 298–9; *HA*, pp. 413–15). The Sahaptin myths first reveal the nature of the spirit of darkness by attributing to him regressive behaviour in respect of cooking: he instils terror into the young hero by swallowing pieces of wood as if they were fish (cf. above, pp. 299–300).

So Wildcat, through being responsible for the reign of night and famine, has committed an offence, which he repeats in the Cowlitz versions when, later, he allows the domestic fire to go out. We can, however, note one difference: darkness is an absence of celestial fire, whereas, on the second occasion, it is a lack of terrestrial fire which prevents the cook from carrying out his function. After the theft of fire from the grizzlies, or from substitute characters, the brothers part, and we might suppose that, as in the Klikitat versions, this disjunction, mitigated by the occasional sharing of food, puts an end to the improper conjunctions for which Wildcat is to blame.

However, after Wildcat's exit, the Cowlitz versions produce another sequence. It is now Mink's turn to make his entrance, and to be guilty of two offences, which both reverse the order in which Wildcat committed his and are antisymmetrical to them in a new register: the register not of fire but of water.

Mink begins by behaving like an *excessive hunter*, whereas Wildcat had proved to be a *deficient cook*. After reaching the shores of a lake crowded with ducks, Mink insists on his adoptive brother shooting them: 'No,' Cougar at first replies, 'they are too far away, you won't be able to go and fetch them.' Finally, he agrees, and Mink swims out to the fallen game, but aquatic monsters rise up, seize him and swallow him. Cougar has to drain the lake and kill the monsters one by one before he discovers Mink, still brandishing his duck, in the belly of the smallest monster (Jacobs 8, pp. 117–18; cf. $M_{216-217}$ and M_{257}). Consequently, just as Wildcat conjoins himself first of all with darkness personified by an ogre, and which is the opposite of daylight and therefore of *celestial fire*, Mink is first of all conjoined to aquatic ogres who, living at the bottom of a lake, represent *terrestrial water* in its negative aspect.

The same relation of symmetry persists in relation to the next offence committed by the two heroes. Wildcat allows the domestic fire to go out, i.e., extinguishes a *terrestrial fire*; Mink unleashes torrential rain, i.e., *celestial water*. Wildcat, through carrying on his back the log he has stolen from the grizzlies, and which contains fire in its wild state, receives burns, the marks of which he still bears. Mink, completely drenched and shivering with cold, is given shelter and protection in the box or case containing civilized fire: the kind which is not stolen from ogres but which is produced by the technical operation of the fire-drill. We see then that the respective offences committed by Wildcat and Mink correspond to each other and form a chiasmus; the first offence of Wildcat and the second offence of Mink are the result of uncontrolled behaviour, excessive or deficient, in respect of hunting or cooking; and the second offence of Wildcat and the first offence of Mink also relate to uncontrolled behaviour, this time of a linguistic nature: Wildcat sings loudly when he ought to remain silent, and Mink bellows out the forbidden place-name. So, the first four sequences of the Cowlitz versions clarify the single sequence of the Klikitat versions; they balance each other to form a coherent system (Figure 21).

So far, the myths seem to operate with a four dimensional matrix; the heroes act: 1) excessively or deficiently; 2) towards fire or water, envisaged 3) according to their terrestrial or celestial modalities; and the offences they commit belong 4) to the alimentary or linguistic registers. We shall see

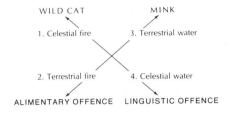

Figure 21. The armature of M_{645}

presently that the following sequence in the Cowlitz myths introduces a fifth dimension, which the story keeps to until the end.

In the course of this sequence, Cougar obtains nourishment, for himself and his brother, from two 'wives': this is his name for the waterholes at the surface of which dishes of steaming, nicely cooked food emerge on request. For native listeners familiar with their myths, this pair of supernatural women would inevitably be reminiscent of others, all of whom, taken together, form a paradigmatic system, in the light of which this apparently absurd and meaningless episode can be interpreted. The mythology of the Sahaptin and their neighbours contains three pairs of supernatural women: the milt-girls, whom Coyote creates from the soft roe of a salmon (M_{375}); the excrement-sisters, whom he ejects and returns to his body at will (M_{606a}); and those to whom it will be convenient to refer as the well-wives, and who, in M_{645}, are associated with Cougar. A complex network of relations can be discovered between these three pairs.

The well-wives belong, in the first place, to a kind of terrestrial water which the myths refer to in its stagnant state (they may be springs, but they look like natural wells or waterholes with no visible outlet). The two other pairs belong to running water, terrestrial in the case of one pair, since the milt-girls form part of the world of fish, celestial in the other case, but in the negative mode: Coyote constantly threatens to send down rain which will cause his excrement-sisters to disintegrate (it may be noted that milts, on the contrary, can stay in water without coming to any harm). Consequently, a relationship of compatibility exists between the well-wives and stagnant water, and between the milt-girls and running water; in both cases this water is terrestrial in origin whereas between the excrement-sisters and running water of celestial origin there is a relationship of incompatibility.

All three pairs have an affinity with food. The well-wives produce cooked dishes, the excrement-sisters are themselves a digested product of cooked food, and the milt-girls a product of raw, unconsumed food: for they were born from the soft salmon roes, which Coyote could not bring himself to cook as he found them so 'white and pretty'.

Each pair has a special kinship relation with its creator. The two creatures born from fish spawn are girls who refuse to become wives: when Coyote addresses them as such, they become incensed and vanish. On the other hand, the well-women conscientiously perform the culinary duties devolving on wives; and the excrement-women are sisters whose physical nature (unlike that of the milt-girls who are the object of sexual desire on the part of their father) prevents them becoming incestuous, for the simple reason that their nature presupposes a close relation with their brother's body, but of a digestive, not a sexual kind.

Lastly, the three pairs are differentiated in respect of the linguistic code. The milt-girls are quick to understand their father's half-implicit suggestion, when he pretends to call them his wives by mistake; the excrement-sisters, as advisers and informants, play a talkative role; as for the well-women, they are silent, or more accurately – and unlike the preceding pair – they suffer from a speech defect. When Mink tries to enter into conversation with them, they can only produce gurgling noises in reply: 'ma'lalalal-alal' (M_{645a}), 'bleblebleble' (M_{645b}), 'belelubelelu' (M_{650a}); according to the Tillamook version (E. D. Jacobs, pp. 135–6), they blow bubbles; in the Clackamas version they can only utter 'noises like girlish giggling' (M_{646a}; Jacobs 2, Part I, pp. 265–6). Mink is surprised: 'You are strange women: you cannot talk.' It is clear, then, that the three pairs can be grouped two by two, according to a series of relevant oppositions: the well-wives and milt-girls are respectively *conjugal* and *non-conjugal*, and the excrement-sisters and well-wives are respectively, as it were, *linguistic* and *non-linguistic* (Figure 22).

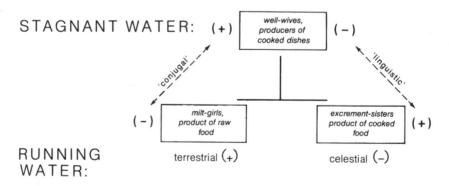

Figure 22. The triad of supernatural women

	well-wives	milt-girls	excrement-sisters
running water/stagnant water	−	+	+
terrestrial water/celestial water	+	+	−
cooked food/raw food	+	−	+
women producers/women as product	+	−	−
conjugal women/non-conjugal women	+	−	−
linguistic women/non-linguistic women	−	+	+

So, however strange and gratuitous it may seem, the story of the well-wives fulfils a clearly defined function. It assembles all the semantic axes that the myth had introduced in turn: *excess/deficiency*, *fire/water*, *terrestrial/celestial*, *alimentary/linguistic*, and it adds yet another, *conjugal/non-conjugal*, the axis along which the last part of the story is to take place. In the preceding parts, Mink's behaviour seemed to be symmetrically opposed to that of Wildcat, but it was always left to Cougar to retrieve the situation. When the code changes, the roles too are reversed. In attempting to marry a Grizzly Woman, Thunder's daughter, Cougar exposes himself and his companion to the hazards of a conjunction no less dangerous than the others, although the myth formulates it in sociological terms, and Mink takes over the role of rescuer. It is impossible to embark on this final phase of the analysis without first introducing the Salish versions.

The Salish-speaking tribes known as the 'Coast Salish' — to distinguish them from those of the Plateau — occupied an area stretching from the western slope of the Cascade Range to the sea. In the Cowlitz valley and in other areas too they were close neighbours of the northern Sahaptin, with whom they enjoyed peaceful relations, based on good neighbourliness, reciprocal visits, intermarriages and commercial exchanges. So, the two linguistic families had in common a great many myths between which, however, contrasts appear, as we move from one group to the other, showing that communities living in close proximity to each other need to feel that they are at once similar and different. Reflection, inversion and symmetry, as they occur in the myths, bear witness to an unconscious effort to overcome contradictory urges: on the one hand, those resulting from territorial nearness and the political and economic advantages inherent in collaboration; and, on the other, parochialism and the need for a collective identity. A precarious balance is established between these conflicting tendencies, and it is this which gives the myths their dynamic force. It is here, too, that we are most likely to find the key to the transformational relationships which determine the different states of any given myth, and which – between groups, and between different sections or distinct periods within the same group – correspond to the twofold necessity to reconcile and contrast what one knows of the other, and what one believes to be peculiar to oneself. I have given examples of this process in another context (L.-S. 5, Ch. XII; 19), but the Salish and Sahaptin provide equally convincing instances.

Like the Sahaptin versions, those of the Coast Salish form a complex system. Firstly, they differ according to the valley in which they originated: Chehalis, Cowlitz or Humptulips. But even among the Chehalis alone, there are two variants which the informants consider to be two quite distinct myths (Adamson, p. 64, n. 1). Without accepting that they are separate, I propose to respect the division between what might be called type I and type II.

M_{648}. Chehalis (Washington). Wildcat and Cougar

Cougar used to hunt and cook for himself and his younger brother Wildcat, whom he allowed only to look after the fire. In spite of Cougar's warnings, once he was left alone Wildcat stubbornly went on throwing pieces of meat directly on to the fire. One day, what Cougar foresaw would happen actually did: the juice from the meat saturated the fire, which grew smaller and smaller and at last went out entirely. Wildcat did not know how to relight the fire, because his brother had taken the fire-sticks with him. Although Cougar had forbidden him to do so, he decided to go and steal some from a house across the river, and succeeded in bringing back a piece of burning wood, not without receiving burns on his head and tail.

When Cougar got back he was angry. Wildcat explained that he liked meat best when cooked directly on the flame, but his brother insisted that he used roasting-sticks. The old man who was master of the stolen fire changed into a floating log, crossed the river and resumed his natural appearance in order to attack Cougar. The two men tore the flesh from each other's bodies as they rose into the air. Wildcat gathered up and laid aside the pieces of flesh, so that he could reassemble his brother, but he put in the wrong liver. Cougar had won, and there was nothing for him to do but to use the liver, for Wildcat had already burnt the old man's body, of which nothing but ashes remained: 'This shall never happen in the next generation,' declared Cougar. 'If anyone should let the fire go out, he will be able to go to another's house and borrow some.'

The brothers went off to camp in another place. One day, when

Cougar had killed a large elk, he sent Wildcat to look for some sharp roasting-sticks. Although he had been told to remain silent, Wildcat began to sing an unwisely worded song. An ogre called Slender Neck heard it; they had to cook for him; he swallowed the meat whole and fell asleep. Then Cougar cut his head off, which did not stop the ogre chasing 'the five Cougar brothers' (suddenly, in this story, one cougar becomes five). They soon disappeared, however (for the four eldest died), but our hero, as the fifth and youngest and only survivor, becomes one again. Wildcat made mountains, but the ogre climbed up them; before the last one he turned himself into a cyclone. It was then ordained, according to the myth, that 'anyone who desires to eat with a man, will do so without molesting his host' [the man].

Cougar and Wildcat met once more and moved to another camp. Wildcat promised to stay there and behave himself. However he went out to the prairie and met two Crane Women, who were singing and digging for button lacamas [*Camassia quamash*]. Wildcat traded his cape made of dried elk skin, which the women wanted to eat, for their stock of lacamas. He cooked the corms and, without telling the women, served them to Cougar, who found them very pleasant. He congratulated Wildcat and told him he had done well. Another time he traded his blanket for the lacamas. Finally, they asked if they could go home with him, and offered to marry Cougar. He hesitated, but let them stay in the house. During the days that followed, he was unable to hunt because the sound of the women singing frightened the game away. 'If they don't stop singing,' said Cougar, 'we'll all starve.' The brothers abandoned the women and fled.

But Cougar had had enough and decided to leave his brother. Wildcat began to weep; he was afraid to look after himself and thought he would never survive. Cougar gave him his oldest bow and told him to hunt. Wildcat could only catch poor game, such as long-tailed mice, moles, gophers and rabbits. Cougar was sorry for him and made him a present of the elk he had just killed and suggested that from now on Wildcat had better follow him. He would always leave some game for him. 'And so it is today: the cougar always covers up some game and leaves it for Wildcat who follows after him' (Adamson, pp. 60–64).

Few myths are as aware as this one of their etiological function, since, after each episode, M_{648} is careful to make its meaning clear. In all instances it is a matter of establishing the rule about sharing; it is applied first to fire, then extended to meals, conjugal relations, and finally to the natural world.

In the first two instances there is no problem: it is explained that fire is something that can be borrowed and meals are intended to be shared. The episode dealing with conjugal relationships is more complex in character, since the crane-women (or wild geese in M_{649b}; Adamson, pp. 67–79) are disqualified in three different ways: instead of giving their harvest they sell it; they take the initiative in proposing marriage; and they make so much noise that hunting becomes impossible. Let us leave aside this last aspect for the moment. It is clear that the first two are complementary to each other, since they state the same truth, one on the economic and the other on the sociological level: unlike commercial transactions, those which lead to and sustain marriages are not reversible. The man courts the woman, not she him (cf. M_{610}) and the woman contributes what she gathers to the couple's food supply without expecting any payment in return. So it can be said that in the first three episodes the myth defines in succession the moral codes relating to the *hearth*, the *table* and *domestic life*. The originality of the fourth episode lies then in the fact that it bases one aspect of the natural order – the sharing of food between predator and carrion-eater – on three particular instances relating to life in society, but in which, exceptionally, sharing rather than exchange is the norm. In moving from culture to nature, M_{648} follows a regressive course, as is evidenced by one of the Humptulips versions (M_{651a}; Adamson, pp. 310–15) which emphasizes that the brothers, after their various misadventures, decided to eat only raw food and thus to assume their animal state. The same version adds that the share of game left to Wildcat by his brothers aroused the bear's greed and that since that time the latter 'steals Wildcat's food whenever he can find it'.

So, M_{648} makes social sharing (with reference to *fire*, *meals*, and *conjugal relations*) the basis of natural sharing. And it also effects a remarkable transformation by substituting roasting-sticks from the bark receptacles mentioned in the Klikitat version, in that the two kinds of kitchen utensil relate to different modes of cooking: boiling in one case and roasting in the other. There is some evidence that the Indians of north-west America held their roasting-sticks in high regard. A Nez Percé myth, which will be analysed later (M_{655a}, p. 327), is partly concerned with this point. The Chehalis of British Columbia, who are distinct from the Washington Chehalis with whose myth we are concerned at the moment, refer to a ritual dance with roasting-sticks to celebrate the return from flounder-catching expeditions (Hill-Tout 2, p. 371). The Cowlitz Indians tried to determine how long they would live by seeing how far they could throw the roasting-stick with the cooked eel's head still on it (Adamson, p. 191). The Alsea, the Chinook and other groups made it a rule that the first salmon of the year should be spit-roasted (Frachtenberg 4, p. 107; Boas 10, pp. 101–10). The Kalapuya, who combine boiling and roasting in their version of the myth (M_{647}; Jacobs 4, p. 246), relate how, in former times, roasting-sticks were not thrown away after use, but were preserved with the greatest care. In the north, the Bella Coola, an isolated Salish group, believed that a woman would give birth to twins if she ate roast salmon straight from the roasting-stick (Gunther 5, p. 171). The Tlingit, who live still farther away, have a myth (Swanton 2, pp. 313–14) which mentions the ritual washing of roasting-sticks.

As for bark, it figures just as largely in the technology and beliefs of this part of America, as it does in those of Amazonia (*HA*, pp. 363–8, 388–92). The Sahaptin and their neighbours need bark mainly as fuel: 'Long ago,' an Indian woman relates, 'the Cowlitz had no matches. They used to take some cedar bark, and would put fire down below in it where it was rotting and take it with them when they travelled to a distance. When they camped for the night, they used to blow and blow on it until it burst into flame, and build a fire with it' (Jacobs 1, p. 226). But bark was also a food: wherever there were conifers, in springtime the Indians used to eat the inner bark of several species, and would scrape the sweet resin from the trunk of the sugar pine (*Pinus lambertiana*). As for the technical uses, all the communities in the area made or used baskets of woven bark fibre, usually 'cedar' (*Thuja gigantea*), dyed red with alder bark (*Alnus rubra*: Haeberlin-Teit-Roberts, pp. 138–9) – this is the bark that Coyote chews in the Karok and Clackamas versions of the myth about the freeing of the salmon (Bright, pp. 206–207; Jacobs 2, Part I, p. 29) in order to bloody his mouth to look as if he had been eating red salmon flesh; by pretending that he is already in possession of the fish, he can more easily set them free. All the tribes knew how to make receptacles with pieces of bent bark. Lastly, the women teased out the fibres of cedar bark to make string; and they also wore short skirts made of woven bark. Bark, being at once a fuel and a food, as well as a raw material for making both clothes and cooking utensils, appears then as a natural substance pervading the whole field of culture. In the beginning, according to the Sahaptin (M_{375p}, Jacobs 1, pp. 139–42), red bark was the demiurge's sole equipment; he only had to show it and game animals died of fright. When his secret was discovered, the demiurge withdrew: 'Now that they have seen me and have learned about me, I had better go far away.' This implies that mankind, having obtained bark, has nothing more to expect from creation.

It will be remembered that the Sahaptin versions exploit an opposition between bark (M_{644}) and green leaves (M_{645}). Bark is used to make three types of utensils: pots, pails and serving dishes; leaves are only put to use as serving dishes. The fact that the respective uses of bark and leaves overlap only in this last respect probably explains why one of the versions (M_{644a}) strengthens the contrast by reserving bark for the first two operations, boiling and drawing water. This brings out the mediatory function of the receptacle between meat and fire, since it holds water into which red-hot stones have been placed; this function is contrary to the relationship of immediate contiguity between cooked meat and the dish on which it has been placed. Consequently, the significant opposition that the Sahaptin versions convey by means of bark and leaves is indicated in the Salish versions by the presence or absence of the roasting-stick. By allowing the meat to be held away from the fire, the roasting-stick also fulfils a mediatory function, which the scullion, however, nullifies not by making a noise, as in the other episode, but by being guilty of messy cooking: he puts the meat directly on to the fire. So the North American myths confirm the existence of that correlational connection between bad cooking and noise, of which the myths of the southern hemisphere have already made us suspect the universality and far-reaching significance (*RC*, pp. 293–6).

But why does the Salish myth substitute the roasting-stick for the receptacle, and roasting for boiling? A River Cowlitz version, which reverts to the bark receptacle in place of the roasting-stick, provides the answer. This version, and another less complete one ($M_{650a, b}$; Adamson, pp. 202–209), are almost identical with those recorded among the Sahaptin, who live higher up the same valley ($M_{645a, b}$), and I propose simply to point out the differences.[3] It is stated at the beginning that Cougar lived along with his brothers, although he had many wives each one of whom lived in a different place. All his adventures take place while he is on his way to visit the latest wife, Buffalo-Woman (M_{650a}), or Grizzly She-Bear, or Thunder's daughter (M_{650b}), whose father is trying to kill him and his brother. A reason for Thunder's hostility, which is not explained elsewhere, is given in M_{650a} by Meadowlark: 'You see,' she said to Cougar, 'you bought the girls some time ago but you did not come for them right away. This made the old man angry. He is a widower and could have got other husbands for the girls.' The second version is even more explicit: 'Cougar

---

[3] One detail in M_{650a} and M_{651a} (Adamson, pp. 203, 312–13) is important in another context to which I have already referred (see above, p. 258): the mistress of the fire stolen by Wildcat kept it hidden in her braids, each one of which consisted of five plaited logs. This detail makes it possible to include, in the same group of myths, the Kalapuya versions about the origin of fire and the Tillamook variant (M_{652a}; E.D. Jacobs, pp. 110–12; cf. $M_{652b, c}$; Edel, pp. 121–4), in which the logs are made of plaited wood.

had not visited his wife for nearly three years, as he had several others living in different places. Because of this, his wife's family was angry and jealous, and to keep him from returning to his other wives planned to kill him' (Adamson, pp. 208–209). Cougar and Mink survive all the attempts on their lives but decide to separate and to change into animals: 'Hereafter mink shall mate with mink and cougar with cougar. They shall always mate with their own kind.' Thunder would always live in a cloud: 'when he was a human being he was very mean' (M_{650b}, *ibid.*, p. 211).

It is clear in what respect these variants are original. The story, which is almost identical to that of the Sahaptin myth, is given the reverse etiological role – the role the Sahaptin attribute, as it happens, to the myth featuring the two she-bears (M_{615}), whose story is an inversion of the one we are concerned with here. Instead of explaining, as M_{645} did, how certain zoological species can live as a community, M_{650} decrees a whole series of separations, similar to the division of the bears according to their species, which was the function of M_{615}. But, for this transformation to be achieved without its outcome being nullified by bringing the group back to the starting-point, it must change to another register. The disunion referred to in the myth about the two she-bears belonged to the alimentary register; the one we are now dealing with belongs to the sexual register: the bear and the grizzly will not eat each other's food, the cougar and the mink will not mate. No doubt they had never mated; but they nearly died of hunger because Cougar had exposed himself (and his brother with him) to the temptations and dangers of marriages so distant that he could no longer fulfil his obligations as an affine. In both cases, consequently, the function of the myths is the same: to mark out, within the social or the natural order, those areas in which the maxim 'fair shares' is replaced by 'every man for himself'. But, whereas the Sahaptin give Cougar and Wildcat the task of defending the first, and She-Bear and Grizzly-Woman that of defending the second, the River Cowlitz Salish, thanks to a change of register, use the first animal pair to demonstrate the point that their neighbours farther upstream entrust to the second pair. This being granted, and taking into account the fact that the inversion of the messages and of the codes has already been established, it only remains to operate a lexical inversion for the transformation to come about. This is precisely what happens with the Chehalis type I (M_{648}), in which the code and message are changed back, while the vocabulary is reversed. In reverting from the maxim 'every man for himself' to that of 'fair shares', the Cougar and Wildcat myth has to change its vocabulary, but without altering the general narrative sequence; thus the terms are changed into their opposites: boiling becomes roasting and the bark receptacle a wooden roasting-stick. As I have implicitly postulated all along, another transformation bears witness to the fact that the return effected by the Chehalis myth (M_{648}) to the formula of the Upper Cowlitz Sahaptin myth (M_{645}) does not result from any direct connection between the two, but must necessarily be an effect of the intermediary agency of the Lower Cowlitz Salish myth. Let us pause to consider this point.

It is clear from what has gone before that the Cougar–Wildcat myth and the one featuring the two she-bears belong to the same transformational group. On the other hand, I have shown (see above, pp. 286–96) that the she-bears myth also belongs to what is known as the bears and fawns cycle. A further proof can be given: in the extreme south of the area of distribution of this cycle, a Pomo version (M_{639}; Barrett 2, pp. 344–9) reconstitutes the armature of the episode devoted to Cougar's marriage, but simply puts the episode at the beginning instead of the end. The symmetry between all these myths is also shown in other ways: in one instance, a doe is married to Thunder, the son of a she-bear; in the other, the Cougar is married to a she-bear, a daughter of Thunder. Also, on each occasion, there is a clash between the relative by marriage and the parent of the other partner. In almost all the versions of the bears and fawns myth, a character called Crane or Heron[4] plays the part of susceptible ferryman. The Chehalis variants $M_{649a, b}$, on the other hand, and certain Humptulips versions (M_{651b}) to which I shall return later, entrust this role to Thunder. But in M_{648}, in which this detail does not occur, Cougar is living with Crane-Women who make an intolerable din; and in M_{649b}, in which it does occur, the cranes are replaced by equally noisy geese, which, however, do not seem to perform the ferryman function in American mythology. I have already drawn attention (see above, p. 291) to the special role attributed to the ferryman in the myths we are considering. I described him as a semi-conductor, whose services are not reversible: he transports one category of passengers quite safely, but the other he intercepts and drowns. The Crane-Women, for their part, are not susceptible, in the sense of touchy: their self-respect is not such as to prevent them proposing marriage, and they have no moral scruples about demanding payment for what they have gathered. M_{648} uses them to show that, contrary to what they seem to imagine, marriage formalities are not reversible. In this field, the accepted approach is uni-directional: from the man to the woman, and not from the woman to the man. Consequently, this rule of behaviour is of the nature of a

---

[4] It is extremely difficult to distinguish between the two birds since, as Ballard (1, p. 77, n. 42) and Godfrey (p. 43) point out, the word 'crane' is often used in ordinary speech to refer to the Great Heron.

semi-conductor, and the action of the Crane-Women is not accidental. These noisy creatures who enter so willingly into their part – which might be called the role of 'non-susceptible ferried ones'[5] – are simply inversions of Thunder in the other versions, who is also noisy but susceptible in the sense of touchy (since he cannot bear anyone to come into contact with his leg when he stretches it from one bank to the other to act as a bridge), and who haggles over the payment for his services; he proves, then, to be as self-regarding as the Crane-Women, when Wildcat bargains with them for their harvest. As a susceptible ferryman, the Thunder in the Salish versions is a transformation of another old man who, in the bears and fawns cycle, is either a crane or a heron; by this means, too, then, the group closes in upon itself.

The episode of the marriage with Thunder's daughter, already encountered in M_{650b}, distinguishes the Chehalis type II from type I (see above, p. 311).

M_{649a}. Chehalis (Washington). 'The Wildcat and the Cougar'

Wildcat was looking for poles on which to cook some meat, and he sang a merry song at the thought of the good dinner he was going to have. An ogre heard him; they had to cook for him and he swallowed the meat whole, then fell asleep. Cougar struck him across the neck and ran off with his brother. The ogre pursued them and killed four of the five cougars which suddenly appear in the story (cf. M_{648}). The fifth got away, but the ogre got on Wildcat's trail. But Wildcat turned himself into several hills, then asked an old man to take him across the river. Thunder (for that was his name) agreed, provided he paid a good price. The ogre came along and he too asked to be taken across. But instead of crossing him over in his canoe, Thunder stretched his legs across the river to act as a bridge. The ogre started to cross; just about half way across Thunder shook his legs, the ogre fell off and drowned. Ever since his head rolls from one side of the coast to the other, and people know what kind of weather it will be according to the noise it makes at one place or the other.

Thunder gave his daughter in marriage to Wildcat, but tried to kill him by all sort of machinations, from which he somehow managed to escape unscathed. At last he ceased to bother him any more (Adamson, pp. 64–7).

---

[5] TRANSLATORS' NOTE: *Passées non susceptibles*: the author is creating an opposition between the active agent, *passeur*, ferryman, and the passive past participle of *passer*, to ferry.

Another version, which combines types I and II (M_{649b}; *ibid.*, pp. 67–9), puts the noisy women episode after the one containing the ogre, and continues with the stolen fire incident and the exchange of livers. As in other contexts, the brothers take leave of each other and Cougar promises Wildcat that he will always keep him a share of his game. However, the ogre continues to pursue him and he seeks shelter in Thunder's house. The latter holds Cougar prisoner, then sets him free on receiving payment for the service rendered. A final and very brief version (M_{649c}; *ibid.*, pp. 69–71) belongs to type II; it likens the noise caused by the ogre's head to the roaring of the ocean: according to whether the noise seems to be coming from the north or the south, the weather will be good or bad.

So we come back once more to the sharing motif, now transposed into meteorological terms; it is significant that the balance established in these versions between winds and between types of weather which henceforth are to alternate also puts an end to a conflict between affines. The Humptulips variants stress this correlation in two ways. On the one hand, they assert the precariousness of food sharing: the bear, even when he is destroyed as a cosmic being in the versions in which Cougar succeeds in killing his grizzly wife, survives as a zoological species according to M_{651a} (Adamson, pp. 310–15): he is still present and, disregarding the sharing rule which prevails between cougars and wildcats, whenever he can he steals the portion set aside by the former for their smaller brother. On the other hand, another Humptulips variant (M_{651b}; *ibid.*, pp. 315–24) develops the meteorological and matrimonial aspects in parallel: the different sounds emitted by the ogre's head in the direction from which they come correspond to three types of weather instead of two; and the hero has to face malevolence on the part of both his father-in-law and his mother-in-law. Finally, he placates them by giving lightning to Thunder, a gift the latter accepts in exchange, so he says, for his daughter. Until then, the myth concludes, *thunder had been noise without light*. As my analyses have confirmed, only in thunderstorms can noise which is incompatible with cooking fire, and light which is also fire, although celestial and not terrestrial, co-exist in harmony and operate jointly.

4   The Proper Use of Excrement

Even night could not separate them: often it would find them lying in the same cot, cheek to cheek and breast to breast, sleeping in each other's arms, with their hands around each other's necks.

J. H. Bernardin de Saint-Pierre, *Paul et Virginie,* 1789

On whatever level the myths operate, cosmic, meteorological, zoological or botanical, technical, economic, sexual or social, etc., they are dominated by concepts of sharing, exchange and transaction. Animal species which do not mate with each other and are careful not to encroach on each other's territories are contrasted with those which, like predators and carrion-eaters, practise a certain form of collaboration. Goods and persons obtained at fairs and markets, or by means of matrimonial transactions, are contrasted with a category of valuable possessions, such as cooking fire and drinking water, which are freely available to all. Thus, the myths we have just examined present what amounts to a typology of the possible modalities of relational life. They analyse and distinguish between cases in which there is neither exchange nor sharing, or exchange without sharing, or sharing without exchange, or a combination of sharing and exchanging. Each myth, in its own way, develops the theory of one of these styles of living, which can be given axiomatic expression in the phrases: 'every man for himself' or 'nothing for nothing', 'fair shares' and 'each for all'. In each instance, too, the demonstration is carried out by means of a different animal pair, the two members of which are partners, adversaries or rivals.

Melville Jacobs, who has devoted his life to collecting all the surviving mythic material in that particular geographical area, has often emphasized that the myths recorded by his predecessors and himself represent only a minute fraction of a vast body of mythology that has vanished for ever. It would, therefore, be pointless to attempt to draw up a systematic table of the animal pairs and their functions. But we can at least single out the most important, those which feature in myths of which we possess several versions. Next, we can distinguish between the pairs formed from antithetical terms (eagle and coyote, eagle and skunk, etc.) and those formed from analogous, but unequally stressed, terms. In this last category I have mentioned the three pairs formed, respectively, by the coyote and the wolf, the brown (or black) bear and the grizzly, and the wildcat and the cougar. In each of these cases, the two animals have an intimate relationship which is abused by one of the two. This leads to conflict, which is resolved, in the first case by the institution of exchange, in the second by that of non-sharing, and in the third by that of sharing. To complete the group we now have to add a fourth pair that has already been mentioned (M_{641a-d}; see above, p. 282). This pair, which consists of Coyote and Fox as elder and younger brother respectively, is a transformation of the pair formed by one or several coyotes and wolves who are strangers to each other and who steal each other's food. In each instance, however, the point is to establish the origin of exchange, in the one case on the commercial and in the other on the matrimonial level. But a further significant difference can be discerned between the two groups.

The conflict between the coyote and the wolves must take place in the spring or at the beginning of summer since, in almost all versions, the wolves are said to be feeding on bird's eggs, which would only be available during this period. A Salish version (M_{614c}; Jacobs 1, pp. 169–71) of the other myth ends with a sequence suggestive of winter: after instituting the use of money in matrimonial transactions, Coyote meets some children who say that their mother is the 'person who gives sudden scares'. The demiurge does not believe them and kidnaps them. Shortly afterwards, however, a bird which was lurking on the ground flies up so suddenly from under his feet that Coyote falls back senseless on the river bank. The bird then comes back and rescues its children. Next the spirit of frost appears and, taking advantage of the fact that Coyote is asleep, steals the bag full of valuables that Coyote had appropriated. Consequently, within the M_{614} group we see the following transformation:

[*bad neighbours* $\Rightarrow$ *bad weather*]

:: [*spatial enemy* = 'Sioux' $\Rightarrow$ *temporal enemy* = 'Frost']

The bird which frightens Coyote is a grouse. In North America the term covers several different kinds of birds, although it would seem that in this part of the continent it is applied chiefly to the *Canachites* and *Bonasa* families, known as grouse or prairie chicken (see below, p. 392 *et seq.*).

Whereas the Salish myth introduces first the grouse then the spirit of frost, and presents them as being objectively in league with each other, the Kalapuya fuse the two characters into one: the bird's call was heard at the time of year when food stocks were exhausted and famine prevailed, and when people were sometimes reduced to eating mocassins. The spirit of the grouse was blamed for the heavy falls of snow which delayed the arrival of spring (Jacobs 4, p. 34). The Nez Percé, for their part, place the adventures of Coyote and Fox during the period of famine at the end of winter (M_{614e}; Phinney, pp. 301–306; cf. Boas 4, 184–5).

It is no doubt possible to find the same seasonal correlations in the other myths in the group, or at least in the one about the two berry-gathering female bears, since berry gathering is a summer activity and the planti-grades sleep during winter. So, in order to complete the cycle, the myth featuring Wildcat and Cougar would have to be set in autumn, and this would be consistent with the habits of animals which live chiefly by hunting. A more explicit indication is given towards the end of M_{644a} (Jacobs 3, pp. 194–5) when Wildcat meets a man fishing for a species of salmon (*Salmo gairdnerii*), known as steelhead trout because of its hard skin. This particular fish swims up river between November and May: many myths belonging to the area indicate that the steelhead trout is fished in winter (Adamson, pp. 163–4; E. D. Jacobs, pp. 167, 177), and consider the steelhead trout and spring salmon as being diametrically opposed to each other (M_{653a-e}; Adamson, pp. 72–4; Ballard 1, pp. 133–4). When considered from this seasonal angle, the Sahaptin myths seem to arrange themselves into a quadripartite group, in which summer is contrasted with winter, just as the cautious attitude Bear and Grizzly adopt towards each other is in opposition to Coyote and Fox's alliance against a common enemy. This first double pair of contrasted terms is inverted to become a second pair, in which autumn is in opposition to spring in the same way as the uni-directional sharing of food between Cougar and Wildcat is in opposition to the reciprocal theft practised by wolves and coyotes.

While the seasonal coding seems plausible in the case of the Sahaptin versions, it cannot be applied so easily to the Cowlitz, Chehalis and Humptulips versions. The gathering of *lacamas* (the Chinook term for camas, *Camassia quamash*), the Crane-Women's occupation in M_{648}, defi-nitely takes place in the spring, since the myth specifies that they are '*Button lacamas*' (Adamson, p. 62), that is, the very early tubers which the Chinook, a little farther south, gathered in March (Jacobs 2, Part I, p. 75). On the other hand, one of the ordeals imposed by old man Thunder on his son-in-law in M_{651b} is the gathering of an enormous quantity of snow. We know, however (see above, p. 320), that the Salish versions are not concerned with any particular period in the year but are meant to explain weather changes occurring in all seasons. Consequently, when we move from the Sahaptin to the Salish, we find that a total transformation brings together within a single and more complex myth meteorological or climatic modalities that the Sahaptin deal with separately, each in a different myth. The same transformation moves the maxim 'every man for himself' from the alimentary to the sexual plane, and that of 'fair shares' from nature to culture. But there is more to it than that, since the order in which the myths have spontaneously arranged themselves – through the mere fact that the interpretation of each one involves bringing another into play – constantly oscillates between transactions of two types, matrimonial and economic, but always based on the concept of permitted or forbidden exchange. Native thought did not separate the two types and made no clear jural distinction between acquiring a wife and obtaining material goods. Sometimes women were even exchanged directly for everyday commodities: the River Cowlitz Salish, 'although they were ashamed of it', used to give a woman in exchange for a selection of freshly picked foods which had been gathered and offered for sale by the Upper Cowlitz Sahaptin (Jacobs 1, p. 245).

After starting with M_{606}, which opens with a family conflict leading to incest and ends with the institution of fairs and markets, I have been led to deal with myths relating to different forms of exchange. In listing and analysing these forms, the myths brought me back to matrimonial problems of the opposite kind to those I studied at the beginning: the myth featuring Wildcat and Cougar deals not with incest but with the dangers inherent in too distant matrimonial connections. According to M_{645}, such marriages can never materialize, and the hero remains a bachelor, but they are successfully achieved at the end of the Humptulips version, M_{651b}, which consequently illustrates the final state of a single transformation. Reducing the matter to its simplest expression, we can say, then, that M_{606} starts with a disastrous marriage concluded between a character called Bow and a grizzly she-bear, whereas M_{651b} ends with the same marriage but which this time is successful; it is still a marriage between a hunter and Thunder's daughter who, according to the intermediary versions, is a grizzly. The woman character and the incidents in which she is involved are gradually shifted from the beginning of the myth (M_{606}) to the middle ($M_{615-642}$), but from M_{645} onwards to M_{651b} it is still the same woman and the same incidents that we find again at the end.

This being so, a Sahaptin myth, which reverses the whole system and provides an *a contrario* demonstration of the previous interpretation, is found to be of particular interest. This myth belongs to a small group, the boundaries of which are ill-defined,[1] and to which American mythographers without reflecting on its meaning and possibilities have given the somewhat colourless title of 'Anus-Wiper'. However, when one is writing in the language of Rabelais, it is no doubt permissible to use a more vivid term.[2]

M_{654}. *Sahaptin (Cowlitz River). 'The adventures of Anus-Wiper and Urinator'*

In former times a grizzly husband and wife were living together. The husband and a young sister, and the wife's best friend was a she-bear. Gradually, Grizzly-Man grew tired of his wife and tried to abandon her. He feigned illness, and spread it around that he was dead. He arranged for his father's dog, which he himself had killed, to be buried in his place . When the wife discovered the piece of trickery, he was already far away.

The enraged Grizzly-Wife devoured all the inhabitants of the village except her little sister-in-law, who became her drudge. Every time she defecated, she used the poor girl's hair to wipe herself. The girl's brother, who had set off to look for her, found her in a pitiable state with her head full of faeces from the wipings. He got inside the house without his former wife recognizing him. The two women were sitting feet opposite feet, with the ogress's cannibalistic food placed on the ground between their widely-stretched legs. On seeing the visitor they quickly folded their legs to hide their privates. The man refused to share their loathsome repast but, although he remained incognito, he spent that night with his wife.

The next morning, on some pretext or other, he made her dig a pit which was so deep that she could not get out of it. He took his bow and arrows and killed her; then he clubbed the she-bear, the dead woman's friend, to death. He ordained that in future wild beasts would be killed in this way.

The man tried to run off with his sister, but she had lived too long

---

[1] They could be extended as far as the Missouri basin, provided the Urinator character is inverted into another, called 'Sternum' or 'Bad Bone' by the Mandan (M_{463}, M_{469b}, Bowers 1, pp. 291–2, 320. Cf. below, p. 336). Nearer Sahaptin territory, cf. the Kutenai myth: M_{656}, Boas 9, p. 125; Okanagon: $M_{656c, d}$, Cline, pp. 201–204, 224–7.

[2] TRANSLATORS' NOTE: The author uses *Torche-Cul* (Arse-Wiper) and *Pipi-au-Lit* (Pee-in-the-Bed).

with the ogress: as they went along she changed into a grizzly, and started to pursue her brother, who fled. She was just about to catch up with him when he took refuge in a house, where there was a small boy. The man asked the boy to help him, but in reply the boy just teasingly repeated what the man had said. This went on until the man addressed the boy as brother-in-law. Whereupon the boy, who in this myth is called Little Urine Person, hid him in a knot of his hair and by magical means made the house shrink. The Grizzly-Sister came along and asked Little Urine Person 'if he had seen the food which she was pursuing'. The boy merely echoed her words; then as Grizzly became angry, he urinated on the bear's body and in her mouth. The urine was poisonous and the she-bear died.

Towards evening, Little Urine Person's five sisters, who were all older than he was, came back laden with edible roots. The boy asked each one in turn if he could sleep with her. The four eldest refused for fear he urinated on them in the night, but the youngest agreed. She knew he had a man hidden in his hair. When he brought him out, the sisters wanted the stranger to become their common husband. 'No,' said the boy to the four eldest, 'you rejected me, so only your youngest sister shall have the man' (Jacobs 1, pp. 186–8).

This curious story would remain incomprehensible if we did not see it as the product of a systematic inversion. The first part can be entirely reconstructed by reversing in turn each narrative cell of the Klikitat myth M_{606}. In that myth, a character called Bow (the hunting weapon of future mankind) is, because of his name, in a complementary relation to his two wives, Grizzly and She-Bear (who are called after future game animals). Here, the situation is reversed: She-Bear and Grizzly are friends, not mutually hostile co-wives; and the relationship between Grizzly and her husband is supplementary not complementary, since he himself is a Grizzly. In M_{606}, natural causes impose a temporary separation on Grizzly-Woman and her husband: she is having her monthly periods. In M_{654}, the husband intends to leave his wife for good and to that end he invents a subterfuge. This gives the following triple transformation:

a) M_{606} *(hostile co-wives)* $\Rightarrow M_{654}$ *(friends not co-wives)*
b) M_{606} *(husband/wife)* $\Rightarrow M_{654}$ *(wife $\equiv$ husband)*
c) M_{606} *(natural, temporary disjunction)* $\Rightarrow M_{654}$ *(artificial, definitive disjunction)*

The Grizzly-Woman in M_{606} has a son and a daughter: her husband is promptly changed into a bow, and nothing more is heard of him. The

Grizzly-Woman in M_{654} has no child: she has, however, two affines, a husband and a young sister-in-law. No further mention is made of her friend She-Bear, except that she is said to have been killed by a blow from a club (an implement forming, with the bow, a pair of correlative and contrasted terms). In M_{654}, Grizzly's affines play a part which is symmetrical to, and the reverse of, the one devolving on Grizzly's children in M_{606}: 1) the relation between them, which is incestuous in M_{606} becomes cannibalistic in M_{654}; 2) this relation is formed after the ogress's murder, not before; 3) the murder is committed by the woman in the one instance, by the man in the other; 4) in both myths, a pit is the means whereby the murder is committed, but the ogress in M_{606} climbs down into a natural pit, since she is suffering from a lack of water (shortage of wet food), the one in M_{654} digs an artificial pit in order, so the myth states, to hide her stock of human bones (excess of dry food); 5) in M_{606} the mother turned grizzly kills her son, while ostensibly delousing him, that is, cleaning his head, a process which is the reverse of the one imposed by the Grizzly-Woman on her young sister-in-law, whom she forces to become her anus-wiper, although she does not kill her: she smears the sister-in-law's hair with her faeces instead of removing lice – a kind of filth – from it.

After the ogress's murder, M_{606} continues with the bird-nester story and M_{654} with the story of Urinator. To continue the comparison effectively, one or two variants must now be introduced:

M_{655a}. *Nez Percé. 'The adventures of Anus Wiper and Urinator'*

A little girl much beloved of the whole village was kidnapped by five Bear-Sisters. Her brother, who was called Red-headed Woodpecker, set off to look for her. He found her in a sorry state: she explained how the bears made her work very hard, wiped their buttocks in turn on her head and gave her nothing to eat. Woodpecker gave her a prairie chicken he had killed, so she could say she had caught it herself, and he covered his sister's head with sharp grass which gashed the bears' buttocks when they tried to wipe themselves. It was their custom to eat nude, and the bears ate their mush very noisily. When Woodpecker came in, they hastily put on their clothes again. He agreed to share their meal, spent the night with one of them, but talked incessantly so that they were all kept awake. When they finally fell asleep out of sheer exhaustion, Woodpecker set fire to the lodge and tried to leave with his sister, forbidding her to take anything with her. But she could not drag herself away from the sight of the bears, whose corpses were exploding in the flames, and she succumbed to her desire to recover their teeth. A fatal decision, for she became contaminated, and having changed into a bear, gave chase to her brother.

The latter sought refuge with five women, whom he called first his cousins, then his sisters-in-law. But they would only listen to him when he called them his wives. They hid him and managed to deceive the she-bear by means of riddles. These women were dangerous wild mountain sheep (*Ovis canadensis*) who, although they allowed the hero to cook his dinner, forbade him to touch the fire with their (roasting?) sticks made of thuya wood. Nevertheless, he used them to stir up the fire. The sticks were the women's 'children', and he had destroyed them. They flew into a rage and started to run after him. He found refuge in a house whose occupant, a boy called Urinator, agreed to hide him at the back of his neck, provided he called him brother-in-law. When the mountain sheep arrived, he sprinkled them with urine and they died.

Soon after, Urinator's five sisters returned from hunting. They upbraided him for having killed their 'cousins', whom they revived by straddling their corpses.[3] Next they prepared their food. Each sister in turn refused to share her portion with Urinator, except the youngest, who shouted: 'The idea of asking them. When did they ever give you a share? Hurry up, come along and eat! We are the only ones who pity each other.' The same scene was repeated when the boy asked each of his sisters to take him in her bed: they all said he stank of urine, but the youngest said: 'As if it were the first time we have urinated on each other in bed! Come along, let us sleep together!' Whereupon, he brought out the boy whom he had hidden on the back of his neck. In spite of Urinator's protests, the sisters seized Woodpecker and made him the husband of all of them.

One day Woodpecker wanted to go hunting. His wives warned him not to cross a certain divide of the mountain, but he followed a wounded buck over the divide. All at once, he was surrounded by a great many small men, who were first of all frightened by his fire. He burnt all his stock of wood, then the game he had killed. As the fire died down, the small men flocked more closely round him. Woodpecker climbed to the top of a large pine which was standing there. By hoisting each other up one upon the other, the small men almost managed to reach him. He broke off a branch and used it as a stake to pierce and burst open their bodies. As the small men fell, they bit one another at random. When morning came, the little men decided to sew each other together, so that

---

[3] For resuscitation by straddling, cf. Spinden 1, p. 153; McDermott, pp. 242, 244 *et seq*.

they formed a solid mass around the pine tree, leaving no room for anyone to pass. However, they fell asleep and slept so soundly that Woodpecker was able to escape, after crushing and bursting open the bodies. When he reached the house, he found Urinator with his eyes swollen from crying (Phinney, pp. 106–12).

This version raises several problems, first that of the title under which the informant's son recorded and published it. He called it 'Young Stars', although there is no mention of stars in the text. Have we to suppose that, as happens in the myths of the Kalapuya to the south (Jacobs 4, pp. 173–5) and the Cœur d'Alêne to the north (Boas 4, pp. 125–6), the leading characters in the myth were transformed permanently into a constellation at the end of the final scene? This is a plausible hypothesis, but it would only be of interest if the stars in question could be identified, and this, unfortunately, is not the case. As for the dwarfs who painstakingly sew themselves together, but are pierced by the hero, it is tempting to compare them with the pygmies referred to in the myths of the Puget Sound Salish: those pygmies are dumb and have such small mouths that they can eat nothing but the maggots on rotten fish (Haeberlin 1, p. 429). Moreover, throughout the area, there are abundant references to supernatural beings who are either blocked above or below, in front or behind, or on several sides at once. They are to be found, for instance, in the myths of the Chinook (Sapir-Spier 2, p. 279; Jacobs 2, Part I, pp. 80–105; Part II, pp. 388–409, cf. M_{598}) and the Tillamook (E. D. Jacobs, pp. 3–9). More often than not, these characters participate in the ordering of the world by the demiurge: he restores them to normal life by piercing the missing orifices. The fact that a comparable action is here presented as being destructive, and that it is carried out when the hero, to escape from a danger of terrestrial if not chthonian origin, has climbed to the top of a tree and is thus both imitating and contradicting the bird-nester character, surely provides adequate proof that this family of myths is a reflection of those – but an inverted reflection – previously studied. And is excrement not the reverse of food?

There can be no question of restarting the enquiry at this level, since the group that has just been illustrated by these two examples is interwoven, in the most complex way, with the whole mythological fabric of north-west America and extends even farther afield. We know that the Salish, the Chinook and their immediate neighbours attribute the ordering of the world to a demiurge called Moon (M_{375}, M_{382}, M_{506}). He carries out his labours in the course of a long peregrination, which takes him back to his own people from the land of salmon, where he had been brought up, and subsequently married by two milt-girls who had stolen him from his cradle. Certain versions state that Moon was conceived in the sky by the woman who wished to marry a star. Unlike her counterpart in the Plains myths, she manages to return to earth, but the rope or ladder that she uses breaks: ever since then, communication between the sky and earth has been impossible (see below, pp. 412–13). The demiurge's saga, in this complete form, which links it to myths that were discussed at length in the previous volume (Parts Four and Five), raises in two successive phases the problem of mediation between the natural and supernatural worlds, and between nature and society. An initial attempt at conjunction along the vertical axis fails: humans will no longer be able to communicate with the sky; however, a second attempt along the horizontal axis is successful, thanks to the demiurge, and the ascent of the salmon, on which men depend for survival, provides periodic confirmation of the myth.

The demiurge's saga, when reduced to these essential outlines, is transformable into the bird-nester story. Both operate in the first place along a vertical axis, no doubt with a view to disjunction and not conjunction in the versions of the bird-nester examined so far; but among the inland tribes (the Nez Percé and the Plateau Salish), we are soon back to the initial formula, since the hero, who has been left stranded at the top of a tree, manages to reach the sky where he experiences various adventures before returning to earth. On the other hand, the peregrinations which lead the *trickster* willy-nilly to the sea, are inversions of those of the *demiurge*, because of their involuntary nature and their direction, but they too precede the freeing (if not the creation) of the salmon.

When the bird-nester myths keep to the disjunctive aspect, we know what happens to the hero on his lofty perch: he suffers hunger and thirst, he wastes away, and birds splatter him with their droppings; his faithful wife or wives who have remained on earth are given only meagre amounts of tainted food by Coyote, their new master. Similarly, in the Salish and Chinook stories, when the demiurge Moon returns to his own people, he finds that his little brother (who was made from his elder brother's urine, and will later become the sun) is being persecuted by a domestic trickster called Blue Jay, who uses him as an anus-wiper. The myths are not simply content, then, to consider straightforward operations such as conjunction and disjunction, and situate them along horizontal or vertical axes, they also distinguish between the *directions* in which these operations occur, and between *degrees*. Corresponding to the *bird-nester*, a weak and incomplete form of a character who succeeds in rising up into the sky, we have the *bear's grave digger* in M_{654}, who is complementary to his anus-wiping relative: a character, so to speak, *buried under a bear*, the bear being the animal incarnation of the chthonian world.

The fact that the misfortunes of Anus-Wiper — a male or female character — represent a chthonian counterpart to the visit to the sky during which a male or female from earth becomes the wife or husband of a star, is also shown by an etiological function common to both groups: they explain the origin of insect parasites, since the relationship of these insects to man (on whom they feed) is the same as that between man himself and the game he hunts. The young Chinook hero, kidnapped by an ogress (M_{598a}), who then brings him up tenderly and feeds him on the foul creatures which form her normal diet (he is in a situation symmetrical to that of Anus-Wiper), kills his adoptive mother and escapes by climbing a tree which takes him up into the sky. There he meets communities which are to become different species of insect vermin, such as bugs, nits and fleas.

Symmetrically, the Clackamas version of the Anus-Wiper myth (M_{656a}; Jacobs 2, Part II, pp. 315–31) relates how a woman, who had already become a grizzly and was soon to turn into an ogress, burst into a village and forced one of the inhabitants to accept her as a co-wife. By giving meat to families of previously vegetarian insect vermin, she instilled in them a taste for blood.

Two remarks are in order here. Firstly, M_{654} and M_{655}, which deal with the origin and technique of bear-hunting (see above, p. 325), could contain inversions of the insect vermin motif in the episode of M_{655} in which the hero climbs to the top of a tall conifer not, as in M_{598a}, in order to reach the sky and encounter creatures which pierce, but in order to escape from the earth, overrun by other dwarf-like creatures that he himself will eventually proceed to pierce. Since these are foundation myths establishing the hunting of bears by humans and not the hunting of humans by lice and fleas, the latter could be appearing in the form of an inversion of insect vermin.

The same point can be made by means of a Thompson myth (M_{655b}; Teit 4, p. 35; 5, pp. 362–5), in which a mother and son, who escape by crossing over an arch formed by a jet of urine emitted by the boy (an inversion of the Urinator character), are pursued and then besieged in a tree by a community of insect vermin. The Nootka version (M_{600f}) of the story about the son born from nasal mucus also confirms this interpretation, since the hero, far from having been stolen by an ogress, is the only one of several children who does not suffer this fate; he can thus set out to look for his brothers and sisters, and eventually set them free. Like his Clackamas counterpart, he climbs up into the sky, where he too marries the sun's daughter. However, there he encounters, instead of piercing insect vermin, beautiful but blind snail-girls, whom he endows with eyes by using his penis as a drill (see above, pp. 242, 281–2). It must not be forgotten that, in a Wishram version of the myth concerning the sun's husband (M_{598g}), we find — on earth this time — the (similarly piercing) counterpart of the insect vermin, in the form of ants, hornets and wasps. Finally, I propose to introduce, at a later stage, a Thompson myth (M_{658b}; see below, p. 325), which is an inversion of those we have just examined, and where the young heroine has a little dog called Vermin: so the role of vermin changes from that of human parasites to that of domestic animals.

If the myth featuring the stolen child who escapes to the sky to become the husband of a heavenly body constitutes, as I have shown, the symmetrical counterpart of the one featuring the wives of the sun and moon, then the reverse myth about the child who *is not* stolen (and who is sometimes the offspring of the *nasal mucus ejected* by a woman or of a *stone* which she *has ingested*) must, in the first of these two forms, constitute the symmetrical counterpart of the important group of studies in the previous volume under the title of 'Stoneboy' (M_{466}, M_{470}, M_{487}, M_{489}), and which, by different means, I had already linked up with the one about the wives of the sun and moon. In the Salish saga about the lunar demiurge, Moon is also described as a kidnapped child, but he is stolen by milt-girls who are the polar opposites of ogresses: they themselves are food, and they give birth either to trees which are useful to humans ($\neq$ the ogress's accomplices in M_{598a}) or to edible fish (the food value of which is unknown to the ogress in M_{598a}). We can thus see how an incredibly complex mass of myths might be organized into a single group (Figure 23).

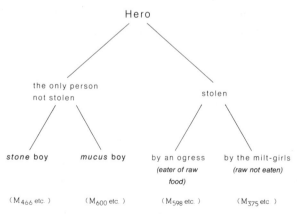

Figure 23. The structure of the Stolen Hero group

All the characters in the diagram have a celestial connotation or counterpart: the Moon or its spots or parhelia, with a corresponding chthonian counterpart or infernal (in both senses of the term) ordeal, which is imposed on characters who will eventually recover their celestial status, and is illustrated in the anus-wiper story. The bird-nester story takes place on an intermediary level: the hero is stranded half-way between earth and sky, and he is soiled not by bears but by birds.

When I first sketched in (pp. 247-8) the outlines of this system, I drew attention to certain Klallam variants of M_{600} in which the mucus boy frees his sister, who has been kidnapped and married by a bear. She goes back to her own people with the offspring of this marriage: a little girl with two heads or two faces, and insolent into the bargain, who offends her uncle by reminding him that he is made of mucus, and thus prompts him to go off into the sky. This girl, who is half human and half bear, and who is particularly dangerous through having eyes at the back as well as the front of her head, and is thus impervious to attack from all sides, makes a brief appearance in a previously quoted Chinook myth (M_{646a}; Jacobs 2, Part I, pp. 262-4), where she is encountered by the son of Thunder and a human woman, who frees future mankind from the extreme danger she represents. She crops up again, a long way from this area, in a myth belonging to the Menomini who live near the Great Lakes ($M_{657a, b}$; Skinner-Satterlee, pp. 305-11; Bloomfield 3, pp. 395-409): here the character is a boy not a girl, the child of a woman who is herself the offspring of a human and a she-bear, and who, for a time, has been reduced by foxes to the function of anus-wiper. The myth ends with the horizontal disjunction of the leading characters, some of whom go off to the north, others to the south, like the people in the Clackamas version (M_{656a}), each of whom sets off in a different direction: the woman becomes a water being and is thus connected with the west; her children and their uncle travel eastwards into the mountains; the husband, on his own, goes off in a third direction.

Another Clackamas myth occupying an intermediary position between the anus-wiper group and the bears and fawns cycle (M_{619}; Jacobs 2, Part I, pp. 156-66) also ends with a tripartition of the 'Myth Age actors': some go towards the rivers, some into the mountains, others into the air; and they become fish, quadrupeds and birds. So, we see the same pattern repeating itself everywhere.

These brief references must suffice. They are enough to show that, despite its bizarre character, the anus-wiper story cannot be passed off as a figment of the farcical imagination of some local story-teller. Moreover, it would be easy to find its paradigm throughout North America, by showing that the motif of the woman victimized by her husband who burns her face with red-hot cinders — a motif widespread throughout the Great Lakes area and farther east — is a transformation of that of the victim whose head is soiled with faeces (see below, pp. 516–19).

I interrupted my analysis to bring in the Nez Percé version, in which the youngest sister of an incontinent hero cordially invites him to share her meal and her bed. This episode is clarified by another version:

M_{658a}. *Cowlitz. 'The story of Urinator'*

Urinator had five sisters. One day he killed a dangerous being, who was chasing a young man, and then concealed the man in his braid of hair. The same thing happened five times in succession with different characters, and so the young hero could give each of his sisters a husband. The eldest had two children, a boy and a girl, who fell in love with each other and ran away. The mother followed them but could not catch up with them. The incestuous couple took refuge with strangers. They had one child. Every day he danced while singing: 'My mother is also my aunty, my father is also my uncle . . .' His father was ashamed lest people should hear him, so he killed the boy. The trickster demiurge arrived on the scene and ordered the incestuous couple to separate; he forced the man and woman to choose a mate for themselves among strangers: 'This is the way it shall be done in the future: as soon as they are old enough to know better, brothers, sisters and cousins will not make love to each other. And so it is today; if a brother and sister act like lovers, it is not nice' (Adamson, p. 226).

Through the motif of the incestuous siblings pursued by their irate mother,[4] this Cowlitz myth links up with the Klikitat story (M_{606}) which was my starting-point. And the latter, in turn, throws light on the Cowlitz story since, although the mother in M_{658a} constitutes a weak replica of the mother turned grizzly in M_{606} (the infanticide remains, but is transferred to the next generation), the marriages of the five sisters with humans take place between too distant partners. On the other hand, a subsequent marriage unites a brother and sister, that is, partners who are too close. This double abuse of an actual disjunction which ought to have been respected, and of a potential conjunction which ought to have been avoided, leads to

---

[4] The study of the Salish group of incestuous siblings belongs more appropriately to a different context which I dealt with in my lecture-course at the Collège de France, 1968–9. Here I only touch on the subject and, for further information, I refer the reader to Teit 2, pp. 340–41; 5, pp. 287–8; Hill-Tout 5, pp. 336–8; 10, pp. 566–74; Cline, pp. 212–13; etc.

the taboo on incest and the institution of a reasonable form of exogamy, uniting partners both of whom are human yet strangers to each other. An intermediary state between the two bears group, to which M_{658a} is linked, is provided by some Thompson and Shuswap myths ($M_{658b, c}$; Teit 4, pp. 72–4; I, pp. 707–709). The heroine, the little sister of four brothers who spend all their time hunting, is the reverse of an anus-wiper since, instead of kidnapping and putting her through the usual ordeal, the four Grizzly-Sisters, whom she encounters in the fields, flatter her and shower her with presents. They want to marry her brothers and, according to M_{658b}, manage to seduce the man by surreptitiously placing some of their pubic hair inside the edible roots which form their staple diet, and persuading the little girl to serve up those roots at the next meal. In other words, we have a triple transformation:

a) (*she-bear's faeces*) $\Rightarrow$ (*she-bear's food*)

b) (*girl's head-hair*) $\Rightarrow$ (*animals' pubic hair*)

c) (*soiled sister*) $\Rightarrow$ (*seduced brothers*)

Once they are married, the she-bears lose no time in killing and eating their husbands. Only the eldest brother manages to escape with his little sister. In spite of the difference in their ages, which makes the incestuous relationship even more reprehensible, he takes her as his wife. Soon she has a child, whom she lulls to sleep by singing: 'Oh, your uncle has gone hunting! Oh, your father has gone hunting!' (cf. M_{658a} and the inversion, correlative with previous inversions, of the direction from which the revelation is made). The eldest Grizzly-Sister, who is still looking for her husband, hears the woman, kills her and eats both her and the baby. The man comes back and recognizes the ogress's voice. He collects all the water from the rivers into a well near the cabin. He comes home, complains of thirst and asks his wife for water, but she tells him that the rivers are dry. He then directs her to the well and, while she is leaning over the edge, he pushes her from behind and drowns her; he then reinstates the proper functioning of the hydrographic system.

It can be seen that the first part of the myth is an inversion of M_{658a}, while the second part is an inversion of M_{606}: here, the sister and her baby die, and the brother escapes unscathed; the reverse happens in the other myth. Furthermore, the cannibalistic she-bear appears as a wife not a mother. Lastly, the ogress is drowned in water which has been made superabundant, whereas the one in M_{606} dies as a result of an absence of water, by falling into a dried-up pit.

In the Shuswap version (M_{658c}), the story develops differently after the episode of the seductive pubic hair. Instead of allowing themselves to be seduced, the brothers decide to kill the bears, but they themselves die in the struggle. Their young sister weeps, blows her nose over the fire, and her nasal mucus becomes a little child. His name, 'Mucus Stone', is in itself a synthesis of the two groups, 'mucus boy' and 'the stone boy', the affinity between which has already been proved independently (see above, pp. 247, 332). On reaching adulthood, he kills the she-bears and brings his uncles back to life.

All these myths, then, belong to one and the same transformational group, and all deal with incest, which they compare with other kinds of union between partners who are either too remote from each other or suitably distant. However, as I recalled on pp. 333–4, in order to establish the connections, I have had to operate by way of myths which express, in terms of relationships between different animal species, the problem that M_{658} reduces to its sociological expression, and which, more importantly, resort to an alimentary code to state the different solutions society can find for the marriage question. It is, therefore, not surprising that the anus-wiper group, which inverts these myths and, in particular, as we saw on p. 327, the two bears myth, should transform the alimentary code into what might be called the excremental code. It, too, in a new register, allows the establishment of a dividing line between what can or cannot be exchanged.

In this respect, the use of others — even slaves — for the purposes that myths $M_{654-657}$ describe, with a kind of horrified fascination, would seem to represent, for the native mind, the ultimate form of degradation. The myths belonging to this area show a genuine delicacy of feeling as regards the performing of the natural functions. For instance, Coyote warns his travelling companion: 'My belly aches. I shall defecate. Do not wait for me. You might smell me' (M_{646a}; Jacobs 2, Part I, p. 264). However, these north-western communities put urine into a entirely different category from faeces.[5] It was collected in pots and used for bodily hygiene. During his celestial peregrinations, the hero of M_{598a-c}, on entering a hut whose

---

[5] The distinction probably supplies the key to the inversion of the group in Mandan mythology that I have already mentioned (p. 325). Instead of wiping her bottom on her victim, the cannibalistic Mandan wife has a protuberant bone which wedges in a crack (≡ anus) hollowed out for that purpose by a young hero called 'Sternum' or 'Bad Bone', whereas, if my interpretation is correct, the name of his Sahaptin or Salish homologue denotes 'good excrement'. The significance of this transformation: *urine* $\Rightarrow$ *bone*, i.e., *liquid excretion* $\Rightarrow$ *solid 'incretion'* is confirmed by the Plains Red Head cycle (M_{463}, M_{469}, etc.), in which the abnormally robust *arm* or *leg* of a man disguised as a woman betrays his identity, just as in the Chinook version of the same myth (Jacobs 2, Part II, pp. 340–41; Hymes 2) he is betrayed by his masculine way of *urinating*.

occupants are absent, goes straight to the pot full of urine and washes his hair. The use of urine as a hair or body lotion, for which there is ample ethnographical evidence, places it in exceptionally marked opposition to the bear's faeces, since urine serves to cleanse the head whereas, according to the myths, it is always the head that is soiled by faeces. On the level of the excretory functions, the bear's behaviour with her slave illustrates a form of reprehensible proximity, which is as shocking as incest would be on the sexual level. Urinator's youngest sister adopts a form of behaviour which, in respect of the excretory functions, comes objectively very close to incest; however, her behaviour concerns urine, not faeces, and on the sexual level, it eventually provides the heroine with a handsome partner, who will make her a good husband. Whether they deal with food or faeces, all the myths are attempting to define the boundaries between what must, or must not be shared.

The arguments just put forward follow on from the observation that, in Sahaptin mythology, the bird-nester myth on the one hand and the Wildcat and Cougar myth on the other have correlative and opposite etiological functions. In its North American forms which we have studied so far, the first purports to explain the origin of fairs and markets, that is, of *exchanges*, and defines them in relationship to culture. The second establishes the origin of *sharing*, which it defines in relationship to nature. Each myth, then, illustrates a symmetrical state of a transformation which develops progressively through a series of states.

However, this progression along a linear axis also gives rise to overtones. Like a melody which follows its own curve, while each note, as it is sounded, awakens the series of its harmonics, so to each stage of the transformation, considered as a succession of states, there corresponds a set of superimposed mythic elements, which together constitute chords. To the character playing the part of mediator, thus ensuring the transition between two states or two worlds, there is a corresponding anti-mediator, who is made inoperative or even rendered capable of a negative effect. The two functions are shared by the hero of $M_{654-655}$ and his sister who, after being forced to act as anus-wiper, is changed into an ogress. The anti-mediator in turn is inverted to become the Urinator character, who comes to the rescue of the first mediator and turns the initially maleficent power of excrement (an inversion of the beneficent power of food) against his opponent.

The dual nature, at once melodic and contrapuntal, of the transformation, which occurs along the two axes of successiveness and simultaneity and which is consequently projected as a sequence of syntagms and a system of paradigms, makes possible the occurrence of delays or anticipations in the manner of what musicians call interrupted or avoided cadences. It sometimes happens that motifs or incidents relating to a previous or a subsequent state of the transformation group are juxtaposed within the same myth, either in the background, or in the form of different myths situated at different levels. When these states are arranged in what might be called, for the sake of convenience, the 'natural' order, the anus-wiper myths definitely come after the bird-nester stories, since it is more economical in negotiating the series of intermediary types to transform the latter into the former than to try to obtain the same result by the reverse process. However, as I pointed out on page 331, the anus-wiper motif was already present by implication in the bird-nester story. In almost all contexts it indicates a critical diachronic phase of the hero's adventure, and it emerges even more obviously when the hero splits up, on the synchronic level, into two characters: his own and that of his young son, who embodies the neutralization of his mediatory function. This is the case in the Yurok versions (M_{557}), where the hero's son serves at a butt for his grandfather, who blinds him with sperm, so as to have no embarrassing witness when he satisfies his incestuous desires: a very obvious transformation of the anus-wiper, since it facilitates the transition from the bird-nester story to the one (M_{598}) about the hero who also climbs to the top of a tree but then goes on up into the sky to become the husband of a solar creature. When he returns to earth with his wife, he discovers that his young brother has been tormented and blinded by Blue-Jay. The transition from one myth to the other is modulated by a third, also belonging to the Chinook (M_{659}; Boas 10, pp. 130–32, cf. below, $M_{712-713}$, p. 447): the hero's companions maroon him on an island in the middle of the sea where they have gone in search of ear-shells (*vertical disjunction* $\Rightarrow$ *vertical conjunction* $\Rightarrow$ *horizontal disjunction*). When he returns to the village, Blue-Jay, a domestic trickster ($\neq$ Coyote, an exotic trickster) appropriates two of the hero's four wives. As in the story of the bird-nester who, in this context, is replaced by a shell-gatherer, the two women remain faithful to their husband. Blue-Jay however also defecates in his victims' house; he forces the son of the house to wipe him with his coat and so ill-treats him that, by the time the boy's father finds him, he has become both blind and bald (cf. M_{767a}, below, p. 514). It is clear from this that certain variants of the bird-nester quicken the tempo so that the bass line of the harmony overtakes, as it were, an alto part which, in other myths, is reserved for a subsequent phase of the message carried by the melody common to all the myths concerned.

Similarly, the bird-nester myth, which comes before the series of animal pairs, which it is connected to by what I have called Overture IV (the mother who changes into a grizzly bear when menstruating), nevertheless has an exactly corresponding equivalent, but one which is transposed into the series of animal pairs. Eagle appropriates the wife of Skunk, his young brother, and takes her off to the sky. Skunk discovers their hiding place but while he is being hoisted up to them, Eagle cuts the rope. Skunk falls and, as he drops, he loses the anal gland which secretes the stinking fluid he uses both for attack and defence. He sets off to look for it, and finds it in the possession of strangers, who are treating it as a toy. By means of a trick, he recovers it, then kills and pillages the communities who have been guilty of a lack of consideration, while sparing those who have shown him respect. Laden with stolen riches, he has an encounter with Cougar, from whom he escapes; then rodents called 'prairie dogs' (*Cynomys* gen.) strip him and reduce him to his present state, which is that of a repulsive but harmless animal which can be frightened off with a mere whistle (M_{660a}; Jacobs 3, pp. 207–15).

Another version (M_{600b}; Jacobs 1, pp. 202–206) makes it clear that the woman stolen by Eagle was originally intended to be his wife; Skunk had appropriated her by means of a trick. The whistling spirit which frightens Skunk off and steals all his riches is, in this case, none other than frost, a detail which allows us to place this group of myths at a point in the series of transformations and very close to those with Fox and Coyote as heroes (M_{614}), and which also state that the stolen valuables are to be used in matrimonial transactions: 'This will be for my affines; this will be for my mother-in-law, and this for my son-in-law. And this will be for my own wedding suit' (Jacobs 3, p. 213). Wolf and Skunk appear in a third version as brothers (M_{660c}; Jacobs 1, pp. 42–5): Skunk is married; Wolf desires his sister-in-law and kidnaps her. Skunk pursues them over hilly ground (*vertical axis* $\Rightarrow$ *horizontal axis*); he trips, loses his anal gland, and having been thus pierced can no longer retain food, since everything he eats passes straight through his body. He blocks his gaping rectum with a wad of straw, and eventually succeeds in absorbing nourishment.

Readers of the first volume of this study will no doubt remember that the hero of the Bororo myth (M_1), who is disjoined in the direction of the high, not the low or the far, undergoes the same fate as Skunk, and also because of incest: his digestive tract can no longer retain food, since he has lost his fundament, and he is forced to go hungry until it occurs to him to stop up the opening (*RC*, pp. 36, 49–50). There is, however, more to it than that, since the hero, pierced below, could be immediately transformed into the one in M_2, who is weighed down from above by a huge and heavy tree which has grown on his body. After getting rid of it, he changes like Skunk in M_{660a-b} into a judge and spares or kills his fellow-countrymen (not foreign communities), according to whether or not they offer him valuable gifts; his behaviour is therefore asymmetrical with that of Skunk, who appropriates the valuables belonging to the people he kills, but respects the persons and property of others who have shown him courtesy.

Let us return now to the simpler contrast between the bird-nester myth and the one featuring Wildcat and Cougar, which appeared (p. 337) through the inversion of their respective etiological functions. There is another parallel inversion relating to colours. The bird-nester's dark-skinned wives are virtuous, the fair-skinned ones are unfaithful. On the other hand, in the Wildcat–Cougar myth, it is light-coloured flesh which is good, and the dark-coloured bad. The relevance of this reversal is clear from another group of myths, whose whole armature, not just their message, is strictly symmetrical with the bird-nester story:

M_{661a-b}. Nez Percé. '*The two brothers*'

In a village, where Coyote was leading man and Eagle the second in rank, there lived two brothers who were great hunters and very wealthy. They preferred to live by themselves. The elder one was married; the younger was unmarried and had a dog, the Grizzly Bear. The wife fell in love with the brother-in-law, who paid no attention to her. One day when they were alone together, she deliberately scratched her face with the claws of a little bird she had asked him to kill. When her husband came home, she claimed that the scratches had been inflicted during her attempts to resist the advances of his young brother-in-law.

Mad with rage, the man broke the arrows that his brother had stayed behind to make and then threw them into the fire. He reproached him bitterly. The boy got up and went away without saying a word. Followed by his dog, he crossed four mountains, and at the top of the fifth, the highest, he undressed, climbed a tree and disappeared into the sky (thanks to the magic power of the dog, M_{661b}). He was never seen again. The dog-bear got tired of waiting for him (M_{661a}) and decided to live in the mountains.

However, the husband now began to reproach himself for having behaved too harshly to his brother, and set off in search of him. Guided by the dog's howls, he came to the place where the animal was. The dog told him the truth, for he had seen how the woman had scratched her own face. The man changed him into a grizzly bear, and told him that henceforth he would be a dangerous animal who would, if necessary, kill people. He himself went back to the village, and without a word of explanation, drew his bow and killed his wife. Then he swallowed all his fine things (clothes and adornments belonging to his brother, his wife and his own people, M_{661b}). He was a tall, good-looking man, but after this strange repast he became ugly, small and pot-bellied. The further he went, the uglier he became. Also, all the women he met laughed and scoffed at him, all except a daughter of Eagle who kindly took him to the house of an old woman, whose grandson he was.

On the following day, Eagle organized a shooting contest and promised his two daughters to the winner. As no one could hit the target, Coyote asked the ugly hero to shoot with him. The little monster's arrow hit the target, although Coyote claimed it was his arrow; but no one believed him. Eagle ordered his daughters to go and be the boy's wives. The younger one willingly complied, but the elder, horrified by the boy's ugliness, decided to marry Raven. After one night during which the hero kept away from his young wife, he sent her away. He asked his grandmother to fasten him to the tent pole head down, and in this position he vomited up all the things he had swallowed. When his wife came back, he had become a handsome man again.

A collective buffalo hunt took place the next day. The hero killed a great many buffalo. When he got back to his village, he drank the water white with clay which his wife handed to him, but refused the water black with coal which his sister-in-law had prepared at the request of Raven, her husband. The latter had gone ahead and picked up the buffalo heads abandoned by the hunters. His father-in-law preferred the good meat given by the other son-in-law. Raven was very angry and imprisoned all game animals of which he was the master. A famine ensued. The hero was the only one who could still hunt.

People wanted to know where Raven had hidden the animals, but because at that time his plumage was white, they could not see which way he flew when he rose up into the sky. Finally, Beaver devised a plan; he would be stretched out like a decaying carcass. Raven alighted on him; he was captured and held above a fire to be smoked. Henceforth, since he was black, people could see which way he flew: but he went off and disappeared behind the horizon.

Having turned himself into a little dog, and accompanied by a few companions who had been variously transformed, the hero succeeded in getting picked up by a raven's daughter. She carried him to the hut, where her parents kept the animals imprisoned. The dog barked so loudly that they (the deer) took fright and started to go out of the tent (Boas 4, pp. 157–64; Phinney, pp. 163–72; cf. Boas 4, pp. 85–90; Cline, pp. 212–13).

What connections are there between this myth and the bird-nester story? Firstly, it illustrates what can be called its 'Potiphar transformation', examples of which can be found in South America (Wagley-Galvão, pp. 146–7; Murphy 1, pp. 87–8; and M_{135}, Koch-Grünberg 1, pp. 55–60, cf. *HA*, p. 275), and which is so widely distributed throughout North America that the whole of the group might be studied afresh from this angle (cf. below, pp. 503–506, 529–30; S. Thompson 3, pp. 326–7).

I shall limit myself to determining what it consists of in the present instance since, in other contexts, it can assume different forms. Instead of the elder of the two men trying to seduce his younger brother's wife or wives, the wife of the older man (father or brother) tries to seduce the younger brother. The tree the hero climbs, and which is the means or the consequence of the reprehensible action, disjoins him from his own people, temporarily in one instance, definitively in the other. His return to earth, if it occurs, requires the intervention of helpful animals, which may be harmless, like the butterflies or the spider in the North American versions, or fierce like the jaguar in the Ge versions. It is significant, then, that M_{661}, a North American myth which is a point by point reversal of the bird-nester story and a symmetrical reflection of it, should present the grizzly bear (the most dangerous wild beast in the north) as the equivalent of the jaguar, while at the same time inverting the function assigned to the second animal in the Brazilian myths: instead of helping the hero in his descent, the dog-bear in M_{661b} conjures up an edible fowl which his master tries to catch and is thus lured up into the sky, from which he never returns.

Like the South American jaguar, which was previously the master of cooking fire, but which has to eat its food raw once it has handed over fire to human beings, the grizzly bear in M_{661}, after being a domestic animal, will henceforth have to live wild. According to a Yurok version of the same myth (M_{661c}; Erikson, p. 287), the crow who has been blackened by cooking fire will henceforth never eat fresh meat but will live on excrement.

In the mythology of the Coast Salish, the Chinook and their neighbours, the Sahaptin, the bird-nester story leads to an episode during which a half-human character called Coyote, before definitively assuming animal form, frees, for the benefit of future mankind, the fish held in thrall by the sea-swallow women (terns, or some other sea birds). In M_{661}, which is symmetrical with the other myth, a half-human character temporarily assumes animal form in order to set free, for the benefit of his contemporaries, game animals which are being held captive by a pair of ravens, which are terrestrial birds.

However, the most remarkable episode in M_{661} is undoubtedly the one in which the hero swallows clothes and adornments, thus changing himself from a handsome, well-proportioned adult into an ugly, infantile creature. To interpret this episode, we should note first of all that the following one, during which the hero is suspended by his feet from the top of the tent – near the smoke-hole, according to the myth – and thereupon vomits everything he has swallowed into the hearth, is an anticipation of the scene featuring Raven in the same situation and being blackened by smoke. In the latter case, an upward movement starting from the hearth, and congruous with smoking, which is a culinary process, blackens and at the same time disfigures a character who had previously been white and beautiful. In the other case, a movement in the reverse direction, congruous with vomiting, the opposite of digestion, restores his original beauty to a character who had become ugly.

However, the eating process, the result of which is nullified when the hero is hung up by the feet, is abnormal in one respect: it concerns not food but clothes. Symmetrically, the hanging of the raven over the fire also presents an abnormal feature, since the bird, instead of being cooked, acquires new attire. This conversion of the culinary code into a vestimentary one would remain incomprehensible if we did not notice that it originates in the North American versions of the bird-nester myth, the transformation of which reaches its final stage in M_{661}.

After he has swallowed the clothes, the hero of M_{661} develops a huge belly and regresses into infantilism. The bird-nester, after being deprived of clothes and food, suffers acute hunger and thirst; he becomes emaciated, his bones stick out and he very nearly dies. We need only glance again at all the North American versions of the bird-nester myth that have been summarized so far to realize that the discarding of the hero's clothes is an invariant feature. By forcing Eagle to undress, Coyote causes him to regress from culture to nature, and, metaphorically speaking, from the cooked to the raw, just as Raven's companions, by forcing him to submit to cooking, transform his original white nudity, which allowed him to merge with the sky, into a distinctive blackness. In addition to these two extreme states of the same transformation, the hero of M_{661} illustrates yet a third: by swallowing his own clothes he can be said to be *dressing himself on the inside*, whereas the bird-nester, who takes his off, is *undressing himself on the outside*; but, for the same reason too, the hero of M_{661} is *taking nourishment from the outside* — since clothes are worn around the body — whereas the bird-nester, who grows thin and has nothing to eat but his own substance, is *taking nourishment from the inside.*[6]

So, as anti-food, the ingested clothes are a transformation of the bird-nester's discarded clothes. They correspond not so much to the lack of food suffered by a naked and starving hero, as to the state of rawness, or even rottenness, to which, in the homologous South American myths, the same hero is reduced before obtaining cooking fire and giving it to mankind. In M_1, the hero covers his body with rotting lizards; the vultures mistake him for a decaying carcass and start devouring him. The same motif reappears, with the reverse function, in M_{661}, where a character (not the hero) changes into a decaying carcass in order to capture the raven. At the other end of the geographical area covered by this study, the Wintu (M_{662}; DuBois-Demetracopoulou, pp. 228–9) have a myth which links, if not the origin of salmon, at least their ritual consumption, with the origin (also dealt with in M_1) of the natural 'potholes' caused in the rocks by erosion (*RC*, p. 137); through a curious coincidence, the lizard-hunting motif is also present in the Wintu myth as an inversion of a real hunt (since the lizards are here called 'deer'), and the protagonists, like the hero of M_1, attach their catch to their belts.

The conversion of the culinary code into a vestimentary one is not, of course, a phenomenon peculiar to the cultures of North America. Many other languages, French included, provide evidence of it, and I have already discussed it from this general point of view (*RC*, pp. 334–9). There would seem to be little doubt, however, that it plays a strategic role in the myths at present under consideration and in which the transition from one code to the other determines the entire series of transformations. As I began to show on pp. 315–16, this is a consequence of two empirical facts: first, the co-extensiveness of bark with the world of culture, because of its various uses as fuel, clothing, food and material for cooking utensils; secondly, the ambiguous nature of shells, whether in their natural state or fashioned into objects, since they could be used at fairs as exchange currency for foodstuffs or elsewhere as money for the purchase of goods or other valuables, or made into jewellery, to be worn on the person or sewn on to costumes. Because of the mediatory function of bark and of shells which were both adornments

---

[6] This does not exclude an opposition, which is brought out farther north between the raven, a stealer of food, and the mouse, that other human parasite, into which the man who eats his clothes is transformed in the mythology of the northern Athapaskan (Jetté, pp. 485–6).

and currency, the vestimentary and the culinary were combined in the native cultures, not only metaphorically but in actual fact.

There is a final argument in favour of this interpretation. Alongside the 'Potiphar transformation' of the bird-nester myth, there exists another which I shall discuss later (see below, p. 429 *et seq*.): it is one in which Coyote, instead of appropriating female affines, tries to seduce his own daughter (for the group as a whole, cf. Schmerler). The point to be noted is that, in most myths of this group, Coyote desires his daughter for the first time when, having climbed on to the roof to put out a fire, she inadvertently displays her pudenda to her father standing below. This incident is clearly an inversion of the one in the bird-nester series in which Coyote sets fire to the clothes of his daughters-in-law in order to force them to expose their pudenda. Raven, his homologue in the Bella Coola and Kwakiutl myths, which contain the same episode, proceeds still more directly (Boas 12, pp. 90–91; Boas-Hunt 1, Part II, pp. 288–91). Consequently, the desired woman, who is an extinguishing agent in the one instance, becomes, in the other, the passive subject of the propagation of fire. Many versions of the myth in which Coyote seduces his own daughter explain how he has recourse to fire in order to accomplish his purpose: he feigns death, after giving orders for his body to be burned; so when he reappears, he is taken for a stranger and is able to marry his daughter, the only person – as he claims in self-justification – capable of lighting his pipe correctly. In some Paiute and Shoshone versions, as a punishment, he is made to eat his own penis, which has been cooked in the hot ashes. If, then, for the reasons I have just explained, this sequence of events all relating to fire is an inversion of the sequence which constitutes the bird-nester myth, it must *a contrario* be the case that the means employed by the same character – the forcing of the son to undress so that his clothes, his physical appearance and his wives can be appropriated – is based on a relation of congruence between the naked and the raw.

The construction of M_{661a} admirably illustrates the relationships of symmetry which both link it to, and contrast it with, the bird-nester myth. Eagle and Coyote appear in both stories, but at the same time as their order of precedence is reversed [(Eagle > Coyote) $\Rightarrow$ (Coyote > Eagle)], the two characters together are reduced from protagonists to incidental characters. By being still present, although now in the background, they serve to show, by this shift of perspective, that the myth has, as it were, swung completely round. It is worth noting, incidentally, that in a Wasco story where they also play small parts (M_{663a}; Sapir 1, p. 233), Coyote and Eagle, his young brother, have a culinary connotation: the two brothers live together: Eagle hunts while Coyote stays at home. Each prepares his own food: Eagle boils the large game animals he kills, whereas Coyote catches mice and roasts them in the hot ash. Coyote kills his brother in a fit of jealousy, and embarks on a nomadic existence: 'Never mind,' he says, 'I shall go to the woods, very soon the Indians will come here.'

The myth is interesting not simply because it asserts the implicit superiority of the boiled over the roast and of the use of the bark receptacle over a culinary technique so rudimentary that it does not even involve a roasting-stick (cf. above, pp. 312–13). By means of the eagle/coyote pair[7]

$$(eagle : coyote) :: (boiled : roast)$$

it expresses what might be called cooking as a universal:

$$(eagle + coyote) = \text{COOKING}$$

But in that case, it follows that the outraged Raven, of M_{661}, who deprives all the inhabitants of the village where Eagle and Coyote are, as it happens, chiefs of the means of cooking (by holding all game animals captive), represents their negative counterpart:

$$raven = (eagle + coyote)^{-1}$$

The Raven's negative culinary connotation is with the smoking he undergoes passively when he is blackened, whereas the Eagle and the Coyote have a positive, active relationship, one with the boiled and the other with the roast. But that is not all. The Eagle and the Coyote can form a pair of correlational and oppositional terms because the contrast between them has two aspects: the Eagle is *celestial* and *predatory*, the Coyote is *terrestrial* and *carrion-eating*. As for the Raven, he can form a triad with the other two animals, since he is *celestial* like the first and *carrion-eating* like the second. This apparently triangular system holds a fourth place in reserve for animals definable in terms of the two remaining relationships: animals which are *predatory* like the Eagle and *terrestrial* like the Coyote. These animals, who also feature in the myth, are the Cougar and the Grizzly Bear: one food-providing, the other cannibalistic, that is, endowed respectively with a positive and a negative culinary connotation.

---

[7] The Thompson myth about the origin of fire (M_{663b}; Teit 5, pp. 338–9) shares out the roles between three animals: the beaver steals fire from the people of Lytton and gives it to the Nicola River and Spences Bridge people; Eagle teaches them how to roast, and Weasel how to boil. Consequently, in this version, cooking as a universal consists of fire plus the roast and the boiled.

It is clear from what has gone before that the myth about the two brothers and the one featuring Wildcat and Cougar, which are inversions of the bird-nester story along different axes, are consistent with themselves when they also invert the respective colour values: black and white or light and dark, which the three myths use to create a significant opposition. In M_{661} in particular, the chromatic opposition occurs twice: water whitened by clay is good, water blackened by charcoal is bad; and the previously white raven turns black. Since the blackening is presented as a punishment, causing the Raven to retrogress from the position of predator to that of carrion-eater, and since M_{663a} establishes the superiority of the former over the latter, we arrive at the following formulation:

	light	*dark*
bird-nester myth:	−	+
Wildcat and Cougar myth:	+	−
two brothers myth:	+	−

This raises a problem: why does the North American bird-nester prefer his dark-skinned wives? The preference is an invariant feature of the group, from the Klamath in the south to the Thompson in the north, by way of the northern Sahaptin, the Chinook and the Cowlitz River and Puget Sound Salish. In the various versions, the light-skinned women are called Squirrel or Fish, Mouse, Cricket, Milt, Duck, Swan, Tern and Finch; and the dark-skinned women Woodpecker, Turtle-dove, Beetle, Cricket, Black Swan, Diver and Mallard Duck. One might be tempted to express the opposition between them in modern terms as a contrast between technophobic and technophilic animals, for two reasons: in several versions the punishment meted out to the light-skinned, unfaithful wives is transformation into wild geese, which henceforth are doomed to live apart from humans, and in M_{661} the same transformation affects the hero's dog when it becomes a grizzly. However, it would be difficult, if not impossible, to supply any empirical basis for this interpretation, since the same animals sometimes change sides from one group to the other. For instance, the cricket and the turtle-dove are black in the Puget Sound, Sahaptin and Salish versions, where they are contrasted with white mice; but in the Cowlitz versions, the white mouse and cricket are contrasted jointly with black turtle-doves. The most that can be said is that mice are always white and turtle-doves always black, although the identity of the various species remains so uncertain, especially in the case of the birds, that there seems to be no hope of discovering an interpretation on the basis of animal habits.

We must try, then, to approach the problem from a different angle. Throughout North America, the opposition between the light and the dark is mainly associated with that between day and night and between the masculine and feminine genders. A myth belonging to the Coast Salish (M_{716b}; Adamson, p. 85) contrasts the 'black' girls of twilight with the 'grey' dawn girls. On the other side of the continent, the north-eastern tribes contrast the dark, ugly child 'born in the night-time' with the handsome light-skinned child 'born in the day' (Speck, 4, pp. 24–5). The Mandan, who are in between, associate white sage with the sun and the white-tailed deer with day, black sage with the moon and the black-tailed deer with night (Maximilian, p. 366; Bowers 1, pp. 304–305). Their Omaha neighbours say that, at puberty, a young man's soul turns white; it is then reborn from darkness, since night is the mother of day (Fletcher-la Flesche, p. 128).

On the other hand, the Wiyot on the Californian coast, whose myths I have already had occasion to quote (see above, pp. 154–6), make a distinction between pipe bowls made from light stone and those made from dark stone, the former being called male and the latter female. These Indians also believe that stars are women who are blind during the daytime (Kroeber 8, p. 39). The same sexual connotation of white and black is to be found among the Kansa in Central North America (Skinner 12, p. 760), and the Omaha, who, however, reverse the Californian formula; the members of the Shell brotherhood considered the white shell of *Olivia nobilis* as being feminine and the darker one of *Olivia elegans* as being masculine (Fletcher-la Flesche, pp. 519–20). However, this classification belongs to a very complex symbolic system, of which it illustrates only one aspect: in the origin myth, the day sky (light, male) and the night sky (dark, male) form a pair correlative with another composed of a different modality of the night sky (dark, female) and the earth (male). On the other hand, shells in the register of the low correspond to stars in the register of the high: therefore both are related to the night sky. Also, according to the origin myth, man found the dark shell, woman the light shell. The sexual relationship of the respective discoverers is therefore just as likely to be one of complementarity as one of homology (*ibid.*, pp. 513–14).

It is scarcely necessary to give further examples; as I showed in *From Honey to Ashes* (p. 422), the relationship of women to night and men to day has an operative value in the thought of the American Indians, and probably in that of other peoples too; this must be the explanation for widespread ritual beliefs, e.g., the taboo on women seeing the rhombs – which would be awkward to interpret otherwise. It will be remembered that in the Puget

Sound area, some versions of the bird-nester story ($M_{606\,c}$; see above, p. 266) identify his white, unfaithful wives with milt-girls, who are described in other myths as being 'very white and beautiful' (Boas 5, p. 156), 'white and pretty' (Jacobs 1, p. 139), etc. And it was because of their colour that the Chinook ironically referred to white people as 'milts' (Jacobs 2, Part II, p. 560). The terms used in Salish myths to describe milt-girls, the future mothers of all fish, are almost identical with those found in a Wasco myth ($M_{601\,a}$), which uses them to describe the selfish mistresses of Salmon: 'they were very bright, they shone more brightly than the sun; their paddles were of white wood, very beautiful' (Sapir 1, p. 266). Here, too, the link between whiteness and the daytime or the sun is evident.

But if women in general, unlike these maleficent sisters, have an affinity with darkness, it follows that pallor, whatever its charms, is an attribute contrary to their real nature: resorting again to a distinction I have already used in another context (L.-S. 2, Ch. XIII), I would say that dark-skinned women are harmonic, light-skinned women disharmonic.[8] If only for this reason, it is understandable that the hero should prefer the former, since they alone are fertile and respect their marriage vows. But why is it that Coyote, in the Salish and Sahaptin myths, shows the reverse preference, and considers the wives his son is most fond of as being 'swarthy and ugly'?

In order to reply to this question we must remember that among the Klamath and the Modoc with whom my enquiry started the roles of the bird-nester and his father devolve respectively upon the two demiurges, Aishísh and Kmúkamch, who have a marked affinity, the first with the moon, the second with the sun. This affinity persists in myths which replace these major divinities by their animal understudies, Marten and Weasel (see above, p. 43), and is also evident in Chinook and Sahaptin mythology, where the roles of the bird-nester and his father are taken over by Eagle and Coyote. However, the straightforward Klamath and Modoc opposition between a bad solar demiurge and a good lunar demiurge becomes more complex here. For the Salish and some of their neighbours, the harmony and proper functioning of the world depend on a satisfactory balance between antagonistic forces, only one aspect of which is expressed by day and night. It is the moon and the moon alone which, by softly illuminating the darkness, illustrates the *reciprocal tempering* of light and dark. The moon belongs, then, to both *night* and *day*; experience shows that the moon is not exclusively nocturnal, since the most nocturnal, and

---

[8] Hence, the often treacherous appeal of blondes, who, as we know, function as home-breakers; but it is an appeal which does not work, even within his own household, for the hero of these myths, a paragon of all the domestic and social virtues.

therefore the darkest, nights are moonless. On the other hand, the myths relate that at the time when the moon claimed to be the day star, it dried and burned up the earth, making life impossible for humans.

The sun, unlike the moon, can preside over day without causing such disasters; but again, experience proves that, unlike the moon, it is incompatible with night. Since it belongs exclusively to day, it is only entitled to a subordinate place in cosmology as a weak replica of the moon, the only luminary in which the two aspects can co-exist harmoniously. This is why, in the Salish myths, the sun is born from urine wrung out of the swaddling clothes of his brother Moon, after the latter has been stolen (M_{375}). The problems raised by this situation would remain insoluble if we did not realize that, as so often happens in myths, the oppositional relationship, from the logical if not the historical viewpoint, is anterior to the things in opposition.

Consequently, in such a system, the character of the bad solar demiurge fades into the background; or, to be more exact, the Salish transform him into a trickster, whose exploits are a parody of the civilizing work of the Moon, the good demiurge and organizer of the world and society; so that Coyote, in his role as trickster, becomes a kind of inverted moon. Moon carries out his task wisely and generously; Coyote completes it, as it were, by default: his positive contributions to the order of the world are the result of accidents, rash behaviour and blunders. Nevertheless, the same oppositional structure, which the Klamath and the Modoc see as existing between the bird-nester and his father, continues to prevail in these northern versions. As a result of his solar affinity, which has been reduced to a negative expression, Coyote retains a predilection for light-skinned women. The bird-nester, through his parallelism with the demiurge—organizer of the world, whom he continues discreetly to echo, retains an affinity with the moon and darkness, and this explains why he has a preference for dark-skinned women.

It is significant that, in order to complete my interpretation of this vast group of myths, I should be obliged to come back to the examples I used as my starting-point, and to apprehend the set as a totality in one all-embracing glance. The story of the bird-nester which is common to the whole group constitutes what could be called its regulator cell. After the bird-nester story, the Salish and the Sahaptin go on to deal with what are for them two essential aspects of the ordering of the world: the freeing of the salmon and the establishment of commercial exchanges. But the Klamath, and even more so the Modoc, lived a long way from the great fairs held along the Columbia River; when they did attend them, it was chiefly to sell captives of war as slaves; sometimes these had been taken by the Klamath and the Modoc operating jointly against the Pit River tribes, and sometimes the Klamath independently, as intermediary agents, had bought them from their southern neighbours and taken them to the north to be sold (Spier 2, pp. 38–43; Ray 3, pp. 134–44). Since, in this case, exchange was a function of war and dissociated from productive activities rather than a condition and a means of ensuring peace, it is understandable that it should not have provided a plausible model for intertribal relationships and should have been even less effective as a solution to the problems that every social order has to solve. So, the regulator cell of the Klamath and Modoc myths, far from leading to the exchange formula, opens the way to another, but symmetrical formula: competitive intertribal games, which also provided a way of avoiding war: not by transforming it dialectically into its opposite, but by offering a less violent substitute.

Besides, the Modoc lived mainly on hunting and gathering. They probably went fishing in the spring and at other times of year, but there were no salmon in their rivers and they had to make do with less nutritious species (Ray 3, p. 192). Such was not the case with Klamath, since salmon and other fish were plentiful in the River Klamath and its tributaries at several periods in the year. However, the Klamath do not seem to have evolved such a complex fishing ritual as their western and northern neighbours. And, according to their myths, the creation of fish dated back to the beginning of time, long before the demiurge quarrelled with his son and changed him into a bird-nester: 'First of all, Kmúkamch created things and beings, and he decided that all species of fish should exist. After which, and having accomplished all that, Kmúkamch commanded his son to climb a

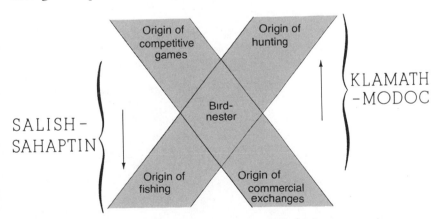

Figure 24. The inverted constructions of the bird-nester myth

tree on the pretext of capturing eagles from their nests' (Gatschet 1, Part I, p. 94). Consequently the liberation of fish is replaced by their creation, which takes place much earlier in the narrative sequence. In fact, as we saw above (pp. 89, 98–107), the Klamath and the Modoc relate the bird-nester story not to the origin of fishing but to that of hunting. Because of its aggressive and adventurous character, hunting, in terms of the quest for food, is opposed to fishing, just as, on the level of intertribal relationships, competitive games, which are also a kind of war, are in opposition to peaceful, commercial exchanges. We thus arrive at a comprehensive picture of the symmetrical values and functions — each of them linked with the empirical substructure — embodied in the bird-nester story in the mythology of the Klamath and the Modoc on the one hand, and in that of the Coast Salish and Sahaptin on the other (Figure 24).

PART FIVE BITTER KNOWLEDGE

Εἴθ ὤφελ' 'Αργοῦς μὴ διαπτάσθαι σκάφος
Κόχων ἐς αἶαν κυανέας Συμπληγάδας.

Euripides, *Medea*, v. 1–2

1 The Visit to the Sky

Grandiras-tu toujours, grand arbre plus vivace
Que le cyprès? – Pourtant nous avons, avec soin,
Cueilli quelques croquis pour votre album vorace,
Frères qui trouvez beau tout ce qui vient de loin!

Will you never cease to grow, great tree more vital
Than the cypress? – Yet we have, with care,
Collected a few sketches for your voracious album,
Brothers who see beauty in all that comes from afar!

Ch. Baudelaire, 'The Voyage', *Les Fleurs du Mal*,
CXXVI, iv

The discussion in the previous chapters centred on the mythology of the Sahaptin and their Nez Percé cousins, but I did not hesitate, where necessary, to draw freely on the myths of both the coastal and inland southern Salish, whose territory was adjacent to that of the Sahaptin, and who were bound to them so closely by trade and matrimonial alliances that it is often difficult to say to which linguistic family a particular version of a given myth should be assigned.

The discussion gradually brought us back to the bird-nester; we ought, therefore, to examine the form it takes to the north of the Sahaptin area, that is, in the vast Salish linguistic family which – with the exception of the two isolated outposts, the Tillamook in the south and the Bella Coola in the north – occupies a continuous area from the eastern section of Vancouver Island to the foot of the Rockies, including the major part of the Columbia and Fraser River basins.

The enquiry will be fraught with special difficulties, which are not entirely due to the fact that Salish mythology is known to us only in fragmentary form, even though the volume of recorded material is quite considerable: in this respect, the situation was much the same in the case of the Sahaptin and their neighbours. The main reason is that the history and ethnography of the Salish tend to complicate the task of analysis. The Plateau Salish were converted to Christianity in the first half of the nineteenth century, sometimes on their own initiative (like the Flathead, who made dangerous expeditions through enemy territory, as far as Saint Louis in Missouri, to request the sending of missionaries, the first of whom was the famous de Smet) and, thanks to their pacific disposition and friendliness towards the Whites, lived in relative tranquillity until about 1870[1] – apart from the havoc caused by epidemics. When, about this time, they were gradually confined to reserves, their traditional culture was already seriously undermined, since they had been subject to influences from the Plains tribes for at least a century before being exposed to that of the settlers. Consequently, ethnologists were unable to observe traditional Salish culture in any real sense, but had to reconstitute it on the basis of the accounts given by the oldest informants, and the evidence of the first travellers and missionaries.

In spite of the diversity of languages within the same family, and the wide divergence in customs, institutions and life-styles between the Coast and Inland Salish (Sapir 6; Ray 5), there is general agreement about the specificity of Salish culture, which underwent internal diversification only gradually through the proximity on the one side of the Plains tribes and on the other of those of the north-west Pacific coast; neither should the influence of the Iroquois be underestimated, since, from the end of the eighteenth century, they acted as guides to the fur traders and aroused the curiosity of the Flathead in relation to Catholicism and the Bible, while at the same time, no doubt, bringing with them certain elements of the eastern myths.

I recalled in the Prologue to this volume, and do not need to emphasize the point again, that this area of America was one of the earliest to be populated, and was inhabited continuously from about 12000 or 13000 B.C. up to the historical period. It forms, between the sea and the Rockies, a kind of corridor, so shaped as to separate off and definitively isolate one or more groups of migrants arriving through the Bering Strait and the inland valleys.[2] Originally the Salish inhabited only parts of their present area of distribution; it is thought that they later spread to the east and the south. But the area itself, taken as a whole, would seem to be filled with, and

---

[1] The situation was not the same near the coast where, to quote only one example, the Puget Sound Nisqually, who numbered several hundreds, perhaps even as many as two thousand, were massacred by settlers in 1855–6. By 1910 they had been reduced to a mere nineteen.

[2] This is to assume that, as Bryan maintains (p. 339), they were unable to move south along the coast: 'Those who have suggested that pedestrians could have moved southwards along the coasts of Alaska and British Columbia have never visited the region of steep-walled fjords where the bases of mountains often jut directly out of the sea with no beach' (cf. above, p. 15).

surrounded by, very early settlements of comparable antiquity and which were continuously inhabited over a very long period. However cautious we should be about accepting the findings of the glotto-chronological school, it is probably significant that, according to its exponents, differentiation of the Salish languages occurred over a period of six or seven thousand years (Swadesh 1, 2, 3, 4, 5, cf. Kroeber 10; Suttles-Elmendorf; Elmendorf 2); the present-day tribes may have extended their previous territory, but they still remain approximately in the same place as the very early occupants of the area.

If the Salish, and perhaps also the Chimakuan along the coast, who form a separate linguistic enclave, are the descendants of a very early wave of migrants, who were shielded from outside contacts for a long time by the Rockies to the east and the Pacific ocean to the west, it would be relatively easy to understand, in spite of the geographical distances involved, that they should have retained, although in locally elaborated forms, a stock of myths that was carried into the heart of South America by other, but contemporary, waves of migrants moving down on the eastern side of the Rockies. As is suggested by a wealth of examples, we might well expect to find, in this remote region of North America, an ideal location for comparing versions of the same myths originating from North and South America. It is a fact and — following in Ehrenreich's footsteps — I have constantly confirmed it from the very beginning of the present volume, that no parts of the New World seem to offer such closely inter-related mythological systems as Central and Southern Brazil, and the area between the Klamath and Fraser Rivers, with which I am now dealing, although as the crow flies they are some ten thousand kilometres apart.

Unfortunately, and to an even greater extent than in the case of the Sahaptin and the Chinook where the problem was similar, the analysis of the Salish myths runs into major difficulties on a level quite different from that of history and geography. These difficulties do not arise from the differences in life-styles, technical skills, social institutions and religious beliefs between Vancouver Island and the coast, the northern coast and Puget Sound, the seaboard, the Strait of Georgia and the interior, or the river valleys and the Plateau; on the contrary, since one might legitimately expect that such variations would offer numerous examples of the way in which the same myths are transformed according to different economic and social circumstances. For instance, the western communities had a strict social hierarchy based on wealth, birth and the principle of primogeniture, and which distinguished between aristocrats, ordinary people and slaves, whereas the social organization of the inland communities was amorphous.

Several of them would have found such concepts as heredity, rank and slavery unthinkable; others — in the east and south — under the influence of the Plains tribes, based their social hierarchy on civic or military merit. Similarly, the people of Vancouver Island, and to a lesser extent those living along the Georgia Strait and the coast of Puget Sound, built probably the largest houses ever observed in so-called primitive societies: these were irregularly shaped constructions, with wooden walls and roofs, and sometimes several hundred metres long. Inland the houses were very different: during the summer, they were no more than crude shelters covered with rush matting and bark; in winter, they were semi-underground lodges, roughly pyramidal in shape, and the framework was covered with earth, then dismantled in the spring. According to the particular community's proximity to the open sea or to straits, rivers and lakes, fishing or hunting was the main economic activity, in addition to the gathering of tubers, roots and wild berries, which was a common practice everywhere. There is a distinction to be made, however, between sea-fishing — for herrings and candle-fish (*Thaleichthys*) — and river-fishing. The five main species of salmon (*Oncorhynchus*), the most important source of food, ran right up only those rivers in which the water was cold, and provided they could get over the falls. Elsewhere, and in all areas in winter, the population had to make do with the much less prized steelhead trout (*Salmo gairdnerii*).

In spite of these considerable differences, a common feature emerges, and marks the whole mythology of the area. With the exception of the eastern groups — the Lakes Indians, the Flathead and the Cœur d'Alêne — among whom, to varying degrees, there was something resembling a tribal organization, obviously imitated from the Plains, the Salish had no concept of the tribe or the state. Doubtless they were aware of a vague feeling of solidarity as between people speaking the same language or the same dialect, but apart from that, their only forms of social order were the extended family among western communities, the semi-nomadic band or semi-permanent village in the north and centre, and the local group in the south. The office of chief, whether hereditary or elective, rarely conferred any real authority. It has even been said (Barnett 3) of certain aristocratic societies of Vancouver, in which precedence and family prestige had constantly to be reaffirmed through lavish entertainments and the distribution of wealth, that there was neither public authority nor state, and that individuals were guided by rules inculcated in childhood and strictly observed.

Whether the groups are to be classified as clans, families, bands or village communities, what we find everywhere are small, autonomous social units which, in the central zone at least (the island and coastal populations and those living close to the Plains tribes had, of necessity, to be more warlike in their behaviour), co-existed and intermingled peaceably, thanks to the generally recognized sociability of the Plateau people. The combination of local particularism and general mobility had an inevitable effect on the myths. For each dialectal group, and in spite of the incomplete nature of the records, we have a great many versions, differing from each other much more than is normally the case, and also in unusual ways. It is, in the first place, as if the substance of the myths had been broken down into tiny fragments, which were then being used capriciously to form a mosaic, containing the same elements in different combinations. As a result, the line of demarcation between the types of myths often becomes difficult, if not impossible, to draw: we are constantly at a loss to know whether we have moved from one variant to another of the same myth, or from one type of myth to another type, with which it had initially been assumed to have no connection.

The instability of the mythic material can also be explained by other factors. Both along the coast and in the inland areas, the Salish often intermarried with neighbouring or distant groups, either to extend their network of political alliances or because the *pax selica* prevailing in the inland area made this kind of marriage as easy, if not easier, than other types, thanks to a kinship system based on bilinear filiation and a taboo on marriages between close cousins. Since trade negotiations were as common as marriage negotiations and since both involved frequent and reciprocal visiting, it is not unreasonable to suppose that, throughout the Salish area, each myth, whatever its source, promptly became common property, although each tiny social unit adapted it in its own way. It follows that the enquiry I am about to undertake is of both theoretical and methodological interest. The question is: can we discover rules governing transformation as well as structure in a complex of myths which, although still recognizable, seems to have been incessantly decomposed and recomposed by tiny communities, whose political amorphousness and reciprocal permeability might lead us to suppose that, by the same token, the great mythic themes they possess in common with the other South American cultures can only exist, with them, in fragmented forms?

It would, however, be appropriate to begin the discussion by returning briefly to the Nez Percé myths. The Nez Percé are northern neighbours of the Salish and linguistically cousins of the Sahaptin, and as such provide a suitable transition between the two families. Besides, the way in which they tell the bird-nester story has several points in common with the Cœur d'Alêne versions, thus indicating Salish influences. I have already referred to the Nez Percé versions (M_{602a-h}, p. 255) in arguing that, contrary to Sapir's view, they link up the myth about the freeing of the salmon with the bird-nester story. The vital difference by which the Nez Percé stories give a foretaste of the Salish myths where the feature achieves maximum importance lies in the fact that this is the first of all the bird-nester stories we have studied in which the hero does not remain stranded at the top of a tree or a cliff, before returning to earth: his perch having risen considerably in the meantime, he reaches, and visits, the celestial world, where he meets with many adventures. This feature is most apparent in M_{602b} (Phinney, pp. 360–81) and M_{602c} (Boas 4, pp. 135–7), which both state quite clearly that the hero, called Young Coyote, first of all passed through the clouds and landed in a world 'just like our earth' according to M_{602c}, and where it was extremely cold.

The first inhabitants he encounters prove to be hostile, but the last are helpful spiders who make ropes which assist the hero in his return to earth. In the other version, the same spiders, who are at first hostile, later change to being helpful. Upon returning to earth, the hero rescues his dark-skinned wife – Cricket or Beetle – who had remained faithful to him, and he changes the light-skinned wife – Duck or Swan – into a wild bird. Next, he takes revenge on Coyote, his father, by sending him to carry a carcass with a strap which keeps on breaking, and also by creating mountains, since formerly the earth was flat. Coyote, whose progress is hampered by these obstacles can go no farther; he grows very tired and, being hot and thirsty, he is tempted to take a swim in the cool waters of a river, which carries him along to the mistresses of salmon. 'He turns into an infant and they take care of him and keep him.' Coyote breaks the dam and sets the fish free (M_{602e}: Boas 4, pp. 137–9; M_{602b}). There follows the episode, which I discussed at length in Part IV, of the reciprocal theft of food ($M_{602f, g, h}$; Boas 4, pp. 139–44) which, in the Nez Percé versions, results in the assigning of their distinctive coats to wolves, foxes, skunks and raccoons: such coats are natural attributes which, unlike possessions and services relating to culture, cannot be exchanged (cf. above, p. 285).

As we shall soon see the gradual emergence of a link between the motif of the visit to the sky and the origin of cooking fire, it is worth emphasizing, especially for readers familiar with the previous volumes of this study, that the Nez Percé are careful to present the bird-nester, even before his adventures, as the inventor of the hearth: 'Coyote had a son, who was a hunting chief, and a good-natured man. He climbed up a mountain near Snake River. One morning he kicked a log and there was a sudden burst of flame. The log has burned since then to warm mankind' (M_{602}). 'Young Coyote was the chief hunter. He would tell his hunters where to start and at the meeting-place he would rush up to a log and kick it: there would be a sudden burst of flame and the wood caught fire. The hunters stood round the fire, while Young Coyote gave out hunting commands and assignments' (M_{602b}). Here, too, there are similarities with the Salish versions, except that the episode, which is absent from the bird-nester story, occurs, in Thompson mythology, in a different story in which father and son are also both called Coyote, and the young hero 'is gifted in magic like his father' (Teit 4, p. 38).[3]

Thus, just at the point when the bird-nester story definitively abandons the prosaic form in which we first encountered it in South America, to take on, with the episode of the visit to the sky, an epic dimension and a cosmological significance (but has not the whole point of my enquiry been to discern, from the beginning, a significance of this kind within what might appear to be no more than a 'just-so story', that is, a story which explains why things are as they are?), at this very point, then, the theme of the origin of fire resounds with solemn gravity in the very first bars of the symphony – whereas in the Ge mythology of Central Brazil (M_{7-12}) it did not make its appearance until the end – thus proving that we are still dealing with the same dramatic issue but caught at that stage in its development when, fire being about to become celestial in origin instead of terrestrial, and at the crucial moment when it is no longer the one and not yet the other – and is consequently lit at the top of a mountain – the final outcome must remain in the balance, and the theme can have no other place than at the beginning. Even so, it should be noted that the Nez Percé and Thompson versions do not describe fire in relation to cooking, but exclusively as a source of warmth for the withstanding of cold and that they deal not with the domestic hearth but with occasional fires lit in the bush during inclement weather.

So, once again we have confirmation of the view I have put forward throughout this study, i.e., the most minute details in the myths are meaningful. In tracing the course of the bird-nester myth from the Klamath to the northern Salish, I have found evidence to the effect that, throughout the area, it undergoes a transformation which sets it apart from the South American versions (the transformation can be detected in South

---

[3] In 1968–9 I devoted my lectures at the Collège de France to an analysis of the group to which this story belongs, and I tried to show how it is linked to the bird-nester myth by a series of transformations. To avoid overloading the present volume, I have decided to omit the analysis here, but hope to publish it separately. Cf. *Annuaire du Collège de France*, 69th year, 1969, pp. 285–9.

America, but only in a latent state, cf. *RC*, p. 75); it consists in the transition from the category of the *raw* to that of the *naked*, and relates culture to the origin of garments rather than to that of cooking (see above, pp. 52, 344). The Nez Percé versions are among those which lay greatest stress on the fine clothes worn by the hero, and that his father forces him to remove before climbing the tree; consequently, after being master of the fire that warms at the beginning of the myth, he changes, in the middle, into a naked man shivering with cold.

We have just seen how the correlation between the Nez Percé myths and the Ge myths is manifested. Since the Ge myths are transformations of the Bororo reference myth (M_1) which was the starting-point for my analysis, it follows that the Nez Percé myths must have, with M_1, a relationship symmetrical to the one I have demonstrated between them and M_{7-12}. This relationship does, in fact, exist: the hero, the inventor of fire as a protection against cold, subsequently takes revenge on his father by creating heat and a lack of water (in the episode where old Coyote suffers from thirst), whereas in M_1 he takes his revenge by creating rain, an abundance of water which deprives his father of fire by submerging and extinguishing all the domestic hearths. On this particular point, too, the Nez Percé myths retain their originality by inverting a message which had remained unchanged from the Klamath–Modoc to the Salish, all of whom, and in a manner homologous with M_1, omit, or merely imply, the origin of fire, while making rain or floods or their functional equivalent the means used by the hero for self-protection or revenge (see above, p. 36).

The comparison with the Salish versions, as illustrated by those of the Nez Percé, does not preclude, then, but rather requires, the appearance of oppositions on other levels. For instance, one of the Nez Percé versions (M_{602f}) states specifically that the salmon held captive by the five sisters were transformed humans, who were restored to their initial state by Coyote when he set them free, an inversion of what happens in the neighbouring Salish (M_{375} etc.) and Sahaptin myths (M_{610}), where anthropomorphic creatures are changed into fish, so that humans can have salmon. Another characteristic inversion concerns the relationship between the terrestrial and celestial worlds. The creation of mountains by the Nez Percé hero (cf. a similar undertaking on the part of the heroine of the Loon Woman cycle, cf. above, pp. 117–20, 125, 132, 135–8, 152), implies that formerly the earth was flat, a feature that the western Salish, on the contrary, believe to be a characteristic of the celestial world; according to the Bella Coola (Boas 12, p. 28), the Thompson and the Klallam (see below, pp. 369, 370, 410), it is flat, mountainless, shrubless, and perpetually windswept. On the other hand, while the Nez Percé maintain that the earth was flat *at first* and then *folded*, the Coast Salish and their Sahaptin neighbours, in the cycle about the Moon as demiurge (M_{375}) to which I have often referred, use the origin of earthquakes to explain why the earth's surface expands and contracts periodically (Adamson, pp. 160, 172, 175; Jacobs 1, p. 140). The mythology of earthquakes would require a special study, which I shall perhaps one day be in a position to undertake.[4]

As I have said, the Nez Percé versions provide a transition between those of the other Sahaptin and the myths of neighbouring Salish groups. I therefore propose to begin my analysis of the latter by quoting a myth belonging to the Cœur d'Alêne, whose territory adjoined that of the Nez Percé to the north.

M_{664a}. *Cœur d'Alêne. 'The bird-nester'*

Coyote's son had two wives. One, dark-skinned and the mother of a little boy, was called Black Swan; the other was fair-skinned and childless, and was called Tern (a small seagull, also known as sea-swallow). Although the dark-skinned woman was generally liked, while no one cared much for the fair-skinned wife, Coyote, charmed by her white skin, fell in love with the latter.

So he asked his son to climb to the top of a fir tree in order to catch some eaglets; blinking and helped by his magic powers, he raised the tree higher and higher until it reached the sky, where the hero landed and found the sky 'just like the earth' (cf. M_{602c}).

He caught sight of a deer, killed it, then cut it up and dried the meat. Night fell; but he was unable to sleep because he was disturbed by the sound of people talking. He realized that two brothers were having a conversation: they were hunters, the elder of whom killed game animals by defecating on them, while the younger, being cannibalistic, hunted human prey in the same way. The two brothers quarrelled and started to belabour each other with canes adorned with the bones of their victims. The hero revealed his presence; he saw that the elder brother was a spider-like animal with very long legs and a small round body. In exchange for deer meat, the Spider promised to protect him from the cannibal and taught him a trick whereby, in case of attack, they would together succeed in cutting off the cannibal's leg.

It started to rain. Beaver women, who used to hunt and feed on this species of rodent, came upon the hero sheltering under a tree but

---

[4] See C. Lévi-Strauss, *La Voie des masques. Edition revue, augmentée et allongée de trois excursions* (Librairie Plon, Paris, 1979).

completely soaked. They took him to their home and married him. The hero used to hunt deer for his wives, but the Spider used to steal his game. He killed Spider and then learned from his weeping wives that he was their father. So he at once brought him back to life. After that he was careful to keep a portion of the game for his father-in-law.

Although he had become the father of a family in the sky, the hero longed to be back with Black Swan. He walked along aimlessly and arrived at the home of two old spinners, who were quarrelling over a stalk of Indian hemp (*Apocynum cannabinum*), which was growing horizontally under the ground and linking the places occupied by each of them. They were probably both blind, because the story states clearly that they were groping about in search of the plant.

The hero called them his father's mothers, and asked them to show him the way back to earth. To repay them, he offered them clothes, then meat, but only the promise of hemp tempted them: 'You talk as if we wore clothes, but it is this rope stuff that interests us.' They put him in a box with a lid, and warned him that he would stop four times before reaching the earth. But if he rolled around every time the box stopped, it would start again.

When he got back to earth, the hero found that his house had been destroyed and that the camp was deserted. He finally found his faithful wife and his child. She told him how her father-in-law had driven her away and set up house with Tern. The hero got Black Swan to take him to the camp, where he killed Coyote, his father, as well as his mother, his brothers and his unfaithful wife (Reichard 3, pp. 77–80).

An older version (M_{664b}; Boas 4, pp. 120–21), although less detailed, gives the son's name: Tôrtôsemstem — the frequentative form of a verb connoting either ascent or descent. Two episodes are absent: the one about the hunting or cannibalistic spiders, and the one about the Beaver women. On the other hand, M_{664b} refers to the two spinners as Spiders, whom the hero addresses not as his grandmothers but as his grand-daughters. He offers them beads, then necklaces, but both are refused; in this myth, too, all they want is hemp.

In relation to the Nez Percé versions, we can note what at first sight seems to be a weakening of the opposition denoted by the names of the two women: Swan and Cricket or Beetle in M_{602}, Tern and Swan in M_{664a}: two water birds rather than one water bird and a terrestrial insect. At the same time the semantic values of the Swan wife are inverted: in Nez Percé mythology, she is fair-skinned, sterile and wicked, whereas in the Cœur d'Alêne myths she is dark-skinned, fertile and good.[5] But does this really represent a weakening of the opposition? If we were better informed about the identity of the birds which, in most of the myths belonging to this area, are originally the selfish mistresses of salmon and, more especially, if we could be sure that the frequently used term 'swallow' referred to terns or sea-swallows, as is suggested by the fact that these birds, in accordance with the punishment inflicted on them by Coyote, later accompany the salmon when the latter swim up the rivers, a significant correlation would appear between the opposition between the two wives and that between the two categories of spiders encountered by the hero in the sky, the latter contrast being much more marked in the Cœur d'Alêne than in the Nez Percé myths.

It will be remembered that, in some versions, the Nez Percé also distinguished two categories of spiders, the first hostile, the second helpful, while in others they refer to one category only, which is initially hostile, and subsequently helpful (see above, p. 360). Yet even in the first group of myths, which are closer to the Cœur d'Alêne version, the opposition seems to be less strongly marked: the first inhabitants of the celestial world encountered by the hero adopt a war-like attitude towards him (they attack him with spears, $M_{602b, c}$), rather than a cannibalistic one (M_{664a}); and, more importantly, the hostile encounters are not described at such length by the Nez Percé as by the Cœur d'Alêne, who attribute various kinds of monstrous behaviour to the inhabitants of the celestial world – hunting by defecation and cannibalism in the case of the Spider Brothers, and homophagy in that of their daughters and nieces – to which behaviour the hero puts an end by providing the Beaver women, who are cannibalistic in respect of their own species, with a more seemly diet, and by keeping their father supplied with game, thus encouraging him to abandon his hunting technique characterized by the improper conjunction of food and faeces.

These differences are important, in that they make it possible to solve a problem raised by one of the Nez Percé versions (M_{602b}): the disjunction of the hero, who is promoted to the position of leader of the hunt from the outset, occurs not – as in all other versions – when he sets off to catch eaglets, but when he climbs the tree to retrieve some game which he has left hanging from a high branch. The Nez Percé versions also differ in the nature of the reward given to the helpful spiders: $M_{602b, c}$ explain that, as a result of constant weaving, the spiders' hands have become sore and tender, and that the hero pays them with meat or deer fat which, as M_{602c}

[5] It is probably the case that terns, which accompany the salmon when they run up the rivers, are looked upon in native thought as occupying a 'lower' position than swans, which undertake long migratory flights.

specifically states, they smear over their scratches. Consequently, versions in which hunting is given the primary role nevertheless make no mention of its alimentary function: they reduce hunting to a mere auxiliary of a different technical activity — hemp weaving — which is related to the vegetable, not the animal, kingdom.

So the Nez Percé try to minimize the gap between hunting and the weaving of textile fibres through regarding hunting less as an alimentary activity related to cooking than as a means of obtaining fat which is necessary as an ointment. It is clear that the Cœur d'Alêne myths adopt exactly the opposite viewpoint: instead of gaining the good will of helpful spiders by making them a gift of meat or fat, the hero, almost immediately on his arrival in the celestial world, comes into conflict with hostile spiders over the game he has been hunting. On the other hand, a twofold opposition appears between hunting and the weaving of textile fibres. In the first place, hunting serves to denote the hostile spiders, weaving the helpful spiders. In the second place, hunting is shown in its basest forms: killing by defecation, cannibalism and homophagy. Whereas the Nez Percé conjoin hunting and weaving, the Cœur d'Alêne disjoin them, and intensify the disjunction by also conjoining animal food and faeces.

Anthropological evidence can help to clarify these differences. They are less obvious as between the Nez Percé and the Cœur d'Alêne, who resemble the other communities to the west of the Rockies in being expert in the weaving and plaiting of vegetable fibres (cf. Teit 10, pp. 47–8), than as between the Nez Percé and their Plains neighbours, who know little or nothing of the textile arts. As it happens, the line of demarcation is represented by the Flathead (Teit 6, pp. 328–30), although they are Salish Indians living immediately to the west of the Nez Percé. A significant passage can be quoted to this effect:

> They (the Nez Percé) were almost always on a peaceful footing with the Flathead, whom they recognized as better hunters. The Flathead could be relied upon to go on to the Plains in winter and return with surplus meat products. Therefore, why should the Nez Percé go so far and risk so much, when they could trade with the Flathead for what they needed? It was not that the Nez Percé did not care for meat: indeed, 'they were just crazy for dried meat' according to an informant; but trade was better than fighting the Blackfoot. The Nez Percé also wanted the superior and more plentiful deerskins of the Flathead mountains, as they considered their own supply inferior and limited . . . Furthermore, perhaps it was in skin-dressing alone that the Flathead excelled the Nez Percé material culture.

Therefore, the Nez Percé looked upon the Flathead as better hunters and skin-dressers than themselves . . . On the other hand, the Flathead did look up to the Nez Percé as the better technologists. They always admired the flat, water-tight basketry bags of the Nez Percé, and were very anxious to have them. They valued them for storage and carrying. But their acknowledgement of Nez Percé superiority, together with the latter's willingness to trade, dampened any desire to learn the process (Turney-High, 2, pp. 136–7).

We might say, then, that the Nez Percé represented the extreme eastern limit of a technique associated mainly with the Pacific seaboard (Spinden 2, p. 190). In this respect, the Cœur d'Alêne were like all their neighbours to the north, the south, the west or the east: i.e., respectively the Lakes Indians, the Palouse and the Nez Percé, the Colville and the Spokane, and the Kalispel or Pend d'Oreilles: 'As most things which the Cœur d'Alêne had were common to all the neighbouring tribes, trading was generally merely an exchange of articles common to all, and depended on the needs and fancies of individuals' (Teit 6, p. 112). On the contrary, in relation to their eastern neighbours, the Nez Percé could regard themselves as champions in the textile arts, since they were well known for their basketwork and the principal raw materials – *Apocynum* and *Xerophyllum* – grew more abundantly in their territory than elsewhere. Their flat bags, which appealed so much to the Flathead, and the hats – shaped like truncated cones – worn by their women, were deservedly famous because of their faultless craftsmanship. It is understandable then that technical activities, such as hunting and skin-dressing, in which they were not particularly proficient, should take second place in their myths to others in which, in comparison with the Flathead, their trading partners, and even more so in comparison with their eastern Plains neighbours, who were also their traditional enemies (Spinden 3, pp. 226–7), they could claim a monopoly; the relative absence or presence of these activities could also be used by them as a measure of the difference between barbarousness and civilization.

But, as I have stressed on several occasions, in this respect the Nez Percé were following the pattern of all the Sahaptin tribes and, as we shall see presently, of the Salish too, In this area of America, where pottery was absolutely unknown, the weaving of fibres can legitimately appear as being co-extensive with culture. No doubt, unlike the Coast Salish, the Nez Percé did not weave blankets, but they certainly possessed some, and although their garments were usually made from hides, the fact that they wore woven hats proves that, even in their culture, basketwork could be connected with dress. It was also used in the construction of dwellings, since rush matting (*Typha* and *Scirpus*) served as roofing; in hunting and gathering in the form of bags, hods and winnowing-baskets; and lastly, in cooking, in the form of watertight baskets in which red-hot stones were immersed during the preparation of certain foods . . . This being so, the weaving of fibres could legitimately claim priority over cooking, on the scale of cultural activities.

Too little is know about the mythology of the communities situated between the Cœur d'Alêne and the Thompson for us to be sure that, as is suggested by the few available documents, these tribes were familiar with the bird-nester story only in a curiously inverted form: inverted first in respect of the ages or generations concerned, since the chief characters are two brothers, not a father and his son — and it is the younger brother who covets his elder brother's wife and plans his death; and then in respect of direction, since the eagle's nest is in each case situated below a rocky cliff, down which the wicked brother makes the other climb before cutting the rope to prevent his return (Sanpoil: M_{665a}, Boas 4, p. 108; M_{665b}, Ray 2, pp. 147–9; Okanagon: M_{666}, Cline, pp. 239–40). In spite of the presence of indisputably native elements (for instance, in M_{665a} the hero's name is Hail-Storm, a reminder of his meteorological function in versions belonging to both North and South America, cf. M_1, M_{557} and my comments above, pp. 156–8), the comparison with certain Shuswap and Thompson stories (Teit 1, pp. 702–707; 4, pp. 63, 87; 5, pp. 371–2) is enough to show that the particular form taken here by the myth is a result of contact with ancient French folklore, which had become known to these Indian communities by the end of the eighteenth century, through the Canadian trappers.

The problem is not, then, so much one of inversion, considered on the level of its formal implications, as of knowing why traditions with origins so remote from each other could so easily converge and fuse around one specific motif. I have dealt with the question in one of my lecture courses and have already explained (see above, p. 361, n. 1) why I propose to leave it aside for the time being.

Let us go back, then, to more specifically American mythic forms, which the Thompson Indians of the Fraser River valley illustrate with a wealth of detail that fully justifies the attention we must now pay to them:

M_{667a}. Thompson. 'The Bird-nester'

At one time very long ago, Coyote lived alone in the world without either wife or children, and he greatly desired a son. He made himself a boy from a lump of clay, but the boy washed, although his father had given him strict injunctions not to do so. No sooner had the disobedient boy entered the water than he melted away until not a trace was left. Next Coyote took gum and made from it a boy whom he told to stay in shady places. However, the child disobeyed, lay down in the sun and melted away. For his third attempt Coyote chose a piece of white stone, probably quartz (jade in Hill-Tout 10) on which neither sun nor water would would have any effect. The boy grew rapidly, and as he was well skilled in all the arts, Loon and Mallard Duck betrothed their daughters to him; they were respectively dark-skinned and fair-skinned.

Coyote fell in love with his daughters-in-law and tried to get rid of his son. He sent him, without any clothes on, to get eaglets from the top of a tree. But the birds proved to be merely his own excrement which he had transformed into a nest, and the tree trunk was so smooth and devoid of branches, except at the bushy top, that the hero was unable to climb back down, particularly since Coyote had caused the tree to grow right up into sky country, in which the young man now found himself exiled.

He set off at random across the celestial world, which seemed to him to be a vast treeless plain where a cold steady wind was blowing. It will be remembered that the hero was completely naked, and so felt the cold keenly. Furthermore he was hungry. He pulled up what he took to be the edible tuberous stalks of a species of wild potato (*Claytonia*) in the hope of satisfying his hunger, and felt the wind from the world below rushing through the holes he had just pierced in the celestial vault, since he had in fact uprooted stars. Still starving, he came to a comfortable under-ground lodge which he entered. Inside he saw no people, only a row of baskets all round the house, which attacked him the moment he tried to take one in order to draw water for his steam bath. He quietened the baskets, then cursed them: 'Henceforth,' he said, 'you will be servants to people for ever.' In the other lodges he visited, similar scenes were enacted with mats, awls, combs and birch-bark vessels, and he denounced them in like manner.

After a while he came to the edge of the bare and barren plateau of which the celestial world consisted, and began to descend an incline, dotted here and there with trees. He came to two old blind women seated one on either side of a fire. One was passing rotten wood over to her friend, for this was their only food, when the hero took it from her. The old women then started to quarrel; they suspected the presence of a man because – so they affirmed – of the powerful stench coming from his sexual organs and particularly because – according to some story-tellers –

in place of the food he had stolen from one of the old women, the hero had put his penis in her hand. Insulted by their remark, he seized one of the women and threw her into some spruce and black-pine trees, where she turned into a fool-hen (or Franklin's grouse), which the hero cursed, saying: 'Henceforth, you shall be a fool-hen and so foolish that women and children will catch you with a stick and a twine noose on the end.' He threw the other old woman amongst some rotten logs and changed her into a ruffed grouse, with a comment that, because of late nineteenth-century American prudishness, is given in Latin in the text: *'et si quando pruris stipite alis tunso gravida fies'*. Not being familiar with confessional manuals, I can only translate this as: 'and if, when you are on heat, wings beat against a log (ablative absolute), you will conceive'. I do not understand why such an innocent observation, which is, moreover, in accordance with the findings of animal ethology – as will be seen further on (p. 395) – should have called for the decent obscurity of a foreign tongue.

He then resumed his journey and, famished and blue with cold, was finally welcomed by a couple of spiders, who gave him clothes and food. They said they were husband and wife, and his grandparents. They spent all their time making twine out of bark with short fibres of poor quality (*Apocynum androsaemifolium*, cf. Teit 9, p. 497). The truth was that they had neither enough game nor bark for their task. It would seem that during his stay with the spiders, the hero was initiated into all their secrets. He acquired great wisdom, killed many deer which he gave to his protectors, and he threw some of the hairs from his pubis on the ground, and there grew up a dense thicket of trees which provided the best quality bark (*Apocynum cannabinum*, cf. Teit 9, p. 498). The spiders thanked him joyfully.

Meanwhile, Coyote, who had put on his boy's clothes and ornaments, passed himself off as his son to his wives. Only the dark-skinned wife had misgivings. Coyote managed to inspect the private parts of his two daughters-in-law. He took a fancy to the fair-skinned one and got rid of the other, who lived on the charity of the people and before long gave birth to a son, for she was already with child when her husband, whom she was now mourning, had disappeared. As summer drew near, the entire community left the village in order to hunt and dig roots.

In the meantime, the hero had grown homesick. The spiders let him down in a basket with a lid, tied to the end of a rope, and warned him that he had to roll over four times in succession without ever opening his eyes when the basket came to a halt – on the clouds first of all, then on the mist, next on the treetops, and lastly on the grass-tops. He would reach earth when he heard crows or meadowlarks calling.

The hero landed on top of a large flat stone which marked the centre of the world, near what is now the town of Lytton. He set off in a northerly direction to look for his own people and, as he had no canoe in which to cross the Fraser River, he made himself one out of horsetail (*Equisetum*, cf. Teit 9, p. 510), which sank the moment it reached the opposite bank. The plant still grows on this spot in the river. He then took the trail for Beta'ni, where he expected to find all his folk. He overtook first of all the Ant, the Beetle, the Caterpillar and other slow-travelling people. He told the Ant that she would cut herself in two if she fastened her sash so tightly. These creatures told him that his family was not far away, so he hastened on and soon came in sight of the wife who had remained faithful to him, carrying his child. The latter was the first to recognize him. They set up camp a little distance away from the others. The hero went hunting during the daytime, and drove all the deer in the region into one secluded and distant place. Coyote and the village people could find nothing to kill; having nothing but roots to live on, they were soon reduced almost to starvation.

The Raven finally discovered that the hero and his wife were living in a state of plenty, while all the rest of the community went hungry. When called upon to reveal where he got the deer fat his children were fighting over, the hero confessed how he obtained his food supplies. Everyone rushed to the hero's house to congratulate him on his return and to feast at his table.

Only Coyote, out of shame at what he had done, held back. His son went to him, ostensibly to give him a deer which, he said, he had killed and hung up from a tree on the far bank of a river. He added that he had also left a fine-looking, highly ornamented packing-line; but this was really just the animal's entrails.

On his way back, the delighted Coyote tried to cross the river: the entrails snapped and Coyote dropped his load and fell into the swiftly flowing waters, which carried him downstream and eventually into the Thompson River, as far as its junction with the Fraser River. In order to escape being drowned, Coyote turned himself into a piece of floating wood.

He floated as far as the mouth of the river, until he came to a fishing dam owned by two old women. One of them picked up the piece of wood and used it as a dish, but when she tried to eat off it, the dish devoured the fish so quickly that the women could not get a fair meal. They became very angry and threw it into the fire, where Coyote at once changed into a baby. One of the women, touched by his cries, took him out and decided to rear him. The boy grew up very quickly, but he was disobedient and hard to rear. Once, while the women were away, he discovered that behind the dam the river was full of salmon, a fish with which neither he nor his people were familiar. He broke the dam, and opened the four boxes which the old women also possessed, and which they had forbidden him to touch. Out of each box there issued in succession smoke, wasps, flies (salmon flies, bluebottle flies, blow-flies) and another variety of insects, meat-bugs, which ever since that time breed and multiply during the salmon season. Coyote went ahead and the fish started swimming up the rivers after him.

After a while, Coyote sat down on the bank to rest and saw, directly opposite him, on the other side, three or four young girls (virgins, according to some versions) bathing in the river. He called out to them and offered them some backbone of the salmon. The youngest shouted 'Yes!'; her companions reproved her, saying, 'You shouldn't have answered him!' Coyote ordered them to stand side by side along the bank, adding, so some say, that they should open their legs wide. Then he stretched out his penis across the river until it reached and penetrated the youngest girl. Her companions helped her out of the water, for she was hardly able to walk, and seemed very ill; but none of the shamans summoned by her parents was able to cure her.

Coyote let the salmon into Columbia River. After guiding them to the head waters of the Okanagon River, he returned and began to conduct them up the Similkameen River. There he saw girls bathing on the opposite bank and offered them some backbone of salmon, which they refused. They said they wouldn't mind having a certain part of a wild sheep (other versions say it was the head, cf. M_{668a}). Coyote concluded that these people did not wish for salmon;[6] he made a great barrier of rock falls which the fish could not get around, and increased the number of wild sheep in the surrounding mountains. Consequently, the people of this area have to travel as far as the Columbia River or the Thompson or Okanagon Rivers in order to obtain their supplies of salmon. Coyote followed the courses of the Thompson and Nicola Rivers and finally reached Lytton.

He dressed himself like a shaman or, according to some versions, in alkali grass (*Elymus triticoides*), to visit the village of the first young girls

---

[6] It should be noted that the basin of the Similkameen River was formerly inhabited by Athapaskan groups.

he had met. The people mistook him for a shaman and asked him to cure the sick girl. He shut himself up with her in a sweat-house and started to copulate with her, in the hope that his penis would become joined to the end which had remained in her vagina, and which was the cause of her sickness. From the patient's cries, everybody realized what was happening. However, Coyote managed to get away and the young girl was cured.

When Coyote was on the Columbia River, he threw in his own daughter, who changed into a rock, with her limbs extended just in the manner in which she fell.

Coyote accomplished many other wonderful feats; he changed the alkali grass *Elymus* and wild cherries into precious shells, fish skins into salmon, and twigs into berry bushes laden with fruit. One day he placed the false fish and the false berries inside the entrance to Grizzly Woman's house and invited her to feast with him, on her own food first, then on his. When all Grizzly Woman's stocks were exhausted, Coyote sneaked away. The next morning, all that was left hanging from the entrance of the house were some dried up fish skins and withered willow branches . . . (Teit 4, pp. 21–9).

A different version (M_{667b}; Teit 5, pp. 205–206) from Fraser Canyon, omits the episode of the artificial sons and starts at the point where the hero is already married. Story-tellers sometimes change the location of the eaglets from a tree ('raw' wood) to a steep cliff ('raw' rock). Therefore in this version the old blind women live not on rotten wood but on rotten rock. Also, it is more explicit than the other in respect of Coyote's long penis, since it states specifically that the young girl, having been penetrated by Coyote's huge member which remains wedged inside her, is unable to walk because of the weight. Her companions try to extricate her, but even by using knives and sharp stones they do not succeed in cutting off the penis; Coyote tells them they will only do so with the help of a kind of swamp grass. Another incident gives a foretaste of the one just described, since, according to M_{667b}, Coyote having been invited to the reconciliation feast (contrary to what is related in M_{667a}) wipes his knife on his brow after eating, but instead of drawing the flat side of the blade over his forehead, he draws the edge over it and makes a large gash right across.

M_{667b} also explains how Coyote becomes the father of a daughter after being accepted as a son-in-law by Wolverine, whom he has met in the area of the Okanagon and Similkameen Rivers. On the other hand, the episodes describing the curing of the sick girl and the visit to Grizzly Woman are absent.

Teit also gives several more fragmentary versions, recorded among the Thompson Indians of the Nicola and Fraser Rivers (M_{668a-d}, Teit 5, pp. 296–300). M_{668a} mentions four instead of three artificial sons; the one made of clay disintegrates in water, the one made from pitch or gum melts in the sun, and the stone one sinks; the fourth, being made of wood, survives. When the helpful spiders bid the hero farewell, they present him with various gifts: four stones which he must throw overboard in turn each time his basket comes to a halt; four articles of clothing made from hide – a coat, a shirt, leggings and mocassins; and four bundles of edible roots or tubers (one of which, *Claytonia*, is a species of the Portulaca family, and another, *Erythronium*, a liliaceous species), which he scatters; this explains how these plants came to exist on earth. The story continues with the hero's return and his act of revenge, the long penis episode, the sharing out of wild sheep and salmon and Coyote's marriage to Badger's daughter. When he goes to visit the village in which the sick girl lives, Coyote is very handsomely attired, and pretends not to understand the local dialect. The short-tailed Mouse, who talked all languages, is called upon to act as interpreter; Coyote, however, will only converse in sign language. After being caught with the young girl, he makes his escape, leaving behind his fine clothes which change into straw, twigs and faeces. M_{668b} relates how Coyote, disguised as a shaman, claims to speak nothing but Kalispel, the dialect of a remote Salish group. Pursued by the Humming-Bird, he escapes by magically conjuring up a thick fog which he creates by rolling over and over on the ground.

According to a third version (M_{668c}), the episode featuring the girls bathing in the river takes place in summer. Every time one of them accepts Coyote's offer of salmon, he allows the fish to swim up the river and his penis at once wriggles through the water like a snake in order to penetrate the girl. Every time his offer is rejected, he blocks the river with rocks or falls, thus making it impossible for the salmon to pass. One day, when he is conducting the salmon into a small tributary of the Columbia River, he meets a family consisting of a father, a mother and their two daughters, who are fishing for tiny fish from an inadequate weir. These people welcome Coyote; by way of thanks, he tells them that there are salmon downstream and explains how they can be caught. He ordains that 'henceforth, salmon will ascend the stream every year and people will always be able to catch plenty of fish at this spot.' Coyote asks if he can marry the two daughters, and the parents readily assent. In a little while each wife gives birth, one to a son, the other to a daughter and both children are able to walk at birth.

Coyote decides to set off on his travels, taking with him the younger of his two wives and his daughter; but on reaching the camp, he remembers

the girl he had injured at Lytton, and decides to pay her a visit. Not wishing
to be encumbered on the journey by his wife and daughter, he throws his
wife into the Columbia River, where she may still be seen in the form of a
rock, leaning over on her back and with her knees sticking out of the water,
which flows over her thighs to form a kind of natural pool: 'Henceforth,' he
decrees, 'this will be a great salmon-fishing place and a plentiful supply of
food will be caught between my wife's legs.' He changes his daughter into a
rock, which can also be seen on the river bank.

In M_{668d}, Coyote appears as a richly attired shaman, whose garments are
fringed with *dentalia*. Even the short-tailed Mouse, who is multilingual
because she has had husbands from many different tribes, cannot understand him. Using sign language, the people beg him to cure the young girl.
After being caught naked copulating with the patient, Coyote flees and, to
the great disappointment of the villagers, the richly embroidered clothes he
leaves behind change into a heap of straw.

Two other versions ($M_{669a, b}$, Teit 5, pp. 301–304) transpose the freeing
of the salmon episode from the Fraser to the Columbia River. The four
mysterious baskets with lids owned by the sorceresses contain three species
of flies (blow-flies, sand-flies and horse-flies) and wasps (M_{669a}); or alternatively, flies, wasps, smoke and wind (M_{669b}). According to M_{669a}, the
sorceresses are young, and when Coyote, having changed into a baby, is
allowed to share their bed, he copulates with them under cover of darkness.
Later he becomes Elk's son-in-law; after his wife leaves him, he changes
their daughter into a rock in the middle of the Columbia River, giving her
the same appearance and the same attributes as those which, in M_{668c} are
assigned to his wife.

Hill-Tout (10, pp. 551–61: M_{670a}) provides as richly detailed a version
as M_{667a}, so I shall do no more than stress the points of difference between
them. Snikia'p, the coyote, makes himself in turn three sons, one from
pitch, one from jade, and one from vegetable fibres. Only the last survives.
His father takes him to visit powerful and dangerous neighbours who, as he
explains, will try to kill them both. Since he has been told what precautions
to take, the young hero manages to escape death by drowning; then, along
with his father, death by fire; in the latter case, they lie down on a
well-beaten path which does not catch fire, since there is nothing for the fire
to feed on. While staying with the friendlier Eagle and Duck people, he
marries their daughters. One has red hair and a red face, the other black hair
and a swarthy face. The hero travels far and wide and becomes a great
hunter, the owner of sumptuous garments and precious shells.

The bird-nester episode follows as in the other versions, but this particular variant clearly states that Coyote covets his son's fine garments as well as his wives, and adds that the hero, after being left naked and shivering at the top of the tree, tries to protect himself from the cold by wrapping his long hair around his body. I shall come back to this detail later (p. 389). In the sky, he hears first of all, then sees, two old blind women pounding up fir branches in a mortar in order to extract and eat the pulp. After their transformation into tetraonidae (in this case willow grouse, perhaps *Lagopus* sp., and black grouse, probably *Dendragapus obscurus*, respectively), which at least gives them the advantage of being able to see their food, although they themselves now become easy prey for hunters when there is no large game to be had, the hero, still naked, is attracted by some pretty flowers which he pulls up and in so doing bursts the thin celestial vault. Next he arrives at the home of the helpful spiders who are very busy spinning *spat'tzin* fibre (*Asclepias speciosa* according to Hill-Tout, but cf. Teit 9, p. 498: *spa'tsen, Apocynum cannabinum*).[7] Since this fibre is already of the highest quality, the hero cannot, as in M_{667a}, express his thanks to his protectors by offering them a superior fibre. So he uses his pubic hair to create gathering grounds which are nearer than those to which the spiders have to travel to collect their fibres. So, supplied with meat and blankets woven from goat hair, and armed with a stone sword, the hero starts his descent, which is thrice interrupted as he passes through intermediary worlds: the country of clouds, the country of water, which is the source of rain, and the country of fog. However, since the wind blowing from these worlds prevents the basket taking off, Spider's wife scarifies her thighs and legs; the blood changes into snow, the weight of which allows the basket to descend.[8]

After landing near Lytton and leaving his sword stuck in a tree (it can still be seen in the form of a knot running right through the thickness of the

[7] However, Teit (9, pp. 470, 498, 513) mentions *Asclepias speciosa* which, according to him, the Thompson Indians called *spetsenêlp* or *spetsenilp*, a name which the Utâmqt group – a community living to the south of Lytton along the middle reaches of the Fraser – extended to *Apocynum androsaemifolium*. Although *Asclepias* and *Apocynum* are separate genera, their flowers have one property in common: they trap undesirable insects by the proboscis, so that the dead bodies are left hanging (Fournier, pp. 865, 867 discusses these two genera, which are native to North America and were introduced into France in the seventeenth century). There could, then, be a significant relationship between the destruction of insects by textile plants, symbols of culture, and their proliferation, which, in a sense, is thought to be the price mankind has had to pay, on the level of nature, for obtaining salmon. As M_{670a} emphasizes, 'He (Coyote) was feeling happy and in good spirits; he has let the salmon up the river and the people above will be able to get them now. There is only one drawback to his feeling of satisfaction: the smoke and flies are troublesome, wasps even more annoying . . .' (Hill-Tout 10, p. 560; cf. above, pp. 371–2, 375).

[8] Compare Cline, p. 159: '(Among the southern Okanagon) part of the technique of weather control was to let blood from one's head fall on the snow . . . (until) the south wind came and washed the snow away.'

trunk) so as to travel more lightly, the hero follows a great many tracks all leading in the same direction. They bring him to two old ladies; as they walk along, they wave fir branches from right to left. Intrigued by this behaviour, he questions them and learns that they are expressing their sympathy for an inconsolable widow whom the hero recognizes as being his wife, Eagle. He reveals his identity, but, although not blind, the old ladies claim they cannot see him. He waves his arms in front of their eyes and immediately he becomes visible. 'You were wrong,' he tells them, 'to walk along like that, but I shall punish you lightly since you were doing it for my wife.' And he changes them into maggots. There follows the reunion scene, during which the hero creates a stream so that he and his wife can wash their tear-stained faces.

Although the couple take the precaution of camping apart from the others, and in spite of the fact that the hero has forbidden the women he has turned into maggots to announce his return, Raven, the unfaithful wife's servant, discovers and reveals the hero's presence. The latter agrees to appear before his people; the next morning he organizes a celebration for the villagers, and distributes the blankets he has brought back. He is proclaimed chief and becomes famous. But he still wants to take revenge on his father and, as in the other versions, he finally succeeds. Then follow the freeing of the salmon episode and the opening of the four baskets containing respectively wind, smoke, flies and wasps. This version offers no explanation of the sick woman incident and her supposed cure, since the story of the long penis is not included. It adds, however, that Coyote, seeking forgiveness for his act of deception, stresses the fact that he has bestowed on mankind salmon and also the wind which now blows up the Fraser River, bringing cool, refreshing breezes during the hot season. I should also mention in passing two short older versions (M_{670b}; Dawson, pp. 30–31; M_{670c}; Boas 13, pp. 17–18), both belonging to the Thompson Indians. M_{670b} describes the four successive stages through which the hero passes on his way down from the sky as the damp world, the cold world, the misty world and the terrestrial world, respectively.

Lastly, I would like to quote the Lilloet version (M_{671}; Teit 2, pp. 306–309), in which the episode containing the reciprocal theft of food precedes that of the bird-nester. In M_{671}, Coyote first of all makes himself four artificial sons – one from clay, one from gum, one from stone, and one from the bark of the balsam poplar (*Populus tacamahacca*, Teit 9, p. 497) – and the story ends with the hero's revenge, for Coyote is carried away by the rising water and drowned; consequently, he is not in a position to free the salmon.

The Cowlitz, who live at the southern end of the Salish zone (M$_{672}$, Adamson, pp. 243–9), tell the story in a rather different way. The hero has four wives: two 'black' and two 'white'. The latter are unfaithful and are later changed into mice. As in M$_1$, the hero takes his revenge by creating rain and floods. Coyote is carried away by the flood water; he tries to grab at overhanging sticks and bushes, and according to whether or not the latter are accessible, he assigns different places to them in the hierarchy of wood species (cf. Chinook, M$_{618, 620}$, p. 286). After freeing the salmon, Coyote does not know how to catch them, and his faeces-sisters (see above, p. 309) teach him to fish and to cook. There follows the episode of the reciprocal theft of food (see above, p. 322). After taking revenge on his opponents, Coyote changes two salmon milts into young girls (see above, p. 309), whom he calls his daughters, although he loses no time in seducing them. They beat him and leave him. Later the girls marry strangers (very nice men) and give birth to the Cowlitz people, who are fair-skinned, as were the girls themselves.

It is interesting that M$_{672}$, in spite of its resemblance to the neighbouring Sahaptin versions that have already been discussed, ends with Coyote's attempt to commit incest with artificial daughters, who consequently are inversions of the artificial sons mentioned at the beginning of the Thompson versions. As it happens, several Salish myths belonging to the Lower Fraser valley or the coast (Chehalis: M$_{673}$, Boas 13, pp. 37–40; Comox: M$_{674}$, *ibid.*, pp. 65–8; Bella Coola: M$_{675}$, *ibid.*, pp. 262–3) retain the two motifs of the visit to the sky and the encounter with the old blind women, but associate them with a hero who wants a celestial wife, the sun's daughter according to M$_{673}$, where the hero himself is the offspring of incestuous siblings. I shall come back to this problem later (see below, pp. 581–2).

The Siciatl, who are Coast Salish, also give the title 'Myth of the sun' to their version of the bird-nester story, of which they present a different transformation:

M$_{676}$. Siciatl. 'The Bird-nester'

There was once an old man whose son had two wives. He was a fine hunter who, in order to warm his chilled companions, went up to a tree which he kicked, making fire spurt out of it (cf. M$_{602b, c}$, M$_{694}$). One day, when he had killed a lot of game, he sent his father to collect his pack. However, on the way back, the strap broke. The old man clutched for it, but the current carried him away. He changed into a piece of floating wood; a woman found it and tried to use it as a dish, but the wood ate up all the food. So she threw it away; it changed into a baby, whom the woman brought up and who became a young man in four days, after which he bade his protectress farewell and set out for his own home.

He was determined to take revenge and changed his excrement into little birds: then he sent his son to get them from the top of a tree. As he climbed, the tree stretched upwards into Sun-land. It was fine country and he set off to visit it. Presently he heard a knocking sound and perceived two old women who were preparing their food. As they were blind, he had no trouble in intercepting the food one was passing to the other. He was hailed as their 'grandson' by the old ladies and he restored their sight by applying the juice of medicinal leaves to their eyes. Then he told them that the river just beyond them contained lots of salmon, and he taught them to fish with a net which he had made by pulling out and knotting a hair from his leg.

A few days later, the old women helped the hero to go back down to earth in a basket. They told him not to open his eyes but to shake the basket every time it stopped. When he heard the crow calling, he would know he was in his country. The hero disobeyed first of all, and the basket immediately returned to the upper land. At last he reached the ground.

The hero found the wife who had borne his child and learned that his father had taken the other wife (Hill-Tout 1, pp. 39–45).

Hill-Tout, to whom we owe this version, thinks plausibly enough that, since the story is somewhat imperfect, M₆₇₆ was probably borrowed from the Thompson by the Siciatl; although he makes no attempt to explain how the imperfections crept in, he himself provides a possible reason by observing, in another context (Hill-Tout 2, p. 316), that in this area salmon could only be fished in Chehalis territory.[9] The coastal tribes, including the Siciatl, who are expressly mentioned, used to congregate in Chehalis territory during the fishing season, and sometimes disturbances and fights would occur. Given the fact that the Siciatl had no salmon in their territory, they could hardly credit one of their cultural heroes with having freed the fish; or, if they did so, he could only perform the action in the sky and not on earth. This major inversion no doubt determined all the others — the son's revenge preceding his persecution, the father's visit to the river women but without the freeing of the salmon, and the discovery of the

---

[9] Hill-Tout is referring to the Lower Fraser Chehalis in British Columbia, whose name he transcribes as 'Stseelis'; the name is also borne by another Salish tribe, on the coast of the State of Washington, and whose myths I have also used.

latter by the son (who finds them but does not free them); the transformation of pubic hair into a fishing net instead of into textile plants . . . This myth is comparable, then, with those I examined in the previous volume (*OTM*, pp. 267–73), where the actual physical absence of an animal, real enough in other areas, could explain its promotion to the rank of a celestial and supernatural creature.

With the Puget Sound Salish, we return to more classical versions. I do not propose to quote the southern ones recorded by Ballard, which are in fact Klikitat and therefore Sahaptin (Ballard 1, pp. 144–50; cf. p. 147, n. 160); they do not include the visit to the sky and are therefore irrelevant to the present discussion. The following one, however, is an authentic Salish version from the north-west of the same area:

M677. *Snohomish. 'The Bird-nester'*

At the time when animals were human beings, there were two friends, Fox and Mink, who thought of nothing else but playing tricks on each other. One day, while they were travelling along together, Mink went off on his own, ostensibly to see what kind of country lay ahead. He urinated into the water and transformed his urine into a trout; then he called to the ever hungry Fox, who hurried to the spot hoping for a good catch. Immediately after eating the fish, Fox felt ill and suspected he was pregnant.

His condition and the cause of it having been explained to him by his excrement-sisters or daughters, he gave birth before long to a son, who grew up fast and became a good hunter. He married two women; one, a plump little duck known as butterball (*Bucephala albeola?*) whom he loved dearly, the other a fowl of indeterminate species for whom he cared little. Fox coveted his son's wives and took him to a tree, in which were perched two birds with white feathers. The hero stripped completely and climbed up the tree; he finally reached the sky, and the birds, who had acted their part very well since they were none other than the excrement-sisters, returned to Fox's body.

The latter put on the clothes which his son had left, so that he looked like him. Only the second wife really thought her husband had come back. Fox set off with his conquest, while the Duck-wife walked behind crying and mourning for her dead husband.

Meanwhile, the hero was wandering about in the sky without meeting a single living soul. He finally came to the house of an old man with large white whiskers, who did not have much to say. He was making twine for fish nets. The hero introduced himself and learnt that his host was a spider and that he was quite willing to send him back to earth; he would, however, have to cross two intermediary countries and force his way through them by rolling over and over until he wore out the ground, which would then give way. The rolling caused all his hair to fall out. When he reached earth, where it was hotter than in the sky, he remembered to tie to the rope the four buckskins he had promised Spider as payment.

The hero found the site on which his village had stood deserted. Still naked and also bald, he followed his people's tracks and finally caught up with the wife who had remained faithful. The packing straps tied round her little bundle were hanging down and dragging on the ground. He stepped on the straps several times, and each time his wife jerked them away. Finally she recognized her husband, and made a motion with her hands which made his hair grow again.

They agreed that she should pack him into her basket. They went to Fox's camp and she claimed that she had as much right to share Fox's bed as the other wife. The young man sprang out of the basket, and refused to accept the clothes which his father wanted to give him back. He sent Fox and his unfaithful wife to fetch some game he had killed, but told the meat to turn into rotten wood and to have the packing strap break. The guilty pair could not imagine what had happened: they had to swim across a river but the current carried the woman away and she was never seen again. Fox managed to reach the other side and called to his two excrement-girls. They told him about two women down below called *witlwitl*, the mistresses of salmon (cf. Ballard 1, p. 146: *witowits*, a kind of snipe). Fox changed himself into a wooden dish, and drifted down the river until he reached the salmon trap. The women tried to use the dish and eat cooked salmon from it, but Fox devoured the fish before they could start eating. So they threw the dish away and it turned into a baby who claimed to be their little brother. One day, after the women had as usual gone to get Indian potatoes (*Claytonia*), Fox had a meal of their salmon, then consulted his excrement-girls, who advised him to tear down the trap so that the salmon could swim up the river and provide food for the people living a long way up, particularly for a woman and her daughter. But, they said, the mistresses of salmon would defend the salmon with great ferocity. Fox, with two vulnerable spots, his head and his anus, had to be careful to protect these two places with baskets.

Fox got the better of the sorceresses, and felt very big and proud as he swam up the river with the salmon following him. He came to the woman and her daughter of whom his advisers had spoken, and pretended that he could only speak Yakima (a Sahaptin dialect belonging to the mountainous area east of Puget Sound), for he wanted to be taken for a great chief of the people of the mountains. Feeling sure that Fox must be a great man, and impressed by all the salmon he had brought with him, the woman offered him her daughter in marriage, in spite of the difference in their ages.

After a few days, the salmon began to get scarce. The young wife left Fox and the baby girl to whom she had just given birth. The baby grew up very fast and Chief Mountain-Sheep asked Fox to let his son marry the girl. Fox let her go off into the mountains (where the sheep lived) with her husband.

Fox was all alone and not very happy, so he decided to go and visit his daughter. He passed himself off as a big chief to the Mountain-Sheep, who were all lords (big chiefs). Hungry as ever, he fancied his grandson's diapers which were made of thin fat. 'It is dirty and your grandson wets it,' said the mother. Fox, however, protested he was just pretending to eat the diapers to show how much he liked the baby and to show that he didn't mind its dirt. His daughter became very ashamed of him.

Fox thought he had better leave, and so went off under cover of night, taking with him a stone mallet. He imagined he was a long way off when he came face to face with his daughter, who accused him of being a thief. He had gone round in a circle all the time and had never left the house. At daybreak his daughter drove him out.

Fox lost his eyes in a stupid game (cf. M_{375}): in order to get them back, he passed himself off as an old woman called Sickness, whom he killed and whose skin he put on. Thus disguised and feigning the feeble motions of age (sitting down the way old women sit), he asked his victim's grand-daughters to carry him on their back: with each girl he tried to copulate from behind. At last he got his eyes back from the villagers, who were enjoying themselves with them. He created a thick fog by means of which he escaped. Then he thought he ought to go back to the country where he had come from, and not try to play any more tricks (Haeberlin 1, pp. 399–411).

After this myth, which presents a curious combination of three themes also present in the Chaco (Fox made ill by the pseudo-food offered him by his companion, the demiurge, cf. M_{210}; *HA*, p. 97; the pregnant demiurge, cf. M_{532}, above, p. 39; and lastly, his unsuccessful attempt to copulate from behind with the woman who is carrying him on her back, cf. M_{218}, *HA*, p. 110),[10] I should mention briefly the vestigial forms of the

---

[10] In support of this particular link, it should be noted that, according to M_{218}, the trickster's attempted copulation occurs with the Sun's daughter. The episode in M_{677}, in which he wanders all night

same myth found among the Tillamook, a branch of the Salish linguistic family, living in isolation on the coast a long way south of the Columbia River estuary (M_{678}, E. D. Jacobs, pp. 139–44). Here, the bird-nester story occurs in a recognizable form in the adventures of the trickster, South-Wind, who wants to get even with a character from whom, in spite of the latter's warnings, he has borrowed a belt made of two snakes which eat into his flesh and almost squeeze him to death. The interest of this transformation lies in the fact that we have already encountered it (see above, p. 282) and shall do so again (see below, p. 439) — Coyote as the borrower of a long penis, which immediately turns on him and which has an obvious relationship of symmetry with the snake belt. The trickster takes his revenge by means of the same device as he uses on other occasions to rid himself of his son and steal his wives — he takes from him, metaphorically, a penis which we can assume (since Coyote is usually described as an old man) to be more impressive than his own. The character who is forced to live in the sky gets his own back in his turn by having South-Wind carried off by a whale. South-Wind escapes and stays for a while at the home of a snake fisherman, who instructs him in the rites for the preparation and cooking of salmon. On reaching the Columbia River, he changes a stranger into a rock and is swallowed by an aquatic monster, from whom he is rescued by the masters of fire-drills, who light a fire in the monster's belly. Without knowing how or why, South-Wind discovers he is pregnant and gives birth to a girl, whom he tries several times to kill; on each occasion, however, she comes back to life. Finally, he agrees to spare her, and he makes her responsible for spreading sickness (cf. old grandmother Sickness, who is killed by Fox in M_{677}). One day, after catching a salmon, he changes the eggs into twin girls, whom he adopts. When they grow up, they refuse to paddle straight, so he becomes furious and calls them 'my wives' instead of 'my daughters' (cf. M_{672}). They take offence and leave him, and then steal the infant Moon, whose saga begins at this point (cf. M_{375}).

Let us see now how the story fares among the inland Salish groups who, in relation to the Thompson Indians, stand in a position symmetrical with that of the coastal communities. The Shuswap are familiar with the bird-

---

round and round in circles in the country of the mountain-sheep while imagining he is escaping with his booty, constitutes the terrestrial, if not chthonian counterpart of those Nez Percé myths in which Coyote, having reached the country of the sky, makes the same mistake, while trying to escape from Moon's lodge: Moon is a cannibal (whereas the mountain-sheep are food for humans) whom he has just killed, or whose son he has killed (Boas 4, pp. 173–4, 186–7). A discussion of this episode would be more appropriate in another context, to which reference has already been made (pp. 361, n.3; p. 368) and which, for reasons already explained, I propose to leave aside. (On the subject of Coyote's pregnancy, cf. Adamson, p. 264; on the subject of his copulating from behind, *ibid.*, p. 253; Jacobs 1, pp. 110, 209–10; 2, Part I, pp. 90–91).

nester myth, but in a weakened form, a fact which confirms my initial impression that the true centre of gravity, as it were, of the northern forms of the myth is to be found among the Thompson Indians.

According to the Fraser Valley Shuswap (M_{679a}, Teit 1, pp. 622–3), Coyote used to live with his son or his nephew Katlla'llst, 'Three Stones', who had two wives, one young, the other old. In order to appropriate these women for himself, Coyote sends Three Stones to the top of a rocky cliff, ostensibly to catch eaglets, claiming that he himself is too old and stiff. Quoting some supposed ancestral custom, he forces the young man first of all to dress in his finest clothes and then to remove them all before undertaking the ascent. After causing the rock to rise higher and higher, so that the hero is trapped on a craggy ledge and unable to climb either up or down, Coyote dons the clothes, stretches his skin so as to appear young, and takes his son's place.

Two Rodent Women (Bush-tailed Rat and Mouse), who are busy gathering hemp on a hillside underneath, hear the hero's cries and, by their magic incantations, cause the cliff to shrink. The hero thanks them by conjuring up a dense thicket of excellent hemp bushes, which he creates by scattering his own pubic hair. When he returns to the camp, Three Stones takes back his fine clothes from his father, and the younger of his two wives. He leaves the older for Coyote and goes off, never to return.

According to another Shuswap version from the Upper Thompson River (M_{679b}, Teit 1, pp. 737–8), an uncle and his nephew each have a wife. The older man falls in love with the younger man's, and gets rid of him by sending him to catch eagles; he then takes his place as the young woman's husband. In this case, the two helpful creatures are called Spider Woman and Mouse Woman. The hero thanks them by supplying them with hemp of a better quality than that which they formerly used.

These versions are weak forms in several respects: the hero is stranded at the top of a rock or half-way up the face of the cliff, instead of being sent up to the sky country; help comes from below, not from above; lastly, the hero, instead of taking his revenge, simply leaves his father or uncle and even allows him to keep one of the wives.

This does not mean that the Shuswap were unacquainted with the other episodes, which the Thompson and coastal groups put together to form a more detailed and coherent story. But, as also happens to a lesser degree in Lilloet mythology (M_{671}), they transpose them into a different context ($M_{680a, b}$; Teit 1, pp. 627–30, 739–41), known to American mythographers as the bungling host story and which we have already encountered several times in the course of this study (RC, pp. 172, 293, n.3; HA, pp. 83–4) and which, for most American tribes, had a highly sacred character, in spite of its farcical and scatological elements. It is easy to understand why this should be so, if the misadventures of the bungling host are a series of symmetrical inversions of the exploits of the demiurge. The latter changed animate or inanimate beings from what they were into what they were henceforth to be. The trickster, on the contrary, acting as bungling host to a whole series of creatures, tries to imitate them as they still were in mythic times, but can no longer be. He thus attempts to extend to different species, and to perpetuate in time, aberrant types of behaviour or manners, and consequently behaves *as if* privileges, exceptions, or anomalies could become the rule, unlike the demiurge, whose function is to put an end to peculiarities, and to promulgate rules universally applicable to every species or category.

The Lilloet version (M_{671}) and the Shuswap versions ($M_{680a, b}$) provide an excellent illustration of the symmetry existing between the two groups of myths. Before or after various adventures, during which Coyote fails in his attempt to imitate improbable devices for the production of food, each one of which, as he is told by the characters on whom he is modelling himself, is their peculiar and exclusive property, there occurs an episode which is the exact counterpart of that featuring the blind old women: it takes place on earth, instead of in the sky; Coyote dupes, then blinds young children whose mothers are described as tetraonidae, instead of first tricking and then restoring the sight of blind old women who change into tetraonidae; the mothers take their revenge, whereas – in certain versions at least – the blind women turn out to be helpful. The act of revenge, prompted by Coyote's harsh treatment of the children of grouse or prairie chickens is identical with that inflicted by the hero of the bird-nester story, Coyote's son, on his father, because of the latter's ill-treatment of him. In both cases, mothers who have a grievance because of their children, or a son who has a grievance against his father, arrange for the culprit, who is always Coyote, to fall into the water.[11] From this point onwards, the two cycles follow the same pattern: the salmon are set free and shared out, the beds of the streams and rivers are rearranged, Grizzly Woman is duped, and M_{680a} transforms the long penis (M_{680b}) into a 'short penis' (since Coyote copulates in the form of a baby) while at the same time combining the episode with the freeing of the salmon. Hence a series of problems which must now be broached.

[11] In connection with this already encountered and very popular episode in the myths of the north-west of North America, cf. above, p. 322. Cf. for other examples Boas 13, pp. 17, 57, 89, 114; Hill-Tout 10, p. 547.

2 The Two Blind Hags

The blind men heard him coming,
Straightway they moved to one side,
And cried out, 'Deal kindly with us,
We are poor beyond any living creature:
He is indeed poor who cannot see.'

'Des Trois Aveugles de Compiengne',
Barbazon et Méon, *Fabliaux et contes des poètes*
français, III, p. 399, v. 30–37, Paris, 1808.

I have given a random sampling from a considerable body of mythic
material which, however, by no means exhausts the Salish variants of the
bird-nester story. But at least it gives some idea of the internal economy of
the myth and of its area of distribution. In both connections, a number of
preliminary observations are necessary.

The inland, as well as the coastal, versions present the hero as having four
distinctive characteristics: he is a master of hunting and therefore of meat; a
master of lavish adornments and fine clothes; a master of warmth providing
fire; and lastly, a master of a destructive kind of water which he unleashes as
an act of revenge. As master of fire (which only he can kindle or knows how
to keep burning) and as master of rain and storms, the Salish hero is
reminiscent of his South American counterpart as we saw him in the Bororo
reference myth. This initial similarity inevitably points to a second, namely
the part assigned, in M_1 and M_{667a}, to edible tubers or roots as stoppers.
The hero of M_1, who is first of all marooned on a high plateau and attacked
by vultures which devour his hindquarters, is unable to retain the food he
eats on his return to earth until it occurs to him to block his gaping anus
with paste made from edible tubers.

I have already pointed out that this motif occurs frequently in north-west
America (see above, p. 339). The Thompson story (M_{667a}), that I am using
as a reference myth at the moment, is an inversion of it: in pulling up what
he supposes to be edible roots but which he cannot eat, the hero makes holes

in the celestial vault and the wind from the earth rushes through the openings. We can take this to be an inversion, since the small Oregon coastal tribes, whose myths are particularly interesting in that they are more likely to have preserved archaic themes because of the isolated position of these Indians, combine the straight form and the inverted form of the myth. According to the Coos, the trickster, being deprived of his entrails and thus unable to retain the fruit he is eating, tries to block his anus with wild parsnip roots (Jacobs 6, p. 192; cf. below, p. 566); but, according to the Tillamook, it is precisely the hollow stem of a wild parsnip that the demiurge uses to evacuate poisonous food which he makes only a pretence of eating (E. D. Jacobs, pp. 9–10). Whatever plant is known as wild parsnip in this area of America, and it may be a *Sium*, a *Heracleum* or a *Lomatium* (= *Peucedanum*), it is in any case an umbellifer, the sacred prototype of which, on the coast and even as far as Kwakiutl territory, is the *Peucedanum*. In the portulaca or purslane family, a similar relation exists between *Claytonia* and *Lewisia rediviva*, which the Flathead, the most easterly representatives of the Inland Salish, also held to be sacred (A. P. Merriam, p. 115). One may suppose, then, the existence of a classificatory system of plants, which are directly represented by their prototypes or by combinatory variants occupying a more modest position within the genus or family. I dealt with this problem in my 1968–9 lectures; to take it up again here would needlessly burden the present discussion.

Another link emerges, peculiar this time to North America, between the Salish myths in which the bird-nester is exiled to the sky country, and those belonging to the star-husband cycle, to which the preceding volume was largely devoted. In each instance, a terrestrial hero or heroine visits the sky and, according to the Algonquin versions ($M_{437, 438}$), is sent back to earth by means of a rope and helped by supernatural protectors, who warn him to keep his eyes shut until he hears the call of a certain named species of bird. The Salish hero lands on a flat rock which marks the centre of the world, an expression which should be taken in the spatial sense; at least one Ojibwa version of the star-husband myth makes it clear that the hole in the celestial vault, through which the wives of the sun and moon find their way back to earth, corresponded to the position of the Pleiades, whose culmination at nightfall marks the new year; in other words, it, too, is a centre of the world, but this time in a temporal sense (M_{444b}, cf. *OTM*, p. 247). The importance of these links will emerge when I come to discuss the Salish and neighbouring versions of the star-husband cycle along with the bird-nester stories in which the hero marries a celestial creature (see below, pp. 566–89).

For the time being, I prefer to concentrate on the more restricted area with which I have been concerned from the beginning of the present volume, but which I would now like to grasp as a whole. It is true to say that, in spite of the geographical gap, we have never been closer to the Klamath and Modoc myths with which our enquiry started than we are with the Thompson and Lilloet versions. In both groups, a demiurge who is also a trickster, undertakes to make himself a son: either he incorporates the child within his own body and gives birth to it after the mother dies in a fire (in Klamath-Modoc mythology and in that of the nearest Salish, cf. M_{565}); or after various attempts he finally obtains a viable son (M_{667a}, M_{668a}, M_{670a}, M_{671}); or the future father becomes pregnant by magic ($M_{532-533}$, M_{677}, M_{678}). In the Klamath and Modoc stories, as in those of several Coast Salish groups, the child is the offspring of an incestuous marriage, an improper conjunction, which, according to circumstances, is intensified, exacerbated or replaced by another conjunction, which is genital, not sexual, and involves one man only.

It will be remembered that the name of the Klamath-Modoc hero, Aishísh, means 'the secreted or secluded one' and refers to his being temporarily enclosed in the demiurge's body. The Salish also give him a name: Tô'rtôsemstem in the Cœur d'Alêne myths (see above, p. 364), Nli'ksentem, Tl'ikse'mtem, N'tlikcu'mtum, N-kik-sam-tam in the Thompson myths, all of which terms, according to the sources (Boas 4, p. 120, n. 1; 13, p. 18; Teit 4, 103, n. 43; Hill-Tout 10, p. 554, n. 1), mean 'raised or lifted up' or 'the climber', and refer to the misadventures of the hero who is sent up by his father into the sky country. Consequently, the two names, or families of names, have a relationship of correspondence: one refers to the conjunction with the father's body, the other to disjunction in respect of this same father, since, the hero, at the two crucial points in the story, finds himself either excessively close to him or excessively remote from him.

From this onomastic symmetry it is already apparent that, within the vast pan-American set formed by the bird-nester myth, the versions I have listed, from the Klamath River basin to that of the Fraser River, constitute in turn a sub-set with all the features of a closed group. This impression is strengthened by the recurrence in both bodies of myths of an initiatory sequence (see above, pp. 68, 70, 116 and M_{667a}, pp. 368–9). It is definitively confirmed by the fact that only the Salish versions enable us to solve a problem peculiar to the Loon Woman cycle which, as I have shown, is a transformation of the bird-nester cycle.

Demetracopoulou, in her study of the first of these cycles and that I have already discussed (see above, pp. 60–61), raises the question of the recurrence, in almost all versions, of a seemingly gratuitous and puzzling detail: the incestuous heroine discovers the existence of her young brother, who is being kept hidden by their parents, thanks to a hair which she picks up and which happens to be longer than the hair of all the other members of the family. Finding no explanation for it, Demetracopoulou concludes that the hair incident must be arbitrary, since it neither 'predicts nor justifies the string of episodes of which it forms a part' (Demetracopoulou, p. 121).

The northern versions of the bird-nester myth also stress the hero's long hair, and give it a relevant function in the story. For instance, in M_{670a} the hero, who is described as shivering at the top of the tree, wraps his long hair round his body as a protection against the cold; in M_{677}, on the other hand, he loses all his hair and returns to earth completely bald; the first act of his wife who has remained faithful to him is to restore his lost hair. Among the Chilcotin, who are Athapaskan-speaking Indians and neighbours of the Lillooet and Shuswap, the bird-nester myth occurs in a form so weak as to be almost imperceptible. Yet the incident is carefully retained: the hero, by weaving feathers from the nest into his long hair, makes a blanket to protect himself from the cold (M_{681}; Farrand 2, pp. 29–30). This can only mean that the hero, who initially is always described as the master of fine clothes, subsequently retains his vestimentary connotation, although in the state of nudity in which he finds himself at the top of a tree or rocky ledge he is no longer clad except *sub specie naturae*. The long hair, a natural covering, is consequently in opposition to manufactured clothes, just as the raw is in opposition to the cooked, and this confirms yet again the transition from the alimentary to the vestimentary code, to which I have constantly drawn attention. It will, however, be remembered that something similar had already occurred in M_1, where the hero, who is in the same situation, starts by hunting lizards in order to appease his hunger; he ties the surplus food to his belt, his armbands and round his legs. Before long, the animals decompose, so that he is clad in a kind of decayed matter, which also belongs to the natural order and provides an unmistakable analogy with the hero's baldness in M_{677}. As I pointed out previously (*OTM*, pp. 182–5), baldness is often associated in American Indian thought with the idea of decay.

All this was already present by implication in the mythology of the Klamath and the Modoc. Not only because the hero invents porcupine quill adornments, which are prominent features of apparel, as his homologue in the Salish myths creates textile fibres – also as a reward for the creatures who helped him to return to earth – but because these southern myths are careful to stress their hero's exceptionally long hair. According to M_{539} (Curtin 1, pp. 95–117), the hidden child's hair reached to the ground, and M_{543} (*ibid.*, p. 28) contains the following remark, which is revealing in the sense that it sets in opposition as homogeneous terms within the same pair the usurpation of fine clothes and the superabundance of game: 'Old man Kumush (= Kmúkamch) lives with Isis (= Aishísh) and sometimes he pretends that he is Isis. He puts on Isis's clothes and tries to sing his song. You must not let him fool you: when Isis is at home, there is always fresh deer meat hanging on the trees near the house.' Consequently, it is normal that in the Loon Woman cycle, which is symmetrical with that of the bird-nester, a richly clad boy should be protected by his family from his sister's anti-social desires, which can only reveal themselves in broad daylight when the natural counterpart of the hero's vestimentary connotation – his long hair – betrays his presence.[1]

I now propose to deal with the Salish myths in detail. The most rewarding versions begin with the trickster's attempts – three or four in number, according to the context – to make himself a son:

Thompson	M_{667a}	: clay	pitch (or gum)	stone	
	M_{668a}	: clay	pitch	stone	wood
	M_{670a}	:	pitch	stone	vegetable fibres
Lilloet	M_{671}	: clay	pitch	stone	poplar bark

If we disregard certain minor differences in the fourth column, which are perhaps to be explained by uncertainties of transcription, only the absence of the 'wooden' son in M_{667a} and of the 'earth' son in M_{671} presents a problem. Of course, in both instances the omission may be due to an oversight; however, to be thorough – and although the effort is perhaps gratuitous – let us try to correlate this feature with others. The narrative defines three sons in relation to water: the first son disintegrates in it, the third sinks to the bottom (except in M_{667a}, where he is not put to this test) and the fourth floats. Only the son made of gum or pitch is defined in relation to solar heat. The relevant opposition is consequently between sky and water. However, the water itself has various connotations: it can be positive or negative, according to whether or not it allows the creature to survive; and it can be defined in respect of the low, the middle or the high,

---

[1] By extending the same argument to a different myth (M_{650a}; see above, p. 316), we can deduce from the fact that hair is assimilated to a natural garment, and from the already established equivalences between the *naked* and the *raw* and the *clad* and the *cooked*, that, in its wild state, fire must have its seat in the hair of the first female who possessed it.

according to whether the creature sinks to the bottom, disintegrates in the liquid or floats on the surface. In M_{667a} — where there is no wooden son and the stone son is viable from birth — the 'high' and 'low' functions of water are absent: there only remains the 'middle' function which, in the absence of the clay son, is the one missing from M_{670a}.

There is, however, another difference between these versions: they give the hero's wives as being, respectively, either the Loon and the Mallard Duck or the Eagle and the Duck. Since, in both instances, the Duck wife plays an unattractive role, the relevant opposition centres on the person of the other wife, Eagle or Loon. Since both are birds, we can disregard their bird nature as an invariant feature and effect a further reduction so that the opposition is now between sky and water. It is obvious that the loon occupies a prominent place among water fowl, as the eagle does among the birds of the upper air.

By widening the wives paradigm, as it is exemplified in the myths being dealt with in this fifth part of our study, we arrive at the following pattern:

	(+)	(−)
Nez Percé:	Beetle, Cricket	Swan, Duck
Cœur d'Alène:	Swan	Tern
Thompson (Teit):	Loon	Duck, Teal
Thompson (Hill-Tout):	Eagle	Duck

Unfortunately, we cannot work in the Lilloet version, where there is nothing by which to identify the hero's wives: all we know is that they come from a basket-weaving community. It is clear, however, in spite of this omission, that the Nez Percé wives, on the one hand, and the Thompson wives in Hill-Tout's version, on the other, illustrate an important distinctive feature: that between a chthonian insect and an aquatic bird, or between a supraterrestrial bird and an aquatic bird. Furthermore, these versions are also in opposition to each other since they present the good wives as being, respectively, either the chthonian one or the celestial one; consequently, they are separated from each other by a gap greater than the one which, in either context, distinguishes each from her co-wife.

On the other hand, the Cœur d'Alène and Thompson versions occupy a middle position in relation to the preceding versions, since they both have one feature in common: they contrast two wives who are both water birds: Swan and Tern, or Loon and Duck. Swans and ducks are migratory: they fly south at the start of the bad weather. But we see from the myths that terns and loons, whether or not they are migratory, are of interest to Indians, because of other aspects of their behaviour: terns accompany the salmon when they swim up river; loons move between the inland lakes and the coast, according to changes in the weather. Consequently, the Loon and the Tern form a pair along an east-west, and relatively low, axis, while Swan and Duck form another along a north-south axis, and they also fly higher at the time of the seasonal migrations. But, since the Cœur d'Alêne and Thompson myths (Teit) reverse the semantic valency of the wives within the pair (*Swan* : *Tern* : *Loon* : *Duck*), it can be said that these myths are inversions of each other in a minor mode in respect of the wives, just as the Thompson myths (Hill-Tout) and those of the Nez Percé are inversions of each other in a major mode.

Let us return now to the artificial sons. If, as the preceding remarks indicate, the identity of the wives is a relevant factor in the myths under consideration, it could be significant that in the one where there is no wooden son the wives are called Loon and Duck, while in the one lacking the clay son they are called Eagle and Duck. In relation to water, the wooden son occupies the high position, which is also the position of the eagle in relation to the sky, and both of them are absent from the same version. Symmetrically, the clay son occupies a middle position in relation to water, and he is absent from the version which, in respect of water birds, makes no mention of those which depend on the lake and river system and which, in relation to the great migratory birds, can be defined as 'median'. There could, consequently, be a connection between these anomalous details.

I move on now to the visit to sky country which calls for lengthy comment. The description given in the myths corresponds accurately to the Salish conception of the celestial world as a great, bare plain, windswept and very cold. In order clearly to grasp how mythic transformations operate, it is worth noting that the immediate neighbours of the Vancouver Salish to the west, that is the Nootka, systematically reverse this view: for them, the celestial world enjoys eternal calm, with canoes ʾloating gracefully on smooth waters, and a total absence of frost and snow (Sproat, p. 209). The Salish, on the other hand, contrast the coldness of the celestial world with the intense heat which once prevailed on earth (Teit 6, p. 176; 10, p. 337). The Tsetsaut, a tiny Athapaskan-speaking community living in isolation along the coast, held similar views (Boas 21, p. 569). So in the beginning, earth and sky were climatically either *all one thing* or *all the other*, and the role of the demiurge or demiurges was to make the earth alternately *one thing and the other*, now that the sky, having become inaccessible, need no longer be imagined, and therefore relinquished, for use by the terrestrial world, the semantic position which, when it was accessible, served to define it in relation to the world below.

According to the Thompson, the celestial plain is like an abruptly terminating plateau except, it would seem, to the north, since these Indians thought of the earth as sloping upwards towards the sky until it reached it in the north (Teit 4, pp. 23, 25, 104; 10, pp. 337, 341). Here again, the cosmological image is reversed by another tribe: the Twana, a Salish community belonging to Puget Sound, believe, on the contrary, that the sky slopes towards the earth and touches it in the west and south (Eells, 3, p. 681).

In sky country, the hero first of all encounters hostile creatures: cannibalistic or warlike spiders, and manufactured objects in revolt against their users. I have already analysed the transformation relating, on the one hand to hunting and cannibalism, and, on the other, to the making of textiles (see above, p. 365). I need only add that, if the hypotheses I put forward are correct, the initial celestial sequences of the story mean that the hero, after being disjoined from mankind by the evil machinations of his father, the trickster, regresses to a pre- or anti-cultural state, which is defined by the equivalence between the raw and the naked. This zero state marks the starting-point of his real task, which is that of mediator; he begins by decreeing that manufactured objects will no longer be able to behave disobediently. Such insubordination would be scandalous in the state of culture, which takes the subservience of manufactured objects precisely as its *terminus a quo*. The more inclusive framework having thus been delineated, the details of the state of culture need only be filled in.

As we shall see later, the next episode, which revolves around the meeting with the two blind women, is very widely distributed throughout North America. However, before taking the broader view, it would be appropriate to study the motif in the narrow context in which it was first encountered. One particularly concise version (M_{670c}; Boas 13, pp. 17–18) makes the essential points: in sky country Coyote's son visits two old grouse-women. One complains that the hero has a bad smell; in a fit of anger he throws them out into the brush, and changes them into birds.

The old women are seated opposite each other on either side of a fire; they are quarrelling over who should have a stalk of bad quality hemp, which is growing lengthwise under the ground between them, and which each one is trying to appropriate (M_{667a}), or they are handing to each other bad food consisting of rotten wood or rotten rock (or rather are failing to do so, because of the hero's sly intervention). He snatches the food from them as they pass it across, and since they cannot see him, because of their disability, they accuse each other of being either clumsy or spiteful ($M_{667a, b}$; M_{670a}; M_{676}). However, although sightless, they can smell, especially since, according to the less prudish versions, the hero replaces the food by his own penis, which he puts in the hand of his unfortunate dupe, who protests that it stinks. It is already obvious that the episode is bringing simultaneously into play several different registers: the technological, the visual, the alimentary, the sexual, the olfactory, etc. Vexed by the old women's offensive remark, the hero throws them into some thickets where, according to M_{667a}, they change into two species of grouse: one is easy to catch, while the other is subject to a very particular mode of impregnation (see above, p. 370).

All these elements are so closely interwoven, and the interpretation of any one is so dependent on the meaning of all the others, that it is very difficult to know where to start. I propose, therefore, to make a number of random observations, in the hope that they will fall spontaneously into place. The word grouse refers, in North America, to several birds of the tetraonidae family, mostly grouse proper and prairie chickens. The term fool-hen would seem to be applied indiscriminately to young grouse and to one particular species, *Canachites canadensis* or *franklini*, 'thus called because of its lack of fear of man: it is often killed by sticks or stones . . . it can sometimes even be caught by grasping one of its feet' (Bent, *Gallinaceous Birds*, pp. 136, 140; Pearson, Vol. II, p. 16). The Okanagon women used to catch these birds by hanging a noose of Indian hemp from a stick, and they feed their young children on them in the hope of making them 'good' (Cline, pp. 24, 120). The Thompson, who were prouder in manner, so it seems, maintained on the contrary that 'eating willow-grouse should be forbidden to the husband of a pregnant woman, for fear the child might be foolish like the bird' (Teit 10, p. 304). The hunting method used by the Okanagon and the Thompson also existed among the Flathead (Turney-High 2, p. 113); its use was doubtless even more widespread, since it was observed among the Similkameen Indians (Allison, p. 307) and still more northerly Athapaskan tribes (Morice, Vol. 5, p. 124). Certain Salish myths describe women who, fleeing for their lives and dependent on what they can find, manage to survive by eating berries and fool-hens (Boas 4, p. 39). Other myths explain that the bird remained timid, because it had originally been human and had been kept in captivity for a long time (Elliott, pp. 174–5). M_{667a} seals the fate of one of the old women by conferring on her the nature of a game bird which even women and children can easily catch; she is changed into a Franklin Grouse in the forests where this species spends the winter (Bent, *loc. cit.*, p. 141). The hero then changes the second old woman into a ruffed grouse, *Bonasa umbellus*, which, according to the ornithologists, differs from the other species in being more suspicious of man (Godfrey, p. 129). So for it, the hero reserves a different fate: it will become pregnant whenever it hears wings beating against a trunk. The male of this species, which is also called the drumming grouse, 'was referred to by some Indians as the "carpenter bird", because they believed it was beating upon a log with its wings to produce the drumming sound' (Bent, *loc. cit.*, p. 143). Audubon, who also refers to the 'drumming log', specifically states that only the male bird drums (*ibid.*, p. 146) and Seton (Ch. II) describes a ruffed grouse 'in a superb pose . . . drumming on a log'.

Although drumming is no more than part of the nuptial display, and the writers just quoted are fully aware of the nature of the operation, in which the log merely acts as a perch, it is clear that, in this instance too, the distinctive characteristic described by the myth corresponds to well-attested native beliefs, based partially at least on empirical data. But why does the myth pick out only two characteristics, and very dissimilar ones at that, in order to define closely related birds which, in the initial human form it ascribes to them, were exactly alike?

In the first instance, we are dealing with a game bird which is abnormally tolerant of physical contiguity with the hunter; and, in the second instance, with a female bird which, no less abnormally, does not need physical contiguity with the male to become pregnant: she conceives at a distance, because her hearing is particularly acute, whereas the other bird, which lets itself be caught by hand, fails to hear the hunter's approach. So in two respects — alimentary or sexual — the birds suffer from a disability relating to the category of contiguity. When the disability manifests itself by excess, as in the case of the auditory fertilization, it leads to the reproduction of the species, and consequently to the propagation of life. When it manifests itself by default, as in the case of the effortless hunting, it has the reverse consequence for the other species: that is, death.

I shall confirm this interpretation later by showing (see below, pp. 537–42), that, in this area of North America, the bird known as the pheasant, but which is in fact a grouse,[2] plays the part of intermediary between the world of the living and that of the dead, since it belongs to both worlds, and is itself, literally, half-living and half-dead. In *The Raw and the Cooked* (pp. 203–207), I arrived deductively at the same pattern in trying, through a series of commutations, to determine the position of the South

[2] 'The early English settlers in North America sometimes called the ruffed grouse the pheasant' (Bent, *loc. cit.*, p. 310). 'Properly grouse (*Bonasa umbellus sabini*), but commonly called pheasant' (Ballard 1, p. 92, n. 80).

American 'partridge' — another gallinacean — in the semantic field formed by the helpful animals; it is extremely gratifying to encounter the same pattern thousands of kilometres away, and to find it confirmed in Salish mythology, this time on the level of actuality, instead of on the potential level, as in South America.

The old blind women, seated on either side of a fire, are quarrelling about a poor quality textile plant, which is growing longitudinally below the ground, or about rotten food, which one is handing over to the other above the ground. In the myths belonging to this area, to offer someone food across a fire is to expose that person to the risk of burning. A myth I do not propose to quote in detail, and of which there are a great many versions (M_{682a-e}; Boas 4, pp. 22–5; Teit 4, pp. 64–6; 1, pp. 673–7; Hill-Tout 8, pp. 158–61; Farrand 2, pp. 41–2), features two brothers, Marten and Fisher, who become involved with a mysterious woman who hands them food over a fire; just as they are stretching across to grasp it, she pulls them by the hand to topple them into the fire. One of the brothers falls, but the other succeeds in leaping over the fire. He knocks the woman over and touches her genitals; this tames her, and she comes spontaneously to the two brothers' camp and agrees to marry her conqueror.

So, while direct contiguity of food and cooking fire has maleficent consequences for the consumer, the consequences of bringing a man and a woman into physical contiguity are, on the contrary, beneficent. All Salish tribes recognized a particular mode of marriage known as 'touching'. The coast communities organized dances which had a religious aspect: while the dance was going on, a man could touch the hand of any female dancer. 'They were then considered married' (Barnett 3, p. 206). The same was true of the inland Lilloet, among whom the 'touching dance' was a prelude to marriage (Teit 11, pp. 268, 284), and of the Thompson (Teit 10, pp. 323–4; Hill-Tout 6, pp. 191–2), among whom the accidental touching of a girl had the same result; similarly with the Flathead (Turney-High 2, pp. 88–9) and the Okanagon: 'If a girl past puberty was seen exposed by a man, or if he touched [her hand], he had to marry her . . . the only alternative was suicide, should so much as her legs be seen . . . Sometimes by means of this custom, boys forced girls to marry them, who might otherwise have refused' (Cline, p. 114).

The existence in Salish society of what one might call a philosophy of contiguity can also be deduced, *a contrario*, from other indications. A Chehalis myth from British Columbia (M_{682f-g}; Hill-Tout 2, p. 340; 6, p. 217) relates how a young grief-stricken widower goes to the land of ghosts in order to look for his wife and bring her back among the living. The dead agree on condition that during the journey back he should not seek to enjoy his marital rights and that he should light a huge fire every evening, on either side of which the husband and wife had to sleep. In real life, Squamish husbands and wives did not sleep side by side but feet to feet. If the bed space was confined, the feet of one would reach to the head of the other, but usually this was not the case (Hill-Tout 7, p. 486).

Blindness is a condition which imposes contiguity on people affected by it: not being able to see, they must use the sense of touch. We can suppose then, that the transferring by the blind women of a form of pseudo-food over the fire constitutes the minimal form — an extremely brief and therefore negative form — of spatio-temporal periodicity, following on the maximum spatial disjunction illustrated by the transferring of the hero from the earth to the sky. This formulation makes it possible to combine into a single pattern the two consecutive episodes of the objects in revolt against their master and the blind women in M_{667a} and M_{664a}, as well as the hunting by defecation on the part of the hostile spiders, which is also an instance of short-circuiting, being a conjunction of food and faeces. Only later, when the hero is staying with the helpful spiders, does he recover his spatio-temporal periodicity, but on condition that during his descent from the sky to the earth (and contrary to what happened during the upward journey) he makes four *pauses*, and, on each occasion, takes his *time*.

Other myths belonging to the area help to illustrate a similar presentation of the problem. At the beginning of the Coast Salish myths M_{375a} and M_{382}, Coyote, being alone, removes his own backside so as to have someone to watch his fish-trap while he himself makes a canoe. However, the backside proves to be incapable of distinguishing between a salmon and, in turn, floating scum, dead leaves or a bit of trash-wood. When it finally manages to catch a fish, Coyote retaliates by eating it all without offering any to his partner, 'who feels very bad about it and his mouth begins to pucker up'. This explains why, henceforth, when Coyote has put it back in its place, the backside has a puckered mouth, to distinguish it from the (other) mouth; in the beginning both had been alike, since the anus as well as the mouth had the gift of speech (Adamson, pp. 158–9). In a second version of the same myth (M_{375b}; Adamson, pp. 173–4), this episode is replaced by another, during which Coyote, who has become blind, makes himself eyes from flowers; they are of very little use, and he exchanges them for those of the snail, who since that time has been totally blind. So, either Coyote disjoins his rear from his front, both of which parts were once equal in the sense that both could speak, with the resulting anatomical differentiation between the mouth and the anus; or he tries to carry out an exchange of eyes, which results in the zoological differentiation between a species endowed with sight and another that is blind. This initial disjunction corresponds, in the Chinook myths I have already discussed ($M_{618, 620}$; p. 293), to the terminal conjunction which occurs when Grizzly Woman, by painting her face with her menstrual blood, unites, as it were, the low and the high. In both instances, a mediate or immediate consequence occurs in the form of anatomical, zoological or botanical differentiation: between parts of the body, and a little later, species of fish in M_{375} (see above, p. 293); and between species of wood in M_{618}, a motif which reappears significantly in the group of myths I am at present discussing (cf. M_{672}, above, p. 378). According to the Salish-speaking Bella Coola who live in isolation much farther north (M_{683a}; Boas 13, p. 241), the differentiation – in other words the introduction of non-contiguity into the animal kingdom – was a prelude to the dispersal of the primeval fog uniting sky and earth and confusing light and darkness, and to the appearance of the visible sun. According to the Thompson (M_{683b}; Teit 5, pp. 313–14), the appearance of an anatomical discontinuity (the different pigmentation of the various native groups) resulted from the theft of the visible sun by Coyote and Antelope, which was a prelude to their own division into two different species (the second species: *Antilocapra*, lived on the eastern slopes of the Rockies). On the other hand, several Coast Salish communities (M_{349}; Adamson, pp. 71, 233, 346, 370) maintain that the fog allowed the stealer of the solar disc to escape, by virtually blinding his pursuers. We can sense, then, the existence of an equivalence between several forms of anatomical disjunction or conjunction – the rear disjoined from the front, the low conjoined to the high, the eyes alternately disjoined or conjoined – and between the high and the low, the sky and the earth, the alternately disjunctive or conjunctive role of the fog: a mediatory term conjoining extremes and rendering them indistinguishable, or coming between them to prevent them drawing closer. The fog can be seen, then, as the reverse of the domestic hearth (*RC*, p. 293).

In the particular instance with which I am now concerned, and which in Salish mythology is illustrated by the bird-nester story, blindness, comparable in its effects to the fog which virtually blinds those whom it envelops, unless, in default of sight, they can touch each other, constitutes one of the various manifestations of contiguity. This contiguity, which is sometimes beneficent and sometimes maleficent, maintains a correlative relationship in the myths with various modes of differentiation, that is, with the introduction of a principle of discontinuity between vegetable or animal species, between human races, or even within some still homogeneous entity, such as space or time. It is a striking fact that in the many available versions of M_{683} there is an invariant feature common to all the tribes, from the Thompson (Teit 4, pp. 32–4) to the Wishram (Sapir 1, pp. 67–75): Coyote's children, who meet their death while taking it in turns to transport the visible sun, which they have stolen, all have names; Antelope's children, however, who complete the exploit successfully, are not named.[3] Coyote's children are individualized, Antelope's are not.

Consequently, in Salish thought, contiguity would seem to be a mode of the more general category of continuity, the theory of which I have already touched upon several times in the previous volumes (see Index under 'chromatism' and 'continuous'). The Salish belief in the connection between contiguity and blindness is also illustrated in the rites: the Thompson insisted that the eyes should be kept closed when invoking the first produce of the season – salmon, fruit or edible roots – as well as during daily prayers. Hill-Tout (2, p. 330; 6, pp. 169–70) observes in connection with the Stseelis (= the Chehalis of British Columbia): 'To keep the eyes closed during incantations and magic performances constituted for the Salish an essential feature of the act, the non-observance of which caused failure. So to ensure this being strictly done, the assisting elders are armed with long wands with which they strike any person found opening his eyes during the incantations in honour of the first salmon.'

Other no less important aspects of the blind women episode emerge when we come to deal with it on the basis of the Tillamook versions. These Salish-speaking Indians, who live apart from the rest of the family to the south of the Columbia estuary, have preserved what are probably archaic elements of a common mythic heritage, while at the same time modifying them to some extent in their own particular way.

The Tillamook relate (M_{684a}; Boas 14, p. 30) how six Indians decide to travel in their canoe all over the world. One day they come to a door which opens and closes with the rapidity and force of lightning. One of the men succeeds in jumping through the door; on the other side, he finds two blind women who possess a plentiful supply of whale meat. The man takes some of the meat and throws it through the swinging door: one piece reaches his companions, another piece remains caught by the closing door. The man

---

[3] In connection with this contrast, which is stressed in the myths, cf. Cowlitz: M_{348}, Jacobs 1, pp. 68–109; Thompson: M_{668a}, Teit 5, p. 296; Cœur d'Alène: Reichard 3, p. 73; Sanpoil: Ray 2, p. 177. According to the Shuswap (Teit 1, p. 597), the nameless stars are earth people who have gone up into the sky and have been killed by the people above. The problem will be reconsidered later from this angle, see below, pp. 466–9.

tries to get back, but when he jumps, half his back is cut off. The wound is healed by means of plasters made from clayey mud.

According to a more recent version (M_{684b}; E. D. Jacobs, pp. 6–7), the hungry demiurge Ice, during his wanderings, meets a community of baskets full of food, which give him a sound beating (cf. M_{667a}). Next, he arrives in front of two little houses: the door of the first house opens and shuts rapidly because the owner talks extremely fast, boasting that she has more whale meat than her neighbour. The latter talks slowly, because she is angry and her door opens and shuts slowly following the rhythm of her speech. Ice succeeds in gaining admittance, eats as much as he can and takes the rest of the meat for his companions. While running through the swinging door, he catches his flesh slightly, and puts some leaves over the sore. The women are two old maids to whom the whalers give a fixed amount of meat, but as one receives a little less than the other, she remains in a constant state of irritation.

So, after a horizontal journey instead of a vertical ascent, the Tillamook hero also encounters two old blind women who live in a perpetual state of disagreement. The difference between the Tillamook story and the more northerly Salish versions lies in the fact that, in the first, the old women are unequal at the start (since one receives more than the other), whereas in the Thompson myths they are made unequal at the finish: they are changed into two distinct species of grouse, although, as I showed, they are also defined in terms of excess or deficiency, in the passive respect of hearing. One has such an acute sense of hearing that the noise of beating wings is enough to make it pregnant; the other is so dull of hearing that it is not even aware of the hunter's approach. In the Tillamook myth the acoustic relationship is active: one woman talks so fast as to be unapproachable, whereas the other talks slowly and, like the first species of grouse, can be more easily approached.

The beliefs of the Puyallup-Nisqually, who are Salish living to the south of Puget Sound, preserve this contrast by applying it to animals, such as owls, squirrels and jays. 'If they talked fast and mad, it meant bad luck; if they talked slow and happy, it meant good luck' (M. W. Smith 2, p. 128).

The symplegades, or swinging doors motif, belongs to an important mythic paradigm, a survey of which has been carried out by S. Thompson (2, p. 298), and which extends over a considerable area of America, in the forms in which we have already encountered it. For instance, in the mythology of the Jicarilla and Lipan Apache Indians ($M_{685a, b}$; Russell 2, pp. 253–71; Opler, p. 185), two old blind women, seated on either side of a fire, wave a stick over the pot to protect their gruel or mush, which is nevertheless stolen by some young boys. The latter replace it by an empty pot, and since this has a hollow sound, the old women, imagining that the water has evaporated and that their gruel is cooked, decide to have a smoke while it is cooling, but their pipe, too, is snatched from them. The old women accuse each other of having smoked all the tobacco, and of having eaten all the gruel. They quarrel and hit each other . . . Even in mythology, two negatives make an affirmative. The hero or heroes succeed in neutralizing the two old women precisely because the latter introduce two negative terms into the system: being in opposition to each other through their negativity, they cannot *together* oppose the hero, just as the swinging doors, because there are two of them, are less difficult to slip through than a door consisting of a single panel, which, not having another to bang against or 'fight' with, would remain permanently shut.

This negative reciprocity, which is an inherent feature of the two blind women mytheme and from which it can be seen to be a borderline form of the swinging doors, also transpires from other versions where it occurs in isolation. I propose to mention only two examples. The Menomini, from whose mythology I have already quoted ($M_{657a, b}$; see above, p. 333), tell the story of two blind men who are carried to the far shore of a lake in order to be shielded from hostile attacks. Since they live all alone and have to take care of themselves, a rope leading from their house to the lake-side guides them when they want to draw water. 'One day, one of the two blind men would do the cooking while the other went for water: the next day, they would change about in their work, so that their labours were equally divided. As they knew just how much they required for each meal, the quantity prepared was equally divided, but eaten out of the one bowl which they had.' Eventually, Raccoon came along; he was a trickster who tried to have sport with them by shifting the rope one of them was using as a guide and by eating all the other's food; he then beat them both. He upset them so much that the two blind men ended by fighting each other. Raccoon laughed and said, 'You should not find fault with each other so easily' (M_{686a}; Hoffman 1, pp. 211–12; cf. M_{686b}: Saulteaux, Young, pp. 26–9; M_{686c}: Ojibwa, Radin 4, p. 80; M_{686d}: Arapaho, Dorsey-Kroeber, p. 227).

The Paviotso, a northern Paiute tribe living in the north and west of Nevada, set the two blind people among the stars, where they were 'seated on either side of a netted rabbit snare, with strings tried to their ears so that they could feel when rabbits ran into the snare . . . When eating, they were in the habit of feeding each other.' Eagle Woman came along and stole all their food. They recognized Eagle by feeling her all over; she doctored their eyes and for a while they were cured. But soon after they became blind again (M_{687}; Lowie 4, pp. 238–9).

The symplegades, in the form of two swinging doors alternately permitting and preventing the transition from one world to another, is a motif widely known throughout the whole of North America, from the Eskimo in the north to the Plains tribes, the Great Lakes tribes and those living in the south-west and south-east, including the coast of Louisiana. It also exists in South America, in particular in Tupinamba and Bororo mythology, where the doors are said to bar the way to the beyond (*EB*, 1, p. 101). The symplegades play an important part in the mythology of the Coast Salish (M_{375a-i}; M_{382}; M_{506}: Adamson, pp. 157–8, 276–84, 356–60; Ballard 1, pp. 69–80; Haeberlin 1, pp. 372–7; Boas 5, pp. 155; etc.) in the form of swinging rocks barring the way into the western world which, for the Salish too, is the kingdom of the dead. It is to this kingdom that the milt-girls (see above, pp. 292–4, 332–3) take the baby demiurge, Moon, after stealing him from two women, one of whom is *blind* and the other a *virgin* (although the latter is the mother of the child through a miraculous conception): here we have two conditions comparable to those attributed to the two old blind women in the inland myths, in which, in exchange for the recovery of their sight, one becomes *deaf* to the hunter's approach, and the other *fertile* without any physical contact with the male.

In the mythic series M_{375} etc., Blue-Jay, the trickster (*Cyanocitta* sp.), manages to get through the swinging doors. However, depending on the versions – which can in this respect be divided into several groups – he loses a few tail feathers (Adamson, p. 161) or his head becomes caught and flattened (*ibid.*, p. 358) or the door clips him on the head and 'knocks his tassel down' (*ibid.*, p. 375; Ballard 1, p. 73; Haeberlin 1, pp. 372–5). Sometimes he manages to hold the doors apart by putting a staff across them (Adamson, p. 175; Ballard 1, p. 73).

If we accept the hypothesis that the two old blind women are a borderline case of the swinging doors, this gives significance to the fact that their visitor can, with impunity, place his penis in the hand of one of them. In the symmetrical series M_{375} etc., which replaces banishment to the sky by abduction across the sea, i.e., an ascent along a vertical axis by a transfer along a horizontal axis, one version at least (M_{375f}; Haeberlin 1, p. 372) describes Blue-Jay in the form of an old grandmother, the back of whose neck has been flattened: this is a threefold inversion of the image of a penis: the creature is feminine and unmarked in respect of the genetic faculties because of her age; she is a grandmother, the back of whose head, through injury, has lost its natural protrusion, whereas the hero's penis, which forms a natural protrusion in front of the lower part of his belly, suffers no injury when entrusted to a grandmother.

It will also be noted that, in the series M_{667a} etc., the blind women visited by the hero recover their sight whereas, in the symmetrical series M_{375} etc., Blue-Jay, the hero's visitor, after flying successfully through the swinging doors has stone chips thrown into his eyes by the hero; he is blinded, and then cured by the demiurge, but is left with a kind of permanent defect, which impairs his sight.

The Tillamook versions ($M_{684a, b}$) occupy a median position between the two extreme states of the transformation. Firstly, because they contain both motifs: the blind women motif and the swinging doors; next, because the blind women have real food (whale meat), and not pseudo-food (sand, stone, or rotten wood); and lastly, because a bit of the hero's hindquarters is sliced off by the swinging doors. This sets him in opposition both to the hero in the Thompson myths who can, with impunity, expose his penis (part of his forequarters), and to Blue-Jay in the Coast Salish myths, who damages either the end of his tail (at the rear of the rear), or his crest on the nape of his neck (which both belong to the high instead of the low).

So, the hero is sometimes 'castrated' as it were, in respect of a high or low posterior part. When he is injured in his vital organs (this is never the case in the M_{375} etc. series, except in the Tillamook versions), he becomes a 'pierced character', theoretically incapable, like the character in the reference myth (M_1), of retaining the food he ingests unless he can find a means of reblocking the orifice. But when, on the contrary, he exposes his penis, without running the risk of real castration, it falls to his blind interlocutors to fulfil the function of 'blocked characters'. This calls for a few explanatory comments.

Certain myths, versions of which have already been encountered (M_{680}; see above, pp. 384–5) and which I propose to study later in their more extended form – which shows them to be connected with the origin of fire (see below, pp. 464–5), a significant point in relation to my argument – relate how Coyote blinds the grouse-women's children by sticking their eyelids together with gum or pitch. In other myths, widely distributed among the Salish and the Nootka, and of which I shall quote only two examples (M_{600f}; Sapir-Swadesh 2, pp. 89–101; M_{688}; Hill-Tout 7, pp. 546–8), an ogress who kidnaps children sticks their eyelids together with pitch so that they cannot witness her culinary preparations. These examples already show that the Salish think of being blind as equivalent to having the eyes blocked.

It should also be noted that, in the mythology of the Puget Sound Salish, the kidnapping ogresses are snail-women (M_{600i-m}; Ballard 1, pp. 106–12). By virtue of a dialectical process with which we are now familiar, the Nootka, who are neighbours of the Coast Salish, reduplicate them, on the one hand, as pitch-ogresses who retain the same function and, on the other, as young and beautiful but blind snail-girls whom the hero meets in the sky. In response to their request, he rubs the tip of his penis over their eyes and thus restores their sight (M_{600f}; Boas 13, p. 117; Sapir-Swadesh 2, p. 97). The creatures thank him by explaining how to reach the abode of the Sun, whose daughter he desires to marry.

This Nootka myth brings us full circle: here we have sky-dwelling girls who, although blind, are also young and pretty instead of old, but towards whom the hero, in both cases by the laying on of the penis, is obviously playing the part of a 'piercing character' – he restores their sight by directing the tip of his penis to their eyes. His piercing function is all the clearer through the fact that, at the beginning of the myth, the kidnapping ogresses blind the older children by blocking their eyes with pitch. On the other hand, some Salish myths (M_{375b}; cf. also a Tillamook source, E. D. Jacobs, pp. 129–30) explain why terrestrial snails ($\neq$ celestial) are blind.

It will be remembered that the reason why the blind women in the Thompson myths can be transformed into grouse is that their infirmity, like the habits of the birds, denotes what I have called (see above, p. 395) a disorder relating to contiguity. It is a striking fact that the myths should come to a similar conclusion in connection with snails. According to the Coos, to tread on and crush a snail's shell turns the person who does so first into an endo-cannibal, then into an exo-cannibal (Jacobs 5, pp. 55–6). The north-west coastal tribes refer in their myths ($M_{689a, b}$; Boas 2, p. 161, cf. pp. 747, 749; Swanton 2, p. 175) to a very coy princess who turns away all her suitors. She is unable to escape from the one who persists in following her about in the guise of a snail: 'Oh this nasty thing! There isn't a time when I go out, but that snail's around the house!' Eells records the following curious detail about the Twana, who are Salish of the Puget Sound area: 'The grouse and mallard duck were not eaten until the whites came; the mallard because it fed on snails.' The taboo on both ducks and grouse occurs sporadically in the coastal region (Drucker, p. 61); however, that on ducks seems to apply only at the major turning-points in the life of the individual, such as puberty, initiation, paternity and maternity, and the loss of a spouse (Barnett 3, pp. 138, 152, 154, 168, 225, 281). More recent sources (Elmendorf 1, p. 144) do not corroborate the evidence supplied by Eells, the significance of which lies in the fact that it includes within the same triad animals into which the two blind women can be transformed.

As yet, we are only familiar with them in the guise of grouse and snails. But from the Nootka on the west coast of Vancouver Island to the Tlingit of

Alaska, the blind women, whom a hero meets in the sky and whose sight he restores, are transformed not into gallinaceans or gasteropods (terrestrial creatures) but into water birds: ducks or geese (M_{675a} and its continuation; Boas gives a list, 2, p. 842; cf. also pp. 883, 907–908; 13, pp. 55, 135, 202, 262–3; 22, pp. 203, 457; Boas-Hunt 2, Vol. I, p. 95; Vol. II, pp. 215, 233–4; Krause, p. 275; Swanton 7, p. 498; etc.). I propose to quote as an example the most northerly Salish version, to which I have already referred (p. 378).

M_{675a}. Bella Coola. 'The old blind women'

In the spring, a certain Indian went to hunt birds with an arrow from which hung a thin string made from a woman's hair. After covering himself with the unplucked carcasses of birds, he asked his younger brother to beat him rhythmically with a stick. Gradually he rose into the air and finally disappeared.

When he reached sky country, he met blind duck-women who fed on roots, which were cooking in a pot. They sensed the presence of a man from his smell. No sooner did he eat some of their food than his mouth became filled with saliva; he spat into the woman's eyes and cured them. As they had an unpleasant smell, he removed their stench and threw them down to earth to be used as food for human consumption. The hero returned home and demonstrated the ability which he had acquired in the sky to catch great quantities of ducks with his bare hands (Boas 13, pp. 262–3; cf. also p. 135).

These birds may be ducks rather than grouse, but they belong to the category of game birds which allow themselves to be approached and tolerate physical contiguity with the hunter. In the case of the ducks, too, the myths establish a relationship between contiguity and blindness. According to the Kutenai (M_{690a}; Boas 9, p. 163), Coyote catches a great many ducks in a net which the birds cannot see, because they have been ordered to shut their eyes. The Flathead (M_{690b}; Hoffman 2, pp. 25 6) mention a different trick; Coyote invited the ducks to a dance, but found a pretext for putting out the fire; being invisible in the dark, he strangled the birds one by one.

It is a remarkable fact that this detail, which is widely present in the myths of the whole of North America, is an inversion of a real-life practice: the ducks, which are rendered virtually blind when the fire is extinguished, stand in a symmetrical relationship to the duck hunter, who blinds himself with the eye-shade he wears to avoid being dazzled by the fire in his canoe that he lights to attract the ducks. This hunting technique, as well as the use of a vertical net that the birds cannot see in the dawn light, or at dusk or during fog (Hill-Tout 6, p. 106; Olson 2, pp. 49–50; Barnett 3, p. 103) have also been reported from the Puget Sound area (Haeberlin–Gunther, pp. 25–6; Gunther 1, p. 205). In Twana society 'the stern paddler used to wear a mat head-dress . . . which rose from the wearer's shoulders to well above the top of his head . . . casting a shadow over the rest of the canoe, the hunter in the bow and the water ahead of the canoe . . . Water fowl swimming out of the shadowed area were attracted by the reflection of the flare which had been lit in the canoe; blinded and frightened, they would swim quickly back; a flock could thus be bunched, or a single bird held in front of the canoe. As an extra precaution both paddles, as well as the canoe, were blackened' (Elmendorf 1, pp. 112–13). The Quinault of the coastal area hunted ducks in their canoes with great torches of resinous wood which blinded the birds and 'made them crazy; they could then be killed with a stick' (Olson 2, p. 50). The Coast Salish living along the strait used to light a fire in the middle of the canoe and put a screen of rushes in the bow of the boat; they would move silently towards the ducks, which congregated in the shaded area, within easy reach of the hunters. Informants said that on stormy nights they could even be caught with the hands (Barnett 3, pp. 95–6). In the Cape Flattery area, when it was foggy, the Nootka-speaking Indians used to light a fire of pitch wood on a platform built at the extreme end of the canoe, and the glare seemed to blind or attract the birds. '. . . In the fall, it is not unusual to find in the canoe a collection of pelicans, loons, cormorants, grebes and ducks of various kinds or other divers. These, after being picked and very superficially cleaned, were thrown promiscuously into a kettle, boiled and served up as a feast' (Swan 2, p. 25). The Lummi living in the Gulf of Georgia did not preserve ducks either; they consumed them on the spot. The Nootka of Vancouver Island used to hunt water fowl mainly during the great seasonal migrations. At the end of the herring season, ducks, flying northwards, disturbed by the light of the fires lit in the canoes, used to seek the patch of shadow cast by a cedar-bark mat with a rod bound to one end, which one of the paddlers held between his teeth. The Nootka would only do this 'on black, stormy nights when there was not a glimmer of moonlight or starlight to reveal the canoe'. The birds, disturbed but not sufficiently alarmed to take flight, swam to the apparent shelter of the shadow under the bow. Then the net was cast and 'it was but a moment's work to wring the necks protruding through the net. In a short time the canoe would be filled with ducks, geese and even swans' (Drucker, pp. 34, 36–7, 42–3).

Lastly, the Kwakiutl of Vancouver Island, 'when catching wild geese, used to light a fire on a clay-covered board placed in the stern of the canoe. The steersman sat in front of the fire holding in his mouth a stick to which a mat was attached. This served as a screen, by means of which the geese were kept in the light . . . It was thus possible to go quite near them. A net stretched tightly over a frame was thrown over the birds . . . Then their heads were twisted. Wet, dark nights were the best for this kind of hunting' (Boas 19, pp. 515–16).

Whether the hunter blinds himself with an eye-shade as a protection against the glare, or whether the birds themselves are blinded, or whether a lack of light prevents them seeing the net, we are nevertheless dealing with a 'blind' hunt, allowing contiguity between the hunter and his game. Among certain communities such as the Makah and the Lummi, and probably among others too, water birds were eaten immediately, whereas most other food produce, such as fish, shell-fish, berries and wild roots, were preserved by a variety of methods. So, in addition to spatial contiguity with the hunter, we find, in temporal terms, a minimal gap between the phases of capture and ingestion. The group of myths featuring the two blind women appears, then, to be homogeneous in this respect throughout its entire area of distribution: ducks and grouse constitute the combinatory variants of a single mytheme which, in accordance with the different features of their respective habitats, the coastal communities define in respect of water (ducks are water birds) and those of the interior in respect of land or earth (grouse live in forests or along the edge of wooded regions).

However, in another respect, ducks and grouse are in opposition to each other. It will be rememberd that grouse are spirits of the cold (see above, pp. 322, 329), and are considered to be specially responsible for frosts and late falls of snow, which delay the arrival of spring and prolong winter famine. Far to the south of the area we are at present considering, the Kalapuya (Jacobs 4, p. 274) also hold the grouse responsible for the appearance of sickness, a detail which should perhaps be compared to the belief, current among the Snohomish and the Tillamook, that Coyote's daughter, or the old grandmother whose skin is donned by Coyote, are responsible for the origin of sickness (M_{677}, M_{678}).

The duck, on the other hand, embodies the power of spring in the dead of winter: 'Everyone believed in the power of the Duck and his wife to make spring come'. Even in midwinter, according to the Okanagon, the duck 'makes a hole in the ice where it sits and is always warm' (Cline, p. 202). The Sanpoil (Ray 1, pp. 184–5, 199) describe the mallard duck, *Anas boschas*, as a handsome young man, the master of warm breezes, known as 'the Chinook wind', which herald the end of winter. The Chinook (Jacobs 2, No. 21) maintain that the Duck is cold in summer and hot in winter. It could be said, then, that Grouse and Duck are diametrically opposed to each other in the sense that one embodies the continuance of winter beyond the normal limit, and the other the early return of spring. In the west of North America, the Duck has, therefore, the same semantic function as that attributed by the eastern Algonquin to the Grebe, another water bird (*OTM*, pp. 247–8). It will also be noticed that, along the east-west horizontal axis corresponding to that between the interior and the coast and between land and water, Duck and Grouse have the same kind of oppositional relationship to each other as the sky and the earth have in Salish mythology, where they connote respectively the cold and the hot (see above, p. 393).

It cannot be categorically asserted, neither, however, can it be denied, that, as I established in the case of homologous myths belonging to the Great Lakes area and the Plains (*OTM*, pp. 241–63), the Salish myths relating to the visit to the sky do not possess, in addition to their spatial dimension, a temporal dimension indicated by the observance of seasonal considerations. On the celestial plateau, swept by an icy wind and inhabited by Grouse who are spirits of the cold, eternal winter seems to prevail; yet the hero leaves the earth at a time when his father could reasonably convince him that fledglings still in the nest were about to fly. It must, then, be the end of spring or the beginning of summer. When the hero comes back down to earth, M_{667a} states quite clearly that it is the beginning of summer, and the start of the nomadic period during which the Indians hunted deer and dug roots (Teit 4, p. 24). It follows that the hero must have spent either a whole year in the sky or only a few days. The second hypothesis hardly seems likely, if we take into account the initiatory sojourn with the helpful spiders, and the birth of a son to the wife who remains faithful. No doubt she could have been already nearing the end of her pregnancy when the hero disappeared; but to accept this, we would have to ignore the fact that the child, born of an earth-dweller, at the time when the husband has temporarily become a celestial being, forms a counterpart to the child whom the sun's wife, also an earth-dweller, conceives, carries and gives birth to in the sky, and whom she has begun to rear before returning to earth (also attached to the end of a rope) – all of which implies a stay of about a year in the sky (*OTM*, p. 201). As it happens, we are about to see that in certain Puget Sound versions of the adventures of Moon, the demiurge, Moon is the son of the woman who went up into the sky in order to marry a star. Consequently, they combine, in consecutive but superimposable sequences, the 'vertical' theme of the ascent and the descent, and the 'horizontal' theme of the peregrination (see below, p. 412).

Even the versions based on the 'bungling host' motif, which might at first sight seem to be composed of arbitrarily juxtaposed episodes, varying in number according to the whim of the story-tellers who were free to add or remove sequences as the fancy took them, appear, on closer examination, to be governed by the calendar. For instance, the Lilloet version of the bird-nester story (M_{671}) lists, in order, five episodes which take place before Coyote makes himself an artificial son: 1) he eats up all Grizzly Woman's food at a time when, outside, there is nothing to eat (winter); 2) he blinds the grouse-children whose mothers take their revenge, as in M_{614c}, where, as I showed on p. 322 *et seq.*, they preside over the late winter frosts and snowfalls; 3) he visits the deer, the hunting of which, as is made plain in M_{667a} and M_{670a}, starts in the spring; 4) he is fed by his host on salmon roe – eggs or milts – which is available in summer or autumn; 5) he eats salmon, which have been caught under the ice, and this brings us back to the beginning of the cold season. Together with his son, Coyote next tries unsuccessfully to hunt swans: 6) 'They saw many swans flying overhead . . . Coyote called on them to fall down . . . They fell like hail on to the lake and remained motionless, as if dead . . . but, when Coyote tried to pick them up, they at once flew away and disappeared' (Teit 2, p. 306). I have quoted this extract, because it corresponds almost word for word to another passage in a Shuswap myth (M_{691}; Teit 1, p. 703), which defines the episode in seasonal terms: 'It was now early spring and the water fowl arrived on their way north. The ice still clung to the edges of the lake and there was very little food left. One day a large number of swans arrived, and the people wished someone could bewitch them and make them heavy so that they would fall . . .'; 7) in the Lilloet version, the bird-nester episode comes next, and it must take place at the beginning or in the middle of summer, since the eaglets are still in the nest; 8) in this version, the wife is already a mother before her husband's disappearance; we can therefore assume that the latter stayed for a shorter period in the sky, and came back down to earth in the autumn, the season when the villagers concentrate on hunting; 9) finally, the rains and subsequent flooding brought about by the hero would appear to correspond to the arrival of winter.

The Shuswap version (M_{680b}; Teit 1, pp. 739–40), although it contains fewer episodes, seems much more explicit. It begins 'in winter', as is quite clearly stated, with a fishing expedition which involved catching fish through holes in the ice; it continues with a visit to Beaver, who feeds his guest on cambium of the cottonwood tree, a substance which is only edible in the spring; and it ends with a visit to the bears, who serve a meal made from the grease from their backs, a commodity with which they are amply supplied only before or at the beginning of the period of hibernation; afterwards they would be lean and raw-boned, having exhausted all their substance; this brings us back to the beginning of M_{671} (see above, p. 409), and closes the seasonal cycle.

A Klallam myth from the north of Puget Sound implies just as clearly the underlying presence of a seasonal code:

M_{692}. Klallam. 'The visit to the sky'

A long time ago, there was only one woman in the world but no man. She made a man of gum, but since, at that time, the sun was much hotter than now, the man melted. His sons were very angry with the sun for this; one of them shot an arrow which stuck in the celestial vault, then a great many more, one after the other, so that they all fitted end to end to form a kind of chain, up which the sons ascended until they reached the celestial world, which looked like an enormous prairie. Geese, which could then talk, showed them the way to the sun's abode. Next, they met two blind women, whose food one of the boys stole while one woman was handing it to the other. He made himself known to the women; they directed him, and gave him a very small basket in which were six berries (*Rubus spectabilis*). After a final meeting, this time with swallows, the brothers arrived at the Sun's abode. The latter was an old man who was piling pitch wood on to a very hot fire, so hot that the visitors thought they would die, and which was what made it hot on the earth. The sun ate the six berries; they swelled within him and killed him. The fire then went down somewhat, and it has not been so hot on earth since (Eells 3, p. 653).

Consequently, and as in the myths devoted more specifically to the bird-nester story, the visit to the sky, a spatial adventure certainly, but one which takes place at a time when extreme climatic conditions prevailed in both the celestial and terrestrial worlds, leads to a form of seasonal mediation: either the previously unbearable heat of the sun is moderated, or the hero causes rain to fall on the earth, which, according to the Plateau Salish, in mythic times was hot, dry and windy (Teit 6, p. 176; 10, p. 337).

The reader familiar with the previous volumes will have no doubt noticed that M_{692} is reminiscent of a Warrau myth (M_{406}; *OTM*, pp. 137–8), in which a remote marriage (between a man and an exotic beauty, instead of between a woman and a male character who is both vegetable and vegetative) precedes and leads up to the corporeal explosion (head or belly) of an old man, with a consequent tempering of the formerly excessive heat of the sun. The two myths of which I propose to continue the comparison later (see below, p. 448), differ in the sense that the narrative of M_{406} unfolds along a horizontal axis, and that of M_{692} along a vertical axis: one deals with a sea journey, the other with an ascent. But on several occasions, I have pointed out the same transformation in Salish mythology by showing that, in the case of the visit to the sky, that is, the ascent, the episode featuring the two blind women is a weak, borderline form of the swinging doors motif. On the other hand, a symmetrical mythic series (M_{375} etc.) exploits the swinging doors motif to the full, and presents the creatures beyond the doors as two young, fertile women instead of two old, sterile ones. What is more, this is not the only difference between the two pairs of women, because the former pair act in collusion with each other, whereas the latter pair quarrel at every opportunity (cf. the blind men in M_{686} and Raccoon's significant admonition); besides, the young women were engendered as milt-girls from raw food, and so present a double contrast with the old blind women, who eat anti-foods, such as gravel, stone or rotten wood.

So, the interception of an anti-food, which is being handed from one to the other by two blind women whose quarrelling eventually leads to actual fighting, corresponds in the symmetrical series M_{375} to the passing of Blue-Jay, who has been half-blind ever since, between two doors which also bang against each other or fight. Blue-Jay's successful flight leads in the end to the granting of the best food to mankind: Moon's saga explains the origin of salmon, the offspring of his union with the milt-girls ($M_{375a,\ 382}$). Conversely, the penis, which is placed in the hand of one of the old women, also implies a sexual union, although in a derisory and even negative mode. The member, which emerges unscathed, has its counterpart in Blue-Jay's tail feathers, crest or neck, or in the piece of flesh from the buttocks of Ice, the demiurge, all of which are either wrenched off or damaged through being caught in the swinging doors. The fact that, in the myth, both blind women are identical yet unequal (since in $M_{684a,\ b}$ one receives more food than the other; and since in M_{667a} each is changed into a different kind of grouse) can be explained in two ways. First of all, the symplegades too are both equal and unequal: they are identical panels swinging at the same rate, but when they come close, one is moving upwards from low to high, the other downwards from high to low. Next, I have established that the double motif of the swinging doors and the blind women is closely related to a third: the motif of 'close hunting' of grouse or ducks, in which, as between the swinging doors and the blind women, there is physical contiguity, although it initially involves beings essentially different from each other — the hunter and his quarry. Between the two motifs of the symplegades and close hunting, that of the blind women provides a transition, through a series of examples (that can be put in logical sequence) ranging from absolute equality to an ever-relative inequality.

So far, we have seen two forms of the swinging doors motif: a maximal form, associated with the horizontal transfer of a hero along an east-west, earth-sea axis; and a minimal form, associated with the vertical elevation of another hero along a low-high, earth-sky axis. It remains to be proved that if the evolution of the motif is looked at on the hither side of its minimal form, it becomes inverted and recovers its original amplitude, but, in so doing, engenders an image of itself which is antisymmetrical with that of the swinging doors it had initially adopted:

M_{375g-h}. *Snuqualmi. 'The kidnapped demiurge and the wives of the sun and moon'*

When the earth was still young and with hardly a tree on it, there was neither sun nor moon: a perpetual half-light prevailed, and humans and animals spoke the same language. Two women, who were busy digging fern roots were discussing whether it would be better for them to marry fishermen or hunters, and whether their stew would taste better with meat or fish. Finally, they wished for stars as husbands, and found themselves in the sky with their husbands. The latter brought back a lot of game but the eldest woman's husband had sore eyes (cf. *OTM*, p. 239).

The celestial world was like the earth except that wind, storms and rain were unknown there. The star men allowed their wives to go on digging fern roots, provided they did not follow the roots too deeply. Before long, the eldest woman gave birth to a son, whom she called Moon. As the two women were bored, they did what they had been told not to do and broke the celestial vault: the wind rushed through the opening and they saw their native earth beneath.

The women made a long rope ladder and escaped. When they arrived at the village, they were greeted with open arms and everyone wanted to go and see the ladder leading to the sky. They made it into an enormous play swing, which swayed from mountain to mountain, moving from north to south and from south to north. As it swept along the ground, the tip of the swing caused the gulches, which still exist today.

During these rejoicings, the woman who had become a mother hired a blind old toad to look after her child. Salmon-woman kidnapped him. When the people realized what had happened, they promptly left the swing and set out to look for him. Only the rat stayed behind; he gnawed the rope and the swing dropped down in a pile, forming a large rock in the Snuqualmi valley.

After several attempts, Blue-Jay succeeded in crossing the great wall, cut horizontally in two with the two halves beating one against the other, which guarded the land of the dead, where the stolen child, now grown to manhood, was living. The young man promised that he would soon return to his own people, and later he distinguished himself by such marvellous exploits as the creation of lakes, rivers and mountains, the division of animals into different species, the invention of fire, and the destruction of monsters . . . Finally he became the moon (Haeberlin 1, pp. 373–7; cf. the Puyallup version, Curtis, Vol. 9, pp. 117–21).

In a Klallam version ($M_{375\ 1}$; Gunther 2, pp. 135–6), the two women have various adventures in the sky; they cross through a barrier of flames, then through swinging doors ['opening and closing rocks']. The rope down which they make their descent swings round in a circle and makes a large coil. It is said to be still visible in the form of a huge rock on Vancouver Island.

Another Snuqualmi version ($M_{375\,j}$; Ballard 1, pp. 69–80) identifies the edible ferns as *Pteridium aquilinum pubescens*, the harvesting of which is always done by women. The celestial swing oscillates along a north-south axis between mountains which are half a day's journey away from each other. After Moon's abduction, his mother creates the future Sun with the urine wrung out of the lost child's diaper. When Blue-Jay finds the demiurge, the latter is already a father, sharpening stone to make flint arrowheads. Moon, annoyed by Blue-Jay's intrusion, throws stone flakings into the bird's eyes and blinds him; then, on learning the reason for his visit, restores his sight. The myth goes on to describe in detail the wonders accomplished by the demiurge, who finally returns to his own people and, with his brother, goes up into the sky, where he becomes the moon and his brother the sun:

People were gathered from everywhere to choose who among all creatures should act as the sun by day and the moon at night. Moon had decided that the celestial swing would be there for ever, and if in future anyone wished to go up to the sky, they could go and get whatever they wanted. But while the trials were in progress, the rat gnawed the rope and the swing fell to the ground taking the rat with it. As a result of this, Moon decreed that people would henceforth have the swing to sport upon, but that it would no longer be so high. And Moon pronounced a curse on the rat, saying that it would be doomed to gnaw and steal what people want, and to destroy whatever is good. All the people sitting around and looking were turned into stone; they are all there yet on the mountain; the stones are like people, breaking all the time. When a stone breaks off, it is a sign of ill-luck and portends the death of a chief.[4]

These, then, are myths which combine into one continuous narrative the story of the wives of the sun and moon, examined at length in the preceding volume (M_{425}, M_{438}), and the saga of Moon the demiurge (M_{375a-p}; M_{382}; M_{506}) that has often been referred to. Moon's exploits take place along an east-west, land-sea axis, and during his wanderings the demiurge travels upstream. Between the earth and the sea, and between the humans and the salmon which provide them with food, stand the swinging doors, which are explicitly described in M_{375h} as a great wall cut horizontally through the middle and the two halves of which move up and down continuously. On the other hand, the story of the sun and moon and their wives takes place along a high-low, sky-earth axis, and, in order to escape, the women use a rope ladder which subsequently serves as a swing as it sways back and forth longitudinally along a north-south axis, and, as M_{375j} states explicitly, across a stream: 'the alighting place is a mountain north of the river, the springing-off place another mountain south of the river' (Ballard 1, p. 72). The swing comes between the sky and the earth, but its purpose is to join, not to separate them; presently, however, the *abduction* of the demiurge *into the distance* (M_{375g-h}) or his *elevation up above* (M_{375j}) leads to the cessation of this means of access to the celestial world. So it is clear that the swing, activated by a horizontal movement along an axis characterized by vertical oscillation, and ensuring a form of communication between the sky and the earth towards the end of the mythic era, provides an exact counterpart to the swinging doors, activated by a vertical movement along an axis characterized by horizontal oscillation, and preventing communication between the earth and the sea before historic times began with the gift of salmon to humans.

The swinging doors theme, which is found all the world over, belongs most certainly to the oldest mythic traditions known to man. The same is probably true of the swing, around which the American Indians built up a whole mythology (Stith Thompson 3, No. 169; Waterman 3); swings existed in real life, particularly among the Salish, whose various dialects distinguished between the cradle-swing — 'suspended from a long thin pole

[4] Like parhelia which, in other contexts, are likened to a 'cleavage' in the sun (cf. above, pp. 242–8).

stuck in the ground and the upper end bent over . . . the weight of the child being sufficient . . . to allow the cradle to swing gently up and down with the movements of the child, which were kept up by a cord attached to the cradle and given to the mother or one of the old women of the household to pull from time to time' (Hill-Tout 6, p. 244; Barnett 3, p. 132) – and the seat-swing, which at least among certain groups had a ceremonial or ritual use, reserved, it would seem, for adult women. However, little is known about this use (Elmendorf 1, p. 228). Hammock-swings were also observed among the Lilloet (Teit 11, p. 261). The swing motif, associated with the moon as in Salish myths, is also found in South America among the Uitoto and the Tacana.

Without going into the place and function of the swing in myths and rites, we can be content with having established that the swing and symplegades motifs form a pair of correlative and opposite terms. The Puget Sound myths, in which these terms are combined, also compress into a single narrative sequence the wives-of-the-sun-and-moon episode and the saga of the demiurge, while providing the latter with a twofold conclusion: the cessation of spatial communication between the terrestrial and celestial worlds, and, with the appearance of the sun and the moon, the compensatory establishment of temporal periodicity.[5]

Whether the Puget Sound myths result from the fusion of two narratives which we have so far encountered as separate entities – the story of the wives of the sun and moon and the exploits of Moon, the demiurge – or whether, on the contrary, the two stories survive as the products of the splitting up of a single myth, the original model of which happens to have been preserved by the Puget Sound Indians, it now becomes clear that the bird-nester myth stands, as it were, 'in the middle' and serves as a link between these two major cycles of American mythology, articulating one with the other. This is already evident from the way in which the hero, after his wanderings in the sky country which correspond, on a smaller scale, to the demiurge's wanderings on earth (compare, for instance, the episode featuring rebellious objects or subjugated monsters in M_{664a}, M_{667a} and in M_{375j}), succeeds, like the wives of the sun and moon, in climbing back down to earth with the help of a rope. But the apparently gratuitous modalities imposed by the plot on the hero's descent provide a transition between the symplegades, which are activated by an oscillatory movement along a vertical axis, and the rope-ladder, which eventually becomes a swing and is therefore activated by an oscillatory movement along a horizontal plane. These two types

---

[5] The formula given in *OTM*, p. 62 can thus be completed as follows: *cradle : swing :: swing : symplegades :: conjunctive : disjunctive.*

of movement are alternating, whereas the bird-nester's descent is continuous, although he has to pause at various stages. While the rope is being lowered the hero is displaced vertically from high to low; and, each time his descent is halted at a certain level, he has to roll over before the basket can be set in motion again. Consequently, the myths subordinate the rate of descent to conditions which relate to both forms of motion.

To confirm the reality of this middle position, it should be possible, after discovering in the bird-nester myth the symplegades motif in the limited form of the old women episode, to find there the swing motif as well, also reduced to its minimal expression. The query has only to be raised for the answer to appear at once with all the necessary supporting details. The Thompson version, M_{670a}, demonstrates the point.

In the sky, the hero meets first of all two old blind women who are preparing their meal by crushing fir branches in a mortar. On his return to earth, the first people he encounters are two old blind women, who are swinging fir branches as they follow the tracks of the villagers who have moved on ahead. The opposition between actions, both of which are carried out with the same instruments — fir branches — seems immediately significant, since one type of action implies a vertical movement from high to low and from low to high, which is reminiscent of the swinging doors, and the other a horizontal movement from right to left and left to right which recalls the swing and which is in fact described in the English transcription of the myth by the use of the verb 'to swing': *'two old women who are swinging fir branches'*, etc.

The swinging of fir branches, while following a trail, could correspond to a real-life custom that has not been recorded. On the subject of fir branches, the only information we have is that pubescent boys and individuals guilty of murder rubbed their bodies with them as a form of purification (Barnett 2, pp. 259, 267, 289), or that pubescent girls or menstruating women, during their periods of seclusion, would travel considerable distances at night, tearing off fir branches which they scattered or hung on other trees (Dawson, p. 13). In view of the fact that small groups of Iroquois had penetrated into the Fraser River area as early as the end of the eighteenth century (see above, p. 356), there might be a connection with one of their rites, which they called 'Waving of Evergreen Branches' (Hewitt 3, p. 942). Professor W. N. Fenton, the eminent Iroquois specialist, has been kind enough to confirm, after discussing the matter with his informants, that unfortunately nothing is known about the rite apart from this one allusion.

However, pure deduction allows us to suggest a much more satisfactory interpretation of the two old women's mysterious behaviour. If my initial hypothesis is correct, we may take as a starting-point the fact that baby Moon was kidnapped while, and consequently because, all the people in the village were enjoying themselves on swings, and had entrusted the child to the ineffectual care of an old blind woman. At the same time, the Puget Sound myths state explicitly that the wives of the sun and moon made their rope ladder, which was later used as a swing, by plaiting conifer branches ('the sisters twisted the branches into a rope', Ballard 1, p. 71; 'the girls twisted cedar twigs', Haeberlin 1, p. 373).

These two indications allow us to deduce that, by swinging conifer branches instead of themselves swinging on ropes made from such branches, women, who are blind in respect of the returned hero (just as the people enjoying the swing are virtually blind to the kidnapping of the demiurge which takes place, as it were, behind their backs), are guilty of a lack of tact: in order to express their sympathy to a young mother whose husband has disappeared, they adopt a form of behaviour which is at once a reflection and an inversion of another form of behaviour which led, in another context, to a young mother losing her child.

By following our particular line of approach, we can explain, then, the tiniest details of a seemingly absurd episode. Moreover, I shall have an opportunity later of showing, in connection with a different myth (M_{762}, p. 504 *et seq.*), that the swing motif, inverted along the vertical axis and reduced as here to its minimal value, depends on a paradigm which is operative far beyond the Salish, and which can always be interpreted in the same fashion. But we have not yet finished with the two old blind women, since their blindness is expressed differently, according to whether they are sky-dwellers or earth people.

The blindness of the terrestrial women, unlike that of the celestial pair who are really blind, only operates in relation to the hero. He is walking along the path in front of them, but they cannot see him although they can make out quite clearly the Thompson River on their right and the Fraser River on their left. They can only see, then, what is *on either side* of a median plane with which they themselves are contiguous. The description of the two celestial old women is an inversion of this pattern: they are sitting *on either side* of the fire and cannot see *each other*; but, although they cannot see the fire, which is in the middle in relation to them — and is undoubtedly symmetrical with the path, since a previous episode of M_{670a} explains why paths do not burn, see above, p. 375; cf. Hill-Tout 10, p. 552 — they perceive it by contiguity, since they are cooking their meal on it.

So, like the respective modes of behaviour of the two pairs of women, their particular forms of blindness are connected with the swing in the one instance and the symplegades in the other (Figure 25): the symplegades are situated on either side of a median plane on which they meet, whereas the swing, oscillating over a deep valley, only touches the ground at two widely separated points, and is farthest from it when half-way between. But the metaphorical expressions used by the myths also involve internal reversals. The celestial old women are symplegades who fail to meet in order to share anti-food, whereas by their junction the symplegades deny humans access to real food. The terrestrial old women can only see rivers which are separated by mountains; the swing only allows its occupants to reach mountains which are separated by a river.

One last point remains to be elucidated: if the two pairs of blind old women are counterparts of each other, in what sense does the transformation of one pair into maggots correspond to the transformation of the other into grouse or ducks?

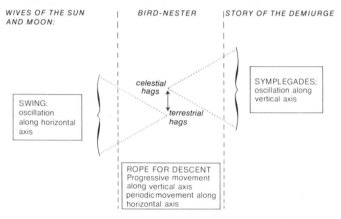

Figure 25. System of the blind hags

As is revealed in one of their rites, these meat-bugs or maggots occupied quite a prominent place in the life and thought of the Thompson Indians:

When a youth wanted to fit himself to become a hardy hunter, he would go down to the river's edge at the close of the salmon run when the carcasses of dead, maggot-filled fish would be found lying along the banks in great numbers. He would thrust his hands up to the wrists in the rotting, maggoty mass and keep them there for hours together. This was said to harden them, so that they became impervious to the cold . . . (Hill-Tout 12, p. 513).

We have already encountered a Klikitat myth (M_{606a}), in which an ogress threatens to stuff Coyote's anus with maggots. Coos myths, which will be summarized later (M_{793}, M_{795}; Frachtenberg 1, pp. 41, 173; Saint-Clair, pp. 35–6; Jacobs 6, pp. 211, 245, 251), mention a sick man whose sores swarmed with maggots, which 'ate up his anus, his face, nose and ears; not long after they ate him all up'. The Coast Salish have myths, not unlike some ancient myths of the Old World ($M_{693a, b, c}$; Haeberlin 1, pp. 428–30; Adamson, pp. 81–3; cf. also Lipan Apache; Opler, pp. 46–7), in which men who have been unjustly accused by their sister-in-law get lost at sea and encounter a community of pygmies who are being raided by a tribe of water birds. The pygmies have very tiny mouths: they are dumb and live on sea-food, sucking out the maggots from rotten fish or the flesh of *dentalia* shells, which are like small concave horns. Like grouse and ducks, which tolerate close proximity between hunter and quarry, maggots, which live in and feed off rotten fish and other forms of carrion, can also be related to the principle of contiguity:

$$(hunter) : (grouse, \ live \ ducks) :: (maggots) : (dead \ fish, \ carrion).$$

The same kind of contiguity, this time between food and adornments, also exists in the case of *dentalia* shells.

It is possible to carry the interpretation a stage further thanks to M_{667a} and M_{668a} (Teit 4, pp. 25; 5, p. 297), in which different characters take the place of the old women who are transformed into maggots. At the same point in the story — that is, when the hero, after returning to earth, discovers the trail of the villagers who are making for their hunting and gathering grounds — he too meets first of all slow-travelling creatures, such as the Ant, the Beetle and the Caterpillar. These animals occupy exactly the same position as the blind women, and are interchangeable with them. The hero, however, behaves differently towards them: he does not change them into animal creatures, since they already have this form in the story; he merely admonishes the Ant, saying, 'Why do you have your sash so tight? You will soon be cut in two!' Other myths can throw some light on this cryptic remark.

Let us recall first of all that the Chinook myths (M_{598a-g}, see above, p. 242) about the origin of parhelia (= sun cut in two), after relating how a hero ascended into the sky and married a luminary, also explained that ants and wasps had small waists because their sashes had become too tight. Some Inland Salish, who share the same belief, add a further detail: 'The ant and the wasp wanted people to die, because they themselves were grave-diggers, as is shown by their being cinched tightly round the waist' (Cline,

p. 167). In Thompson mythology, too, the Ant is included with the spider and the fly among the creatures which bring death. Like the hero in M_{667a} (who has a special understanding with spiders), the Spider says to the Ant: 'You'll cut yourself in half if you pull your sash so tight, and soon you will die.' The Ant replies that she will not really die, but will very soon come back to life again. According to the Puget Sound Indians, the Ant pulled her sash too tight, at the time of the discussion about the alternation of day and night. The same motif occurs throughout the whole linguistic area and beyond, as far as the Kutenai who live in the foothills of the Rockies: they relate how the Ant pulled her sash too tight when she was getting ready to bury the first dead man (Okanagon: Cline, p. 167; Thompson: Teit 5, p. 329; Puget Sound: Ballard 1, p. 57; Kutenai: Boas 9, p. 213).

Like parhelia (see above, pp. 242–8) and gallinaceans (see above, p. 395; see below, pp. 537–43), ants and other insects are, then, bipartite creatures, in whom the waist, although reduced to its simplest expression, nevertheless holds the two halves together; in native thought, these halves correspond to other pairs, equally inseparable although composed of terms in opposition to each other: day and night, and life and death. On the other hand, ducks which are associated with water and grouse which are associated with trees (cf. M_{667a}: prairie chickens with conifers, and the ruffed grouse with willows and alders) are in opposition to the group of the terrestrial old women, which is composed of creatures all living at ground level or below ground: maggots, ants, beetles and caterpillars – a point which is still further strengthened by the Thompson belief in an underground world, inhabited by the Ant people (Teit 4, pp. 78–9, 116, n. 253; 5, pp. 214, 373). We can compare this aspect with the role played by the Rat in the Puget Sound versions: he too cuts something in half – the rope ladder, which ensures communication between the two worlds, and in order to describe his action, M_{375j} has recourse to terminology which repeats, and at the same time reverses, that used in the same myth to define the celestial world: humans climb up the ladder to the sky because there 'they can get whatever they want'. On the other hand, to curse Rat, the hero says to him, 'You will gnaw and steal what people want.' He thus sets him very strongly in opposition to the sky, the place where all desires are granted, whereas the chthonian function of the Rat will be to thwart desire. The swing, too, is linked to the earth, since its movements create hills and valleys; and the symplegades which, in one version at least (M_{375l}) are situated in the sky, are associated in all versions with the far, of which the sky provides the ultimate example, since the freed Salmon will ensure communication along the horizontal axis between the sea and the earth, but, after the breaking of the rope-ladder, communication between earth and sky will be abolished for ever.

What we see reappearing here, then, is in fact the origin of man's mortality (see above, p. 174) and of periodicity (taken simultaneously in a cosmological and a biological sense), which are suggested in turn by the grave-digging ants and the maggots, symbols of organic decay. However, the origin of man's mortality is transferred to the bird-nester cycle, whereas in South American mythology it is part of the cycle concerning a mortal's star-wife, which cycle, by means of a simple sex inversion, reproduces the North American cycle of the wives of the sun and moon, which in turn establishes the periodicity of biological rhythms (cf. *RC*, pp. 147–63; *OTM*, pp. 216–25). Certain Salish versions of the bird-nester cycle take up the same motif again, transposed into sequences that I am now about to discuss, and where the origin of sickness is personified by an old woman whose skin is donned by the trickster and who is called Sickness (M_{677}), or where he himself assigns the pathogenic mission to his own daughter by making her responsible for the spreading of epidemics (M_{678}).

The fact that the bird-nester myth acts as a connecting link between the most important mythic cycles common to both parts of the American continent helps to explain why I felt compelled to adopt it at the outset as reference myth, although I was not yet aware of its strategic role, which has only become apparent through a prolonged analysis spread over four volumes. The bird-nester cycle, like the other two between which it serves as a link and a means of transition, is pan-American in its distribution. In the dual form of the wives of the sun and moon, and the star-wife of a mortal, I have identified one cycle in both hemispheres, and followed the stages of its transformations. As for the saga of Moon, the demiurge, we encountered it in the first place in South America, in Baré mythology (M_{247}), and we cannot but be struck by the fact that it recurs, in almost identical terms, in the north-west of North America, for instance, among the Salish of Puget Sound, the Klallam and the Nootka (M_{375j-o}; Ballard 1, pp. 69–80; Gunther 2, pp. 143–4; Boas 2, pp. 903–13, Curtis, Vol. 8, pp. 116–23; Sapir-Swadesh 2, pp. 45–51). It would be difficult to find a more convincing illustration of the underlying unity of American mythology.

3 *Cosmopolitanism and Exogamy*

Young knights, shunning the bonds of marriage for fear of being deflected from their profession, considered it their duty, during the first years after their entry into the Order, to visit distant lands and foreign courts, so as to turn themselves into Perfect Knights. *The green in which they were clad denoted the freshness of their youth, as well as the robustness of their courage.*

La Curne de Sainte-Palaye, *Mémoires sur l'ancienne Chevalerie*, Paris, 1759, Vol. II, p. 8

There once was a young man of Greenwich
Whose balls were all covered with spinach;
So long was his tool
That it wound round a spool
And he let it out inach by inach.

W. S. Baring-Gould, *The Lure of the Limerick*, New York, 1967, p. 88

There was a tribe whose chief had a son, a young man who was very lazy. He did not desire anything at all, and lay down all the time. So his father said to him: 'If one is a man one usually travels. Do you travel. Go with young men of your own age and travel. Pay attention to the women you see, and do at least take one of them for a wife.'

From an Omaha myth (M_{649c}) in: J. O. Dorsey, 1, p. 185

Using almost the same terms as those employed in the Chinook and Nez Percé versions already discussed ($M_{601-602}$, see above, pp. 225–7), the Salish versions of the bird-nester myth include the episode of the freeing of the salmon; generally speaking, it occurs after the point when Coyote, having fallen into a rushing stream, is eventually washed ashore near the dam guarded by the selfish mistresses of salmon. However, in addition to this etiological narrative, the Salish have other stories which explain the origin of salmon in their own way.

Since I mentioned them towards the end of the previous section, let me first refer back rapidly to the last Salish myths {M_{375}, M_{382}, M_{506}} devoted to the saga of Moon, the demiurge and organizer of the world. After Blue-Jay succeeded in passing through the swinging doors and in obtaining the promise that the demiurge would soon return to his own people, the latter, having married the milt-girls, who had kidnapped him while he was still a baby, and having become the father of a large family, instructed his children as to what their respective missions were to be. The children of the eldest sister were trees and shrubs; Moon assigned a function to each species, as firewood, as wood for manufacturing purposes, as a source of bark or vegetable fibre, as edible plants, etc. The youngest sister created all fish, of which the myth lists, in addition to the five species of salmon, seven or eight other varieties. In the case of each species or family, Moon decided what the migratory period should be, as well as the season for fishing and the techniques used, and the mode of cooking. He then went on long journeys during which he made mountains and valleys, instituted various crafts, created several species of edible plants and quadrupeds, changed the swing which sent people to their deaths into a pleasurable sport, destroyed an ogress who used to kill children by pretending to play dolls with them, and rendered this pastime harmless. He did the same for steam-cooking, which had previously been used only for cannibalistic feasts, escaped from a fire lit by flame-spitting women by lying down on a non-burnable path (cf. M_{670a}), got the better of a seductress with a toothed vagina, and decreed that henceforth women should no longer be dangerous, apart from widows, whom young men should refrain from marrying . . . Then, he created the woodcutter's tools and also fish-traps, which had once been made of human victims, destroyed an evil echo in the form of a tapeworm, decreed that henceforth if people shout across a river, asking to be ferried to the other side, their request should be granted, and borrowed a magical bark cap which stuck tightly to his head and could only be removed by an ugly female Toad. As he had promised to marry the person who could take it off, the marks on the moon can still be recognized as the Toad-woman carrying her little bucket. This misadventure is the origin of ill-assorted marriages (cf. $M_{399-400}$, *OTM*, pp. 74-7, 103-104). When he got back to his old home, Moon punished Blue-Jay who had ill-treated and humiliated his parents (cf. above, p. 337); then he went up with his younger brother into the sky, where they have been shining ever since 'as the day moon and the night moon'. Moon's mother still travels all round the world; an earthquake occurs every time she completes her circuit. Moonless nights are caused by Moon's wife putting her hands from time to time over his eyes, and eclipses by a monster trying to devour either the sun or the moon (M_{382}, cf. OTM, p. 75; Adamson, pp. 158–72).

Keeping to the subject of the origin of fish, we may note that the myth presents this episode as one of the first great works accomplished by the demiurge, on a par with the creation of ligneous plants. His other achievements are noted one after the other in no apparent order, so I shall leave the problem of their elucidation to others, since it would involve comparing all the lists of seemingly heterogeneous exploits attributed to the demiurge in the many versions of this chronicle. Instead of singling out the genus *Oncorhynchus* for special mention as the bird-nester myth does, the saga of the demiurge stresses the diversity of species, and more especially the fact of their diversity, by emphasizing the parallelism, in this respect, between the vegetable and the animal kingdoms.

So true is this that M_{382}, far from considering salmon as a separate case, incorporates them into a group which, in theory if not in fact, includes all species of fish: 'all the fish on this earth', according to the myth; it does the same with the ligneous plants. Another difference in relation to the bird-nester myth is that M_{382} deals with the origin of fish in general, but makes no attempt to relate their origin to the problem of why fish are not equally distributed between the rivers, a problem with which the other myth is particularly concerned. Instead, M_{382} raises a problem which, as we shall see later, is closely linked to the first one: the origin of ill-assorted marriages, and how it can happen that ugly women have handsome husbands. By now it is clear that, on the sociological level, this phenomenon is symmetrical with the other. In the one instance, it is a matter of explaining why only certain communities possess salmon; in the other, why all men, and not just some, have wives (with the exception of those men who would be well advised to prefer celibacy to marriage with a widow), the reason being that one can choose between various forms of diet, such as meat or fish (see above, p. 372), whereas there is only one form of domestic life: the married state, the need for which, being felt by all, does not allow everyone to be as selective as he or she would no doubt like to be.

The mythology of the Cœur d'Alêne raises different problems, since it distinguishes as two separate narratives the bird-nester story – followed by the hero's visit to the sky, then his return to earth and his revenge ($M_{664a, b}$, see above, p. 363) – and the one about the freeing of the salmon, which is prefaced, as it were, by a sequence not found elsewhere:

M_{694}. *Cœur d'Alêne. 'The freeing of the salmon'*

A good hunter called Crane lived far from the village with his grand-mother. Coyote was chief of the village but only Crane had any game. So Coyote sent his daughters to propose marriage to him. The door of the house was dotted with cooked camas, on which the hungry young girls threw themselves greedily. Crane invited his visitors in and asked his grandmother to serve them a dish of fat meat.

When each woman had given birth to a child, they went on a visit to their parents with their husband. Crane loaded up vast amounts of meat which, by magical means, he reduced to tiny pieces. Thanks to his son-in-law's generosity, Coyote was able to offer his people a feast. The next morning, Crane took everybody hunting. By simply kicking a tree trunk, he set fire to it (cf. $M_{602, 676}$). Coyote subsequently tried to do the same, but always bungled it and so brought back very little game. However, he grew weary, and feeling thirsty on the way back he jumped into the river to cool himself. He amused himself by floating down over the falls, and overheard a conversation between people on the bank about four cannibalistic girls, named after water birds and mistresses of a dam, in which all fish were kept in captivity.

The story cheered Coyote up and gave him the idea of changing into a baby and floating downstream as a slat ('riffle'). The young girls picked him up and fed him on a kind of salmon mush. At the first opportunity, Coyote assumed his own form, burst the dam and led all the fish upstream.

Soon he felt hungry, so he clubbed a salmon and roasted it on a spit. Some wolves and a fox stole it while he slept, and burned him [with the stick] round the nose and eyes. Coyote was first of all shocked by his ghastly appearance when he saw his reflection in the water; then he took his revenge on the thieves by leaving his excrement in place of the birds' eggs the animals had gathered.

Coyote took the salmon to various places, but saw to it that he left none where the inhabitants refused to give him one of their daughters in marriage. At last, he obtained a Nez Percé wife and changed into a rock (Reichard 3, pp. 98–105).

So the Cœur d'Alêne disjoin the story of the visit to the sky from the one about the release of the salmon, while giving the latter an unusual form. They had good reasons for so doing: since the visit to the sky belongs to the realm of the imagination, each community has as much right as any other to claim it proudly as its own, whereas the presence or absence of salmon is an empirical fact and therefore more intractable: the territory of the Cœur d'Alêne lay above the Spokane Falls, which the salmon, apparently, could not get beyond. As a result, the tribe were obliged either to procure dried fish from their Spokane neighbours, or to obtain permission to fish below the falls. However, at an earlier period, before the introduction of the horse or roughly about that time, the Cœur d'Alêne were in the habit of fishing more to the south-east, in the mountain torrents of the Clearwater basin, i.e., in Nez Percé territory (Teit 6, pp. 107, 112–13). One Okanagon version (M_{697a}; Boas 4, p. 69) also credits Coyote with the creation of Spokane Falls, in consequence of which 'the Cœur d'Alêne have no salmon'. A Flathead myth already quoted (M_{608}) formulates the problem in the same terms: the Spokane Falls were created to prevent the salmon reaching the Pend d'Oreilles 'who were not willing to allow their daughters to inter-marry with other tribes'.

Consequently, the Cœur d'Alêne who, like the Siciatl (see above, p. 378), were forced to fish in foreign territory, found a different solution to the philosophical and moral problem which the absence of salmon in their respective territories inevitably posed for both tribes. The Cœur d'Alêne did not opt for the 'celestial' solution chosen by the Siciatl; on the contrary, they gave the freeing of the salmon an even more overtly terrestrial connotation: and they made up for the admission that it was mainly of benefit to foreign communities (such as the Nez Percé) by explaining that it was the consequence of a miraculous hunt, which took place under their aegis. In the Cœur d'Alêne version, the freeing of the salmon and the art of fishing are presented only as makeshift measures which had to be accepted by a character who had previously proved himself to be a bad hunter.

This being so, it seems significant that the 'upstream' versions which, in respect of salmon, establish an opposition between the Cœur d'Alêne and the Pend d'Oreilles on the one hand and the Nez Percé on the other, should not be constructed according to the pattern of the other Salish versions of the bird-nester story but should offer something of a contrast with the 'downstream' versions originating along the lower reaches of the Columbia River. For instance, in M_{601}, Coyote, inspired by a sexual appetite for his daughters-in-law, sends his son Eagle off along a vertical axis. In the Cœur d'Alêne version, however, prompted by an alimentary appetite awakened in him by a future son-in-law called Crane, he sends his daughters off along a horizontal axis. Whether or not the bird referred to is a real crane, or more probably a heron (in this part of America the term crane is applied to the Great Blue Heron, *Ardea herodias*, cf. above, p. 318, rather than to the Canadian Crane, *Grus canadensis*), it is a large stilt-bird with a loud voice and, as a water bird, is in opposition to the high-flying Eagle.

But the explanation of why we can move from son to son-in-law, or from Eagle to Heron, by means of a straightforward commutation, lies in the identical power that the Nez Percé ($M_{602b, c}$) attribute to the one and the Cœur d'Alêne (M_{694}) to the other: each is a hunting chief who, by kicking a fallen trunk can cause warmth-giving fire to spurt forth. The transformation which changes Coyote from a father sexually mad about his daughters-in-law into a father who is alimentarily mad about his son-in-law, is, therefore, the same as the one I studied and discussed at length in connection with the South American myths (*HA*, pp. 226–32). Furthermore, the motif of the hungry daughters in search of a food-providing husband refers back to a transformation of the bird-nester myth previously encountered in Modoc mythology at the beginning of the present volume (M_{543}, see above, p. 81).

In the 'normal' versions of the bird-nester story, Coyote, in order to be able to *consummate* incest with his daughters-in-law, disjoins his son towards the high. In the Cœur d'Alêne version, in order to be able to *consume*[1] the meat possessed by his *son-in-law*, Coyote disjoins his daughters towards the far. It is stated quite clearly in the myth that the hunter-hero lives a long way from the village of which Coyote is the chief, and perhaps towards the south, according to certain indications. The Shuswap (M_{695}; Teit 1, pp. 723–4) mention the Sā'tuen, a community of cranes or herons who live in a southern area and migrate annually to the north; several myths in the group $\{M_{375}, M_{382}\}$ relating to the origin of the sun and moon, tell how the bird called Crane or Heron was tried out in the role of sun, but was rejected because he made the days too long (Sanpoil: Ray 2, p. 137; Okanagon: Cline, p. 178). The journey to the south undertaken by Coyote's daughters, who are called after terrestrial squirrels, clearly corresponds to the ascent into sky country made by Coyote's son – known in the southern versions as Eagle, the name of a celestial bird – just as the incident of the house dotted with camas, edible tubers which the girls attack greedily but on which they cannot appease their hunger (since what they want is meat) reproduces and transforms the episode in M_{667a}, in which the hero uproots other edible

---

[1] TRANSLATORS' NOTE: As has already been pointed out, in French the verb *consommer* has the two meanings: to consume and to consummate.

tubers from the celestial vault in the hope of appeasing his hunger, a vain hope since the tubers are really stars.[2]

The heroines are taken into the lodge and given a feast of meat such as they have never had before; they hesitate to eat the precious fat and wish to keep it for use as an ointment. Here, too, we have an obvious allusion to the visit to the sky, since the Cœur d'Alêne versions attribute the same reaction to the helpful Spiders, who enable the hero to return to earth, after which he regains his native village, whereas Coyote's daughters, wishing to see their family again, take their husband to their own village, not to his: so the two movements along the horizontal and vertical axes are counter-reflections of each other. In M_{694} the link-up with the freeing of the salmon is achieved by means of sequences belonging to the bungling host cycle, replacing the act of revenge which, in this case, would be unmotivated. I have already discussed this transformation in connection with the Lilloet and Shuswap versions (see above, pp. 384–5) and I do not propose to mention it again, except to note that the cannibalism attributed to the mistresses of salmon who are also, in M_{664b}, the last creatures encountered on the horizontal axis, corresponds to the cannibalistic hunting by defecation, attributed by the Cœur d'Alêne versions to the hostile Spiders, the first creatures encountered on the vertical axis.

An Okanagon myth (M_{697e}; Cline, p. 237) also makes mention of a hero called Crane or Heron, a great hunter, but who, unlike his Cœur d'Alêne homonym, does not succeed in finding a wife to his liking among all the women who present themselves, and persists in remaining a bachelor. Why does a character, who is alternately conjoined or disjoined in respect of *marriage* on *earth* (the water bird in this case being a hunter, not a fisher), have the same name as the one who, in the myths of North America, usually plays the part of susceptible ferryman (cf. *OTM*, pp. 445–6), in other words, is both conjunctive and disjunctive in respect of a *journey* across *water*? The answer to this little problem will appear presently (see below, p. 445).

The Sanpoil and Okanagon, who live at the centre of the Plateau, tell the story of the freeing of the salmon in such similar forms that it would be wearisome to discuss them in detail. Nevertheless, certain curious incidental differences do emerge, and deserve brief mention. For instance, the Sanpoil, whose permanent villages once occupied the terraces along the

---

[2] If it is true that the motif of the door dotted with camas belongs to a transformational group, other states of which are known to exist, Reichard's suggestion (3, p. 4, n. 2) that this detail was borrowed from European folklore should be treated with scepticism.

middle reaches of the Columbia River, sometimes used to incorporate the salmon episode into a series of adventures (M_{696a}; Boas 4, pp. 101–103) which begin with Coyote meeting and killing a beautifully attired warrior called Sparrow. Decked out in his victim's fine feathers, he sets off downstream travelling close to the river so that he can gaze at leisure at his reflection and admire his handsome appearance (cf. M_{694}, see above, p. 425, in which Coyote's first reaction is one of horror, when he sees the reflected image of his ugly face). Soon he sees a tent and hopes that there will be a beautiful maiden to admire him; but only the willow-grouse's twelve children live there. In reply to Coyote's question, they all answer in a language he does not understand.[3] Coyote, believing that he has been insulted, blinds them with pitch and goes off (cf. M_{680}, see above, pp. 385, 403–404). The parents return; determined to have their revenge, they hide and scare Coyote, who is so frightened he falls into the river where he changes into a basket which drifts downstream. Sisters, the mistresses of salmon, salvage the basket and use it to hold their cooked salmon, which the basket promptly devours. So they throw it into the fire, where Coyote at once changes into a little boy whom the women keep and bring up. He loses no time in breaking their dam and turning his adoptive mothers into a water-snipe and a killdeer plover, both fish-eating birds. Later, Coyote offers a salmon to a pretty little girl, but takes the fish back when she refuses to marry him; wherever he is similarly scorned, he creates falls to keep the salmon from running upstream.

Other stories, restricted to the freeing of the salmon, are all variations on one theme (M_{696b-e}; Ray 1, pp. 72–3; 2, pp. 167–77). Coyote gives salmon only to those people who offer him a daughter in marriage and he refuses salmon to the others, by various devices: he creates impassable falls downstream, destroys the fishing dams, or changes the course of the river. One rather more elaborate variant (M_{696d}) places the reciprocal theft of the food (already discussed above, p. 276) after the freeing of the salmon and follows it with a new episode:

M_{696d}. Sanpoil. 'Coyote and his daughter'

While travelling upstream in the hope of finding a wife, Coyote built several fishing dams in succession, and tore them down every time his suit was rejected. At last at Kettle Falls, he managed to get a wife. This wife, Gopher, gave birth to a daughter who, when she grew up, inspired

---

[3] The fact that the texts of the myth remain homologous, even when they seem most divergent, is proved by the constant symmetry of the narratives: [*Coyote pierces from afar, below, creatures for whom he is unintelligible*] ⇒ [*Coyote blocks at close range, above, creatures whose speech is unintelligible to him*].

incestuous desires in Coyote. He pretended he was about to die and decreed that after his death his daughter should marry a stranger from Kutenai country. He lost no time in presenting himself in this guise and, as he spoke only Kutenai, the multilingual Mouse acted as interpreter. Coyote married his daughter; the Prairie chicken brothers realized what had happened, and were determined to tell what Coyote had done. The young woman was so ashamed she turned into a rock in the middle of the river. Since then, every once in a while, men have tried to live with their own daughters (Ray 2, pp. 173–5).

We have already encountered the motif of Coyote's incest with his daughter (see above, p. 345) as well as that of the woman or girl who is changed into a rock in the middle of a river (see above, pp. 373–5). The reasons for their being combined in this context will become apparent later. I must first continue with the account of the Plateau versions.

The Okanagon ($M_{697a, b}$; Boas 4, pp. 67–71) relate how Coyote, who has changed first of all into a dish which devours food, then into a non-libidinous baby (unlike the one in the Sanpoil version M_{696d}, since here the women call him 'nice younger brother'), succeeds in letting the salmon pass up the river. Then he visits all communities in order to find a wife and withholds salmon from those who refuse their daughters in marriage or who, as a way of rejecting his advances without offending him, claim never to eat fish, but only the back of the head of the mountain-ram. Conversely, every time the parents accept him, even though the girl herself is unwilling, Coyote causes the river bed to contract so as to facilitate the capturing of salmon, or alternatively, the freeing of the salmon episode follows on from the one in which Coyote, thanks to his long penis, copulates on the opposite bank with girls who have rashly accepted his offer of salmon backs; the offer is immediately withdrawn if the girls demand sheep's necks in place of fish.

In the Hill-Tout version (8, pp. 146–7; M_{697c}), which is more or less contemporaneous with the preceding versions, Coyote is swept away not by currents but by a great windstorm and, having been changed into a wooden dish, he himself decides to land; the mistresses of salmon adopt him as their little brother after he has assumed the appearance of a baby. Coyote breaks down the weir, sets the salmon free, escapes and later marries Wolverine's daughter (cf. M_{667b}, in which the same incident is set in Okanagon territory); he creates falls upstream from his new abode, so that salmon cannot reach the land of the mountain-sheep, and decrees that, in future, no salmon will ever come up Similkameen River.

Finally, let me mention two more recent versions ($M_{697d, e}$; Cline, pp. 214–18), one of which includes the episode involving the reciprocal theft of food, as a sequel to which the Wolf and the Fox on the one hand, and the Coyote on the other, gave each other their present-day appearances (with shorter or longer tails, muzzles and legs, more or less pointed snouts and slit eyes). Coyote travels everywhere to lakes and rivers, confers the benefit of salmon, and flat, rocky banks from which to fish more easily, on communities which offer him their daughters in marriage, but refuses these favours to people who reject him or declare a preference for wild goat meat rather than fish; this explains why there are falls in various places to prevent the salmon running up. The other version continues with Coyote's incest with his daughter (cf. M_{696d}), who is so ashamed that she throws herself into the river, and is perhaps changed into a star.

Alongside the 'normal' versions (M_{667}–M_{670}), which I have chosen as my point of reference, the Thompson stories refer to the time (M_{698a}; Teit 5, pp. 347–50) when salmon did not yet run up rivers and game was scarce. So the birds made a war-party against an aquatic monster which held all fish captive. Having been swallowed by the animal, the birds succeeded in killing it from the inside (cf. M_{678}, see above, p. 383). Their victory led to the present day distribution of fish in lakes and rivers, regular seasonal migrations, and the initiation of all inland communities in the art of fishing with spears and dip-nets. The war of the birds against fish is similar to other stories of the same type, e.g., the war between river fish and sea fish – Trout against Salmon and Sturgeon – the events of which explain why the Sturgeon has few bones and why members of coastal communities seldom marry those of inland communities (M_{698b}; Teit 5, pp. 350–52); the war between fish and land animals, which is won by the latter who inflict a disorderly rout on their opponents, with effects that are still to be seen in the present-day distribution of fish (M_{698c}; Teit 5, pp. 352–3); and the war of the fish with the Okanagon, which had the same outcome (M_{698d}; Teit 4, p. 77). One variant (M_{698e}; Teit 5, pp. 231–2) describes a triangular conflict which started when a salmon carried off an Indian woman. Then the land animals in turn kidnapped her when she returned to visit her parents, with the result that the Fish declared war on the land animals, by whom they were speedily vanquished and put to flight; this explains their present distribution in the rivers. As in M_{698c}, Salmon's surviving son determined to avenge his people, killed several land animals and freed his mother whom they were holding prisoner.

All these myths, then, postulate a bipartite division of creatures – Fish and Birds, coastal fish and inland fish, Fish and Land Animals, and Fish and

Humans; or a tripartite division of the animal kingdom into humans, land animals and fish. At the same time, they explain why fish are unevenly distributed among the various rivers. A complete study of this group should be made; I have done no more than single out a few typical instances; it is curious, to say the least, that the group should describe the natural order according to a model analogous with that used by certain North Athapaskan in the organization of their society: the Western Athapaskan were divided into exogamous phratries, called respectively Bears and Birds; the Kutchin and the Loucheux had three: Birds, associated with fair people, Land Animals, associated with dark people, and Fish, associated with people who were neither dark nor fair but between the two. In former times the Carrier had four, if not five, phratries which bore the names of the Grouse, the Beaver, the Toad, the Grizzly Bear or the Raven (Hill-Tout 6, pp. 144–5).

It will be remembered that the Lilloet tell the story of the bird-nester, but omit the episode about the freeing of the salmon (M_{671}; see above, p. 377); the episode is treated by them as a separate myth (M_{699}; Teit 2, pp. 303–304), in which it is tempting to recognize the influence of the Iroquois, who have stories of the same kind. Two brothers live at the sources of the River Lilloet; one of them falls sick; no food agrees with the invalid, and after four years he is nothing but skin and bone. His brother takes him with him in a canoe and they travel downstream giving names to all the places as they pass and making the waters navigable all the way. They reach the Fraser River, then the ocean, and come at last to the land of the salmon. The strong brother hides while the sick brother changes into a beautifully carved wooden dish and, in this form, is driven ashore at the foot of the dam inside which the salmon are kept. A man picks it up and gives it to his daughter. Everything she leaves on the plate disappears, but she does not care because salmon are plentiful in her country. Thanks to his diet of salmon, the sick brother becomes fat and well again. When he has completely recovered, the two brothers break the dam and let the salmon swim out into the streams of the interior. Then they return to the sources of the Lilloet in the Cascade Range: there they find hot springs which they can use in cooking their food.

From the nature of the tasks assigned to the two brothers, it is clear that the Lilloet myth presents an inversion of the normal forms: they make the river navigable, whereas Coyote creates impassable obstacles in the rivers he visits; they cut right through the middle of a rocky cliff barring their way so that their canoe can pursue its course. The stone arch, which is said to be still visible, is symmetrical with the solid rock in several of the normal versions, that Coyote sets up in mid-river, thus forcing the water to divide into two streams. The freeing of the salmon episode is found in both contexts, but it will be noted that M_{699} ends with the origin of a natural means of cooking the fish, in the boiling water of certain hot springs which are a feature of Lilloet territory. The inverted nature of the myth is accentuated by the fact that salmon, instead of being a food of prime importance for mankind, which had previously been short of sustenance, takes on the function of a curative substance used to restore the health of someone who is an invalid, in spite of enjoying a copious and varied supply of food.

Everything that happens in the myth is related to the concept of ease: the heroes refashion the river bed to make the river navigable all the way, whereas Coyote, in the symmetrical versions, creates falls which are impassable for both salmon and canoes. The masters of salmon demonstrate their liberal-mindedness by not objecting to the fact — they have, in any case, a surplus of food — that the two brothers (who, for their part are undemanding enough to make do with leftovers) appropriate the remains of their meal. These remains, when scattered, are enough to stock 'all the streams and rivers with fish', says the text, as if it were eager to avoid the restrictive clauses carefully enumerated in the 'normal' versions. Lastly, cooking is possible without fire, thanks to the hot springs.

The geographical distribution of the Lilloet groups, as it was observed at the end of the nineteenth century, no longer corresponded to the previous state of affairs (Hill-Tout 3, pp. 126–8); however, one myth suggests that, in former times, one of the two main sections of the tribe had no salmon. After the transformer gods — whose saga is reflected, although on a reduced scale, in M_{699} — have travelled up the Lilloet, two of them go off in opposite directions and then return, one from the south, the other from the east. Their companions who have stayed behind greet the first, calling him Li'luet, and then the second, calling him Sla'tlemux; they add that henceforth the Li'luet will travel up the Fraser River into Sla'tlemux country to buy salmon and hemp fibre. Then they carve a sign in the rock to mark the tribal boundary (M_{700}; Teit 2, pp. 292–6). Even if, as this myth implies, salmon did not get as far as the upper reaches of the Lilloet, the presence of a great many hot springs in the mountains could suggest the utopian idea of a land of plenty, where all material problems would be miraculously solved, in the same manner as the labour of cooking. Just as M_{699} is an inversion, in this respect, of symmetrical myths about the freeing of the salmon, M_{700} is an inversion of the coastal myths about the origin of salmon (M_{375}, M_{382}, M_{506}), because of the way in which it describes the pierced rock incident, also present in M_{699}: 'As they proceeded up the lake the Transformers came to its head, into which the river Lilloet flows. They saw flat ground like a bog which moved up and down continuously, hindering the canoes from ascending the river. They made it into firm but swampy land and left a channel by which canoes might reach the river' (Teit 2, p. 295). In both cases, whether we are dealing with a stone arch spanning a river or with a swamp bisected by a canal, the image of an obstacle hollowed out through its centre, and allowing the waters to join up again, stands in opposition to that, present in the symmetrical versions, of an obstacle set up in the centre, and forcing the waters to divide (Figure 26).

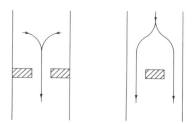

Figure 26. The two obstacles

These patterns are not merely reminiscent of those brought to light by our analysis, in the celestial register, of the oppositional and correlational relationships between moonspots and sunspots, on the one hand, and parhelia and paraselenes, on the other (see above, pp. 247–8). The state of affairs described by M_{700}, before the Transformers or the heroes of M_{699} put an end to it by the means illustrated on the left-hand side of Figure 26, is a direct reminder of the symplegades, which also bar the way to the land of the salmon (cf. M_{699}) and are subject to vertical oscillations (cf. M_{700}). We can thus also postulate a certain homology between the right-hand side of Figure 26 and the swing, which, like the river in the latter case, is subject to a divergent movement. The point will be established later (see below, pp. 444–5). For the moment, it will suffice to have shown that the two structures, being mutually opposed, involve the consequence that those myths in which either is featured to the exclusion of the other are in opposition to each other. And, since M_{699} develops the theme of abundance, it follows, as has already been suggested by syntagmatic analysis (see above, p. 444), that the symmetrical versions concerned with the freeing of the salmon develop the theme of scarcity. They lay less stress on the abundance of salmon in certain privileged areas than on their absence elsewhere. And it is above all the absence of salmon that they set out to explain.

It is important, then, to examine jointly the two sequences, in which the theme of scarcity takes exactly opposite forms; as it happens they follow on from each other. After freeing the salmon Coyote sets out to look for a wife; he approaches the river communities in turn, gives salmon to those who accept him as a son-in-law, but refuses salmon to those who reject him. From this point onwards, the versions develop differently: either Coyote falls in love with his daughter and succeeds in marrying her, by feigning death and then reappearing in the guise of a high-born stranger speaking an unintelligible language (M_{696d}); or he calls to young girls who are bathing and copulates across the river with those who accept his offer of salmon, but withholds salmon from those who declare their preference for meat. The end of his mutilated penis having remained in his victim's vagina, he manages to recover the missing part by using the trick which, in a different context, allows him to seduce his own daughter: in this respect, the two versions coincide. However, their conclusions differ: one explains why the mountain people who prefer meat will henceforth be deprived of salmon; the other, why certain river communities will catch an abundance of fish quite easily; at the point where Coyote's daughter, transformed into a rock, is set in the middle of the river, the water will divide and a deep, calm pool will form between her legs.

We can already distinguish, then, two types of women towards whom Coyote behaves in the same manner, having adopted the guise of a high-born foreigner. In the one case the woman is his own daughter, in other words, too close a relative to be his wife; in the other, she is a complete stranger whose remote position as a future wife results from the fact that Coyote sees her, and then talks to her, from the other side of the river in a language she does not understand; and he is able to copulate with her across the water because of his abnormally long penis. However, to go no further than this simple opposition would be to disregard the fact that Coyote had already had dealings with women of another type: the mistresses of salmon.

Almost all the available versions bring out a fundamental contrast between the mistresses of salmon and the pretty bathing girls: Coyote meets the former, usually in the sea, after a long journey *downstream*; but he encounters the latter when he stops to rest after travelling a long way *upstream*, and they are on the opposite bank. The contrast between the two types of women could perhaps best be expressed by the two adverbs 'along' and 'across'; the first women are in the direct line of the river, or parallel to it, whereas the others are at right angles to it.

Once the contrast has been perceived, it can be confirmed and reinforced by further details. Coyote proposes first of all to the bathing girls that he should feed them from a distance with food that they either do not possess or do not want. Then, thanks to his long penis, he copulates with one of them. With the mistresses of salmon, his behaviour is both similar to this and the reverse: first, after changing into a voracious dish, he ingests, through direct contact, food which they possess and he covets; then, after changing into a baby, in some versions he is chaste, in others lewd; i.e., in the one instance he has no penis, and in the other his penis may be presumed to be short on two counts: because it belongs to a baby, and because copulation takes place, not at a distance and in broad daylight, but at night and in the intimacy of the bed which his protectresses allow him to share.

Let us go one stage further or, to be more accurate, let us go back to the beginning of the myth we are now discussing. The correlational and oppositional relationship that I have just pointed out between the two groups of women encountered by Coyote during his aquatic adventures was already present between the two groups of characters encountered by Coyote's son during his wanderings through the sky country. The two old blind women, who are sitting on either side of a fire across which they hand each other bad food (gravel, stone or rotten wood) are prefigurations of the respective positions of Coyote and the bathing girls, who are on the opposite banks of a river, across which the passing of good food (salmon back) leads to sexual consummation and the partial amputation of the bad penis (it makes the girl ill) — whereas, in the first case, the partial removal of the bad food was followed by the direct insertion into the hand of one of the old women, i.e., at close range, of a good penis (it cures blindness). Whereas the old celestial women are blind, the young bathing girls are hard of hearing: they fail to understand, or positively misunderstand, what Coyote is shouting across to them from a distance and in an unfamiliar language (M_{667a}, M_{668a-d}, M_{680b}, M_{696d-e}): 'Hereafter, young girls shall not ask travellers what they have in their packs. Old people may do it, but not young people' (Adamson, p. 263).

If the first women encountered in the sky come into the 'across' category, it should follow that the helpful Spiders, who are visited next by the hero and who bring him back down to earth by means of a long rope (in contrast to the short stalk in M_{664a}, also part of a hemp plant, linking the blind old women horizontally across the fire), come into the 'along' category, although the expression must apply in this case to the vertical axis, with the Spiders at the top, at the opposite end from the earth, and not to a horizontal axis, one end of which, in mid-ocean, is the abode of the mistresses of salmon, while the other end joins up with the land or earth.

Just as the blind old women are 'on the side of' (*du côté de*, in the Proustian sense) the swinging doors, the helpful Spiders must inevitably be 'on the side' of the swing; and the fact is that, in the Puget Sound versions, the long rope linking sky to earth becomes a swing. Consequently, 'on the side of' the swinging doors, we have two women in the 'across' category, and another two in the 'along' category; the same is true 'on the side of' the swing (Figure 27). Each mechanism combines the two aspects: both the symplegades and the swing — the first vertically, the second horizontally — oscillate 'across'; but the first are in the sea, at the entrance to the distant country of the salmon, while the second is on the earth, in the heart of the territory which will become the home of people who eat salmon.

This ambiguity, peculiar to the two basic schemes from which the myths were generated, emerges even more strikingly, when we observe that, in M_{382}, a version of the saga of the demiurge Moon, the episode of the swing — still deadly but later to be used only for sport — occurs just before the one in which the demiurge gets the better of a creature with a toothed vagina, and ordains that, henceforth, the female organ will no longer be armed with stone knives but will be made of flesh only. Three other episodes are inserted between these two: the first is devoted to dolls, consequently to another game (see above, p. 423), probably by analogy with the swing as a form of play, while the other two, significantly perhaps, account for the origin of cooking and the domestic hearth.

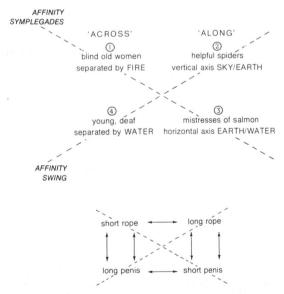

Figure 27. Women belonging to the two categories 'along' and 'across'

A woman with a toothed vagina amounts to an anatomical equivalent of the symplegades, just as the long penis is an anatomical equivalent of the rope linking the sky and the earth, and which is, in its turn, transformable into a swing. Moreover, in M_{700}, we find a more direct equivalence, since the woman desired by the heroes is not on the opposite side of a river, that is, in the 'across' category, but at the top of a cliff overhanging the river, and consequently in the 'high' category, the high, as we have seen, being a mode of the far. They try to reach her with their penises, but fail: they succeed only in spattering the vertical rockface with sperm. Only after stuffing themselves with sage (a detail which clearly confirms the inverted character of this myth, cf. L.-S. 9, pp. 63–9) can they lift their penises to the required height.

It is revealing, then, that the myths of this part of America should make a point of splitting up the motifs of the long penis and the toothed vagina. Of both they present complementary images illustrating respectively their 'symplegades' aspect and their 'swing' aspect, both 'along' and 'across'. Although, as we have just seen, there exist women whose vaginas contain sharp stones, and are thus comparable to the symplegades, the pretty bathing girls with whom Coyote copulates *trans flumen* are certainly not in this category. It is only because Coyote's penis is huge and heavy that it remains wedged in the distended vagina. Furthermore, all the versions stress one point: no object in any way whatever resembling a toothed vagina – for instance, the knives and sharp stones used by the victim's companions – is of the slightest avail in the attempt to truncate the long penis. Coyote himself has to suggest the use of a sharp-edged leaf or blade of grass. This is tantamount to stating that the young girl's vagina *is not toothed*; it is she who falls gravely ill because of the segment of penis lodged inside her, whereas, if her vagina had been toothed, her male partner would have perished.

Consequently, the motif of the untoothed vagina plays just as important a part in the myths as its contrary; the image of a normal vagina is therefore situated between the two. The same observation is valid in connection with the long penis: in the examples I have just referred to, the problem is how to cut it, whereas in other versions the penis itself is a cutting instrument. According to the Sahaptin myth M_{611a} (see above, p. 282), Coyote exchanged his own penis for another, which was able to fell trees like an axe, but it turned against its borrower's vital organs, when there was no wood for it to attack. In Chinook mythology, the wood-eating penis is the same as the organ with which Coyote tries to copulate across the river (M_{611b}; Jacobs 2, Part I, pp. 87–9). The Chehalis of Washington State (M_{701c}; Adamson, pp. 152–4) believe that it belonged to Wren, the smallest bird; Coyote tries to trade his organ for Wren's, but the penis devours all his meals. So he takes it back to its owner and decrees that in future the penis will not eat people's food. Man shall use it only for urinating and copulating. According to the Cowlitz River Sahaptin ($M_{701a, b}$; Jacobs 1, pp. 102–103, 243–4), it is after borrowing the Wren's penis, which is so long that it fills five baskets and which is fed on odorous ants (cf. *ibid.*, pp. 76, 108 for the inverted forms), that Coyote undertakes to copulate across the river.[4] We shall see later (see below, p. 469) that the Wren, who is here credited with a long penis, is, in other myths, the only creature capable of attaching to the celestial vault the long chain of arrows which allows the mythic animals to conquer fire for the good of mankind (Jacobs 1, pp. 145–6; cf. 3, p. 175).

However, this does not exhaust the list of transformations relating to the long penis. Sometimes, Wren's penis changes into a short one, and moves from the category of the low to that of the high when its owner wrenches out an aching tooth from a stranger who agrees, in exchange, to mend his nose, the point of which has been almost cut off so that it is hanging down and dangling in mid-air (Siciatl: M_{703}; Hill-Tout 1, pp. 38–9). Coyote, who has borrowed a food-consuming penis, also sometimes devours his own penis when he is hungry, and his arrows, unlike those of Wren, the rightful owner of the large member, later fail to reach the sky (Klikitat: M_{703}; Jacobs 1, pp. 61–2). A final state of the same transformation can be observed among the Tahltan, who are northern Athapaskan and neighbours of the Tlingit; their myths mention a male organ which is not only inordinately long but also has sharp teeth and a cannibalistic appetite (M_{704}; Teit 7, pp. 245–6): it is, then, a *penis dentatus* symmetrical with the *vagina dentata*. All the possible transformations are so methodically illustrated that it seems legitimate to interpret the long piece of rope that, in most versions of the bird-nester myth, the faithful wife — for reasons unknown — leaves trailing behind her and that the hero steps on several times in order to jolt her to a standstill and thus force her to notice his presence (M_{602b-c}; M_{606a-c}, M_{677}, etc.), as an inverted image – going from the woman to the man – of the long penis used by Coyote at the end of his aquatic adventures, which are closely parallel to the celestial and terrestrial adventures of his son.

---

[4] My colleague, Pierre Maranda of the University of British Columbia, points out that, according to information obtained from Melville Jacobs, these creatures, which are known as 'pissing ants', emit a powerful stench of urine when they are squashed. This probably explains why the long penis is so fond of them. According to native informants, their smell resembles that of bears rather than of urine; the Indians used to put crushed pieces of the ant-hills outside their houses, because marauding animals were frightened away by the smell.

We saw that along the lower reaches of the Columbia River the bird-nester story leads up to the freeing of the salmon, followed by the origin of fairs and markets. Farther south, the same story is inverted and transformed into the Loon Woman cycle, which deals with incest and periodicity, viewed from a temporal rather than a spatial angle. If any conclusion is deducible from my preceding remarks, it must be that, to the north of the Columbia River, in the basin of Fraser River, the bird-nester story remains unchanged, but associates the episode of the freeing of the salmon on the one hand with the problem of the *distribution* of fish in the system of lakes and rivers, and on the other, with that of *exogamy* as a characteristic feature of the system of matrimonial alliances.

Such is the literal meaning of the myths, when they explain the presence or absence of salmon by the positive or negative responses made to Coyote's marriage overtures by the communities he visits; this is also their symbolic meaning, which is illustrated by a series of images arranged on several levels: the symplegades and the swing as barriers or as a means of free communication between the near and the far, and the low and the high; mutilating or mutilated vaginas, and long penises either eager or reluctant to cross the river, in response to declared preferences for fish or meat; lastly, the image of the ideal suitor, who is sure of winning a wife if he succeeds in presenting himself as being metaphorically a 'long penis', that is, a high-born foreigner speaking a language intelligible only to the polyglot Mouse who, throughout her long life, has had a series of husbands from all countries.

It is a fact that both the coast and inland Salish were very keen on exogamous marriages; generally speaking, these Indians used to choose wives from foreign tribes rather than from their own. It is difficult to say whether they were prompted by political motives, or by a more or less conscious interest in the biological advantages; the first supposition is the more likely. In fact, they would boast about being of mixed stock. 'The expression "I am half Snokwalmu, half Klikitat," or some similar one, is of everyday utterance. With the chiefs, this is almost always the case' (Gibbs, p. 197; cf. too the grandmother's reply, see above, p. 170). According to more recent evidence, these same Coast Salish 'made an effort to obtain wives from as many villages as possible . . .; a variety of alliances afforded protection and hospitality outside the territory of [their] local group' (Barnett 3, p. 182). 'Exogamous marriage . . . was the recognized method of bridging the suspicion existent between villages' (M.W. Smith 2, p. 42; cf. pp. 165–7). The Chilcotin, who were Athapaskan living next to the Salish, often entered into marriages with their Bella Coola, Shuswap and

Lilloet neighbours; about 1855, it was estimated that the Shuswap living in the gorges of the Fraser River were at least half Chilcotin (Teit 1, pp. 762–3). Certain myths of the inland Salish provide similar evidence. The Thompson describe the discovery of an unknown people living just a short distance away, but on the far side of a long impenetrable forest: 'These groups had been living for generations within a mile or so of each other, yet neither knew of the other.' They knew no language other than their own. Two young men made contact, and each was at once given a wife by his hosts. They set to work and cleared the riverbed and banks and made trails leading to the villages. As soon as communication by land and water had been established, 'intercourse became frequent and they intermarried' (M$_{705a, b}$; Teit 5, pp. 279–80).

The communities in question live along the banks of either a lake or a river. The practice of exogamy does not, however, extend beyond the watershed between two river basins. The Nez Percé who, as I pointed out earlier (see above, pp. 367–8) represents an outpost of the culture of the Plains and the coastal area over towards the Rockies, took a pessimistic view of matrimonial alliances with their Plains neighbours, into whose territory they occasionally ventured in order to hunt buffalo. Having been promised a wife, so the story goes, Coyote helps an old Buffalo to get back his ten wives, who have been carried off by a younger rival. He receives his reward, but has to promise to remain chaste during the ten days of the return journey. However, on the eighth day, the Buffalo Woman changes into a female Coyote, thus making her new husband even more impatient. On the tenth night, being unable to sleep, at dawn he creeps in beside his new wife, who at once resumes her original animal form and returns to her own country. 'It will ever be thus,' concludes Coyote; 'If a man tries to take away a wife from this country, she will leave him before even reaching his house.' Coyote experiences the same misadventure with a young mountain Goat, whom he has cured, then married: she leaves him for someone else. Since then, women from the buffalo country often leave their husbands (M$_{706a, b}$; Boas 4, pp. 190–92). Similar instances (Cline, pp. 236–7) are quoted in Okanagon sources.

The Quileute, who lived along the sea coast, also disliked distant marriages and, in support of their view, would quote the example of a young wife of their tribe who, while on a visit to her own people, refused to return to her too-distant husband: 'This is why the Quileute try to marry women of their own tribe. Should they marry a woman from another tribe, and she ever gets home again, it is difficult to get her to return to her husband's house' (Reagan, pp. 58–60).

Although the exogamous enthusiasm of the plateau and coastal people stopped short at marriage with quadrupeds or, to put it more realistically, with women belonging to communities which, unlike themselves, preferred hunting to fishing, it would seem that imaginatively at least they were not averse to the vegetable kingdom. Salish myths describe several marriages between a woman and a root, or between a man and trees. I do not propose to include them among the myths to be studied here, since they could be dealt with more appropriately in an analysis of the plant system, the possibility of which I have already mentioned (see above, p. 387), but which is beyond the scope of the present volume. I need only refer to the fact that an important mythic cycle common to the Cœur d'Alêne, the Thompson, the Shuswap and the Lilloet concerns a demiurge, who is the son of a human woman and a *Peucedanum* root (Teit 1, pp. 644, 651–2; 4, p. 95; Hill-Tout 10, pp. 564–6; Dawson, p. 31; Reichard 3, pp. 57–67; etc.); and that a group of other demiurges give Coyote, in place of his wives made from tree branches, more satisfactory spouses made from alder and poplar; their contrasting skin and hair colour determined the differences in physical appearance observable among the Indians today (Teit 2, pp. 357–8; 4, p. 44; Boas 4, p. 19; 13, pp. 17, 23).

The importance of these themes, illustrating what might be called a form of vegetable exogamy, can be understood in the light of the point already made (see above, p. 424) to the effect that myths relating to the organization of the world by the demiurge give pride of place to the origin (of the diversity) of ligneous plants and to the origin (of the diversity) of fish. In thus stressing a homology between the vegetable and the animal kingdoms, they emphasize the fact of the diversity rather than the concrete modalities in which it is manifested in different areas. This attitude of mind is understandable in a region where the rivers cross vast stretches of semi-desert land, in which there is very little wood either for making things or for fires, and where, consequently, an uneven distribution of shrubs and trees poses the same problem as the uneven distribution of fish. However, by introducing a third kind of homology, this time with uneven exchanges of women between groups or tribes, according to whether or not they possess salmon and are more dependent on hunting or fishing, the myths are trying to solve a more specifically philosophical problem, since they are likening the presence or absence of matrimonial alliances between the groups, or the unequal proportions of such alliances, that is, quantitative data, to the diversity of animal and vegetable species, which is a qualitative phenomenon. In short, what they are doing is transmuting certain deficiencies of the social order into positive properties of the natural order, and behaving as if the absence of organization and the amorphous nature of the Salish groups, which I stressed at the beginning of the discussion (see above, p. 358), reflected – in spite of all evidence to the contrary – a natural order for which loose societies felt a kind of nostalgia.

This ideal social order, which purports to correspond, in the manner of a sunk carving, and even by its omissions, to the positive aspects of the natural order, nevertheless meets with certain external limitations when it comes up against the problem of the incompatibility of environments and modes of life. In this respect the solution adopted by the Salish differentiates them from their more southerly neighbours who, as we have seen, solve the same problem by the organization of fairs and markets: consequently, the latter accept, and even advocate, the exchange of women between communities who have quite different ways of life, but who meet periodically to trade their raw materials, manufactured objects and foodstuffs. The Plateau Salish, who were more distant from these trading centres, although they might go there occasionally, liked, as a community, to keep themselves to themselves, and their myths explain that they exchanged women mainly with people who had the same diet as themselves.

However, these exchanges also meet with an internal limitation which is brought out by Coyote's incest with his daughter, although the incest is penalized in various ways. According to the Cowlitz River Salish (M$_{707}$; Adamson, pp. 262–3), the girl runs off with an Indian to a place known as The Falls, near Nesika: 'And so it happens in this place, if a girl wants a man, she runs away with him; her parents do not choose for her. But among the Cowlitz a man must not buy his wife. And so in this section of the country parents never choose their children's mates.' In other versions, and these are more numerous, the girl is so ashamed that she throws herself into the river and changes into a rock: she is made stationary in one place instead of being removed to a distance: 'She jumped into the river facing upstream. Coyote called to her to face downstream and spread her legs apart so that the fish can jump up'. According to another version, also belonging to the Sanpoil, Coyote, who had been refused a wife, destroyed a waterfall: 'A huge boulder rolled out into the middle of the river making falls on either side. Then Coyote called out. "My daughter, oh, my daughter, don't face upstream, face downstream". The big rock turned completely round. The part above water on the side facing downstream had a large oval-shaped crevice in it. "From now on," Coyote continued, "whenever the salmon come upstream to spawn they will jump into your vagina in trying to get over the falls" (M$_{696}$; Ray 2, pp. 173–5). In a Nez Percé variant (M$_{708}$; Boas

4, pp. 189–90), the middle section of Coyote's long penis is transformed into a ledge: Coyote himself cuts off that part of the penis near his body, while his victims cut off the other end. The Okanagon (M_{709}; Boas 4, pp. 72–4) explain why women sometimes commit suicide: they are imitating Coyote's daughter who was transformed into a rock. Conversely, the Kutenai blame Coyote's conjugal frustrations for the disappearance of the navigable channels which are said to have once existed between the lakes and the Kutenai River, and for the subsequent laborious carrying of canoes between the two waterways (M_{710}; Boas 9, pp. 81, 179).

We can see, then, that the myths set three internal limits to exogamy, at the same time as they attempt to formulate exogamy as a system: incest, sudden love and female suicide. In all three cases, the young girl is removed, or removes herself, from the matrimonial transaction: she upsets the mechanism of conjugal exchanges. But at the same time, the myths are extremely careful to differentiate between, on the one hand, the relatively unimportant anomalies which may occur within the system without permanently preventing its operation, and, on the other, the much more serious disruptions brought about by one social group persistently refusing an offer of marriage made by another. Only the latter eventuality creates an irremediable situation, quite different from such minor and strictly localized incidents as when young people choose each other as partners in defiance of the marriage policies of their families or tribes (M_{707}), or such rare occurrences as a young girl's impulse to commit suicide (M_{709}), or incestuous relationships which, as M_{696d} significantly emphasizes, are no more than episodic: 'Since then, every once in a while, in time to come, men will try to live with their own daughters . . .' (Ray 3, p. 175). Whether serious impediments or mere mishaps which temporarily disorganize the normal working of marriage arrangements, all these sociological phenomena are coded by the Salish myths in terms of the lake and river system, in which the accidents of nature produce either an abundance or a dearth of fish, according to whether the falls slow down the fish's progress or stop them altogether; in either case, the downstream communities benefit and the upstream communities are deprived.

Borrowing the language of phonemics, we can say, then, that the falls act as *occlusive mythemes*: their relative position determines the presence or absence of fish. On the other hand, the rock, which is a result of incest, and which the myths describe as being in the middle of the river, partially blocking its course and yet allowing the water to flow freely on either side, does not interrupt the salmon run, but slows the fish down and drives them nearer the river banks. Again, using the same terminology, we can say that the rock functions as a *lateral mytheme* — and, as happens with lateral and fricative phonemes — is in contrast with the *fricative mytheme* (in the case of fricatives, as the phoneticians explain, the tongue curves up at the sides to form a narrow passage), illustrated in the left section of Figure 26, which shows the water being forced through a narrow passage by bands of rock on either side, whereas the right-hand section shows it striking against a central obstacle, which divides it into two streams. In neither case is the obstacle absolute, like a waterfall; it is a semi-obstacle, congruous with the symplegades as regards the fricative mytheme, and with the swing as regards the lateral mytheme.

As linguists might also say, the two mythemes are vibrating or rolled: one along the vertical axis, and the other along the horizontal axis. But they can be differentiated from each other by their respective affinities with occlusion pure and simple, and the absence of occlusion. If the constriction producing the fricative mytheme — the narrow navigable channel cutting through a rock or a swamp — is carried to its extreme limit, it becomes equivalent to a waterfall as a form of total occlusion. So, in varying degrees, the falls and the channel are unmistakably connected with the symplegades. Moreover, according to M$_{700}$, the navigable channel was the result of a transformation of marshy symplegades. For the people living upstream, the falls prevent the arrival of salmon, just as a long way downstream the rocky symplegades act as a barrier to the country of the salmon.

The cosmic swing, on the contrary, is non-occlusive; while it existed, it formed a link between the sky and the earth, and on the earth itself, between widely distant mountains. This twofold function was only possible because of its longitudinal movement, which, in relation to its starting-point, caused it to diverge alternately in either direction, just as a river, coming up against a central obstacle, divides into two streams, which diverge to flow past simultaneously.

I have thus confirmed the existence of a system that, at an earlier stage (pp. 378–9), I could only suggest as a hypothesis. The complete group of relations is shown in diagrammatic form in Figure 28, which the reader

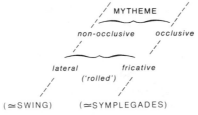

Figure 28. The system of obstacles

might like to compare with the diagrams on p. 339 of *RC* and p. 248 of *HA* in order to appreciate the conclusions that may appropriately be drawn. There is a contrast between the lateral movements of the swing and the vertical movements of the symplegades through their respective frequencies, with the result that the *slow/fast* opposition is present in the three cases.

The ultimately positive value of the semi-obstacle emerges very clearly from a Puget Sound myth (M_{711}; Haeberlin 1, p. 396), which envisages the complete absence of any obstacle only in order to reject the possibility as undesirable: the rivers might have flowed in both directions and this would have made navigation easier. But no sooner would the salmon have swum upstream than they would have come down again, and fishing would have been impossible. It is better, then, that rivers should flow only one way. It is striking to find applied to fish — in myths which establish such a close correspondence between the laws of fishing and those of exogamy — the same argument as was formulated in terms of matrimonial exchanges by South American myths, which also envisaged the possibility of rivers flowing both ways (cf. *OTM*, pp. 159–74, 180–81).

The tentative synthesis just suggested makes it possible to solve another problem that was raised on p. 428 by the reappearance, in this group of myths, of a character called Crane or Heron, divested, however, of the role of susceptible ferryman usually assigned to him in the myths of North America. We had already encountered the same problem in connection with other myths (see above, p. 318), and I remarked at that point that this ferryman operated as a partial conveyor or semi-conductor: he gets half his passengers over safely and drowns the other half during the crossing. Consequently, he too is a semi-obstacle placed along an axis which is perpendicular to the course of the river. But in the myths we are now considering the relevant axis, which is that of the ascent of the salmon and of the visits to the people living along the banks, becomes parallel to the course of the river. It is understandable, then, that the Crane or Heron character should love his function as a semi-obstacle, when this function occurs along an axis in opposition to that along which he normally operates; and why, along the latter, he should be replaced by Coyote's long penis copulating *trans flumen*, in the form, however, of a total conveyor, which is then changed into its opposite when the girls decline his ambiguous offer of communication: in the Thompson version M_{668c} (Teit 5, p. 298), Coyote makes the pretty bathing-girls a deliberately incomprehensible proposition: if they accept, he copulates with them across the river; if they refuse, he builds — also across the river — a rock barrier which prevents the salmon running upstream. When transposed to a different axis and given a different embodiment, the susceptible ferryman function is perceptible in Crane or Heron only because of the persistence of an ambiguity inherent in his original nature: either he is a great hunter, and this one skill (the reverse of the fisherman's) enables him to obtain exogamous wives from afar, whom he accepts as soon as they appear (M_{694}) — it will be remembered that the Cœur d'Alêne had to make a virtue of necessity, since they had no salmon — or, on the contrary, he is an indecisive bachelor unable to choose between many, immediately present, marriageable maidens (M_{696}).

This interpretation is confirmed by an important group of Plains myths (which also extends as far as the west coast, cf. M_{659}, M_{712}), that I have already used to solve another difficulty (see above, p. 338). In this group, the bird-nester story, still recognizable in the form of what I called (p. 342) its 'Potiphar transformation', moves from a vertical axis of disjunction to a horizontal axis of disjunction. On the pretext of gathering the eggs of water birds (instead of eaglets from the top of a tree), the bird-nester's father, brothers or companions leave the hero marooned on a remote island (cf. below, $M_{762-767}$; M_{769a-d}. Cf. also Caddo: Dorsey 8, pp. 26–7; Biloxi: Dorsey-Swanton, pp. 99–107). He returns from the island, before or after experiencing various adventures, on the back of an aquatic monster who, as a ferryman, proves to be highly susceptible to atmospheric disturbances and, in all other respects, in accordance with a prototype which, as I have already pointed out (*OTM*, pp. 444–6), is strictly the same in both the Plains myths of North America and the myths of the Amazon basin.

As has already been noted, these myths can only combine the bird-nester and the susceptible ferryman stories into a single narrative by converting the major axis of disjunction from the vertical to the horizontal. This being so, let us hark back to the very beginning of our enquiry. The helpful jaguar in M_{7-12}, who assists the hero in his *descent*, surely belongs to the same paradigm as the aquatic monster in the group {M_{460}, M_{469}, M_{503}, $M_{766-769}$, etc.}, who helps the hero *across*. Because of the change of axis, the 'ferryman' who operates between the high and the low must also change his nature: unlike his fellow ferryman operating along a horizontal axis, he is *non-susceptible*, a characteristic which I interpreted as a 'show of indifference' in the restricted paradigmatic context of the first volume (*RC*, pp. 81–3); this context can now legitimately be widened. In the Bororo myth (M_1), which is an inversion of the Ge myths (M_{7-12}) along a different axis (the axis of fire and water, the vertical axis remaining constant), the 'ferryman' role devolves on carrion vultures; they perform this function in respect of a character who, for his part, embodies the absence of susceptibility, since he is incapable of reacting when the birds devour his posterior.

Even without going back so far, anyone who has read the previous volume will be aware that the Salish myths present the problems in a manner very similar to their treatment in the Amazonian myths analysed in *OTM*. In both cases, the lake and river system, its intrinsic properties (such as the opposition between upstream and downstream with the ensuing practical consequences), and the natural accidents which characterize it at different points, provide a kind of grid which serves to code, in homogeneous terms, certain technical and economic particularities (navigation and fishing) of communities whose mode of life is associated with water, as well as other particularities connected rather with the social order, and chief amongst which are political relationships and the rules governing exogamy.

When I was considering these phenomena in the context of the Amazonian myths, they could all be reduced to one and the same pattern: an opposition between two types of marriage, one near (and in the extreme case, incestuous) and the other so remote that it could only be illustrated by exotic relationships, and even encounters with supernatural creatures (cf. *OTM*, pp. 135–69). Since then, we have frequently come across the same pattern in North America; in the Plains mythology, for example, the close wife, associated with agriculture, is contrasted with the distant wife, associated with hunting (*OTM*, pp. 314–17; 371–5); in the mythology of the north-west coast, Asdiwal's celestial wife is opposed to his countrywoman, whom he misguidedly prefers (L.-S. 6). Only a few examples are needed, then, to demonstrate how important a role the Salish and their neighbours assign to a hero who hesitates between two wives, one distant and one near, and whose adventures quickly assume a cosmological nature.

Like the Warrau of Venezuela (M_{406}; *OTM*, pp. 137–8), the Kwakiutl link up the pattern of the two wives with what I have called the 'Potiphar transformation'. In this case, the close wife is a relative, for instance, the elder brother's wife, with whom the younger brother has an illicit relationship. The husband, thirsting for vengeance, throws the traitor into the river and leaves him to drown. However, Thunder-Birds rescue him and he marries their daughter. He changes into an eagle, kills his elder brother, takes up his permanent abode with the Thunder-Birds and becomes their chief (M_{712}; Boas–Hunt 1, Part II, pp. 365–74). The Comox have a very similar story: the hero who has committed adultery is seized and thrown into the water. He is miraculously saved and marries the daughter of the Eagles. He brings her on a visit to his own people and, in spite of her warnings, he allows himself to be seduced by a village girl. His wife leaves him and he follows her; she grows weary of his importuning, turns round towards him and gives him a baleful glare; he sinks below the waters, and this time is drowned (M_{713a}; Hill-Tout 1, pp. 54–7). For a reason which will soon become clear, it should be noted at this point that this tragic tale begins and ends with what might be called a journey in an anti-canoe. At the outset, the hero is thrown into the river, after being glued with pitch to the bed in which the adultery has been committed; he drifts along until the heat of the sun melts the pitch, and thus frees him from the uncomfortable craft. At the conclusion, when his Eagle-wife leaves him, she does not deign to use the canoe but walks on the waters. Her grief-stricken husband does likewise, and it is only when she turns round and looks at him that he feels the water is no longer supporting him and sinks to the bottom. The Lilloet have an almost identical story (M_{713b}; Teit 2, pp. 319–21), whereas the Bella Coola make their hero hesitate between the love of a she-wolf and that of a fellow countrywoman (M_{711a}; Boas 12, pp. 103–10), or explain that the disappearance of salmon was caused by Raven's infidelity to his wife Fish, whom he left for a fellow countrywoman (M_{714b}; Boas 13, p. 246).

It will be remembered that the canoe journey of the sun and moon, which symbolizes simultaneously diurnal and nocturnal periodicity, seasonal periodicity and the periodic return of fish, is the operator used by the Amazonian myths to reconcile the contradiction between close and distant marriages (*OTM*, pp. 170–95). The same motif, with exactly the same characteristics, can be found in the mythology and ritual of the Salish. To be accurate, the South American myths were never absolutely clear on this point, and I could only infer from them that the sun and the moon must be the prototypes of the passengers in the canoe. However, the Salish go much further in this direction than the Amazonian Indians.

When, in 1808, Simon Fraser sailed down the river which now bears his name, the Thompson Indians, who had never seen a white man before, thought he was the sun and called him by that name (Boas 4, p. 64). There exists a mythic account of the shipwreck in which Fraser lost his life, and Teit remarks in connection with it (5, p. 416 and n. 1) that the incident may have become confused in the minds of the Thompson Indians with a real mythological tale about the moon: 'When the new moon appears with the whole disk dimly visible, they say that it is the moon holding her canoe.' The shipwreck in which Fraser died is described by the Thompson Indians as follows ($M_{715a, b, c}$; *ibid.*, p. 416): Long after Coyote had taken part in the organization of the universe, he reappeared on the river in a canoe with six companions: the Sun, the Moon, the Morning Star, Kokwela (the demiurge who was the son of a *Peucedanum* root, cf. above, p. 442), the Diver and the Arrow-Arm Man. Moon, who was steering the craft from the stern, sank with the canoe (cf. M_{354}; *OTM*, pp. 24–60), and the other passengers swam to a rock overhanging the river. At night Moon reappears with his canoe. Others say that the canoe sank with all its passengers, and that the Morning Star was seen to emerge at dawn, to be followed by the Sun at midday. According to a final version, there were two canoes; the first was carrying seven celestial characters: Sun, Moon, Morning Star and another four who remain unnamed and may have been stars; the second contained seven mythological beings: Coyote, Nli'kisentem (in other words, our old friend the Bird-nester, whom we should not be surprised to find in such good company), Kokwela, who has already been mentioned, a character called 'the Ancient One', and lastly three individuals called Ntcémka, Skwia'xenemux, and Enmui'pem. All came ashore, sat on a rock and looked into the distance until the evening. We know from another context (Boas 4, pp. 49–50) that Ntcémka is 'a man of very large stature and a great hunter and warrior', and that Skwia'xenemux is the name of the Arrow-Arm character (who is also a hunter and warrior and able to fly like a bird), mentioned in the other version. A Lilloet myth (M_{715d}; Teit 2, p. 350) mentions him along with Coyote, the Sun, the Moon and Muepem, who is probably identical with the Enmui'pem of the Thompson; as the term means 'diver' in Lilloet, it is probable that the character merges with the Diver in the first version (cf. also Boas 13, pp. 19, 45, 56, 63, 76; Hill-Tout 2, p. 360; 7, p. 518).[5]

As regards the respective positions occupied by the canoe passengers, the details are particularly interesting in that the Coast Salish, like the Amazonians and the Great Lakes Indians (*OTM*, p. 149), had very definite ideas about the placing of the sexes when a man and a woman travelled together in the same craft: 'following the custom, [the woman] would always take the stern' (Adamson, p. 284). The Lilloet, however, contravene this rule during the bride's honeymoon journey to her husband's village (Hill-Tout 3, p. 132; 6, pp. 184, 185, 187). An important Humptulips myth, which I do not propose to analyse in detail, except to point out that it inverts the usual values of the close wife and the distant wife – since it concerns a heroine who is more attached to her brother than to an exotic lover – starts with a young girl's impregnation in a canoe, an action which is mistakenly attributed to her brother, and ends with them being turned into birds: so

---

[5] Given these equivalences, as well as the bird-nester's and his persecutor's respective lunar and solar affinities, it should follow that the character known as 'the Ancient One' can only correspond to the Morning Star in the other canoe in M_{715c}, and in the single canoe in M_{715a}.

they return to a state of nature and announce that they will live 'homeless and eat their food raw' (M_{716a}; Adamson, pp. 284–93). The auto-fecundation is the work of a supernatural character, described as a bird from the north, who brings it about by creating a thick fog. The moisture collects on the surface of the haliotis-shell nose-ring worn by the girl and drips on her lips. She conceives by licking up the moisture with her tongue. The extraordinary nature of this incident is clarified by a Coast Chehalis myth, in which the hero escapes from the amorous attentions of the Daughters of the Night, 'from whose noses hung an elongation shaped like a male organ' (M_{716b}; Adamson, p. 85). In a canoe sailing *along* the river (Chinoose Creek, according to the text), this ultra-short penis – anatomically contiguous with the mouth, which here plays the part of a sexual orifice for fecundation – is consequently opposed to the long penis which, instead of the promised food, Coyote throws *across* the river in the direction of a distant vagina. Furthermore, the incident concerns a chief's daughter who is both passionately fond of hunting (she learns to shoot with a bow almost before reaching puberty) and also of her brother's company, since she never leaves his side, even when they are travelling in a canoe. All this is strictly against the rules, for the Coast Salish kept a close watch over their high-born, marriageable girls; they would even seclude them from childhood onwards in an enclosure inside the house. Being forced to remain in a sitting or squatting position with absolutely nothing to do, the girls grew pale and weak and became incapable of any kind of work; when released, they could hardly walk. In the eyes of their suitors, their continued inactivity marked them out as aristocratic and gave them a languid charm (Barnett 3, p. 180).

Consequently, even in an 'excessive' narrative like that of the Humptulips myth, the canoe journey retains the character that we discovered it to have in South America; it symbolizes the striking of a balance between the near and far. The regressive nature of the myth, which returns the main characters to the animal state and deprives them of domestic life and the enjoyment of cooking fire (fire being congruous with the canoe, through the transformation *earth/sky* $\Rightarrow$ *near/far*, cf. *OTM*, p. 187, where the point was established), can be explained by the fact that, in this particular instance, the near was too near – the sister is brought too close to her brother for tasks unsuited to her sex – and the far too far; it is a northern icebound country, inhabited by man-killers, and the heroine, having changed into a horned and hairy aquatic monster, never returns from it . . .

In all other contexts, the canoe journey remains linked to the normal manifestations of spatial/temporal periodicity. It was while sailing up

Fraser River in a canoe that the six Lilloet Transformers carried out their tasks and established order in the world (M_{700}). It was also in a canoe that Raven, already master of daylight, embarked with his four servants, Worm, Flea, Louse and Little-Louse, to go and seize fire held captive by the fish. But for the daylight, he would not have seen the smoke which indicated where the fire was kept. Raven then sold fire to every family that wished for it, and each paid him by giving him a young wife (M_{717a}; Teit 2, pp. 300–30). In this case, exogamy in exchange for cooking fire stolen from the fish replaces exogamy in exchange for fish.

The theme of temporal periodicity, which we know to be linked with the periodicity of matrimonial exchanges (*OTM*, p. 158), reappears in another Lilloet myth (M_{718}; Elliott, pp. 176–7), where two cousins, sons of the brothers Sun and Moon respectively, come down to earth and undertake a canoe journey, during which they accomplish many marvels, in the company of a man they have raised from the dead, as well as of Beaver who had undertaken to chew a hole for them in the celestial vault. Eventually they go back to their celestial progenitors. The Cœur d'Alène also have a myth (M_{719}; Boas 4, p. 126), in which the characters connected with the canoe are changed into celestial bodies. Five men are making a {bark} canoe. One is at the prow, one at the stern, two at the sides, and the fifth is 'standing between one of the end men and one of the side men'. In this position they are all transformed into stars, perhaps the constellation the Thompson call 'Bark Canoe', that is Orion (Teit 6, p. 179). In connection, precisely, with myths relating to the canoe, we have observed the same transformation in South America, where it led from the moon and the sun to Orion (*OTM*, pp. 89–92).

In the Puget Sound area, several Salish groups – Squamish, Duwamish, Snuqualmi, Snohomish and Skokomish – gave ritualistic expression to the canoe journey. During a ceremony performed in winter, and which is known only through the accounts given by informants, the shamans and their assistants would set up fretted panels painted with emblematic patterns. These panels were meant as the framework of one or two symbolic canoes, in which they would take up their positions and pretend to paddle to the land of the dead, in order to retrieve the vital force, stolen by the ghosts from some unlucky man or invalid (Dorsey 10; Haeberlin 2; Waterman 5; M. W. Smith 2, 5). The timing of the ceremony can be explained by the belief that in the country of the dead day and night, the rising and ebbing of the tides, winter and summer, are reversed in relation to the world of the living. Winter is therefore summer in the Beyond, so that souls or guardian spirits, beguiled by the pleasant weather, are easier to capture.

Haeberlin, although unable to be more explicit (2, p. 257), points out that 'there seems to be a certain association between the course of the sun and the journey of the shamans to the land of the dead'. The image of the canoe associated with a ritualistic celebration must be deeply rooted in the American mind, since it also occurs among the Ojibwa. Two of the main officiants in the brotherhood known as Midéwiwin were called, respectively, *naganid* (foremost man) and *wedaged* (hindmost man), which were the terms commonly used in connection with positions in the canoe (Landes, pp. 54, 114–15, 119, 240–41; Hoffman 1, p. 84).

However, it was among the Bella Coola, who lived far to the north of the other Salish, among the different communities of the north-west Pacific coast, that the canoe journey motif reached its highest development both in myths and rites. Atlquntäm, one of the chief figures in an extremely complex pantheon, was connected with the Sun, 'which he can enter and use as if it were his canoe . . . or self-propelling, radiant boat with windows through which he looks forth' (McIlwraith, p. 33). One myth (M_{720a}; Boas 12, pp. 38–40) relates how the quadrupeds and the birds set out to achieve the conquest of salmon in a canoe in the stern of which sat a divinity called the Hermaphrodite.[6] Each bird captured one particular species of salmon, after being warned by Mink to be sure, in each case, to obtain a male and a female. On their return they released the fish in the rivers. The Indians believe that the beneficent canoe comes back every year from the land of the salmon, stays with them for about nine months and then goes back again. It is then that the canoe bringing the winter ceremonial arrives, carrying all the divinities of the pantheon who normally live in the House of Myths. When this second canoe leaves, the first one comes back from the land of the salmon.

However, the mutual convertibility of the horizontal axis leading to the land of the salmon and the vertical axis at the summit of which the gods live in the House of Myths in the sky is demonstrated in another version (M_{720b}; Boas 13, pp. 252–3). Five brothers, who are running away from an ogress, whom the youngest has imprudently helped across the river and who, during the night, sucks out the brains of sleeping humans by means of her extensible, tube-like mouth (an anti-symmetrical image of the long penis through the following transformations: *active crossing of the river* ⇒ *passive; man* ⇒ *woman; 'consumed' penis* ⇒ *consuming mouth*), escape and ascend into

---

[6] Like the moon in the Thompson versions $M_{715a, b, c}$. In connection with the hermaphroditic moon, cf. *OTM*, pp. 176–7, 195, etc. The Bella Coola Hermaphrodite could perhaps correspond to the 'resuscitated dead man' – death and resuscitation being another mark of ambivalence also illustrated by the moon – mentioned in the Lilloet myth M_{718}, see above, p. 450.

the sky where they meet Atlkundam (*sic*), master of the solar canoe, and the ogress's son. They have first to pass through the Symplegades which, being situated in the sky, have also undergone a change of axis. On hearing about his mother's misdeeds, Atlkundam kills her, burns her body on a pyre, and causes mosquitoes to spring from the ashes. While the youngest brother is engaged in seducing Atlkundam's wife, thereby – contrary to the European belief – causing the husband to be unlucky in gambling, the other brothers challenge him and win salmon from him. At the same time, they obtain an elixir of long life made from the wife's urine, and, on their return to earth, use it to revive those of their relatives who had been killed by the ogress.

It follows from this whole body of remarks that the Salish canoe, carrying divinities, the foremost of whom are the sun and the moon, belongs, as a mytheme, to a horizontal axis which links the near and the far, and is convertible, as in the myths of tropical America, into a vertical axis linking the earth and the sky. It can be noted in support of this generalization that M_{720b} reproduces a sequence of the Warrau myth M_{28}, in which a fish-eating ogress follows the bed of a river instead of crossing it, pursues brothers, one of whom is sitting astride a branch overhanging the river, and tries in vain to catch his reflection in the water (*RC*, pp. 109–10). M_{28} is a myth explaining the origin of stars which inhabit the high, just as M_{720a} is a myth explaining the origin of salmon which inhabit a 'far', commutable with the high in the variant M_{720b}.

We can conclude, then, that certain mythic patterns, fundamental to American Indian thought, and the adumbration of which, even as hypothetical possibilities, required a lengthy analysis of a whole set of South American myths, are now directly verifiable and assume a tangible form in North American myths which express them 'in clear'. The parallel I have just drawn has, then, an experimental value, in that it confirms the virtues of the method used and corroborates the relevance of its results.

PART SIX GOING BACK TO THE SOURCES

'Wie macht' ich den andren,
der nicht mehr ich,
und aus sich wirkte,
was ich nur will?

> R. Wagner, *Die Walküre*,
> Act II, Scene II

1 Fire and Rain

In tal guisa i primi poeti teologi si finsero la prima favola divina, la più grande di quante mai se ne finsero appresso, cioè Giove, re e padre degli uomini e degli dèi, ed in atto di fulminante; si popolare, perturbante ed insegnativa, che'ssi stessi, che sel finsero, sel credettero e con ispaventose religioni, le quali appresso si mostreranno, il temettero, il riverirono e l'osservarono.

G. Vico, *La Scienza nuova seconda*, II, I, I, Ed. Nicolini, Bari, 1967, p. 146

The ogress in M_{720b} creates darkness by quenching the flames of a domestic fire in order to facilitate the perpetration of her crimes, and her celestial son, master of the solar canoe, punishes her by burning her on a pyre. Having been neutralized on earth, cooking fire is inverted, then, into destructive celestial fire, in a myth which attributes to salmon a celestial, and therefore imaginary origin, whereas other myths (M_{375}, M_{382}, M_{720a}), which keep closer to experience, locate the origin of salmon far to the west, in the sea from which the fish do, in fact, come every year. At the cost of over-simplifying, one could say that Salish thought establishes an inversely proportional relationship between the origin of cooking fire and the origin of fish intended as food: depending on the particular instances and the tribal groups, salmon are said to come from the 'far' and fire from the high; or conversely, fire is said to come from the 'far' and salmon from the high. We shall see, however, that in reality things are more complex since certain myths attribute the same distant origin to both fire and salmon.

We have already encountered an example of the common origin of fire and fish in a Lilloet myth (M_{717a}, see above, p. 452), where Raven, who has become master of daylight through stealing it from his friend Seagull, sees a column of smoke indicative of the whereabouts of the primordial fire, which is jealously guarded by the fish. Raven approaches in a canoe, captures a little girl and demands fire as her ransom. He then shares it with those families who agree to give him a wife in exchange.

Let me mention briefly a number of variations on this theme. The Indians of the lower reaches of the Fraser River relate (M_{717b}; Boas 13, p. 43) how Beaver and Woodpecker robbed the chief of the salmon of both fire and his baby daughter who was still in her cradle; when the child and the cradle were thrown into the river, salmon appeared. Beaver then gave fire to the spirits, from whom Mink in turn stole it, after cutting off their chief's head; he later gave it back in exchange for the fire-drill. Two versions belonging to the Nanaimo, who are Vancouver Island Salish ($M_{717c, d}$; *ibid.*, pp. 54–5), attribute the possession of the first fire to an unknown people, or to the spirits of the dead. In both cases, Mink kidnaps a baby and, as its ransom, demands either fire or the fire-producing implement. A Comox variant (M_{717e}; *ibid.*, pp. 80–81) replaces Mink by a deer, who obtains possession of fire or the fire-drill after passing through symplegades. The Kwakiutl (M_{717f}; *ibid.*, p. 158) say that Mink stole the child of the chief of the spirits and gave him back in exchange for fire. According to the Klallam (M_{717g}; Gunther 2, pp. 142, 146), fire, and fine weather which is favourable to fishing, were obtained from the dead as a ransom for one or several children kidnapped by the demiurge. A Skagit myth from the north of Puget Sound comes closer to the Lilloet version (M_{717h}; Haeberlin 1, pp. 391–3); according to it, Raven and Mink stole daylight from the people of the east.

The Thompson (M_{663b}; Teit 5, pp. 338–9; cf. above, p. 346) refer to a very remote period when wood did not burn and fire was in the possession of a community living near the estuary of the Fraser River. The people living upstream sent Beaver, Weasel and Eagle to steal it by means of a ruse (see below, pp. 484–5). On their return, Beaver explained how to light a fire, Eagle how to roast meat, and Weasel how to cook by throwing red-hot stones into water. A particle of fire was inserted into all the different kinds of wood; since that time, all wood can burn. Another version (M_{663c}; *ibid.*, pp. 229–30) states that before the theft of fire, the sun was very much hotter than it is now; food was exposed to the sun's rays and people prayed to the sun when they wanted their food to be cooked (cf. *RC*, p. 289, n. 2). The Nicola River Thompson relate (M_{663d}; Boas 4, p. 2) how Coyote sees from the top of a mountain far away to the south the light of the fire of which an unknown people are the masters. He travels to their country with a few companions and deliberately allows his head-dress made of wood shavings to catch fire when he goes too close to the flames; then he runs away. The masters of fire cause a great wind to rise and the fire spreads all over the country. Coyote retaliates by releasing heavy rainfall, which puts out the fire. Since then, there have been fire and smoke together everywhere in the world; and, just as in the myth the wind makes fire blaze up, people today blow on fire to make it burn more brightly.

Unlike the preceding myths, certain Thompson versions (M_{663e}; Hill-Tout, pp. 561–3) place the theft of fire in the far north and, significantly no doubt, credit it to Beaver and not Coyote, thus linking up with the Plateau Salish myths, according to which the conquest of fire took place in the sky (see below, pp. 461–3), that is, was an event relating to the 'above', not to the 'far', It is no less significant that, contrary to the myths concerned with the celestial theft of fire, whose regressive function – in view of the primordial continuity of the different natural kingdoms – I have stressed and shall stress again (see above, p. 398; below, pp. 464–8), the versions just mentioned credit Beaver with a further exploit after the theft of fire; he obtains a magic blanket (M_{663f}; *ibid.*, pp. 563–4) decorated with paintings representing all the utensils, tools and weapons which were part of Indian culture before the arrival of the white man. Beaver carefully cut out these patterns and his companions used them for the making of every type of object; but the owner of the blanket took his revenge and changed Beaver into the animal he has been ever since.

More clearly still than the Thompson (cf. M_{698a-e}, above, pp. 431–2), the Shuswap establish a link between the conquest of fire and the conflict between the animal species for the possession of salmon. As in the Lilloet myth M_{616a}, the land animal heroes of the Shuswap myths (M_{621a-b}; Teit 1, p. 669) steal fire from the fish. At the same time, they kidnap a pregnant woman whom they turn into their slave, and who soon gives birth to a son. Having been informed by his mother of his origins and the misfortunes of his people, he asks for, and obtains, thunder and lightning as his guardians; with the help of celestial and destructive fire, he exterminates the murderers of his people.

A vast group of myths, covering an area which stretches from the Chinook in the south to the Nez Percé in the east and the Thompson in the north, and is also known to the Coast Salish, deals with a triangular conflict, in which humans, fish and land animals fight over a young Indian girl who has been kidnapped by a Salmon and whom land animals – usually Wolves – abduct in turn when she pays a visit to her native village (Cœur d'Alêne: Reichard 3, pp. 119–21; Sanpoil: Ray 2, pp. 142–5; Thompson: Teit 5, pp. 231–2, 236–41. Cf. also Haeberlin 1, pp. 383–4; Jacobs 1, pp. 159–63; Boas 10, p. 77; Phinney, p. 222; Adamson, p. 110; etc.). After being eventually defeated, the Wolves assume their animal nature, become harmless to humans, give up cooking fire and eat their food raw (Reichard, *loc. cit.*; Adamson, pp. 191, 307, 337).[1]

Unfortunately, it would not be possible to make a thorough study of this group of myths, already briefly mentioned in connection with M_{698c} (see above, p. 431), without going into other problems that I have alluded to more than once,[2] only to explain why I must regretfully leave them on one side, at least until some future date. At this point I shall make only two observations. First, the war between the prototypes of the animal species and humans, following the kidnapping of a human girl by a fish, is obviously the counterpart of the peaceful sharing out of the animal species among humans, which assigned a particular food to each group (salmon to some, goats and mountain-sheep to others) after a test, the object of which was to separate out those who agree from those who refuse to exchange their daughters *among themselves*. In opposition to the abduction of a human girl by a salmon, we have the granting of salmon to humans, provided they agree that henceforth women will be exchanged, not stolen. The myths hypostatize the terms of these alternatives by envisaging two extreme cases: one in which the theft of a woman seems all the more outrageous in that it is committed by animals, not humans; and another in which the exchanging of wives, the reverse of abduction, is established and maintained within the confines of the human.

Secondly, the opposition between theft and exchange can be fitted into a larger system along with another motif establishing a correlation between salmon and fire, which are respectively the raw material and the means of cooking, and which both originate from the world of the dead or of the spirits. In this system, food and fire are commutable: their presence, once achieved, makes exchanges possible, just as their absence, when it has to be suffered, requires theft to make good the lack. The child of the masters of terrestrial fire, i.e., the spirits of the dead — who is the counterpart of the son born of the union between a salmon and a human girl, the master of a celestial, destructive fire which brings about the death of his abductors — and who is himself abducted and then ransomed at the cost of fire, would seem consequently to be deducible, through a series of transformations, from a global armature in which, in view of the compact and limited distribution of the motif, he can be assigned a derivative position in relation to the more general theme of the theft of fire pure and simple.

---

[1] The formula is reversed farther south in Tillamook mythology (M_{652}), in which the wolves are masters of an inextinguishable fire.

[2] See above, pp. 361, n. 3, 368, 382, n. 10, 387.

Those myths which locate the wresting of fire from the spirits of the dead or from fish in some distant place belong mainly to the area between the north of the Georgia Strait and the southern shore of the Juan de Fuca Strait. All around the area are to be found other myths, according to which the conquest of fire took place in the sky. These myths are all the more certainly in a relationship of symmetry with the preceding ones in that, for the latter, the initial absence of fire is to be explained by the original incombustibility of wood. But, according to the former, the reverse situation prevailed at the beginning: the people of olden times had the benefit of continuous fire, which burnt without wood, and they lost it through their own imprudence.

The Tillamook, whose isolated position in relation to the rest of the Salish family perhaps explains why their myths retain many archaic features, believe that this miraculous fire existed at a time when the rules governing exogamy also operated in reverse:

M 722. *Tillamook. 'The miraculous fire'*

'In myth-age times, women were always hunting husbands.' One of them noticed one day that smoke was coming out of the roof of a house; she concluded that the occupier possessed fire and decided to marry him.

In the hope of being accepted, she brought him a large basket filled with edible roots. The man was undoubtedly a good fisherman because the house was full of salmon. When the visitor entered, she saw no one, but a fish kept dropping down on to her head from where it was hanging on a beam, although she was always very careful to put it back. She did not realize that the fire burning in the centre of the house was telling her that she could cook the fish and eat it; for the fire was none other than the main occupant's mother. As the young woman was hungry, she roasted some of her roots in the hot ashes. The fire-mother in turn, believing mistakenly that the stranger was offering her food, ate the roots – in other words, she burnt them. The woman became angry; she poked the fire and scattered it all about. The fire started to go out, but she managed with great difficulty to get it to burn up again. Meanwhile the man returned, explained the reason for all these mysterious happenings, married the visitor and taught her how to obtain ready prepared meals. All she had to do was to say, 'Mother, cook this for me!' He also explained to her that this would involve no hard work on her part. She could obtain from the fire-mother as many baskets as she liked merely by burning reeds and spruce roots, the usual raw material used in the making of mats and baskets (E. D. Jacobs, pp. 93–5).

Since the myth states clearly that, by scattering the hot ashes with the poker, the woman nearly blinded the fire-mother, a relation of symmetry exists with myths in which the hero, in the sky and not on the earth, cures his supernatural protectresses of blindness by piercing eyes for them with the tip of his penis (M_{600f}; see above, p. 404; as regards the phallic connotation of the poker, cf. below, p. 529). And in fact, the situation he encounters in the sky, where he shivers with cold and where basketwork objects — symbols of culture, like domestic fire — attack him when he tries to use them to prepare a steam-bath in which to get warm, is diametrically opposed to the one described by M_{722}: here we have a situation in which culture is self-engendering, thanks to a maternally solicitous fire which warms its children, feeds them, and without requiring any effort on their part, supplies them with as many ready-made household articles as they need. A second correlation can also be seen — although along a different axis — between M_{722} and a Nez Percé myth (M_{655a}), in which the hero marries mountain-sheep women whose 'children' (wooden spits) he kills through his clumsiness when he tries to use them as pokers. This myth, too, is a transformation of the bird-nester myth (see above, pp. 327–8).

The Green River and Puyallup Indians of Puget Sound have similar stories:

$M_{723a, b, c}$. *Puget Sound. 'The conquest of fire'*
In former times, people enjoyed a fire which never went out. It burned without wood and its human embodiment was the mother of a great fisherman called Land-Otter. A young woman went to his house and married him. One day, although she had been warned not to do so by her husband, she used a poker. The fire went out because the wife had unwittingly killed her husband's mother, and at the same time all the fires in the world also died down. No one had fire any more. A great meeting was called and it was decided to organize an expedition to sky country to get fire.

Only a 'little bird' succeeded in shooting an arrow into the celestial vault, where it became implanted; then it shot others, all of which connected to form a kind of chain. When the latter reached the earth, Raven climbed up it and made steps so that all the people could follow him. Since Beaver seemed to be the only one who would not laugh even when tickled, he was told to pretend to be dead and allow himself to be captured by the masters of fire. While the latter were busy skinning their game, the attackers rushed at them and killed them all. Beaver seized the fire and placed a small piece in every species of tree. The conquering animals came back down to earth, but the ladder broke and two snakes of different species fell, one into Yakima country, the other in the Puget Sound area. The latter, a rattlesnake, was thus able to make himself teeth from poisoned arrowheads, since the Puget Sound Indians had more poisoned weapons than other people. Snakes of this species have an understanding with the Puget Sound Indians. Rattlesnakes will not attack an Indian from Puget Sound, but will molest an Indian from the other area (Ballard 1, pp. 51–4).

I shall return (see below, p. 467) to the creating of the ladder, which the myths explain by the grotesque and clumsy behaviour of Bear Woman and Cougar Woman (M_{723c}) – in some versions, the sisters Bear Woman and Grizzly – or by an over-energetic triumphal dance performed by the four shamans, Black Bear, Grizzly, Cougar and Wild Cat ($M_{724a, b}$; Haeberlin 1, pp. 389–91, 411–12). I shall also return to the episode in which certain animals were slowed down or dispersed by this accident – the snake and the lizard, according to M_{724b} – and to other peculiar features of this version, which is of Snohomish origin and in which the inhabitants of the sky start the hostilities by capturing the only carpenter (a canoe maker) who existed on earth at that time, because he persisted in working at night and thus disturbed them by the din he made. So, the noisy carpenter, who upsets the alternation of day and night, is a counterpart to the noisy scullion, who provided the theme and the title of Section 3 of Part IV.

An initial expedition to the sky country to recover the irreplaceable craftsman revealed to the brothers Summer-Robin and Winter-Robin that the celestial inhabitants possessed fire, which at that time was unknown on earth. Hence a second expedition for the conquest of fire which is as successful as the first: after ensuring the liberation of their carpenter, on condition that he will stop working at night, the mythic animals, the predecessors of the human race, obtain cooking fire and the boats they need for travelling long distances in order to fish and hunt water fowl. In the Skagit version, M_{721a}, Woodpecker and his grandmother Snail are given, respectively, the tasks of making, then strengthening, the chain of arrows.

To keep for the moment purely to birds, we can see that we are dealing with several species. The versions $M_{723b, c}$ are not specific about the identity of the bird which connected the chain of arrows; in M_{723c} (Ballard 1, p. 53) it is called *tsitses*, and is described as 'the smallest bird of all'.

A River Cowlitz myth, recorded in the Sahaptin dialect but probably of Salish origin (M_{725}, Jacobs 1, pp. 145–6), states that the task of making the chain of arrows was shared by two very similar little birds, the Wren and another called *t'si'datat*. This duality, which was already apparent in M_{723b}, but in a less marked form, is also evident between the 'little bird', the hero of that myth, and Raven; between Woodpecker and Snail his grandmother in M_{724a}; and between the two robins in M_{724b}. On the other hand, the Klikitat, who are neighbours of the Cowlitz, say that *one bird only*, the sapsucker – a small woodpecker of the *Sphyrapicus* genus (Bent, *Woodpeckers*, pp. 145, 151, 154; Godfrey, pp. 278–80) – has the task of fixing *two* chains of arrows to the sky in parallel, like the sides of a ladder (M_{726}; Jacobs 3, pp. 175–81).

Let us turn now to the Plateau Salish. In the mythology of the Kalispel, or Pend d'Oreilles (M_{727}; Boas 4, p. 118), Wren makes the chain of arrows which Grizzly Bear breaks; as a result of the breaking, Flying Squirrel acquires his membranes, and the Sucker fish (*Catostomus*) has his bones broken into tiny pieces, and this explains why bones are found in all parts of his flesh now; another fish ('whitefish': *Coregonus?*) puckers up his mouth in fear, which explains why to this day he has a small, round, puckered mouth.[3]

According to the Sanpoil (M_{728a}; Boas 4, pp. 107–108), after torrential rain which puts out all the fires, the animals go up into the sky the following spring to bring back fire. The Chickadee (*Parus* sp.) shoots the arrows; Musk-rat, Beaver and Eagle steal the fire. Since Grizzly, on account of his weight, has broken the ladder, the animals are taken back to earth, each on the back of a bird. Coyote, who has stayed above, makes himself wings and becomes a bat. The Sucker fish breaks its bones, which accounts for the many bones in its flesh. Very similar variants ($M_{728b, c}$; Ray 2, pp. 152–7) add that the celestial people urinate on the thieves to try to put out the fire they have stolen. In consequence of which, the latter, who have already gained possession of fire, invent garments which will protect them from the rain, as well as the art of building up food reserves for use during bad weather.

In addition to M_{728}, the Sanpoil have another more complex version:

M_{729}. *Sanpoil. 'The theft of fire'*

Chickadee, on his way to a big gathering where, so he had been told, people intended to shoot arrows at the sky, was jeered at by Coyote. Regarding this as a provocation, he killed him, but Fox quickly brought his companion back to life.

---

[3] Coregonids have such small mouths that they can swallow only minute creatures and plankton.

During a second encounter, Coyote challenged Chickadee in a gambling game, and won all his weapons and all his garments. A little while later, he cooked the two children of the Grouse or Prairie Chickens, because they only grunted instead of replying to his questions. Chickadee, who had then arrived on the scene, promised the weeping parents that he would resuscitate their children, provided they helped him to recover all that Coyote had taken from him.

The Birds set up an ambush along the road taken by Coyote, and frightened him by suddenly flying out in front of his face. He lost his balance and fell to his death in a gully. Once again, Fox revived him, but Chickadee managed to rescue his weapons and clothes, after which he took part in the competition and succeeded unaided in implanting in the celestial vault the first of the arrows to form a chain which the other animals completed.

The great ascent began. Grizzly was the last to climb but, as he was carrying a great deal of food for himself, he was too heavy: he broke the ladder and had to remain below. The other animals, who had failed to make such provision, found nothing to eat in the sky.[4] Starving, and without a ladder, they assumed the form of various objects and floated slowly back down to earth. Only two pairs of comrades remained in the sky: Beaver and Woodpecker on the one hand, Dog and Faeces on the other. Dog ate his companion and went back down to earth. The other two stole fire, but it was put out by a flood – all except one ember, which a magpie managed to save.

In order to escape from his pursuers, Woodpecker hid behind a pile of branches where he was found by an old terrestrial woman. At this time, Woodpecker was red all over: 'He was the king of small birds.' The old woman married him to her grand-daughter, but as a son-in-law she found him too pretty. So she lit a great fire of pitchwood, and the wind carried black smoke to the place where Woodpecker was sitting. He was soon covered with soot, and wondered how he could save his bright feathers: but he was only able to protect his head. This explains why he now has a red head, while all his other feathers are black (Ray 2, pp. 157–60).

---

[4] It would seem, then, that this version is dealing with the origin of food supplies to be taken on a journey; these should be adequate but not excessive, unlike the winter foodstocks mentioned in the other Sanpoil version (M_{728a}; see above, p. 464), and which raise no problem of limitation. The contrast between the two types of foodstocks can perhaps be explained by the fact that the hero of one version is Wren and of the other Chickadee, two birds associated respectively with the bad and the good seasons (see below, pp. 486–7, 495–6).

The regressive nature of the Kalispel and Sanpoil myths, which is already obvious from this last episode, is also indicated by the observation that, in the mythic age, the animal species were not only more beautiful than they are now, but more numerous too. Many were destroyed by the sky people and transformed into stars; those we have today represent only the survivors of the war (Boas 4, p. 118, n. 2). The Okanagon held the same belief, and also made Chickadee responsible for the chain of arrows. However, they attributed the breaking to a quarrel between Black Bear and Grizzly Bear about their respective weights ($M_{730a, b}$; Boas 4, pp. 85, 92).

A third Okanagon version (M_{731}; Hill-Tout 8, p. 146) calls the bird who made the chain of arrows *tsiskākena*. So again it is the Chickadee, as is confirmed in more recent versions ($M_{732a, b}$; Cline, pp. 218–22), where the native name of this bird is transcribed as *tcuckakína*. In this version, when the two pairs of friends are left in the sky, Water Snake eats Frog, and Dog eats Faeces. In the Sanpoil versions, only the first pair is featured, and again Water Snake eats Frog. In both cases the Fish break their bones or their skulls in falling, hence the nature of their bones and the strange shape of the mouth of Catfish, and of the head of Sucker.

On the other hand, it may be that, in an older version (M_{733a}; Gatschet 2, pp. 137–9), Wren retained his role as heroic bird. This, at least, is what Boas says (9, p. 283), and he must have had his reasons. But, in Gatschet's text, the bird is identified as *Zonotrichia intermedia*, and is therefore a sparrow. On the other hand, the native word *tskan* or *tseskan* is more like the word for Chickadee quoted in the preceding paragraph, and Gatschet's description, 'a black-headed bird with white markings on the sides of the head', could apply equally to the Chickadee or to certain sparrows characterized, but to a lesser degree, by the same contrast between black and white. Although the bird known as the Chickadee is the same throughout America (see below, p. 437), uncertainties such as these show the advisability of caution as regards the exact identity of the animals mentioned in the myths.

Be that as it may, the bird in M_{733a}, like the Chickadee according to the Sanpoil (M_{729}), possesses a bow and arrows of exceptional power, to which he owes his success; Coyote and the Grouse involve him in the same adventures as those attributed to the Chickadee in the Sanpoil myth. This is also the case in a Kalispel myth (M_{733b}; Boas 4, pp. 114–15), which ends with Coyote's death at the hands of the Grouse, and with his second resurrection.

I have already commented on the Thompson myths in which fire is stolen from afar ($M_{663b, c}$, see above, p. 458). These Indians also have myths which make no mention of the conquest of fire, but in which the earth people nevertheless make war on the inhabitants of the sky, but for different reasons: through love of adventure, or because of their warlike temperament (M$_{734a}$; Teit 5, p. 334) or from a desire to avenge the abduction of a woman (M$_{734b}$; *ibid.*, p. 246). In this last mentioned version, the earth people include several birds, since the text refers to Swan as the wronged husband, and to Wren as the sole maker of the chain of arrows. In a shorter version (M$_{734c}$; Boas 13, p. 17), the birds are even the members of the terrestrial community responsible for the opening of hostilities.

The sky people, on the other hand, include Grizzly Bears, Black Bears and Deer; this involves a radical inversion of the previously studied myths, in which Black and Grizzly Bears represented the heaviest earth-dwellers, and were responsible for the breaking of the ladder, and consequently debarred from the sky. The two Thompson versions both stress the fact that the earth people were routed and forced to beat a disorderly retreat to their ladder, which broke under their weight. Many were killed as they fell; others, who were above the point at which the rope broke, scrambled back into the sky, where they either perished or were made prisoner. This explains why there are fewer mammals and birds on earth than in the past. Most of them died in the sky, or were changed into stars.

A curious version originating from the lower reaches of the Fraser River (M$_{735}$; Boas 13, p. 31) indicates a possible link-up with the bird-nester story, and the remainder of this volume will show more clearly why. Two brothers called Woodpecker and Eagle each had a son (cf. M$_{718}$; see above, p. 452). Coyote, in a fit of jealousy, tried to get rid of them. He changed his wife's faeces into a beautiful water bird; the two cousins went after it and it led them up into the sky. Their fathers organized an expedition to release them, but only the young man with a woodpecker grandmother — who helped him by keeping time with her magic song (cf. M$_{724a}$, in which a grandmother imposes a rhythm on the spatial continuum by completing the cosmic ladder) — succeeded in shooting his arrows up to the sky. All the warriors climbed up, vanquished the inhabitants and freed the two boys. But they knocked the chain of arrows down before the snail had time to reach the ground; the unfortunate gasteropod fell and broke his bones, and this explains why he is so slow today. At the same time, then, as the episode of the injured animals is inverted (since here it is the Snail who loses his bones, instead of certain types of fish acquiring bones), the conquest of fire motif is replaced by the freeing of a hero, after a series of misadventures which echo those undergone by the bird-nester.

I shall conclude my survey of this series of myths with a Shuswap version (M$_{736}$; Teit 1, p. 749): Black Bear and Wolverine, respectively chiefs of the

Fishes and Birds,[5] assemble all the earth people in order to make war on the inhabitants of the sky. Only Wren, the smallest bird, is able to fix his arrow in the celestial vault. Other informants attribute this exploit to Humming-Bird or Chickadee. Be that as it may, all the birds line up in order of size, each in turn shoots an arrow, and all the arrows form a ladder reaching right down to the earth. The warriors climb up, leaving the two chiefs below to protect the rear. The chiefs start jeering at each other and pushing each other against the ladder, which collapses.

The earth people attack the celestial people. At first, they are victorious, then their luck changes. The earth people are routed and flee in great disorder in the direction of the ladder: but it has gone, and their retreat is cut off. Some make a stand against the sky people, others throw themselves into the void. The birds are able to fly down to the ground; however, several fish miss the lake into which they are trying to throw themselves and are wounded on the rocks. Since that time, one species has a flattened skull, another a broken jaw, a third a bloody mouth (in connection with this last mentioned fish, cf. Adamson, p. 163); the Sucker (*Catostomus*), since it had broken all its bones, has bones scattered throughout its flesh. Those earth people who remained in the sky were either slain or changed into stars.

There are several indications in the myths that these stars, the smallest visible in the sky, are also stars which do not feature in the named constellations. So, in the astronomical register, they represent a kind of residual continuum, in opposition to the constellations, for which the Salish not only have descriptive terms, but which they deal with in special myths explaining the origin and configuration of each: frozen in characteristic poses, terrestrial people are transported to the sky where they hold their positions, as in a *tableau vivant*. I have already given examples of this (see above, p. 229; cf. M_{719}, p. 452). Those birds which can fly emerged more or less unscathed from their celestial adventure, but mammals were reduced in number, from which it can be inferred that the differential gaps between the remaining ones became more marked. As regards fish, the myths seem to exclude the different species of salmon and trout which are a staple part of the native diet; and mention only three or four species, some inedible like the *tcoktci'tcin*, a small fish with a red jaw (Teit 1, p. 692, n. 1; p. 749, n. 3), and others little appreciated, like the Sucker ('small, poor fish, such as suckers' is the expression used in the Okanagon myth M_{697a}, Boas 4, p. 69). Consequently, in this instance too, the myths are trying to explain essentially privative aspects of creation. From the whole range of fish, whose origin is described in the saga of Moon, the demiurge, they

[5] For an explanation of why Wolverine is a master of the birds, cf. L.-S. 9, pp. 67–72.

mention only those which are not salmon, unlike the bird-nester story which, in Salish mythology, is concerned solely with salmon (see above, p. 425).

But the first problem raised by the myths about the war between the two worlds, whether or not the motive was the conquest of fire, stems from their differences or uncertainties concerning the identity of the little bird, the only creature able to attach the chain of arrows to the sky, or to build it in its entirety. The choice of the Wren could easily be explained by the commutation, along the vertical axis, of the long penis, attributed to him in several myths (M_{701a-c}; see above, p. 439), into a ladder of arrows, and would thus provide an additional argument in support of the reciprocal convertibility of the horizontal and vertical axes, joining respectively the near and the far and the low and the high, that different reasons had already led me to postulate. But there is more to it than that; the long penis, which is conjunctive along the horizontal axis, is a homogeneous, smooth-surfaced object, whereas the chain of arrows, conjunctive along the vertical axis, is composed of discrete elements requiring articulation into a whole. The myths stress this second aspect when they state that a collaborator or protector had to intervene in order to make steps (M_{723}), fasten the various pieces securely together (M_{724a}), give a rhythm to the constructor's work by means of a song (M_{735}), or when they say that the chain of arrows formed a sort of ladder (M_{726}), which is how it is described in almost all versions. Compared with the long penis, a natural organ which, like nature itself, belongs to the continuous, the chain of arrows, an artificial creation, illustrates what I referred to in Volume 1 as chromatism (*RC*, pp. 246–81, 319–27), which, in American Indian thought, is tantamount to a category of the understanding: through an accumulation of short intervals, the ladder of arrows uses discrete elements to create a continuum. It is significant, then, that the arrow-ladder should allow people to ascend to the sky but not to descend – since it is destroyed before they can do so – whereas in the bird-nester myths, another cultural product, the hemp rope – a result of weaving – a peaceful technique opposed to the arts of hunting and war associated with the arrows – allows descent from the sky without previously being used for the ascent. And, as it happens, the Puget Sound myths about the wives of the sun and moon, commemorating a time when it was possible to make the journey both ways, refer to the device used as being a woven object, like the rope which serves for the descent, but as taking the form of a ladder, like the chain of arrows which serves only for the ascent.

Why, then, do certain myths feel the need to replace the Wren, whose role would seem to be so perfectly appropriate, by other birds? If we disregard the Humming-Bird, which is mentioned by some Shuswap informants, perhaps because it is very small – smallness, as we shall see, being in itself a category with a relevant function – these birds can be reduced to two types: on the one hand, the red-headed Woodpecker or the *Sphyrapicus* sp., closely related genera which can be assumed to have the same semantic function,[6] and on the other the Chickadee. Let us begin with the Chickadee, which is dealt with in myths whose action, as is sometimes explicitly stated, takes place before the war expedition to the sky for the conquest of fire.

M 737. *Sanpoil.* '*The origin of the Chickadee*'

An old woman and her grandson lived near a river. The grandson wished to cross the river and called to an old Deer to take him across on his back. While they were in the water the boy cut the buck's throat and killed him (an inversion of the susceptible ferryman; see above, pp. 445–6).

The grandmother started to cut up the beast. Drawn by the scent of the meat, five wolves planned to steal it. The old woman dressed a piece of rotten wood to make it look like her grandson; she placed it in a conspicuous position, then, by magic, she wished herself and her grandson and their food to be carried to a ledge on the face of a cliff. The wolves attacked the tent, but found that what they believed to be a boy was only rotten wood. They tried to jump up to the ledge but were unable to reach it, it was so high. Weary of trying, they gave up and asked for some of the meat. The old woman told her grandson to throw hot stones wrapped in suet into their mouths. All the wolves died except the youngest who, not being able to swallow the huge stone, only had the sides of his mouth burned [by the fat]. This is why wolves have dark masks at the side of their mouths.

The grandmother and grandson continued to live on the ledge. When he had used up all his arrows, the boy looked for feathers to make new ones. He caused two eagles to quarrel; they fought and the boy gathered the fallen feathers. He himself was transformed into a chickadee and left his grandmother to join the people who were going to make war on the sky (Boas 4, p. 107).

Less explicitly than the Okanagon myth M$_{733a}$, in which the hero, by

---

[6] All the more certainly since identification of the first bird remains doubtful: the true red-headed Woodpecker (*Melanerpes erythrocephalus*) is not normally found in the extreme west of North America (cf. Godfrey, pp. 276–7), and the *Sphyrapicus* genus includes certain red-headed species. The references may be to one and the same bird.

killing a deer, obtains the rib with which he makes himself a bow, this Sanpoil version is nevertheless dealing with the origin of the magic weapons, thanks to which the hero will later succeed in shooting his arrows up to the sky. In this instance, however, the hero is a Chickadee, whereas in the Okanagon myth he was a different bird. At the same time, his character is an inversion of that of the bird-nester, in the sense that the disjunction towards the high is a rescuing process, and also allows him actually to obtain eagle feathers. According to the previously quoted Okanagon version, the bird *tskan* obtained the feathers for his arrows by means of a trick which combined the bird-nester's adventures with a motif linked with the conquest of fire: he disguised himself as a decaying carcass, and allowed himself to be carried off by an eagle, which took him to its eyrie at the top of a steep cliff; the hero was then able to capture the eaglets.

Lastly, the sequence just quoted, which precedes the war against the celestial people, has a relationship of symmetry with the latter: after climbing to a high place, although not right up to the sky, the hero mutilates the wolves' jaws, thus giving the species their distinctive physical appearance. This significant disfigurement is caused by the throwing of red-hot stones (congruous with fire) from the high on to bodies below; whereas, in the myths about the celestial war, the jaws of certain fish (instead of land animals) are mutilated when they fall from the high on to the stones below which, since they surround a lake, are congruous with water. Hence, in this case too, the introduction of a specific difference within another family of vertebrates.

The Shuswap and the Thompson explain the origin of the Chickadee in a context which brings us even closer to the way in which the Plateau Salish tell the bird-nester story (see $M_{667a, b}$):

M_{738}. *Shuswap. 'The origin of the Chickadee'*

An old Grizzly Woman, who lived in an uninhabited part of the country, tried to make herself a daughter. She made one with gum which melted in the sun, one with stone which sank to the bottom of the river, one with clay which dissolved in the river because the girl itched and scratched herself so much, and finally she made one with wood who survived because she could stand heat, could float and could scratch without dissolving. One day while she was bathing, she admired a trout and wanted him to be her husband. The fish changed into a handsome young man and carried her off to the bottom of the lake: this proved no easy task because every time he dived with her into the lake his wooden bride rose to the surface again.

After many long years in the land of the fishes, she allowed her son and daughter to visit their maternal grandmother. But, to begin with, the children were frightened by her grizzly-bear appearance: three times in succession they came away, leaving behind tracks which the old woman was able to interpret. So, on the fourth occasion, she set up a tall stick on the hillside and hung her basket and robe on it; it was her own likeness, clearly visible on the hill. She hid in the house which the children entered, thinking their grandmother had gone to look for edible roots a long way away. But suddenly she appeared and sprinkled them with a magic decoction of herbs. The fluid covered the boy and he assumed human form, but only a few drops of the medicine fell on the girl who was transformed into a small female dog.

The old woman called the boy Chickadee and taught him to hunt. She warned him not to beat the dog when she took her share of the game. But one day, after the dog had devoured a fine bird of prey which had only just been shot down (a 'chicken-hawk': *Accipiter?*), the boy grew very angry and thrashed the dog severely. The dog revealed who she really was and fled to the mountains, in spite of the hero calling out: 'Oh, my younger sister!' To this day the Chickadee goes round calling for his younger sister.

Shortly afterwards, the hero, forgetting his grandmother's warnings, rashly climbed to the top of a tree to recover a lost arrow. The tree rose up into sky country, a great empty plain covered lightly with snow. The hero, not knowing which way to go, shot an arrow which would show him which direction he should take. Before long, freshly cut wood chips indicated the presence of woodcutters. He came to a lodge where he was greeted by a lame old man, who told him he was his grandfather (or great-grandfather, according to some versions, the husband or father of a grandmother). He added that, not far away from there, people were living in an underground house; they were the people who gave him food, water and fuel. Their chief had a daughter who was as good as she was beautiful, but who turned away all suitors. The old man promised to help the hero to win her, but only on the very strange condition that he got inside the old man's body: during the day, he would live inside the old man; at night, he would leave his hideout and the old man would instruct him in his magic. And so both lived in this manner, until the day when the chief summoned the suitors and promised to give his daughter to the first one who could shoot an arrow into the little owl perched on top of the ladder inside the house. The old man's arrow sped straight to the target, even though he was blind and unable to stand up without support. In spite of everyone's disgust, the chief was true to his word and gave his daughter to the pitiable winner. Every night, the hero emerged from his ugly outer covering of flesh and the young woman was wonderfully contented with her husband. The village people, still thinking him to be a lame old man, jeeringly obliged him to go hunting with them. Since he had no weapons, each one made him a present of either a good or a bad arrow. The hero secretly emerged from his skin and killed all the game. To each of the other hunters, who had all returned home without having seen any deer, he gave an animal and the arrow which had killed it. Those who had given a good arrow were entitled to nice, fat bucks, the others to does; Coyote, who had given a bark arrow with leaves instead of feathers, received only a yearling. The hunters were curious and questioned the young woman, finally extorting her secret from her. They killed the old man, skinned him and succeeded in extracting the hero. He lived for a long time in the upper world with his wife. He was a great deer hunter. Afterwards he was transformed into a Chickadee (Teit 1, pp. 691–6).

The Thompson versions (M$_{739a-c}$; Dawson, pp. 34–5; Teit 4, pp. 77–8; 5, pp. 355 9) sometimes replace trout by salmon, and clarify the episode of the transformed children by explaining that the latter had been, from birth, half-bear and half-fish. Depending on the particular version, the sister who is changed into a dog and beaten later takes on human form or resumes her original bear/fish nature, or is transformed into a Chickadee. She then ascends into the sky, followed by her brother, who fails to find her. Or else, the brother willy-nilly finds himself in the sky after losing his four arrows in trying to shoot down a red-headed woodpecker. He climbs up a tree to look for them: the arrows had become implanted at right-angles to the trunk and, in order to reach the highest one, the hero uses the lowest as if they were the rungs of a ladder. But no sooner have his feet left one arrow than it falls out of its own accord and implants itself above him. The hero is forced to climb higher and higher and finally arrives in the celestial world.
Piles of wood shavings or freshly cut logs lead him to the house of an old man called Spetlamulâx, 'Weed' – like himself, as he notices with surprise – and who is none other than his grandfather, in exile in the sky through the evil spells of his wife Grizzly: perhaps he too, like his grandson, was inveigled into the sky through the search for a lost arrow. The hero hunts for the old man and builds up reserves of wood and water for him. The inhabitants of the neighbouring village, surprised to see how well-supplied the old man is, discover the stranger's presence and offer him their daugh-

ters in marriage, at first without much success. He finally marries one of them, by whom he has four children. Some say he never went back to earth, others that he did go back but changed into a Chickadee, perpetually searching for his sister and calling to her with his cry.

These myths, a real hotch-potch of Salish and Sahaptin themes, are to some extent irrelevant to the present discussion, since the sequence about the visit to the sky reproduces in every detail sequences in other myths which take place either on the earth or in the chthonian world, and which belong to parallel series, including the one about the origin of wind or fog that, for reasons already indicated (see above, p. 360), I cannot go into here.[7] Postponing discussion of them for the moment, I would only like to draw attention to a particular aspect of the physical 'incorporation' theme in the celestial sequence, because it is a reminder of the bird-nester cycle where the hero is 'incorporated' by the demiurge, according to the Klamath-Modoc, or created by the trickster, according to the Thompson. However, these operations take place on earth, before the disjunction of the hero towards the sky, whereas, here, the 'incorporation' occurs in the sky, and after the disjunction of the hero in circumstances reminiscent of those endured by the bird-nester. At the same time, the role of fabricator on earth of an artificial child (a daughter in this case, not a son) passes from Coyote, the trickster, to a Grizzly Woman, who also figures in the Salish versions of the bird-nester, but as the victim of Coyote who deceives her either at the beginning (M_{671}) or at the end (M_{667a}) of the story, or sometimes in a separate narrative (M_{680c}), and always in connection with the seasons of the year.

The Thompson, Lilloet and Chehalis of British Columbia have myths in which the same solitary old woman, a Wolverine instead of a Grizzly, also replaces Coyote, but this time in a twofold capacity: as the creator of the milt-girls in relation to the mythic series M_{375} containing the saga of Moon the demiurge; and in relation to the group $M_{696-697}$, where Coyote tries to marry his own daughter, whose mother is sometimes a Wolverine.

M 740. Thompson. 'The grandmother disguised as a man'

An old woman called Skaiyā'm lived all alone. She created two grand-

---

[7] In these myths, an ulcerous old man fertilizes a chief's daughter by spitting or urinating on her from the top of a ladder at the foot of which she is lying asleep (cf. L.-S. 20). It is therefore clear that the single arrow which speeds straight to its target — a symbolic representation of the young girl — stands in the same relationship to the chain of arrows in the other mythic series as the jet of urine, compensating for the impotence of a sick old man, to the long penis. An indirect and *a contrario* demonstration thus again reveals the principle of the reciprocal convertibility of the long penis and the chain of arrows, which we had already brought to light by other means. We shall see later (p. 486) that the relationship of the owl to the heroine, which in this instance is metaphorical, becomes metonymical in other contexts.

daughters for herself out of fish roe. When they became adult they desired to have husbands. Their grandmother feigned death and fixed herself up to resemble a man; she tied the loose skin of her breasts under each armpit so that she acquired a man's flat chest; for penis and testicles she hung between her legs a chisel made from deer-horn and a stone hammer with a handle in the middle. She passed herself off as a young stranger and, at nightfall, slept with the young girls. Bruised by the hard, artificial member, they suspected some ruse and tickled their lover, forcing him to laugh. As soon as the stranger opened his toothless mouth, they recognized their grandmother ($M_{741, 742}$). They were angry with her for deceiving them, and threw her into the river. The old woman drowned; she laughed as she sank and made the kind of bubbles which can often be seen rising to the surface of a river or lake (cf. Gunther 2, p. 166).

The young women travelled down river, and stole a baby which was being nursed by its blind grandmother. They put a piece of rotten wood into the cradle in place of the child. When the old woman realized what had happened, she called her husband who was away fishing, and their son. All three set off in pursuit of the kidnappers. From time to time the old woman drew up the loose skin of her breasts into a bunch and at once the distance between pursuer and pursued became shorter. The distance increased every time the tired old woman let go of her skin. The kidnappers were not overtaken.

The old woman made another child with the rotten wood in the cradle. He quickly grew up, learned to hunt, and one day met his elder brother who had married the roe-women who had abducted him. After a farewell visit to their grandparents, the brothers returned together to the mountains; the elder gave one of his wives to his younger brother. Thus the women each had a husband (Teit 5, pp. 283-5).

The different versions of this myth remain easily identifiable thanks to the old woman's name, Kaiyam in Lilloet and Kaiam in the language of the Chehalis of British Columbia, i.e., Wolverine. In the Lilloet version (M_{741}; Hill-Tout 3, pp. 177-89), her husband, who is called Skwaskwaset, at first carries her on his back; but, becoming annoyed at the fact that the kidnappers gain ground every time fatigue forces him to set down his burden, he changes his wife into an edible plant called *tsúkwa*, probably bracken, *Pteridium aquilinum*, also called *tsúkwa* in the Thompson dialect (cf. Teit 9, p. 482; see above, p. 412).

The mother of the stolen child makes herself another child with urine wrung from his garments. One day, while the second son is hunting in the mountains, he meets his elder brother and reveals to him that they are akin. The elder, who has married his kidnappers, changes them into two she-bears, one black, one grizzly. He sets fire to a piece of pitch and burns his house, destroying all his possessions; then he returns to his own people.

The versions belonging to the Chehalis of British Columbia ($M_{742a, b}$; Hill-Tout 2, pp. 342–54; Boas 13, p. 30) allow us to interpret the husband's name, Skwáskwustel, which is almost identical with the name in the Lilloet version; it means 'Cooking-stone': the kind of stone which, when red-hot, is plunged into water-filled bark or basketwork receptacles in order to bring the water to the boil, or to heat earth ovens. After discovering the identity of their disguised grandmother – who has stretched her skin in order to look like a young man, but who, being old and toothless, cannot chew her food properly – her two grand-daughters tickle her until she dies: 'Hereafter,' they say, 'when people tell this story, the weather will always be calm on the lake.' Then they steal a baby from his blind grandmother, but contrary to what happens in the Lilloet version, it is not her husband, Cooking-stone, who takes her on his back, but her daughter, the mother of the stolen child, who hopes to travel more quickly and reduce the distance between herself and the kidnappers; but the distance increases whenever the daughter becomes exhausted and sets her mother down. Weary and dis-couraged, she abandons the pursuit and changes her mother into an edible plant. She throws her father into the river, where he becomes the kind of stone for salmon to hide under. She then wrings out the baby's garments and a child comes into existence from the urine. Later, he finds his brother in the mountains and tells him who he is. Having been informed of the wicked conduct of the kidnappers who had since become his wives, the elder brother burns them on a fire made from pitch; he transforms the younger, who is good and kind, into a light, fleecy summer cloud, and the unpleasant elder sister into a dark, lowering winter cloud. He also changes the son he had by the younger sister into a robin (*Turdus migratorius*) – the American robin is a handsome, graceful bird with a red breast – and the son he had by the elder sister into a black, croaking raven. The sparks rising from the fire become snow birds (cf. above, pp. 83–4). The two brothers go back to their mother, who decides to change them into stars. The younger, who is called Sk.wumtcetl, becomes the sun, the elder, the moon. According to one variant the two women are changed into Sturgeon and Sucker (*Catostomus*), after which the brother made from urine melts in the heat of the fire.

It is clear that these myths partially reproduce the story of Moon the demiurge, which also ends with the metamorphosis of the two brothers, who become, respectively, the day star and the night star. But the fact that we are dealing here with versions which might be called perpendicular rather than parallel is shown by the triple transformation: a female Wolverine instead of a male Coyote, the daughters are born from *eggs* and not the *milts* of fish (M$_{742a}$, Hill-Tout's version, is very definite on this point: *keleq*, 'the roe or eggs'; if the Salish term excluded milts, a point about which I cannot be sure, the two transformations would be redundant);[8] last but not least — since in this case there is no room for doubt — the abduction of the elder son to the mountains, not the sea, towards terra firma and not water, to the east not the west, with a concomitant transformation of women (in other contexts congruous with salmon) either into she-bears or clouds, or into estuary or lake fish. But at the same time, we know from the 'normal' versions of the demiurge's story that the woman — the mother or grandmother of the stolen child — able to make the earth alternately contract and expand, represents earthquakes, which cause folds in the earth's crust (see above, p. 423). A Coast Salish version (M$_{743}$; Boas 5, p. 156) presents another possibility: she urinates and creates lakes, liquid concavities, which are inversions of mountain peaks.

The transformation of the male Coyote into a female Wolverine, both of them characters who, in order to commit incest with their daughter or daughters — one of whom has been conceived normally and the others engendered from raw food — feign death and assume the appearance of a handsome stranger, is reminiscent of the freeing of the salmon episode, where Coyote's incestuous machinations are directed towards the granddaughter of a woman who is invariably described as a mountain animal, sometimes even as a Wolverine, and whose son-in-law he becomes. But in the myths we are concerned with now, Wolverine Woman undergoes a double transformation: not only does she change from a close relative into a stranger, but first of all and for a good reason, from a woman into a man, because she wants to seduce her own daughters or grand-daughters. She is, then, a *lewd grandmother*, which brings us back to a theme we have already encountered and that a lengthy discussion (see above, pp. 163–89) allowed

[8] Mrs Kew, the wife of a professor at the University of British Columbia, and to whom I take this opportunity of expressing my thanks, has been kind enough to explain, in response to an enquiry made on my behalf by Professor P. Maranda, that the distinction exists in Cowichan, her native language: *galax*, 'salmon eggs', *slgey?*, 'milts'. Kuipers' dictionary gives, in Squamish, *t'amk'°*, 'salmon eggs', *sλ'amk'°*, 'preserved salmon eggs for winter consumption' (pp. 269, 291); on p. 282 there is a reference to *sp'ə'l?xˢm*, the meaning of which would seem to be 'lung' or 'milt', according to informants (cf. Cowichan and Musquan *sp'šl?xʷəm*, 'lung', Elmendorf-Suttles, p. 20). The distinction also exists in Coos: *heléyîs*, 'eggs', *meqLōu*, 'milt' (Frachtenberg 1, p. 34). Concerning the semantic position of the bracken, cf. my article in *Mélanges en l'honneur d'André G. Haudricourt*.

me to articulate with others which had led me to it. As it happens, the story of the lewd grandmother already exists in this initial form in the mythology of the Thompson, the Lilloet and the Shuswap ($M_{563b, e}$; Teit 1, pp. 678–9; 2, pp. 323–5; 4, pp. 66–7; 5, pp. 247–8). These Plateau Salish treat it as a separate story, or incorporate it with others, but they always relate it to man's mortality, that is, to the impossibility of rejuvenating old men or resuscitating the dead: this is made clear by the toothless mouth motif, which is present in all contexts to demonstrate that, in spite of all possible tricks and artifices, aging is an irreversible process.

Alongside this etiological function, which is latent rather than actual, the disguised grandmother myths just introduced have a further, and much more explicit, one: they deal with the origin of other phenomena, also periodic but telluric or meteorological in character, related to the earth's crust and to atmospheric conditions; in other words, to the median world: the origin of earthquakes, which periodically change the earth's contours, or, as in M_{742a}, the origin of calm or stormy weather (see above, p. 477), which is analogous to seismic disturbances but concerns the atmosphere and not the land surface. Only a few versions mention the episode explaining the origin of the sun and moon; it is, then, less firmly a part of this group of myths than of the demiurge's saga (M_{375}, M_{382}, M_{506}), where it constitutes an invariant feature.

This being so, we can understand the reasons for the emergence, between the saga of Moon the demiurge and the lewd grandmother cycle, of these apparently heterogeneous mythic forms, which partake of both, since the chief character is a lewd grandmother who disguises herself as a man so that, like Coyote, she can seduce the milt-girls. In the case of Coyote, the action leads to the origin of the sun and moon, i.e., periodicity envisaged from the astronomical point of view. In the case of the lewd grandmother, the action, as we have seen, leads to the origin of biological periodicity, which is rendered inevitable by the impossibility of slowing down, for the benefit of one generation, the rate at which all must succeed each other. Between these two forms of periodicity, and between two protagonists, a male and a female, are intercalated certain mixed forms, in which the female protagonist assumes both sexes, and which, between the two extreme manifestations of periodicity that they continue to hint at obliquely by a less regular and less forceful expression of the motifs, bring out a third manifestation: seasonal periodicity (M_{742a}), associated with the less regular periodicity which, at the contiguous levels of the ground and the air, is demonstrated by earthquakes and weather changes (Figure 29).

It is significant, then, that the myths concerned with the exploits of

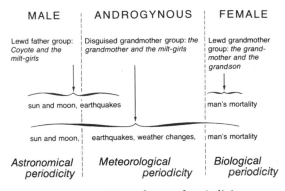

MALE	ANDROGYNOUS	FEMALE
Lewd father group: *Coyote and the milt-girls*	Disguised grandmother group: *the grandmother and the milt-girls*	Lewd grandmother group: *the grand-mother and the grandson*

sun and moon, earthquakes   man's mortality

sun and moon,   earthquakes, weather changes,   man's mortality

| *Astronomical periodicity* | *Meteorological periodicity* | *Biological periodicity* |

Figure 29. Three forms of periodicity

Moon the demiurge and which regard Coyote as the creator of the milt-girls, should as it were, pull earthquakes in the direction of astronomical periodicity (M_{382}; see above, p. 423), whereas, in one at least of those featuring the disguised grandmother, the emphasis shifts towards weather changes which, it is said, will be brought about by the mere telling of the story. Similarly, on the extreme edge of the lewd grandmother group, certain Nez Percé myths (M_{571a-c}; see above, p. 187) connect Coyote's loss of teeth with the origin of the periodicity of winds. Lastly, some Okanagon myths ($M_{744a,\,b}$; Cline, pp. 228–9) explain how ducks, who, as we know, are the masters of spring (see above, p. 407), originated from teeth lost in the river by one or several ogresses, who were subsequently changed into owls, and one of whom was cooked in an oven. In this way, the meteorological code effects a kind of compromise between the astronomical and biological codes.

The frequent allusions, in all these myths, to the earth oven, raise the problem of its ritual function. I dealt with this subject in my lectures at the Collège de France during the 1968–9 session, when discussing what I have referred to more than once as the parallel series, which cannot be fully examined in the present study. However, the myths relevant to my immediate purpose make it possible to suggest a partial but adequate solution, purely on the basis of the syntagmatic chain.

Fern rhizomes were cooked in earth ovens; they were then pressed into loaves or cakes which kept for a very long time. A dish considered as one of the greatest delicacies throughout the entire coastal region (from the Kwakiutl in the north to the Puget Sound communities, by way of the Bella Coola; cf. Boas-Hunt 2, pp. 343–4; Eells 1, p. 216; Haeberlin-Gunther, p. 24; Curtis, Vol. 9, pp. 52, 58; McIlwraith, Vol. II, p. 451) consisted of fern rhizomes and salmon roe: it would be difficult to imagine a more paradoxical *plat garni* or conjunction of foodstuffs, since the two products were harvested in diametrically opposed conditions: the rhizomes in autumn when, with the start of the cold season, the plant stopped growing (Gunther 3, p. 14; Haeberlin-Gunther, p. 20), and the salmon roe when the fish were spawning — that is, when the species was multiplying.[9] Through the connection with cooking, we can already explain the twofold association of a Fern Grandmother with Roe Women, on the one hand, and with a husband called 'Cooking-stone', on the other. But this grandmother is also old. It would seem that young women were forbidden to harvest ferns, for fear they fell sick, both in the north and the south of the Salish area, among the Kwakiutl (Boas-Hunt 2, p. 616) and the Coos: 'The young wives picked berries and fruits; those who were a little older dug rhizomes, fern roots or tubers, wild carrots and camas' (Jacobs 5, p. 84).[10]

The fact that a woman who, in other myths, is responsible for earthquakes and, in this one, causes the earth to extend and contract, and then becomes the Bracken (*Pteridium aquilinum*), may be a result of special features of the fern harvest. The Bracken has a slender, woody rhizome, with irregular deep-rooting ramifications (Abrams 1, p. 23). In M_{741} it is also described as a 'creeping vine'. The elderly women harvesters had to break open the ground with their digging sticks over a wide area, and their labours could well produce an effect not unlike a miniature earthquake. This is not an idle supposition on my part; Salish groups as far apart from each other as the Bella Coola and the Tillamook, both of whom have long been cut off from the main body of their linguistic family (and in opposite directions), make the link-up in almost the same terms, although the Bella

[9] The opposition is not exactly between summer and winter. According to the species, the spawning period for salmon can extend from August to November and even to December (Netboy, p. 48); the Chehalis of British Columbia called the months October and November by names which mean 'spawning season' (Hill-Tout 2, p. 334). However, they also referred to a period from the end of July to the beginning of October by an expression meaning roughly 'the coming together or meeting of the two points of the year', and the end of this intermediary period also had a special name: 'the time of the dying salmon', since, as is explained in the same source (*ibid.*, p. 335), 'the creeks are full of dead and dying salmon which always die after spawning'. Consequently, the spawning season heralds the end of a calendrical cycle and, in theory at least, the harvesting of fern roots belongs to the following cycle.

[10] But not, perhaps, in the Puget Sound area, if we are to believe $M_{375g, h, j}$, where two young women, while harvesting ferns, express a wish to have stars for their husbands (see above, p. 412). Unless, of course, this occupation, like their decision to sleep in the open in unseasonable weather, indicates an infringement of customary practices which could be the chief, or incidental, cause of their subsequent misadventures.

In connection with the winter connotation of ferns, cf. Frachtenberg 3, p. 81: the Indians of the Lower Umpqua relate how formerly 'they ate mostly dried fern roots during the winter: this is how they kept alive in winter'.

Coola believe it to be of recent origin, whereas the Tillamook quote a myth to justify it. 'Not many years ago,' say the Bella Coola, 'a number of women were collecting bracken roots when one which had been gathered began to turn into a snake. The women were alarmed and puzzled . . . As they stood watching, the ground in front of them fell away under their feet as if there had been an earthquake, and they realized that the snake-root had been the "mother" of the ferns' (M_{745a}; McIlwraith Vol. I, p. 92). The Tillamook (M_{745b}; E. D. Jacobs, pp. 176–7) relate how a man tried to eat the 'mother of ferns', which had been dug up by his wife and resembled a snake. The earth and the very house in which he was living started to shake.

The Alsea, who are southerly neighbours of the Tillamook, make the same association between snakes and ferns, but express it metonymically, not metaphorically, through the character of a Snake Woman who digs up fern roots (Frachtenberg 4, pp. 129–31, 141–3).

The taboo on fern gathering by young women, which has been already mentioned as existing along the edges of the Salish area, might be explained, then, by the link that the Salish themselves established — at a sufficiently early date for it to have persisted in two completely isolated groups — between ferns on the one hand, and, on the other, earthquakes as telluric disorders affecting periodicity, so that only elderly women past the menopause could be involved in the fern harvest without becoming contaminated and thus endangering the proper functioning of the universe (cf. *OTM*, pp. 506–507).

Thus, a human mistress of earthquakes, able to cause them at will and according to her needs becomes the 'mother' of a food plant, which however — on pain of provoking an earthquake — a human must not consume, even though, according to M_{745b}, the plant is particularly tasty (it will be noted that the Bella Coola who have secularized the myth, maintain on the contrary that women were not afraid to eat the snake-like rhizome once they realized that it was the 'mother' of ferns). A symmetrical transformation affects the husband: he changes from a 'cooking-stone' into a 'raw stone': 'one of those rocks in a river bed which provide a cover for fish' (M_{712a}). After being a culinary utensil used in the preparation of a particular food (incidentally, a plant on which, according to the myths, bears like to feed), he becomes an obstacle hindering the search for food: when salmon hide under stones they cannot be caught. And the salmon is, *par excellence*, a food for humans: animal by nature, associated with water, not with the earth; and, as far as we know, the Indians did not cook it in ovens but grilled, boiled or dried it. The transformation appears to be of the same type as the one affecting the old man in M_{739c}, who is banished to the sky by Grizzly his wife, and whose name is Weed: this plant, unlike the fern, is inedible, and therefore never other than raw.

This apparent digression about ferns and the earth oven was necessary for the elucidation of certain aspects of the myths, and it will contribute to my overall interpretation of them. However, it must not be forgotten that I introduced the disguised grandmother group with a precise purpose: to understand the myths about the origin of the Chickadee, which are connected with it by some obscure link that needs clarification.

Let us return, then, to the Chickadee. According to the different versions of the myth explaining the origin of this bird, either a brother eternally searching for his lost sister, or the sister first, then the brother, changed into chickadees without ever being reunited. These characters are themselves the offspring of the marriage between a bear-wife (her mother was a grizzly bear) and a fish — a trout or a salmon — that the girl saw in the lake at the edge of which she lived. The pattern of the encounter echoes that of the wives of the sun and moon, since, in both cases, a young woman admires a supernatural being and rashly wishes he were her husband. But this time, there is no question of overcoming the opposition between sky and earth, or even that between the near and the far (since the heroine's abode is by the lakeside). From being cosmic or socio-geographical, the opposition shifts into a different category; it concerns the taxonomic differences between two animal families which Indian thought conceives of as being widely separated, not only because the bear is terrestrial or even chthonian and the salmon aquatic, but also because all the myths belonging to this region of America present salmon which are *par excellence* a food for humans, as anthropomorphic or even superhuman beings, and bears, which are often cannibalistic, as sub-human beings. In this twofold respect, the wolverine (L.-S. 9, pp. 67–72) seems to be an only slightly less marked counterpart of the bear.

The two antithetical natures, symbolic of an extreme disjunction within the animal kingdom, are incorporated in the children who have the two physical appearances: according to M_{739}, they are half bear, half fish. Their grandmother does not succeed in transforming them completely: the boy becomes human, but the little girl is changed into a dog and thus remains half-way between animality and humanity (see above, pp. 471–2).

Fortunately, to interpret this incident, we can keep to the syntagmatic chain without bringing into play the very considerable set of myths belonging to this part of America and dealing with a woman whose husband was a dog, and who was also only partially successful in her attempt to force her dog-children to keep their human form, which they only assumed privately when they thought no one was looking. The relationship between the *human/dog* pair and the *bear/fish* pair is easily understandable. They conjoin terms which, in the first instance, are extremely close, and in the second, very distant. Moreover, the brother and sister at birth were both bear and fish; each, therefore, embodied an *internal difference*, but since there were two of them, their identical make-up created an *external resemblance* between them. After the transformation, the pattern is reversed: one character becomes human, the other a dog; consequently, an *external difference* is introduced between them, although being, as we say, 'of the same blood', each is marked by an *internal resemblance*: and it is precisely this resemblance that the grandmother urges the boy to take into account by allowing the dog to appropriate its share of the game.

The myth therefore illustrates the following pattern:

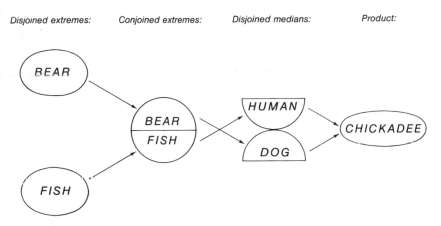

Disjoined extremes: *Conjoined extremes:*   *Disjoined medians:*   *Product:*

Figure 30. The origin of the chickadee, according to M₇₃₉

We have here two attempts at mediation, one impossible through being contrary to nature, the other consonant with culture, but nevertheless unsuccessful in its turn because of a misunderstanding: the young hero interprets as a maximum difference (although the maximum difference has been abolished) the minimum difference that has replaced it: he singles out the 'beast' aspect of the dog, refusing to recognize the 'sibling' aspect, and makes the mistake of taking as an absolute difference between his sister and himself what is, in fact, their relative identity. The transformation into a chickadee of both the children or of one of them, then, is the consequence of two successive mediations, the first on the level of nature, and the second on the level of culture. No doubt the chickadee is able to retain a positive role, but only as a semi-mediator: on the temporal and meteorological levels which, as I have suggested, stand in an intermediary position between two more overt types of periodicity, one astronomical, the other biological; or again, the chickadee, when called upon to play the part of spatial mediator between the sky and the earth is only half successful (just as the grandmother, as a taxonomical mediator, is only half successful): the arrow-ladder which the bird alone, out of all the animals, is able to attach to the celestial vault makes ascent possible but not descent; in most versions this is because of the bears, who thus demonstrate their negative efficacity when faced with the problem of mediation. After which, the inhabitants of the earth suffer a disaster and obtain cooking fire – when they do finally obtain it – only in exchange, as it were, for a reduction in their numbers and, above all, in their variety: henceforth, the zoological species will be separated by those differential gaps which the union between a she-bear and a fish wilfully disregarded, in defiance of all verisimilitude.

As I have already hinted, the episode about the origin of ferns, although anecdotal in form, respects and strengthens the same pattern: the *plat garni*, the rhizome and roe dish, the contents of which combine a temporarily sterile product of the earth with an essentially fertile product of water, is broken down into its constituent parts: the old woman who is destined to *become* a fern fails in her pursuit of the young women who have *come from* salmon roe; if only in gastronomical terms, the new year will never catch up with the old (see above, p. 480, n. 9); the oven stone, the mediatory action of which ensures the preservation of rhizomes from one season to the next, becomes a stone in the natural state in running water which cannot be heated; a refuge for fish against the fisherman and the gatherer of salmon roe.

The semi-mediatory function of the chickadee and his partial success, which brings about an irreversible distortion in the order of the world, explain why the story of the bird duplicates that of the bird-nester in one respect, and is in opposition to it in another. The point is made all the clearer by the fact that, in Salish mythology, the bird-nester is entirely deprived of the functions that are attributed to him elsewhere as master of fire and inventor of cooking and the arts of civilization. The successful visit to the celestial world and the return to earth tend to be reduced to purely formal achievements. The credit for the conquest of fire – by a character simulating a dead game animal in accordance with a pattern I first pointed out in Tupi mythology (*RC*, pp. 139–42) – is usually attributed to the

Beaver[11] acting alone or in a team with the Eagle and the Weasel (i.e., a triad relating to water, air and earth); whereas, in the myths of these same Salish tribes, the origin of cooking motif splits up, as it were, in the hands of a trickster, into two themes: the origin of salmon and the origin of fairs and markets: the first lies on the hither side of cooking, since it is concerned with the very existence of food, and the other on the far side, because markets were used for the exchange of food produce that had been stored for the purpose and had often undergone some initial processing.

Even though the myths about the origin of the chickadee, such as M_{737} and to a lesser degree M_{733a} (see above, pp. 466, 469–70), tend to link up with those relating to the bird-nester, there is no inversion of the regression from oven stone to stone in river; instead of a transformation of the oven stone along the axis linking culture to nature, we find another which simply leaves the stone in its natural state but attributes to it a destructive instead of a constructive function; the first transformation is related to the natural order, the second to the cultural order. This use of oven stones for lethal purposes, leading up to the conquest or reconquest of cooking fire, is reminiscent of the Ge myths, particularly M_7 and M_8, where the hero, before receiving terrestrial fire from a helpful wild animal ($\neq$ before wresting celestial fire from fierce enemies), injures deliberately or accidentally – by throwing stones in place of raw birds – the potential wild beast which, in social terms, is what a brother-in-law always amounts to, since he has taken away your sister; whereas, in M_{733a} and M_{737}, the hero kills or wounds actual wild beasts by hurling oven stones at them, 'coated', to use a culinary term, with cooked meat, because they were trying to steal from him game obtained in a moment of intimate bodily contact, a kind of incest transposed to the hunter/game relationship, and – according to the Okanagon version M_{733a} – consisting in a physical penetration of the animal through the anus, a form of penetration which, in the related lewd grandmother series, becomes the incidental cause of real incest (M_{562e}, M_{564}), transposed from the horizontal axis of siblings to the vertical axis of alternate generations.

[11] It would be worth trying to verify whether the Beaver forms a pair with the Land-Otter; the latter loses primordial fire which burned without wood (M_{723b}; see above, p. 462), the former achieves the conquest of fire and then places it in the various kinds of tree. M_{723a} indeed suggests that they are a pair: old Fire-Woman has two daughters, one married to Beaver, the other to Land-Otter; the two husbands are in opposition to each other, one being an eater of wood, the other an eater of fish. Otter's wife, incensed by the fact that her husband keeps the biggest fish for his mother, kills the latter by furiously stirring the fire. There is no fire left anywhere, except in a distant house, from which Beaver succeeds in stealing it by means of his usual trick. He places it in the trees, and since that time fire can be obtained from the fire-drill, an implement made of two pieces of wood which are rubbed one against the other (Ballard 1, p. 51).

Much farther north, the same link is to be found between the bird-nester group and the lewd grandmother cycle: in a Kaska myth (M_{746a}; Teit 8, pp. 462–3) a mother, in order to assume her daughter's physical appearance and appropriate her two husbands, disjoins the girl by sending her to the top of a tree where she turns into an owl (cf. above, pp. 473, 474 n. 7). A widely distributed Eskimo myth, which I shall quote only in the Greenland version, since it is the most remote (M_{746b}; Rink, pp. 442–3), refers to a woman who hates her son, a bad hunter, and abducts his wife. After changing into a man, she becomes her daughter-in-law's husband, and lives with her until her son discovers their hiding place and kills her.

But why the chickadee? In *The Origin of Table Manners* (p. 255), I replied in advance to this question by showing that for the North American Indians, the chickadee is linked with temporal periodicity:[12] the notches in its tongue mark the months on the year, and its song heralds the spring or the summer. It is also believed to be the harbinger of spring or summer in the western part of North America. The Lilloet maintain that there are people who can forecast the kind of weather according to the movements and song of the chickadee (Teit 11, p. 290). Like their neighbours who live along the eastern slopes of the Rockies, the Kutenai maintain that the chickadee is singing 'Spring! Spring!' (Chamberlain, p. 580; being an Englishman by birth, he uses the word 'tomtit' instead of the American Chickadee, cf. Boas 25, p. 326). In one of the myths we are concerned with (M_{728a}, see above, pp. 463–4), the archery competition in which Chickadee triumphed took place in the spring. Other myths ($M_{729-733}$), though less explicit, tend to prove the same point, since they place the conquest of fire after Coyote's misadventures at the hands of the prairie chickens or grouse who, according to certain versions, function precisely in this context in their capacity as spirits of the cold, who hold back the spring (cf. M_{614c}, and see above, pp. 322, 339).

Thus the myths establish a twofold connection between the chickadee and the arrival of spring on the one hand, and the conquest of fire, on the other. They also establish a clear opposition between celestial fire and celestial water in the episode in $M_{728b,\ c}$, where the people above urinate on the earth people, causing a downpour which puts out the stolen fire.

---

[12] Even though the names of the chickadee are obviously onomatopoeic in character, one cannot but be struck by the resemblance between them in widely different parts of North America and in communities speaking quite different languages; for instance, in Cherokee *tsikilili* (Mooney 1, p. 281), in Jicarilla Apache *tcitc'ike* (Goddard 2, p. 237), and in Thompson *tcîski'kik* (Teit 4, p. 76); these terms are also similar to the name of the unidentified 'little bird', *tsitses* and *t'si'dadat*, in the mythology of the Puget Sound Salish and their Sahaptin neighbours (see above, pp. 463–4).

Approaching the problem from this angle, we can extend and elaborate the interpretation of the Chickadee's role already suggested by enquiring, as usual, whether or not the bird is transformable into some other species in those myths which commute spring with autumn or winter, and fire with water or rain.

Leaving aside for the moment the Chickadee's transformation into a Wren, since the two birds share the same function, I propose to begin by noting that other birds appear alongside them in the myths. Some versions originating to the south of Puget Sound (M₇₂₃, see above, p. 462) refer to collaboration between a 'small bird' and a Raven. Others, from the northern part of the area, say that the summer robin and the winter robin, a dioscuric pair, were sent as scouts to the sky (M₇₂₄ᵦ, see above, p. 463). In the related series concerned with the origin of the Chickadee, certain Chehalis versions from British Columbia (M₇₄₂ₐ, see above, pp. 475–6) present a series of transformations featuring birds, meteorological phenomena or fish: the milt-girls change into clouds, white in summer and black in winter; the son of one of the women is changed into a handsome robin, the son of the other into an ugly raven; the sparks from the fire, or the children themselves, change into snow-birds; the two heroes become the sun and the moon; and, according to one variant, the milt-girls change not into clouds but, respectively, into a sturgeon and a sucker.

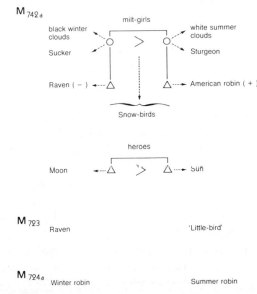

Figure 31. Correspondence between binary oppositions

As this recapitulation shows, the American robin *Turdus migratorius*, which is notable for its reddish breast, is on the same side as the sun and summer. Yet, in the myths, it is given an ambiguous relation with fire and heat. According to the Nootka, the Quinault and the Kathlamet (M_{784}: Boas 13, pp. 100–10; M_{804}: Farrand Vol. 1, p. 109; M_{756b}: Boas 7, pp. 67–71), the Robin – being infirm of purpose, say the Alsea (Frachtenberg 4, p. 63) – does not succeed in stealing the celestial fire because, feeling very cold, it tries to warm itself instead; but it goes too near and its red breast is lasting evidence of the heat of the fire. On the other hand, according to the Sanpoil and the Cœur d'Alêne (M_{588}: Ray 2, pp. 135–7; M_{748b}: Teit 6, p. 177; Reichard 3, p. 63), the Robin, when he was first tried out as the sun, was got rid of because he burned up the earth. Either, then, the Robin feels too hot, as in the coastal myths, or he himself is too hot, as in the inland myths.

Almost everywhere in North America, the American robin has a firmly established reputation as 'the harbinger of spring . . . almost all these birds migrate, but their places are taken by other birds who have bred farther north, so that the species is usually well represented even in the dead of winter' (Pearson, Vol. III, pp. 236–9). Even in most parts of Canada, the robin is said to arrive early in the spring, when the snow is beginning to clear, and so is undeniably a sign of spring (Godfrey, p. 340). The Indians also attribute a meteorological function to the robin, although they seem to associate it with rain. 'Soon it will rain!' is the significance of the robin's call, according to the Kutenai (Chamberlain, p. 580), and the Flathead maintain that rain can be caused by people annoying robins (Turney-High 2, p. 25). The Tsimshian believe that such rain occurs at the end of winter, causing the thaw which the robin, as harbinger of summer, summons by his call (M_{354b}; Boas 2, p. 181; 23, p. 201). If the link between the robin and the thaw prevails throughout the area, the bird must be seen as functioning in correlation with, and opposition to, another bird of the turdidae family, known as the swamp robin, probably the solitary thrush, more often referred to as the hermit thrush (*Hylocichla guttata*; in connection with the synonymy, cf. Pearson, Vol. III, pp. 234–6), and which can be distinguished from the other thrushes by its reddish tail and light-coloured breast speckled with dark brown (Godfrey, pp. 342–3). In a Thompson myth, where the bird is called *s'xoyi'k*,[13] it is presented as the creator not of the warm rain which occurs at the end of winter, but of the refreshing rainstorms characteristic of midsummer (M_{747e}; Teit 5, p. 233). This being

---

[13] Whereas the Thompson call the true robin *qa'léq'a?*, as Professor Maranda kindly checked with native informants, at my request.

so, it is tempting to identify with the hermit thrush the bird called robin in a Coos myth (M_{747d}; Jacobs 6, p. 233), where it is the sole survivor of a civil war between birds, although (unlike the robin in the Salish myths) it was the ugliest bird of all, since its breast was speckled with reddish spots – a description which fits the thrush better than the robin. Since certain myths (M_{724b}) make a distinction between the summer robin (*Turdus migratorius*) and the winter robin (*Ixoreus naevius*) – the harbinger of snowstorms, according to Brasher (Vol. III, p. 111), and to which I shall return later (see below, p. 491) – we cannot exclude the possibility that the common term 'robin' may in fact refer to three different birds. It would seem that in Cowichan and Musqueam the same word *skʷqɛq* refers to both species of 'robin' (Kuipers, p. 294; Elmendorf-Suttles, p. 24). At the same time, a correlation and oppositional relationship could exist between the robin and the chickadee, because the latter calls for its lost *sister* and the robin, according to certain Coast Salish ($M_{747a, b}$; Adamson, pp. 30, 369), is also calling for a lost relative, but in his case it is his *wife*.

Be that as it may, the fact that snowstorms, the warm rain at the end of winter and the refreshing rain of summer are all attributed to birds which are lumped together under the same name explains the ambiguous role of the 'Robin' in respect of the sun, heat and fire: without rain, the summer would be too hot; although the summer rains are heralded by 'white clouds', instead of the 'black clouds' which bring the winter rains (cf. M_{742a}), they are in opposition to the sun shining alone in a clear sky.

Apart from its meteorological function, the American robin has another one, related to a different form of periodicity. A Cœur d'Alêne myth, that I shall not study in detail since it belongs to the parallel series on the origin of wind and fog to which I have frequently alluded, ends with the transformation of its two main characters, a mother and her son, into a robin and a diver (probably a grebe). 'As for me,' says the woman, 'I will be a ghost. I will sit on a tree near the houses of people and make my sound there when people have a death' (M_{748a}; Reichard 3, p. 170). The role of psychopomp thus attributed to the robin is even more clearly evident in the mythology of the Carrier, who are Athapaskan neighbours of the northern Salish. They say (M_{749}; Jenness 2, p. 100) that the village of the beyond is divided into two portions by a river: on one side, the houses are red, on the other, black: 'the black houses were the homes of the dead, the red of the robins which dwell on earth during the day and go back to the underworld at evening'. But the fact that there is continuity between the two functions, that is, from meteorology to biology, is shown by the Tsimshian myth I have already quoted (M_{354b}) in which the humans who have been invited to the robins' village discover that the chief's house is divided into two halves: a winter half and a summer half (Boas 2, pp. 182, 760).

Let us carry the analysis a stage further. The Carrier, one of whose myths I have just quoted, establish a correlational and oppositional relationship between the robin and a bird called Song-Sparrow, probably *Melospiza melodia*: 'both come in March. The Robin sings throughout both spring and summer, but the Song-Sparrow does not begin until May, for it works during the months of March and April. So in winter when Robin had nothing left to eat, while his neighbour had plenty of food, he tried to buy food from him in exchange for his red leggings; but Song-Sparrow refused' (M_{750}; Jenness 2, p. 254).

This American Indian version of the fable of the grasshopper and the ant is of particular interest since it associates and contrasts two birds, between which the same semantic function is interchangeable, depending on whether the myths concerned belong to the northern or the southern limits of the Salish area. We have seen that, in the north, the Carrier attribute to the robin the power of travelling between the world of the dead and that of the living. In the extreme south, the Tillamook, who, unlike the Carrier are Salish, although cut off from the main part of their linguistic family (whereas the Carrier live close to it), attribute this same power to the Song-Sparrow, while at the same time they place the world of the dead in the sky: 'The Sparrow has an awful power: he will go to the spirit land and then he can get back here' (M_{751a}; E. D. Jacobs, p. 12), whereas for the Carrier it is chthonian. In another myth from the same source (M_{751b}; *ibid.*, pp. 98–9), the Sparrow plays the part of ferryman on the river dividing the world of the living from the world of the dead.

The identity of the bird may seem uncertain since, in both the source-texts, the word used is 'sparrow'. However, by arguing once again on the basis of commutations, we can be confident that the bird in question is indeed the same 'sparrow' (a bird of the Fringillidae family).

The Tillamook myth begins in winter. The sparrow cannot bear the cold and pesters Ice, the demiurge, by always coming to get warm at his fire. The demiurge in exasperation marks the bird's breast with a fire-brand, whereupon the sparrow, as I have said, flies up to the sky to complain to the spirits.

So, because he feels cold in winter, the Tillamook sparrow has a black mark on his breast, made by charred wood. As it happens, the Puget Sound Indians tell a very similar story about a bird called *spetsx*, who is harshly treated by his brothers-in-law (his wife's brothers). When they force him to gather firewood, he laboriously chops up a dead, half-burnt tree, and his brothers-in-law protest that he never washes the grimy soot from his face. His wife adds her reproaches to theirs; for the sake of peace and quiet, Spetsx goes to the river, turns towards the south-west, and, addressing the sky, starts his ablutions. At once rain falls, the rivers rise and flood the valley, and all the inhabitants die, all except Spetsx, who flies off and takes up his abode with his ancestor, the south-west wind, the rain wind. Now, if the bird is taking a bath on a sunny day and looking south, this is a sign of rain (M_{752a-d}; Ballard I, pp. 49–51; cf., too, p. 63).

There is some uncertainty about the identity of the *spetsx*, which according to some sources, is similar to the Oregon junco, while others state categorically that it is the marsh sparrow (*Melospiza georgiana?*; Ballard I, p. 49, n. 2, p. 50). The Cowlitz, who called the lewd grandmother Spi'tsxu, associate the bird of the same name with the snow-bird, probably the junco (M_{562a}; Adamson, p. 220; cf. M_{752h}; *ibid.*, p. 178). The Chehalis of Washington State also speak of the *spi'tsxu* bird, and Adamson (M_{752e-g}; pp. 1–3) renders the name in English as 'thrush': it is probably, then, the varied thrush (*Ixoreus naevius*, cf. above, p. 489); this hypothesis seems the most plausible, since this winter bird with the 'weird and mysterious note' (Pearson, Vol. III, pp. 240–41) could well be the 'Robin', the harbinger of death, into which the heroine of the Cœur d'Alêne myth (M_{748a}) is changed, after she has covered her body with *dentalia* shells: hence the variegated plumage — tawny, black and white — which makes the winter robin (the varied thrush) so different from the summer robin.

The disagreement among the Puget Sound informants is, in itself, instructive. *Junco oregonus* is the scientific name of the snow-bird, which has already appeared in the myths discussed (cf. above, pp. 83–4, 427–8). This bird has a *mahogany brown* back (Pearson, Vol. III, pp. 46–7, *Names of Birds*, etc., p. 20), and thus can form a correlational and oppositional pair with the red-breasted American robin.[14]

On the other hand, the sparrow who, in Tillamook mythology, is *cold* in winter and has, on his breast, a black mark made by a *red-hot* poker, also forms a pair with his fellow in the Puget Sound mythology, whose *face* is marked by wood which is still *cold*, and who unleashes the south-west wind which, as we know from other contexts (M_{754a-g}, see below, p. 492), puts an end to the harsh winter weather by bringing rain and *warmth*.

[14] It should also be noted — although without jumping to any hasty conclusions — that, among the eastern Algonquin, the name junco or snow-bird suggests effervescence or bubbling (Speck 5, pp. 368–9), that is, a type of phenomenon mentioned in M_{740}, where the grandmother is transformed into air bubbles which burst on rising to the surface of the water. We have seen already that, in the Cowlitz version, the lewd grandmother and the junco have the same name: Spi'tsxu.

We are dealing, then, with two pairs of birds. In one pair, the junco, 'a true winter bird indeed' (Pearson, *loc. cit.*), is in opposition to the robin, associated with summer, because it has russet markings on its back and not on its breast. In the other, a sparrow, blackened on the breast by the 'hot' because it cannot stand the cold, is opposed to a sparrow which is blackened in the face by the cold, with the result that the bird itself produces the hot. The apparent disagreement among the informants could therefore be a consequence of the fact that, in quite separate respects, the Junco and the Sparrow are commutable within a pair in which one or the other can be in correlation with, or in opposition to, the Robin.

In any case, as we move from south to north and from the coast inland, the robin and the sparrow replace each other in the same roles: on the level of biological periodicity as psychopomps and, on the level of seasonal periodicity, as birds responsible for the coming of spring. I have already mentioned the Flathead belief that to vex robins will cause rain; the Puget Sound Indians say exactly the same about sparrows (Ballard 1, p. 63, n. 33).

However, as rain-makers, the birds do not act in the same way. The sparrow is well-prepared for the severity of winter because, instead of singing like the robin from the beginning of spring, it first builds up supplies of food (M_{750}). So it prolongs the benefits of summer into winter, unlike the robin, which sings very early to bring about a thaw and thus hasten the transition from winter to summer (M_{354b}). Further south, certain Chehalis and Skokomish myths ($M_{747a, b}$) make the point that the robin suffers a lack of food for the common good; the bird is reduced to a state of famine because of his wife's habit of peeling off all the camas she gathers, so that she always returns empty-handed. In order to punish her, he burns her face so severely that she throws herself into the river, where the stones stick to her warm body. She changes into a grub which lives in a sheath of compressed sand. Here again, then, we see a relationship of correlation and opposition between the robin and a creature who is burned on the face or breast.

One cannot help noticing that as regards their plumage all the birds under consideration have mixed colouring, through the contrast of black and white or the partial presence of red. In the first group, we can put the chickadee with its black head and white cheeks, and the sparrow with black markings on its face or breast or, according to M_{752c}, round its eyes. Some Indian languages made the parallel between the two birds even closer. The species known as the 'white-throated sparrow' (*Zonotrichia albicollis*) is referred to in Blackfoot by an abbreviation of the word for the chickadee (Schaeffer 2, p. 43); it is called 'the Great Chickadee' in the language of the eastern Algonquin, which in fact does not always distinguish clearly between the two birds (Speck 5, p. 368).

In the second group we find the red-breasted American robin, the russet-backed junco, the hermit thrush with its speckled breast and reddish tail, as well as various members of the woodpecker family, to which I shall return: the red-headed woodpecker of the genus *Sphyrapicus*, which also has red markings on its head; and lastly the rosy woodpecker or red-shafted Flicker (*Colaptes cafer*) whose egg becomes the sun in a Shuswap myth about the origin of this heavenly body (M_{753}; Teit 1, p. 738).

In order to summon rain when the weather was very cold and the ground was thickly covered with snow, the Puget Sound Indians used to make bull-roarers with boards painted black on one side only, and young boys would whirl them to make a noise that was believed to bring the south-west wind; or alternatively, they would blacken a sparrow so that as soon as it was released it would fly off to the river to wash its face and call the south-west wind (Ballard 1, p. 63, n. 31). Such practices link up not only with myths M_{752a-d}, but also with a whole other group that I do not propose to study in detail, since it contains inexplicable contradictions which seem to be due to lapses of memory or slips of the tongue on the part of the informants (M_{754a-g}; Ballard 1, pp. 55–64; M_{754h}; Haeberlin 1, pp. 398–9). Rain could be brought on by telling the myths, which describe a conflict between the north-east winds and the south-east winds, following the marriage of a man belonging to one of these wind people with a 'mountain beaver' woman, *Aplodontia rufa*,[15] or with a porcupine, both of whom might, or might not, be members of the rival community. The son born of this marriage, who is himself called Storms (March rainstorms; cf. Ballard 3, p. 81), rescues one female relative, the only survivor of the community of the south-west, whom the Raven, a member of the other community, is persecuting by soiling her face with excrement. Rain starts to fall when the

---

[15] The aplodontia is not a beaver, but the only surviving representative of a very archaic genus of rodents, 'half-beaver, half-squirrel' according to the dictionaries, which exists only in this limited area of America, where it lives in forests and dense thickets, digging burrows which may be two or three hundred metres long. This animal appears so seldom in the myths or – which amounts to the same thing – it is so rarely mentioned by name, that I hesitate to suggest that it might be part of a system which would make it commutable with two other rodents: the porcupine, of which it is in this instance a combinatory variant, and the beaver, which resembles it. Such a circular permutation would, however, be very interesting, since it would offer an additional means of consolidating the myths about the conquest of fire, and those featuring the wives of the sun and moon, where the heroes are, respectively, the beaver and the porcupine (*OTM*, pp. 226–73; see below, pp. 581–8). I shall do no more than propose, as a working hypothesis, the following triad, homologous with those on pp. 479, 499:

Beaver:	*Aplodontia:*	*Porcupine:*
Spatial periodicity	Spatio-temporal periodicity	Temporal periodicity

hero signs to her to wash herself, and the ensuing flood scatters, or almost completely destroys, the enemy camp. This is the origin of the alternation of the seasons.[16]

The interest of these myths lies in the fact that they are convertible. Whereas in the preceding versions the action develops along a horizontal axis, the poles of which are north-east and south-west, in some Coast versions the war between the winds is transposed along a vertical axis. According to the Washington Chehalis (M_{756a}; Adamson, pp. 75–6), the south-west winds decide to wage war on the north-east winds which are causing unbearable cold. But the latter live in the sky and can only be reached through the snow-bird pulling the sky down to earth. The Kathlamet of the Lower Columbia area and other Chinook tribes tell the same story, but in their version the south-west winds are in the sky and are responsible for destructive storms (M_{756b}; Boas 7, pp. 67–71). I propose, then, to disregard the Chinook and to confine myself to the Salish.

The latter put the sky, north-east winds, dry weather and cold on the same side, in opposition to water, south-westerly winds, rain and hot weather. At the same time, the junco's action of pulling the sky down to earth is an obvious inversion of the operation carried out by the wren or the chickadee who, by means of the chain of arrows, build a ladder from the earth to the sky. It follows, firstly, that the sparrow in the Puget Sound myths (M_{752a-d}) belongs to the low when he turns towards the south-west to summon rain, and is thus in opposition to the chickadee and the wren who turn towards the high to obtain not water but fire; next, that the junco, who is congruous with the sparrow (see above, p. 491), is himself in opposition to the other two birds. However, we also know that for the

---

[16] I cannot at this point embark on a consideration of the theme of twins, which looms large in the myths of this area, because it belongs rather to the parallel series about the origin of wind and fog I have already alluded to. In support of the dual nature of birds endowed with a meteorological function, I shall merely note that, inland, or in more northerly coastal areas, certain motifs present in myths M_{754a-h} are concerned with twins. In the inland area, the Shuswap credit twins with the ability to bring fine weather by whirling a kind of bull-roarer (Boas 16, p. 644), the function of which is symmetrical with that assigned to the instrument by the communities to the south of Puget Sound. On the other hand, among the Coast Nootka, twins, like the sparrow farther south, are believed to bring rain by washing their faces which have been previously blackened (*ibid.*, p. 592).

A short Cœur d'Alêne myth about the origin of death (M_{755}; Boas 4, p. 125) confers on twins the same ambivalence in respect of life and death as the Carrier assign to the robin and the Tillamook to the sparrow: twins, probably a girl and a boy, fell into a faint one day and remained unconscious for a long time. At least this is what was believed, for when they were alone they argued secretly with each other inside the lodge about the respective advantages of life and death, one defending life, the other death. Their mother stole upon them unawares and interrupted their discussion. Since then, people have died from time to time. Some are born, while others die, and there are always some living and some dead. If the twins had been able to finish their argument, today there would be neither life nor death. A Chehalis myth from Washington State (M_{716b}; Adamson, pp. 83–7) refers to Siamese twin brothers who always walk and shoot arrows in opposite directions to each other.

Salish — and especially in this group of myths — the seat of cold weather is in the sky, whereas in mythic times the earth was hot and dry. In this sense we can say that the hibernal junco brings winter (corresponding to the high) closer to summer (corresponding to the low), whereas the chickadee and the wren perform the same operation in reverse. All these birds, then, effect a semi-mediation, successful only in one direction, and corresponding to the singular function I attributed, on different grounds, to the robin and the sparrow.

We may seem to have too many birds, but to those already considered, we must now add woodpeckers. It will be remembered that they play the part of conquerors of fire in certain Klikitat or Salish myths: Sahaptin (M_{726}), Skagit and Sanpoil (M_{724a}, M_{729}). In North and South America alike, woodpeckers act as spatial mediators because they spend most of their time on tree trunks, between the sky and the earth (*RC*, p. 203; *OTM*, p. 289). There is a suggestion in Ballard (3, p. 85) that, in the Puget Sound area, the small woodpecker of the genus *Sphyrapicus*, the hero of the Klikitat myth, might also have a temporal function. When questioned about the native calendar, an informant defined the period from the end of January to February as follows: 'The ducks get stuck in the ice; the steelhead can't travel; sapsucker is here.' Whether or not 'here' means 'still here' or 'already here', it associates the bird with winter. In connection with various Picidae with red markings (therefore well-qualified to conquer celestial fire) found in this area of America, it has been observed (Bent, *Woodpeckers*, pp. 145, 151) that at the end of autumn they move from the most exposed parts and settle in sheltered localities. Like the varied thrush which in winter comes down from the mountains into the valleys, and like the junco which remains in the same latitudes all the year round (Pearson, Vol. III, pp. 46–7, 240–41), woodpeckers, or some species of them at least, would appear, then, to have a marked affinity with winter.

It may seem less easy to come to a conclusion about the wren, since in American English the name covers a considerable number of species, and even different families of birds. But if the myths refer to the species which is commonest in this part of America (*Troglodytes Troglodytes pacificus* Baird) and indeed is present everywhere — cf. Hill-Tout (6, p. 11): 'This bird can be seen throughout the whole of British Columbia, and is found even in the densest forests where no other bird save the woodpecker is to be seen' — and moreover simply moves into the sheltered valleys in the winter (Bent, *Nuthatches, Wrens, etc.*, p. 175), then this wren, which is also given the epithet *hiemalis*, must have the same affinity with winter as the birds previously mentioned.

The point can be proved *a contrario* thanks to certain Blackfoot myths (M_{701d}; Josselin de Jong 2, p. 25), which are inversions of the Salish stories about Coyote, the trickster, borrowing the wren's long penis in exchange for his own (M_{701a-c}; see above, p. 439). According to the Blackfoot, it is 'the Old Man' himself (corresponding to the trickster) who has the long penis and who, to avoid suspicion, exchanges it for that of *nepumaki*, the 'bird of spring' or 'bird of summer', i.e., the chickadee (Schaeffer 2, p. 43). It follows from this that:

(*long penis* : *short penis*) : : (*Wren* : *Chickadee*) : : (*winter* : *summer*).

It should be recalled, however, that the myths in this group establish the contrast not so much between winter and summer in the absolute as between meteorological phenomena which act as semi-mediators, in other words, the warm rains of late winter, and the cool refreshing rainstorms of summer: the former, as it were, introduce *summer into winter* and the latter *winter into summer*. Although the milt-girls in M_{742} are disjoined from each other in order to embody contrasting seasons, they do so in the same form, since they both turn into rain-bearing clouds.

Be that as it may, one cannot but be struck by the fact that the myths, although so careful to establish Chickadee's origin and to give a detailed account of his adventures right up to the conquest of fire, show very little interest in the Wren's past (see above, p. 171). The Bella Bella, who are coastal neighbours of the Bella Coola but not themselves members of the Salish family, consider the wren to be the instigator of death, since it would build its nest on the undersides of coffins which these Indians were in the habit of placing on a platform or in trees (M_{757a}; Boas 24, p. 29). The Comox-speaking Squamish credit the wren with the power of causing berries to ripen out of season (M_{757b}; Hill-Tout 7, p. 529). Generally speaking, however, in the area with which we are concerned, the wren is not described as possessing any special talent: the myths simply contrast it with the other species as being 'the smallest of all the birds'. It is clear that smallness is taken to be its most relevant feature since the expression is often used periphrastically as a way of naming it. If we suppose an axis along which all the birds are arranged in order of size, the wren, as an unmarked term, is situated at one of the poles. Its tiny frame contrasts with the immense space between sky and earth, which nevertheless it alone is able to span. It is clear from this that the wren, as the embodiment of a spatial pole, is placed in correlation with, and opposition to, the chickadee, another very small bird, but one whose origin and adventures the myths describe and to whom they assign the role of temporal mediator (see above, p. 486), before it becomes a spatial mediator, on a par with the wren, and like it (but in different versions) the only creature capable of attaching the chain of arrows to the sky. It follows that the wren and the chickadee have a dual function, one on the spatial axis, the other on the temporal axis. This is a consequence of their commutability not only in respect of the chain of arrows which allows ascent but not descent, but also in the lewd grandmother cycle, where either one or the other plays the part of initiator of man's mortality (see above, pp. 169–70, 477–8). On one side of these median operators are the woodpeckers, who are associated only with the origin of fire and not with that of man's mortality. The mediation they carry out is therefore spatial, and since it relates to the conquest or reconquest of cooking fire, it provides humanity with a means of heating which belongs to the realm of culture.

On the other side of the diagram, we can place the sparrow which, by bringing winter to an end with warm rain, effects a temporal mediation and bestows on mankind a kind of heating which, unlike the other, belongs to nature. In this last respect, the function of the median operators — Wren and Chickadee — is also seen to be twofold: as the makers of the chain of arrows enabling the conquest of fire, they are agents of culture; but as grandsons of the lewd grandmother and responsible for man's mortality, they are agents of nature.

If we bear in mind that the term robin probably covers three birds: the American robin, the varied thrush and the hermit thrush, all three harbingers of atmospheric phenomena (late winter rains, midsummer rains and snowfalls), the only birds which have not yet been defined are the syncretic 'robin' and the junco. We know, however, that these birds cannot be placed in a separate category, since each one is commutable with the sparrow: at opposite ends of the Salish area, the function of ferryman between the world of the dead and the world of the living, as well as that of initiators of spring, fluctuates, as it were, from the sparrow to the robin, or from the robin to the sparrow (M_{345b}; M_{749}; M_{751}); whereas, in the centre of the area (M_{752a-d}), the function of temporal mediator guaranteeing the alternation of the seasons is, for the reasons I have already given, attributed either to the robin or the junco or else to the sparrow.

It follows, then, that three etiological functions, relating to the origin of fire, rain and man's mortality, are reciprocally commutable and, depending on the particular area (probably through that dialectical process which prompts each group to want to be both like its neighbours and different from them by having the same myths but telling them in its own way), the mythic operators are also commutable between the functions. Taking into account, very roughly, the geographical distribution of the mythic themes, we arrive more or less at the following table:

MAN'S MORTALITY (*through CHICKADEE*)

RAIN (*through SPARROW*)   FIRE (*through CHICKADEE*)

FIRE (*through WREN*)

MAN'S MORTALITY (*through WREN*)

MAN'S MORTALITY^{-1} (*through SPARROW*)

At the bottom left-hand side of the table, the transformation of man's mortality into its opposite refers to the Tillamook myth M_{751b}, in which the sparrow, as ferryman of the dead, brings about a resurrection.

The general armature of the system is tripartite, following a pattern which is worth comparing with those on pp. 429–30 and 493. The obvious correspondence between them is further confirmed by the name of the lewd grandmother in M_{562a}, since it is the same as the one attributed sometimes to the sparrow and sometimes to the junco.

Apart from one exception in Shuswap mythology (M_{753}), to which I have already alluded, and in which a woodpecker of a particular species, not mentioned in other myths, succeeds in becoming a solar divinity, albeit separate from the visible sun which is later born from one of its eggs, the woodpecker proves, on the whole, to be as unfitted as the robin to play the part of the sun (see above, p. 488). There can be no question of either the sparrow or the junco assuming the role, because of their direct association with winter and the rains which herald winter's end. Consequently, the woodpecker and the robin are both inadequate when it is a question of obtaining warmth, the first in respect of nature – since he is only able to conquer cooking fire – and the second in respect of fire, not water (in connection with the woodpecker, unusable as the sun through being either too hot or devoid or light, cf. M_{758a-c}; Sanpoil: Ray 2, p. 137; Puget Sound: Ballard 1, pp. 79–80; Okanagon: Hill-Tout 8, p. 145, and Boas 2, pp. 727–8).

We must not forget, then, that these irreversible acts of mediation entail serious adverse consequences: first, a quantitative impoverishment of the natural order – in time, by the limit imposed on human life, and in space, by the reduction in the number of the animal species after their disastrous celestial escapade; and also a qualitative impoverishment, since through

WOODPECKER	WREN/CHICKADEE (unmarked) (marked)	SONG-SPARROW
	$\underbrace{\qquad\qquad}$	Commutation $\begin{cases} \text{external : ROBIN} \\ \text{internal : JUNCO} \end{cases}$
Origin of fire	$\begin{cases} \text{Origin of fire (}\textit{culture}\text{)} \\ \text{Origin of man's} \\ \quad \text{mortality (}\textit{nature}\text{)} \end{cases}$	Origin of rain
Cultural warmth		Natural warmth
Spatial mediation	*Spatio-temporal mediation*	*Temporal mediation*

having conquered fire the woodpecker loses most of his decorative red feathers (M_{729}); and since the red breast acquired by the robin takes the form of an anatomical injury, resulting from his failure during the same mission. So, either through the destruction of an original harmony, or through the introduction of differential gaps which impair that harmony, mankind's accession to culture is accompanied, on the level of nature, by a form of deterioration entailing a transition from the continuous to the discrete.

2 Junctions

However different the roads they take, all travellers arrive at the same meeting-place.

Chateaubriand, *Voyage en Amérique*, Introduction

In the earlier part of this work, my analysis of South American mythology had already brought out the various themes with which we have just been dealing: the transition from the continuous to the discrete, the conjugation of the origin of fire and rain with that of man's mortality, a phenomenon which, in the temporal dimension, interrupts the demographic flow and, by dividing it into generation levels, introduces differential gaps comparable to the differences between the animal species, in the sense that what might have remained an undifferentiated fabric is fragmented into separate entities.

In the present volume, attention has been concentrated on a limited area of North America, not so much because its mythology has certain features in common with that of Brazil and the neighbouring regions, but rather because in the two areas the mythic field is organized in the same way. Not only do the individual myths resemble each other; there is also, more importantly, a resemblance in the relationships between the myths. On several occasions (see above, p. 99 *et seq.*, p. 158 *et seq.*; *OTM*, p. 410), we have seen that if, in tropical America, there is a myth B which is a transformation of a myth A and a myth C which in turn is a transformation of myth B, a myth A′ homologous with A has only to exist in the northern region west of the Rockies for us first to deduce, and then to confirm, that myth A′ implies B′, which is a transformation of it just as, in South America, B was a transformation of A. The same thing happens in the case of C and C′ and the parallels can sometimes be carried even further.

It must not be supposed that similar observations would be impossible in the case of other areas. However, the mass of material is so great that a truly exhaustive study of North American mythology would require a whole lifetime, if not several. I am obliged, therefore, to limit myself to the partial approach adopted in the present volume, as in the preceding one. However, if only to avoid errors of perspective, I should give some rough indication of the roads by which, in regions of North America other than those studied so far, we might be led back at least to the bird-nester story, which I have used consistently as my reference myth; the reason for the choice, which has gradually become clear to me, has to do with the median, if not central, position of this myth, as the hinge-point of a whole system, so much so that, wherever we find it, we can be sure of also finding the same mythological set articulated around it.

In a manner which is not entirely arbitrary, I propose to begin this rapid investigation with the Arapaho, and shall thus follow the same order as I adopted in *The Origin of Table Manners* (p. 207) in studying the mythic cycle about the wives of the sun and moon, which, it must not be forgotten, stands in an immediate transformational relationship with that of the bird-nester. I may add that the Arapaho myths to which I have already had occasion to refer in the present volume (see above, p. 417), show striking affinities with those of the Salish. In spite of the present geographical distance between the tribes, this should not seem surprising, since the Arapaho, the most southerly members of the great Algonquin linguistic family, came down from the north. And during the long migration which took them from an area probably situated to the west of Lake Superior to what are now the States of Colorado and Kansas, they must have stopped for a time in Wyoming where, during the historic period, the most conservative section of the tribe still lived. It seems more than likely that the Arapaho must have lived there in contact with the eastern Salish since, in former times, the latter had spread beyond the Rockies in the direction of the plains (see above, p. 356).[1]

Between the Salish and Arapaho versions of the bird-nester myth, the differences are minimal:

M 759. Arapaho. 'The bird-nester'

There was once an Indian who was married and the father of a boy and a girl. The Trickster, who wanted to appropriate his fine garments and his wife, persuaded him to go and fetch eaglets from the top of a high peak. The Indian took off his clothing and started to climb up the cliff, which

---

[1] It would be interesting to know what philologists think about the apparent similarity between the Arapaho name for the trickster, transcribed as *Nih'änçan* by Dorsey-Kroeber, and that of a rival and competitor of the trickster, in Cowlitz mythology, called *Nəxántci* in Adamson's transcription (pp. 230–33), after 'an (unidentified) animal with a reddish coat bearing some resemblance to a mouse'.

he found quite an easy task, since the way to the nest was like a stairway. But the Trickster commanded that the peak increase in height. He made the sides completely smooth so that the Indian was unable to come back down and remained stranded at the top.

The Trickster did not attempt (as in Salish mythology) to assume the outward appearance of his rival. He related what had happened but said nothing of the part he himself had played, and claimed that the hero, before disappearing, had told him to take care of his wife and children. The wife consented but it was not long before her new husband started to scold his stepchildren without cause or reason. Such is the feeling with the stepfather or stepmother for children. The woman, who loved her children and was unhappy to see them being ill-treated, decided to divulge the suspicious circumstances in which her husband had disappeared. Everybody went to the foot of the peak which was strewn with beads; these were the tears shed by the hero who had wept for days and nights. They called upon the wild geese to help: they flew to the top, put the man on their backs and landed him safely. He was at once comforted and cared for; he recovered his health and strength.

He then set off to look for his wife and children; he found them again and gave them food, for his rival had deprived the children of food in the hope that they would quickly die of hunger. The hero then hid in a meat sack, jumped on the Trickster and killed him. The corpse was cut up and the pieces scattered.

However, the Trickster came back to life. He went away and stopped to rest by a lake, and meditated on death: should death be final or not? On seeing that a stick, then a buffalo turd, and lastly a piece of pith remained afloat after he had thrown them into the lake, he opted for resurrection. However, when a pebble sank, he reversed his decision. It was better that people should die, he concluded, otherwise the earth would quickly become overpopulated. Since that time, people only live for a certain period and die for ever (Dorsey-Kroeber, pp. 78–81).

The reader will have recognized that the last sequence is the same as that devoted to the fabrication by the Trickster of an artificial son ($M_{667a, 668a, 670a, 671}$) in the most complete Salish versions of the bird-nester story. But in the Salish myth, the problem consisted in creating life while freeing man from biological constraints, whereas in this case it is a question of setting a limit, through the introduction of irrevocable death, to human life, which will henceforth be subject to the same constraints, but at the end instead of the beginning. The Arapaho myth, a perfect example of indissoluble fusion of form and content, therefore transfers this sequence from the beginning to the end of the story. It thus maintains consistency with the Salish versions, and furthermore with the Klamath and Modoc myths studied at the beginning of the present volume, and with which the Arapaho version also has in common the motif of the origin of adornments: the beads formed from the tears shed by the hero during his exile take the place of the quill embroidery he invents while recovering in the home of the life-saving sisters. The different position allocated to the porcupine in the mythology of the Plains Indians (*OTM*, pp. 207–13) made the substitution necessary.

Lastly, it should be noted that the Arapaho – who are less interested in the origin of fire than in the technical improvement brought about by the invention of the fire-stone, which was much easier to use than the fire-drill (M_{760}; Dorsey-Kroeber, pp. 8–9) – include in the same myth a discontinuous means of ascent to, but not descent from, the sky, succeeded by a continuous union, but which, however, is given a negative function by the very fact of its continuity (see above, p. 469). The cliff face, which was easy to climb because it formed a natural stairway, is reminiscent of the ladder or chain of arrows in the Salish myths about the theft of fire; but its transformation by the trickster into a uniformly smooth column is reminiscent of the same trickster's long penis (here transposed from the horizontal to the vertical axis) in the Salish myths, where it is assigned a similarly wicked function, that is, the conquest of a woman who would otherwise be out of reach. The long penis motif as such is not absent from the Arapaho myths ($M_{761a, \, b, \, c}$; Dorsey-Kroeber, pp. 63–5) but, contrary to what happens in Salish mythology, the Trickster comes to a tragic end, since he bleeds to death when his penis is cut off. Ever since, a man's penis has been reduced to modest proportions, and attempts at rape, such as groups of young men in the Plains tribes sometimes went in for, have been severely punished (*OTM*, p. 388). A motif which, in other contexts, is given a much broader, symbolic meaning, is used here, then, for moral and practical purposes in connection with a matter of public order.

On the other hand, the bird-nester myth was invested with an important symbolic significance relating it to the myth about the wives of the sun and moon (cf. *OTM*, pp. 213, 252–3), since both had a place in the liturgy of the sun dance. Inside the ritual lodge a forked stick set in the ground with the two tips pointing respectively east and west had on it the dead body of a small unidentified bird, turned towards the north. This emblem symbolized the hero's descent on the backs of the geese (Dorsey-Kroeber, p. 80; Dorsey 5, p. 86), a detail which will be of some importance for the concluding part of my analysis (see below, p. 595).

Alongside this 'normal' version of the bird-nester myth, the Arapaho have another, less recognizable, variant which deserves close attention, for reasons which will soon be evident.

$M_{762a, b}$. *Arapaho.* '*The two brothers*'

A great chief had a young brother called Lime-Crazy or White-Painted Fool (a perhaps meaningless compound-name). This boy was lazy and untidy. One day, his elder brother told him he should be ashamed, and ordered him to wash his face, comb his hair and perfume himself; he lent him some decent clothing and sent him to join the young women getting water at the springs.

The hero was only too eager to follow these words of advice. He made a practice of seducing and enticing the women by his charm, and made so many conquests, even among the married women, that he was soon regarded as a regular nuisance. A delegation went to the village chief and promised him that, if only he would consent to kill or expel his brother, he would be regarded as the only ruling chief, and that he would have the best of things.

Tempted by this prospect, the chief agreed. On two successive occasions, the brother was bound and thrown into deep water, but he emerged safe and sound and went on annoying the wives of headmen and warriors. Finally, his elder brother took him hunting. As soon as he had killed and cut up a buffalo, he ordered the young man to stay where he was and wave branches to drive away the flies, while he went to the village to seek help so that they could carry the meat home. But he never came back, and the hero, faithfully obeying his orders, continued going round and round the meat and fanning it with the branches. Several years passed in this way. As there was no news of him, the people concluded that he had starved to death.

But the inhabitants of the village had only wanted to be rid of the troublesome brother. Having achieved their ends, they turned against their chief, abused his authority, took all his possessions and drove him out. Despised and rejected, he lived a wretched existence with his wife outside the camp circle. One day, his wife suggested that he should go and look for his brother. He found him where he had left him, three-quarters buried in the ground, from which only his head emerged and the branch which he was still waving. When he was asked to come out of the ground, he refused and continued to drive away the flies as he had once been ordered to do.

The wife added her own entreaties to those of her husband. Every time they returned together to visit the hero, the latter had sunk even further into the ground; but he was still waving his branch, so the meat had remained in good condition in the circular pit worn away by the hero as he walked round and round the pieces of game. Finally, his sister-in-law, who had always loved him tenderly (M_{762b}), painted such a pitiful picture of their hardships that he consented to jump out of his hole and go along with them; but in place of the branch he carried a club-board.

When they entered the camp, the young men were dancing (M_{762a}) and the elders of the tribe were beating the drum (M_{762b}). The hero asked his sister-in-law to announce his return; first of all they insulted her and drove her away, then they threw tallow at her which greased her last dress. Finally, the hero revealed his presence; he ordered everyone to sit erect in a row and keep their legs stretched out in front of them; then he told his sister-in-law to strike their shin-bones with the club-board. After this punishment, the former chief and his wife were allowed to retrieve their reserves of food and their other possessions. Once again they were treated with respect by all and had servants.

However, people continued to hate and fear the hero. His rivals in amorous adventures (M_{762a}) or his brother himself (M_{762b}) persuaded him to go on a hunt and made him cross a great river, ostensibly to capture eagles in the rocks overhanging the far bank. While the hero was picking up feathers, his companions fled in the one and only boat. Fortunately, a bird of prey, a buzzard or hawk, advised him to ask for help from the Father-of-the-Waters who, in return for gifts of eagle feathers, would take him half-way across the river. At this point, he was directed to make a very piercing sound on a bone whistle, and take a sudden leap into the air as high as the sky; the water would spurt beneath him without reaching him, causing a widespread flood; he, however, would land safe and sound at the top of a hill. Everything happened as the bird had forecast, and when the waters receded, the hero went back to the camp circle (M_{762a}). When he went on a journey again, the white owl – that is, a snowstorm – killed him, but others say it was the lightning (M_{762b}) (Dorsey-Kroeber, pp. 23–31).

Since it was at this point that I concluded my analysis of M_{759}, let me observe first that, in the present myth, the eagle feather offered to a horned monster is reminiscent of one of the sun-dance rites (Dorsey-Kroeber, p. 28n.; Dorsey 5, pp. 201–2). This establishes an initial link between M_{759}, M_{762} and the cycle about the wives of the sun and moon.

More importantly, it is clear that M_{762} is connected with what I have referred to several times as the 'Potiphar transformation' of the bird-nester myth, although I have only sketched it in rough outline. A first proof is that the hero's disjunction occurs at a great distance; this is a characteristic feature of the transformation from the central Algonquin (as we shall soon see) to the Chinook (M_{659}), except in the instance I have already discussed (M_{661}; pp. 340–45), where the conversion of the culinary code into a vestimentary code justifies the retention of the vertical disjunction, which, however, becomes definitive – a sign of its non-relevance in this changed context.

In M_{762}, however, the Potiphar transformation is systematically inverted so as to present a reverse picture of itself even down to the finest details. Instead of a well-behaved hero who refused to commit incest with his father's or his brother's wife, or who is unjustly accused of committing incest while remaining totally ignorant of his female relative's intentions, in this myth, a ne'er-do-well, corrupted by his elder brother (who in other contexts plays the part of injured husband), behaves like a veritable Don Juan outside, not inside, the family circle. We shall see presently that, in the Algonquin versions, one of the men who plot to kill the hero (in collaboration with the latter's father or brother) also appropriates his possessions; so the aggression of which the hero is a victim also reduces him to poverty. But in M_{762b}, where his brother and his other relatives, whether close or distant, have to pay heavy fines to his victims' families, especially if married women have been involved, the impoverishment – not of himself but of his kinsfolk – is caused by his own acts of aggression. On the other hand, the plotters in M_{762} promise the hero's brother all kinds of riches provided he agrees to co-operate in their scheme. The hero of this myth is, to start with, so destitute that he has to be lent clothes. Here, too, collective jealousy is directed against a man who has incited to sexual excess a brother from whom his own wife has nothing to fear. So, instead of jealousy operating from within outwards, it is operating from without inwards.

The Potiphar transformation disjoins the hero on an island, that is, land surrounded by water; in M_{762}, an initial attempt at disjunction fails although the hero is twice thrown into a deep river, that is, water bordered by land on both sides. The only purpose of this episode seems, then, to be the exclusion of the other formula through its inversion, so that the later, successful disjunction can be of a purely *terrestrial* nature, since it takes place during a *buffalo hunt*, which replaces the expedition to gather *water-bird's* eggs. But by hollowing out, through persistent walking, a circular ditch full of meat which remains fresh, the hero creates an empty space surrounded by land, i.e., an inversion of the island – a terrestrial eminence surrounded by water — where, according to the 'straight' versions, there was nothing to eat.

The hero of M_{762}, who sinks deeper and deeper into the earth, is also an inversion of the bird-nester character exiled to the sky, and his disjunction towards the low is added to, and intensifies, the disjunction usually inflicted on the heroes of the Potiphar transformation which is towards the far. I have already shown (p. 416) how the branch swung from the low to the high to drive away the flies in stubborn obedience to an order is in opposition to the plaited rope which in the bird-nester cycle allows the hero to come back to earth on condition that he scrupulously obeys orders; there is a similar opposition with the Salish versions of the wives of the sun and moon cycle, in which the wives transform their rope ladder into a swing, the lower part of which swings — unlike the branch — from a fixed point situated above.

In the Potiphar transformation, after the hero's banishment, the chief culprits become rich; in the Arapaho myth they become poor. And whereas in the first instance a wife full of hatred for her brother-in-law or son-in-law is responsible for his disjunction, in the second the same woman, by demonstrations of affection, succeeds in obtaining his conjunction. When she is soiled with fat — i.e., a *food* — by her fellow villagers, she echoes the *excrement*-soiled victim encountered in the group $M_{654-657}$, and who will reappear in the Algonquin versions of the Potiphar transformation, thanks to a double inversion affecting both the mode of aggression and the symbolic value of the mode used in this instance (see below, pp. 511–12). We shall also see that the punishment inflicted on the wicked in M_{762} — a beating which, if carried a little further, would have broken their legs at a time when they were engaged in dancing or sounding the drum — is an inversion of the fate meted out to them in an Omaha version of the bird-nester story (M_{771a}; see below, p. 520) by means of a magic *drum*, the sound of which first lifts them into the air, then brings them down with a crash to the ground so that their bones are broken — whereas, according to M_{762}, the hero owes his life to a magic whistle which lifts him into the air above the river and brings him comfortably down again to a safe landing. Moreover, M_{762} reveals its direct link with the bird-nester myth in a final sequence, where the hero's enemies take him to capture eaglets on the other side of a great river (this negates the island in the middle of a lake of the Potiphar transformation) and so disjoin him along the horizontal axis (an inversion of the vertical axis of disjunction, which is an invariant feature of the bird-nester cycle). Contrary to what happens in the latter cycle, the hero collects a great many eagle feathers, with which he pays an aquatic monster to ferry him across the river; the monster is, then, a transformation, along the horizontal axis, of the vertical ferrymen represented by the geese in M_{759}: they, too, are aquatic creatures, but birds, i.e., creatures living above water not below, and it is their wings, that is, feathers, which carry the hero.

M_{762a} tells us nothing about the hero's subsequent fate. In M_{762b} he either dies in a snowstorm or is killed by a thunderbolt: the latter is celestial fire, the former intense cold, but both are in opposition to the method used by the hero himself, in the Algonquin version of the Potiphar transformation, to destroy the culprits: he brings intense heat out of the earth and causes the rivers to boil.

My reason for first introducing the Arapaho myth was to explain, by reconstituting its paradigm, the incident (in itself incomprehensible) involving blind old women who wave conifer branches, in a Thompson version of the bird-nester story (M_{670a}). In doing so, I was also seeking to demonstrate the operative value of a pair of correlational and oppositional terms: the swing (an inverted image of which is presented by the branches swinging from low to high) and the symplegades which, as I also postulated, are suggested by another pair of blind old women, this time celestial. I have just shown that M_{762}, which contains the waving branches motif, is an inversion of the Potiphar transformation, which in its turn is a transformation of the bird-nester myth. If the hypothesis put forward on pp. 414–18 is correct, it follows that the straight versions of the Potiphar transformation must contain the symplegades motif. Proof of this is to be found in certain Siouan and Algonquin myths.

Although the Blackfoot and the Cree belong to the Algonquin family and the Assiniboine to the Siouan family, the three tribes occupy adjacent territories, and those of their myths with which I am concerned here are so similar that they can legitimately be grouped together.[2] They also provide examples of intermediary types between the bird-nester myth and the Potiphar transformation. There is an unmistakable link between the first group and a Blackfoot version (M_{764}; Josselin de Jong 2, pp. 60–63), in which a man who, because he covets his friend's possessions, makes him climb down a cliff face to fetch an eagle's nest, then abandons him. The

---

[2] I propose to leave aside a brief moralizing transformation found among the Arapaho and the Gros Ventre ($M_{763a, b, c}$; Dorsey–Kroeber, p. 262; Kroeber 6, pp. 118–20), in which the young man, whether or not he has yielded to the advances of his sister-in-law (brother's wife), soon discovers that she prefers a passing stranger, with whom she plots to kill him. The hero defeats the stranger and takes the wife back to his brother. He subsequently confesses his own guilt and obtains his brother's pardon. Together they kill the unfaithful wife.

eagles turn out to be helpful and, when the young are fully grown, the mother bird carries the hero back to level ground. It only remains for him to avenge himself by killing the traitor, which he does. Two points are particularly notable in this version: the hero, as the eagles' guest, manages to survive by cooking the portion of meat given him by the birds through exposing it to the sun. Because of his disjunction towards the low, he is brought back, then, to a pre-cultural condition, to the state of nature, as it were; whereas, in the South American versions of the same myth, the hero, through being disjoined towards the high, obtains cooking fire and the arts of civilization; he thus achieves a state of culture. In both cases, the people, and his father in particular, explain his return in almost the same terms.

According to the Serenté myth (M_{12}), the hero at first remained hidden and only showed himself to his people at a feast commemorating the dead (RC, pp. 34–74). In the Blackfoot myth (M_{746}), the father, on first seeing his son again, says 'that he seems to have come back from the world of the spirits'. It will be remembered that the reference myth M_1, which is an inversion of the Ge versions, gives a double form to the father's vengeance on the son guilty of incest: before exiling him to the sky, he tries, but without success, to cause his death by sending him westwards to look for noisy ritual instruments *in the aquatic kingdom of the spirits*. This double disjunction, first towards water which is far away, then towards the sky which is high, brings together, within one and the same myth, two patterns of possibility between which the North American tribes we are at present discussing hesitate, according to whether myths, otherwise very similar, link up with the bird-nester cycle rather than with the Potiphar transformation of this same cycle. What, it may be asked, is the difference between the two types? It lies in the fact that the plot of the bird-nester myth, when the hero obtains cooking fire for mankind, is based on an antagonism between *affines* and, more particularly, between the giver of a woman and the taker, which gradually weakens to become a vague relationship of friendliness (compare M_{179} and M_{764}); the Potiphar transformation, on the other hand, rests on an antagonism between *close relatives*, a father and a son, or an elder and a younger brother. The reason why the armature of the bird-nester myth, as it can be observed from the Klamath-Modoc to the Salish, appears to be in contradiction with this contrast, is that it exploits a different potentiality of the system:

$$\text{Bororo} \quad \begin{pmatrix} \bigcirc = \triangle \\ | \\ \triangle \end{pmatrix} \Rightarrow \quad \text{Klamath-Modoc, Salish} \quad \begin{pmatrix} \triangle \\ | \\ \bigcirc = \triangle \end{pmatrix}$$

In *The Raw and the Cooked* (pp. 71–2, 92–3), I showed that the reference myth M_1 is situated at the point of intersection of these two types. It is based on an antagonism between father and son, but because matrilinear descent operates in Bororo society, the son belongs to his mother's social group, which is in the position of giver, in relation to the father. It is clear, then, why the reference myth makes use of the two disjunctive schemes which American Indian thought as a whole seems to be unanimous in attributing to forms of antagonism which are themselves in opposition to each other.

I gradually came to the conclusion that, in the mythological system of both North and South America, the bird-nester myth serves as a point of articulation. However, we can now envisage the possibility of carrying the analysis a stage further. If the bird-nester myth splits up into two formulae, one respecting a prototype (initially identified in Ge mythology), the other culminating in the Potiphar transformation,[3] between the two the reference myth M_1 itself serves as an initial element of articulation; and I now understand still more clearly why, of all the available American myths, this particular one should have forced itself upon me before I knew the reason why.

The Assiniboine versions also hesitate between the two formulae ($M_{765a, b, c}$; Lowie 2, pp. 150–54 and cf. M_{504}, *OTM*, p. 445): either the hero's father disjoins him far away on an island in the middle of a lake, or his elder brother does the same, or disjoins him at the top of a tree on the pretext of capturing eagles; however, since the brother cuts down the tree, thus causing the hero to fall into the river, the opposition between the two types of disjunction is very considerably weakened. This phenomenon occurs in conjunction with another: the emergence, alongside the jealous relative (father or brother) of a wicked affine in the person of the hero's sister's husband, who in M_{765c} ill-treats the sister so that the hero, after being rescued by an aquatic monster, takes his revenge twice: on an affine first of all, then on a relative. The Assiniboine versions therefore confirm the analysis in the preceding paragraphs.

They confirm it in another way, too. There is a feature of these versions which is also to be found among the neighbouring tribes, who are members of the Algonquin linguistic family. Almost all the heroes of the Potiphar transformation take their revenge by similar means: either by bringing the

---

[3] These lines were written before the publication of the second volume of the *Encyclopédia Bororo*, which contains a hitherto unpublished variant of M_1. Provided it is not simply an editorially inspired reworking of the story, it is very close to the Potiphar transformation, since it concerns not a son who rapes his mother, but a stepmother who seduces her stepson (*EB* Vol. II, pp. 303–59).

sun closer to the earth (M_{765a}) or by ordering the ill-treated sister to light a huge oven, or by themselves creating intense heat which changes water into steam so that the traitors are scalded to death (M_{765c}); the means, then, is destructive fire of terrestrial or celestial origin, with the difference that, in the latter case, the sun approaching the earth is an inversion of constructive cooking fire, which takes the sun farther away from mankind; fire too, the obtaining of which, according to the bird-nester cycle, freed man from the harsh alternatives facing them: either to eat their food raw or to cook it directly in the sun's heat, thus running the risk of being consumed by fire themselves. But the analysis can be taken further; in both Assiniboine and Cree mythology ($M_{766a, b}$), the hero treacherously advises his father to protect himself from the imminent conflagration by smearing himself with fat — bear fat, in some contexts — a dangerous precaution which makes him even more inflammable. Since fat is a food, and furthermore the part of the meat that is considered most nutritious (see above, p. 539), the destructive fire conjured up by the hero is undeniably the reverse of cooking fire. Furthermore, the transformation to which I drew attention on p. 507, as occurring between the $M_{654-657}$ group where a hero or heroine is soiled by *excrement* (bear's excrement, as it happens), and M_{762} where the heroine is soiled by fat, i.e., a *food*, is continued in this context by means of the same fat, which is *burnt up* instead of being *cooked* or *excreted*; in other words, it moves from the category of the *rotten* to that of the *cooked*, and then to that of the *burnt* (cf. *RC*, p. 294).

One last aspect of the Assiniboine versions is also worthy of note: M_{765} relates how the hero, on his way back home sees two chasms, the sides of which are rapidly moving away from each other and then coming together again. He succeeds in getting beyond them by throwing a tiny fish into each one, and by taking advantage of the moment when the earth closes up to swallow it. As I had already postulated (p. 508), the Potiphar transformation restores, then, the motif of the symplegades which are here neutralized by the offering of small fish made by a human, and are transposed from the vertical plane to the horizontal, thus effecting a double reversal of the real symplegades in the group M_{375}, M_{382}, etc., which deny the right to eat large fish to those humans who have not succeeded in getting through them.

Several Algonquin versions give the hero or his father various names which appear to have something in common: Ayatç (M_{766a}), Aïoswé or Aïswéo (M_{766b}), Ăyāsä (M_{767a}), Aiasheu (M_{767d}), or A'katahōneta (M_{505}), which is less similar. Petitot (1, p. 451, n. 1) translates the first form as 'stranger', and suggests that it is derived from two roots one meaning 'bound' or 'tied', the other 'covered' or 'buried'; this would make it an inversion of the meaning of the bird-nester's name in the Thompson myths, which is said to be 'the raised one' (see above, p. 388). Michelson, who was probably a better linguist, translates the last form (in: Jones 3, p. 77) by 'the One-Left-Behind', a meaning of which is equally consonant with the mythic analysis, since it stresses the horizontal axis of disjunction characteristic of the Potiphar transformation, whereas the Thompson name of the hero refers to the contrasting vertical axis of disjunction characteristic of the bird-nester cycle.[4]

If it were possible to confirm these similarities of name, the point would be of great interest, especially since the Algonquin versions support, in other respects, the hypothesis I put forward in connection with the Salish myths: that the old blind women are a celestial counterpart of the symplegades. This was a deduction, but certain Algonquin myths now corroborate it with empirical proof: they replace the horizontal symplegades which obstruct the hero's progress in the Assiniboine version (M_{765a}) and the Cree version where they are referred to as 'the earth's mouth' (M_{766a}; Petitot 1, pp. 451–9), by two old blind women whose forearms and elbows are spiked with bones as sharp as daggers (M_{766b}; Skinner 1, pp. 92–5), or by two old women who try to suffocate the hero under their knees, which are swollen with pus, then by two others, also blind, whose elbows are armed with awls (M_{767a}; Jones 2, Part 2, pp. 381–9); or again (M_{505}; Jones 3, pp. 75–89) by two cannibalistic cougars which also occur in Assiniboine mythology (M_{765c}), then by two blind old men between whom the hero provokes a quarrel and who finally kill each other, in accordance with a pattern already exemplified in other Algonquin myths, as well as in Athapaskan and Ute myths where it exists as a separate element ($M_{685-687}$, see above, pp. 400–401). The symbolic correspondence between the two blind people and the symplegades results not only from the fact that, from one tribe to the next the two motifs are commutable in the same myths (and in Cree mythology, from M_{766a} to M_{766b}), but also from the way in which the myths describe the destruction of the ogresses by the hero:

He thought of a plan by which he might dupe the old women into killing each other. Instead of going himself and sitting between them, he got a large parchment and, fixing it to the end of a pole, he poked it in between

---

[4] On the other hand, the form *āyāsä*, the name of the hero's father in Ojibwa (cf. naskapi, *ayas.i*; Speck 11) is puzzling, since Jones translates it by 'filcher of meat', an expression the meaning of which can be elucidated in the light of similar myths (see below, p. 514) but which does not seem to have any etymological relationship with the other forms.

them . . . The old women heard it rattle and thought it was the boy himself coming to sit between them. They both turned their backs [to the skin] and began to hit away at it with their elbows. Every time they stabbed the skin they cried out exultantly and at last got so near to each other that they began to hit one another calling out all the time [cries of victory addressed to their supposed victim]. They finally stabbed each other to death . . . (Skinner 1, p. 94).

On the island where he is marooned, the hero of M_{766a} and M_{767a} either lives on raw eggs or fails to find anything whatever to eat. Consequently, he has no fire either. After being taken across the river by an aquatic monster, he meets first an old woman who supplies him with food from an inexhaustible kettle, then the two ogresses, who die in the manner just recounted. According to M_{766b} and M_{767a} (the versions $M_{767b, c}$, Radin 4, pp. 27–31 are much less detailed and I mention them only for the sake of completeness), the hero must also avoid causing the human bones hanging across the path to rattle against each other. Otherwise, strangers, masters of fierce dogs, will hear the noise and kill him. The hero is careless enough to knock against the bones, but he escapes by digging an underground tunnel, at the entrance of which he places a stuffed ermine, to give the impression that it is just an ordinary burrow. The dogs that are pursuing him allow themselves to be taken in by the ruse; their masters are furious, accuse them of deceit and complicity, and kill them. According to M_{767a}, a magic pouch, made from the skin of a dead woodchuck, bores a tunnel to by-pass the bones, but it surfaces too soon and bumps into them, causing them to rattle. Whatever the details, this episode, during which the hero is exposed in the land of the dead to a mortal danger symbolized by *bones which must not make any sound*, and who owes his life to *underground* animals, although they are not always quite up to the task entrusted to them, is strikingly reminiscent of the experience of the hero in the Bororo reference myth (M_1), who is sent off to the land of ghosts to bring back ritual jingle rattles and gourd rattles *which must not make any sound*; he succeeds in his mission with the help of *aerial* creatures, the last of which, because it is slow rather than clumsy, narrowly escapes death (*RC*, pp. 35–6). The similarity becomes even clearer when we note that, according to M_{767a}, the bones were in fact shoulder blades, i.e., ritual objects for Indians who practised scapulimancy (Cooper 2); gourd rattles also were ritual objects which, in South America, made the wishes of the spirits audible, as in this case, or allowed them to be divined, as in the other instance.

On returning to his village the hero of M_{767a} finds his mother completely naked and blind, as a result of ill-treatment by his father. He gives her clothes and restores her sight by blowing on her eyes. In M_{505}, on the contrary, he punishes her for having adopted a child after his disappearance and forces her to burn the substitute son.

In M_{766b}, the father, who is a great bear hunter, thinks he can escape the fire by hiding under his stores of fat. This proves a vain precaution, and the only people who survive the conflagration are the hero and his mother, who, respectively, change into a gray jay (*Perisoreus canadensis*) and an American robin (*Turdus migratorius*). This conclusion is reminiscent of a Cœur d'Alêne myth (M_{748a}, see above, p. 489), where the mother also turns into a robin, and the son into a grebe. We noted that these two birds are given periodic functions along the temporal axis, as heralds of imminent death in the one instance and bad weather in the other. But the Cree myth establishes a correlational and oppositional relationship between the robin and the gray jay, a bird which, among the eastern Algonquin at least, had a well-founded reputation as a camp pilferer and meat thief. It was referred to as the 'greedy' or 'thieving' bird, and aroused such feelings of hatred in the Indians that they used to harass it remorselessly and pluck it alive as soon as it was caught (Speck 5, pp. 365–6; Desbarats, p. 66). As it happens, the hero of the Kickapoo version (M_{505}) changes his traitorous servant into a crow, also a thief and carrion-eater, and the hero's father in the Ojibwa version M_{767a}, who, contrary to what happens in the other versions, is spared by his son for unknown reasons, is called 'filcher of meat' (see above, p. 512, n. 4). This is enough to elucidate the semantic function of the gray jay. If the role of psychopomp that the Cœur d'Alêne and the Carrier attribute to the robin is also found in Cree mythology, the two birds would be both correlated with, and opposed to, each other as 'subtractors', one of food, the other of years of human life. As far as a gray jay is concerned, this function would seem to tally with its name in eastern Algonquin, which the English settlers transcribed as 'whiskey-jack', homonymous with the name of the trickster god, Wiskedjak (Speck 5, p. 365).

Further confirmation is supplied by a Cree myth (M_{768}; Skinner 1, pp. 107–108), which begins just after the universal conflagration was started (or, is here, simply foreseen and foretold) by a hero whose father, with whom he has quarrelled and who dies in the fire, is called Aiacciou, a name deriving probably from the common root which I have mentioned (p. 511) as occurring frequently in myths belonging to this group. According to M_{768} too, the hero marks out a patch of ground into which he invites all those whom he wants to spare. Whereas, in the preceding myths, only the mother is granted this favour, or occasionally the father and a few privileged persons (M_{767a}), in this instance all the creatures are given refuge. After the fire, the hero endows each animal species with its distinctive features, and thus forestalls the confusion which would have occurred if any particular species had tried to appropriate those of another. He also gives each inhabitant of the village a name. According to the informant, he calls his mother Robin 'because she is loving' and himself Blackbird (*Agelaius?*) 'because this bird only comes every spring'. This is also true of the American robin whose early return is also mentioned by Speck (5, p. 372; 7, p. 79), as well as its meteorological role as a harbinger of rain, when it sings during the day (see above, p. 488). Although there is a shift to the seasonal code in this myth, the two birds are nevertheless responsible – together with another bird (the hero's sister who has changed into a golden woodpecker) for the introduction of differential gaps between the animal species and also between humans, on each of whom a proper name confers 'a distinctive mark', as is specifically stated in the text (cf. L.-S. 9, Ch. VII). In short, in this continuation of the Potiphar transformation, the hero's banishment to a far country leads to a destructive terrestrial conflagration, followed by the establishment of specific differences. It will be remembered that the Salish myths associate the second consequence with the constructive conquest of celestial fire – an expedition towards the high – and explain it as the effect of subtractions modifying an original zoological continuum (see above, pp. 466–7, 498–9).

To sum up, the Potiphar transformation of the bird-nester myth (which is itself a transformation along another axis of the saga of Moon the demiurge) is accompanied by a whole series of direct topological operations, of which the following are the most important:

1) *vertical disjunction* $\Rightarrow$ *horizontal disjunction*;
2) *non-susceptible ferryman* $\Rightarrow$ *susceptible ferryman* (see above, p. 447);
3) *vertical symplegades* $\Rightarrow$ *horizontal symplegades*
   (*in the sky*: the old blind women) $\Rightarrow$ *horizontal symplegades*
   (*on earth*: blind old women, and chasms with moving sides);
4) *the swing* (oscillating from high to low) $\Rightarrow$ *boughs* (swinging from low to high).

In this way the transformation combines within a single myth themes which, to the west of the Rockies on the one hand and in tropical America on the other, are shared between two: the bird-nester myth along the vertical axis, and the Moon's saga along the horizontal axis (M_{375}, M_{382}, etc.) or, in Amazonia, the story of Poronominaré (M_{247}) and other related myths, among which – as I now realize – can be included the Serenté myth featuring Asaré, that I discussed at length in *The Raw and the Cooked*, if we grant the following secondary transformation (secondary, that is, in respect of the preceding ones): *the origin of the moon* ⇒ *the origin of Orion and the Pleiades*. This follows, on the one hand, from my previous discussion of a Blackfoot myth M_{591} (see above, p. 224),and, on the other, from the fact that the myth in question – which is a transformation of the Asaré myth and also explains the origin of the Pleiades – tells of a conflagration (comparable to the one in previously discussed myths in that it causes rivers to boil) which is brought to an end by the arrival of rainy weather. This change of sign affecting a conflagration of terrestrial or celestial origin, in one context carried to its ultimate conclusion, and in the other stopped in good time, is accompanied by a return to a vertical axis of disjunction, and thus completes the cycle of transformations, at least in this respect.

The affinity between the Siouan versions and those just discussed is already clear from the title of a Dakota myth: 'The nation of birds', which the text does not explain, because the informant suffered from a lapse of memory and ended the story abruptly:

M_{769a}. *Dakota. 'The jealous relative'*

A wealthy Indian family had a boy and a girl: the latter was very pretty and Iktomi, the trickster, wanted to secure her. So he plotted with a kinsman who was jealous of the many horses his young cousin possessed. The brother was abandoned by this accomplice on an island, where they had gone together to collect eagle feathers. A horned aquatic monster brought him back to the shore. The hero found his sister married to Iktomi, who was abusing her by picking up coals of fire and sticking them in her face. He killed this wicked brother-in-law, and also his thievish cousin, trimmed up his lodge with the eagle feathers he had brought back from the island, and made out of them the first . . . Here the text ends (Beckwith 2, pp. 411–13).

In an older version (M_{769}; Wissler 1, pp. 196–9; cf. also M_{769c}, Riggs 2, pp. 139–43) the hero has a wicked sister-in-law (the wife of his elder brother, who falsely accuses him of incest) and a no less wicked brother-in-law, the sister's husband who tortures her as soon as he has won her as a reward for his collusion. The hero, abandoned by his treacherous brother-in-law on a desert island, lives on berries and wild roots which push up noisily through the ground. A horned aquatic monster takes him across the lake and is killed by a thunderbolt: so, like the character in the Algonquin versions, this monster, too, is a ferryman susceptible to atmospheric conditions. The hero encounters, in turn, mice living in a buffalo skull who are bewailing their 'grandfather's' death, and all of whom he kills; an old woman who tries to kill him by crushing him under her abnormally large leg; however, he kills her and burns her corpse; 'If he had not done so, women would still have the power to increase the size and strengh of their legs to such an extent that they could kill men with them.' Next he visits a woman who tries to poison him by offering him her own brains to eat (she has extracted them through a hole at the top of her head); however, a friendly gopher manages to make a hole in the bottom of the pot so that the food runs into the ground. The hero kills the wicked woman by taking a hot stone from the fire and dropping it into the hole in her head. He then burns the body: 'If he had not done this, women would still mix the poison of their brains with the food they cook'. Then the hero arrives at the house of a hospitable old woman, the mother of two very pretty daughters who each have a bed at opposite ends of the lodge. They each invite the hero into their bed, but he does not move, and they fall to disputing which he will choose. They have teeth in their vaginas which can be heard grating. The hero takes his crane's bill (or heron's bill) and kills one, then the other: 'If he had not done this, women would be dangerous to their lovers'. After this adventure he is pursued by animals of every species. He disguises himself as an old man. A woman, although she is with the persecutors, takes pity on him and tells him that he will find old, weak skunks, porcupines and badgers in the rear that will serve him as food: 'this is the way people came to eat the flesh of animals'. When at last he returns home, the hero finds that his sister has aged prematurely because of her husband's cruelty towards her. He strikes the husband down, and because he did this, 'it came to pass that cruel husbands are punished by their wives' relatives'. The hero returns to his father, who drops down dead from the excitement of seeing his son, and to his own people. He goes out hunting for them and kills buffalo, the possession of which is being fiercely contested by great numbers of birds and other animals. All the people are destroyed in the struggle: 'This is why animals now eat the flesh of man' (Wissler 1, pp. 196–9).

This unexpected conclusion adds a final etiological function to those previously mentioned. The animals referred to are probably carrion-eaters, animals which feed on corpses, and are the only survivors of a time of primaeval chaos when the women played the part of stranglers, poisoners and castrators, although they spared old men. A version belonging to the Canadian Dakota (M_{769d}; Wallis 1, pp. 78–93), like the one recorded by

Riggs (M_{769c}), tells how the hero is forced by the trickster (called Spider in this myth) to drink his own urine and eat his own excrement. On his way back home he also has various encounters: three hospitable old women, then two cannibalistic women who try unsuccessfully to smother him under blankets woven from human hair; they subsequently have their monthly periods, after which he marries then. Each gives birth to a son. When the boys reach adulthood, they take their father and mother to visit their father's family. The hero discovers that his sister is married to Spider, who is ill-treating her and burning her face with red-hot pokers. It is now his turn to force the cruel brother-in-law to drink his urine and eat his excrement, after which he burns him to death, causing a universal conflagration in which everybody dies except his father and mother (in the Riggs version he has to resuscitate his parents who have been killed by his brother-in-law, and he burns only the brother-in-law to death).

In moving from Algonquin to Sioux mythology, we may note several transformations. First, the pouch made from a woodchuck's skin (M_{767a}) becomes a pocket gopher[5] (*pouch as container* $\Rightarrow$ *pouch as content*). In the one instance, an animal, or its animated skin, tunnels a passage to by-pass maleficent *bones*; in the other, on the contrary, by making a hole in a cooking-pot, the animal releases a soft substance, *brains*, which is in opposition to the hard bony tissue in the same way as marrow, which is absent from the shoulder-blades mentioned in M_{767a}. In M_{766b} and M_{767a}, the problem is how not to make a noise, and the hero or his helpful animal are unsuccessful in dealing with it. In M_{769b}, on the contrary, the hero is able to remain silent when the two women contend for his favours and, on two occasions, he owes his life to a noise: the sound made by the sprouting wild parsnips which serve as his food on the island; and later the grating of the toothed vaginas of the seductresses — a warning noise which ensures that he himself is not eaten.

The ogresses, who are congruous with the swinging doors in the Algonquin myths, are armed with sharp, outward-facing weapons: pointed bones or awls (apart from the pus-infested knee in M_{767a}, which is, in this particular instance, an inversion of the poisoned brains in M_{769b}). Except in M_{769c}, which brings the two types together, those in the Dakota myths are armed with blunt or inward-facing weapons: legs capable of vice-like pressure, or toothed vaginas, or smothering blankets made from human hair (M_{769d}), which are in opposition to the bone spikes, as the soft is to the hard, that is, as the brains to the bones with no inner marrow. The episode

---

[5] TRANSLATORS' NOTE: 'Pouch' and 'pocket' correspond to a single term in French: *bourse*, *rat à bourse*.

of the mice in the buffalo skull, illustrating a paradoxal contrast between life and death, could also connote the preceding opposition. But the point could only be proved by an investigation of the paradigm to which this motif belongs, and which, in Plains mythology, appears to be commutable with many others. I propose, then, to leave aside this aspect of the myth.

Let us enquire, rather, into the reason for the transformations I have just listed. The Riggs version (M_{769c}) and the Canadian Dakota version (M_{769d}) develop, and at the same time duplicate, a transformation which I have followed throughout the myths of the group from $M_{654-657}$ (where the victim's head is soiled by faeces, see above, pp. 325–31) to M_{765a}, $M_{766a, b}$, where the traitor is burned through the intermediary agency of foodstuffs, by way of M_{762}, where a victim is soiled with cooked food. Here, in this context, first a victim (the hero) and then a traitor are forced to eat excrement, and another victim, the hero's sister, has her face burned with red-hot pokers. The major opposition: (*faeces* : *food*) :: (*destructive fire* : *constructive fire*) is between the beginning of the myth, where the traitor forces the hero to drink his urine and eat his faeces, and the end of the same myth where the hero kills everybody by fire, but not before taking a double revenge on his principal enemy in the penultimate episode; this revenge brings together, synchronically, the categories of the *rotten* and the *burnt*, which the narrative sets in opposition to each other diachronically, by putting one at the beginning and the other at the end.

By arranging their myth in this way, the Canadian Dakota seem, then, to have effected a synthesis of traditional versions, peculiar to the tribal group from which they originally sprang, with the versions found among the Algonquin. The latter end the story with a conflagration, which destroys the whole community, and in particular the hero's father, although he has tried to protect himself with a covering of fat, a detail which makes him comparable to cooked food. The fullest available version, which belongs to the Plains Dakota (M_{769b}), ends in exactly the opposite way: the father, a blameless character, dies from the shock of seeing his son again, and the son, while hunting for food for his kinsfolk, unintentionally causes their death, since the animals fight with them for possession of the meat, kill them and feed off their corpses. So, instead of moving towards the category of the burnt, like the Algonquin versions, this Dakota version moves towards the category of the rotten, which is that of rapidly decaying corpses. Furthermore, this progression would seem to be consistent with the rest of the myth, since the hero's first encounters suggest, either directly or metaphorically, sexual activity involving young creatures, but in connection with which the hero is in danger of being eaten alive; whereas his last encounter, before he returns to his village, leads to the eating of cooked meat (first by himself and by the human race after him), but because he has assumed the guise of an old man. After passing from youth to old age, the myth moves on to death and to decay. The Algonquin myths follow quite a different pattern, since the hero's encounters are emphatically concerned with the land of the dead, from which he returns in order to take his place among the living. These remarks can be summarized in the form of a diagram:

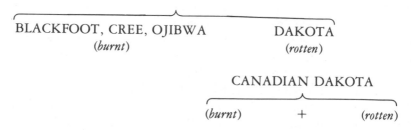

Let us now see what happens among other tribes belonging to the Siouan linguistic group. The Ponca and the Omaha have a very modified version of the meeting with supernatural beings congruous with the symplegades. In their mythology (M_{770}, an Omaha variant of a myth already discussed, cf. *OTM*, M_{469c}, J. O. Dorsey 1, pp. 185–6, 201–206) we find cannibalistic Thunderers, for whom the hero makes himself invisible (thus rendering them blind in respect of himself). He steals, not their food, as in the Salish versions, but their lit tobacco pipe and uses it to inflict on them burns, for which they blame each other. In the end the hero reveals his presence and persuades the Thunderers to abandon cannibalism and eat game. Since that time, thunder, instead of destroying humans, has been of help through bringing refreshing rainstorms during the heat of summer. As might be expected, at the same time as there is a return to the meteorological code, the axis of disjunction moves from the horizontal to the vertical. This brings us back to the bird-nester myth. It exists among the Omaha, since they have a myth (M_{771a}; J. O. Dorsey 1, pp. 586–609) about a poor, despised orphan boy who is the only person to shoot a 'small very red bird' with his first arrow,[6] and thus wins a competition, the prize being the chief's daughter. His disappointed rival, the trickster Ictinike, takes him

___

[6] The Arapaho have a very similar story (M_{771b}; Voth, p. 43). The bird, perhaps a redstart (*Setophaga ruticilla*), which is called 'little fire' by the eastern Algonquin (Speck 5, p. 369), could perhaps be the unidentified bird in the Arapaho sun-dance rites symbolizing the bird-nester's successful descent (see above, p. 503). Another witness of the rites describes a forked stick holding a tuft of sage brush (replacing the bird mentioned by Dorsey), 'with in addition something red, apparently cloth' (Kroeber 3, p. 286). In connection with this emblem, cf. below, p. 595.

off to hunt wild turkey, and, on the pretext of recovering a lost arrow, forces him to remove his clothes and climb a tree. The tree rises up into the sky: the hero is stranded and then rescued by four birds: the eagle, the buzzard, the crow and the magpie, who take him back to earth in relays. He returns to the camp, recovers his magic clothes and organizes a communal dance to the sound of the drum. The dancers are all hurled into the air, then crash to the ground and break their bones. This brings us back, then, not only to the bird-nester cycle but also to the conclusion of the Arapaho myth M_{762} (see above, pp. 504–508), and the entire Algonquin-Siouan set is thus rounded off.

I shall conclude this brief eastward sally with the Iroquois. According to different versions of the same myth ($M_{772a, b}$; E. Smith, p. 85; Cornplanter, pp. 167–81), either a man or a woman detests the son of his or her spouse born of a previous marriage. He or she gets rid of him by imprisoning him in a large hole or in a porcupine's burrow, ostensibly to capture the cubs. M_{772a} relates how the hero weeps for a long time, then falls asleep, and wakes up in the animals' den. The latter deliberate as to how they should feed their guest, since, unlike themselves, he cannot eat raw food. M_{772b} misses out this sequence and carries straight on with an episode featuring a she-bear who lives in the den and rears the hero along with her own cubs. Of all the animals, only bears have a diet acceptable to humans: dried fruit, nuts and honey from honeycombs . . . Several years go by, then one day a hunter discovers the bear's lair and kills her as well as the cubs. He captures the hero who has turned into a wild beast, teaches him to speak and re-educates him. According to M_{772b}, he is taken back to his father, his wicked stepmother having died in the meantime, and he teaches mankind the rites of the bear dance as they have existed ever since. In M_{772a}, he marries the daughter of his guardian whose wife complains that he never brings home 'tender bear meat'. So he resolves to kill a bear, in spite of his feelings for his adoptive mother's people. Retribution quickly follows: on his way back, he is impaled on a stake and dies.

This myth, in which the birds are inverted to become porcupines and the celestial world becomes the chthonian world, seems very far removed from those with which we started. And yet, it refers back, in a most striking way, to an episode of the Timbira myth, M_{10}, which was an essential element in my early interpretations (RC, pp. 71, 149–54). In that myth, the hero, who is rescued by a jaguar, arouses a stepmother's hatred. Being pregnant, and because of this prone to irritation, she is exasperated by the noise the hero makes in eating roast meat. The stepmother is complaining, then, that the meat he is eating is *too hard*, whereas in the Iroquois myth, she complains that the meat he has given her to eat is not *tender enough*. As a consequence of which, in the first case the hero pierces the jaguar-woman's paw with an arrow; in the second case, he himself is pierced and dies.

This myth belonging to the north-east of North America is, then, on two counts, an inversion of the South American versions, since the helpful animal in M_{10} — whether a jaguar or a bear — can feed the hero according to culture — the South American jaguar being the first master of cooking fire at a time when humans ate their food raw — whereas, in M_{772a}, the helpful animal is the only creature able to feed the hero according to nature, since only bears eat raw foods compatible with a human diet.

The relationship of inversion between these myths belonging one to the northern, the other to the southern hemisphere, is itself a function of another inversion observable between North American myths, according to whether they originate in the extreme east or the extreme west. It is worthy of note that the she-bear in M_{772b}, in order to bring out her affinity with humans, should choose to contrast herself, not with other wild animals, but with dogs: 'We, the bears, are the most closely related to your people. Our habits are almost the same as your people's. Some people say that it is the dog that stands next to man . . . But . . . you cannot eat the food that dogs live on, nor can you live as they do in winter-time' (Cornplanter, p. 174). It is a fact that bears hibernate in dens which resemble houses and which protect them from the cold; also, they eat dried fruits and nuts.

We need only refer to the myths from the west coast which have already been summarized and discussed (see above, pp. 50, 165–8, 201–202, 266–7, etc.) to gauge the importance of the reversal: among the Salish and the Sahaptin, she-bears are featured as ogresses. But dogs, which are situated half-way between humanity and animality, were said to have given man cooking fire (like the South American jaguar) as well as the implements with which to kindle it (see above, pp. 117–18, 158); and although bears hibernate, dogs usher in the warm spring winds (Jacobs 1, pp. 30–33). The Iroquois, as is well-known, had an ambivalent attitude towards dogs, which were used as propitiatory offerings and burnt in mid-winter to implore the sun's return (Hewitt 3). It follows that, from east to west, the system remains the same, although all the terms are reversed: the physical contiguity which, on the west coast, establishes a meteorological affinity between dog and man, disappears in the west to be replaced by a metaphorical resemblance between the respective modes of life of bears and humans. Not unexpectedly, the crux of the reversal occurs at the half-way point: in Blackfoot mythology (M_{591}), where dogs, the friends of man, extinguish a fire (among the Iroquois, fire was the means used to sacrifice them to the sun) by imploring and creating rain: this is the origin of the Pleiades, the culmination of which at dusk (Shimony, p. 174) signalled, for the Iroquois, the time for the dog sacrifice:[7]

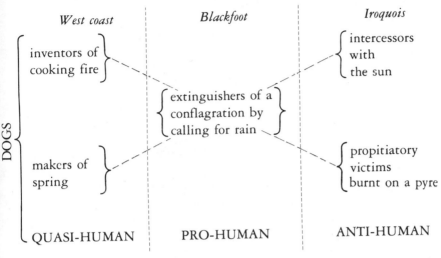

This double parallel between the north-east of North America and Central Brazil, on the one hand, and the east and west of North America, on the other, strengthens the conviction that American mythology forms a whole.

Looking southwards, along the frontiers of the area where, as I showed in the early sections of this volume, the bird-nester myth changes into the Loon Woman myth, what we find first are weak forms. Among the Takelma, a small linguistic group in South Oregon surrounded by Athapaskan, the story of the bird-nester is simply inserted as one episode among Coyote's other adventures (M_{773}; Sapir 5, pp. 83–4). We have

---

[7] Between the Blackfoot and the Iroquois, an additional transition is provided by a Cree myth, M_{766b}. It presents dogs as fierce beasts in the service of killer-spirits, who accuse them of deceit and slaughter them, after the hero, by means of a trick, has succeeded in escaping from them (see above, p. 513). This means that dogs, although already anti-human, have behaved objectively as if they were still pro-human. Other transitional myths are to be found elsewhere; among the northern Athapaskan, who believed that it was possible to bring on thunder by biting a dog's ear so that it howled (Jetté, p. 351), and among the Yokuts and the Mono, who held the opposite belief that the celestial dog, the master of storms, would stop the rain on hearing the howls of a dog being beaten on earth, for this purpose (Gayton-Newman, p. 29; cf. also pp. 48–50, where twins reared by a bitch become the thunderers). Lastly, it should be noted that the myth about present-day humanity having originated from the union of a human woman and a dog, which is very widely distributed to the west of the Rockies, takes on a symmetrical and opposite form in the eastern part of the North American continent, in the mythology of the Montagnais who believe that thunder sprang from the marriage of a male, superhuman character, the demiurge, with a female musk-rat (Perrot, p. 160).

already noted (M$_{636a, b}$; see above, p. 290) that the Maidu transfer the bird-nester theme to the bears and fawns cycle. On the other hand, it has a prominent place in Ute mythology. The Ute linguistic group occupied a vast stretch of territory — the Great Basin area, which corresponds to present-day Utah, with in addition parts of Wyoming, Colorado and Nevada. The Ute lived as small nomadic groups, depended on gathering and collecting rather than hunting, and were expert in exploiting the resources of their semi-desert terrain, which differed from the neighbouring regions just as much as their language — a branch of the Uto-Aztec family — their social organization and their way of life set them apart from the adjacent communities: the Sahaptin to the north, the Californian tribes to the west, the Navajo and Pueblo to the south and the Cheyenne and Arapaho to the east.

A twofold peculiarity can be observed in the mythology. The bird-nester myth is reconstituted almost completely and at the same time it is fused with the complementary story, that is, the Potiphar transformation. This dual process is carried out with such elegance and precision, and with such an ingenious use of means, that it is worth dwelling on a little, especially since the Ute, as a community, appear never to have been properly appreciated either by the early white settlers or by anthropologists.

Actually, a tendency towards syncretic treatment is already apparent among the Mono, the eastern section of whom belongs to the same linguistic family as the Ute. In their mythology (M$_{774a}$; Gifford 1, pp. 338–9), Coyote sends one of the dioscuri, his matrilateral nephew and son-in-law called Baumegwesu, to collect eagles in a deep hole, into which he pushes him. Another of the hero's maternal uncles, the Junco or snow-bird, manages to get him out, but only after the nephew has demanded that he first of all give proof of his skill and strength by hauling up a huge rock. It will be remembered that some much more northerly myths (M$_{756a}$) credit the Junco with the ability to lower the celestial vault in the direction of the earth, in contrast to the wren and the chickadee, who proceed differently by building the chain of arrows. Similarly, in this context, the Junco is an inversion of the other helpful animals common to the bird-nester cycle: he carries the hero from the low to the high, instead of helping him down from the high to the low. And he is also in opposition to Coyote, who pushes the hero downwards, instead of raising him up into the sky.

According to other versions more closely resembling those found in Ute mythology (M$_{774b}$; Gayton-Newman, pp. 45–8, cf. pp. 75–8, 94–6 and Steward, p. 406), the hero Pumkwesh invented arrows and the tool used for straightening them, as well as war, bear-hunting, sororal polygamy and the domestication of animals. Coyote, being jealous of his sister Junco's son-in-law, pushes him into a deep hole. Eagles look after him and a bat, the 'grandfather' of the unfortunate victim, who in this version bears the same name as the Tohi bird (*Pipilo* sp.?), lifts him up out of the hole, after a demonstration of strength. We shall come across this last incident again in the Navajo versions. Meanwhile, it would be appropriate to introduce the bird-nester myth as it occurs in Ute mythology:

M₇₇₅. Ute (Uintah). 'The bird-nester'

One day, Coyote, feeling he was dirty, had a swim in the river. Then he ate, fell asleep and dreamed of birds. When he awoke, he saw a number of wild geese with whom he entered into conversation. He asked them if they would agree to carry him to the sky. They were afraid that he would make a noise, but finally they gave him some feathers and agreed to take him along with them, provided he made absolutely no noise. However, Coyote could not help crying out loudly; the geese took back their feathers and Coyote fell to the ground.

A little later, the geese visited the Ute, who were engaged in a great fight with the Sioux. Coyote slept through the fight. When he awoke, the geese gave him a young Indian woman, whom they had rescued from her enemies.

Soon, a snowstorm began. The woman tried to build a brush house but a pointed stick, which Coyote had carelessly left stuck in the ground, penetrated her anus. Coyote called Duck, who was a famous healer, to cure his wife. Duck, on the pretext that he needed another doctor to help him, sent Coyote to look for one. As soon as Coyote had left, Duck diagnosed the cause of the sickness, pulled out the stick and poked it into the bottom of the fire.

Coyote returned home alone. Duck did not tell him that he had cured the young woman, but sent him to fetch water which he had to take, he carefully explained, from the bottom of the lake at the middle. Coyote tried in vain to cheat by bringing back water he had taken close to the shore. After several fruitless trips to and from the lake, he discovered that both the healer and the woman had gone.

Puzzled, Coyote sat down; after a while he heard a noise which seemed to come from the fire. It was the stick trying to catch his attention. Coyote pulled it out and ate it all up. Then he knew all that had happened in his absence.

The next morning he got up and started out to look for his wife. The first person he met was Duck's young son. Coyote returned the latter's bow and arrows, which he had found a short while before, and was thus acknowledged as the child's stepfather. He stayed in Duck's camp and persuaded the latter to go after little eagles at the top of a rock. While his companion was climbing up the cliff face, Coyote dug away all the earth from around the rock, so that the Duck could not get back. He had nothing to eat or drink; he grew thin and soon he was nothing but skin and bones.

Coyote took his wife back and went off. He became the father of a great many little coyotes and told his wife to take care only of them, and not of Duck's boy, whom he hated.

Duck was still marooned at the top of the rock, where he was spotted by some Ute Indians. They told him to jump, assuring him that they would catch him in their arms, but the hero was afraid of getting hurt and wanted the Indians to try first to catch a rock. Eventually, he let himself drop; an Indian caught him, took him home and fed him; 'then he greased him all over', until he was all right again and ready to start out anew.

Duck's rescuer told him all the dreadful things that had happened; he no longer had a wife, and his son was being ill-treated. Why should he not kill Coyote by making a great storm, a great cold? Duck set out to look for his own folk and, when he found them, he froze Coyote's children to death, and then killed Coyote himself with a big stick. The wife, having been forewarned, saved their son from death. After inducing a miscarriage to get rid of the baby coyotes in her womb, Duck took his wife and son home (Mason, pp. 310–14).

The rehearsal preceding the actual rescue links the Ute myth with the Mono story ($M_{774a, b}$). On the other hand, the ill-treated son-in-law motif is reminiscent of the Arapaho myth (M_{759}; see above, p. 502), which explains the origin of the hatred often felt by a step-parent for stepchildren. M_{759} and M_{774} belong to the bird-nester cycle, the plot of which is reversed in the Ute myth: the victim is a complete stranger and not a close relative, and it is the kidnapper and not the injured husband who occupies the position of bird-nester into which he is put by his rival, in retaliation for the abduction that the rival has suffered, and not so that the rival himself may become a wife-stealer. Concomitantly, the rock with the eagle's nest does not rise up into the sky; on the contrary, the ground is hollowed out below; the result, however, is still the same: in either case the rock grows, increasing in size either upwards or downwards.

In versions belonging to more northerly tribes, the Sahaptin and the Chinook, the two main characters, father and son respectively, are called Coyote and Eagle (M_{601a}, M_{606a}, M_{610}, etc.). In the Ute myth, they are respectively client and healer, and are called Coyote and Duck. The duck is a water bird and, as such, is in opposition to the eagle, a bird of the upper air. In M_{759}, the Indians admit that they cannot recover the hero and call upon the geese, which are also water birds. I would like to add one last observation: the bird-nester, usually a human character saved by helpful animals, is given an animal's name in the Ute myth, and is rescued by humans.

The helpful goose episode in M_{759} also exists in M_{775}, but in a doubly inverted form: on the one hand, the geese carry the persecutor and not the persecuted individual; on the other, instead of bringing their passenger back safe and sound, they drop him and cause him severe injuries. This episode is worth looking at more closely for a variety of reasons.

It occurs in a series of Nez Percé myths already discussed, and to which the first part of M_{775} bears a striking similarity. The Nez Percé myths ($M_{571a, b, c}$; see above, pp. 187–8) begin with an episode during which Coyote loses his teeth through having eaten tainted meat and becomes an old man. There is nothing like this in the Ute myth, except that at the beginning Coyote – and this detail of the story is unintelligible unless interpreted in the light of other myths – feels that he is dirty, that is, impure, and decides to wash himself. So he is rejuvenated, just as in M_{571c}, where his youth is restored by a young woman who gives him a new set of teeth, and it so happens that this unknown young woman is the geese's sister. From that point onwards, the stories converge, although M_{571c}, which is more explicit than M_{775}, explains that Coyote falls not only because he cannot resist making a noise, but because he is too heavy; being very greedy, he has not been able to bring himself to do as the geese do, and leave behind the entrails of the game they have caught. Consequently, from being dirty at the beginning of the geese episode in M_{775}, Coyote becomes dirty at the end of the same episode in M_{571}. The filth adds to and exacerbates the noise (cf. HA, pp. 309–11, 384, etc.) in circumstances in which, on the contrary, no noise should be made (cf. M_1, M_{9-10}, M_{766b}, M_{767a}; see above, p. 513).

The Nez Percé myths place this sequence next to a visit to the daughters of winter or the cold wind. In the Ute myth, it occurs before a snowstorm. We may suppose, then, that the geese carry Coyote in autumn, when they fly southwards (as is specifically stated in the Ojibwa version, cf. Jones 2, Vol. II, p. 435). If, as I have suggested, the sequence is an inversion of the one in M_{759}, in which the geese rescue the hero, we should find that this rescue operation coincides, in turn, with the spring migration of the geese northwards. It will be remembered that one of the rites of the Arapaho sun-dance consisted in placing in the sacred lodge a forked stick supporting a small bird which, according to the Indian informants, was a symbol of the hero's rescue by the geese in M_{759}; this little bird was facing northwards (see above, pp. 503, 520). But there is a further point to be mentioned; the bird's role can only be understood in the light of a belief that was held right across the continent, from eastern Canada to the Rockies (and in the Old World, too, since Buffon mentions it), the belief, perhaps partly grounded in fact, that 'the small birds arriving in the north with the spring tide of migration ride upon the backs of wild geese or loons, and return to the south by the same accommodating means in the fall' (Speck 5, pp. 375–80). Since it is the bird-nester, and not Coyote, who is represented in the sun-dance by a small bird, we must conclude that his cycle constitutes the 'straight' form, of which the Nez Percé and Ute myths, where he is replaced by his opponent, constitute the inverted form.

The rest of M_{775} confirms this interpretation. The sequence about the girl rescued from the battle – then impaled, nursed back to health and kidnapped by a healer, whose crime is revealed to Coyote when he eats the sharp stick which had pierced the girl's anus – would remain incomprehensible, were we not able to see it as the product of a systematic inversion of the long penis episode which the northern neighbours of the Ute include in the bird-nester cycle.

In the Salish myths, the young girl is injured by the long penis because she alone, and not her companions, accepts an offer of food: that is, enters into a type of transaction which, in this area of America, ensures the establishment of friendly relations between the various communities attending fairs and markets. In the Ute myth, the girl is injured by a sharp stick, planted vertically into the ground ($\neq$ thrown horizontally across the river), by a man to whom she is already married, following a battle between hostile tribes. The sharp stick on which she is accidentally impaled remains in her anus and makes her seriously ill, just as the previous heroine becomes sick when the long penis is caught in her vagina. In order to remove the piece of penis and restore its physical integrity, Coyote himself has to pretend to be a healer. In M_{775}, on the contrary, it never occurs to him to play this part and he loses no time in calling on a third person, who removes the stick and changes it into a fire-poker, a tool which, as I have already stressed, has a phallic aspect (see above, p. 462). That is not all: here, instead of copulating in the literal sense with a girl who accepts a purely metaphorical offer of food, Coyote eats the poker: he thus reintegrates into himself what was in fact merely a metaphor for the penis, through eating it in the literal sense. As they pass into M_{775}, the constituent sequences of the bird-nester myth are redistributed in a different order along the syntagmatic chain; and all the paradigmatic groupings are maintained at the cost of a lexical reversal.

A myth belonging to the northern Shoshone, who are close neighbours of the Uintah and members of the same linguistic family, confirms this interpretation. This myth (M_{775b}; Lowie 12, p. 250) inverts the preceding one in two ways: Coyote plays the role of seducer, and with regard to the daughter of his friend Duck. The tip of his penis remains inside the young girl and makes her ill. Duck, who was a healer in M_{775a}, has here to appeal to another specialist, Humming-Bird, who removes the length of penis, which he first uses to club Coyote (the penis thus is likened to a stick), and then throws into the fire, where it is completely burnt, unlike the wooden poker which, although also a stick, has the peculiarity of being fire-resistant.

The same interpretation also holds good for the Potiphar transformation. M_{775} does not use blood relations or affines as leading characters, nor are the protagonists friends, as we have seen to be the case in certain myths belonging to both North and South America (see above, pp. 509–10), but complete strangers, between whom a different kind of relationship is established: that of healer and patient. However, in order to appropriate his client's wife, the healer proceeds in the same way as the character in the Potiphar transformation, who is convinced that his son or brother has already appropriated his wife: they both try to rid themselves of their rival by disjunction through water. In the Potiphar transformation, the operator of the disjunction is an island in the middle of a lake, that is, a place where the immersed land bulges towards the high. In this case, too, the operator is the middle of a lake, but because water has to be drawn from the deepest part, where the lake bottom is most markedly concave. The Potiphar transformation ends with a universal conflagration, whereas M_{755} ends with a snowstorm and a severe cold spell – a pattern we have already encountered in the Arapaho myth M_{762} (where, however, it is the hero and not his persecutor who dies of cold). In analysing that myth, I pointed out that, like the reference myth M_1, it effects a synthesis between the bird-nester story and the Potiphar transformation, and we have just confirmed that the same is true here. In the three myths, M_1, M_{762} and M_{775}, there are homologous transformations: cooking fire into torrential rain which extinguishes it (M_1); or a conflagration, which turns water into steam and burns up the earth, into a cold wave (M_{762}) which also extinguishes domestic fires (M_{775}).

The mythology of the Navajo, Athapaskan Indians who moved down from the north less than ten centuries ago, is a vast body of material that I do not intend to broach,[8] not only because of its abundance and complexity, but also because successive generations of native thinkers have given it a theological and liturgical elaboration which would compel the analyst to adopt a different approach. However, the Navajo are the immediate neighbours of the Ute to the south, and it must at least be pointed out that their version of the bird-nester myth, which is integrated with the saga of the dioscuri (cf. the Mono myth M_{774a}), has close links with the Ute versions. This is shown by the way in which the Navajo retain and transform the fire-poker episode.

In Navajo mythology, the story of the bird-nester belongs to the category of emergence myths: the action is set at the time when the dioscuri were busy destroying monsters — including eagles — which were destroying the earth. With the help of three rodents, the gopher, the mouse and the ground squirrel (tamia?), one of the dioscuri kills a horned monster. He has a disguise made for himself with the bloody viscera, and uses the stomach as a mask. Thus attired, he sets off to provoke the eagles in their eyrie at the top of a rock, which then grows so high that the hero cannot climb back down. He suffers from hunger and thirst. Two pretty girls with fair skins and black-ringed eyes come along and feed him with corn mush. They are Turtle-doves. An old Bat Woman then comes on the scene, and after demonstrating her strength by carrying four huge rocks in her hod, conveys the hero back down to the ground. He has, incidentally, to protect his person from the short-tempered old woman who is trying to cut the calves of his legs. Together they approach the dead eagles, which Bat Woman sets about plucking. Later, she disregards the hero's warning not to enter a deep valley where wild sunflowers are growing; she loses all the feathers, which fly into the air and change into little birds (M_{776a}; Haile-Wheelwright, pp. 73–5).

In one variant (M_{776b}; *ibid.*, pp. 108–109), the elder of the twins, after being turned into Coyote through the evil spells of a member of the coyote species, regains his original appearance, thanks to magic performed by humans while he is their guest. However, the Coyote his enemy, takes him eagle hunting and increases the height of a rocky cliff on to which he has ventured. A small bird called Tsehnutl-Tsosi helps him to climb back down

[8] I shall leave aside Pueblo mythology for the same reason. But it will be remembered that, as early as 1951, my first attempts at interpretation were centred on Pueblo myths (L.-S. 21). The work has been continued by J.-C. Gardin in unpublished material relating to Zuni mythology, and by the late L. Sebag, in an important study of the Keresan (*L'Invention du monde chez les Indiens pueblos*, F. Maspéro, Paris, 1971).

(cf. Haile, p. 162, *tsenaolchosi*, 'canyon wren', *Catherpes mexicanus*). Later, the hero takes his revenge on Coyote by making him swallow red-hot stones, which have been sprinkled with edible pollen to make them seem appetizing. The Coyote dies, prophesying that a miracle will occur at his resurrection. On the appointed day, the seven Dilgeheh stars appear (cf. Haile, pp. 38, 44: *dilyehe*, 'The Pleiades').

The third version, which is also the most complex (M_{776c}; Haile-Wheelwright, pp. 112–18), features a human hero different from the dioscuri, but who has also been changed into a Coyote by an animal of the coyote species who seizes his mask and weapons, usurps his identity and appropriates his wife and children.

The hero is saved by a squirrel, regains his original form and and sets off to look for his kinsfolk. But there is nobody left in the camp. A fire-poker which has been left behind, calls out to him, advising him to go eastwards. On the way, the hero encounters other domestic implements or utensils – a cooking-pot, an earthenware bowl and a hairbrush – which direct him. He eventually finds his wife and children, as well as the Coyote who makes a pretence of welcoming him. However, under pretext of looking for feathers to re-plume the mask and the arrows he has usurped, Coyote takes the hero to raid a nest of supposed eagles, which turn out to be only locusts. As in the other versions, the rock increases in size, but in addition the hero is transported to the sky by a thunderbolt; the rock shrinks, leaving him stranded. The divine twins are informed of this by their messenger, Dontso, the large fly, and set out to look for the hero. They eventually find him imprisoned 'in the house of darkness', and guarded by a fierce fire, which is kept going by two devils. They extinguish the fire, render the two devils harmless and revive the unconscious hero. After teaching him all their songs, the dioscuri take him back to his home, and recommend him never to allow Coyote to speak first.

The hero asks his wife for some flour known as *gloh- deh- glohtsosi* (cf. Haile, pp. 185, 209; *tl'o'dei-*; Elmore, p. 44; *tl'ohteei'tsoh, Chenopodium*), and sprinkles it over red-hot stones which he then gets Coyote to swallow; the latter dies. He then gives his wife an emetic, and purifies both her and his children.

Shortly after, however, the hero is wafted to heaven by the wind. He is greeted by a Spider-Woman, whose children have been eaten by wasps. Since he has a fire-drill, he kindles a fire with faggots and destroys the wasps, all except four, the ancestors of the present-day insects. The text of this myth, which if fairly obscure, appears to indicate that the Spider-Woman teaches the hero to use the drill, and to light the first fire. Then she brings him down from the sky by means of her thread. After returning to earth, the hero is invited to attend a competition between day animals and night animals to decide whether day or night is to prevail on earth. But the result is a draw and, ever since, light and darkness have alternated (cf. Eaton, pp. 219–20). Then there suddenly appear two skulls belonging to twins who were killed long ago by an enemy tribe (Taos). Black ants collect the blood and flesh of the Twins, and all supernatural beings join forces in order to reconstitute and revive the bodies. This is the origin of a ceremony.

The reader will have at once noted that the ants play a part which is an inversion of the grave-digger role, attributed to them farther north by the Salish and the Kutenai (see above, p. 419). Here, the power to resuscitate the dead, which founds a healing rite, appears, however, to be a function of daily periodicity, instituted a little while earlier: according to the Puget Sound Indians (Ballard 1, p. 75), ants also had a part to play in this, because of their anatomical make-up; since their bodies consist of two halves, they can readily connote a pair of correlative and opposite terms: day and night, or life and death. If, as appears to be the case, the Navajo hero learns the art of making fire during his stay in the sky, we have come back very close indeed to our starting-point: the bird-nester myth, after being subjected to various reversals by the Ute, has its theme reconstituted by the Navajo. However, the link with the Ute versions is maintained in various details: preliminary proof is demanded of the helpful animal's strength; and, more importantly, an identical role is attributed in both myths to the fire-poker, which the Navajo include in a series of equally helpful domestic implements; and this – by means of a simple inversion – brings us back to the rebellious utensils which the Thompson hero encounters in the sky and which he commands henceforth to serve their future users.

Since sunflower and chenopodium seeds were used for making flour (Bailey; Vestal), we should no doubt link up the feeding to Coyote of red-hot stones sprinkled with chenopodium flour, and the warning given to the Bat that, in her own interests, she should not go near the sunflowers, which, in Navajo territory, bloom in the lowlands during the rainy season (Elmore, p. 11). Because she disregards the warning, the Bat loses the eagle feathers, whereas, in a Dakota version, the hero managed to salvage them and use them to decorate his house or his tent (M_{769a}; see above, p. 516).[9] The feathers lost by the Bat turn into small birds, and although M_{769a} breaks off before the end, the title 'the community of birds' suggests that

---

[9] In support of this link-up, it should be noted that the beak of the crane or the heron, the Dakota hero's magic weapon (see above, p. 517), occupied an important place in Navajo liturgy (Haile 2, pp. 22–3).

the feather-decked house has some connection with the origin of the birds. It is a fact that all the versions of the Navajo myth, other than those previously quoted (M$_{776d}$: Matthews, p. 119; M$_{776e}$; Haile 1, pp. 123–5; M$_{776f}$: Wheelwright, pp. 89–92; M$_{776g}$: O'Bryan, pp. 87–92), stress the loss of the ornamental feathers, as a result of going through a sunflower field. An explanation of this unusual episode is perhaps to be found in a remark made by Vestal (p. 51): 'Horsehair traps were hung on sunflowers to capture blue birds and yellow birds for their feathers.' M$_{776e}$ states quite clearly that the eagle feathers so carefully collected by the Bat turned into birds, which were first grey, then of various colours. Both myths seem, therefore, to be dealing with the origin of ornamental feathers.

We can conclude, without spending any more time on the Navajo stories, which are inseparable from the rest of Navajo mythology, that these versions of the bird-nester myth are very closely linked with those belonging to neighbouring or distant communities. For instance, the garment made from entrails that the Navajo hero puts on to attract the eagles, i.e., to conjoin them with himself, is reminiscent of the deer entrails which, according to the Nez Percé versions (M$_{571c}$), Coyote refuses to relinquish, with the result that he is so heavy the geese have to get rid of him. Similarly, the two demons who hold the Navajo hero prisoner are reminiscent of the symplegades; and the reason why he has to protect his legs from the Bat, who might cut them in a fit of temper, is that the Bat, although a helpful animal, retains some connection with the two old blind women, congruous with the symplegades, whose elbows are armed with pointed bones and who are said by the eastern Algonquin to be the ancestors of bats (Speck 5, p. 373).

I would like to end with one last observation. In the Navajo myths, as in those of the Dakota (M$_{769b}$), the Maidu (M$_{636a, b}$), the Sanpoil (M$_{737}$), the Assiniboine (M$_{765a, c}$) and the Cree (M$_{766a, b}$), the traitor – sometimes smeared or larded with fat – either dies in the fire, or swallows red-hot stones covered in fat or flour, which turns him metaphorically into an earth oven. Coyote, after receiving the same treatment, brings about the rising of the Pleiades (M$_{776b}$), a detail which leads us back to previous remarks about this constellation, which, either in the temporal register of the calendar or in the spatial register of stellar configurations, marks sometimes the period, sometimes the place, at which communication can be established between sky and earth. In certain myths belonging to the cycle of the wives of the sun and moon, the Pleiades actually represent the gateway to the sky (M$_{444b}$).

It is legitimate, then, to wonder if the Pleiades, whose origin is explained in so many North and South American myths – from the Matako and the Macushi to the Wyandot (*RC*, pp. 241–2), the Iroquois (M_{591g}: Beauchamp, pp. 281–2) and the Thompson (M_{591f}: Boas 13, p. 21) – by a refusal of food, are not a counterpart to the earth oven: the constellation being a hole in the sky resulting from the absence of food, the earth oven a hole in the earth where an abundance of food is concentrated: and a paradoxal place, too, where a fire of celestial origin finds a repository in the chthonian world. What is more, the celestial fire is solar in nature, whereas, as was shown in the previous volumes (*RC*, p. 158; *OTM*, pp. 39–40), the Pleiades have an affinity with the moon. I shall return to this interesting problem in my concluding remarks.

PART SEVEN THE DAWN OF MYTHS

Has omnes, ubi mille rotam volvere per annos,
Lethaeum ad fluvium deus evocat agmine magno:
scilicet immemores supera ut convexa revisant,
rursus et incipiant in corpora velle reverti.

Virgil, *The Aeneid*, VI, v. 748–51

What are we to think of a law that asserts
itself only by periodical revolutions?
It is just nothing but a law of nature
founded on the want of knowledge of those
whose action is the subject of it.

F. Engels, note *in: Capital*, Vol. 1, p. 46, translated by Samuel Moore and Edward Aveling, 1946 reprint

I   *Binary Operators*

It is as if, throughout the length and breadth of the New World, communities whose languages, modes of life, customs and habits presented no
common features, persistently tried, in very varied environments, to identify certain forms of life in the animal kingdom (and no doubt phenomena
belonging to the other kingdoms as well) and to trace them through, as it
were, working in wherever possible different species, genera, or families, in
order to ensure that one or other of the latter continue to function as algorithms to be used by mythic thought for the carrying out of the same operations.

I have several times drawn attention to such instances, e.g., the role
played by otters, either the sea or the river variety, from Alaska to southern
Brazil (*HA*, pp. 200–205); and again, in both North and South America,
the importance attributed to certain birds, the Icteridae, as watchmen,
protectors, or advisers (*OTM*, pp. 41–2, 229–39). At several points in the
present volume, we have had irrefutable evidence of similarities between
the semantic function attributed in North American myths to certain
tetraonidae – prairie chickens, grouse and ptarmigans – and analogous
functions ascribed to the tinamidae in South America. As so often happens,
we are dealing here with creatures which differ as regards species, genus and
family, but nevertheless belong to the same order; in this case, they are
gallinaceans. It is as if the classifications were being made according to
some obscure lore, although the criteria on which they are based are of quite
a different nature from those used for more scientific taxonomies.

But the case of the gallinaceans is instructive in other respects too. When, in *The Raw and the Cooked*, (pp. 203–23), I put forward the hypothesis that the inhambu bird (*Crypturus* sp.; now called: *Grypturellus* sp.) had an ambiguous semantic function on the borderline between life and death, I was able to do so only on the basis of what I have called elsewhere (*HA*, pp. 38, n. 6, 245–9, 396; *OTM*, pp. 209–10; L.-S. 14) *a transcendental deduction*. Empirical observation of the habits of these birds does not suggest anything of the sort, and the conclusion emerged indirectly and of its own accord while I was attempting to reduce several zoemes to their invariants. Beginning with the hypothesis that a Serenté myth, M_{124}, was a transformation of a Bororo myth, M_1, I noted, among other clues, the presence in both myths of a triad of helpful animals. In M_1, the creatures are, in the first place, the Humming-Bird and the Pigeon, who form a correlational and oppositional pair in respect of water, and then an insect, the Grasshopper, which, because it flies more slowly and nearer the ground, is in danger of perishing during a mission it carries out in common with the two birds: nevertheless, it returns victorious, although half-dead. As the Serenté myth (M_{124}) also includes a pair of arboreal creatures, woodpeckers and monkeys, who are in correlation and opposition to each other in respect of fire — celestial and destructive fire in the case of the woodpecker, terrestrial and constructive fire in the case of the monkey — it had to follow (through the application to a simplified instance of a canonical formula suggested at the outset of my researches, cf. L.-S. 5, p. 252; *HA*, p. 249) that the transformation involving the first two terms of each triad was closed, and that an identical transformational relationship must therefore characterize the third term in both myths. In M_{124}, the third term designates 'partridges', that is — in South America, where there are no phasianidae — birds belonging to the family of the tinamidae.

From the point at which it could be supposed, hypothetically, that the tinamidae occupy an ambiguous and equivocal position on the borderline between life and death, it became possible to discover, in their make-up and behaviour, as well as in the myths and beliefs relating to them, features which, if considered separately, would not have suggested any interpretation of this kind, but to which it was possible to give a meaning in the light of the hypothesis just mentioned. The tinamidae are different from other aerial creatures in being clumsy fliers; in the category of the high, they occupy a relatively low position. The black and white feathers of the birds were used by the ancient Tupinamba to make their war regalia. Certain tinamidae and cracidae are supposed to repeat their call at such regular intervals through the night that the Indians regard them as a kind of forest clock; they are associated, then, with very brief forms of periodicity. Furthermore, the myths stress the affinity between these birds and night, at the same time as they present them as inferior game, yielding a bitter broth, the only food that a secluded boy was allowed, etc. However, these details in themselves, fragmentary and tenuous as they are, would not be enough to confirm the hypothesis; still less would they have suggested its formulation.

Thanks to North American myths from the area west of the Rockies, I am now in a position to provide proof of what I put forward on the basis of myths belonging to tropical America. To establish the point, I should first of all mention a number of further details, strictly consistent with those just summarized. Since there are no tinamidae in North America, these details relate to another family belonging to the gallinacean order — the tetraonidae, which we have encountered on several occasions in Sahaptin and Salish myths.

In a Mundurucu myth (M_{16}; RC, p. 85), a bad hunter who only catches inhambu birds is contrasted with his sisters' husbands who can catch wild pigs, a superior form of game, in exchange for which he successfully offers his inhambu fowl. Another myth from the same source (M_{143}; RC, p. 260) quotes the case of a bad hunter who brings back only inhambus for his wife and is chided by her in consequence. The Great Lakes Ojibwa begin one of their myths in exactly the same way: a man, a husband, and father of a great many children, proves to be such a hopeless hunter that he cannot even bring back such insignificant and easily caught game as a ruffed grouse to feed his family. His luckier brothers-in-law make fun of him. The next day, his mother-in-law makes, not a bitter broth — as in M_{143} — but a soup which is so hot when she hands it to him that he spills it over himself and burns his chest. Demoralized by this incident, he no longer has the heart to hunt and, when he returns with nothing but a prairie chicken his wife drives him out (M_{777}; Jones 2, Vol. II, pp. 443–51). The myth also explains why the Ruffed Grouse is such an inferior fowl: its white flesh is lacking in fat; the rest of the story tells of the desperate search for a more fatty kind of meat. It is probably significant that the search, which is finally successful, is placed next to the story of the trickster who is first carried then dropped by the geese, since in certain western versions already discussed (see pp. 187, 525) this episode is followed by another in which the trickster, after committing an alimentary error, loses all his teeth and is unable to eat his food.

But let us keep to the prairie chicken. The reference to its white flesh is in accordance with a view held by many Indians; the Ten'a, who are north-western Athapaskan, say that the cooked flesh of the willow-grouse (another of the tetraonidae) is extremely white (Jetté, Part I, p. 306). Still on the strictly alimentary level, an inherent ambiguity characteristic of the tetraonidae is indicated by the name the eastern Algonquin give to the Ruffed or Pinnated Grouse; the Penobscot and the Malecite value its flesh highly, but at the same time they refer to it as 'the bad bird'; the reason is, according to an elderly informant, the shocking fact that such good meat should be so lean (Speck 5, p. 358). These opinions are in keeping with a remark about the inhambu made in Brazil by a European traveller, Maximilian de Wied: 'its flesh is very good . . . almost gelatinous; it contains hardly any fat' (*in*: Brehm 2, Vol. 4, p. 494). Looked at from this angle, the ambiguity that the Indians of both North and South America considered as being characteristic of the gallinaceans would appear to be of the same kind as that which gave rise to the debate, during the early years of Christianity, about whether or not it was right to eat fowl as well as fish on fast days (Hastings, Vol. 5, p. 767a).

But there is more to be said: the myths of both hemispheres exploit the ambiguity in the same way. The Chinook classified the tetraonidae, along with *bitter* roots (Jacobs 2, Part I, p. 77; cf. M_{143}), among foodstuffs eaten only during periods of famine; they also used the flesh of the fowl to make a broth for the sick, a practice which also existed among the Coast Salish, since in the Humptulips version of the story of Moon the demiurge (M_{375c}; Adamson, pp. 276–84), the mother of the stolen child, is changed into a 'pheasant' (i.e., Pinnated or Ruffed Grouse, cf. above, p. 395), and made to utter the following last words: 'Hereafter, I shall live in the bushes because I have been made very sad. I shall be humble all my days. When a person takes sick, they will give him my flesh to eat – the only meat a sick person can keep in his stomach. Should a very sick person eat pheasant meat and throw it up, it is a sign he will die.' She then set to and cut her hair short except in the middle, as if she were wearing a hat as a sign of sorrow. She changed her own mother into a Grebe who would henceforth live in lakes.

All these characteristics – absence of fat, mournfulness of temperament, suitability as a food for the sick, and the association with death – are also found together in South American myths. It will be remembered that the North American myths in the area we are concerned with present the grouse in addition as a spirit of the cold which, because of the snowstorms it creates at the end of winter, delays the arrival of spring and prolongs famine. The Kalapuya regard it as one of the masters of sickness (Jacobs 4, pp. 272–4). The Sanpoil forbid couples who are about to have a child to eat its flesh 'in case the child cried until it was out of breath and had convulsions' (Ray 1, p. 124).

Consequently, the Salish and their neighbours go further in their treatment of these birds than their fellow-Indians of South America, and we shall soon see why. Among the Salish, the distinctive features attributed to the 'Pheasant' or the Grouse rest on a clearly stated mythic foundation. The communities living to the south of Puget Sound (M_{778a-g}; Ballard 1, pp. 128–32) have a myth in which a rejected suitor kills a 'pheasant'-girl. Her father, also a pheasant in some versions but a marsh sparrow in others, goes to look for her in the land of the dead. His mission fails because the dead refuse to admit him. 'However, Pheasant does not return permanently; for at a certain season of the year, he is missing. He then goes on his yearly visit to the dead.' This explains why some people do not eat pheasants for fear of dying before their time (*loc. cit.*, pp. 129–30). It will be remembered that the Tillamook regard the Sparrow as a go-between linking the world of the living with the Beyond, and that farther north the Carrier attribute the same function to the Robin, stressing his daily comings and goings (see above, p. 489). By placing the 'Pheasant' in the same category as the Sparrow, the Puget Sound Salish are simply changing the daily rhythm into a seasonal one, while clearly remaining within the framework of a system which extends into South America with the attribution of a nocturnal function, also linked to daily periodicity, to the gallinaceans in their capacity as forest clocks. In this connection, it is significant that one of the Salish versions uses the Pheasant's journey to the kingdom of the dead – he tries unsuccessfully to bring back two of his grandchildren, and has to be content with rescuing only one – to explain how it was at one time customary to kill twins, who were thought to be monstrosities. The myth concludes: 'For future people it shall not be well to have two children at one time' (Ballard 1, p. 131). Two children born at the same time were thought to constitute a kind of abnormality disrupting biological rhythms.

A native informant adds the following commentary to this group of myths: 'Pheasant's daughter is blind in one eye. She looks with her blind eye, talking to the spirits. An Indian never eats the head of a pheasant, because half of it is dead. When the girl looks to the right she is talking to the living. The head was ghostly' (Ballard 1, p. 133).

While working on certain South American myths, I inferred from them (although they themselves made no such statement) that the semantic function of the 'gallinacean' zoeme could only be understood if one assumed that it connoted the point of intersection between life and death, and movement from one to the other. This proposition, which I arrived at through pure logical necessity, now appears in an explicit form in North American myths where it is accompanied by an ample explanatory commentary. I could wish for no better proof of the validity and fruitfulness of my method. Not only does it enable us to solve apparently disparate problems by the use of a single solution — thus realizing that economy of means to which any would-be scientific research aspires, and which gives it confidence that it is achieving its aim — but also, and more importantly, through the unforeseen embodiment of the symbol in an image, it produces a kind of self-evident proof which can rightly be called apodictic, since the image, already present millions of kilometres away in the overt discourse of societies, remote both in language and culture from those which served as our starting-point, gives concrete form to a pattern which was both abstract and concealed. This being so, it may now seem superfluous to add the following indirect confirmation.

In certain previously discussed Chinook myths (M_{566}, see above, pp. 176–7) belonging to the lewd grandmother cycle, Raccoon, who has been beaten by his grandmother because he has spoiled food intended for them both, takes his revenge by making her swallow balls of crushed fruit filled with thorns. She chokes and asks for a drink: he offers her water in a hat with holes. The old woman turns into a gallinacean and flies away. As I noted at the time, the myth has its exact counterpart in Bororo mythology (M_{21}; *RC*, pp. 94–5): wives who have been kept short of food by inefficient husbands give them prickly piqui fruit (*Caryocar* sp.) to eat; they choke and utter grunting noises like wild pigs and, indeed, change into these animals; this is the origin of wild pigs. We now know that whereas wild pigs provide a superior form of meat in South America, in both North and South gallinaceans are considered the lowest form of game. In spite of the geographical distance between the two areas, we are dealing then, with the same myth; there has been a simple reversal of the respective values ascribed to the victims of each metamorphosis.

The second confirmation is supplied by the Thompson myths belonging to the bird-nester cycle. It will be remembered that the old blind women whom the hero encounters in the sky change into two species of tetraonidae, one capable of being fertilized *from afar* through the sense of hearing, and the other easy to capture since it tolerates the *close* proximity of humans. As the first characteristic concerns the perpetuation of life in the case of the one species, and the second the premature cessation of life in the case of the other, the duplication of the species is tantamount to a demonstration of the same type of ambiguity but by different means. In the person of the 'pheasant', half of whose head is living while the other half is dead, life and death, normally kept separate by the individual life-span, are paradoxically brought together.

This approach confirms that the Pheasant or Grouse, like other American gallinaceans, is a bird within which life and death are conjoined. The Wichita (M_{370}; *OTM*, p. 58) transpose the same ambiguity to the Prairie Hen (*Tympanuchus* sp.).[1] These birds, when they assume human form, are particularly dangerous enemies, because they are ambidextrous, and can shoot arrows with either hand. Their hands are therefore twin hands and, like the first twins born to Pheasant's daughter in the Puget Sound Salish myth, they are dreaded precisely because they are twins.

Throughout the area with which we are dealing, from the Alsea and the Tillamook in the south and up the coast to the Tlingit in the north, one of the most popular stories features the Skate. It is occasionally replaced by another fish, the species of which is not easy to identify; although the Chinook language has precise names for fish, others, such as Alsea, a member of the Yakonan family, often refer to the sole, the skate, the halibut and the flounder by the same term — *hulō' hulō* — which is also the word for a mythic character who acts as a go-between or ferryman (Frachtenberg 4, pp. 70, n. 10, 72–253). These linguistic uncertainties are not very important since, as we shall see, all these fish figure in the myths for the same reason: they are flat-fish, and consequently the underside of their bodies, which rests on the bottom of the sea, is of a different texture from the upper side. A description of the group can be found in Boas 2, pp. 658–60 and p. 842.

The Tillamook describe a duel between the Skate and the Deer (M_{779}; E. D. Jacobs, p. 11). The latter feels sure he will win, since his opponent is so wide that every arrow must inevitably hit him in the middle. However, on each occasion the Skate manages to stand sideways just at the right moment, and when his turn comes to shoot, it is the Deer who is killed. A Kathlamet myth I have already quoted (M_{756b}; see above, p. 494) tells of a similar episode in the sky: the animals in league against the South-West Winds try to dissuade Skate from fighting on their side, when the battle is about to begin. They explain that, being so wide, he will offer too easy a target; it would be better if he returned to the village. However, Skate demonstrates his skill in avoiding arrows and is allowed to stay.

According to a myth belonging to the Salish on the south side of Puget

---

[1] Prairie hens are also tetraonidae, which the Shuswap (Teit 1, p. 629) put into the same group as other members of the family. I dealt with the problem of the gallinaceans in my Collège de France lectures of 1965–6.

Sound, it was because of this skill that the animals chose the Skate to lead them in the war against the South Wind, whom they spared after their victory on condition that he promised not to blow all the time (M_{780a}; Ballard 1, p. 69). In Klallam mythology, the animals make war against the North Wind. The Skate is confident that he can resist the Wind by standing sideways, but when the Wind blows he swings round and has to cede the honour of victory to the Wren, who wrests from the Wind the promise that he will never blow more than seven days at a time (M_{780b}; Gunther 2, p. 121).

Although the Quinault and the Quileute spoke different languages, they lived close together along the sea coast. They say ($M_{781a, b}$; Farrand 1, pp. 108–109; Reagan-Walters, p. 319) that in the war waged by the terrestrial people against the celestial people, the Skate avoided the Raven's spears by turning edgewise, and then managed to pierce his opponent's beak. The Quileute add that an inhabitant of the sky urinated on the Skate; or that an earth-dweller killed a skate, laid it near the door of one of his celestial enemies and returned to his own camp on the other side of the river. A little later, he came back with fire to cook his fish. But meanwhile one of the people of the sky had come out of his house in the night, and not seeing the skate, he threw slop all over it and the skate tastes of slop to this day (M_{782a}: Farrand-Mayer, pp. 264–6; M_{782d}: Reagan, pp. 51–4; M_{782c}: Reagan-Walters, p. 319).

A similar story is to be found among the Nootka of Cape Flattery:

M₇₈₃. Makah. 'The war against the South Wind'

Formerly, the land animals and fish paid a visit to the South Wind. They found him asleep and thought they would frighten him. The Cuttle-fish hid under the bed, the Flounder and the Skate lay flat on the floor at the foot of the bed, and the Mouse bit the sleeping Wind's nose. The latter jumped out of bed and, in so doing, slipped on the two flat-fish and fell. The Cuttle-fish twined its tentacles round the Wind's legs. This so enraged the Wind that he began to blow with such force that the perspiration rolled down his forehead and formed rain. Finally, he succeeded in blowing all his tormentors home again. But, out of spite, he came back down to earth at intervals to torment his enemies, for the land animals are very uncomfortable in rainstorms and many fish are thrown up on the shore by the big breakers and perish (Swan 2, p. 92).

The various themes we have so far encountered separately are combined in the myths of other Nootka and Kwakiutl groups, especially those of Vancouver Island.

M_{784}. Nootka. 'The origin of tides' (cf. M_{593}–M_{597})

Formerly, the wind blew unceasingly; low tide did not exist, and it was impossible to gather shell-fish. So people resolved to kill the Winds. Several animals who had been sent on ahead failed in this mission: one of them was the Winter Robin, who succeeded in entering the Wind's house, but forgot what he was there for as he warmed himself in front of the fire, which burnt him and gave him red spots (cf. M_{756b}). The Sardine was no more successful, and came back with his eyes closer to his snout than to his gills. Finally, the Seagull, in spite of his weak eyesight and his broken arms, crossed the cape swept by violent winds which guarded the entrance to the enemy village. The Skate and the Halibut took up their position near the door; the Winds, as they came out, slipped on the Halibut, and fell and tore themselves on the Skate's barbs. Only the West Wind offered any resistance; he promised however that, in future, he would bring fine weather with gentle breezes and cause the tides to ebb and flow twice a day, so that humans could catch edible shell-fish. On this condition, his life was spared (Boas 13, pp. 100–101).

M_{785}. Vancouver Island Kwakiutl. 'The pacified wind'

In order to put an end to the violent wind which blew unceasingly, the animals waged war on him, although several fell victim to his stench. Finally, the halibut stretched out in front of his door. When the wind tried to go out, he slipped on the fish and fell. The animals took him prisoner and only released him on condition that he promised to be more gentle (Boas 13, pp. 186–7).

$M_{786a, b}$. Nootka. 'The duel between the Raven and the Skate'

The Raven wanted to eat the Skate and challenged him to a duel. However, the latter avoided the attacks by turning sideways. According to M_{785b}, the Raven did likewise by jumping up and down on the spot; he insisted that the Skate should lean forward, but the latter succeeded in wounding the Raven by doing the unexpected thing and withholding his fire until the Raven's feet had touched the ground again. After being pierced by his opponent's javelin, the Raven gave up the fight (Boas 13, pp. 107–108; Sapir-Swadesh 2, pp. 26–9).

Apart from a very few exceptions, I have not extended my enquiry to cover the tribes of the north-west Pacific coast. It will be enough, then, to mention that the Halibut's trick of causing the hostile wind to fall by using the contrast between the two sides of its body, one rough, the other slippery, is found in the mythology of the Kwakiutl, the Bella Bella, the Tsimshian, the Haida and the Tlingit (M_{787a-g}; Boas 22, p. 227; Boas-Hunt 1, Vol. I, p. 358; Vol. II, p. 98; Boas 24, p. 32; 2, pp. 79–81; Swanton 9, p. 129; Krause, p. 189).

Among the myths just summarized, several (M_{756b}, M_{781a}, M_{782b}) state that the skate remained in the sky as one of the animals left behind, who died and were changed into constellations. The Quinault called one constellation *djagage'h*, 'the Skate'; it was probably Orion (Olson 2, p. 178). The one that the Twana called the Skate – *kwikwä'äl*, in their language – was apparently next to the Great Bear (Elmendorf 1, p. 537). Although the Makah gave different constellations the names of various fish – the Whale, the Halibut, the Skate, the Shark, etc. – they have not been identified, because these Indians disliked pointing them out. They 'seemed to have a repugnance to do so, and though at times they would talk about the stars they preferred cloudy weather for such conversation' (Swan 2, p. 90). The belief that some constellations are transformations of fish is found even among the Tlingit, who called the Pleiades 'the Sculpin', and gave the name 'the Halibut Fishers' to an unidentified constellation (Swanton 2, p. 107).

I have mentioned that the Skate is among the animals left behind and eventually changed into stars, who have already been discussed in connection with the myths in which they appear (see above, p. 466). These myths, which also deal with a cosmic battle, are inversions of those in which the Skate is featured, in the sense that they deal with the domestication of fire, not with wind or rain, and with the taming of the icy North winds instead of the storm-bearing South Wind.[2] They replace the Skate episode by another, in which the leading characters are more often than not the Snake and the Frog. The first episode takes place before the cosmic battle, the second afterwards when the animals come back down from the sky: 'They saw the Snake jump, fall and break all its bones. Frog danced for joy, and angered Snake so ever since snakes have eaten frogs' (M_{725}; Jacobs 1, pp. 145–6). In the Chehalis myth (M_{756a}; Adamson, p. 75, cf. also p. 77), which deals with the war between the South-West Wind and the North-East Wind, Snake is put in charge of operations; he is a great warrior and cross-eyed. No one on the South-West Wind's side is killed, but Snake is

---

[2] It is true that, in the Klallam myth (M_{780b}), the Skate goes to fight the North Wind, but the battle ends in defeat, not victory.

missing and assumed to be dead; but he eventually finds his way home and hears his little sister, the Frog (Toad), wailing his loss while making unkind remarks about his squint. He kills and eats her; ever since snakes have been enemies of frogs. The same incident occurs in a Puget Sound version of the myth about the conquest of fire (M_{723b}; Ballard 1, pp. 52–3).

The Snake, like the Skate, is characterized, then by an anatomical peculiarity. But whereas, in the case of the former, this consists in a twofold opposition between full-face and side-face, and between the upper and lower surfaces, in the case of the latter the peculiarity relates to eyes with crossed lines of vision. The myths provide proof of the fact that these two kinds of ambiguity are commutable.

A Chehalis version of the adventures of Moon, the demiurge (M_{382}; Adamson, pp. 173–7), transfers the story of the conquest of fire to the horizontal axis; and consequently tells it in reverse. In other contexts, the north-east winds are the celestial masters of cold, and therefore of anti-fire. In the Chehalis story, a community of prairie hens lives on earth – but in the east where it is cold – not in opposition to fire, but because they are unaware of its existence: to cook their meat they dance on it, an activity which takes up all their time. Moon, the demiurge, visits them and gives them a fire-drill and teaches them to cook in a wooden receptacle filled with water brought to boiling point by the immersion of red-hot stones. This episode, which reintegrates the gallinaceans (see above, pp 537–43) into a far-reaching system, the unity of which we are now beginning to grasp, precedes another, during which Moon encounters the Salmon and the Flounder who are blind. He restores their sight, but the Flounder remains cross-eyed.

In a note (p. 176, n. 2), Adamson, who says she finds this incident vague and strange, points out that her informant did not repeat it in the native-language version of the story he later gave to Boas. However, it appears almost unchanged in the Nootka myth about the war against the winds and the origin of tides (M_{784}; see above, p. 545), where the Sardine, after failing in his mission, returns with his eyes set close to his snout instead of being separated as before: in other words, he squints. His failure and the anatomical peculiarity resulting from it put him in opposition to the Halibut, who later succeeds in causing the winds to fall through slipping on his slimy surface. It is normal, then, that in the Chehalis version, which is an inversion both of the war for the conquest of fire and the fight for the taming of the cold winds, the Flounder, a combinatory variant of the Skate and the Halibut, should have a squint, like the successful Snake or the Sardine in the 'straight' versions: the Sardine is, admittedly, a different fish, but like the Snake it is round, not flat, and unlike the Skate, the Flounder and the Halibut, it fails in its mission.

The myths which include the Skate episode explain that the fish, who were left behind in the sky, became a constellation. There are good reasons for supposing that the same is true of the Snake. A Snohomish version adds the detail that the Snake and the Lizard, who are left behind in the sky because the breaking of the ladder cuts off their escape route, cannot come down until the spring (M$_{724b}$; Haeberlin I, p. 412). This detail seems to indicate that the names of the two reptiles were given to winter constellations. We might conclude, then, that the flat-fish, whose semantic position, as we have just seen, is in a symmetrical relationship to theirs, represent summer constellations. But to do so would be to disregard another transformation, which could easily remain undetected, did we not bring into play a mythic paradigm common to both North and South America, and which makes it possible to dispel to some extent the uncertainty mentioned on p. 546 about the constellation referred to as 'the Skate'.

It will be remembered that the Snohomish version presents an anomaly in relation to the other myths dealing with the conquest of fire (see above, p. 462). It is the sky people who open hostilities against the earth, because they are exasperated by the noise made at night by a carpenter building canoes; they abduct him and hold him prisoner. The terrestrial animals go up into the sky and obtain his freedom in return for the promise that he will work only during day time. This episode, which begins before the expedition to the sky, occupies the same position in the syntagmatic chain as that allocated to the Skate episode in the myths about the war against the Wind, who is taken prisoner through a ruse on the part of a flat-fish and later set free on condition that he promises henceforth to blow intermittently.[3] It is hardly necessary to emphasize that the Carpenter, by working night and day, produced a continuous noise, which is the equivalent, on the acoustic level, of an equally continuous storm, since it is clear, in any case, that the two sequences of events are symmetrical, provided the respective values of the Carpenter and the Winds are inverted. Consequently, we may further ask if the Carpenter, who, after his release, is to be silent at night and noisy during the day, is not a transformation of the Skate who, before being captured and changed into a constellation, is thin in profile and broad full-face. The correspondence is made still more plausible by the fact that the Carpenter in M$_{724b}$, who works continuously, is *foul-smelling*, and the

---

[3] We can thus remove a difficulty which worried Boas (2, p. 660) in connection with a Haida version (Swanton 9, pp. 32–4), intermediary between the two types.

Skate, through being present in the sky, becomes foul-smelling, according to $M_{782a, b}$. Here again, then, we have a case of the equivalence of din and stench, the reality of which has already been established several times and by means of different data (RC, pp. 293–6; HA, pp. 366–421; see above, p. 527); the last instance was in connection with the story of Coyote who is carried up into the sky by the geese, and then dropped because he offends them by the noise he makes, whereas here, the reverse happens: it is because of the noise he makes, that the inhabitants of the upper world take the Carpenter off to the sky.

On the strength of these intuitive certainties, let us now take a bold leap – but one which will be amply justified in the subsequent stages of my argument – to the south of tropical America. The Matako, who live in the Chaco, relate in one of their myths (M_{788}; Métraux 3, pp. 59–60) that an Indian one day heard a noise at the bottom of a lagoon. He dived in and saw people building a large house under the direction of a master carpenter. This carpenter was none other than the skate, who taught the Indian the art of house building. This explains why Matako houses are skate-like in shape.

We are following the same path, then, as we did in the case of the gallinaceans, but in the opposite direction. The South American myths provided me with the principle of a transcendental deduction, empirical proof of which was to be provided by North American myths through their embodiment, in concrete images, of what was previously no more than an abstract and theoretical pattern, produced by pure speculation. Now, on the contrary, it falls to North American myths to provide the starting-point of a deduction which can then be validated by South American ones containing the explicit statement that the skate was the first carpenter. It is true that he is building houses, not canoes. However, I have pointed out (OTM, pp. 188–9) that the mobile canoe and the non-mobile house are commutable not only in America, but in other parts of the world too. The relationship of the Snohomish carpenter with the canoes he makes is one of contiguity, whereas that of his Matako colleague with the Matako houses is one of similarity. This torsion in the system suggests that since the North American carpenter who is a transformation of the skate in the symmetrical myths belonging to the same area, agrees to limit his activities to day time, the type of periodicity he is submitting to must be daily in character. In which case, the corresponding constellation should be visible all the year round, except of course during the day, and it is more likely to be in the neighbourhood of the Great Bear than of Orion.

Furthermore, if the two commutable sets – Skate on the one hand, Snake and Lizard (or Frog) on the other – refer to constellations which are in opposition because of the distinctive type of periodicity characteristic of each – diurnal and nocturnal only, or seasonal as well – we can conclude that this opposition forms a system with another, which we have already identified in the same myths (see above, p. 398). This gives the following formula:

(*permanent constellations : seasonal constellations*) :: (*unnamed stars : named stars*).

Anonymous stars are also permanent, by definition as it were, since there are always stars in the sky which are equivalent to each other, through the sheer fact of not having been given a name. We can thus see once again that, as I have shown elsewhere (L.-S. 9, pp. 226–86; cf. above, pp. 398, 515), to name is to classify, and therefore to introduce discontinuity.

This is not the first time we have encountered the Skate during the course of the present study. In *From Honey to Ashes* (p. 309, n. 19), I pointed out that the Warao and the Baniwa of South America and the Yurok of North America compare the Skate to the uterus or the placenta: 'A Skatefish looks like Woman's insides', according to the Yurok (M_{292d}; Waterman 4, p. 191; Erikson, p. 272). The Wiyot, the Tolowa and the Hupa have myths similar to those of the Yurok, in which a Flounder Woman, or another supernatural creature called Maiyotel, captures her lovers and sends them into exile across the sea (M_{292e-h}; Kroeber 7, p. 97; Goddard 1, pp. 116, n., 132). Recently available information about South American beliefs corroborates the view expressed in the Warao and the Baniwa myths. The Tukano compare the Skate to the placenta (Reichel-Dolmatoff 4, pp. 21, 77). The Trumaï of Central Brazil echo the Yurok in one of their myths (Monod, MS. source): ' "Might not this Skate be the same thing as a woman?" an Indian wonders, and then continues: "Yes, it is the same", and he lay down on top of it . . .' Another piece of evidence, that I only put forward tentatively, might however be significant. In the Nootka myth M_{786a}, the Raven is very keen to eat the Skate's liver, since the Skate, according to M_{786b}, is a very fatty fish. The Carib-speaking Kalina of Guiana call the Skate *ereimo*, perhaps from *ere* 'liver', with the suffix *imo*, which is used to form the names of dangerous animals (see Ahlbrinck, under 'ereimo' and 'imo'). The connection might appear accidental, if we did not know from other contexts (*HA*, p. 365) that many South American Indians believe that the liver is composed of coagulated blood, and that it acts as a reservoir for menstrual blood. The identification of the Skate with the liver, which may be based solely on external similarity, could possibly relate to the fish's 'uterus function', of which there is ample evidence in various contexts.

It will also be remembered that there is an Amazonian myth (M_{147}; *RC*, p. 263), in which a lunar and civilizing heroine kills hostile animals by smoking them with a resin fire, but has to make two attempts before getting the better of the Wild Pig, the Tapir, the Great Snake and the Skate. Although the text is by no means explicit, it would seem that, as in North America, it credits the Skate with a certain talent for evasion. On the other hand, the Tacana of Lower Bolivia, who believe that the Skate was born from sanious body fluids (compare M_{782c}) exuded by a god as he emerged from a snake-monster who had swallowed him, deny the Skate the ability to spin quickly round, that is attributed to him by the Salish. On the contrary, in the Tacana story, the Skate observes frogs or tadpoles, who are greeting a thunder shower with songs and dances and, filled with admiration, he tries to imitate them. However, being unable to spin round, he falls down and dies (M_{195}, M_{789}; Hissink–Hahn, pp. 107–109, 165–6). The Tumupasa believe that skate are the head-dresses of the spirits of water, and that they symbolize the moon (*ibid.*, pp. 66–7).

Consequently, in both parts of the American continent, we can observe the same association between the Skate and, on the one hand, the female reproductive organs – the matrix and the placenta – and, on the other, manufactured objects such as canoes, houses, and head-gear, all of which, in their different ways, have an enveloping and protective function and, as we know from other contexts, are in fact looked upon as symbols of the uterus in several South American communities (Reichel-Dolmatoff 1, 4, *passim*).

Furthermore, in the Salish myths, the Skate is commutable with a pair of terms formed by the Snake and the Frog; the former – for reasons I have already given – probably connotes a constellation visible all the year round because of a simple diurnal-nocturnal periodicity, and the latter a constellation visible only during one half of the year. This triad of complementary or antagonistic terms reappears in the Tacana frog-dance myths, which obviously also have a seasonal character. In one variant, the snakes and the frogs dance together, and are thus in opposition to the Skate who cannot imitate them, because his anatomical constitution does not allow him to keep his balance when he tries to spin round. From this point of view alone, it is already clear that there is a major opposition between the Skate and the Snake: one is flat and diamond-shaped, while the other has the form of an elongated cylinder. But the symbolical connotations with which, as I have shown, the Skate is invested in both North and South America, make it possible to develop the opposition on other levels too. Whereas the Skate is a uterus-like creature, the Snake has an affinity with the penis, and this is systematically exploited in a vast group of myths (M_{49-52}; $M_{150-159}$; $M_{255-256}$, etc). The Skate, who is helped or hindered by his inability to keep his balance, and the Snake who squints, appear, then, as the final phases of a transformation which we have followed through from its initial phases, which were illustrated in the previous volumes by two motifs – the woman with the large vagina, the mistress of a snake and transformable into an opossum (foul-smelling like the Skate), and the man with the long penis, transformable into a tapir seducer endowed with large testicles (*RC*, pp. 249–50; *HA*, pp. 411–12; *OTM*, p. 83). At the same time, we know that the Frog occupies an intermediary position between these two series: as a 'clinging wife', she forms a counterpart to the man with the long penis (*OTM*, pp. 54–85). Yet, on the other hand, as it were, the Frog who is afflicted with urinary incontinence and is responsible for menstruation, who clings to Moon's face and is the mistress of a magic hat (M_{382}; *OTM*, p. 75), also has a relationship of complementarity with the Skate, a uterine or placenta-like creature, who is urinated upon and is used as a hat by lunar spirits (Figure 32).

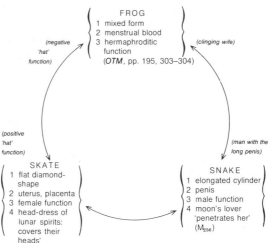

Figure 32. The Skate, the Frog and the Snake

I have stressed more than once that the myths dealing with the war waged by the earth-dwellers against the inhabitants of the sky or against the winds have a subsidiary function. They explain not only the conquest of fire in the one instance, and the establishment of the wind system in the other, but also the origin of the stars; or, to be more accurate, they show why the stars are divided into two categories: on the one hand, the smallest and most numerous, which form an anonymous mass and, on the other, the constellations, all of which, like the animal families from which they originated, have a distinctive shape and a name. We have also seen that, in all cases, the mythic narrative singles out a pair of protagonists from the main body. Depending on whether they come into action before or after the fight, these include the Skate, in opposition to another animal, the Raven or the Deer; or the Snake and the Lizard, or the Snake in opposition to the Frog. Since the Snake presents an image symmetrical to that of the Skate, we can say that the Skate is present in all contexts either positively or negatively.

There is an important Bororo myth, already summarized and discussed in *From Honey to Ashes* (M_{292a}, pp. 308–28), where the Skate plays a decisive role and whose etiological function is to explain *the origin of the names of the constellations*. In relation to the astronomical code, this Bororo myth stands in the same position, then, as the North American myths featuring the Skate, the only difference being that the opposition between named and unnamed stars, which in Salish mythology takes a synchronic form — some have names, others are nameless — in Bororo mythology takes a diachronic form: originally the constellations were nameless, but now they have names.

The Bororo myth, like those to which I have compared it in the course of the discussion, opposes a son with a celestial polarity (a bird in M_2; a bird of ill omen in M_{292a}) to a father with a terrestrial or aquatic polarity (a tree-bearer and creator of water in M_2; a hunter who abandons game for fish in M_{292a}; a man who is changed into a skate and forced to live in mud, M_{292b}). Consequently, in one sense, these myths, like the Salish stories, deal with a conflict — between the terrestrial or aquatic camp and the aerial or celestial camp — but with the difference that the poles are reversed: the Bororo myths, unlike the North American ones, take the side of the character with celestial affinities. This reversal is accompanied by another, which directly concerns the Skate. In the Quileute versions ($M_{782a, b}$; see above, p. 544), the Skate acquires its stench through having been *soiled* with the '*wet*' — urine or dirty water. In the Bororo myth (M_{292a}), the Skate *soils* through being impregnated with hot ash, which belongs to the category of the *burnt*. It will be remembered that the father, thoroughly irritated by his son's impatient calls, throws the half-cooked fish in his face; the boy is burnt and blinded by the embers sticking to his flesh.

The analysis can be taken further. When, in a Quileute version, the Skate becomes foul-smelling, the reason is that its owner has, at first, no fire to cook it with. When, in the Bororo myth (M_{292a}), it soils, this is also through lack of fire, but in time and not in space: instead of the fire having to be brought from *elsewhere*, it is present, but it does not cook *quickly enough*. The consequence is not a *stench*, but a terrible *din*: the cries and rumblings in the forest, which echo the child's sobbing. It follows that the rules governing transformation that I defined in order to make the transition from the Quileute Skate, which is rendered foul-smelling, to the Snohomish carpenter, the creator of noise (and who is a Skate in Matako mythology), have been respected in their entirety during the movement from North to South America.[4] The analogy will appear more striking still when we see that, in the North American myths, the Skate and the Snake/Frog pair commutable with it, play a part in the conquest of cooking fire or the taming of storms and rain. The two functions – master of storms and rain, and master of fire – are attributed in Bororo mythology to one and the same person – the hero of M_1, who shares with the hero of M_{292a} the characteristic of being disjoined from his father as a result of real or metaphorical incest – sexual in M_1 and alimentary in M_{292a} (since the hungry child tries to conjoin with a still raw fish, which is moreover a uterine symbol); and, in both cases, the disjunction takes place towards the sky. It should also be noted that there is a correspondence between the child whose face is covered with burning ash by his father through the intermediary agency of an *undercooked* fish, and the child in M_{292b} who is showered with jeers because he has eaten a *cooked* rat – as a consequence of which the father is transformed into a skate – and in M_{782b}, *uncooked* skate, as a consequence of which the skate itself is drenched with dirty water and transformed into a foul-smelling fish. Here too, as was already demonstrated in *From Honey to Ashes* (pp. 305–33), insults are, on the linguistic level, the equivalent of stench and noise.

Let us turn now to another animal family, the sciuridae. In South America there is a small arboreal squirrel of the genus *Sciurus*, which is called *acutipuru* or *coatipuru* in the Amazonian basin, and *serelepé* or *caxinguelé* farther south. The etymology of the two latter terms is uncertain and that of the first two a subject of controversy. Each term is made up of two morphemes, the first of which is the name of other small quadrupeds, agouti or coati.

---

[4] So also has the transformation rule already defined in *OTM*, p. 389 and above, p. 248, governing the metamorphosis of a celestial object – the moon or a constellation – into a light-coloured terrestrial stone, in a Quileute version, which brings us back to the Potiphar transformation by inverting the carpenter myth (M_{724}; Reagan, pp. 71–84): here, the carpenter, the creator of a disjunction towards the far instead of being the victim of a disjunction towards the high, changes his miserly (not incestuous) brother into a white calcite rock.

The second morpheme is a suffix used in the *lingua geral* to form the names of plants or animals which bring good luck: e.g., uirapuru, a bird notable for its song, tajapuru, a plant propitious for fishermen and lovers, and manakapuru, a tree the roots of which are used in the brewing of an intoxicating drink, an aid to successful hunting. The Squirrel enjoys a high reputation because of its silky coat, its long tail, its agility,[5] and more especially for a further reason: the squirrel is said to be one of the very few animals – incidentally, along with the coati – able to come down from the highest trees head first. An Amazonian lullaby credits it with the power of lulling small children to sleep; also in Amazonia it was believed that when the corpse finally decomposed, the soul left it and went up into the sky in the form of an acutipuru (Rodrigues 1, p. 288; Stradelli 1, p. 362; Câmara Cascudo, 1, p. 11; Ihering, under 'serelepé').

In the part of North America with which the present volume is concerned, a similar role as psychopomp, but with sinister connotations, is often attributed to another of the sciuridae, the Flying Squirrel or Palatouche, of the genus *Glaucomys*. This rodent cannot actually fly, but it glides, with the help of the supple and extensile skin joining its feet from back to front. According to the Okanagon (Cline, p. 171), the Flying Squirrel was a harbinger of imminent death, and the belief was shared by the Klikitat, as can be seen from certain myths ($M_{790d, e}$; Jacobs 1, p. 45; 3, p. 207); they add that the Flying Squirrel was formerly a cannibalistic monster, the equivalent of which is also found in the Puget Sound area (M_{790f}; Haeberlin 1, pp. 427–8). Farther north, the Tsimshian regarded the Flying Squirrel as a dangerous animal, which delighted in throwing pine kernels down from the tree tops in order to terrify passers-by (M_{790h}; Boas 23, p. 205). The Nootka-speaking Makah, on the contrary, considered that Flying Squirrels brought good luck; they never hunted them deliberately, but if they caught one by chance, they regarded its capture as a windfall (Gunther 6, 116). In both hemispheres, then, sciuridae, which are sometimes on the side of life and sometimes on the side of death, connote in like fashion the margin between them. Several Carrier myths (including M_{749}; Jenness 2, p. 99) refer to a young girl who dies of laughing on seeing a

[5] The coati-puru (acutipuru), however, plays an extremely ambiguous part, which I do not propose to investigate further at this point, in a group of Cashinawa myths (M_{790a-c}; Abreu, pp. 209–26), where it provides magic food for starving Indians, who have been reduced to eating earth. After which, it seduces a woman, then changes into a bat, and castrates her husband. All the Indians join forces to attack it. It manages to escape, taking with it the food it had given the Indians. Dr Pierre Clastres has pointed out to me that, in certain Guayaki rites, the coati plays an important role, which appears to be determined by ideas similar to those current farther north in connection with the acutipuru. He suggests, incidentally, that the suffix 'puru' could be the same as the Guarani 'mburu', which, according to Cadogan (4, pp. 18, 59), connotes a state of religious fervour (cf. above, p. 550, the Kalina suffix 'imo').

squirrel descend from a tree. According to the Hoh and the Quileute (Reagan, pp. 66–7, 80–81), a woman stranded at the top of a tree is rescued, sometimes by a squirrel, sometimes by a comic character. Could the comic effect produced by the squirrel, or by a creature playing the same part, not be a result of the fact that, like its South American counterpart, it comes down head-first? A Quileute version (M_{790g}; Andrade, pp. 58–63) maintains that this is the case, and explains the woman's rescue by this feature of the animal's behaviour. The Cœur d'Alêne believe in the existence of supernatural dwarfs who climb up and down trees with great celerity, and always head-first. They appear to be all red and carry their babies upside down. People whom they approach lose their senses and, when they come out of their stupor, they find themselves leaning upside down against a tree. There are other communities of dwarfs who dress in squirrel skins (Boas 4, p. 127, n. 1; Teit 6, p. 180). Although we are dealing here with two distinct races of dwarfs, the double reference to garments made from squirrel skins and to the head-first descent from trees, also transposed to the way of carrying babies and the treatment of human victims, clearly indicates that native thought postulates a very close affinity between dwarfs and sciuridae.

Consequently, in South as well as in North America, animals belonging to different genera of the sciuridae are thought of as supernatural beings capable of lulling children to sleep and of causing adults to lose consciousness; in North America, they are harbingers of death, in South America conveyors of the soul when it leaves its mortal remains for its permanent abode in the world beyond. And, in both hemispheres, these parallel beliefs are linked with the characteristic mode of movement of the sciuridae, which climb down trees head-first.

It will no doubt have been noticed that the three types of animals whose role in the myths we have just examined are only given a part to play in so far as each is worked into a binary opposition. Such oppositions, which are connected with anatomy, physiology or social customs, depend on observable phenomena, and consequently on empirical deduction. This was true in the case of the ants and the wasps encountered on pp. 242 and 419 and whose narrow waists seem to divide their bodies into two halves, so that the insects can be given the role of separators establishing the alternation of day and night and of life and death: they can be used all the more convincingly for this purpose since, as is suggested in an Alsea myth (M_{799b}; Frachtenberg 4, p. 141), some of them seem to go on living even after having been cut in two.

Similarly, gallinaceans paradoxically combine two opposite characteristics: the presence of meat and the absence of fat. And flat-fish seem abnormally broad when looked at from the front, but extremely thin when seen in profile. Lastly, unlike other quadrupeds, some of the sciuridae make a right-about turn when changing from an upward to a downwards direction.

Mythic beliefs, however, do not accept the limits of observable data. To the results of empirical deduction, that is binarism, they added a transcendental deduction which, going beyond any mere abstract concept of arbitration between those supreme opposites, life and death, proceeds to create a whole series of images, which it then reincorporates into the real world; e.g., the Grouse's head, which is alive on one side and dead on the other; the supernatural gnomes who give explicit expression to the empirically evident peculiarities of the Squirrel, by means of imagined behaviour patterns of the same type in respect of their children and their enemies; the permanent constellations, whose distinctive feature is that, while always present in the sky, they are invisible by day, like the Skate in profile, and fully visible at night, like the Skate seen 'full-face'.

That we have reached the heart of the problem is evident from a commutation affecting the character of Skate Woman, which emerges as we move from the coastal to the inland communities. According to the Yurok, the Wiyot, the Tolowa and the Hupa (M_{292d-f}; see above, p. 550), this demonic woman, or some other equivalent creature, gripped the demiurge firmly between her thighs during copulation, and took him away across the sea. The Nez Percé tell a similar story ($M_{542a, b}$; see above, p. 80), in which the same demonic role is attributed to a Butterfly Woman. In view of the correspondences I have just suggested between animals common to myths of both North and South America, it is remarkable that the Amazonian Tucuna should tell the same story as the Nez Percé, only substituting the stomach for the penis. They say (M_{292i}; Nim. 13, pp. 122–3; cf. *OTM*, p. 119) that a jaguar killed and ate the demiurge (or, to be more accurate, the father of the demiurges, although he shares the role with his sons); with his victim's stomach, the animal makes a trumpet, and plays upon it. The sons succeed in knocking it out of his hands, but owing to their clumsiness, fail to prevent it flying away. The stomach, after experiencing various adventures, comes to rest on the open wings of a blue butterfly of the genus *Morpho*, to which the Amazonian tribes attribute maleficent powers. The insect folded its wings over the demiurge's stomach and refused to give it up. To force it to do so, a hole had to be burnt in its wings.

The Butterfly lends itself to the role of binary operator in the same way as the Skate; when it opens out its wings, it is very broad and when it closes them and is looked at from the front or back, it is very narrow. And just as the Wichita stress the ambiguity of the gallinaceans by imagining the Prairie Hen as being ambidextrous in its human guise (see above, p. 543), the Kutenai have a myth (M_{791}; Chamberlain, p. 578) in which a Butterfly in human form is at first taken for a woman, although it belonged to the opposite sex.

The transformation of the Skate Woman into a Butterfly Woman, which can be observed as we move from the Yurok to the Nez Percé, is continued in Navajo mythology, where it is accompanied by a change of sex. In a myth ($M_{792a, b}$; Pepper, pp. 178–83; O'Bryan, p. 163), the heroines of which are none other than the secluded daughters who have already figured in this volume (see above, p. 42), the girls yield to the advances of a butterfly man, who abducts them and treats them harshly. One version (M_{792b}), repeating the Yurok theme of exile across the sea, explains that the maleficent character 'stole the wives and lured their husbands across the water and killed them.'

The preceding remarks about the Skate Woman and the Butterfly Woman or Man suggest another hypothesis. By exiling his victims across the sea, the character fulfils a function which is complementary to that attributed by the Salish, in the M_{375} series, to the symplegades: the prevention of the return of a hero who has been exiled to the land of the dead on the other side of the water. So here again, the relevant opposition is between the dead and the living.

The exile, which the symplegades prevent being brought to an end, is deliberately provoked by the Skate Woman precisely because *she is not symplegades*: she closes up and refuses to open. In the myths about the war against the celestial people which takes place along the vertical, not the horizontal, axis (although, as I showed on p. 494, the two axes are convertible), the Skate has a correlational and oppositional relationship with the squinting Snake; and are not the symplegades, in a sense, squinting stones? We thus glimpse the possibility of welding, into a single group, the symplegades motif, which belongs to the saga of Moon, the demiurge, the Skate motif, which belongs to the earth-dwellers' fight against the celestial people, and lastly, the role of anti-symplegades performed by the Skate and the Butterfly. At the same time, the Skate in the Quileute myths ($M_{782a, b}$), which is soiled on one side, but left clean on the other, at a time when it is establishing a certain type of seasonal periodicity, presents a striking analogy with the bull-roarers, blackened on one side but unmarked on the other, that the Puget Sound Indians whirled round in the air to cause rain and the spring thaw; and with the grandmother in the corresponding myths, as well as with the Sparrow, featured in neighbouring myths, whose face is first blackened or soiled, and then washed clean.

We thus return to the concept of the binary operator. It is to this concept, it would seem, that we must attribute the almost incredible single-mindedness with which the Indians of both North and South America, throughout the centuries and over vast expanses of territory differing in geological structure, climate, flora and fauna, strove to preserve, rediscover or replace, the zoemes they deemed indispensable for certain operations (Figure 33). Of course, all mythemes of whatever kind, must, generally speaking, lend themselves to binary operations, since such operations are an inherent feature of the means invented by nature to make possible the functioning of language and thought. But it is as if certain animals were more suited than others to fulfil this role, either because of some striking feature of their make-up or behaviour, or because of an equally innate natural tendency of the human mind to apprehend properties of a particular type more quickly and more readily. However, the two explanations really come to the same thing, since no feature is significant in itself: it is perceptive analysis, already by definition combinatory and capable of logical operations on the level of the sensibility which, when relayed through or backed up by the understanding, bestows a meaning on phenomena and turns them into articulate statements. We can say, then, that the binary operators are those operators which are already perceptible to empirical deduction as algorithms, before transcendental deduction has intervened to produce its effects.[6] They are thus the basic constituents of the vast combinatory apparatus, which is what any mythic system amounts to.

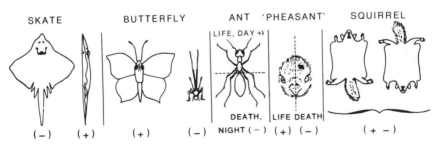

Figure 33. The binary operators

[6] However, the analysis to which sense experience lends itself does not always take a binary form. For instance, the myths of this particular area divide birds of prey into three different categories, according to whether the species or genus concerned feeds on birds, fish or small quadrupeds. Birds of prey have, then, an initial, triple valency, linking them to air, water and earth. These elements, in their turn, are sometimes classed together as a triad, and sometimes contrasted with each other, two by two, in a high/low pair, the second term of which then requires a subsidiary dichotomy between earth and water.

The fundamental role they play explains why the communities who peopled North and South America in successive migratory waves, moving along the coasts or inland, through rain forests or deserts, over the plains or into the mountains, struggled, consciously or unconsciously, to ensure that the essential elements of their system should be neither lost nor scattered; they did so by rediscovering and identifying species, genera or families wherever possible or, in the absence of the known ones, looking for those others best suited to allow the re-establishment of the invariant relationship with entirely new forms of animal and vegetable life, a different distribution of fauna and flora, and the new exploitation of animals and plants made possible by techniques and life-styles that were also in process of change.

2 One Myth Only

A minute freed from the temporal order has recreated within us, to appreciate it, a being freed from the temporal order.

Translated from M. Proust, *Le Temps retrouvé*, II, p. 15

At the beginning of *The Raw and the Cooked*, in the 'overture' to what was to be a very long enquiry, I explained that I would proceed by working, again and again, 'outward from the centre' (*RC*, p. 4). It is a fact that, in the course of these four volumes, I have followed, partially or completely, many circular itineraries — some with a narrow and some with a broad radius — bringing in each time widely scattered myths and linking them up with others, which in turn were incorporated into groups merging to form ever larger, but also less numerous, entities.

The first of these itineraries, which gave rise to all the others, established a link between the Bororo myth about the origin of water (M_1) and the Ge myths about the origin of fire (M_{7-12}). Together, they entered a larger circle to join up with myths explaining the origin of man's mortality and that of cultivated plants (M_{87-92}). All these myths, which are characterized by the use of a vertical axis of disjunction, were then incorporated with others involving two axes of disjunction, one horizontal and the other vertical ($M_{124-125}$). In a final foray, I established a link-up between the original myths I had started from, M_1, M_{7-12}, and the last, $M_{171-175}$, $M_{178-179}$, to which the argument of *The Raw and the Cooked* had led us. In the second volume I followed the same procedure, but cast the net more widely. By way of M_{21-27}, M_1 and M_{7-12} were grouped, first of all, with new myths, $M_{188-191}$ (*HA*, p. 62). Similarly, with $M_{216-217}$ and $M_{259-266}$ (*HA*, pp. 222–8). A series of to-and-fro movements, which brought us back each time to the starting-point, then established links between M_{7-12} and M_{273} (*HA*, p. 252), M_2 and M_{292} (*HA*, p. 308), and finally M_1, M_{7-12} and $M_{300-303}$ (*HA*, p. 346).

After showing, in the first part of *The Origin of Table Manners*, that certain link-ups, no less imperative than the others — between M_{130} etc. and M_{354}, between M_{354} and $M_{365-385}$, and between all of them and $M_{393-394}$ (pp. 25–113) — made it essential to refer to North American motifs, I was able, and indeed felt obliged, to describe a circle wide enough to include myths belonging to the northern hemisphere. This extension of the enquiry took place in two stages: first, by means of a further South American itinerary, more comprehensive than the previous ones, and also in a sense recapitulatory, linking M_1, M_{7-12}, and $M_{405-406}$; then, by means of another, which extended from a South American myth (M_{10}) at the beginning to North American myths (M_{428}, M_{495a}) at the end (*OTM*, pp. 305–306, 424–7). The double journey thus accomplished through the mythology of North and South America was illustrated, in diagrammatic form, in Figure 41 (*OTM*, p. 467).

Readers will have noticed, since the beginning of the present volume, that the procedure which consists in threading on to the same argument myths from both North and South America, has not only been continued; its rhythm has been intensified. More rapid cross-references, together with an increase in the number of points of view and angles of approach have made it possible to consolidate into a whole what might at first have seemed to be a loose and precarious assemblage of odds and ends, all dissimilar in form, texture and colour. Careful stitching and darning, systematically applied to reinforce weak spots, has finally produced a homogeneous fabric, clear in outline and harmonious in its blend of shades; fragments which at first seemed disparate, once they have found their appropriate place and the correct relationship to their neighbours, come together to form a coherent picture. In this picture, the tiniest details, however gratuitous, bizarre, and even absurd they may have seemed at the beginning, acquire both meaning and function.

This being so, certain fundamental questions arise: how did the picture originate? Why did it come into being? What is its history? How can it be representative of something and have a meaning, when it is the work of countless painters, separated from each other by millions of kilometres, speaking different languages and imbued with different traditions, and who, without any possibility of intercommunication, have each conceived and executed only one infinitesimal fragment? Through what mysterious collusion do the fragments happen to fit together, correspond to each other or echo each other? And what does the picture itself consist of? Is it repeating the same image hundreds of times over? Does it express an accidental harmony and equilibrium, originating from some random collaborative effort which, precisely because of the number and diversity of the participants, has produced an apparent orderliness through the reciprocal neutralization of multiple differences? Or again, are we to conclude that, throughout the entire American continent, there is only one myth, which all the populations have evolved through some mysterious impulse, but which is so rich in details and in the multiplicity of its variants that several volumes barely suffice to describe it?

It must be possible to suggest at least a tentative reply to these questions. It would be a beginning if we could show that the major themes of this picture, as we have tried to decode them and understand them — with the help of some eight hundred myths, or almost twice that number if the variants are taken into account — are to be found in certain communities in the same order and with the same meaning as I have attributed to them. The fact is that I myself have been evolving a myth on the basis of myths, whereas the actual stories, which are clearly situated in time and space, are like a body in its natural state that I am trying to synthesize in laboratory conditions, and about which I can only postulate that my synthesis must correspond somewhere to a real object. If, however, the real object proved to be no more than an unconscious pattern, generating the same phenomena in both South and North America, the hypothesis would remain unverifiable, and the reasons for adopting it would depend solely on its usefulness in explaining apparent incoherencies, resolving contradictions, elucidating anthropological problems and achieving economical solutions in these various fields. The situation would be quite different, if, at the heart of the closely defined area towards which the spontaneous drive of my investigation has irresistibly carried me, there were certain specific myths representing a concrete realization of the hypothesis; this would be no less gratifying than the experience of an astronomer who, after calculating the existence of a hitherto unknown heavenly body, suddenly sees it through his telescope at the place where it ought to be and with the mass and the momentum required to confirm all the apparent anomalies of the system to which it belongs, as being so many proofs in support of its existence.

As it happens, in the area of North America with which this volume is concerned, such myths are to be found to make the demonstration possible. They all belong to coastal groups living along a narrow band of territory, extending from the south of the Oregon River to beyond the Fraser River, that is, a region characterized by the smallness of the communities who live there, the restricted area occupied by each, and great linguistic diversity. In addition to maritime Salish, such as the Quinault and the Tillamook, and coastal Salish such as the Cowichan, the Lkungen, the Lummi, the Klallam, and the Twana, etc., there are a few Athapaskan groups cut off from the main body of their linguistic family, as well as the only known representatives of some tiny isolated families: the Coos, the Yakonan (today attached to the Penutian family), and the Chemakum . . . Virtually nothing is known of these last groups, whose traditional culture collapsed at an early stage when their numbers dwindled. Such is especially the case with the Coos, of whom there were about 1,500 in southern Oregon at the beginning of the nineteenth century. I have chosen to begin the last part of my enquiry with them, because, as the most southerly element in the small sample to which I have tried to confine myself, they lived almost in the same latitude as the Klamath; the territories of the two tribes were between a hundred and two hundred kilometres apart. Since, in the present volume, I started with the Klamath, and moved gradually northwards, I propose to follow the same pattern in studying a mythological microcosm which contains, in a condensed form, all the major themes broached since the beginning of my enquiry; the mythology of the area to which the present volume has been devoted in itself presents a reduced model of these themes, but we are now about to see a very much smaller one still, which will allow us to extract the quintessential mythic formula.

M_{793a}. Coos. 'The bird-nester'

An old Indian had a son who was married to two women, by whom he had two children. The father-in-law desired his daughters-in-law. He placed his blood-stained faeces at the top of a small conifer (spruce, *Picea* genus; *Epinette* in French-Canadian) and arranged for a pretty woodpecker with red feathers to come and peck them. As his grandchildren coveted the feathers, he persuaded them to get their father to go and shoot the bird.

While the hunter was climbing up towards his target, the tree rose high into the air, set him down in the sky and disappeared. The wicked old man assumed the appearance of a young man, and took possession of his daughters-in-law.

The celestial world was a vast and beautiful plain: 'just one prairie spread out'. There was no wind and no food. The hero spotted two 'blue cranes' (probably herons); he tried to shoot at them, missed, and ran after them. When he caught up with the birds, they had assumed the appearance of two elderly humans. They welcomed him and gave him shelter, for they were well-supplied with all kinds of food. These two old men lived 'on the end of the world'. They warned the hero that every day Sun Woman stopped at their house to eat people's stomachs, for she was a cannibal. So they hid him when she arrived, preceded by a great noise and blazing red heat. After her usual repast, she set off once more on her travels. The hero followed her, went up to her and managed to copulate with her by means of a penis made of ice, which modified his partner's excessive ardour once and for all. Henceforth, Sun Woman behaved with greater clemency towards the living.

Next, the hero arrived at the house of unlucky hunters of sea otters; there, two sisters fell in love with him. They were nocturnal travellers, and the elder, a nice, kind girl, explained that they had come from another country: 'Whenever we get anywhere,' she added, 'the women have their monthly periods; we travel here for the same length of time as we do in the other country, and this is why you always see me.' The hero married the two women. His evil father-in-law forced him to undergo various ordeals, all intended to cause his death: however, he emerged triumphant. He then decided to visit his own people, and promised his wives that he would return in two days. The elderly helpful Herons loaded him with gifts and provisions – a belt, a whale (*sic*), a shield, a feather band – and dropped him to earth in a basket suspended from a rope.

He was reunited with his earthly women and children. His father, having been warned of his return, lost no time in becoming an old man again. The hero forced him to put on the magic belt which he had brought back from the sky: by means of this evil spell, the old man was carried out to sea in the company of a whale. His son climbed back into the basket with his kinsfolk and installed his earthly family in the sky, along with the other family he had left there.

Meanwhile, the hero's father, who spoke all kinds of languages, including the language of whales, ordered the cetacean to swallow him and take him home. He emerged from the monster's entrails, completely bald and reduced to a skeleton; only his heart was left. He found willow leaves, and presented them as herring to small hunchbacks, the whale's subjects, thus making them believe that it was summer, and time to emerge from their winter sleep. Then he commanded the whale to take him along the coast, shouting as loud as he could so as to attract the attention of the inhabitants.

At last he reached his own country, where it was so intensely cold that he nearly died. He warmed himself for a while in the sun and suddenly he recalled that the world had such a thing as food. He crawled everywhere and found a few manzanita berries (*Arctostaphylos* sp.). He stuffed himself with these for a whole day but never 'got satiated'; the reason was that he had no sooner ingested them than they dropped out of his body. He plugged some grass into his anus and could then assimilate food in the normal way.

He built a small house, lit a fire and remembered the existence of skunk cabbage (*Lysichiton*; an early flowering Aracea) and the technique of roasting. The cabbage, however, just dried up in the fire; instead of roasting, it remained raw. Gradually, the old man rediscovered the art of making an earth oven and he succeeded in cooking a meal, which he divided into equal portions. Although he had no one with him, he assigned each portion to an 'ideal' relative: uncle, brother, elder brother, aunt, sister-in-law, younger brother . . .

Soon the salmon arrived. The old man speared them and boiled them. But it was exhausting work and he invented (or reinvented) the fish trap. Every morning he went to collect the salmon caught during the night, and put them out whole to dry – including the head, the heart, the gills, the tail, and the 'milter'. Summer came, and the old man considered that he had greater stocks of food than he needed. Yet, downstream, there were people who were starving. The old man tried to take food to them: as soon as he started off, all he possessed in the way of dried fish jumped into the water and disappeared. Since that time, fish swim up the river every year (Frachtenberg 1, pp. 21–37).

There are more recent versions of this myth, which form part of a cosmological system ($M_{793b, c}$: Jacobs 6, pp. 184–6, 188–92, 210–22). The Coos, like other coastal communities, believed that a dynasty of five trickster demiurges once reigned in succession over the world, leaving behind evidence of their exploits. The plot of M_{793c} features the fifth demiurge in the role of bird-nester, and his father, the fourth, in the role of persecutor.

At that time, it is said, the father and son visited a community which had neither cooking fire, water, nor food, since the chief of the village where the fourth demiurge lived had sole possession of these necessities of life and refused to part with them. Answering an appeal from the fifth demiurge, all the animals joined forces and, by means of various ruses, defeated the chief in a gambling contest, winning fire, which they placed in the wood of trees, water which spread everywhere, and all kinds of food. Henceforth people could quench their thirst, and cook food on a fire instead of putting it under the arms of young men and making them dance until it was warm.

At this point, the fifth demiurge married two wives and went to live with them in his father's house. Next follows the bird-nester episode, with the one modification that the father changes his blood-stained faeces into a small woodpecker of the genus *Sphyrapicus*. While chasing after the bird, as his father had commanded him to do, the hero disappears into the sky. The old man takes possession of his daughters-in-law, and blinds his grand-children with his sperm. This is the origin of purulent discharges which have affected eyes ever since.

In the sky, the hero stays at the home of a pair of poisonous Spiders. The skulls of both husband and wife are half eaten away by the heat which Sun Woman radiates during her daily visits. She stops at their home every day for a meal, but regularly lifts the food to the sides of her lips since, to her great annoyance, she can never find her mouth. By means of his penis, which is made of ice, the hero moderates the Sun Woman's heat; the Sun then resumes her daily course, and sends the hero off to marry her younger sister Moon who, she says, has the advantage of being able to stay at home from time to time.

The helpful Spiders make various recommendations to the hero, which will enable him to overcome the ordeals imposed on him by his parents-in-law. As in the other version, he goes back to earth to look for his wives and children, who tell him how unhappy they are. The entire family go up into the sky, except the father, who is disowned by the hero and condemned to become a coyote.

Regretfully, I must leave to one side certain aspects of these myths. Sun Woman's predilection for human stomachs belongs to a paradigm common to the Coos, the Salish, and particularly the Nez Percé, who relate how Coyote decapitated or punished Moon, who at that time was a cannibal feeding on human testicles (Boas 4, pp. 173–5, 186–7). Since Moon is a male character in these myths, a link-up can be made with M_{793a-c} by means of a triple transformation: 1) *moon* $\Rightarrow$ *sun*; 2) *male* $\Rightarrow$ *female*; 3) *testicles* $\Rightarrow$ *stomach*. But any discussion of these myths would be out of place here: a more appropriate context, as I showed in my 1968–9 lectures at the Collège de France, would be with the parallel series on the origin of wind and fog, to which I have already referred (see above, pp. 360, 369, 491). It is already clear from the way in which M_{793c} begins (see above, p. 565), that the Coos myths are situated on the side of water and fire. On the other hand, Sun Woman, who fails to reach her mouth when she eats, seems to be afflicted with a kind of blindness; however, the myth does not say this explicitly, and other interpretations are possible, especially since certain Cashinawa myths, to which, by a curious coincidence, I had to refer only a few pages earlier (M_{790a-c}), deal, like the Coos myths, with all sorts of food that a supernatural being (the acutipuru in the Cashinawa context) obtains, by magical means, for a community so deprived that its members have to eat earth in order to survive. When presented with their first meal of fruit and vegetables, these people behave exactly like Sun Woman with her cannibalistic meal: being unable to find the way to their mouths, they stuff the food up their noses. If all these myths formed part of the same set, in spite of the geographical distance between them, the clumsiness of the characters could be a simple expression of their gluttony. As it happens, the next Cashinawa myth in Abreu's collection refers to another supernatural and gluttonous character: a toad who devours the dishes along with the food they contain (M_{390}; *OTM*, p. 80).

Be that as it may, an obvious relationship between M_{793} and certain South American myths emerges from the sequence in which the trickster demiurge, who has no fundament, cannot retain food until he has the idea of blocking his posterior with a wad of grass. I have already referred to this incident (see above, p. 339), in order to show that the versions of the bird-nester story found in this northern region of America lead back to the reference myth (M_1), where a similar mishap befalls the hero, when the putrefied lizards with which he has covered his body give him the appearance of carrion, and he is attacked by vultures which devour his hindquarters. In the Coos text, the same effect is produced by a sojourn inside a whale's belly; the demiurge emerges in a similiarly putrefied state, without any outer covering of flesh and completely bald. It is, of course, true that, in this case, the character is the father, not the son, the persecutor and not his victim. However, this calls for two remarks: by placing the characters in a dynastic series of five demiurges, the Coos make them more readily commutable. Secondly, like M_1, M_{793} is situated at the point of intersection of two mythic series: that of the bird-nester proper, and the one I have called the Potiphar transformation (see above, p. 515). From one series, it borrows the vertical disjunction of the son in the direction of the sky, and from the other, the horizontal disjunction of the father across a stretch of water. In the case of M_1, I explained this special construction by the dual etiological function attributable to this myth, which accounts simultaneously for the origin of celestial water, in the form of windy rainstorms, and for the origin — or if not the origin at least the recovery — of domestic fire. In *The Raw and the Cooked* (pp. 64–5), I said that M_1, was a myth about the origin of cooking; this is surely also true of M_{793a-c}, where the demiurge, who has reverted to a state of nature through contact with a whale (whose semantic function will be defined more clearly later), and is thereby reduced to a state of putrefaction, reconstitutes — in an amazing instance of anamnesis — the dietetic pattern of mankind along with the techniques for obtaining and cooking man's principal foods. In this respect it is not without significance that the rediscovery should start with berries, which can be eaten raw, and should continue with skunk cabbage; this foul-smelling aracea, which is still closer to the category of the rotten, is the first plant to flower in the spring, even before the snow has finished melting. At that time of year, it was often the only food the Indians had to save them from famine, and the Kathlamet say in one of their myths (M_{794}; Gunther 3, pp. 22–3) that before discovering salmon, humans lived almost entirely on skunk cabbage. In M_{793}, the discovery of salmon follows that of the skunk cabbage; the myth observes, then, a twofold natural and cultural progression: (*berries, raw*) → (*araceae, roasted in oven*) → (*salmon, boiled*).[1]

The dual etiological function I postulated for M_1 was put forward in *The Raw and the Cooked* in a hypothetico-deductive form, which the Coos myths now confirm empirically. M_{793c} differs from the other versions in putting the bird-nester sequence before the rediscovery of cooking – whereas M_{793a} puts the rediscovery at the end – and it includes in the process fire, water and foodstuffs. This also happens in myths concerned more particularly with the origin of fire and water:

M_{795}. *Coos. 'The origin of fire and water'*

Formerly, people lived in a mixed-up fashion; they had neither fire nor water. Whenever they intended to eat something, young men would put it under their arms and dance with it; old people would sit on it. They decided to visit a foreign land where a famous cook kept fire and water, and to win them from him in a gambling contest. The match began and the visitors enlisted the help of maggots, which started devouring their chief opponent. Soon, he was no more than a fleshless skeleton, yet he went on gambling. At last, a snake, which was trying to enter his nose, scared him and forced him to run away. The visitors immediately seized the fire and released the water. Since then, humans possess fire and rain falls on the earth (Frachtenberg 1, pp. 39–42; 5, pp. 422–9).

The acquisition of fire and water, like the rediscovery of food and cooking

---

[1] It is possible that a correlational and oppositional relationship existed between skunk cabbage and ferns. Kwakiutl recipes regularly treat skunk cabbage leaves and dried ferns as being interchangeable (Boas-Hunt 2, Vol. I, *passim*). In a Tillamook version of the journey across the sea (M_{684a}; Boas 14, pp. 27–30), the hero encounters women harvesting skunk cabbage instead of fern rhizomes, as in the other Salish versions; and again in Tillamook mythology (M_{800}; Boas 14, pp. 136–7) even when the encounter takes place in the sky. This gives the formula: [(*earth-water horizontal axis*): (skunk-cabbage)] :: [(earth-sky vertical axis) : (fern rhizomes)] :: [spring : autumn] (cf. above, pp. 479–80; see below, p. 576).

in M_{793a}, is here related to the decomposition affecting one of the characters: the fourth demiurge before his rediscovery of the art of cooking, or his substitute (the chief of his village, according to M_{793c}), who has to be made to hand over the means of cooking. One rots *inside* a whale's body, of which he is the content, whereas the other rots in his capacity as container, when the maggots eat their way *inside* his body. This remarkable inversion points to another: during the attack by the cannibalistic maggots, the master of fire and water (the means of cooking), remains unperturbed when a snake tries to enter his mouth (Frachtenberg 1, p. 43; 5, p. 426), and *only takes fright* when the reptile threatens to penetrate his nose. On the contrary, according to M_{793a-c}, Sun Woman, mistress of fire in a destructive and anti-culinary form (since it burns up her hosts' skulls), *flies into a rage* when she fails to lift her cannibalistic meal to her mouth, and reaches her nose instead – as we can suppose, if we complete the sense of the myths. Myths $M_{793a, c}$ contrast hyperbolic forms of fire (the Solar woman) and water (the penis made of ice); M_{795} links temperate forms of fire (domestic hearth) and water (celestial rain), yet these myths are nevertheless part of the same system.

This being so, we can understand why the spiders in M_{793c} are poisonous; they are in league with the hero against the sun, who was at that time destructive and cannibalistic, and are commutable with the snake in M_{795}, the ally of the animals against the master of domestic fire who, by withholding it from everyone, was behaving in an equally barbarous way. We still have to explain how spiders with *burnt skulls* come to be changed, in M_{793a}, into large herons, birds which normally have *their feet in water*. This small problem can be solved in two ways.

M_{793} effects a conjunction between solar fire and water in the form of ice, leading to a positive result: the advent of a temperate, beneficent sun. M_{795}, on the other hand, effects a conjunction between celestial water in the form of rain and domestic fire, also leading to a positive result: the advent of cooking. In this respect, the Coos myths differ from the Bororo M_1, instead of resembling it; in the Bororo myth, the conjunction of celestial water with domestic fire leads to a negative result: the extinction of all fires, except that belonging to the hero's grandmother, and – in the case of the other inhabitants of the village – the temporary loss of cooking. If, then, there is a transcontinental mythic system, it should include a Bororo myth about the tempering of the sun's heat. There is, in fact, such a myth (M_{120}; *RC*, p. 193); it tells how two brothers, named Sun and Moon, spill the water of which aquatic birds are the masters, with the result that the sun's heat becomes unbearable. The birds fan themselves to keep cool, causing such a powerful wind that the two brothers are carried up into the sky, where they have remained since, at a reasonable distance from the earth. In both contexts, then, the aquatic birds have their appointed place in the system and we could simply note the parallelism without trying to understand it.

However, it is possible to carry the analysis further by extending the Coos paradigm to include a neighbouring version belonging to the Alsea who, like the Siuslaw, whose territory bordered on that of the Coos, belonged to the Yakonan linguistic family.

M 796. *Alsea. 'The bird-nester'*

Seúku the transformer (a character different from Coyote the trickster) set off on his travels with his son. They stopped in a village, in which the young man took two wives who each bore him a child. While his son was away, Seúku assumed the appearance of a young man and tried to seduce his daughters-in-law. The hero, having been advised of this by one of his wives, took his father along with him wherever he went.

One of the children fancied a bird perched on a twig. The hero climbed up the tree, which kept on growing taller, and left him in the sky, then contracted downward and finally disappeared.

In the sky, the hero met five helpful Thunders. They wrapped him in a whale-skin (*sic*), and let him back down to earth at the end of a rope. When he returned home, his children chewed the tasty outer covering and offered their grandfather a share. The latter lost no time in resuming the appearance of an old man. The hero, however, wrapped him up in the skin, which he placed on hot stones. The whale-skin shrivelled up around him until not a single part of his body showed anywhere. The bundle was thrown into the sea, and the east wind carried the 'whale' out to sea where it could be seen spouting water. The transformer decided to take advantage of this means of transport to examine the world thoroughly, and organize it. First he went southwards, then northwards. He landed one day, and sent the whale back to sea. He told the whale that, once a year, it would be washed ashore at a place inhabited by rich people and provide food for the inhabitants.

The transformer supplied himself, by magical means, with a bow, quiver and arrows. He had a sudden fit of hunger, knelt down and began to munch red Kinikinnick berries (probably *Arctostaphylos uva ursi*, cf. M 793a). However, he could not satisfy his hunger, for the berries kept dropping through his armpits. He blocked his armpits with grass, and that is why people have hair under their arms.

Next, he created salmon, sturgeons and whales, together with instruments for fishing, and ordained that salmon should be roasted. He named the localities, created seals and other mammalian pinnipeds, shells and edible tubers, and wherever he placed these things, they are found there today (Frachtenberg 4, pp. 77–91).

Instead of rotting inside a whale's belly like the trickster demiurge in the Coos myth, the Alsea transformer could be more accurately described as roasting inside it. No sooner has he emerged, than he declares the whale a primary food, after which come raw, edible berries, and next salmon, roasted and not boiled as in the Coos myths. What does this progression signify? From evidence recorded among neighbouring groups – those along the Lower Umpqua, who are also members of the Yakonan linguistic family, and close neighbours of the Coos and the Alsea; and, farther north, the Hoh and the Quileute – we know what it meant to these maritime communities for a whale to be washed ashore, since, unlike the Nootka, they did not hunt the large cetaceans.[2] 'Sometimes, in winter,' according to an informant belonging to the Lower Umpqua area, 'a whale came ashore. People from every direction assembled there, and no matter how many people there were, they could all store up lots of grease. That was why these people were glad when a whale came ashore . . . To people living long ago it was a very great boon' (Frachtenberg 3, p. 83). The Hoh-Quileute were even more eloquent: 'The smell of whale-meat is pleasing to the gods' (Reagan, p. 44). So, the whale, a heaven-sent gift in a period of famine, forms a counterpart to the skunk cabbage in the Coos myths, the fetid smell of which contrasts with the whale odour, just as whale meat, the richest of all foods, is in opposition to the skunk cabbage, which is the poorest. Moreover, M_{796} associates the grounded whale with monetary wealth (see above, p. 571), which, in the Oregon communities, took the form of *dentalia* shells.

This first inversion: *skunk cabbage/whale*, is followed by another. In the Coos myths, the armpits make raw food digestible, since that is where it is cooked. In the Alsea myths, on the other hand, the gaping armpits allow the food to escape before it can reach the stomach: consequently, they prevent digestion. A third inversion concerns salmon; in another Alsea myth (M_{797}; Frachtenberg 4, p. 107), it is stated that the fish must be 'cut open and roasted on a stick': 'This is why', the myth concludes, 'salmon is

---

[2] With the exception of the Quinault and Quileute, who did so to some slight extent, in imitation of the Makah.

done thus today.' There is a suggestion in the Alsea myths that, like many other tribes, these Indians believed in an affinity between the boiled and the rotten (*OTM*, pp. 481–3).[3] The myth already quoted, in which the leading characters are the five Thunders, who also figure in M_{796}, tells how they are taken prisoner by cannibals and dropped into the cooking-pot. The youngest emerges unscathed from the boiling water, and sets about reviving his brothers by ordering them to open their 'rotten eye'. Frachtenberg (4, p. 299) confirms the meaning of the word *pi'lqan* (= rotten) used in the text. The rediscovery of cooking in M_{793} is therefore situated between two related terms, the rotting in the whale's belly at the beginning, and the boiling of the salmon at the end. The rediscovery described in M_{796} is also situated between two related terms: roasting on hot stones at the beginning, and later the roasting of salmon on a spit.

At the same time, the food system changes from one myth to the next:

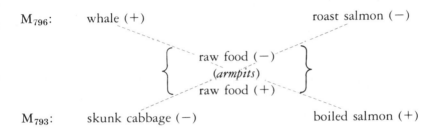

M_{796}:   whale (+)   roast salmon (−)

           raw food (−)
           (*armpits*)
           raw food (+)

M_{793}:   skunk cabbage (−)   boiled salmon (+)

As a remedy for famine, the whale is superior to the skunk cabbage; so, in order to balance the system, the boiled must be superior to the roasted. This confirms an order of preference already noted in connection with the Chinook myth, M_{663a} (see above, p. 345). It thus follows that the Coos myths, which start lower down the culinary scale but attain a higher level, are stronger versions than the Alsea one.

This, indeed, was already implied by the total absence from the Alsea version of any mention of the hero's celestial adventures. Instead of describ-

---

[3] Another example, this time from French-speaking Abenaki Indians, can be added to those already quoted. 'A "*remède échaudé*" is a vegetable product that has been scalded or boiled. When he (the informant) says: "*Les pétaques ont été sumées trop de bonne heure, elles ont été échaudées*", the biologist interprets this as meaning that the tubers, through being killed by the frost, have rotted or fermented. From the informant's point of view, they have behaved like scalded tubers' (Rousseau 1, p. 148). A saying recorded by Seton (Ch. 32) in the Canadian north reflects a similar attitude and gives a perfectly orthodox definition of what I have called the culinary triangle:

> Fried meat is dried meat,
> Boiled meat is spoiled meat,
> Roast meat is best meat.

ing his involvement with Sun Woman and his marriage to Moon, followed by ordeals during which he gets the better of his parents-in-law, M_{796} reduces his stay in the celestial world to the single encounter with the Thunders, who lose no time in sending him back to earth. The Thunders therefore concentrate, in their five persons, the antithetical roles which, in the Coos myths, are shared out amongst helpful animals and a hostile cosmic family.

If we postulate that the Alsea version is the weakest of all, it can serve as the starting-point for a series in which the Coos versions follow on from it. In this case, we can say that M_{793a}, although stronger than M_{796}, is weaker than M_{793b}, which thus represents the strongest of the three versions. This classification is based on considerations of three different kinds.

Firstly, among the helpful animals, the herons, *noisy* birds associated with *water*, are closer to the thunders than to the spiders with burnt skulls; the latter, being the victims of a fire of solar origin, are in opposition to thunderstorms rather than in correlation with them.

The cosmic family in M_{793a} is also weaker than the one in M_{793b}: Sun Woman, the most strongly marked term in the system, is not included, and only the father-in-law is a persecutor. In M_{793b}, on the contrary, Sun Woman and Moon Woman are sisters and their mother is hostile towards the hero in the same way as her elder daughter, of whom she is, in fact, a doublet within the family cell.

Lastly, M_{793a} mainly emphasizes the origin of monthly periods of which Moon Woman is the instigator; these represent a relatively short form of biological periodicity. M_{793b}, on the other hand, is silent on this theme, and concentrates all its attention on the tempering of solar heat, i.e., periodicity on the astronomical level (see the following table).

As regards meteorological periodicity, it should be noted that an already quoted Alsea myth explains how the five Thunder brothers, who formerly lived on earth, were driven out. Not knowing where to go, they took refuge in the sky and that is why, so the myth concludes, they 'shout back from above' (M_{797}; Frachtenberg 4, p. 109). This interpretation reconstitutes an armature already encountered in Salish mythology (see above, pp. 479, 498). But there are also certain differences which need to be explained. At the same time as biological periodicity changes from being long in Salish mythology to short in Coos mythology (*human life-span* $\Rightarrow$ *interval of a lunar month between the menstrual periods*), in the Coos-Alsea group it takes on the role of connecting link between astronomical and meteorological periodicity that is attributed in the Salish myths to meteorological periodicity as connecting link between the other two forms. By fusing

COOS		ALSEA

M_{793b}:	M_{793a}:	M_{796}:
Sun, Moon: sisters; hostile parents-in-law	Sun, non-sister of two Moons; only father-in-law hostile	
		Helpful Thunders
Helpful poisonous spiders with burnt skulls	Helpful water birds	
Astronomical periodicity	*Biological periodicity* (menstruation)	*Meteorological periodicity*

together the two diagrams on pp. 479, 499, we arrive at the following system for the Salish:

$$\begin{bmatrix} \text{astronomical} \\ \text{periodicity} \\ \\ \textit{male} \\ \\ \text{spatial} \\ \text{mediation} \end{bmatrix} \Rightarrow \begin{bmatrix} \text{meteorological} \\ \text{periodicity} \\ \\ \textit{transvestite} \\ \textit{character} \\ \\ \text{spatio-temporal} \\ \text{mediation} \end{bmatrix} \Rightarrow \begin{bmatrix} \text{biological} \\ \text{periodicity} \\ \\ \textit{female} \\ \\ \text{temporal} \\ \text{mediation} \end{bmatrix}$$

It is clear that, in Coos mythology too, the male aspect remains linked to astronomical periodicity, since the hero institutes the latter by copulating with Sun Woman, and the female aspect to biological periodicity, in the form of female monthly periods, under the aegis of Moon Woman. But what are we to say of the transvestite character?

The Coos, the Alsea and their neighbours, the Tillamook and the Takelma, have a myth – which, incidentally, can be linked with others studied in *The Origin of Table Manners* ($M_{482-486}$) by following a route that I propose to leave unexplored – and in which transvestism plays an important part. The Coos versions ($M_{798a, b, c}$; Frachtenberg 1, pp. 149–57; Saint-Clair, pp. 32–4; Jacobs 6, pp. 235–8) relate how, one day, a stranger cuts off the head of a canoe-making carpenter. The latter's younger brother discovers the body and realizes – since the victim's dog is looking up at the sky and barking – where the act of aggression has originated. He shoots his arrows one after the other: they all fit into each other and form a ladder, by means of which he climbs up into the sky. There he meets the killer's wife, who is harvesting fern rhizomes, and he plies her with questions to find out what she does, and how she spends her time. After which, he kills her, removes her skin which he himself dons, and passes himself off as her. Although well-informed as to his victim's habits, he very nearly betrays his identity on several occasions, particularly when he offers rhizomes to an elderly couple to whom the woman never used to give any (cf. M_{656a}, see above, p. 331). After nightfall, he decapitates the killer, takes his brother's head and flees. As he pierces holes in all the canoes, he cannot be pursued, and he climbs back to earth down the chain of arrows. When he returns to the village, the inhabitants assemble, stand the carpenter's corpse upright by leaning it against a small conifer, and stick the head back on again. The man revives. The celestial people cannot climb down to earth in order to take their revenge. The people below become woodpeckers, whose heads are red because of the blood that has flowed from the severed neck.

In the most recent version, the carpenter has four brothers and two sons, and the latter are given the task of retrieving the severed head. These seven characters are all small birds of prey which, as is explained in one of the Alsea versions to which I shall refer later, kill other birds by cutting their heads off. Since there are two brothers, they meet two women in the sky, marry them and disguise themselves in their clothes. In order to cross the river separating them from the killer's village, they need a ferryman, a role which, in the Alsea saga about the exploits of Seúku, the transformer (see above, p. 571), is given to a skate or some other flat-fish (*hulō'hulō*), but always in connection with the recovery of a severed head (Frachtenberg 4, pp. 71–3). When the brothers return to earth, they realize that their father's head, since it has been smoked over a fire by the celestial people, is no longer usable. So, instead, they stick on the killer's head, which is smaller. This is the reason why birds of prey have very small heads.

Between $M_{798a, b}$ which deals with the origin of woodpeckers, and M_{798c} which replaces them by small birds of prey, the Alsea versions ($M_{799a, b}$; Frachtenberg 4, pp. 125–49) act as a link. They are more logical in presenting the celestial head-severers as birds of prey and the earth people as woodpeckers (the white-necked woodpecker, in one version, because of the white clay used to stick the head back on again). But, contrary to what happens in the Coos-Alsea group, M_{793} and M_{796}, in this instance the Alsea text is the stronger: it attributes to the carpenter a dog-wife, as well as two children, human in form, who have extremely complex adventures in the sky. They meet a first group of informants, whom they change into flies (those same flies which continue to move even when cut in two, cf. above, p. 556), then the killer's wives, snake-women who are gathering fern rhizomes (cf. above, p. 481). They kill them and put on their skins: this is why ever since snakes have sloughed their skins. Because all the inhabitants, and not just an elderly couple, refuse the ferns offered by the disguised heroes, the latter change them into lice (M_{799a}). According to M_{799a} too, it is the two heroes who change their father into a woodpecker; they themselves become dogs.

Another version belongs to the Tillamook, a group cut off from the main body of the Salish linguistic family, and living on the coast next to the Alsea (M_{800}: Boas 14, pp. 136–8). As in the second Alsea version, only one of the hero's two sons has a dog for his mother, and in appearance, he himself is half-man and half-dog. Here too, his father is a hunter. When questioned by the two brothers, the women they encounter in the sky point out that they never give fern rhizomes to large grubs, who live in one of the houses in the village. The heroes kill the women and simply put on their clothes, not their skins. However, they make lots of mistakes, and 'a man called Qä'tcla', about whose identity there will be more to say later (see below, p. 580), suspects them of being imposters, and very nearly unmasks them. On their way back, the heroes revive their two victims and marry them. They mend their father's head with strips of bark, but the head remains red because of the blood that has been spilled, and the man turns into a woodpecker.

The Takelma, who live inland, have a myth (M_{801}; Sapir 5, pp. 155–63) which can be brought into line with the preceding ones by means of a number of transformations:

1 (*earth*/*sky* axis) $\Rightarrow$ (*earth*/*water* axis);
2 (canoe builder/terrestrial hunter) $\Rightarrow$ (fisherman);
3 (dog-wife) $\Rightarrow$ (spirit of the waters-wife);
4 (kidnapped head) $\Rightarrow$ (kidnapped heart);

5 (snake-women) $\Rightarrow$ (bird-women);
6 (fern rhizomes) $\Rightarrow$ (tree resin);
7 (red-headed or white-necked woodpeckers/small-headed birds of prey) $\Rightarrow$ (black-coated otters).

This Takelma version would seem to represent a borderline form of the system, and I propose to leave it aside. On the other hand, I should like to recall at this point a Tsimshian myth that I summarized in *The Raw and the Cooked* (M_{170}, p. 301), where its sudden appearance among South American myths may have seemed somewhat inappropriate. One has only to re-read it, however, to be convinced that it forms part of the same group as those with which I am now concerned. In quoting it then, at a very early stage in my enquiry, I was simply gauging the extent of a pattern of interconnections, the definition of which I hope shortly to be able to conclude (see below, p. 581).

Disregarding the Tillamook version, which is undeniably the weakest of all the coastal versions, it can be noted that, in the others, the hero is a canoe builder. This carpenter is an old acquaintance, whom we first encountered in a Snohomish myth about the conquest of fire (M_{724b}; see above, p. 463), where the celestial people, without going so far as to decapitate him, abduct him and hold him prisoner because they have been disturbed by the noise he makes through working night and day. In the Alsea version, on the contrary, it is the sky people who make a terrible noise around the severed head, and the two heroes, guided by the din, are able to discover their whereabouts. On the other hand, whereas the Snohomish carpenter works even at night, his Alsea homologue carefully refrains from doing so. The myth states explicitly that he comes home every evening, and goes back to his labours at dawn. It is also during the day, and always at the same time, that he hears a sinister noise heralding the approach of his killer. The version M_{799a} refers several times, on the same page, to this regular sequence of events (Frachtenberg 4, p. 125). In fact, it is so insistent about the matter that we are entitled to bring into play a major principle of structural analysis: when a myth takes such care to stress a seemingly gratuitous detail, this can only mean that it is seeking to set itself in opposition to some other myth, which is to be found elsewhere, and usually not far away, and which has definite reasons for stating the opposite about the same subject.

Let us remind ourselves of the conclusion of the Snohomish myth. It ended, on the one hand, with the institution of daily periodicity (either with the skate of the other Salish myths, who is commutable with the carpenter, representing a permanent constellation; or with the carpenter in opposition to the skate as a permanent constellation in opposition to a seasonal one, see above, p. 550); and, on the other hand, with the acquisition of cooking fire, the only remaining evidence on earth of a conjunction with the sky, which was a unique occurrence, never to be repeated. The only thing that can be said, since the collapse of the ladder of arrows ensuring communication between the two worlds, is that cooking fire is below as the celestial luminaries are above. Daily periodicity, characterized by the regular alternation of day and night, which the carpenter promises henceforth to respect, bears witness to the fact that a spatial opposition between the two most distant poles conceivable to man — the sky and the earth — was for one brief moment overcome, in the temporal realm and in an extremely short form. In M_{724b}, and consequently in the other myths in the group, Salish thought moves from spatial discontinuity to temporal continuity.

One has only to look at the decapitated carpenter myths in Alsea mythology to see that they follow exactly the reverse process. There, too, the skate replaces the carpenter in a symmetrical series, but instead of being terrestrial in origin and remaining disjoined in the sky in the form of a constellation, it plays the role of *ferryman* on the river dividing the two worlds, that is, it ensures a two-day transition from one to the other. Similarly, according to M_{799b}, the flies which have been cut in two remain alive, and snakes avoid the inevitability of death by growing a new skin every year. Although the skate does not actually appear in $M_{799a, b}$, the two myths refer to it *a contrario*; in the Quileute myths ($M_{782a, b}$), it is a terrestrial creature or one acquired by an earth-dweller, whom an inhabitant of the sky soils with dirty water or urine. The Coos and Alsea myths, in turn, reverse the roles by relating that the celestial people believed at first that they were being defiled with urine by their terrestrial visitor, when they were splashed with the blood of the man who had been decapitated by his supposed wife.

All these themes — the keeping open of a passage between the world of the living and that of the dead, the flies which remain alive although cut in two, and the snakes resuscitated by the annual shedding of their skin — deny mortality as an expression of biological periodicity, in the longest form known to man; Alsea thought moves from the denial of the biological periodicity of man's mortality towards the no less illusory denial of the insuperable distance separating sky and earth. Their myth concludes not with *real temporal alternation* but with *false spatial union*; the arrow-ladder stays in place long enough to allow the heroes to climb back down to earth, and the decision to cut it is taken by them in order to protect their retreat;

however 'there is one mountain somewhere in this world that almost reaches the sky' (Frachtenberg 4, p. 147). By sticking back on to a body which has remained terrestrial a head which is by nature (M_{798c}) or by destination (in other versions) celestial, the heroes are symbolically asserting the virtual interconnection of the two worlds, although in fact it is as utopian as the resurrection of the dead, the possibility of which is referred to in the myths only to be rejected; as a consequence of having achieved it momentarily, the chief characters lose the benefit of their human nature; they are transformed, some into woodpeckers or small birds of prey living between sky and earth, others into dogs, domestic animals half-way between nature and culture, just as cooking fire (which was procured by dogs, according to the Wiyot, cf. M_{559}, see above, p. 158) is the consequence of the 'domestication' of celestial fire by earth-dwellers.

I shall not at this point — although the exercise would be instructive — follow up the series of interconnections linking these myths about a human married to a dog-woman to another large group found in the same area (see above, p. 482) and dealing with a human woman who took a dog as her lover. This last union — a transformation of incest between a sister and a brother — is truly conjunctive, since it engenders children who look like dogs at first, but very quickly become humans. Here, the reverse happens: the children start as humans and change into dogs at the end. However, it is clear that their disjunction is a moderate one: the differential gap between dogs and woodpeckers (with which M_{799a} ends) is much smaller than the one (in the M_{793} series) between a celestial fire which is feminine and destructive and the penis made of ice — the modality of water at the opposite pole of the same axis — which succeeds however in mastering the fire. The link between these two pairs of terms is nevertheless apparent, as can be seen from a Tillamook version (M_{800}), in which the only named celestial character is called Qä'tcla, 'Ice', like the trickster demiurge who, in Tillamook cosmology, presides over the first mythic age and is then replaced by South Wind, the counterpart of Coyote in the myths of the other Salish tribes (E. D. Jacobs, *passim*).

As is the case in the bird-nester series, the Coos-Alsea carpenter cycle has as protagonists a mature man and his younger brother, or his son, or sons. In the one instance, the son is disjoined towards the sky by his father's wickedness; in the other, the kindness of a brother or sons (one of whom, incidentally, plays a major part) brings back to earth an elder brother or a father whom the sky had disjoined from his own people. We can see that we are dealing with the same pattern even more clearly from the fact that in the Coos-Alsea bird-nester series *the transformation of blood-stained faeces into a woodpecker constitutes the means of disjunction*, and, in the carpenter series, *the transformation into a woodpecker as a result of the blood streaming from the severed head controls and determines the conjunction*. The mythic texts are very explicit on this point, since the same small conifer, here covered with the blood-stained faeces, allows the woodpecker to make its appearance and, by growing taller, causes the hero's disjunction; and in the other myth – but because it is exactly the same in size (M$_{798b}$; Saint-Clair, p. 34) – provides a support against which the decapitated body can be propped for the fitting on of the head.

Consequently, in this area of North America, we can observe a phenomenon on which I dwelt at some length in *The Raw and the Cooked*, in connection with South America (*RC*, pp. 147–95). In both hemispheres, a simple transformation ensures the transition between the bird-nester cycle, in which the interposition of cooking fire sets the sun at a reasonable distance from the earth, and another cycle, concerned with man's mortality.[1] In South America, the first cycle operates from the low to the high since, in order to obtain fire, the hero must first of all ascend; the second cycle, on the other hand, operates from the high to the low, since the introduction of cultivated plants and man's mortality are a function of a star's coming down to earth to marry a mortal. The North American myths which have just been examined observe the same pattern: in the one instance, the hero takes his terrestrial family off to the sky; in the other, according to one of the Coos versions (M$_{798c}$) as well as the Tillamook version, the heroes bring back to earth the wives they have married in the sky.

At the beginning of the discussion of the Alsea myths, I pointed out that those relating to the bird-nester were weaker than the Coos versions, in the sense that their hero neither encounters, rapes nor marries any celestial creature. The corresponding sequence in the Coos versions brings into play a new factor, the importance of which needs to be stressed. In *The Origin of Table Manners*, I was concerned to prove (this, indeed, was one of the main aims of the volume) that the myths featuring the wives of the sun and moon were transformations of the bird-nester ones, and that all together they constituted a single myth (cf. *OTM*, pp. 305–306). The point I established

---

[1] And, in Coos mythology, even with a significant echo of the *hearing/not hearing, seeing/not seeing* pattern, used by both North and South American myths to suggest this motif. 'I will send ten sounds round the world,' the trickster demiurge said to the ancestors, 'and you must shut your eyes then, otherwise you will have no knowledge.' If all communities are not equally endowed in these two respects, the reason is that some opened their eyes too soon during the ringing sounds made by the demiurge (Jacobs 6, pp. 225–6).

deductively in that context is now confirmed empirically by the Coos myths: the bird-nester goes up into the sky, and unites first with a cannibalistic Sun Woman, then with a Moon Woman who is well-disposed towards humans. He therefore fulfils a double function, symmetrical with the roles that the myths featuring the wives of the sun and moon divide between two terrestrial heroines, one of whom marries the cannibalistic sun, and the other the moon who is well-disposed towards humans. Thanks to kindly parents-in-law, the latter heroine receives an education during her stay in the sky. The reverse happens in the Coos myths about the bird-nester: although the parents-in-law, whom the terrestrial hero acquires in the sky, are very ill-disposed towards him, the net result of his stay is that Sun Woman — not the terrestrial wife of Mister Moon — acquires an education.

It would be wrong to conclude, from what has just been said, that the Coos were not familiar with the myth about the wives of the sun and moon. But it is in keeping with my interpretation that the Coos versions should be extremely brief ($M_{802a, b, c}$: Frachtenberg 1, pp. 51–3; 3, pp. 38–41; Jacobs 6, pp. 169–70). They are little more than short moralizing tales about young scatterbrained girls who spend their time stargazing, and one of whom learns to her cost that appearances are deceptive. This confirms that the most meaningful part of the mythic message lies elsewhere.

This no longer hypothetical, but actual, union between myths initially encountered in a disjoined state, and which achieve the synthesized form in a very small area of North America, is still more clearly visible among coastal groups situated to the north of the Columbia estuary, near the Puget Sound Salish, and themselves members of the Salish or Chemakum families.

The corpus of myths available in the case of the Quinault, who are maritime Salish, is so inconsiderable that only very tentative conclusions can be drawn from it. But at least we must be struck by the fact that these Indians seem to reverse the relative positions attributed by the Coos on the one hand to the cycle about the wives of the sun and moon and, on the other, to the cycle that I have just identified as being symmetrical to it — the one dealing with the marriage between a terrestrial hero and a female sky-dweller. Although this symmetrical formula is found in Quinault mythology, it occupies a secondary place in relation to that of the wives of the sun and moon, to which the Quinault accord the dominant position. Furthermore, this weak form is still further enfeebled by the fact that the wicked father-in-law is the Thunder, i.e., a term which, as I have already noted in dealing with the Coos and Alsea versions (see above, p. 574), is not as far removed from the earth as the Sun. At the beginning of the Quinault myth (M_{803}; Farrand 1, pp. 113–14), the hero is already living in the sky and married. After accomplishing various tasks set him by his father-in-law, he is sent down by the latter to the chthonian world (that is, he suffers a vertical disjunction from high to low as a consequence of his marriage, instead of a disjunction from low to high leading incidentally to the marriage) with instructions to conquer lightning which, at that time, did not yet accompany storms. The hero accepts the mission, and his agreement is enough to effect a reconciliation between the two men: the Thunders help the hero by creating torrential rain, which puts out his pursuers' torches. Once he has conquered Lightning and brought it back, Thunder is able not only to produce it at will, but to share out the surplus light he has at his disposal among all those animals and birds — woodpeckers in particular — which since then have had partly or entirely red fur or feathers.

At the same time as it transforms a warmth-giving celestial fire into a light-giving chthonian fire, this myth introduces a relation of incompatibility between chthonian fire and rain, thus inverting the compatibility postulated by the Coos myths between rain and domestic fire. The Quinault myth transfers this compatibility to lightning: a form of celestial fire compatible with celestial water, as experience shows. We have already met with, and discussed, this transformation which is typical of myths belonging to the Sahaptin tribes and certain Coast Salish groups (see above, p. 328).

On the other hand, it will have been noticed that this borderline instance of the bird-nester story leads us back to the origin of the colours of birds, connoted by the partially red plumage of the Woodpecker, as in a previously discussed Sanpoil myth (M_{729}; see above, p. 465), but with two differences: in the one case, the red feathers are the result of an addition, in the other, of a subtraction: and a surplus of celestial fire is responsible for the first, while an excess of terrestrial fire is the cause of the second. So we are still concerned with the same pattern; but here, however, the origin of the colours of birds is linked to a major event in the realm of meteorology, the institution of the stormy season. This is to say that, by means of myths that are this time in close proximity to each other, I can verify the validity of the pattern I outlined in *The Raw and the Cooked*, on the basis of myths geographically far apart. I have already noted on p. 578 that myths I introduced there led back to the Tsimshian myth, M_{170}. It is to the Parintintin myth (M_{179}) that we now return (cf. *RC*, pp. 313–14), since it allows us to link M_{803} with M_1 and M_{7-12}, by way of a whole series of intermediary myths discussed in *The Raw and the Cooked* ($M_{171-175}$, M_{178}) as well as in the present volume ($M_{643a, b}$, M_{651b}; see above, pp. 296, 320). Whether the story concerns sky-dwellers disturbed by noise at night – a time when light is absent – as in the Tsimshian myth and those relating to the carpenter, or whether, on the contrary – as in the Humptulips myth (M_{651b}) and the Quinault myth (M_{803}) – it concerns the noise – thunder – made by the sky-dwellers themselves, and which needs to be accompanied by flashes of lightning, we are still dealing fundamentally with the same problem of arbitration between celestial fire and noise, where the solution in North as in South America makes possible the introduction of an order which, according to the level at which the various myths operate, may be cosmological, zoological or cultural.

I have already pointed out that, of all the versions relating to the marriage between a human and celestial woman, the Quinault story is the weakest. Conversely, the Quinault version of the myth about the wives of the sun and moon is particularly strong, since the abduction of these heroines to the sky is presented as being the incident which precipitates the war for the conquest of fire:

M_{804}. *Quinault. 'The wives of the sun and moon'*
Once Raven's two daughters went out on to the prairie to dig roots; night came on before they knew it and so they had to camp where they were. They lay down together and gazed up at the stars. The younger sister wished she were up there with a big, bright star; the elder wished to be there with a little star. However, when they found themselves in the sky country, the younger of the two girls found that her husband was a feeble old man, whereas the one chosen by her sister was young and strong. Furthermore, the old man's eyes were sore and running and he used his wife's hair to wipe away the pus. The miserable young woman begged a spider to take her back to earth. The old woman agreed, as soon as she had spun a long enough rope. The heroine, however, grew impatient and wanted to leave immediately: when the rope was stretched out, it left her hanging in the air. After several days in this uncomfortable position, she died; first of all her clothes fell to pieces and landed in front of the house where she had been born. Her father recognized them and summoned all the animals, birds and fishes to go up to the sky and avenge his daughter.

A small bird failed to bring the sky down close enough (see above, p. 494). In order to reach it, a chain of arrows had to be hung from it. Only the Wren 'the smallest of birds' reached the sky, guided by the Snail, who at that time was very keen-sighted. So the Sea Eagle or Fish Hawk (*Pandion haliaëtus*) borrowed his eyes, and finding them very good, kept them. Ever since this time, the Fish Hawk has excellent sight, whereas the Snail is blind.

At this point, there occurs the fight between the Skate and the Raven; then comes the ascent into the sky, where it was winter and icy cold. In their attempt to keep warm, the animals entrusted the Robin, the Dog, and the Puma in turn with the task of stealing a fire-brand from the celestial people, but, for various reasons, they all failed (in connection with the series of incidents, cf. above, pp. 488, 497–8). The Beaver was more successful; he brought back the fire, but the eldest girl, who was still a prisoner in the sky, had not yet been set free.

Rats and mice gnawed through the bow-strings belonging to the sky men, the girdles on their clothes, and everything they could find in the way of bindings or fastenings. When the time for the attack came, the sky-dwellers could not shoot their arrows, nor could their wives dress in order to run away. They rallied with great difficulty, and beat back and routed the earth-people, some of whom climbed back down to earth by means of their ladder, taking with them the wife they had come to free. But the ladder broke, leaving the last people hanging in the sky where they became stars (Farrand 1, pp. 107–109).

The Quileute are Coast Chemakum and neighbours of the Quinault, and their versions (M_{782a-c}; Farrand-Mayer, pp. 264–6; Andrade, pp. 71–83; Reagan, pp. 54–6) differ only slightly from the one I have just summarized. In M_{782a}, the heroines are friends, not sisters; they marry two stars, one of which is red and an old man, the other blue and a handsome young man. On the other hand, in M_{782b}, the heroines are sisters and camp with their mother; the younger falls in love with a little star, which turns out to be an old man; the elder prefers a large star and obtains a fine young man for a husband. In M_{782a}, the star-men's hearts are softened by the tears of the girl who has made a bad match, and they themselves arrange for their wives to go back down to earth. This does not prevent the earth-dwellers from declaring war on them; the first bird entrusted with the task of stealing fire has a red breast and is a robin, according to M_{782c} (but in M_{782b} a snow-bird); through being exposed too long to the heat, it received burns which leave speckled marks on its chest. This detail, which we have already encountered in Coos mythology, suggests the hermit thrush, rather than the American robin or the junco. Moreover, it is clearly stated in M_{782a} that the red-breasted bird, called *tedod*, is not a robin (see above, p. 489).

M_{782b}, which is close to the Quinault version, relates how one of the women escapes, with the help of the spider. In this story, too, she dies as she dangles from the end of the rope, but her corpse is immediately changed into a star. When called upon to free the elder girl, his wife, the husband refuses, and is slaughtered by his father-in-law: 'Thus the chief who had come from the earth killed the chief who lived in the sky.' There follows a general conflict, from which the earth-dwellers emerge victorious. Their arrow-ladder breaks before they can all reach the ground: all those remaining in the sky are changed into stars; hence the origin of these heavenly bodies.

For us to be able to work out the micro-system of these variants, our documentation about the mythology and ethnography of the Quinault and the Quileute would have to be much more abundant than is unfortunately the case. I shall therefore confine myself to a few general remarks. Since the beginning of this study, I have linked together many themes. First, the story of the bird-nester with the origin of fire; then the origin of fire with that of meat and tobacco: these origins jointly with those of cultivated plants and man's mortality; and lastly, as the conclusion to the first volume, the creation of a cultural order expressed in cooking and the other arts of civilization, correlative with the creation of a natural order expressed by specific differences between animals, and especially the colours of birds.

Here, we have just discovered, side by side and concentrated within a very restricted area, myths which effect these connections directly in pairs, and which, furthermore, are all linked with each other. Some associate the bird-nester story with the origin of alimentary produce and cooking; others associate the earth-dwellers' war against the celestial people (which leads to the acquisition of cooking fire) with the origin of human mortality, and of specific differences between animals. Others again provide concrete evidence of the symmetrical relationships I had inferred between the bird-nester story and that of the wives of the sun and moon. Finally, the last myths to be introduced combine, in a single narrative, the story of the wives of the sun and moon and that of the earth-dwellers' war against the celestial people, which results in the acquisition of fire.

What has just been said makes it still more significant that we should also encounter, in this area of North America, one of the very first themes I studied at length and which was to give a decisive orientation of the course of my argument. The Stseelis or Chehalis, who are Salish belonging to the Cowichan group living along the lower reaches of the Fraser River, relate how (M_{805}; Hill-Tout 2, pp. 345–6) Mink tries to visit his father, the Sun. His grandmother, who has brought him up since his birth, tries in vain to dissuade him from going. The young hero starts off, arrives at his father's house, and is given a warm welcome, although he is warned never to put anything on the fire that crackles and sends out sparks. Mink is nevertheless surprised that his father's wife avoids looking at him and, to attract her attention, does the opposite of what he has been told to do. The wife happens to be thunder and lightning combined; when the fire begins to crackle, she turns round suddenly to see where this unaccustomed noise is coming from. Her flashing eyes alight on Mink; he is scorched and instantly shrivels up, so that only his burnt skin and bones remain.

On returning that evening, Sun finds his son dead and he loses no time in restoring him to life. To prevent him committing further foolish acts, he sends him to light up the world in his place. During the first three days, Mink performs his task correctly; on the fourth day, desiring to rest and in spite of his father's warnings about not climbing up on to the rafters, he goes up to the roof and lies down. He finds the genitalia of a woman hanging there and has coition with them. When he comes down again, he finds that his stepmother is dead. Sun revives her, and clubs his son to death. He subsequently resuscitates him, but then throws him out for good. Mink returns to his grandmother.

So, thousands of kilometres from the area where we first noted it in a Ge myth (M$_{10}$; RC, pp. 71, 148–9), we rediscover the same theme: a *stepmother cannot bear her husband's son, or adoptive son, to make a noise.* The coincidence will seem less startling, if we remember that twice already I have had occasion to make the same kind of transcontinental connection: the last time by means of an Iroquois myth (M$_{772a}$ see above, p. 522), and before that by means of a Menomini myth (M$_{495a}$; OTM, pp. 406–407, 427–8), in which the Sun takes up into the sky an Indian he has saved, but whose eating habits are not tolerated by the Sun's sister. This woman, who may be the wife or the sister of the Sun — the master of celestial fire — has a cosmic personality in her own right: she is either the hostile modality of the moon, or thunder and lightning combined. There can be no doubt that she is a faithful echo of the jaguar's irritable wife in the heart of Central Brazil. In South America, the jaguar is the first master of cooking fire; and, in North America, humans have to go up into the sky in order to obtain fire. Lastly, in so far as a disagreement arises between two celestial characters about an earth-dweller in the North American versions, we can say that the action of these myths is set in motion by a quarrel between the sun and the moon, and that they are thus linked by an additional strand to the cycle of the wives of the sun and moon of which, as we know, the bird-nester cycle is a simple transformation.[5]

---

[5] It should be noted in this connection that, like the Plains versions of the myth about the wives of the sun and moon, the Lilloet version of the bird-nester myth (M$_{671}$; Teit 2, pp. 306–309) entrusts the Meadowlark with the task of calling to the hero to signify to him that he has landed successfully.

In the area we are concerned with here, this relationship between the two cycles can be verified in another way. As it happens, there exists a whole group of myths which I do not propose to examine in detail, since their rightful place is with the parallel series about the origin of wind and fog, to which I have often referred. These myths, which are fully present among the Thompson and have a still recognizable form among the Lilloet, the Chehalis of the Lower Fraser and the Lkungen in the south-east of Vancouver Island (M_{806a-c}: Teit 4, pp. 53–5; Boas 4, 43–4; 13, p. 15; Teit 2, pp. 336–7. $M_{807a, b}$; Hill-Tout 2, pp. 354–7; 5, pp. 346–8), confirm the marriage between the sun and mankind, which takes place after a terrestrial visitor brings to the sky human women (sometimes water fowl), whom he offers in marriage to the sun and his son. In consequence of which, the sun, who until then has been a cannibal, agrees to become humanized: after being too near the earth, he takes up his position at a reasonable distance from it, and humans, who used to cook their food by exposing it to the sun's heat, are now obliged, and able, to cook it on a domestic fire (cf. Teit 5, p. 229, n. 3). In short, these myths prove that it was not without reason that the Kayapo, along with the more southerly Ofaié, said that the jaguar's wife was a human (RC, pp. 57, 82–3). No doubt, in mythic times, humans were indistinguishable from animals, but between the non-differentiated beings who were to give birth to mankind on the one hand and the animal kingdom on the other, certain qualitative relationships pre-existed, anticipating specific characteristics that were still in a latent state.

It would not be enough to say that the North American myths I have just quoted transform the bird-nester motif into that of the wives of the sun and moon. They actually unite the two motifs, since the hero who is ill-treated by his own people, and reduced to a state of wretchedness which makes him an outcast from his native village, suffers a disjunction, the causes of which are moral, not physical, but which is not different from the disjunction suffered by the bird-nester. In one of the versions originating from the British Columbia Chehalis, the hero encounters, in the sky, blind and helpful creatures whom the text identifies first as tetraonidae, then as Herons: this version bears witness to the unity of the extreme forms (M_{667} and M_{793}) assumed by the myth in the north and south, in the inland areas and along the coast. And it is self-evident that the hero of these latest myths to be studied ($M_{806-807}$) takes on a synthetic function: he is simultaneously the bird-nester in a very slightly transposed form, the man who introduces the wives of the sun and moon into the sky, and the initiator of a cosmic reformation, of which the art of cooking is both the price and the prize.

Thus, in the course of the present volume, I have identified the bird-nester myth and classified all its modalities in an area of North America lying to the west of the Rockies, approximately between 40° and 50° parallel. At the centre of this region, that is, in the basin of the Columbia River, the myth ends with the freeing of the salmon and the establishment of fairs and markets, that is, with the natural, then the social, origin of the food supplies ensuring the subsistence of mankind.

In changing, farther south, into the Loon Woman cycle, the same myth modifies its etiological function: on the social level, it deals with *incest*, which is a rejection of the principle of exchange; and, on the natural plane, with the institution of *periodicity*, which it formulates in terms of time rather than of space. On the other side of the Columbia River, that is, to the north in the Fraser basin, the reverse phenomenon can be observed: there, the bird-nester myth retains its original form but deals with *exogamy* — real or symbolic — rather than with incest; and it lays greater stress on the sharing out of fish within the *existing space* of the lakes and rivers system than on their release at a particular moment *in the past* and their *seasonal return*. The problem of the origin of fire, the fundamental theme behind all these myths, is related, in the south, more to culture and the state of society; in the north, to a system of cosmological oppositions embodied by the sky people and the earth people, from whose quarrels fire, and indeed the whole human race, originate: every Coast Salish group liked to claim that it was descended from some ancestor who had fallen from the sky (Hill-Tout 1, 2, 3, *passim*). The myths about the origin of fire set the earth people, who were once animals, in opposition to the inhabitants of the sky, where many earth people died and changed into stars. The Quileute are presenting this pattern in their own particular way, when they declare that 'animals were on earth first. From the union of some of these with a star which fell from heaven came the first people. These first people were the ancestors of (present-day) Indians who were all created at the same time on Vancouver Island' (Reagan-Walters, p. 306).

We find, then, some extremely strong versions of our myth concentrated in this narrow coastal strip, barely five hundred kilometres in length and a few dozen in width. To gauge the amount of ground covered by our analysis, we need only compare the first and last forms of the bird-nester myth as they have appeared to us: we were at first dealing with a village quarrel, or even a family one, between a father and his son who is guilty of incest (M_1), or a quarrel between two brothers-in-law about eaglets which are, or are not, in the nest (M_{7-12}); in North America, on the contrary, in the area just defined, the issue is a conflict of cosmic proportions between the sky and the earth, a veritable war of the worlds, and to wage it, both sides mobilize all their forces, which comprise in fact the whole of creation ($M_{802-804}$).

If, as I believe, we are dealing with one and the same myth, these extreme forms must each find their place in the general picture of it that we can draw up. Going right back to the beginning for the last time, let us say that *The Raw and the Cooked* established two points, essential to this picture. In the first place, the South American versions of the bird-nester myth diverge, according to whether they deal with the origin of fire (M_{7-12}) or the origin of water (M_1). In the second place, the bird-nester myth itself originates in the bifurcation of a much larger system, the other branch of which (M_{87-92}) leads to the origin of man's mortality. This too schematic summary of a very long process of analysis reveals two characteristic properties of the South American myths. Firstly, those concerned with water and fire adopt the standpoint of spatial periodicity – since, in this case, it is a question of effecting mediation between the low and the high, the sky and the earth, the sun and mankind – whereas the group of myths relating to man's mortality adopts the standpoint of temporal periodicity. Next, and most important of all, the myths dealing with the origin of fire and water – in other words the bird-nester myths – occur in South America in a very weak form: their ostensible content can be reduced to the temporary abandonment of a minor affine at the top of a tree or rock. Myths about the origin of mortality, on the contrary, are more strongly expressed, since they involve a star, a supernatural creature, who renounces the celestial world to come down to earth and marry a mortal. It is already apparent from this provisional analysis that the spatial dimension of the South American myths conceals a strong content inside a weak form, and that their temporal dimension conceals a relatively weak content inside a strong form. In one instance, the disjunction of the sky and the earth, in order to achieve mediation, assumes the appearance of a humble family quarrel. In the other, the assigning of a reasonable span to human life demands that there must have been a time when the earth and the sky were conjoined.

If, in the case of North America, the overall picture appears at first glance more complex, this is because, as I showed earlier (*OTM*, pp. 226–41), the cycle featuring the wives of the sun and moon – the South American counterpart of which is the Star-wife cycle – itself divides up into two forms, one weak and the other strong. In the first, which is found throughout what I have called the northern crescent, the two wives are allowed to come back down from the sky safe and sound, and are then exposed to a series of adventures leading ultimately to the institution of seasonal periodicity, a phenomenon belonging essentially to the temporal order. The Plains versions illustrate the second form, according to which the escapade involving the wives of the sun and moon ends in disaster, with the death of the heroine while trying to escape; the rest of the action concerns her son who, after experiencing various adventures, goes up into the sky where he changes into a heavenly body. Actually, however, the Plains versions represent a mixed form, since they also deal with biological periodicity, in the form of the institution of monthly periods, and the determining of the normal period of pregnancy. On the other hand, the successive two-way movements of the heroine and her son along the vertical axis, bring out the spatial aspect, although they are also linked to seasonal periodicity (*OTM*, pp. 262–3); it follows that these relatively strong forms of the myths have spatio-temporal co-ordinates.

If we ask now where, in North America, the strongest forms are to be found, the answer is: precisely in that coastal area of the states of Oregon and Washington, where the transformation of the bird-nester myth into that featuring the wives of the sun and moon is directly evident, and where the second myth takes on the dimensions of a war of the worlds, such as we have seen in Quileute and Quinault mythology; the result is, of course, the conquest of fire, but also, along a more specifically spatial axis, the definitive disjunction of the sky and the earth, the origin of the stars – the celestial counterpart of the fire, for which many earth-dwellers had to be sacrificed so that it could become terrestrial – and subsequently, the origin of present-day humanity, which came into existence through the marriage of a stellar character with female earth-dwellers.

In North America, then, we can distinguish a weak form of the myth about the wives of the sun and moon, culminating in seasonal, therefore temporal, periodicity, which is illustrated by the versions from the northern crescent; and a strong form culminating in a cosmic disjunction mediatized by the acquisition of fire (thereby bringing us back to the bird-nester story). So, in North America, the weak form – the celestial, then terrestrial, misadventures of scatterbrained young ladies – conceals a strong content: the advent of annual and seasonal periodicity. The strong form on the other hand – that is, the war between the two worlds – conceals a content which, by comparison, is weak: the origin of domestic fire. Between these two extreme modalities, the Plains versions occupy a median position, the composite character of which I have already emphasized.

There is still more to be said. Although the South American cycle concerned with a mortal's star-wife reflects the strong form of the North American cycle about the wives of the sun and moon, it only does so by inverting all the terms since, in the one case, a celestial woman comes down to earth and in the other, terrestrial women go up into the sky. Turning now to the weak forms, we can observe a different kind of inversion, which occurs when we move from one hemisphere to the other. North American mythology expresses these weak forms by means of the story about the wives of the sun and moon, whereas South American mythology does so by means of the bird-nester myth. We can say, therefore, that the first inversion concerns complementary structures, the second supplementary structures, and that they lead to different results. In the case of the complementary structures, the inversion which affects, from within, the matrimonial relationship uniting two characters, who are respectively terrestrial and celestial: $\begin{pmatrix} \triangle & \bigcirc \\ | & | \\ \bigcirc & \triangle \end{pmatrix}$ functions so as to transform a spatial category (*sky/earth*) into a temporal category (*life/death*). On the other hand, the inversion of the story of the wives of the sun and moon into that of the bird-nester functions so as to transform a natural category (that of periodicity, both astronomical and biological) into a cultural category (represented by cooking and the other arts of civilization). During this transformation, as a necessary intermediary phenomenon, there occurs the establishment of the zoological order, which depends on nature at the outset, but then, by making nature accessible to conceptual thought through the introduction of the discontinuity between the species, allows culture to assert a hold over nature and to overcome its absence of differentiation (Figure 34).

Let us agree to choose, as the initial state of this transformational group, the strongest version offered by the myths, that is, the one in which a conflict occurs between the sky people and the earth-dwellers, as a consequence of the abduction of one or several women, who are stolen from the earth-dwellers. The latter launch a war-like expedition against their celestial enemies. Whatever the outcome of the fighting, the result is that communication between the two worlds henceforth becomes impossible. However, in the form of the stars in the sky and cooking fire on earth, there survives a twofold proof of the fact that the high and the low were once united.

The story of the wives of the sun and moon, as it exists in Plains mythology, keeps very close to this pattern, expressing it in a weakened form, which is, however, stronger than the version of the same myth to be found throughout the northern crescent. The South American versions of the bird-nester story occupy an even weaker position and, in the light of what has just been said, the reason for this is clear. In relation to the myth

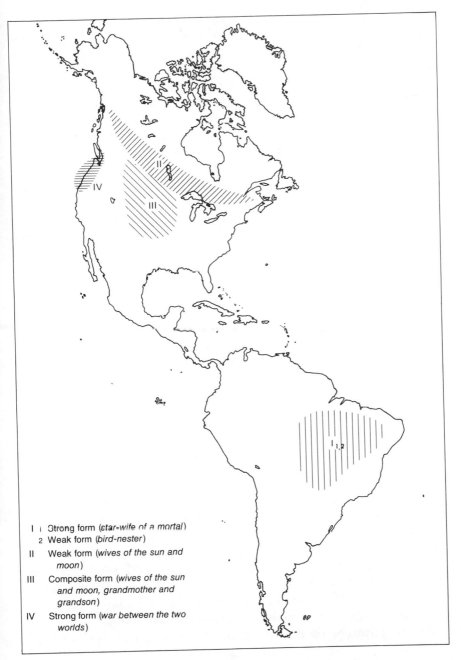

I 1 Strong form (*star-wife of a mortal*)
2 Weak form (*bird-nester*)

II Weak form (*wives of the sun and moon*)

III Composite form (*wives of the sun and moon, grandmother and grandson*)

IV Strong form (*war between the two worlds*)

Figure 34. The reference myth: strong and weak forms

about the wives of the sun and moon, the South American versions illustrate a state, not just of transformation, but of partial collapse. The hero, instead of rising up into the sky, is stopped on the way: at the top of a tree or rocky cliff, from which he soon descends to take his revenge, with the proviso that he subsequently re-ascends to the median region of the sky where he changes into the master of meteorological or seasonal phenomena.

If, then, the character of the bird-nester is an inversion of that of the wife of the sun or moon, it is in the same way as an eroded anticline takes on the deceptive appearance of a syncline: it presents an inverted image of itself, although geological history can explain the transition from one to the other, and how an apparent reversal may result from a continuous process (Figure 35). In South America, the part which has disappeared is projected, in the negative mode, as it were, and in an inverted form, as the star-wife of a mortal, but it acquires — as a compensation, one might almost say — a positive content: in the origin of cultivated plants, the counterpart of man's mortality, and complementary to the positive function which devolves on the bird-nester as the provider of cooking fire for mankind.

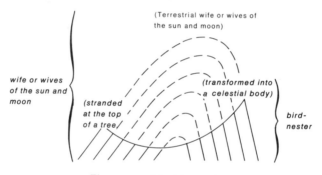

Figure 35. Mythic erosion

We have seen that in North America, on the contrary, the mythic fold survives in its entirety: the strata which have disappeared in the other hemisphere are still intact; and it is precisely in them that we find a very dense distribution of forms intermediary between the South American bird-nester myth and those, more specifically North American, myths which deal with the wives of the sun and moon. The study of the Salish versions enabled me to catalogue these intermediary forms, in which the bird-nester first goes up into the sky, and then manages to come back safely to earth.

So, he both resembles, and differs from, the sun's human wife; according to the Plains myths, she fails to get back to the earth, and comes to a wretched end as she falls. Her son, who falls at the same time as his mother, and who is covered with the stench of the decomposing corpse, is rescued and cleansed by a protectress in human form (M_{425}, of which this sequence is the continuation; cf. Dorsey-Kroeber, pp. 324–5); he is thus unlike the bird-nester, who is made foul-smelling by bird droppings during his sojourn in the sky, and who is helped back to earth, then cleansed, by a protective animal.

The parallels between the two cycles can be taken further. In the Algonquin versions of the myth featuring the wives of the sun and moon, the two heroines are first of all taken up into the sky, and then brought back down to the top of a tree, where their real troubles begin. Consequently, they are in the same position as the South American bird-nester, whose adventures, being less dramatic than theirs, take place entirely between the ground and a tree-top, where, at one point in the narrative, he too is stranded.

The Plains heroine falls from a greater height: but, after her death, her son carries on in her place and, in the role of organizer of creation, takes over from the bird-nester. So the two cycles are partly homologous, partly complementary, as can be seen from the diagram in Figure 36, the significance of which will be immediately obvious.

The relationship between the two cycles is expressed in exactly the same way in the Arapaho Sun-Dance Ritual, but by means of emblems and symbols. The central pole of the ceremonial lodge, which is also, of course, the tallest, is attributed to the sun's wife: a digging-stick, placed horizontally at the top, represents the one the heroine placed across the hole in the celestial vault to hold the rope she used to climb back down to earth (OTM, pp. 175, 207). But, as we have seen above (pp. 503, 520, 528) at a lower level, there is also a forked stick stuck in the ground – a kind of miniature central pole since both are forked – which bears the effigy or remains of a small bird, the symbol of a different return to earth, i.e., the bird-nester's descent. The Arapaho are aware, then, of a structural homology between the two myths, while being also conscious of a difference in scale which, however, as in my diagram, relates only to physical dimension.

If the correspondences I have just established between the North and South American forms of the same myths have a basis in reality, another consequence must ensue. We know that, in South America, the versions of the bird-nester myth concerned with the origin of water are stronger than those concerned with the origin of fire. According to the latter, the hero, after being temporarily disjoined at the top of a tree, returns home safe and sound, and we are told nothing about his future life after these events. The former, on the other hand, describe how he makes a dangerous expedition to the kingdom of the souls, and then becomes the master of meteorological or seasonal phenomena, perhaps in the form of a constellation (M_1); he certainly changes into a constellation according to other versions (M_{124}, which is a transformation of M_1; cf. above, p. 223).

We have just verified that the strongest North American myths, that is, those concerned with the war between the worlds, relate primarily to the origin of fire, and only secondarily to that of water (M_{793c}, M_{795}). Simplifying a complex system in order to facilitate the demonstration, I propose to confine myself to those aspects of it, the strongest and the weakest respectively, which constitute its boundaries, as it were. The symmetrical interrelationships between the myths of North and South America then require that the weakest North American versions should have some connection with water.

Which are these weak versions? As I have explained, they are those versions of the myth about the wives of the sun and moon which originate in the northern crescent, especially in eastern Canada, where, as is also the case at the other extremity of the North American continent (M_{782a}), the celestial husbands are moved by their wives' tears and agree to send them back to earth. According to one version belonging to the eastern Algonquin (M_{437a}; Leland, pp. 140–46, cf. *OTM*, pp. 237–9), these women are aquatic spirits or water-girls (cf. M_{801}), who marry sea birds after completing their celestial, then terrestrial, adventures.

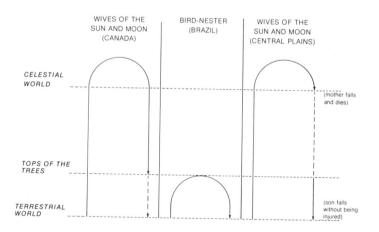

Figure 36. The bird-nester and the wives of the sun and moon

The aquatic connotation, already undeniable in Algonquin mythology, becomes more marked still in the Ojibwa myths, where the heroines also end by marrying water birds, who, however, bring about the spring thaw or even a universal flood, which submerges and drowns all the inhabitants ($M_{444a, b}$; *OTM*, pp. 244–7).

There is still more to be said. The Ge hero, stranded at the top of a tree and covered with bird droppings, is rescued by the jaguar, who asks him to climb down, then cleanses and revives him, in return for a food offering; the hero has thrown down to him the eaglets that were in the nest. A perfectly symmetrical picture is presented by the Algonquin myth, where the heroines are stranded at the top of a tree, and ask the wolverine to help them to climb down in return for the sexual offering of their persons, lodged on high as in a nest; later, they break their promise, deceive their rescuer and sometimes soil him with urine (M_{447}). If the South American jaguar is the master of terrestrial fire and of cooked meat, the North American wolverine is the victim of cooking fire and the master of raw meat.

These two characters are both to be found in the myths of north-west Canada. The Tahltan, who are Athapaskan-speaking neighbours of the Tlingit, have a myth ($M_{808a, b}$; Teit 7, pp. 246–8) about the wolverine, who was a cannibal at the time, being vanquished by the master of fog (− a mode of water). They also relate how the wolverine steals all the game from his wife's brothers who, fearing that they may be reduced to famine, throw hot grease over him, beat him with sticks and break his back. Ever since, the wolverine has had reddish fur, a burnt smell and, because of the injury to his genitalia, has been impotent. Being a stealer and polluter of raw meat (by urinating on it), the wolverine is an enemy of cooking; so, in relation to him, cooking fire has a destructive function. As was supposed in my

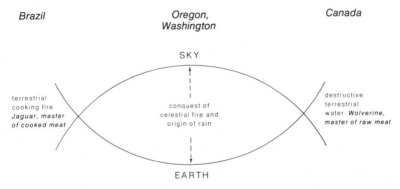

Figure 37. The conquest of fire in the sky and its limits

hypothesis, the wolverine in North America and the jaguar in South America, both of whom rescue human prisoners from a tree-top, are therefore diametrically opposed to each other as regards their respective etiological functions (Figure 37).[6]

This rounds off my analysis of a vast system, the invariant elements of which can consistently be represented in the form of a conflict between the earth and the sky for the possession of fire. Sometimes this conflict involves whole peoples, that is, the respective inhabitants of the two worlds; or it may take the more modest form of the temporary exile – in the direction of the sky, at least – of the hero at the top of a tree or a rocky cliff, from which he eventually redescends to become the master of fire (M_1, M_{7-12}). However, even in these extreme instances, certain features remain constant: one, which is sociological in nature, rests on an analogy between enemies and relations by marriage. In the strongest versions, the war between the two worlds is the consequence of the abduction of terrestrial women by celestial men; so one community is a taker of wives, the other an unwilling giver. In both South and North America, the same relation exists between the two main characters of the bird-nester myth: in the Ge stories, the protagonists are brothers-in-law, in the Bororo and Salish ones, they are a father and his son; but, in a matrilinear system like that of the Bororo, father and son are affines; and in both the Klamath-Modoc and the Salish myths, the demiurge puts himself in the same type of situation through his desire to appropriate his son's wives, which transforms the son willy-nilly into a giver of women. As the Kayapo and Ofaié maintain (see above, p. 588), the wife of the South American jaguar must be human since, in accordance with the strongest North American versions of the myth, the jaguar gives cooking fire to mankind in exchange.

---

[6] The wolverine neutralizes cooking fire by soiling raw meat with urine. According to a Menomini myth (M_{809}; Bloomfield 3, pp. 132–53), the mother of the dioscuri dies while giving birth to the second twin, who is made of sharp pieces of flint which tear her body. These flints explain the origin of fire-stones, and consequently of terrestrial fire; however, the mother, as she bleeds to death, quenches the domestic fire, so that the dioscuri grow up in a fireless world, and the elder twin has an urge to reconquer fire.

At the same time as, from the Tahltan to the Menomini, it is possible to trace the transformation: *neutralized cooking* [by conjunction: *raw meat, masculine urine*] ⇒ [by conjunction: *domestic fire, feminine blood*], cf. *OTM*, pp. 418–20, there is another to be noted: [*origin of celestial fire*] ⇒ [*origin of terrestrial fire*], as we move from the Machiguenga (M_{299}; *HA*, pp. 320–21) to the Menomini (M_{809}), by way of an intermediary Taulipang form in which terrestrial fire changes its origin: [*fire given birth to*] ⇒ [*excreted fire*]. No doubt, it is not simply for euphemistic reasons that 'to have one's monthly periods' is expressed in Menomini by the phrase 'to light one's fire out of doors' (Bloomfield 3, p. 191 and n. 1). I merely mention this series of interconnections in passing; if followed up, it would bring to light a further link in the transcontinental system.

The other invariant is cosmological in nature, and is to be found in all the versions of the myth, even the weakest; the Klamath-Modoc protagonists have celestial affinities, one with the sun, the other with the moon; and these affinities persist even in the Ge myths, where the sociological moiety that each individual character belongs to includes either the sun or the moon among its emblems (see above, pp. 44–7; *RC*, pp. 75–6).

The only difference that has to be pointed out between the myths in this respect relates to the fact that the strong or hybrid versions establish the chief opposition between terrestrial creatures on the one hand and celestial creatures on the other, whereas the weak forms — weak, that is, in this respect — confine it to two terrestrial protagonists who, however, take on, by metaphorical means, celestial connotations that have become detached from their original points of reference. In these weak forms, the cosmological opposition between earth and sky which, in other contexts, is concretized in separate characters or groups of characters (humans as opposed to celestial bodies in the myth about the wives of the sun and moon) takes the form of a rhetorical opposition between the literal and the figurative meanings, each of the two extant characters being entrusted with the task of conveying these two aspects. In this case, we have already seen that, in North America, the persecutor symbolizes the sun and his victim the moon. The latter, however, as I explained in *The Origin of Table Manners* (p. 397, n. 1) has a greater affinity than the sun with earth-dwellers, and the myths indicate this relative proximity by various characteristics, ranging from the clumsiness, inefficiency or mortality of the lunar hero (Bororo and Ge), to his generosity and organizing power elsewhere (Baré, Salish, Nootka, etc.).

In Bororo and Bakairi mythology, as well as in that of the Ge and the Salish, these same two heroes with a celestial vocation or affinity are represented by terrestrial and masculine characters. So, on the grounds of parity, we may expect to find a group of symmetrical American myths in which the same opposition is assigned to a feminine, instead of a masculine, pair. An initial opposition between the sky and the earth, and man and woman, was first of all reduced, in an initial phase, to an opposition between the sun and the moon in the form of celestial masculine characters ($M_{425-430}$). Any change of sex should, then, entail the appearance of a new dichotomy, affecting one of the poles of the preceding opposition. So, by a process of deduction, we come back to a well-authenticated mythic series devoted to the conflict between the two moons, and that I have already referred to (*OTM*, p. 422).

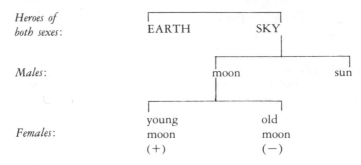

Any doubts that one might have about this derivation can be dispelled by considering the North American versions of the myths which refer overtly or implicitly to the conflict between the two feminine characters. I have already given one example, taken from Ojibwa mythology (M_{499}; *OTM*, pp. 410–11). It will be remembered that this myth, as well as the one immediately preceding it in Jones's collection (2, Vol. II, pp. 609–23), relates how Sun welcomes into his home a young, helpless, terrestrial woman; but his wicked old wife, Moon, takes a dislike to her and tries to kill her by making her fall from a swing. The young heroine gets the better of her persecutor, brings about her death and succeeds her in the role of the nocturnal luminary, which henceforth will be favourably disposed towards humans. The same pattern, transposed to the terrestrial world, makes it possible for another myth, also of Ojibwa origin, to fuse motifs from the bird-nester story and that of the wives of the sun and moon into one narrative:

M$_{810}$. *Ojibwa. 'The two moons'* (2)

There was an old hag of a woman living with her daughter-in-law and son and their infant son and a little orphan boy, whom she was bringing up. When her son came home from hunting, it was his custom to give the choice bits to his wife. These she would cook until they were crisp, so that she made a noise with her teeth as she ate them. This kind attention of the hunter to his wife excited the old woman's envy. She asked her son's wife to come out and swing her, forced her to undress and to tie herself to the swing with a leather thong. When the swing was in full motion and sweeping over a precipice, the old woman cut the cords and let her daughter-in-law drop into the lake below. The old woman put on her daughter-in-law's clothing, and counterfeited her appearance and duties in order to be given the dainty morsels. She eagerly ate them but, on giving the grandchild the breast, found that the milk would not draw.

In the meantime, the orphan boy mentioned his suspicions to the husband. The latter placed his spear upside down in the earth and requested the Great Spirit to send lightning, thunder and rain. A storm blew up over the waters of the lake but, contrary to the man's expectations, his wife's body did not arise from them.

The wife in fact was not dead; a water-tiger had twisted his tail round her body and drawn her to his lodge at the bottom of the lake, where she became his wife. On hearing her young son cry, she would nevertheless come back from time to time in the shape of a gull in order to suckle him. When the child again cried, the husband took advantage of his wife's appearance to break the monster's tail with his spear. When the old woman looked up and saw her victim again, she changed into a bird, flew out of the lodge and was never heard of more (Schoolcraft *in*: Williams, pp. 258–9).

This myth presents a twofold interest. On the one hand, the heroine, who makes it a point of honour to chew roast meat noisily, corresponds to the one in the myth about the wives of the sun and moon who has the same ability (*OTM*, pp. 277–323); this ability is nearly the undoing of the Ge hero, when his adoptive father's wife (and not the husband's mother) cannot stand the noise he makes while chewing meat too crisply roasted, the same kind of meat that is here coveted by another wicked old hag precisely because of its crunchiness. According to M_{10} and M_{428}, etc., this alimentary dilemma is the consequence of a vertical disjunction, operating from low to high by means of a tree; in M_{810}, it is the cause of an equally vertical disjunction, but one which operates from high to low by means of a swing: and once again we confirm (see above, pp. 415, 505–508) that the swing constitutes a mytheme symmetrical with the one about going up to the sky by means of a chain of arrows, or a magically growing tree or rock. Lastly, it is clear that the old woman's stratagem, in forcing the daughter-in-law to take off her clothes before disjoining her from her husband and appropriating her garments in order to assume her identity as the son's wife, corresponds, in an inverted form, to that of the bird nester's father when he behaves in a similar way in order to appropriate his son's wives. The son allows himself to become temporarily disjoined from his father through being attracted by a celestial bird. The heroine of M_{810} succeeds in being temporarily conjoined to her son by herself assuming the appearance of a water bird.

Far from being peculiar to the Ojibwa, this mythic pattern based on a conflict between the two moons is almost as widespread throughout North America as the myths of which it is a transformation. The motif, which is referred to by North American folklore specialists as the 'swing trick', and the distribution of which has been plotted by Waterman (3; cf. also Barrett 2, pp. 487–8), can almost always serve as a clue for the identification of myths of this type. Similarly, the disguised mother motif links the lewd grandmother group with the one about the two moons. We have already encountered this motif in Eskimo mythology (M_{746b}), and it can be followed south as far as the Osage ($M_{811a,\,b}$; Dorsey 9, pp. 25–6), by way of the Assiniboine (M_{811c}; Lowie 2, pp. 155–7) who have a version very similar to the Ojibwa one.

In a recent work on the formal analysis of myths, Buchler and Selby maintain (p. 68) that it is possible to formulate rules which allow all mythic transformation to be deduced in succession from any one of them, provided this particular one is taken to be 'non-recursive' or 'undecidable'. This is no doubt true, if each myth is considered separately; but I have often shown that these sequences, which are undecidable in respect of any particular myth, can be reduced to reciprocal transformations, perpendicular, as it were, to several superimposed mythic narratives (*HA*, pp. 353–8). Buchler and Selby's statement can be accepted as valid, then, provided the analysis is confined to one specific myth or group of myths; however, it is in the nature of any myth or group of myths to refuse to be treated as a closed entity: there inevitably comes a point during the analysis when a problem arises which cannot be solved except by breaking through the boundaries that the analysis had prescribed for itself. The same interplay of transformations which makes it possible to reduce the sequences of a given myth one to another, extends more or less automatically to the undecidable sequence, which is nevertheless reducible, outside the myth to other undecidable sequences, originating in myths in connection with which the same problem arose.

In the last resort, there is only one absolutely undecidable sequence in the case of each mythological system. When reduced to its essential features through a series of transformations, this sequence boils down to the expression of an opposition, or, to be more accurate, to the expression of the opposition as being the initial datum. In the last part of this volume, it has been demonstrated that several hundred stories, apparently very different from each other, and each extremely complex in itself, proceed from a chain of interlinked statements: there is the sky and there is the earth; between the two there can be no conceivable parity; consequently, the presence on earth of that celestial phenomenon, fire, is a mystery; since celestial fire is now present here below on the domestic hearth, it must have been brought down from the sky by an expedition which went up from earth to fetch it.

It follows from all this that the absolutely undecidable sequence boils down, if not to the empirically decidable assertion that there is a world (whereas instead there might have been nothing), at least to the statement that this 'being of the world' consists of a disparity. It cannot be said purely and simply of the world that it is: it exists in the form of an initial asymmetry, which shows itself in a variety of ways according to the angle from which it is being apprehended: between the high and the low, the sky and the earth, land and water, the near and the far, left and right, male and female, etc. This inherent disparity of the world sets mythic thought in motion, but it does so because, on the hither side of thought, it conditions the existence of every object of thought.

An arrangement of matching opposition in-built, as it were, in the human understanding, begins to function, whenever recurrent experiences, which may be biological, technological, economic, sociological, etc. in origin, activate the control, to produce effects like those in the innate behaviour patterns said to be characteristic of animals, and the phases of which unwind automatically as soon as an appropriate conjunction of circumstances sets them in motion. Similarly stimulated by empirical contingencies, the conceptual apparatus begins to operate; from every concrete situation, no matter how complex, it unflaggingly extracts a meaning, and turns it into an object of thought by adapting it to the imperatives of formal organization. In the same way, it is through the systematic application of rules governing opposition that myths come into being, develop, and are transformed into different myths which in turn also undergo transformation; and the process continues until insurmountable cultural or linguistic barriers, or the inherent inertia of the mythic machinery itself, allows the production of only smudged, barely recognizable forms, because the properties peculiar to myth have become blurred, and are giving way to other means of processing reality, which, according to circumstances, may be closer to the novel, or legend, or the fable, conceived as a vehicle for some moral or political lesson (*OTM*, pp. 114–31; L.-S. 20).

The problem of the genesis of myth is inseparable, then, from that of thought itself, the constitutive experience of which is not that of an opposition between the self and the other, but of the other apprehended as opposition. In the absence of this intrinsic property – the only one, it is true to say, that is absolutely *given* – no act of consciousness constitutive of the self would be possible. Being, were it not apprehensible as a relationship, would be equivalent to nothingness. The conditions which allow the emergence of myth are therefore the same as those of all thought, since thought itself cannot be other than thought about an object, and since an object, however starkly and simply it is conceived, is an object only in so far as it constitutes the subject as subject, and consciousness itself as the consciousness of a relationship.

For a myth to be engendered by thought and for it in turn to engender other myths, it is necessary, and sufficient, that an initial opposition should be injected into experience and, as a consequence, other oppositions will spring into being. That between the high and the low admits of three modalities, according to whether the movement from one pole to the other occurs in one direction, in the opposite direction or in both. The axis of reference which is sometimes kept vertical, sometimes changed to the horizontal, and sometimes partakes of both at once, may have, as its poles, the sky and the earth, the sky and water, or land and water. In the category of the celestial bodies, individual luminaries such as the sun and moon may be in opposition to the constellations, and the latter, or the named celestial bodies taken as a group, to the mass of anonymous stars. Considered in their reciprocal relationships, the sun and the moon themselves may be both male, or both female, or of different sexes; they may also be strangers to each other, friends, blood relations or affines. Similarly, whoever the characters are, the kinship link, conceived in the mode of consanguinity or marriage, will be ascendent or descendent, straight or oblique, and envisaged from the point of view of takers or givers of women. At each oppositional level there will be further corresponding speculative attempts to confer meaning on the particular cross-sections of reality thus selected for consideration.

We still have to ask ourselves why, in this particular case, all the various strands running through these many operations seem to converge on one very restricted area of North America, to which anthropologists have not paid any special attention, at least in this respect. Yet it is here that we find, side by side, the weakest forms of the myth about the wives of the sun and moon, at times reduced to the level of a mere village tale (M_{802a-c}) – the weakest state of the generally weak set of versions known as the northern crescent versions – and those strong forms which can be regarded as the strongest of all, and which have as their theme the war waged by the earth-dwellers against the celestial people for the possession of fire.

This peculiarity is not the only one which strikes us in studying what, in the interests of simplification, I shall call the Oregonian area. It is here too that we find the largest number of very small tribal groups living side by side, each occupying a limited territory and differing from its immediate neighbours in language, traditions, and often in culture too. To mention only the variety of languages, along the Pacific coast and in the immediate hinterland between $40°$ and $50°$ parallel, very different linguistic families occur within a few kilometres of each other: Penutian, Hokan, Athapaskan, Algonquin, Chinook, Salish, Chemakum, Wakashan . . . That is not all. If one looks at a map showing the areas of distribution of the tribal and linguistic groups, like the now classic one drawn up by Driver, Cooper, Kirchhoff, Massey, Rainier and Spier,[7] one cannot but be impressed – whatever one's reservations about the inevitably arbitrary nature of the divisions and classificatory conventions – by the general appearance, which is reminiscent of a histological cross-section through living tissue. The whole area between the Rockies and the Pacific, especially in its middle section, seems to be made up of very small cells, all different in form and organization and whose extremely dense and lengthwise distribution makes one think of some deep germinative layer, whereas the cross-section from west to east presents an increasingly loose assemblage of cells, which looks much more like connective tissue. In this respect, the involuted coastal pattern formed by the Georgia Strait, the Juan de Fuca Strait and Puget Sound, around which the Oregonian singularity is organized, seems like a kind of original centre of North American cultures, the point at which in the past they were perhaps all linked to what we might call – giving concrete expression to an abstract idea – their umbilical cord.

If this hypothesis, which I put forward only tentatively, were true, the myths discussed in the last part of this study would represent the best preserved, the richest and still living, forms of a system which gradually broke up as it spread eastwards and northwards, so that what we found in the heart of South America was no more than its scattered remains, as they were after being carried for centuries on successive waves of migration. In gathering up the pieces and setting them end to end in the course of my study, I may be seen as having patiently reconstituted the system by moving back step by step to its source, where I have at last rediscovered it in a relatively unaltered state.

However, the situation might also be interpreted differently. Instead of seeing the Oregonian singularity as the point in space-time where all the strands of a primaeval mythic system, which have become broken and confused elsewhere, survive intact and still hold together, we could suppose that stories, originally distinct, came to fuse and unite within it, as the elements of a possible system brought into being by an act of synthesis. Myths, which elsewhere were potential – mere modalities of the system – must, then, have succeeded on one occasion and in one place, in organizing and articulating themselves so as to give birth to a living myth.

---

[7] In: H. E. Driver and W. C. Massey: 'Comparative Studies of North American Indians', *Transactions of the American Philosophical Society*, n.s., Vol. 47, part 2, Philadelphia, 1957.

Yet it is also clear that, from the point of view of the analysis, the two hypotheses merge, since I could have started from either one or the other and, given a general inversion of all the signs, my procedure would have been exactly the same. Because of the fact that the totality I set out to reconstitute is a closed system, it comes to the same thing whether one explores it from the centre towards the periphery or from the surface inwards: in either case its intrinsic curvature ensures that it is covered in its entirety. In a situation of this kind, it is impossible to tell whether one is following the time sequence or running counter to it.

It is true that particular analyses make it possible to establish sequential relationships between certain mythic transformations, as I have shown on several occasions (*RC*, pp. 223, 307–11; *HA*, pp. 344–58; *OTM*, pp. 356, 364–72, 389; and in the present volume, pp. 202, 217, 219–20, 233, 317–18, 326, 337–40, 460, 528). But when the analysis is raised to a level of generality which makes it possible to look at the system from without, and no longer from within, historical considerations lose their relevance and there are no longer any criteria enabling us to distinguish between states of the system as coming before or after each other.

Thus it could be that this arduous quest has reaped its own reward: it may have located – without having looked for it or actually reached it – the site of that long-promised land where relief is to be found for the impatient, threefold awareness of a 'later' that has to be waited for, a 'now' that slips through the fingers, and a voracious 'yesteryear' that draws to itself, disrupts and collapses the future into a present already confounded with the past. If this is so, my enquiry has not been simply a search for time lost. The category of time revealed by the study of the myths is, in the last resort, none other than that which the myths themselves have always dreamed of. Time which is more than just regained, time abolished: time as it would be experienced by someone who, although born in the twentieth century, felt increasingly as he grew older that he had had, in his youth, the good fortune to live in the nineteenth century in the company of his seniors who had belonged to it – although he was not then aware of the sensation – as they themselves had had the good fortune to be still living in the eighteenth century, through having been intimately acquainted with people belonging to that century – although they were not aware of the fact either; so that if we all combined forces to weld together the links in the chain – each period endeavouring to keep the preceding one alive for the benefit of the next – time would be cancelled out. And if all of us, the whole of mankind, had known this from the beginning, we could have organized a conspiracy against time; such an aspiration persists at the heart of contemporary civilization, as is shown, sometimes in a rather pathetic way, by the love of books and museums and the liking for antiques and curios; a desperate, and inevitably vain, aspiration to halt time and reverse its movement.

The interest we think we are taking in the past is, in fact, only an interest in the present; by binding the present firmly to the past, we imagine we are making it more durable, and are pinning it down to prevent it slipping away and becoming itself part of the past. As if, through being brought into contact with the present, the past itself would, through some miraculous osmosis, become present, and the present be protected from its fate, which is to become part of the past. And, no doubt, that is what the myths claim to be doing, in respect of what they are dealing with; but the amazing thing is that they actually do so, in respect of what they are.

If taken to its logical conclusion, the analysis of the myths reaches a point where history cancels itself out. Like the Dakota Indians of Canada, who have modified the traditional version of a tribal myth in order to neutralize the contradiction between the Sioux and Algonquin ideologies, which they actually experienced during a recent and historically attested migration, (see above, p. 519), all the Indian peoples of both North and South America seem to have conceived their myths for one purpose only: to come to terms with history and, on the level of the system, to re-establish a state of equilibrium capable of acting as a shock absorber for the disturbances caused by real-life events. How, otherwise, are we to explain the fact that those elements of the system which I have called binary operators — gallinaceans, flat-fish, butterflies and other insects, sciuridae, etc. — retain their semantic function throughout both hemispheres, and that their persistence can be discussed without any reference to the countless demographic and cultural upheavals which have occurred over the centuries?

The unity and solidity of the system would seem totally inexplicable, if we did not take a more accurate view of the peopling of America and of the historical and geographical relationships between the different population groups, than that to which our own position as so-called civilized communities would incline us.

In the first place, the speed of modern, worldwide transport, which we tend to regard as a recent achievement, can lead us to underestimate the vast distances that small bands of hunters, or even of gatherers and collectors, are able to cover in a few decades or centuries, provided they have the desire to keep going. One of the most striking results obtained by archaeological research in the New World is the approximate coincidence of the dates suggested for the earliest human settlements in both hemispheres. For both North and South America, the estimated dates of human occupation have gradually been moved back at the same rate and, at the time of writing, they have been established in both cases at approximately 13000 B.C. It is certain that they will be moved further back still, but there is every reason to believe that they will remain in step. From the time when men first entered America unwittingly by way of the land bridge on the site of the Bering Strait, they set about systematically occupying the whole extent of the New World, and even taking into account halts lasting for months or years, a few centuries were probably enough to allow bands capable of walking a few dozen kilometres a day to spread out at greater or lesser distances from each other, from Alaska to Tierra del Fuego. What might be called the first distribution of population took place over the whole continent, and in a relatively short time.

However, I am not making the absurd suggestion that, after these first settlements others did not follow. Even allowing for the fact that ice movements made communication possible between the Old World and the New only during two periods of the Upper Pleistocene – around 25000 B.C., and then approximately between 13000 and 10000 B.C. (Müller-Beck, pp. 374–81) – these 'windows' were wide enough to admit several successive waves of migrants, spread out over hundreds or thousands of years. Each wave could take advantage of temporarily abandoned territory, or drive out or destroy previous occupants. As I also recognized in the previous volume (OTM, p. 70), it may well be that, throughout this long stretch of history, certain communities retraced their steps, since there is no reason why they should have always moved in the same direction.

At the time when the discovery and colonization of both parts of the continent were, in a sense, about to shatter and then completely destroy its independent historical development, such population shifts were still taking place, and during the subsequent centuries they were either checked, put off course or precipitated by the presence of the white settlers. In South America, particularly among the Tupi, they continued intermittently until the twentieth century, as qualified observers were able to testify. All this is true. Nevertheless, it follows from what I said previously that both parts of the continent, taken at any point in their history, were nine-tenths empty (with the exception of Central America, Mexico and the Andean region) and yet constituted a solid or saturated world. Not, of course, in the sense that the words would have in a modern context of dense over-population, but in the light of the fact that very small human groups, forced by rudimentary technology to exploit vast empty spaces for the purposes of hunting, gathering, collecting and even shifting cultivation, do in effect fill them by ranging ceaselessly across them, even though their presence bears more resemblance to the way in which a minute quantity of gas expands and distributes its molecules throughout the entire volume of a balloon than to the cramming together of human individuals in a modern conurbation. In spite of their small numbers, so-called primitive groups are able to make their presence felt over a whole stretch of territory, as far as the boundaries created by the balance of forces between communities. Consequently, instead of imagining the New World in pre-Columbian times as virtually empty space where tiny human groups lived in isolation hundreds of kilometres apart, we should think of it rather as a compact assemblage of large, non-dense cells, yet each diffusely populated throughout its entire volume, so that the contiguous cell-walls acquire a degree of firmness.

If we consider the situation in this light, it becomes conceivable that any original creation occurring in one place should, through direct contact, produce repercussions in the other places, and that a dislocation of the system at one point should lead to its gradual and complete reorganization. The science of metallurgy shows how even the slightest 'play' in the molecules of a rigid body is enough to cause an overall rearrangement, when tension exceeds a certain limit at a given point, although the appearance and external properties of the body itself remained unchanged. Meanwhile, the body in question may be involved, from without, in all kinds of chemical or mechanical processes which modify its shape, its consistency, its colour, its properties and the purposes for which it can be used; the two types of phenomena are not of the same order of magnitude and occur on different levels.

It is high time that anthropology freed itself from the illusion gratuitously invented by the functionalists, who mistake the practical limitations imposed upon them by the kind of studies they advocate for the absolute properties of the objects with which they are dealing. An anthropologist may confine himself for one or more years within a small social unit, group or village, and endeavour to grasp it as a totality, but this is no reason for imagining that the unit, at levels other than the one at which convenience or necessity has placed him, does not merge in varying degrees into larger entities, the existence of which remains, more often than not, unsuspected. At the very least, we must distinguish between separate levels of activity in the life of peoples without writing. There is, on the one hand, what we may call the field of strong interactions, which, precisely because they are strong, have received most attention: i.e., migrations, epidemics, revolutions and wars, which occur intermittently in the form of profound upheavals, with far-reaching and long-lasting effects. But there is, at the same time, the neglected field of weak interactions, which are much more widespread and occur at shorter intervals, in the form of friendly or hostile meetings, visits or marriages. It is these interactions which keep the field in a state of perpetual agitation. The constant activation of the social surface means that weak, low-powered, local vibrations gradually extend to the limits of the field, independently of demographic, political or economic changes, which occur less often, and produce their effects more slowly and at a deeper level.

Consequently, there is no contradiction in recognizing that each American community had its own independent and extremely complicated history, whose dramatic events it constantly tried to neutralize by reshaping the myths, in so far as this was compatible with the constraints of the traditional moulds into which they always had to fit. A story already altered by such internal developments reacts externally on similar productions; adjustments are made or fresh oppositions come into being, transposing the constant pattern of similarities and contrasts on to different levels. During intertribal encounters, such as marriages, commercial transactions, or the taking of prisoners, all these rectifications are sparked off in sequence, and spread in a counter direction much more rapidly than those major occurrences which seal the destiny of peoples. The system has only to be disturbed at one particular point for it immediately to seek to re-establish its equilibrium by reacting in its totality, and it does so by means of a mythology which may be causally linked to history in each of its parts, but which, taken in its entirety, resists the course of history and constantly readjusts its own mythological grid so that this grid offers the least resistance to the flow of events which, as experience proves, is rarely strong enough to break it up and sweep it away.

Yet even in history itself, certain elements persist, and provide a solid anchorage to which the myths can attach themselves. Looking back over the themes that have been the driving force of the present study since the outset, we can perhaps say that certain modalities of culinary technology are of this nature. Not that I wish to suggest the operation, in this connection, of a form of determinism that would be of a singularly petty kind, but because it is impossible to give an exhaustive analysis of the ideology of any human group without taking into account its concrete relationships with the world; the ideology expresses these relationships, at the same time as the relationships in turn translate the ideology. There is no need to appeal to ethnography to arrive at the conclusion that eating habits are the form of behaviour by which people choose most often to assert their originality in relation to others. Ordinary people judge a foreign country in the first place by its cooking, and the persistence of this criterion even in our industrialized civilization, is surely convincing proof that, independently of any biological considerations, it expresses in a most profound way the links which bind each individual to one environment, one way of life and one society.

The 'short symphony', which concluded Part Two of *The Raw and the Cooked*, and which had three movements devoted to the Ge, the Bororo and the Tupi respectively, implied that a sort of culinary-conditioned counterpoint might underlie the different ways in which these adjacent communities explain the origin of fire. I pointed out that the Bororo occupy an intermediary position between the Ge, who regard *raw + rotten* as a natural category, and the Tupi, for whom *raw + cooked* represents a cultural category, and I added that this 'needed to be explained' (*RC*, p. 143). Now that we are familiar with the myths, and have been enlightened by the culinary considerations which have frequently arisen in the course of the discussion, we may be able to relate these differences to the respective customs of the three communities. The Tupi made pottery and practised cannibalism, that is, they exercised a technical skill and followed a custom, which were either unknown to, or forbidden by, the Ge. The Bororo were potters like the Tupi, and non-cannibalistic like the Ge. Moreover, whereas the ancient Tupi used to smoke or roast meat over a low fire, the Bororo usually boiled it. This preference is not clear, it is true, from von den Steinen's account, but he saw the Bororo away from the traditional villages, in a camp where they had been put by the military authorities, who, however, left them quite free to observe their own rites and customs: the German anthropologist notes (p. 624) that the Indians roasted game without even skinning it, and put only the guts into the stew-pot. On the other hand, the Salesian missionaries were struck, as I myself was in 1935, by the liking shown by the Bororo for boiled food: 'The flesh of wild animals and birds is usually boiled in cooking-pots called *aria* . . . Only on very rare occasions do they grill meat on wooden sticks placed near the fire . . . Large fish are cut into pieces and boiled' (Colbacchini 3, pp. 66–7; cf. pp. 126–7 in connection with the rites of exorcism in respect of boiled game). According to the *Enciclopédia Bororo* (Vol. I, p. 34; cf. pp. 322–8), the women cook meat 'almost always in water', and they use the stock to make a vegetable soup which they carry to the men's house. The Bororo also eat corn in the form of a mush, as the Tupi did, and still do, in those areas where they survive. In this respect, these two communities are in opposition to the Ge, who, according to Banner (1, p. 54), 'drink pure water and do not like the corn mush, of which the Tupi are so fond'.

In the case of the Bororo, these culinary preferences correspond to their mythology which, as I showed (*RC*, pp. 193, 292), constantly stresses the primacy of water over fire, a point moreover clearly indicated by a comparison of the Ge myth (M_{163}) and the Bororo myths ($M_{120-123}$), where the following terms are commutable: *woodpeckers* $\Rightarrow$ *water birds; clumsy Moon* $\Rightarrow$ *clumsy Sun; fire spilt* $\Rightarrow$ *water spilt: sun brought closer* $\Rightarrow$ *sun moved farther away*; etc. With the exception of M_{55}, which deals with the origin of fire in its cultural form, it can be said without exaggeration that all the Bororo stories on this theme deal, not with the lighting of the first fire, but with its extinguishing by water.

If we bear in mind that, in the case of South America the Ge myths, and in the case of North America the Salish myths, have, as it were, formed the backbone of the argument developed in this study, we can attach even greater importance to the presence in the two communities of the earth oven, associated in both cases with very similar ideological patterns, whereas its absence among the adjacent peoples — who were certainly not unaware of its use by the Ge or the Salish — may, by reaction, have prompted the invention of compensatory ideologies. These ideologies are, therefore, just as much part of the system as the others.

In Salish society the earth oven was associated invariably and exclusively with the female sex. The Flathead considered everything to do with digging roots or edible tubers and caring for the pit women's work. 'In fact, the presence of men was tabooed . . . lest bad luck and famine overtook all' (Turney-High 2, p. 127). Among the Cœur d'Alêne the same taboo applied especially to bachelors: 'The tubers would spoil or would not cook properly, if a man came too near the oven' (Teit 6, p. 185; 9, p. 509). A similar, and complementary, taboo existed in Okanagon society, where women were not allowed within half a mile of the fishing dams (Cline, p. 17). 'When tubers and roots are to be baked, so the Thompson declare, women only must do it' (Hill-Tout 10, p. 513). The inland Shuswap and the Twana along the coast of Puget Sound similarly forbade men to have anything to do with earth ovens (Boas 16, p. 637; Elmendorf 1, p. 133). So, throughout the whole of the Salish zone, this is a universal rule. The symmetrical taboo, mentioned in connection with the Okanagon, would suggest that the rule is based on a twofold opposition: between men and women on the one hand, and between water and earth (or fire) on the other.

The Ge, unlike their Bororo and Tupi neighbours, used and still use, a kind of earth oven which has been described in detail in anthropological literature. Stones, or fragments of anthill of comparable hardness, are heated on a wood fire until they are red-hot; the site of the fire is then swept, and on it are placed green leaves, to serve as a base for a round, leaf-wrapped pie, more than a metre in diameter, made of manioc with a meat stuffing. The still scorching stones or anthill fragments are piled on top (or placed underneath, according to Maybury-Lewis, p. 45), and the whole thing is covered with old matting and earth dug from the fire area; the general appearance is that of a funeral mound (Nimuendaju 5, p. 34; cf. also 8, p. 43; Banner 1, pp. 54–5; Dreyfus, pp. 34–5; Maybury-Lewis, *loc. cit.*). With the exception of the Apinayé, among whom the men helped with the earth oven (Nimuendaju 5, p. 16), the Serenté, the Timbira, the Kayapo and, so it would seem, most of the other Ge tribes, like the Salish, considered it to be an exclusively feminine concern. Among the Xikrin, who are northern Kayapo, the earth oven which is built with a roof over it, at the opposite end of the village from the men's house, seems to be in opposition to it as a private place where only women can assemble (Frikel 3, pp. 15–16). The Kayapo name for the earth oven, *Ki*, which is common to most languages of the same family, becomes *ki-kré*, 'lodge', with the addition of a suffix, and the Indians do in fact believe that the shelter built to protect the oven in wet weather is the prototype of their houses (Banner 1, p. 55).

The Kayapo had myths explaining the origin of the earth oven, but unfortunately only fragments of them are extant. They are linked to the cycle of the dioscuri, the founders of the men's house and the initiators of hunting rites, a cycle I have had occasion to discuss in previous volumes (M_{253}, $M_{225-227}$; *RC*, p. 259, *HA*, pp. 119–49). According to one version (M_{812a}; Banner 1, p. 55), one of the two heroes, although the myth does not specify which, asks for a round manioc loaf to be made, clasps it in his arms and orders a fire to be lit all around him. Before the fire dies down, the Indian has changed into a stone, on to which the women pour water to prevent it cracking. But the loaf has had time to cook, and the man resumes his natural appearance. However, his skin has changed from white to red, and it is since then that stones have been used to heat the oven.

The other versions ($M_{812b, c}$, *ibid.*; Dreyfus, pp. 85–6) relate how a man becomes furious with fire which has burnt his nephew. He orders his sister to prepare an oven. 'But where is the meat?' she asks. The man replies, 'With me,' and he lies down on the burning stones, which roast him. Whereupon, he gets up, walks to the river and (having changed into a cayman, M_{812c}) disappears into the water. A long time afterwards, he comes back safe and sound, bearing no trace whatever of the ordeal he has endured. He relates how he has lived in the land of the fish and, as proof, shows all the small fish which have been caught in his long hair. They are, in fact, women, who a long time previously gave up their human form (cf.

M_{153}, RC, p. 266). He teaches the Indians the ritual songs he has learnt from the fish (M_{812b}), and shares out among the different households the ceremonial 'fish' names which are part of Kayapo culture (M_{812c}).[8]

However defective the text of the Kayapo myths may be, several observations can nevertheless be made about them. Within the same cycle, they are obvious inversions of M_{142}, in which women sacrifice the hero by pushing him into the still glowing embers of an earth oven (HA, p. 121), whereas, in the Kayapo myth, they pour water on him to prevent him being destroyed by the fire. Yet, in both cases, the hero is responsible for the creation of oven stones and the anthill, fragments of which serve the same purpose as the stones. I showed in *From Honey to Ashes* that M_{142} belongs to a group concerned with the education of women. The women in M_{812a-c} are well-trained, since they can prepare food and supervise its cooking, both of which tasks are essentially feminine; in creating stones and pieces of hardened earth, the hero provides them with the means of exercising their skill.

I would like to digress for a moment, and return briefly to North America. The Kalapuya, who used to form a separate linguistic group between the Salish and the Sahaptin, and who had a great belief in the curative properties of deep cauterization,[9] insisted on a shaman walking barefoot over the red-hot stones before each women placed her harvest of tubers in the collective earth oven: he would cover the whole area of the oven in this way, then would inspect the soles of his feet to check that they were unharmed, and would promise that the camas would soon be cooked (Jacobs 4, pp. 18–19; cf. pp. 29, 30, 36). So here too – although in the form of a rite rather than a myth – a consecrated man has to be 'cooked', so that the women can entrust the gathered tubers to the oven with every hope of success.

M_{812b}, on the other hand, presents itself openly as the foundation myth of a ceremony in honour of fish. A similar celebration existed among the Timbira, who performed it during the years when there was no initiation ceremony for young men, and alternately with a feast in honour of birds (Nimuendaju 8, pp. 212–30). As it happens, the foundation myth of the bird ceremony, known as *pepkaha'k*, is exactly symmetrical with M_{812b}. An Indian, so the story goes, suffered from a serious infection through an ant attaching itself by its mandibles deep inside his auditory canal. The

---

[8] Perhaps these Ge myths are echoed by those of the Ayoré of the northern Chaco, who believe a terricolous insect with a painful sting to be the inventor of the oven, the red-hot embers of which turned its breast red; it is also a harbinger of plentiful harvests when it is seen burrowing into the earth in cultivated fields (Muñoz-Bernand, p. xlii).

[9] So, too, had the Puget Sound Salish, who treated rheumatism by burning a hole in the flesh right to the bone (Eells 1, p. 218).

infection spread to his whole body, which became covered with abscesses. Since he was unable to move, he was left on his own with a supply of food. Birds of prey swooped down to eat what they believed to be a corpse. On discovering their mistake, they got the long-beaked humming-bird to remove the cause of the infection, and instructed the vultures to eat the worms and pus. Then the great vulture took the man off to the sky and fed him, not on carrion but on roast meat and manioc cakes. When he was cured, the birds of prey instructed him in their rites, which, on his return to earth, he himself taught to his kinsfolk and fellow-tribesmen, who had believed him to be dead (M_{813a}; Nimuendaju 8, p. 247; cf. the Apinayé versions $M_{813b, c}$; Oliveira, pp. 80–82; Nimuendaju 5, pp. 184–6). Consequently, the sky and the birds act as saviours and initiators in respect of a putrefied man, just as, in M_{812b}, the water and the fish do so in respect of a burnt man, thus inverting the sign of the functions which, in the Bororo and Tupi myths, associate fire with the sky and putrefaction with water:

$$(sky \simeq fire) \Rightarrow (rotten^{-1})$$
$$(water \simeq rot) \Rightarrow (burnt^{-1}).$$

Furthermore, the birds in M_{813a} are male, whereas the fish in M_{812b} are embodiments of the female sex. I would like to dwell on this point for a moment.

Woman have an affinity with water, which is weak in M_{812a}, and strong in M_{812b}: they either drench the hero with water or, having themselves a fish-like form, they take him to live in water. Conversely, the masculine hero has an affinity with stone – which he becomes in one version – and with fire, to which he entrusts himself in both versions. Stones are comparable to hardened earth and, in the technology of the oven, earth hardened by ants can replace stone. In this respect, there exists both a resemblance and a difference between the earth oven and pottery: both consist of baked earth, but in the first case the earth is on the side of fire, and consequently similar to a natural element; in the second, it is on the side of food, which, being a receptacle, it contains, and is therefore a cultural artefact. Consequently, cooking in the earth oven and cooking in clay pots brings into play the same three elements – fire, baked earth or stone, and food – but establishes different relationships between them. In the earth oven, the stones or pieces of previously 'cooked' earth (they are heated until they are red-hot) are on the side of fire and nature: in cooking by boiling, the baked earth (of which the receptacles are made) is on the side of culture and cooked food:

earth-oven: (fire + stones or pieces of baked earth) // food
pottery: fire // (baked earth + food).

The displacement of one term, observable between the two formulae, is symmetrical in form with that which seemed imperative in the course of the analysis of the myths about the origin of fire, belonging respectively to the Ge and the Tupi (see above, p. 611):

Ge: (rotten + raw) // cooked;
$Tupi$: rotten // (raw + cooked).

The Ge used the earth oven, but did not make pottery and did not practise cannibalism; consequently, they are in opposition on three counts to the Tupi, who are potters, cannibals and non-users of earth ovens, which can be said to be replaced in their culture by smoking. The fact that the presence or absence of cannibalism is part of the system results, on the one hand, from the Tupi myths about the origin of fire in which the hero turns into a decaying carcass and pretends to offer himself as food for the vultures (M_{65-68}), and on the other, from the Ge myths about the origin of the earth oven, in which the hero simulates self-sacrifice by pretending to be roasted like meat intended for a feast. So the Ge — although only on the level of mythology — set against the genuinely war-associated cannibalism practised by the Tupi, who used to eat the flesh of their enemies, a humane, metaphorical form of cannibalism. Far from expressing an outward-turned ferocity, it reflects the closest form of social and family solidarity known to the Kayapo: that which exists between maternal uncle and nephew, through the transmission of ceremonial surnames, the origin of which is founded by M_{812c}. Furthermore, a reversal occurs, because of the kind of supernumerary torsion, which I pointed out at the very beginning of my enquiry as being a property peculiar to mythic transformations, (L.-S. 5, p. 252): contrary to logical expectation, the hero's self-cooking does not turn him into food, but into oven stones, that is, into a means of cooking.

Between the two extreme formulae illustrated by the Ge and the Tupi, it becomes clear, then, that the Bororo, who are potters like the latter and non-cannibalistic like the former, occupy a median position. On the other hand, although they do not possess earth ovens 'like funeral mounds' (see above, p. 612), they have an inverted equivalent in the form of what could be called 'a rotting mound', in which the well-soaked corpse, while awaiting a second burial, rots away and becomes fleshless. So, for these Indians, who practise cooking by boiling, water possesses a twofold function: it ensures both cooking and putrefaction. There seems to be little doubt that the Ge too practised double burial (Nimuendaju 5, p. 153; 6, p. 100; 8, pp. 134–5; Dreyfus, pp. 59–60) with the difference that the deceased's bones, after being washed and painted, were interred and not thrown into a lake or river, as was the Bororo custom.

We have seen that the myths, M_{812a-c}, presuppose a double affinity between women and water on the one hand, and men and fire on the other. Among the Bororo, since water ensures the preservation of the bones which have been painted and decorated with feathers (and thus covered, as it were, with incorruptible flesh), the reverse affinities prevail: there is a congruence between water, the abode of souls, and the society of men who embody the souls of the dead on earth: 'The woman must always give way to the man, for during ceremonies men represent the souls' (Colbacchini 3, p. 139). It is not possible to cook in the men's house; but in the family hut, husband and wife eat from the same dish, although sitting back to back. Men and women, disjoined by cooking, are conjoined by its opposite: when her husband is present in the hut, the wife is not allowed to leave it, not even to relieve nature (cf. Colbacchini, *ibid.*, pp. 68, 139).

On the other hand, the Ge myths about the origin of the earth oven conjoin the sexes symbolically, since they show both men and women participating in the same cultural activity, the men on the side of fire, and the women on the side of water. In real life, however, the opposite is the case, since only the women deal with the earth oven. But, as with the Okanagon,[10] this rule has a counterpart: the women are excluded from the rites connected with collective fishing expeditions which, in Kayapo society, are a male preserve, women only being allowed to look on (Dreyfus pp. 30–31).[11] If men are excluded from the collective oven ($\simeq$ fire) and women from collective fishing ($\simeq$ water), it is understandable that, to mediatize the opposition, the myths should associate women with fish, the passive objects of fishing, and men with oven stones, the passive means of cooking (Figure 38).

Let us return for a moment to North America and to the Coos myths. M_{793a-c} (see above, pp. 564, 569), in which I noted a double hierarchical progression leading, as regards the raw materials of cooking, from berries to

[10] And probably farther east too: 'The people of La Baye . . . made it clear to the Outaoüas that, if they stayed away from their wives for a long time, the latter would go hungry, since they did not know how to catch fish' (Perrot, p. 134).

[11] Nimuendaju (5, p. 94) records contrary evidence in the case of the Apinayé, and says that men, women and children all took part in fishing by means of poison. Maybury-Lewis, on the other hand, maintains that, among the Shavanté, the women never do any fishing. In *The Raw and the Cooked* (pp. 276–8) I put forward various reasons for believing that, throughout most of Central Brazil, fishing was an exclusively male occupation. The available evidence does not allow us to decide with certainty whether the taboo on the participation of women no longer applies farther north, or whether it takes the weak form of a division of labour – the men preparing and spreading the fish poison, and the women simply collecting the drugged fish in their baskets.

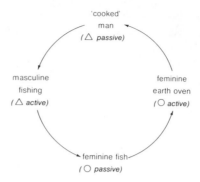

Figure 38. The origin of fish

salmon by way of roots and tubers and, as regards the means of cooking, from the raw to the boiled by way of preparation in the earth oven. Similarly, the Wasco myth M_{663a} (see above, p. 345) proclaims the superiority of the boiled over the roasted, roasting being understood as direct contact with the glowing embers. In South America, the Bororo, who do not have earth ovens, rate boiling as being superior to all other modes of cooking; and the Ge, who do not boil food since they do not make pottery, and rarely heat water with red-hot stones except to warm and soften the fruit of the bacaba palm (Nim. 5, p. 96; Lowie 13, p. 383), regard the earth oven as a refined method of cooking, which confers on its practitioners an undoubted superiority over their less civilized neighbours (according to a personal communication from T. S. Turner).

We can dismiss at once the outmoded theory that the absence of pottery among the Ge and the North American communities living to the west of the Rockies and in the Plains was due to a lack of technical ability, or to the impossibility of finding suitable clay. In case of need, the Okanagon would dig holes in clayey soil, fill them with water, and use them for cooking food by dropping in heated stones (Teit 6, pp. 230, 278); in 1929, the Sanpoil could still point out along the banks of the Columbia River excellent white clay which had previously served them for the making of jars that they dried in the sun, lined with fish skin, and used exclusively for drawing water.

The Arapaho, who have figured largely in my argument, made pottery until quite recently (Kroeber 3, p. 25), and shards have been discovered in territory now occupied by the Ge (Lowie 13, pp. 386–7). Those communities which are so backward technologically that they are incapable of making pottery can be counted on the fingers of one hand, and the explanation appears quite absurd when applied to the Ge, the Sahaptin or the Salish. On the contrary, the whole trend of my analysis of the images and beliefs relating to the earth oven has tended to show that the reason why certain tribes with earth ovens do not make pottery is that they sense, more or less consciously, what might be termed a philosophical incompatibility between the two techniques.

This natural philosophy, which prevails over vast and widely separated areas of the New World, is not present in certain more restricted regions, such as the Chaco, where pottery was in general use, but where several tribes – Matako, Choroti, Ashluslay, Tsirakua and Ayoré – built earth ovens, sometimes with chimneys running obliquely through them to provide ventilation. In the north of the Argentine, where the art of pottery was highly developed in prehistoric times, there are ample traces of underground constructions, which were probably ovens, although it is impossible to say whether they were used for cooking food or for the firing of ceramic objects.

We cannot claim, then, that pottery and earth ovens were incompatible in this area of America. But there is an aspect of the structural approach that I must emphasize, particularly in these concluding pages: far from trying to establish the singleness and all-pervading nature of any mythic pattern, I recognize that a particular pattern, however basic it may appear to be, usually gives rise to its opposite, either through an immediate, mirror-image effect, or as the ultimate outcome of a process of elaboration. It is appropriate, then, to find room to mention here a transformation that I cannot discuss thoroughly, since to do so would make this volume quite unwieldy; its basic premises – which involve far-ranging enquiries – were established in my 1964–5 lectures at the Collège de France. Suffice it to say that this transformation, which can be observed in the Chaco area of South America and along the middle reaches of the Amazon, is also to be found in Central America and in North America among the so-called Plains village tribes. Whether or not it makes pottery and the earth ovens compatible with each other – and its consequences are not worked out to that point by all the communities concerned – it rests on a more general pattern involving a shift in the emphasis of mythic thought; the emphasis moves from the earth-dwellers' conquest of fire in the sky to the granting, to earth dwellers, of clay and the mysterious art of pottery by supernatural beings, who are both aquatic and chthonian. The earth oven and pottery, which are incompatible in respect of the earth-sky axis, become compatible then in respect of an axis which has the earth as one of its poles and water and the chthonian world as the other (cf. RC, pp. 247–8, 321–3; OTM, p. 77, n. 7).

Where the incompatibility exists, it does not affect cooking by boiling either, if such cooking is done in wooden, bark or watertight basketwork receptacles, into which heated stones are plunged. As happens with the oven, the stones or fragments of baked earth function in this case as if they belonged to nature and fire, and not to food and culture. It is, then, as if the earth oven were an operator which reversed the respective values attributed elsewhere to the roast and the boiled; this is because it represents a superior culinary technique more closely allied to boiling by means of heated stones than to cooking directly on red-hot embers. Although the latter method is objectively a form of roasting, the earth oven, as it were, attracts the other technique to itself, and thus gives this particular form of boiling precedence over roasting pure and simple.

Consequently, the Ge, who do not boil food, consider oven-baking to be superior to roasting over an open fire or on hot ashes. The Salish and their neighbours, who boil food in containers made from bark, wood or basketwork, into which red-hot stones are placed, consider that boiling is superior to oven-roasting, and oven-roasting superior to roasting on hot embers. In this meta-system, the Bororo again occupy a median position:

$$Salish, \text{ etc.:} \quad \text{boiling} > \text{oven-roasting} > \text{direct roasting;}$$
$$Bororo: \quad \text{boiling} > \quad O \quad > \text{direct roasting;}$$
$$Ge: \quad O \quad > \text{oven-roasting} > \text{direct roasting.}$$

On the level of the myths, this conceptualization of the infrastructure is expressed by an ideology in which the conquest of fire alone may be taken as reflecting the primacy of the earth oven, and the combined conquest of fire and water the primacy of cooking by boiling. The Ge myths express the first, the Bororo myths the second, and the Salish – who possess the most complete culinary system – have myths which combine both types of narrative.

But, throughout the vast mythic field we have explored, it is undoubtedly the earth oven which, by its presence or its absence, acts as a pivotal factor. In several Ge versions of the bird-nester myth (M_7, M_8, M_{12}), the hero throws a stone (which he has sometimes taken from his mouth, M_{12}) at his brother-in-law, instead of the young birds he has been sent by the latter to obtain from the top of a tree. According to M_8, he throws down stones he has found in the nest, and the myth states clearly that these stones are round. One observer (Frikel 3, p. 15) notes, in connection with the Xikrin, another Kayapo group, that 'oven stones are always smooth, round or oval in shape, and are taken from the river bed', in other words, they have been rendered smooth through being rolled together in the water. These seemingly trifling details take on an increasingly definite significance as we survey the whole North American field. The Arapaho myths, for a start, describe the projectile hurled by the moon at his human wife in order to kill her and prevent her descent from the sky to the earth as a 'heated stone' (M_{428}; Dorsey 5, p. 223); it is obviously the sort of stone that the Arapaho, who had lost the art of making pottery, used for boiling water in a hole made in the ground (therefore congruous with the earth oven), and lined with raw hide (Kroeber 3, p. 25). In versions of the same myth originating among the central and eastern Algonquin ($M_{437-438}$, M_{444}), the hero called Loon or Clad-in-Wampum is killed by a red-hot stone being thrown into his mouth while he is asleep. This motif – the introduction of a red-hot stone into the body of a character who is thus symbolically transformed into an earth oven – occurs at various points, sporadically no doubt but with astonishing persistence, in all the modalities of the great mythological transformation to which the four volumes of this work have been devoted: from the Maidu of California (M_{636}) to the Assiniboine and the Cree ($M_{766a, b}$), by way of the Okanagon (M_{733}) and the Sanpoil (M_{737}); and southwards, as far as the Dakota (M_{769b}) and the Navajo (M_{776b}). Even along the frontiers of the transformational group, the earth oven is embodied by a chthonian or trickster character: for instance, in the Klamath versions of the bird-nester (M_{538}); in the Cowlitz versions of the quarrel between the two bears where Grizzly Woman's father is called Hot-Rock, or Bake-on-hot-rocks (M_{615b}: Adamson, pp. 211–13; M_{615c}; Jacobs 1, pp. 159–63); and lastly, in the Navajo myth M_{775b}, where Coyote perishes through swallowing a red-hot stone coated with food, while the Pleiades appear in the sky as a stellar counterpart of the glowing embers in the earth oven, the use of which was known among the Navajo (Franciscan Fathers, pp. 207, 208, 218).

It will not have passed unnoticed that, in all the examples I have quoted, the image of the earth oven is presented in a negative form, as the cause or effect of a disjunction, and as the means of destroying an opponent, often a man-eating, chthonian monster. We are dealing, then, with an oven which is operating, as it were, in reverse: we might call it an anti-oven, and indeed the use of this term can immediately be justified.

In so far as all these myths belong to the bird-nester cycle, they refer, directly or indirectly, to a period when cooking fire did not yet exist. Consequently, at this stage, the image of the earth oven as a supreme manifestation of culinary art, could be no more than potential: only the conquest of fire could make it actual. It follows that the anticipatory image of the earth oven proposed by the myths about the origin of fire is therefore inverted, in relation to a real object which has not yet come into being, like the image of an object placed outside a *camera obscura*, and the light rays from which fuse and intersect, as they pass inwards through the aperture. The latter is a spatial metaphor for the major event which, in the time of the myths, marks the transition from the state of nature to the constitution of society.

This event, crucial for the life and future of mankind, is, as we know, the theft of fire from the sky by a terrestrial hero who, by going there either voluntarily or against his will, brings into play an opposition which is deemed essential in mythic thought and is perhaps the root-source of other religious images, including those of our own culture. 'In the last resort', writes M. E. Benveniste (Vol. II, p. 180), 'the only thing that the Indo-European community can be credited with is the idea of "god". It is widely in evidence in the form *deiwos*, the literal meaning of which is "luminous" and "celestial"; in this respect, gods are opposed to human beings, who are "terrestrial" (this, indeed, is the meaning of the Latin word *homo*).'

But if the opposition is so widely accepted, this must be because it has a basis in reality. In recognizing the fact we are in agreement with a thinker who cannot be suspected of having any nostalgia for the distant past:

> In spite of the gigantic liberating revolution in the social world which the steam-engine is carrying through . . . it is beyond all doubt that the generation of fire by friction had an even greater effect on the liberation of mankind. For the generation of fire by friction gave man for the first time control over the forces of nature, and thereby separated him for ever from the animal kingdom . . . how ridiculous it would be to attempt to ascribe any absolute validity to our present views, is evident from the simple fact that all past history can be characterized as the history of the epoch from the practical discovery of the transformation of mechanical motion into heat up to that of transformation of heat into mechanical motion (Engels, *Anti-Dühring*, p. 159, The Foreign Language Publishing House, Moscow, 1954).

To take one last example, equidistant from America and Europe, the pygmies of the mountains of New Guinea say that the first man came down from the sky by means of a rope, and discovered on earth all the animals, which he proceded to cook in an earth oven. He then noticed that the rope had been cut. His wife, whom he had left behind in the sky, heard his lamentations, and threw fire and edible plants down to him. Among the plants were four cucumbers which turned into women, whom he then married; they planted his garden, and bore him two daughters and two sons, who were the ancestors of humanity (Aufenanger 2, pp. 247–9). Consequently, in this case too, future mankind receives cooking fire *in exchange* for the interruption of the communication which once existed between the earth and the sky.

However, we also know that, in America at least, this cosmological pattern is accompanied by a sociological pattern, to which it closely adheres. If the matter is looked at in this light, givers and takers of women are in opposition to each other on the social axis, just as, on the world axis, the earth is opposed to the sky, and the earth in turn to the underworld. So, if primaeval fire is found on the side of the sky, and its necessary receptacle – later to become the oven – on the side of the earth, it follows that the women exchanged through the process of matrimonial alliances, perform, between givers and takers, the same mediatory function as that which, by virtue of the inherent logic of the system, they must also assume between fire and earth. It is they, then, who must look after the oven.[12] To assert their presence in the system, men must choose one of two alternatives: either they can play a passive role in women's work, in the form of stones or fire, which they embody in certain myths, or they can claim an exclusive and active role in the area complementary to that of the earth oven – that of the raw and of water. In this case, they alone have the right to take part in collective fishing, at the same time as the myths allow them to transform women symbolically into fish, i.e., the passive objects of the activity.

Of all culinary techniques, cooking in the earth oven would appear, then, to be the one which reveals most meaningfully a close and formal homology between infrastructure and ideology. Because of its often considerable complexity of structure, its nature as a collective undertaking, the traditional knowledge and attention needed to ensure its correct functioning and the slowness of the cooking process, which sometimes lasted several days, and was accompanied until the final moment by uncertainty as to the outcome – an uncertainty rendered all the more acute by the fact that enormous quantities of food, representing the provisions of one or more families and their only hope of surviving the winter, were irredeemably entrusted to it, on, or even in, the earth – the oven bears witness to the presence and power of fire; every time it is lit, it contributes a majestic commemoration of the primaeval conflict, which was an anticipatory image of all those subsequent conflicts, culminating eventually in the conquest of fire. So, as a technique, it remains closely allied to a heroic mythology, as

---

[12] The situation is different in certain areas of New Guinea, where the ritual use of the oven is restricted to men, perhaps because, in New Guinea, women are given a celestial polarity.

can be sensed by anyone who has experienced the joyful and fervently ritualistic atmosphere of a clambake on some New England beach. Because of its heroic character, such a mythology — at least among the Ge, the Sahaptin and the Salish — is opposed to, and even incompatible with, the use of earthenware vessels for the boiling of food, these utensils being symbolic of what might be called fruitful but stay-at-home cooking. The opposition is also suggestive of others, such as that pointed out by M. Dumézil (2, pp. 135–59) between heroic death, followed by cremation of the corpse, and fertile death by drowning or followed by burial.

So, at the same time as we glimpse a system of categories which lends itself to many and various transformations and which, in its essence, may indeed be universal (since it probably also includes initiation ordeals or rites of passage, involving either symbolic removal of flesh by means of scarification, flagellation or poisonous insects, or, on the other hand, symbolic cooking, cf. *RC*, pp. 334–7), we come to understand how the modest account of a family quarrel that I took as my starting-point, contains the whole system in embryo, and how the, for us, insignificant act of striking a match to kindle a flame perpetuates, in the very midst of our mechanized civilization, an experience which, once for the whole of mankind, and even now for a few last survivors, was, or remains, invested with great solemnity, since it is a symbolic gesture holding in balance the most profoundly meaningful oppositions that it is given to the mind of man to conceive: between the sky and the earth on the level of the physical world, between man and woman on the level of the natural world, and between relations by marriage on the level of the social world.

Finale

. . . lastly, all the chapters are prefaced by strange and mysterious epigraphs, which considerably enhance the interest of, and give character to, each part of the composition.

Victor Hugo, *Han d'Islande,*
Preface to the first edition

Throughout these pages, the 'we' the author has deliberately adhered to has not been meant simply as an expression of diffidence.[1] It also indicated a deeper concern to reduce the subject to what, in an undertaking of this kind, he ought to try to be – if indeed he can ever, in any circumstances, be anything else: the insubstantial place or space where anonymous thought can develop, stand back from itself, find and fulfil its true tendencies and achieve organization, while coming to terms with the constraints inherent in its very nature. If there is one conviction that has been intimately borne upon the author of this work during twenty years devoted to the study of myths – these volumes cover only the last eight years – it is that the solidity of the self, the major preoccupation of the whole of Western philosophy, does not withstand persistent application to the same object, which comes to pervade it through and through and to imbue it with an experiential awareness of its own unreality. For the only remnant of reality to which it still dares to lay claim is that of being a 'singularity', in the sense in which astronomers use the term: a point in space and a moment in time, relative to each other, and in which there have occurred, are occurring or will occur events whose density (itself in turn relative to other events, no less real but

[1] TRANSLATORS' NOTE: The first person plural pronoun, *nous*, is commonly used in French academic writing instead of the singular, *je*, because of the conventional belief that it is more modest and objective. It is, of course, a purely rhetorical device, since the adjectives qualifying it are put in the singular, not the plural. In English, the corresponding use of the plural, the 'editorial we', tends to sound more stilted, and so, from the outset, we have often translated *nous* by 'I', and can only continue to do so in this final section. But, in the original, the author has consistently avoided *je*.

more widely dispersed) makes possible its approximate definition, always remembering of course that this nodal point of past, present and probable events does not exist as a substratum, but only in the sense that phenomena are occurring in it, and in spite of the fact that these phenomena, of which it is the place of intersection, originate from countless other sources, for the most part unknown.

But why, it may be asked, should one have such reservations with regard to the subject when dealing with myths, that is, with stories which could not have come into being unless at some moment — even though, in most cases, that moment is beyond the reach of enquiry — each of them had been conceived and narrated in the first instance by a particular individual? Utterance is a function confined to subjects, and every myth, in the last resort, must have its origin in an individual act of creation. This is no doubt very true but, in order to achieve the status of myth, the created work must cease precisely to be individual and, in the process of generalization, must lose the essential part of those factors determined by probability with which it was infused at the outset, and which could be attributed to the particular author's temperament, talent, imagination and personal experiences. Since myths depend on oral transmission and collective tradition, the probabilist levels they include are continuously eroded, because of their lesser resistance to social attrition, than those levels which are more firmly organized, through corresponding to shared needs. It will be readily agreed, then that the difference between individually created works and myths which are recognized as such by a given community is one not of nature but of degree. In this respect, structural analysis can be legitimately applied to myths stemming from a collective tradition as well as to works by a single author, since in both cases the intention is the same: to give a structural explanation of that which can be so explained, and which is never everything; and beyond that, to seek to grasp, in varying degrees according to circumstances, another kind of determinism which has to be looked for at the statistical or sociological levels, i.e., in the life-story of the individual and in the particular society or environment.

Let us recognize, then, that all literary creative work, whether oral or written, cannot, at the outset, be other than individual. When it is immediately taken over by oral tradition, as is the case in communities without writing, only the structured levels will remain stable, since they rest on common foundations, whereas the probabilist levels will be subject to extreme variability resulting from the personalities of successive narrators. However, during the process of oral transmission, these probabilist levels will rub against each other and wear each other down, thus gradually separating off from the bulk of the text what might be called its crystalline parts. All individual works are potential myths, but only if they are adopted by the collectivity as a whole do they achieve 'mythic' status.

It can be seen from this how far genuine structuralist interpretations differ from those practised by psychoanalysis or by schools of thought which claim to reduce the structure of a collective or individual work to what they mistakenly call its genesis. Not that I am unaware of the fact that every structure must have a genesis. In his recent and excellent little book on Structuralism, Piaget says I am unaware of this (p. 97), but his criticism seems to arise from a misunderstanding. It can be readily admitted that every structure has a genesis, provided we also recognize that – as Piaget's book demonstrates – each anterior state of a structure is itself a structure. 'It is not obvious why it should be unreasonable to think that the ultimate nature of reality is a constant process of construction instead of an accumulation of ready-made structures' (Piaget, p. 58). Indeed, but the process consists of structures which are undergoing transformation to produce other structures, so that *structure itself is a primordial fact*. Less confusion would have occurred in connection with the concept of human nature, that I continue to use, if it had been realized that I do not take it in the sense of a heap of completed and immutable structures, but rather with the meaning of matrices giving rise to structures all belonging to the same set, without necessarily remaining identical throughout any individual existence from birth to adulthood, or, in the case of human groups, at all times and in all places.

However, psychoanalysis and the so-called genetic schools of thought take a different view of genesis from that about which Piaget and myself might more easily reach agreement. Far from recognizing that, as Piaget puts it, 'in reality as in mathematics, every form is a content for the forms comprising it and every content is a form for the contents it contains' (p. 95), these people try to explain types of categories by reducing them to contents which are not of the same kind and which, through the operation of a remarkable contradiction, are supposed to modify their form from without. Genuine structuralism, on the contrary, seeks first and foremost to grasp the intrinsic properties of certain types of categories. These properties do not express anything external to themselves. Or, if it is felt that they really must refer to something external, that point of reference has to be the organization of the brain envisaged as a network whose various properties are expressed by the most divergent ideological systems in terms of some particular structure, with each system revealing, in its own way, modes of interconnection of the network.

But this philosophic caution, which makes it possible to avoid the pitfalls of reductionist interpretations, is also a strength. It supposes that each suggested new interpretation of a myth – and this means, for a start, my own interpretations – takes its place in sequence after the already known variants of that myth (L.-S. 5, p. 240). But, it will be asked, does this not shut you off inside a circle where each form, having been immediately transformed into a content, requires to be explained by another form, thus creating an infinite regress? On the contrary, it follows from the preceding argument that the criterion of structural interpretation avoids this paradox, since only structural interpretation can account both for itself and for the other kinds. In so far as it consists in making explicit a system of relationships that the other variants merely embodied, it integrates them with itself and integrates itself with them on a new level, where the definitive fusion of content and form can take place and will therefore no longer lend itself to new embodiments. The structure of the myth, having been revealed to itself, brings to a close the series of its possible developments.

It can thus be seen how the elimination of the subject represents what might be called a methodological need: it corresponds to the scrupulous desire to explain no part of the myth except by the myth, and consequently to exclude the point of view of an arbiter looking at the myth from outside and therefore inclined to propose extrinsic causes for it. On the contrary, it must be recognized as a fact that behind each mythic system there loom others, which were the dominant factors in determining it; it is these other systems which speak through it and echo each other down the ages, if not indefinitely at least as far back as that irrecoverable moment in time, hundreds of thousands of years ago – or perhaps even longer ago still, as may one day be claimed – when mankind, in the beginning, produced its first myths. This is not to say that, at each stage of this complex development, the myth, in passing from one community to another, has not been modified by the proximity of different techno-economic infrastructures which exert an attraction on it. It has to adapt to their mechanisms, and I have shown again and again that, in order to understand the differential gaps between versions of the same myth belonging to different communities, sometimes close neighbours, sometimes geographically remote from each other, the infrastructure has to be taken into account.

Each version of the myth, then, shows the influence of a twofold determinism: one strand links it to a succession of previous versions or to a set of foreign versions, while the other operates as it were transversally, through the constraints arising from the infrastructure which necessitate the modification of some particular element, with the result that the system undergoes reorganization in order to adapt these differences to necessities of an external kind. But there are only two possibilities: either the infrastructure is identical with the kind of things which it is supposed to bring into play and, in that case, it is as inert and passive as the things themselves, and can engender nothing; or it belongs to the realm of lived-in experience and is therefore in a perpetual state of imbalance and tension: in this case, the myths cannot derive from it through a causality that would very rapidly become tautological. They should be seen rather as constituting local and temporary answers to the problems raised by feasible adjustments and insoluble contradictions that they are endeavouring to legitimize or conceal. The content with which the myth endows itself is not anterior, but posterior, to this initial impulse: far from deriving from some content or other, the myth moves towards a particular content through the attraction of its specific gravity. In each individual case, it alienates, in the process, part of its apparent liberty which, looked at from another angle, is no more than an aspect of its own necessity. The origin of this necessity is lost in the mists of time; it lies in the depths of the mind, and its spontaneous unfolding is slowed down, accelerated, deflected or bifurcated through the action of historical constraints which couple it, so to speak, with other mechanisms that its effects have to be reconciled with, but without involving a departure from its original direction.

The subject, while remaining deliberately in the background so as to allow free play to this anonymous deployment of discourse, does not renounce consciousness of it, or rather does not prevent it achieving consciousness of itself through him. Some people pretend to believe that the criticism of consciousness should lead, logically, to the renunciation of conscious thought. But I have never had any other intention than to further knowledge, i.e., *to achieve consciousness*. However, for too long now philosophy has succeeded in locking the social sciences inside a closed circle by not allowing them to envisage any other object of study for the consciousness than consciousness itself. This accounts, on the one hand, for the powerlessness of the social sciences in practice, and on the other for their self-deluding nature, the characteristic of consciousness being that it deceives itself. What structuralism tries to accomplish in the wake of Rousseau, Marx, Durkheim, Saussure and Freud, is to reveal to consciousness *an object other than itself*; and therefore to put it in the same position with regard to human phenomena as that of the natural and physical sciences, and which, as they have demonstrated, alone allows knowledge to develop. Recognition of the fact that consciousness is not everything, nor even the most important thing, is not a reason for abandoning it, any more than the principles professed a few years ago by the Existentialist philosophers obliged them to lead a life of debauchery in the cellars of Saint-Germain-des-Prés. Quite the opposite, in fact, since consciousness is thus able to gauge the immensity of its task and to summon up the courage to embark upon it, with the hope at last that it will not be doomed to sterility.

But this assumption of consciousness remains intellectual in character, that is to say it does not substantially differ from the realities to which it is applied; it is these very realities arriving at their own truth. There can be no question, then, of smuggling the subject in again, under this new guise. I could have no tolerance for a form of deceit in which the left hand slips under the table to restore to the worst kind of philosophy what the right hand claims to have taken from it above board, and which, through simply replacing the Self by the Other and by sliding a metaphysics of desire under the logic of the concept, deprives this logic of its foundation. By substituting for the Self on the one hand an anonymous Other, and on the other hand an individualized desire (individualized, because, were it not so, it would signify nothing), one would fail to hide the fact that they need only be stuck together again and the resulting entity reversed to recognize underneath that very Self, whose abolition had been so loudly proclaimed. If there is a point at which the Self can reappear, it is only after the completion of the work which excluded it throughout (since, contrary to what might be supposed, it was not so much the case that the Self was the author as that the work, during the process of composition, became the creator of an executant who lived only by and through it); then, it can and must take an overall view of the whole, in the same way as the readers who will peruse the text without having found themselves in the dangerous situation of feeling prompted to write it. This finale, headed by an epigraph which is unlike the preceding ones and is meant as a commentary on them, is itself in the nature of a commentary on a completed work, from which the writer is trying to deduce his own conclusions, now that his mission is over and he is again free to speak in the first person singular.[2]

When I look back over my work, there is one thing that strikes me, and all the more sharply in that it was not intentional on my part. In beginning my enquiry with myths of the southern hemisphere, and gradually shifting it to the northern and western areas of the northern hemisphere, I have gone, as it were, against the grain of American history, since the peopling of the continent clearly took place for the most part in the opposite direction. Was this procedure useful or necessary, independently of the personal reasons

[2] TRANSLATORS' NOTE: From this point onwards, the author uses *je* instead of *nous* in the original.

which made it easier for me to deal with the myths of communities I had myself observed? I think so, but largely for a different reason, connected with the peculiar nature of ethnographical enquiry: the South American mythic corpus, being far less rich than the North American, is more appropriate for preliminary study, because it can be looked at as if from a distance: it is simplified, and its very poverty reduces it to its essential features. The North American corpus, on the other hand, appears so abundant, complex and detailed that, had I begun with it, my analysis might have been side-tracked. The investigation of South American sources, although apparently less rewarding, made it possible to save time. But I have often wondered whether, had I begun at the other end, the result would have been the same. I would probably not have chosen the same reference myth: the material used by the North American versions is so rich and varied that the myth does not stand out so sharply from the corpus. On the other hand, is it certain that since South America was peopled by way of North America, the South American versions of the reference myth represent more recent and defective forms? The contrary could be the case if the same myth, while being worked upon at length and transformed in North America, had preserved more of its initial freshness and simplicity in South America. If this is so, the sequence chosen corresponds to the sequence in reality. But it is very important that the order of ideas in these four volumes should not be seen as a linear programme. By means of myths introduced in the second volume, and following on from those presented in the first, we moved, in the third volume, from South America to North America, thanks to *inverted* myths with *identical* meanings. In the fourth volume, we have come back from North America to South America thanks to *identical* myths (since $M_{524-531}$ correspond to M_1, M_{7-12}) with *inverted* meanings. The astronomical code gives particularly clear expression to this two-way movement, since it has allowed us to show how a hero who, to start with, personifies the *Corvus* constellation (M_1) first assumes the functional role attributed to Orion ($M_{557-558}$), and then is finally identified with the latter constellation in phasal opposition to the former (M_{575}), which is personified, in South America (M_{124}) by a hero whose adventures are also in opposition to those of his North American counterpart.

But it is not on ethnographical grounds that my critics, for the most part, have chosen to attack me. They have usually raised methodological objections, some of which are so feeble that it would be unkind to mention the names of their originators. I propose to deal with them rapidly to clear the ground before moving on to more serious matters.

I have been accused of basing my analyses on summaries of myths, without first submitting the myths to textual criticism. Let me begin with the second point. No one with the slightest knowledge of the subject can have failed to notice that, in spite of the abundance of the material dealt with, it represents only a tiny fraction of the myths of both hemispheres that I might have used. Perhaps it is thought that I chose my documentation at random or according to personal convenience. Behind the thousand or so myths or variants of myths that I have commented on lie many others that I have examined, briefly analysed and have not included for various reasons, in which textual criticism had its part, but always kept in check by the conviction that, except in those cases where there is glaring evidence to prove the point, myths do not exist in 'good' and 'bad' versions; at any rate, it is not the analyst's business to decide the issue in the light of criteria foreign to the object he is studying: it would be truer to say that the myths criticize and select themselves, opening up, through the confused mass of the corpus, certain paths which would not have been the same, had one particular myth rather than another been the first to emerge. But not only have I, for my own enlightenment, constantly criticized my sources, without feeling the need to keep the reader informed of these preliminary phases of the enquiry, which were not his concern; also, whenever possible, that is, whenever the native text was available in languages for which there were also dictionaries and grammars, I have taken care to check the translation with the original, and this has sometimes enabled me – for instance, in the case of the Klamath myths recorded by Barker (see above, pp. 52, 60, 73, 83–4) – to throw light on certain points that were not clear in the version as printed.

As for the summaries which, I admit, have often given me more trouble than the actual commentaries, they have never been used as a basis for exegesis. They are intended for the reader and give him a general view of each myth, until such time as the discussion gradually brings in details and shades of meaning which could not be included in the body of the summary. I have too great a mistrust of summaries to admit that they could serve any other purpose; experience has taught me how impossible it is to grasp the spirit of a myth without steeping oneself in the complete versions, however diffuse they may be, and submitting to a slow process of incubation requiring hours, days, months – or sometimes even years – until one's thought, guided unconsciously by tiny details, succeeds in embracing the essential nature of the myth. The summary, as I use it, has no analytical function, but only serves as the starting-point for a synthetic account which enriches it with additional detail, until the complete myth has been successfully reconstituted and interpreted as an organic whole.

No less inadequate are those critics who claim to show that I am contradicting myself because I am supposed to have asserted, on the one hand, that the analysis of myths is endless and that the myths themselves are *in-terminable* (*RC*, p. 6), and on the other (*passim*) that the group of myths I have studied constitutes a closed system. To argue in this fashion is to fail to understand the difference between the mythic discourse of any community, which, like any discourse, remains open-ended — every myth can have a sequel, new variants may appear or new myths come into being — and the 'language' (*langue*) brought into play by the discourse, and which, at any particular moment, forms a system.[3] It is in relationship to itself, and considered as a discourse unfolding diachronically, that a mythology remains unclosed. But the open-endedness of this *parole*, in the Saussurian sense of the term, does not mean that the 'language' on which it depends is not closed in relation to other systems, also envisaged synchronically, rather in the way a cylinder might be said to be a closed surface, and would remain so, even if it were extended indefinitely through time at one end: an observer could claim to have seen round it and to be able to work out the formula for the calculation, at any moment, of the volume involved, even if he never succeeded in following it along its whole length.

Other critics have claimed that the method I use has shown a constant regression from one book to the next, and that this is evidence of its inadequacy. The argument has been applied to the first three volumes of this *Introduction to a Science of Mythology* on the curious ground that tables and diagrams, of which abundant use was made in the first volume, became less frequent in the second, and still more so in the third, before — as will now be pointed out — disappearing almost completely from this last volume. But these tables and diagrams are illustrations, not a means of proof, and their function is primarily explanatory. Once the reader has been sufficiently enlightened by their use, he does not need to have them inflicted upon him at every turn. If he finds it a useful exercise, as I myself have done throughout the work, he is free to take pencil and paper and, at every comparison of two or more myths, to convert into diagrammatic form the elucidation that I have thought fit to give in discursive prose in order to save time and space (a diagram never absolves one from the explanation, without which it would be unintelligible), and also, to be quite frank, to reduce printing costs. But throughout the whole process of analysis, I have never stopped drawing up such tables and diagrams for my own guidance, and as frequently as at the beginning, the only difference being that I no longer

[3] TRANSLATORS' NOTE: The author uses *discours* and *parole* as synonyms, in opposition to *la langue*, in the Saussurian sense.

thought it useful to include them in the text. However, any attentive reader will notice that each time I compare two or more myths, I am describing, and commenting on, an implicit table or diagram in which the homologous terms of several syntagmatic chains are superimposed, item by item.

Some critics have gone further still in accusing me, rather inconsistently, of using symbols borrowed from the typographical language of logic and mathematics to compose formulae which, for them, are devoid of any validity or significance – although I discussed this point frankly at the outset (*RC*, p. 31), when I made it clear that these formulae are not instruments of proof but shorthand patterns or expressions – while at the same time reproaching me with having changed my ground between 1955, when I wrote an article welcoming the general introduction of mathematics into the social sciences (L.-S. 22), and the end of the overture to *The Raw and the Cooked*, where I confessed my inability to deal with myths in a logico-mathematical fashion. Such critics thus betray a total ignorance of matters about which they boldly claim to express opinions. My 1955 article dealt with the treatment of kinship systems by means of set theory, which was initiated by André Weil in one of my books (L.-S. 2, Ch. XIV), and which quickly started a new trend; since 1949, so many volumes and articles have followed up this theme that there now exists what might be called a mathematics of kinship, to the inception of which I claim to have made no other contribution than to have formulated the problems in a style capable of attracting the attention of mathematicians and encouraging them to take over from anthropologists, who had reached a point where the complexity of the problems defeated their rudimentary methodology and brought them to a halt.

However, the study of myths raises much more difficult issues and which do not arise simply from the fact that, of this vast field, we can never hope to know more than certain fragmentary and partial aspects which, before they come into our ken, have already been subjected to all kinds of upheavals and phenomena of erosion. Each particular body of myth, even if we supposed it to be ideally intact, although reality offers no such example, can only be apprehended in a process of becoming and, for reasons already explained (see above, p. 626), it carries along with it, and engenders in the course of its oral transmission, probabilist levels which, at best, will only make it possible to single out and define restricted areas where phenomena are completely determined. This state of affairs need not lead to discouragement, since it is not so very different from that which physicists have to deal with in studying the most stable and highly organized forms of matter. As one of them has written: 'At the beginning of the century physicists were busy pointing out that crystals are orderly arrays of atoms, ions or molecules. More recently, they have been just as busy insisting that the order is limited, and that imperfections are always present because of impurities or native irregularities' (Henisch, p. 30). Nevertheless, crystallography exists, and the prospects for the structural analysis of myths are not jeopardized by the knowledge that it can only fully operate on certain favourable aspects of its subject matter.

The difficulties in the way of a logico-mathematical treatment of myth, which can nevertheless be seen to be desirable and possible, are of a different order. They are linked in the first place with the problem of arriving at an unequivocal definition of the constituent elements of myths either as terms or as relations; according to the variants being considered and the different stages of the analysis, each term can appear as a relation and each relation as a term. Secondly, these relations illustrate types of symmetry which are different from each other, and too numerous to be described in the limited vocabulary of contrariness, contradiction and their opposites. This second difficulty is still further increased by the fact that the elements defined as such for the purposes of the analysis are, themselves, more often than not, complex entities that the analyst has been unable to break down for want of the appropriate techniques. Thus it is that mythological analysis, without always being fully aware of the fact, is dealing not so much with simple terms and relations as with bundles of terms and bundles of relations which it classifies and defines in an inevitably crude and clumsy fashion.

It was through being conscious of these obstacles that I felt unable to promise, for the structural study of myths, the same rapid progress on the logico-mathematical level as was accomplished twenty years ago in the study of marriage rules and kinship systems. Since then, both in France and the United States, mathematicians have drawn my attention to the fact that a recent development of their subject, known as category theory, might make it possible to treat myths by means of the same methods as are applied to kinship data (Lorrain 1, 2); I have been given to understand that promising work along these lines has already been done on the basis of *An Introduction to a Science of Mythology*. The definition of categories, as systems formed both by a set of terms and by the set of relations between these terms, corresponds closely to that which can be given of myth, and the concept of morphism, which expresses nothing more than the existence of a relation between two terms without any indication of its logical nature, seems to overcome the same kind of dilemma as was solved for me twenty-five years ago when, after I had been told by a famous mathematician of the old school that he could not help me to clarify kinship problems because he was acquainted only with addition, subtraction, multiplication and division, and marriage could not be likened to any of these operations, a young mathematician to whom I have already referred by name, assured me that it was a matter of indifference to him to know what marriage might be, mathematically speaking, provided it were possible to define the relation between the different types of marriage.

The caution I expressed at the beginning of this new venture was, then, in no sense a recantation. It is to be explained by the emergence of new problems, the difficulty of which I realized at the outset, when I admitted that I was trying to blaze a trail in an area where 'everything, or almost everything, still remained to be done before there could be any question of genuine scientific knowledge' (RC, statement on the back cover of the original French version); I was incidentally convinced that others, helped perhaps by the fact that I had cleared the ground, would shoulder the task of solving these problems by the use of new logico-mathematical instruments, more finely tuned than those which have already proved effective in less complex areas.

It is true that, in order to imprison me within a contradiction of another kind, a prejudicial objection has been made to my openly expressed desire for the use of logico-mathematical instruments. These instruments, it is said, belong to the epistemological equipment of our own culture; in wishing to apply them to material deriving from different societies to improve such knowledge as we can have of these societies, I am said to display a naïve ethnocentrism and to be transposing, on to the level of knowledge, the ethnocentrism I claim to be breaking free from by seeking, in the underlying logic of the myths, the rules engendering the authentic discourse of each community. But – and I shall have occasion to return to this point (see below, p. 639) – cultural relativism would be puerile if, in conceding the richness of civilizations different from our own, and the impossibility of arriving at any moral or philosophical criterion by which to decide the respective values of the choices which have led each civilization to prefer certain ways of life and thought while rejecting others, it felt itself obliged to adopt a condescending or disdainful attitude towards scientific knowledge which, however harmful it may have been, and further threatens to be, in its applications, is nevertheless a mode of knowledge whose absolute superiority cannot be denied. It is true that scientific knowledge came into being, and has developed, with a total disregard for other modes of knowledge, because of their practical inefficiency in respect of the new aims which it had in view. For too long, this intellectual divide has, perhaps inevitably, caused us to lose sight of certain aspects of reality that are now almost forgotten, and that the forms of knowledge best adapted to them formulated in terms of genuine problems, which scientific knowledge brushed aside as being insignificant, when in fact its initial lines of development did not allow it to understand the interest of these problems, and still less to solve them. Only during the last few years has science taken a different turn. By venturing into areas close to human sensibility, areas which may seem novel but which in fact it is only rediscovering, it is proving that, from now on, knowledge can progress only by broadening out to comprehend other forms of knowledge; and to comprehend should be taken here with the meaning of to understand and to include. It follows that the development of knowledge goes hand in hand with a gradual widening of the framework traditionally assigned to science: science now overlaps with, incorporates and in a sense legitimizes forms of thought that it previously considered as being irrational and beyond the pale. To adopt the viewpoint of scientific knowledge is therefore not equivalent to smuggling in the epistemological framework peculiar to one society to explain other societies; on the contrary, as I realized for the first time when I was studying the kinship systems of the Australian aborigines, it is to accept the fact that the newest forms of scientific thought may be on a par with the intellectual procedures of savages, however lacking the latter may be in the technical resources that scientific knowledge, during its intermediary phases, has allowed us to acquire. It is, therefore, at least on this particular level, to reconcile the undeniable fact of the progress of science with the possibility of recovering a great wealth of knowledge that scientific progress itself began by sacrificing; and finally, it is to take one's stand in an area where abstract thought and theoretical knowledge, as they go forward, realize that, through a retrograde movement in no way incompatible with their advance, they are simultaneously rediscovering the inexhaustible lessons of a realm of sensibility that they originally believed they should deny. Nothing could be more false than to postulate opposite types of knowledge, mutually irreducible throughout the ages, with a sudden and unexplained switch from one type to another. While it is true that seventeenth-century thought, in order to become scientific, had to set itself in opposition to that of the Middle Ages and the Renaissance, we are now beginning to glimpse the possibility that this century and the next, instead of going against the immediately preceding ones, might be able to achieve a synthesis of their thought with that of more remote times, whose themes, as we are now beginning to realize, were not entirely nonsensical.

Other criticisms are more philosophical in nature, and are based on the philosophical element that some readers claim to find in my books. But although, from time to time, I take the trouble to indicate briefly in passing the philosophical implications that seem to arise from my work, I attach no importance to this aspect of it. I am more concerned to deny in advance what philosophers might read into my statements. I do not set my philosophy in opposition to theirs, since I have no philosophy of my own worth bothering about, apart from a few homely convictions that I have come back to, less through the development of my own thought than through regressive erosion of the philosophy I was taught, and that I myself once taught. I am averse to any proposed philosophical exploitation of my work, and I shall do no more than point out that, in my view, my findings can, at best, only lead to the abjuration of what is called philosophy at the present time.

This negative attitude is dictated by circumstance. In reading the criticisms that certain philosophers formulate against structuralism, accusing it of demolishing the human person and its traditional values, I am just as flabbergasted as if they were to attack the kinetic theory of gases on the ground that, by explaining why hot air expands and rises, it endangered family life and the morality of the family hearth, whose warmth, being thus demystified, would lose its symbolic and emotional overtones. The social sciences, following the example of the physical sciences, must grasp the fact that the reality of the object they are studying is not wholly limited to the level of the subject apprehending it. These appearances are underlaid by other appearances of no greater value, and so on, layer by layer, as we look for the ultimate essence of nature which at each level escapes us, and will probably remain forever unattainable. These levels of appearance are not mutually exclusive or contradictory, and the choice of any one or of several depends on the problems one is dealing with and the various properties one wishes to perceive and interpret. The politician, the moralist and the philosopher are free to take up their abode on whichever storey they deem the uniquely honourable one and to barricade themselves in, but they should not try to shut away everyone else along with themselves and forbid us, when we wish to tackle problems different from theirs, to adjust the microscope and change the focusing so as to bring into view another, different object, behind the one in whose contemplation they are totally engrossed.

We have, indeed, to conclude that their object of study is not the same as ours, since several philosophers seem to agree in accusing me of having reduced the living substance of the myths to a dead form, of having abolished the meaning and frantically endeavoured to work out the syntax of 'a discourse which says nothing'. But seriously, if the myths really said what some people seem to expect from them, they would not repeat themselves endlessly throughout the world, and they would not produce unlimited series of variants oscillating around the same armatures. Those societies which, during hundreds of thousands of years, or even longer, depended on the myths for the solution of their theoretical problems, would not have been restricted to the technical procedures, forms of economic life and types of social institutions which, however varied they may have been, have nevertheless made it plausible to assert that the human condition has undergone greater change between the eighteenth and the twentieth centuries than it did between the neolithic period and modern times. The fallacious complaint that the myths have been impoverished hides a latent mysticism, nourished in the vain hope of the revelation of a meaning behind the meaning to justify or excuse all kinds of confused and nostalgic longings, which are afraid to express themselves openly. I too, of course, look upon the religious field as a stupendous storehouse of images that is far from having been exhausted by objective research; but these images are like any others, and the spirit in which I approach the study of religious data supposes that such data are not credited at the outset with any specific character.

We have to resign ourselves to the fact that the myths tell us nothing instructive about the order of the world, the nature of reality or the origin and destiny of mankind. We cannot expect them to flatter any metaphysical thirst, or to breathe new life into exhausted ideologies. On the other hand, they teach us a great deal about the societies from which they originate, they help to lay bare their inner workings and clarify the *raison d'être* of beliefs, customs and institutions, the organization of which was at first sight incomprehensible; lastly, and most importantly, they make it possible to discover certain operational modes of the human mind, which have remained so constant over the centuries, and are so widespread over immense geographical distances, that we can assume them to be fundamental and can seek to find them in other societies and in other areas of mental life, where their presence was not suspected, and whose nature is thereby illuminated. In all these respects, far from abolishing meaning, my analysis of the myths of a handful of American tribes has extracted more meaning from them than is to be found in the platitudes and common places of those philosophers – with the exception of Plutarch – who have commented on mythology during the last 2,500 years.

But philosophers pay little attention to the concrete problems that ethnographers themselves have striven with in vain so long that they have practically given up all hope of solving them; these problems have cropped up one after the other at every turn in my analysis, which has proposed for them solutions as simple as they are unexpected. Being incapable, through ignorance, of recognizing and appreciating these problems, philosophers have preferred to adopt an attitude whose real motives, however, are much more dubious than if they were the mere consequence of a lack of information. Without being fully conscious of this reaction, they hold it against me that the extra meaning I distil from the myths is not the meaning they would have liked to find there. They refuse to recognize and to accept the fact of their deafness to the great anonymous voice whose utterance comes from the beginning of time and the depths of the mind, so intolerable is it for them that this utterance should convey something quite different from what they had decided in advance should be its message. In reading my work, they feel a sense of disappointment, almost of grievance, at being supernumeraries in a dialogue – far richer than any so far entered into with the myths – which has no need of them and to which they have nothing to contribute.

Whither, then philosophy, and in present circumstances, what can it possibly find to do? If the prevailing tendencies continue, it is to be feared that two courses only will be open to it. One, incumbent on the philosophers following in the wake of Existentialism – a self-admiring activity which allows contemporary man, rather gullibly, to commune with himself in ecstatic contemplation of his own being – cuts itself off from scientific knowledge which it despises, as well as from human reality, whose historical perspectives and anthropological dimensions it disregards, in order to arrange a closed and private little world for itself, an ideological Café du Commerce where, within the four walls of a human condition cut down to fit a particular society, the habitués spend their days rehashing problems of local interest, beyond which they cannot see because of the fug created by their clouds of dialectical smoke.

The other possibility for philosophy, when it feels stifled in this confined space and longs to breathe a fresher air, is to make its escape into areas previously forbidden to it and where it is free to disport itself. Intoxicated with its new-found liberty, it gambols off, losing touch with that uncompromising search for truth which even Existentialism, the last embodiment of metaphysics in the grand style, still wished to pursue. Becoming an easy prey for all sorts of external influences, as well as a victim of its own whims, philosophy is then in danger of falling to the level of a sort of 'philosop'art' and indulging in the aesthetic prostitution of the problems, methods and vocabulary of its predecessors. To seduce the reader, woo his interest and win his custom, it flatters their common fantasies with shreds of ideas borrowed from a now antiquated but still respectable heritage, using them to produce surprise effects, more connected with the art of display than with the love of truth, and whose occasional felicities remain purely sensuous and decorative.

Between these two extremes, I may mention various phoney activities pursued by fishers in troubled waters: one example is that 'structuralism-fiction', which has recently flourished on the philosophico-literary scene, and whose productions, in relation to the work of linguists and anthropologists, is more or less equivalent to the contents of certain popular magazines flirting with physics and biology: a debauch of sentimentality based on rudimentary and ill-digested information. The question even arises whether this so-called structuralism did not come into being to serve as an alibi for the unbearable boringness of contemporary literature. Being unable, for obvious reasons, to defend its overt content, this structuralism may be trying to find hidden justifications for it on the formalistic level. But if so, this is a perversion of the structuralist aim, which is to discover why works capture our interest, not to invent excuses for their lack of interest. When we give a structuralist interpretation of a work which has had no need of our help to find an audience, we are supplying additional reasons in support of a successful effect which has already been achieved in other ways; if the work had no intrinsic interest on the levels at which it is immediately open to appreciation, the analysis, in reaching down to deeper levels, could only reduce nothingness to further nothingness.

It is unfortunately to be feared — and here we have a link-up with another kind of philosophy — that too many contemporary works, not only in the literary field but also in those of painting and music, have suffered through the naïve empiricism of their creators. Because the social sciences have revealed formal structures behind works of art, there has been a rush to create works of art on the basis of formal structures. But it is not at all certain that these artificially arranged and conscious structures are of the same order as those which can be discovered, retrospectively, as having been at work in the creator's mind, and most often without any conscious awareness on his part. The truth is that the long-awaited renascence of contemporary art could only result, as an indirect consequence, from the clarification of the laws inherent in traditional works, and which should be sought at much deeper levels than those at which the analysis is usually content to stop. Instead of composing new music with the help of computers, it would be more relevant to use computers to try to understand the nature of existing music: to determine, for instance, how and why we need to hear only two or three bars by a particular composer to recognize his style and distinguish it from others. Once the objective foundations had been reached and laid bare, artistic creation, liberated from its obsessions and phantasms by this new awareness and now face to face with itself, might embark on a new development. It will only succeed in doing so if it first realizes that not every structure can automatically have significance for aesthetic perception because of the mere fact that every aesthetic signifier is the sensory manifestation of a structure.

The social sciences have, then, an ambiguous status in the mainstream of contemporary thought: sometimes, philosophers reject them out of hand; at other times, like writers and artists, they presume to appropriate them and, by carving off fragments according to the dictates of their fancy, produce compositions as arbitrary as collages, while imagining that this dispenses them from reflecting on, or practising, the social sciences, and above all from following the line which these sciences prescribe for themselves in the scrupulous search for truth.

They are, in fact, forgetting that the social sciences do not exist on their own or in their own right. Like the moieties in dualist societies studied by anthropologists, they are simultaneously united to, and subordinated to, the exact or natural sciences by a relationship of reciprocity, which does not exclude, but on the contrary implies, a constitutive dissymmetry. In the resulting dialogue, the social sciences have taken over from philosophy, which is doomed to stagnate unless it turns itself into reflection on scientific knowledge, an ambitious enough programme. The social sciences are no doubt comparable to the physical and natural sciences in the sense that neither achieves direct apprehension of reality, but only of the symbols in terms of which the mind perceives reality in accordance with the constraints and thresholds of our sensory system. However, there is a fundamental difference between them, arising from the twofold fact, firstly, that the physical and natural sciences operate on the symbols of phenomena while the social sciences operate on the symbols of phenomena which are themselves symbols in the first place, and, secondly, that, in the former instance, the adequate approximation of the symbol to the referent is demonstrated by the 'grip' exercised by scientific knowledge on the world around us, whereas the practical ineffectiveness of the social sciences – apart from the teaching of a problematical wisdom – does not allow us, at least for the time being, to assume any adequate correspondence between the representative symbols and the represented symbols.

Looked at in this perspective, the social sciences take on the appearance of a shadow theatre, the management of which has been left to them by the natural and physical sciences, because the latter do not yet know the location or the constitution of the puppets whose silhouettes are projected on to the screen. As long as this provisional or definitive uncertainty lasts, the social sciences will retain their peculiar and double function, which is to soothe the impatient thirst for knowledge by approximate suggestions, and to provide the natural and physical sciences with an often useful, anticipatory simulacrum of the truer knowledge which it will one day be their task to formulate. Let us beware, then, of too hasty analogies: it may be that the attempt to decode the myths has a resemblance to the work of the biologist in deciphering the genetic code, but the biologist is studying real objects and he can check his hypotheses by their experimental consequences. We are doing the same thing as he is, the only difference being that social sciences worthy of the name are no more than the image-reflection of the natural sciences: a series of impalpable appearances manipulating ghost-like realities. Therefore, the social sciences can claim only a formal, not a substantial, homology with the study of the physical world and living nature. It is precisely when they try to come closer to the ideal of scientific knowledge that it becomes most obvious that they offer no more than a prefiguration, on the walls of the cave, of operations that will have to be validated later by other sciences, which will deal with the real objects of which we are examining the reflections. Neither philosophy nor art can, then, give in to the illusion that they have only to try to commune with the social sciences, often with predatory intent, to achieve their own redemption. Both of them, often so contemptuous of scientific knowledge, ought to realize that, in appealing to the social sciences, they are entering into a dialogue with the physical and natural sciences, and thus rendering homage to them, even if, for the time being, the homage is indirect.

None of the objections that I have just briefly reviewed goes to the heart of the problems that these volumes try to elucidate. A much more serious one, worthy of greater attention, has been made by certain linguists who reproach me with having, only in exceptional cases, taken into account the diversity of the languages in which all these myths were first conceived and formulated, although not invariably recorded. Even though I have referred to the original language in a few instances where it was not too difficult to do so, I cannot claim to be linguistically competent, and even among the specialists there is probably no one capable of undertaking the comparative philological study of texts originating in languages which, although all American, differ as much among themselves as those of the Indo-European, Semitic, Finno-Ugrian and Sino-Tibetan families.

Philological analysis has to be resorted to in the case of the dead languages, where the meaning of each term can only be determined by looking at it in several contexts. The situation is not exactly the same when the stories have been taken down directly from informants still speaking their language and who were able to clarify a good many doubtful or ambiguous points. In most cases, unfortunately, there is no original text, and the myth is known only in translation, or even through several successive translations made by interpreters capable of understanding a foreign language and who made versions in their mother tongue, which was not always that of the person recording the story.

Hic Rhodus, hic salta: if, in spite of the decisive part played by philology in Professor Dumézil's outstanding works, from which I have learned so much, I had made it a preliminary condition that I would study the myths only in the original languages, my project would have been unrealizable, not only by me, since I am not a philologist with expert knowledge of the Amerindian languages, but by anyone else. I had therefore to commit myself to a double wager, first in making do with such instruments as I could improvise, not of course as a substitute for philological study, the lack of which will always remain obvious, but to offset to some extent the impossibility of having recourse to philology; then in deciding to await the result before coming to a conclusion about the fundamental problem. The result is now available; I myself at least am convinced that this enquiry, which was undertaken in the face of limitations serious enough to make it theoretically unfeasible, has on the contrary proved most fruitful. This is an accomplished fact we must now argue from, even if at first sight it seems to constitute a mystery, which calls for explanation.

The key to the enigma is, I think, to be found in the myth creation process revealed by my study, and which it alone could demonstrate clearly by being carried through to its conclusion. If, as is shown by the comparative analysis of different versions of the same myth produced by one or several communities, *conter* (to tell a story) is always *conte redire* (to retell a story), which can also be written *contredire* (to contradict), it is immediately understandable why it was not absolutely essential, for the purposes of the rough sorting out I had in mind, to study the myths in the originals, instead of in a translation or a series of translations. Properly speaking, there is never any original: every myth is by its very nature a translation, and derives from another myth belonging to a neighbouring, but foreign, community, or from a previous myth belonging to the same community or from a contemporaneous one belonging to a different social sub-division — clan, sub-clan, descent group, family or brotherhood — that some listener tries to plagiarize by translating it in his fashion into his personal or tribal language, sometimes to appropriate it and sometimes to refute it, and therefore invariably distorting it. A particularly striking instance of this phenomenon is supplied by the Hupa myth about the origin of fire that the demiurge is said to have tried initially, and unsuccessfully, to produce by percussion, and then by inventing the first fire-drill. The person who recorded this story states specifically that it was produced with the intention of giving the lie to a myth belonging to a neighbouring tribe and which asserted that the first fire had been obtained by theft (Goddard 1, p. 197; cf. above, p. 158).

These oppositional relationships between the myths, which can only rarely be observed at their actual inception, are brought out strongly by comparative analysis. Therefore, the reason why philological study of the myths is not an absolute precondition is to be found in what might be called their diacritical nature. Each of their transformations results from a dialectical opposition to another transformation, and their essence lies in the irreducible fact of translation *by* and *for* opposition. From an empirical point of view, every myth is simultaneously primary in relation to itself, and derivative in relation to other myths; it does not exist *in* a language and *in* a culture or sub-culture, but at their point of articulation with other languages and other cultures. Therefore a myth never *belongs to its language*, but rather represents an angle of vision on to *a different language*, and the mythologist who is apprehending it through translation does not feel himself to be in an essentially different position from that of the native narrator or listener. I pointed out this aspect of the problem at an early stage in my research when I emphasized that 'the substance of the myth is neither in the style nor in the form of the narrative, nor in the syntax, but in the *story* that it tells' (L.-S. 5, p. 232).

This is not to say, of course, that a knowledge of the original language, supposing the text to be available, is superfluous, and that philological study would not make it possible to arrive at a more exact and complex definition of meanings, to correct mistakes and give more depth and scope to the interpretation: these are tasks for the people who come after me. But once all these advances and corrections have been made, it will no doubt be seen that, except in exceptional circumstances, philological study adds extra dimensions to the myth and gives it more substance and character, but does not essentially affect the semantic content. The gain will be rather on the literary and poetic side; it will make it easier to appreciate the aesthetic properties of the text, whose message – given the fact that translation allows the myth to be understood as myth – will hardly be modified.

Contemporary philosophy, being imbued with a mysticism that is rarely openly admitted and more often concealed under the appellation of humanism, and always hoping to discover a gnosis that would allow it to mark out for itself a private area inaccessible to scientific knowledge, has taken fright on seeing mythology, which it wanted to be full of hidden meaning, reduced to what some people take to be the vacuity of a series of translations without any original text. This is to fail to see that the same might be said about an area where, however, mystical aspirations and sentimental outpourings are given fairly free rein; I am referring to music. The truth is that the comparison between mythology and music, which was the *leitmotif* of the 'overture' to this work, and which was condemned as arbitrary by many critics, was based essentially on this common feature. The myths are only translatable into each other in the same way as a melody is only translatable into another which retains a relationship of homology with it: it can be transcribed into a different key, converted from major to minor or vice versa; its parameters can be modified so as to transform the rhythm, the quality of tone, the emotive charge, the relative intervals between consecutive notes, and so on. Perhaps, in extreme cases, it will no longer seem recognizable to the untutored ear; but it will still be the same melodic form. And it would be wrong to argue, as some people might be inclined to do, that in music at least there is an original text: famous composers have proceeded in the way I have just described; starting from the works of their predecessors, they have created works stamped with the mark of their own style, which it is impossible to confuse with any other. Research into the recognition of forms, which is henceforth feasible thanks to computers, would no doubt make it possible, in many instances, to discover the rules of conversion that would show styles of popular music or those of different composers to correspond to various states of the same transformational group.

But while one can always, and almost indefinitely, translate one melody into another, or one piece of music into another piece, as in the case of mythology one cannot translate music into *anything other than itself* without falling into the would-be hermeneutic verbiage characteristic of old-fashioned mythography and of too much musical criticism. This is to say that an unlimited freedom of translation into the dialects of an original language forming a closed system is bound up with the radical impossibility of any transposition into an extrinsic language.

The fundamental nature of myth, as it has been revealed by my enquiry, confirms, then, the parallel between mythic narrative and musical composition that I indicated at the beginning. Now that my study has been brought to a close, it would seem that the relationships between them can be formulated more clearly and convincingly. I propose to assume, as a working hypothesis, that the field open to structural study includes four major families of occupants: mathematical entities, the natural languages, musical works and myths.

Mathematical entities consist of structures in a pure state, free from any embodiment. In this respect, they are in a correlational and oppositional relationship to linguistic phenomena which, as Saussure showed, exist only through their double embodiment in sound and sense, and arise in fact from the intersection of these two phenomena.

This axis having been established, with mathematical entities and linguistic phenomena at the two poles, it is immediately obvious that the other families, in relation to it, occupy positions on a different axis, transversal to the first. In the case of music, the structure which is, so to speak, detached from the sense, adheres to the sound; in the case of mythology, the structure is detached from the sound and adheres to the sense. As far as mythology is concerned, this is precisely what I have tried to demonstrate in the preceding pages in connection with the problem of translation.

Let us postulate, then, that mathematical structures are free in relation to both sound and sense; and that linguistic structures, on the contrary, are concretized in their union. Musical and mythic structures, being less completely embodied than the latter, but more so than the former, are biased, in the case of music, in the direction of sound (without sense) and, in the case of myth, in the direction of sense (without sound). This way of looking at the relationships between them has several consequences.

In the first place, if music and mythology are each to be defined as language from which something has been subtracted, both will appear as derivative in relation to language. If this supposition is correct, music and mythology become by-products of a structural shift which had language as its starting-point. Music no doubt also speaks; but this can only be because of its negative relationship to language, and because, in separating off from language, music has retained the negative imprint of its formal structure and semiotic function: there would be no music if language had not preceded it and if music did not continue to depend on it, as it were, through a privative connection. Music is language without meaning: this being so, it is understandable that the listener, who is first and foremost a subject with the gift of speech, should feel himself irresistibly compelled to make up for the absent sense, just as someone who has lost a limb imagines that he still possesses it through the sensations present in the stump. It is the same in the case of myth: the shift which takes place in the direction of sense explains how the myth, when reduced – or raised – to the status of a pure semantic reality, can, as a vehicle of meaning, become detached from its linguistic base, with which the story it tells is less intimately connected than ordinary messages would be.

So far, I have defined the relationships between music and mythology as if they were perfectly symmetrical. It is obvious, however, that there is a dissymmetry because, unlike music which borrows only the sound element from natural language, myth needs the whole of language to express itself. The comparison I have just suggested only remains valid if we see each myth as a score, which, for its performance, requires language to serve as orchestra, unlike music, the means of realization of which are the singing voice (produced in physiological conditions totally different from those required for speech) and instruments.

It cannot be claimed, then, that myth is as completely free from language as music, since it remains involved with it. However, its relative detachment expresses itself, in the mythic narrative, by attempts to recapture sound, attempts comparable to the impulse that leads the listener to try to give sense to a musical work. The myth is attracted towards sense, as if by a magnet: and this partial adhesion creates a potential void with regard to sound that the narrator feels the need to fill by various devices, such as vocal effects or gestures which diversify, modulate and reinforce his speech. Sometimes he chants or intones the myth, sometimes he declaims it; and his recitation is almost always accompanied by stereotyped formulae and gestures. In addition, he imagines the scenes vividly, and he knows how to make them equally present to his listeners: he sees them as if they were happening there and then, he relives them and communicates his experience with appropriate mimicry and gesticulation. It can even happen that the myth is recited by several voices and thus becomes a theatrical performance. The defective relationship to sound is thus compensated for by a redundancy of verbal formulae, repetitions, *da capos* and refrains. Alliterations and paronomasia produce a wealth of assonance and recurrent verbal sounds which excite the ear, as the meaning invested in music by the listener excites his intellect. Something remains, then, of the disparity recognized at the beginning of this paragraph, in spite of the re-establishment of symmetry at the cost, however, of an inner torsion. In music, the coalescence of a global metaphorical significance around the work makes up for the missing aspect, whereas the myth reintroduces sound by metonymical means. In the one case, the sense restored to music corresponds to *the totality* of the sound; in the other, sound is added as *part* of the sense.

Symmetry exists, however, but it assumes a more complex form than I allowed at first, so as to simplify the argument. As has just been said, in myth something of the sound persists in the sense and cannot be expelled from it, if only in so far as the language in which the myth is narrated loses much of its specific relevance in relation to the sense, which survives when entrusted to different linguistic vehicles. In music, on the contrary, the sense is outside the sound and cannot be reintegrated into it, unless Baudelaire is right when he says (pp. 1210–14) that music is a common form into which an unlimited series of significant contents can be fitted according to the personality of the listeners. Consequently, myth, a sense-system, adapts to the unlimited series of linguistic vehicles used by successive narrators, in the same ways as music, a sound-system, adapts to the unlimited series of semantic charges that its successive listeners care to put into it. In the last resort, the reason for this parallelism lies in the fact that the signifying function of the myth is exercised not within language but above it (L.-S. 5, p. 232): the contingent language of each narrator is always good enough to transmit a system of meanings evolved by meta-linguistic processes and whose operational value remains more or less constant from one language to another. Symmetrically, the signifying function of music proves irreducible to any part of it that might be expressed or translated in verbal form. It operates below language, and no discourse whatever, not even that of the most inspired commentator, could ever be profound enough to make it applicable.

To me, at any rate, it appears certain — since I embarked on this *Introduction to the Science of Mythology* in full consciousness of the fact that I was trying, in a different form and in an area accessible to me, to make up for my congenital inability to compose a musical work — that I have tried to construct with meanings a composition comparable to those that music creates with sounds: it is the negative of a symphony of which, some day, some composer could well try to produce the positive image; I leave it to others to decide whether the demands that music has already made on my work can be said to prefigure such an image.

The adherence of structure to sense, which is characteristic of mythology, is clearly demonstrated by the specific constraints it imposes on the quad-ripartite groups I discussed on several occasions in Volume Three (*OTM*, pp. 356–8, 382, 403, 420). We saw then that myths or variants of myths were arranged like Klein groups including a theme, the contrary of the theme and their opposites. This gave sets of interlocking four-term struc-tures, retaining a relationship of homology with each other. These were, in the instances examined and following the order in which the interlocking took place: 1) non-sister, misbehaving sister, sister-instructress, wife; 2) return of spring, separation of the seasons, end of summer, conflict of the seasons: 3) wounded man, lame woman, hunchbacked man, menstruating woman; 4) sap, resin, urine, menstrual blood. But we also saw that these groups were not independent of each other, that none was self-sufficient as an entity in its own right, as it would appear to be if it could be envisaged from a purely formal angle. Actually, the ordered series of the variants does not return to the initial term after running through the first cycle of four: as through an effect of slippage, or more accurately through an action comparable to that of the gear-change of a bicycle, the logical chain is jolted loose and engages with the initial term of the immediately following interlocking group, and the process is repeated right through to the end. The variant-producing cycle thus takes on the appearance of a spiral, whose progressive narrowing disregards the objective discontinuity of the interlocking levels. This is tantamount to saying that, in the case of myth, the periodic distribution of the group structures becomes inseparable from the semantic levels that the analysis brings to light. Unlike mathematics, myth subordinates structure to a meaning, of which it becomes the immediate expression: as on a television screen, when we say it is out of order, but only because the parameters of reception are being altered through contingent reasons instead of being governed by a law, we are dealing in all cases with images which are inverted from positive to negative or are reversed from right to left or from top to bottom; all of which transformations are similar to the mechanism of the pun which, when properly used, causes a word of a sentence to display, as if in the manner of a negative, *the other meaning* that the same word or sentence might take on, if transposed into a different logical context.

Transformations of this kind constitute the basis of all semiology. If, as I wrote some time ago, meaning is the operator of the reorganization of a set (L.-S. 9, p. 30), it follows that the search for the meaning, for the meaning hidden behind the meaning and so on, is limited only by what we might call — broadening a concept invented by Saussure — 'the anagrammatic capacity' of the signifying set. It is well known that Saussure himself did not carry his discovery through to its conclusion, because of a difficulty he came up against and that he was unable, or lacked the will, to overcome: if anagrams play an essential part in the poetics of the most ancient literatures, how is it that rhetoricians and poets themselves never mentioned them or gave any sign that they were conscious of using such a device? The generalization I am proposing might perhaps supply an answer. If such anagrams represent a particular application of a device which is both archaic and fundamental, it could conceivably have been perpetuated not by conscious observation of rules, but through unconscious conformity with a poetic structure that was perceived intuitively through experience of previous models evolved in the same conditions. After all, the objection that I come up against, on the part of conservative thinkers who refuse to accept that poetic inspiration depends on the play of a combinatory system, itself has its roots in a very old mysticism which, since the earliest times, may have consistently relegated the true mechanisms of aesthetic creation to the unconscious.

Perhaps because the involvement of musical expression with the intellect is less overt, musicians do not seem to have been similarly shy about recognizing and expounding the logical basis of their art. Treatises on counterpoint and harmony show how different structural distributions can only come into existence and be perceptible if they are distinguished from each other by differences of key, pitch, quality of tone and rhythm. Musicians have long known that they have two main means of composition: they can contrast structures with structures, or they can maintain the same structures while transforming their sensory expression: this is called development.

But also as they were becoming more and more clearly conscious of this latter device, and succeeded in listing and even codifying its possibilities, musicians very quickly weakened, banalized and sterilized the art of development to such an extent that its facile abuse eventually compelled them to emphasize the first means at the expense of the second. But then a new phenomenon occurred, when music began insidiously dissociating the phase of structure elaboration from the process of providing the structures with a sensory vehicle, both operations having been previously indistinguishable. These two aspects of the work of musical creation tended from then on to separate off from each other, the link between form and sound became weaker, and the sensory system itself became one means, amongst other equally possible ones, of coding intelligible structures which have not first been conceived by the imagination as sound systems. The language of music has thus gradually broken away from what used to constitute its distinctive character — the fact that its latent structures were always a function of the sensory vehicle, and not the opposite. It is only through the variations in the sensory vehicle that the structures of traditional music preserve their individuality. As always and in all circumstances, the structure only becomes accessible by dint of a homomorphism, made possible by a redundancy of levels: a musical work is a sound system capable of inducing meanings in the mind of the listener.

The counterpart of the traditional conception of music would consist, then, of structures of meaning left in suspense, even if only theoretically, while waiting to be imbued with sounds. This is a fairly accurate definition of certain contemporary musical experiments which, rightly or wrongly, give the impression of using sounds to code systems of meaning which seem to have been imagined and worked out before being transposed into a musical form. It would not be incorrect, and in any case not at all belittling, to say that these experiments represent an anti-music; mythology, because of its bias in the direction of language, lies half-way between traditional music and this anti-music.

What I said above about the relationship of symmetry uniting mythology and music on either side of the transversal axis opposing mathematical entities to linguistic phenomena needs to be tempered and restricted by an important reservation: the symmetry is only valid, and has only continued, in the case of a particular kind of music, that which came into being in the sixteenth and seventeenth centuries, and is now on the wane, after exhausting its possibilities for the reasons I have already mentioned. Far from enjoying any absolute existence, this symmetry is peculiar to a period of modern, contemporary history, and we may ask ourselves how it came into being, and why it is now tending to disappear.

It would seem that the point at which music and mythology began to appear as reversed images of each other coincided with the invention of the fugue, that is, a form of composition which, as I have shown on several occasions (*RC*, pp. 147–63, 240–55, and in this volume, pp. 115, 182, 337), exists in a fully developed form in the myths, from which music might at any time have borrowed it. If we ask what was peculiar about the period when music discovered the fugue, the answer is that it corresponded to the beginning of the modern age, when the forms of mythic thought were losing ground in the face of the new scientific knowledge, and were giving way to fresh modes of literary expression. With the invention of the fugue and other subsequent forms of composition, music took over the structures of mythic thought at a time when the literary narrative, in changing from myth to the novel, was ridding itself of these structures.[4] It was necessary, then, for myth as such to die for its form to escape from it, like the soul leaving the body, and to seek a means of reincarnation in music.

[4] In *The Raw and the Cooked* (p. 15), when I was not yet looking to musical forms for anything more than what might be called methodological inspiration, I suggested that they preceded mythic forms, and it is true that these forms were first clarified in musical theory. We can measure, then, the distance covered between the overture to the first volume and the finale of the fourth: it has brought home to us the fact that we could not have looked for the structural modes of mythology in music, if mythology itself had not already found them.

In short, it is as if music and literature had shared the heritage of myth between them. Music, in becoming modern with Frescobaldi and then Bach, took over its form, whereas the novel, which came into being about the same time, appropriated the deformalized residue of myth and, being henceforth released from the constraints of symmetry, found the means to develop as a free narrative. We thus arrive at a better understanding of the complementary natures of music and the novel, from the seventeenth or eighteenth centuries to the present day: the former consists of formal constructions which are always looking for a meaning, and the latter of a meaning tending towards plurality, but disintegrating inwardly as it proliferates externally, because of the increasingly obvious lack of an internal framework; the New Novel tries to remedy the situation by external buttressing, but there is nothing left for the buttressing to support.

With the death of myth, music becomes mythical in the same way as works of art, with the death of religion, are no longer merely beautiful but become sacred. The aesthetic enjoyment they afford, even in the supreme cases, is out of all proportion to the exaggerated prices paid for them; at the same time, the category of the artistic is broadened at the lower end so as to include all sorts of utilitarian objects belonging to the pre-industrial era, or even to the early phase of industrialism when it still respected the traditional canons and strove to follow them in practice — or, as with *art nouveau*, to revitalize them — instead of obeying the dictates of economy and functionalism, as has been the case since. Following the pattern of communities without writing who, in their most sacred rituals, do not use European or even local instruments if they are man-made, but knives consisting of a sharp stone, a mollusc shell or a splinter of wood, and utensils cobbled together out of scraps of bark or twigs, of the sort that mankind must have used when still living in the state of nature, contemporary man, in similarly surrounding himself with precious objects or antique junk to which he accords an identical sacred status, is soothing his nostalgic longing for the secondary natural state that was lost after the primary one, and which is recalled by these surviving remnants of ages that have now become venerable through the sheer fact that they are gone forever. The different phases of culture take over from each other and each, when about to disappear, passes on its essence and its function to the next. Before taking the place of religion, the fine arts were in religion, as the forms of contemporary music were already in the myths before contemporary music came into being.

It was doubtless with Wagner that music first became conscious of the evolutionary process causing it to take over the structures of myth; and it was also at the same point that the art of development began to flag and mark time, while waiting for a renewal of the forms of composition to be initiated by Debussy. This assumption of consciousness also marked the beginning, and was perhaps even the cause, of a new stage of development, in which music was to have no other choice but to rid itself in turn of the mythic structures, which now became available so that myth could assume self-consciousness in the form of a discourse on itself. This being so, there is a correlational and oppositional relationship between my attempt to retrieve the myths for modern thought and the endeavours of modern music which, since the serial revolution, has on the contrary broken definitively away from myth by sacrificing signification to expressiveness and through a radical decision in favour of asymmetry. But, in so doing, it is perhaps only repeating a previous phase of development. Just as the music of the seventeenth and eighteenth centuries took over the structures of a dying mythology, might it not be the case that serial music, anticipating more recent developments, was simply taking over the expressive and rhapsodic forms of the novel, at the point at which the latter was preparing to empty itself of them in order to disappear in its turn?

Mythology and music have in common the fact that they summon the listener to a concrete form of union, with the difference, however, that myth offers him a pattern coded in images instead of sounds. In both cases, however, it is the listener who puts one or several potential meanings into the pattern, with the result that the real unity of the myth or the musical work is achieved by two participants, in and through a kind of celebration. The listener, as such, is not the creator of the music, either through a lack of natural ability or through the incidental fact that he is listening to someone else's music, but a place exists inside him for the music: he is, then, like the reverse, hollowed-out, image of a creator, whose empty spaces are filled by the music. The phenomenon is inexplicable, unless we admit that the non-composer has at his disposal a multiplicity of meanings, all at the ready and otherwise unused, which are attracted as if by a magnet to attach themselves to the sounds. Thus, the union of the sound proposed by the composer, and of the meaning present in a latent state in the listener, is reconstituted in a pseudo-language. When they encounter the music, meanings drifting half-submerged come to the surface and fit together according to lines of force analogous with those determining the patterning of the sounds. Hence a sort of intellectual and emotional coupling of the composer with the listener. They are both equally important, since each represents one of the two 'sexes' of the music, whose carnal union is realized and solemnized in the performance. Only then do sound and sense meet up with each other to create a unique entity comparable to language, since in this case too there is a coming together of two halves, one consisting of a superabundance of sound (in relation to what the listener could have produced on his own) and the other of a superabundance of meaning (since the composer had no need of it to compose his work).

In both cases, the supplementary sound and the supplementary meaning are in excess of the needs peculiar to language, which uses sounds other than musical ones (so much so that it has been said that an ear for language and an ear for music are in inverse proportion to each other), and which is never able to give expression to the ineffable emotions and meanings that music arouses in its devotees. We can say, then, that musical communication and linguistic communication both suppose the union of sound and meaning; but it is also true to add that the sounds and meanings exploited in musical communication are precisely those that are not used in linguistic communication. In this respect, the two types of communication are in a relationship of supplementarity.

The comparison can be taken further. Within any community, the category of myth excludes all dialogue: the members of the group do not contest its myths, but transform them while believing that they are repeating them. Sound and meaning, united in the mythic discourse, move together, step by step, down the line of successive narrators, instead of exchange or union occurring between them, as is the case with music, in or by the act of communication. On the other hand, the exchange peculiar to language also has as its medium molecules charged with both sound and meaning, but which move between speakers whose utterances take the form of statement and answer. In the musical field, exchange certainly occurs, as is the case in articulate language but not in mythic discourse. But music is like mythic discourse, not like articulate language, in that the exchange does not have as its medium bivalent and identically constituted molecules which, as we have seen in the case of myth, are transmitted in one direction only. The exchanged values are of a different kind: they consist of two sorts of monovalent molecules, some charged with sounds (music) or images (mythology), the others charged with meaning. When they meet, each sort communicates to the other sort the complementary charge which it lacked. Union which had previously been potential is achieved as if through an effect of copulation.

There has no doubt never been a better description and analysis of the pleasure to be obtained from music than in those parts of *Un Amour de Swann* where Proust writes about 'the little phrase' and Vinteuil's sonata, and shows how music involves the listener's soul, filling it completely and taking over the flow of his ideas which it then adapts for a time to its own sinuous course, as, in an aircraft, the automatic pilot substitutes its decisions for those of the captain, only returning the controls to him and restoring his reflective consciousness to itself at the end of the journey, throughout which a higher wisdom has relieved it of the harsh necessity of thought. However, Proust does not attempt to fathom the mysterious reasons for the fact that a melodic line or a harmonic combination provide such enjoyment; he merely describes this enjoyment as being 'special' and as producing a 'noble and precise' state of happiness, which, he adds, remains 'unintelligible' (I, p. 283).

But any attempt to understand what music is stops half-way if it does not explain the deep emotions aroused by works which may even be capable of moving the listener to tears. We can guess that the phenomenon has an analogy with laughter, in the sense that in both cases a certain type of structure external to the subject, in the one instance a pattern of words or actions, in the other of sounds, sets in motion a psycho-physiological mechanism, the springs of which have been tensed in advance; but what does this mechanism correspond to, and what is happening exactly when we weep or laugh with joy?

The phenomenon is even more curious; as Proust shows so well, the pleasure of music does not stop with the performance and may even achieve its fullest state afterwards; in the subsequent silence, the listener finds himself saturated with music, overwhelmed with meaning, the victim of a kind of possession which deprives him of his individuality and his being: he has become the place or space of the music, as Condillac's statue was a scent of roses. Music brings about the miracle that hearing, the most intellectual of the senses, and normally at the service of articulate language, enters into the sort of state that, according to the philosopher, was peculiar to smell, of all the senses the one most deeply rooted in the mysteries of organic life.

Meaning, escaping from the intellect, its habitual seat, is directly geared on to the sensibility. The latter is, then, invested by music with a superior function, unhoped for on the part of the subject: hence his feeling of gratitude towards the music flooding him with joy, since it suddenly transforms him into a being of a different kind, in whom normally incompatible principles (incompatible, at least, according to what he has been taught) are reconciled with each other and, in the process, arrive at a sort of organic unanimity. This organizing function with regard to the sensibility was made most clearly manifest in Romantic music, from the time of

Beethoven, who raised it to incomparable heights; but it was present in Mozart and had begun to appear in Bach. The joy of music is, then, the soul's delight in being invited, for once, to recognize itself in the body.

Music brings to completion, in a relatively short space of time, something that life itself does not always manage to achieve and, when it does, only after months or years or even a whole existence: the union of a project with its realization, and this, in the case of music, allows the fusion of the two categories of the sensory and the intelligible, thus simulating in an abbreviated form that bliss of total fulfilment which is only to be attained over a much longer period through professional, social or amorous success, that has called into play all the resources of one's being; in the moment of triumph, tension is relaxed and one experiences a paradoxical sensation of collapse, a happy sensation, the opposite of that produced by failure, and which also provokes tears, but tears of joy.

Koestler, I think, was the first person to explain the mechanism of laughter; it arises from a sudden and simultaneous awareness of what he calls 'operational fields' between which experience suggested no connection. An example that has often been used, but always wrongly interpreted, is that of the mirth aroused by the sight of a formally dressed gentleman, walking along with great dignity, who is suddenly sent sprawling into the gutter. What actually happens is that the two immediately juxtaposed states in which the gentleman appears to us could not occur in normal conditions without being connected by a complicated series of intermediary states, which have been eliminated or short-circuited by the treacherous presence of a banana skin. The onlooker's symbolic faculty, which is subconsciously brought into play to reconstruct and interpret what has happened, and which is prepared to make great efforts to arrive at a synthesis of the two disjoined images, grasps in a flash the unexpected term which allows it to reconstitute the logical chain most economically.

The human mind is always, potentially, in a state of tension and at any moment it has reserves of symbolic activity at the ready to respond to any kind of speculative or practical stimulus. In the case of a comic anecdote, a witticism or an amusing conundrum – all of which allow the interconnection of two semantic fields, which seemed very remote from each other, by means of a link-up that the listener cannot suspect – this surplus energy (which the skilful teller of a funny story seeks in the first place to condense) has nothing to which to apply itself: having been suddenly released and not being able to expend itself in intellectual effort, it is deflected into the body where the ready-made mechanism of laughter can allow it to exhaust itself in muscular contractions. This is the function of spasms of mirth, and the state of well-being which accompanies them is caused by the gratification of the symbolic faculty, which has been satisfied at a much smaller cost than it was prepared to pay.

Laughter, thus explained, is the opposite of anguish, the feeling we experience when the symbolic faculty, far from being gratified by the unexpected solution of a problem that it was prepared to struggle with, feels itself, as it were, being strangled by the need, in vitally urgent circumstances, to achieve a synthesis between operational or semantic fields, when it is without the means of doing so. The cause may be an immediate threat of aggression or the urge to restore the balance of a way of life that has been upset by the death of an irreplaceable loved one. Instead of a theoretically laborious roundabout journey being avoided by the short cut of the comic, what happens is that the inability to find a short cut produces the kind of painful paralysis which grips the mind, when it is terrified by the inevitable difficulties and vicissitudes of the stages of life looming ahead. This interpretation is confirmed indirectly by physiology. The so-called anxiety neuroses are accompanied by an increase in the quantity of the derivatives of lactic acid in the blood (Pitts). It is well known that the production of lactic acid is normally the result of muscular effort, of which the straining of the symbolic faculty to the limit could be the equivalent on the mental level. Anxiety would, then, be the expression, in emotional language, of a state of physiological obstruction affecting the calcium which transmits the nervous impulses and thus paralysing them, this state being brought about in the body by the homology between the mental and physical situations. When the obstruction is a result of too great a mechanical effort, it finds a sensory outlet in cramp and muscular stiffness, of which anguish in the pit of the stomach is the equivalent, in the form of an embodied metaphor.

Once we have managed to work out an adequate relationship between laughter and anguish, we can see that musical emotion is the result of a third possibility, which borrows something from each of them. It is true that this emotion causes tears, like mental suffering, but, as is also the case with laughter, the shedding of tears is accompanied by a feeling of joy. We weep with laughter, when the muscular contractions, which at first were limited to the area of the mouth, spread to the eyes and the whole face through the effect of a feeling of jubilation aroused by some particularly rapid and telling ellipsis. But the tears of joy produced by listening to music result, on the contrary, from the course that the music has actually followed, and brought to a successful conclusion, in spite of the difficulties (which are only such from the listener's point of view) that the inventive genius of the composer, his need to explore the resources of the world of sound, has caused him to accumulate, together with the answers he has found for them. Carried along panting in his wake, the listener, by every melodic or harmonic resolution, seems to be put in possession of the result and hurried forward. And since he has not himself had to discover or invent these keys that the composer's art furnishes him with, ready-made at moments when he is least expecting them, it is as if an arduous path had been followed with an ease of which the listener, left to his own devices, would have been incapable – as if it had, in fact, through some special favour, been by-passed thanks to a short cut. Every arduous path has existential connotations, on the conscious or the subconscious level. The real arduous path, the one against which the listener measures all others, is his life, with its hopes and disappointments, its trials and its successes, its expectations and its achievements. Music offers him the image and the pattern of his life, but in the form of a model (L.-S. 9, pp. 34–6), which not only simulates its events but also speeds them up, crowding them into a period of time that the memory can grasp as a whole, and which moreover – since we are dealing with masterpieces such as life itself rarely knows how to produce – leads them to a successful conclusion.

Each melodic phrase or harmonic development proposes an adventure. The listener, in embarking on it, entrusts his mind and his sensibility to the initiative of the composer; and if, at the end, he sheds tears of joy, this is because the adventure, which has been lived through from start to finish in a much shorter time than any actual adventure would have taken, has also been crowned with success and ends with a felicity less common in real-life adventures. When a melodic phrase appears beautiful and moving, this is because its form seems homologous with that of an existential phase of life (doubtless because the composer, in the act of creation, made the same projection, but in the opposite direction), while showing itself capable of solving with ease, on its own level, difficulties homologous with those that life, on its level, often struggles against in vain.

This being so, there are grounds for maintaining that music, in its own way, has a function comparable to that of mythology. The musical work, which is a myth coded in sounds instead of words, offers an interpretative grid, a matrix of relationships which filters and organizes lived experience, acts as a substitute for it and provides the comforting illusion that contradictions can be overcome and difficulties resolved. This entails a consequence: at least during the period of Western culture when music takes over the structures and the functions of myth, every musical work must assume a speculative form, must look for and find a solution to the difficulties which constitute its true theme. If what has just been said is correct, it is inconceivable that there should be any musical work that does not start from a problem and tend towards its resolution – this word being understood in a broader sense, consistent with its meaning in musical terminology.

It is surprising, then, to come across a statement by a theoretician, who is himself a composer, to the effect that Ravel's *Bolero* is an example of a 'process of simple transformation, developing in one direction without ever doubling back upon itself . . . an extreme case of perfectly continuous and uninterrupted directionality . . . (which goes) from one extreme to the other . . . both having in common the fact that they are *extremes*, that is, it is impossible to go further and that continuation would involve coming back again' (Pousseur, p. 246). Such a description seems to be contrary to any reasonable conception of music and, in this particular instance, it disregards the modulation which occurs towards the end of the work and gives the listener a feeling not only of conclusiveness, but of a decisive answer having been given to some obscure problem that was posed at the outset, and for which the musical discourse has vainly put forward and tested several solutions in turn. Even though Ravel himself defined *Bolero* as an instrumental crescendo and pretended that it was no more than an exercise in orchestration, it is clear that the work involves much more than that; in the case of music, poetry and painting, analysis could never be carried very far if we felt ourselves to be bound by what the creators themselves say, or may even believe, about their works.

The score of *Bolero* is divided into sections numbered from 0 to 18, corresponding to a series of homologous statements, but within which more subtle divisions are immediately perceptible. For reasons of convenience and although the expression is literally inaccurate, the work can be considered as a sort of fugue 'unpicked and laid out flat',[5] so that the different parts are set end to end in linear sequence, instead of chasing each other and overlapping. It is then possible to distinguish a subject and an answer and a counter-subject and a counter-answer, each occupying eight bars. The subject and the answer, and the counter-subject and the counter-answer are repeated twice over with, in the interval between these sequences, two bars in which the rhythm – which remains constant throughout the work – comes to the fore because the melody is held in suspense; the same thing happens after each ending of the second counter-answer and before each

---

[5] TRANSLATORS' NOTE: The metaphor, in inverted commas in the original, is *'mise à plat'*. *Mettre à plat* is a dressmaking expression, meaning to unpick a garment.

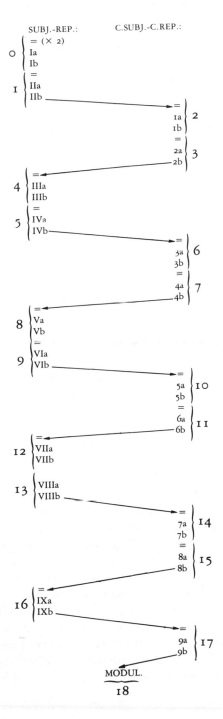

SUBJ.-REP.:   C.SUBJ.-C.REP.:

return of the subject. There are, then, in all two consecutive sequences each made up of the subject and the answer and which are repeated four times, alternating with two consecutive sequences made up of the counter-subject and the counter-answer similarly repeated; this goes on right to the end of the work where, as if forming a stretto also 'laid out flat', the subject and the answer, the counter-subject and the counter-answer follow each other without duplication and lead into a modulation. This modulation occurs fifteen bars before the end, and resolves the ninth and last presentation of the counter-subject.

The double opposition of the subject and the answer, and of the counter-subject and the counter-answer, included within a major opposition between the two pairs of sequences; the reduplication of these pairs in regular alternation, separated each time one from the other, and from the complementary sequence, by a two-bar interval – all this clearly indicates symmetrical patterning, frankly binary in its inspiration. Moreover, a kind of horizontal binary opposition persists throughout the work, which unfolds simultaneously on two levels, one melodic and the other rhythmic. However, the whole piece is written in three-part time, although, in listening, one is often uncertain whether there are three or two beats to the bar. From the preceding remarks, a fundamental aspect of the work has already become clear: it lies in the ambiguity between the binary patterning and repatterning of the musical discourse and the ternary beat running through it; between the complex symmetry characterizing the construction and the simple asymmetry of the exposition.

Let us now consider the horizontal opposition, consubstantial with the work, between the melody and the rhythm. It too displays the same kind of ambiguity. Unlike the melody, whose uneven arabesque breaks the regularity of the ternary rhythm through the frequent use of syncopation, the percussion, which is restricted at the beginning to the drum, respects the ternary rhythm according to the strict letter of the score. But, in fact, it includes several kinds of binary formulae: opposition between two rhythmic motifs which always follow each other in the same order; opposition, within these motifs, between two isochronal elements (a quaver and a triplet); opposition, within the first motif, between two pairs (quaver + triplet) followed by two quavers which themselves form a pair; in the second motif, a similar opposition between two pairs (quaver + triplet), this time followed by two triplets forming a pair, so that, from one bar to the next, the function of expressing duality moves from the quaver element to the triplet element, which are the two constituent units of the whole rhythmic system. So, while the melody tends towards an asymmetry in excess of that implied by the ternary rhythm, the rhythm itself tends in the reverse direction towards binary oppositions which are symmetrical with each other, and cumulative in their effect.[6]

Thus the melody and the rhythm both stand in an ambiguous relationship to the time-pattern. It is the intrinsic rhythm of the melodic discourse which breaks the time-pattern. The percussion, on the other hand, whether reinforced or not by other instruments, respects the triple time, but its rhythmic motifs – in other words, its discourse – produce the opposite effect. The ear does not hear the percussion as it is written, or rather it hears an additional something which is not in the score, whereas this is not the case with the melody, whose syncopated pattern is in the actual text. After the two initial pairs (quaver + triplet), the ear does not pause on the last of the two quavers preceding the bar line: the previous triplet attracts the first quaver of the next bar, which forms a triad with the other two; and for the opposite reason, the second motif, which begins immediately afterwards, demands that the three consecutive triplets should be rounded off with the first quaver of the following bar. The tympani, which come in at Section 12, reinforce the effect by accentuating the first and last beat of each bar; but they are not responsible for creating the effect.

The phenomenon is to be explained partly by causes connected with the rhythm, as we have just seen, but also and perhaps chiefly by the fact that, from the beginning of the work, not just one rhythm but two are in operation: there is the rhythm of the drums, which has just been analysed, and, in the background, the *pizzicati* of the string instruments which, for the time being, are limited to the cellos and violas. These *pizzicati* indicate, however faintly, a melodic line; and they accompany the ample rhythm of the drum with a simpler one, which sounds like a reduction of it: three crotchets, then two crotchets followed by two quavers, which together form an uneven rhythm marked, from one bar to the next, by the same alternation of ternary and binary as has already been pointed out. However, there is more to be said; the string instruments, by going straight into the fifth, followed by a double octave suggestive of unison, remove the accent from the first beat and transfer it to the second and the third, which then, as through an effect of anacrusis, appear to open the bar. The tonal and rhythmic intervals combine to create the impression that there are two ternary time-patterns, out of step with each other. The rhythm, going hand in hand with a melody that is forever in a state of expectancy and often

---

[6] TRANSLATORS' NOTE: In the original, the expression is *plusieurs fois démultipliées*. The author changed it on reading the translation in order to clarify the meaning.

anticipates the next bar through syncopation, proceeds contrariwise so as always to seem one beat behind. The harp, which is used as a percussion instrument but has more expressive power, admirably emphasizes this aspect: it comes in, in Section 2, with crotchets on the second and third beats; the same accentuation then passes to the violins and the woodwind (6 and 7); the harp comes in again, in 8, on the second beats with quavers, which are replaced, in 10, by crotchets forming chords of three, and then four, sounds, but only on the second and third beats. So, through this whole passage and beyond (the effect is taken up by the trombones and reaches its paroxysm in the last six bars), the second beat is stressed and contrasts with the first, which is unstressed, or less heavily stressed, than the other two.

In the course of the work, the two rhythms, which are out of phase with each other, and one of which is fully deployed while the other is condensed, undergo two types of transformation. Firstly, each in turn comes to the fore and dominates the rhythmic pattern; the synthetic rhythm, after being subordinate at the beginning, is amplified by the growing intervention of the quartet, reaches parity towards Section 11, triumphs towards 13, then gradually dies away and is obliterated, in Section 16, behind the analytical rhythm, which reaffirms its predominance through being supported by the strings. Secondly, each rhythmic type, in asserting itself, defends and illustrates a contrary metric option: the synthetic rhythm tends towards a simple ternary time-pattern, and achieves it to the full in the first five bars of Section 13, before starting to diminish; whereas the analytical rhythm, although also ternary, simulates, so to speak, binary transfigurations, and this is expressed by the harp when, in Section 16, it moves abruptly from triads of crotchets to alternating pairs of crotchets and quavers, at the very point when the analytical rhythm, invading the foreground again as at the beginning, monopolizes all the strings — except the first violins — as well as the majority of the wind instruments.

Let us now ask what these rhythmic transformations correspond to on the melodic level. While the rhythm oscillates between binary and ternary patterns, the melody, for its part, oscillates, with faster periodicity, from the subject-answer sequence to the counter-subject-counter-answer sequence; in so doing, it moves alternately from the flattest and solidest of the key-signatures — that of C major — not, actually, into a different key, but into the same key, so profoundly modified by an influx of flats that it comes close to the minor sub-dominant, without however falling into it, since, after the prolonged and panting repetition of the assertive D flat of the counter-subject, the counter-answer, as if exhausted by this vain effort, resigns itself and accepts a return to the status quo. There is not, properly speaking, an opposition between two tonalities, but rather a 'regular and periodic' swinging of the pendulum (to quote the phrase of *L'Heure espagnole*), which moves the melody away from a clear and stable key-signature, and then brings it back again, thus reconstituting a sort of equivalent of the rhythmic opposition between binary and ternary, and of the simultaneously rhythmic and melodic opposition between symmetry and asymmetry.

If this is accepted, it becomes obvious that the work as a whole is an attempt to overcome a complex set of oppositions, interlocking, as it were, one with another. The main opposition, which is stated at the outset, is between the melody, announced in the smoothest and most even tone – and therefore entrusted to the flute, the instrument with the most appropriate timbre for this purpose – and two interwoven rhythms, one of which seems to be always trying to move on ahead, while the other insists on lagging behind. The melody, by its tonal oscillations and the rhythm, by its internal duality, vary between symmetry and asymmetry, expressed respectively by the hesitation between binary and ternary, and between serene and anxious tonalities.

To reconcile these contradictions, the composer appeals immediately to the only musical feature not yet involved in the debate: the different instrumental timbres. The instruments are first brought in singly, then are associated two by two, and later combined in increasing numbers until it becomes clear, at the *tutti*, when quality changes into quantity, that no solution has been found and that the use of the total possible volume has been of no avail. But then, at the moment when the frustration of the orchestra reaches a climax, its very impotence suddenly brings about the right solution, in an area where one would have never thought of looking, if previous failure had not led towards it. The orchestra, having lost all hope of achieving its end, and being unable to increase the sound still further, as if in a last despairing attempt, rises to a modulation, the famous tonal modulation which occurs fifteen bars from the end, but which as we must at once emphasize, has been prepared for, and introduced by what could be called a rhythmic modulation: the harp which, from Section 16 onwards, has been supporting the binary rhythm, returns for an instant to a frankly ternary rhythm before the tonal modulation during which, in the last six bars, the rhythmical synthesis is achieved.

This modulation – into E major – has as its relative the key of C sharp minor, the enharmonic of D flat which belongs to the key of F major (the minor sub-dominant of C), towards which the counter-subject was vainly striving. A solution existed, then, in the area of tonality; the key of E major triumphs, by eliminating two incompatible tonalities (incompatible, because one of them never came out into the open) and by effecting a tonal modulation which, as a consequence, allows the superimposition, and even the temporary fusion, of the binary and ternary rhythms, since the latter opposition was the counterpart to the former. During the last six bars, the analytical rhythm, a combination of binary oppositions, joins with the other rhythm, which is reduced to its simplest expression through the use of three instruments, the bass drum, the cymbal and the gong, which each mark a beat: the first expresses rhythm without timbre, the second timbre without rhythm, and the third represents a synthesis of rhythm and timbre. During four bars, the ternary rhythm dominates, and is marked by the *glissandi* of the trombones in the second and third beats; in the last two bars, everything is reversed, so that the penultimate bar displays a binary division into two motifs, whereas the final one, reduced to a single strong beat, provides the rhythm with the point of rest that had previously eluded it. Lastly, the tremendous dissonance of the second half of the second-last bar, which is made up of steady notes and rising and falling scales all jumbled together, signifies that nothing any longer has any importance, neither timbre, rhythm, tonality nor melody.

Thus, like a myth, even a work the construction of which at first sight seems so transparent as to need no comment, is telling simultaneously on several different levels a very complex story, for which it has to find a conclusion. As is also often the case in myths, the simultaneous levels are, here too, those of the real, the symbolic and the imaginary. The rhythmic opposition between binary and ternary is very real. One cannot say the same about the opposition between symmetry and asymmetry, since it remains implicit, and the task of symbolizing it concretely is entrusted to contrasts which are sometimes rhythmical and sometimes tonal, or which arise between the rhythm of the melody and the line of the rhythm, the latter being made melodic by the *pizzicati* of the strings incorporated into the percussion together with the harp. The imaginary is represented by the opposition between the frank and simple tonality of C major and the ambiguous tonality characteristic of the counter-subject, since in fact it never arrives at any definable key signature.

It was therefore not completely inaccurate, at the beginning of this analysis, to compare *Bolero* to a fugue, as I said, 'laid out flat'. The expression is inappropriate, in the sense that it would be impossible to reconstitute a true fugue by means of the content of the work. But does the fact that this content can exist only in the form of a linear series not prove precisely that it involves incompatibilities which rule out any tighter, stratified organization? Yet it is also these very incompatibilities which, to achieve their own reconciliation, create a true fugue, an abstract and purely formal one, which rises like a spiritual entity from the prostrate and extended limbs of the actual music. Consequently, as in an actual fugue, the superimposed levels of the real, the symbolical and the imaginary, chase each other, catch each other up and partially overlap up to the point of the discovery of the right tonality, although it had seemed a utopian ideal throughout the whole duration of the work. Thus, when the modulation finally brings together and ensures the coincidence of the categories of the real and the imaginary, the other oppositions are resolved: the binary and ternary principles become compatible through being superimposed, for the same reason as the apparent incompatibility between symmetry and asymmetry is healed through the effect of a mediation realized on the tonal level. After a final tumultuous outburst, instantly quelled, the score ends on the telling silence that marks the completion of work well done.

The apparent digressions I have allowed myself in the preceding pages have a part to play in this finale. They show that, contrary to what certain critics have said, I do not underestimate the importance of the emotions. I merely refuse to give in to them and to abandon myself, in their presence, to the kind of mysticism which proclaims the intuitive and ineffable character of moral and aesthetic feelings, and even sometimes asserts that they heighten awareness, independently of any apprehension of their object by the intellect; on this basis it has been said that, in describing and analysing 'savage thought', I have misunderstood and misrepresented its true nature because, in the account I give of it, 'the aesthetic faculty as well as the emotions have practically disappeared' (Milner, p. 21).

Any reader with a modicum of sensitivity, who has gone through my books from *The Elementary Structures of Kinship* to this *Introduction to a Science of Mythology*, by way of *Tristes Tropiques* and *The Savage Mind*, will realize the inaccuracy of this statement. Certainly, none of these works is lacking in feeling. On the other hand, it is true that I try to discern, behind emotional phenomena, the indirect effect of changes occurring in the normal course of the operations of the intellect, instead of accepting intellectual operations as being secondary in relation to emotional phenomena. It is only those operations that we can claim to explain, since they are of the same intellectual nature as the activity which is endeavouring to understand them. Emotions not deriving from intellectual operations would be strictly unknowable as mental phenomena. In postulating the existence of such emotions as a basis for intellectual operations, in relation to which they would have the privilege of priority in time, we would merely be deluding ourselves with empty words (since meaning, by definition, lies beyond), and substituting magic formulae for the exercise of reason. Any phenomenon of the life of the emotions which does not reflect, on the level of consciousness, some important event hindering or accelerating the work of the understanding, is not a matter for the social sciences; it belongs rather to biology (L.-S. 8, pp. 99–100), and its discussion must be left to others.

In various quarters, but mainly in England (Fortes, pp. 8–9; Leach 4, p. 8; 5 *passim*), I have been accused of reducing the intensely lived experiences of individual subjects to emotionally neutral symbols, like those used by mathematicians, whereas the thought of communities without writing is said to have recourse to concrete symbols, highly charged with emotional values. It is added that the gap is unbridgeable, given the stance I have assumed. My preceding remarks about the nature of musical emotion prove the contrary, but it remains to be established that the same type of interpretation can apply to phenomena more relevant to anthropological research, and especially to ritual.[7] I have been challenged with the impossibility of linking up ritual chiefly with the operations of the intellect (Beidelman, p. 402), on the grounds that – in the words of another author who shares the same point of view –

> the symbols and their relations . . . are not only a set of cognitive classifications for ordering the universe . . . They are also, and perhaps as importantly, a set of evocative devices for arousing, channelling and domesticating powerful emotions such as hatred, fear, affection, grief. They are also informed with purposiveness and have a 'conative' aspect. In brief, the whole person and not just the mind . . . is existentially involved in life and death issues (V. W. Turner 3, pp. 42–3).

This may well be so; but when it has been said, and pious lip service has been paid to the importance of the emotions, we have not advanced one step nearer an explanation of how the strange activities characteristic of ritual, and the symbols relating to them, can produce such fine results.

Anthropologists mainly concerned with ritual start from a fact which, in itself, is undeniable: like the Ndembu studied by Turner, some societies 'have remarkably few myths, and compensate for this by a wealth of item-by-item exegesis . . . There are no short-cuts through myth and cosmology to the structure . . . of religion. One has to proceed atomisti-

---

[7] The following ideas about ritual were originally put forward in English, in the Frazer Lecture, which I delivered in Oxford on November 19th, 1970.

cally, and piecemeal . . .' (V. W. Turner 3, p. 20). However, when the matter is presented in this way, no account is taken of the fact that mythology exists in two clearly different modalities. Sometimes it is explicit and consists of stories which, because of their dimensions and internal organization, rank as works in their own right. Sometimes, on the contrary, the mythic text is fragmentary, and is made up, as it were, only of notes or sketches; instead of the fragments being brought together in the light of some guiding principle, each remains linked to a particular phase of the ritual, on which it serves as a gloss, and it is only recited in connection with the performance of ritual acts.

But, just as a novel and a collection of essays, in spite of being conceived differently, both belong to literature, explicit mythology and implicit mythology are two different modes of an identical reality: in both cases, we are dealing with mythic representations. The error of contemporary theoreticians of ritual arises from the fact that they do not distinguish between these two modes of existence of mythology, or do so only incidentally. So, instead of taking as a whole the problems raised by mythic representations, whether explicit or implicit, and making a separate study of ritual, they draw the dividing line between explicit mythology on the one hand, arbitrarily reserving the name mythology for it, and, on the other, the glosses or commentaries on ritual, which belong to the category of myth, but which they link up with, and confuse with, ritual proper. Having mixed up the two categories inextricably, they find themselves dealing with a hybrid entity about which anything can be said: that it is verbal and non-verbal, that it has a cognitive function and an emotional and conative function, and so on. By endeavouring at the outset to give a specific definition of ritual distinguishing it from mythology, they leave in the former all sorts of elements which rightly belong to the latter, and get everything thoroughly confused.

If we wish to study ritual in itself and for itself, in order to understand in what sense it exists as an entity separate from mythology and to determine its specific characteristics, we should on the contrary begin by removing from it all the implicit mythology which adheres to it without really being part of it, in other words, those beliefs and representations which are connected with a philosophy of nature, in the same way as the myths; and when trying to bring out 'the non-verbal language of ritual symbols' (V. W. Turner 3, p. 39), we should avoid putting outselves, like Leach (3, 4), in the position of asserting simultaneously that the concrete symbols of primitive thought are steeped in emotional values, and that the function of ritual is to ensure the transmission and communication of a complex set of information about the natural world, which is exactly the opposite. Besides, all these commentators, who see the emotional aspect of ritual as being central to it, and who expatiate on the anguish created by taboos, make one think irresistibly of some anthropologist from another planet who, in his monograph on earth-dwellers, might describe the superstitious terror which prevents motorists from crossing the symbolic limit marked simply by a line along the road, and even from infringing the taboo ever so slightly; he might also give a horrifying account of the penalty, which is collision with another vehicle . . . But we have no feelings of this kind; we respect the white line as part of our everyday routine without attributing any emotional value to it. As is the case with so many ritual actions, performance is automatic on the part of the people involved, because they are only aware of it as an intrinsic part of their conception of the world.

This is not to say that I underestimate the specific nature of ritual, or — although I feel that the point is often exaggerated — the anxiety states that may prompt ritual actions when they are not, on the contrary, caused by these actions. The initial question of which causes which was left undecided, after a famous controversy between Malinowski and Radcliffe-Brown (L.-S. 8, pp. 96–9); it will become clearer later why both theories can be disregarded. Be that as it may, the very fact that the study of ritual obliges one to discuss its relationship with anxiety proves that the comments I am about to make had to be preceded by my preliminary remarks about anxiety or anguish in the broadest sense, without reference to the particular circumstances in which it occurs. These remarks were prompted by the attempt to define the reciprocal relationships between mythology and music, and I shall therefore begin by considering whether ritual can be given a place in the total system I indicated.

We have seen that myth, which has articulate language as its vehicle, remains bound to language; only music, defined as a system of sounds, breaks completely free. This is mainly true in the case of instrumental music; vocal music, which was probably the earliest form, is comparable in this respect to myth: vocal music also has articulate language as its vehicle, although in each particular case the signifying function is out of phase, being always above or below the linguistic level proper. From this point of view, it can be said that the respective fields of articulate language, vocal music and myth intersect. In the area where they overlap, they have an affinity which is demonstrated by the fact that myths are often chanted or sung. The affinity gradually diminishes, and eventually disappears, as we move from pure vocal music to singing or chanting with an instrumental accompaniment, and finally to pure instrumental music, which is outside language. The same gradation can be observed, on the hither side and the far side of myth, between explicit mythology, which is literature in the full sense of the term, and implicit mythology in which fragments of discourse are bound up with non-linguistic actions, and lastly pure ritual which, in its extreme forms, can be said to lose all contact with language, since it consists either of sacred formulae – incomprehensible for the uninitiated, or belonging to an archaic tongue that is no longer understood, or even of utterances devoid of any intrinsic meaning, such as are often used in magic – or of physical movements or of the selection and handling of various objects. At this point, ritual, like music at the other extreme of the system, moves right outside language, and if we wish to understand its distinctive nature, we have obviously to consider this pure form, not the intermediary states.

How, then, are we to define ritual? We can say that it consists of words uttered, gestures performed and objects manipulated, independently of any gloss or commentary that might be authorized or prompted by these three forms of activity, and which would belong not to ritual itself but to implicit mythology. This being so, to discover the distinctive properties of ritual, we should not compare it with mythology, particularly since the comparison would hardly be possible as regards gestures (these are not totally absent from myth, but, as I showed on p. 648, they have a metonymical function, instead of the metaphorical role they play in ritual), and totally impossible as regards objects. On the other hand, the three forms of activity are present in everyday life; the problem posed by the nature of ritual can, then, be formulated as follows: firstly, why, in order to achieve the results aimed at by ritual, is it necessary to utter words, perform gestures and manipulate objects; secondly, in what way do these operations, as carried out in ritual, differ from similar operations which also occur in daily life; in other words, and without raising the question of content, which would inevitably bring us back to mythology – thus giving rise to the illusion that we were defining ritual when in fact we were talking about the accompanying myth – we can ask three questions, the answers to which must underlie any theoretical interpretation of ritual: what distinctive manner of speech is used in ritual? What gestures? And what special criteria govern the choice of ritual objects as well as their manipulation?

As regards gestures and objects, all observers have rightly noted that, in ritual, they are given a function additional to their practical use, and which sometimes replaces that use: gestures and objects serve *in loco verbi*; they are a substitute for words. Each is a global connotation of a system of ideas and representations; by their use, ritual condenses into a concrete and unitary form procedures which otherwise would have had to be discursive. The gestures are not being performed, or the objects manipulated, as in ordinary life, to obtain practical effects resulting from a series of operations, each following on from the preceding one through a causal link. Instead, ritual uses gestures and things to replace their analytical expression (L.-S. 9, pp. 203–204). The performance of gestures and the manipulation of objects are devices which allow ritual to avoid speech.

This observation faces us immediately with a paradox, since, in fact, there is a great deal of speech in ritual. Whenever a ritual ceremony has been recorded and transcribed in its entirety, as has been the case in North America among the Iroquois, the Fox, the Pawnee, the Navajo and the Osage (L.-S. 9, pp. 79–80, 187–97), and also in Africa and Polynesia, we see that the complete text, which may take several days to recite, may fill a whole volume, sometimes a very large one. But here again, we must refrain from asking what the ritual words *are saying*, and restrict ourselves to the question of *how they are saying*. On this point, there is a twofold observation to be made, and it applies both to the choice and manipulation of objects and to the performance of gestures. In all cases, ritual makes constant use of two procedures: parcelling out and repetition.

Parcelling out, in the first place; within classes of objects and types of gesture, ritual makes infinite distinctions and ascribes discriminatory values to the slightest shades of difference. It has no concern for the general, but on the contrary goes into great detail about the varieties and sub-varieties in all the taxonomical categories, whether it be those of minerals, animals and plants, or those, for which it is itself largely responsible, of raw materials, forms, gestures and objects. The same type of gesture takes on a different role and a different meaning, and its place in the ritual is altered, according to whether it is performed from right to left, high to low, or inside to outside. The same is true of speech. As early as 1949, in studying a particular rite (L.-S. 5, Ch. X; cf. 9, p. 17), I emphasized that each procedure was described with extreme minuteness, and broken down into as many minimal sequences as could be found through the most pernickety analysis. It is probably not without significance in this connection that when some Navajo Indians were given a movie-camera by anthropologists and asked to make films, they produced works all of which had the common feature of giving more importance to the movements of the actors from one place to another than the chief activity intended as the subject and defined in the title: the actors were shown in great detail walking along with a view to doing something, much more than actually doing it; the promoters of the experiment rightly saw a parallel between this feature and certain Navajo stories, which they referred to as myths, but which are in fact songs chanted during the rites, and made up interminable sequences enumerating the various ways of walking in the minutest detail, and describing the inner feelings experienced by someone in the course of such peregrinations. The observers were also surprised to see that the Indians could do the montage of their films with greater rapidity than any technician would have been capable of; they cut and rejoined the lengths of film apparently at random, but it later turned out that, without checking, they were able to remember some particular image from among the thousands or tens of thousands that had been photographed (Worth-Adair, pp. 23–30). It is well known that Navajo ritual is exceptionally rich and varied, and that it plays an important part in the individual life-cycle and the collective life of the community. It is not surprising, then, that they should have transposed the process of fragmentation, combined with the capacity to perceive the smallest distinctive units, to the material discourse recorded on the film, in order to produce a form of presentation different from that to which they were traditionally accustomed.

At the same time as ritual indulges in these subtleties, emphasizing the slightest phases of procedures so that their performance, through its infinite attention to detail, is carried to aberrant lengths, and gives the impression of 'slow motion' camera-work marking time to the point of stagnation, it uses another, no less striking device: at the cost of considerable verbal expenditure, it goes in for a riot of repetition: the same formula, or formulae similar in syntax or assonance, are repeated at short intervals, and are only operative, as it were, by the dozen; the same formula must be repeated a great many times running, or alternatively, a sentence containing a very slight meaning is sandwiched, and almost concealed, between accumulations of identical and meaningless formulae. The Iroquois and Fox rituals provide striking examples of such repetitions of the same formulae: thrice, thrice, four times, once, thrice . . . during a single phase of the ritual, the same formula may be uttered consecutively in blocks of ten, twelve, twenty and twenty-five repetitions (Michelson 8, pp. 72–3, 149–67; 5, pp. 96–115).

At first sight, the two devices of parcelling out and repetition are in opposition to each other: in the one case, it is a question of finding differences, however small, between operations which could seem identical, and in the other, of repeating the same statement indefinitely. But, in fact, the first procedure is equivalent to the second, which represents, so to speak, its extreme development. Differences which have become so small as to be infinitesimal tend to disappear in quasi-identity; and this brings us back to the reference to cinematographic film, which breaks movement down into such small units that consecutive shots are hardly distinguishable one from another and appear to be repetitions, so that a film editor has to use markers to make sure of getting his cuts right, unless he happens to be a Navajo Indian, that is, someone long accustomed, through the practice of ritual, to distinguishing the limit-values of identity and differentiation.

What, we may now ask, are the fundamental reasons which cause ritual to resort systematically to the complementary procedures of parcelling out and repetition? G. Dumézil's famous studies of archaic Roman religion throw light on the problem, and allow us to suggest a solution. Dumézil distinguishes two categories of Roman gods: the major divinities, who are few in number, arranged in a triad of distinctive oppositions and each in charge of an aspect of the order of the world, thus forming a functional set, whose relationship with other functional sets reconstitutes the total structure of the universe and human society; and a pleiad of minor divinities, who are numerous enough to be assigned to the various phases of ritual or to the successive, and minutely distinguished, stages of some aspect or other of practical life, such as the periods and successive operations characteristic of agriculture and cattle-breeding with their accompanying rites, and also perhaps the incidents of childbirth (Dumézil 3, pp. 363–85; 4, pp. 253–304).

It would be easy to make similar observations about the cults of Ancient Mexico or of various areas of South-East Asia and Africa. Only the major divinities can be directly related to the myths. How are we to explain, then, this opposition between major divinities, few in number and each corresponding to a major segment of the universe and society, and minor divinities numerous enough for each of them to be entrusted with particular responsibility for a concrete aspect of practical life?

The two categories result from the movement of thought in two different and complementary directions. The fluidity of the real is such that it constantly tends to escape through the mesh of the grid that mythic thought has placed over it so as to bring out only its most contrasting features. Ritual, by fragmenting operations and repeating them unwearyingly in infinite detail, takes upon itself the laborious task of patching up holes and stopping gaps, and it thus encourages the illusion that it is possible to run counter to myth, and to move back from the discontinuous to the continuous. Its maniacal urge to discover the smallest constituent units of lived experience by fragmentation and to multiply them by repetition, expresses the poignant need of a guarantee against any kind of break or interruption that might jeopardize the continuance of lived experience. In this sense, ritual does not reinforce, but runs counter to, mythic thought, which divides up the same continuum into large distinctive units separated by differential gaps.

On the whole, the opposition between rite and myth is the same as that between living and thinking, and ritual represents a bastardization of thought, brought about by the constraints of life. It reduces, or rather vainly tries to reduce, the demands of thought to an extreme limit, which can never be reached, since it would involve the actual abolition of thought. This desperate, and inevitably unsuccessful, attempt to re-establish the continuity of lived experience, segmented through the schematism by which mythic speculation has replaced it, is the essence of ritual, and accounts for its distinctive characteristics that were brought out by the analysis conducted in the preceding pages.

We must therefore now turn our attention to this primary schematism of mythic thought, which is in itself a complex phenomenon.

Mythic thought operates essentially through a process of transformation. A myth no sooner comes into being than it is modified through a change of narrator, either within the tribal group, or as it passes from one community to another; some elements drop out and are replaced by others, sequences change places, and the modified structure moves through a series of states, the variations of which nevertheless still belong to the same set. Theoretically, at least, there is no limit to the possible number of transformations, although, as we know, myths too can die (L.-S. 20); and this being so, it must be possible, without in any way relinquishing the principles of structural analysis, to detect on occasions, within the myths themselves, the seeds of their decay (OTM, pp. 114–31). However, from the purely theoretical point of view, there is no way of deriving, from the concept of transformation considered in the abstract, any principle from which it would follow that the states of the group are necessarily finite in number: any topological figure lends itself to alterations as small as the imagination cares to make them and, between any two distortions taken as boundaries, we may suppose an unlimited series of intermediary states, which are an integral part of one and the same transformational group. If, between one variant and another of the same myth, there always appear differences expressible, not in the form of small positive or negative increments, but of clear-cut relationships such as contrariness, contradiction, inversion or symmetry, this is because the 'transformational' aspect is not the whole story: some other principle must come into play to determine that only some of the possible states of the myth are actualized, and that only certain apertures, not all, are opened up in the grid which, theoretically, could accommodate any number. This additional constraint results from the fact that the mind, which is working unconsciously on the mythic substance, has at its disposal only mental procedures of a certain type: if it is not to wreck the logical armature which supports the myths, and therefore to destroy them instead of transforming them, it can only subject them to discrete changes, discrete in the mathematical sense of the term, which is the opposite of its psychological meaning: the characteristic of a discrete change is to be indiscreet.[8] In addition, each discontinuous change necessitates the reorganization of the whole; it never occurs alone but always in correlation with other changes. In this sense, it can be said that mythic analysis is in a symmetrical and inverted relationship to statistical analysis: it tends to replace quantitative precision by qualitative precision, but in either case precision is only possible as an aim because both forms of analysis have at their disposal a multiplicity of cases which display the same tendency to organize themselves spontaneously in space and time.

The preceding remarks help to explain why Dürer's speculations in *Vier Bücher von menschlicher Proportion* and those of Goethe in *The Metamorphosis of Plants*, which were revived, generalized and given scientific status by D'Arcy Wentworth Thompson, still retain their significance. The British biologist showed that by varying the parameters of a system of co-ordinates, it is possible, by means of a series of continuous transitions, to move from one living form to another and, with the help of an algebraic function, to deduce the outlines or external differences – I am almost tempted to say the irreplaceable graphic form or style – which make it possible to distinguish at a glance, from their shape, two or more kinds of leaves, flowers, shells or bones, or even whole animals, provided the creatures concerned belong to the same botanical or zoological class (Figure 39).

It is no doubt true – and the objection comes spontaneously to mind – that, contrary to what is supposed in the myths (*RC*, pp. 50–55, 280–81, 319–20), present-day specific or generic differences are not the result of the ideal segmentation of a virtual continuum, but are directly linked with the discontinuities of the genetic code which, like language, proceeds by the combination or distinctive opposition of a small number of elements. D'Arcy Wentworth Thompson was well aware of this obvious truth, the principle of which was no doubt unknown in Goethe's day (although Rousseau, it will be remembered, defined botany as the study 'of combinations and relationships') but could already be glimpsed at the time when he himself wrote: 'A "principle of discontinuity", then, is inherent in all our classifications, whether mathematical, physical or biological; and the infinitude

[8] TRANSLATORS' NOTE: The pun is more telling in French, since the single form *discret* covers the two meanings: 'discrete' and 'discreet'.

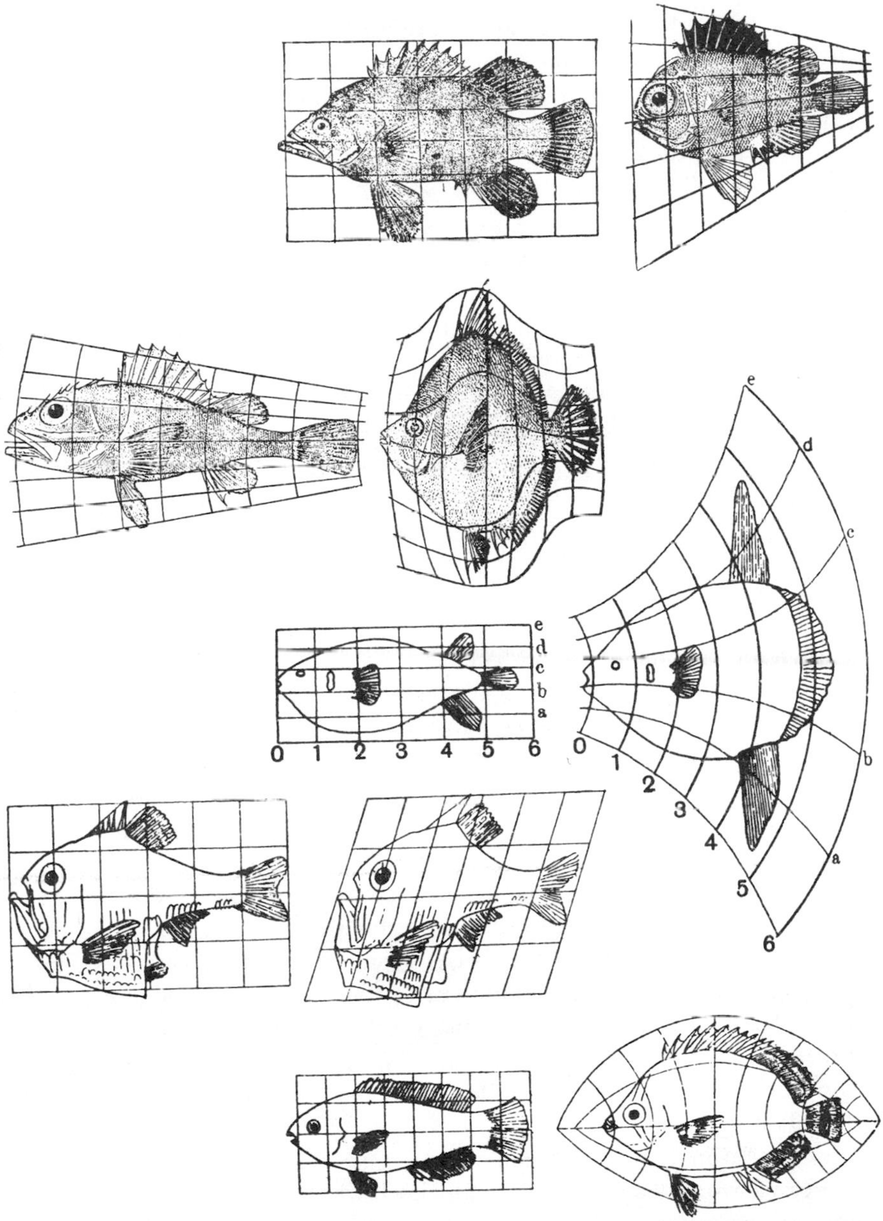

Figure 39. Zoological transformations: *from left to right and top to bottom*, *Polyprion*, *Pseudopriacanthus altus*, *Scorpaena* sp., *Antigonia capros*, *Diodon*, *Orthagoriscus*, *Argyropelecus olfersi*, *Sternoptyx diapthana*, *Scarus* sp., *Pomacanthus*. (From D'Arcy Wentworth Thompson, II, pp. 1062–4)

of possible forms, always limited, may be further reduced and discontinuity further revealed by imposing conditions – as, for example, that our parameters must be whole numbers, or proceed by *quanta*, as the physicists say' (Thompson, Vol. II, p. 1094).

With the discovery of the genetic code, we can now see the objective reality behind this theoretical requirement for a principle of discontinuity operating in the processes of nature and in the constructions of the human mind, to limit the infinite scale of possibilities. Only in a mythic universe, as we saw in the stories quoted above (pp. 463–9), could the species be so numerous that the differential gaps between them became imperceptible. And if the myths themselves conform to a similar principle of discontinuity, this is because, in reconstituting the properties inherent in the world of the senses, but whose objective foundations they could not be aware of, they were simply making a general application of the processes according to which thought finds itself to be operating, these processes being the same in both areas, since thought, and the world which encompasses it and which it encompasses, are two correlative manifestations of the same reality.

But thought can never be directly in mesh with the external world. To consider for a moment only the faculty of sight, a process of analysis occurs even in the retina, and precedes the reactions of the brain. I shall come back to this point (see below, p. 692), but let me emphasize for the time being that the eye does not simply photograph visible objects; it codifies their relationships, and what it transmits to the brain is not so much figurative images as a system of binary oppositions between immobility and movement, the presence or absence of colour, movement occurring in one direction rather than in others, a certain type of form differing from other types, and so on. On the basis of this range of discrete information, the eye or the brain reconstruct an object that, strictly speaking, they have never seen. No doubt, this is especially true in the case of the eyes of certain vertebrates with no cortex, such as the frog; but even in the case of cats or primates, in which the analytical function is largely taken over by the cortex, the brain cells merely follow up operations, the original seat of which is in the sense organ.

In other words, the operations of the senses have, from the start, an intellectual aspect, and the external data belonging to the categories of geology, botany, zoology, etc., are never apprehended intuitively in themselves, but always in the form of a *text*, produced through the joint action of the sense organs and the understanding. Its production occurs simultaneously in two divergent directions: through progressive decomposition of

the syntagm and increasing generalization of the paradigm. One corresponds to what may be called a metonymical axis; it replaces each relative
totality by the parts it discerns in it, and treats each of the parts in turn as a
subordinate relative totality on which the same operation of decomposition
can be performed. Thus, behind each primary oppositional couple, there
appear secondary couples, and then, behind these, tertiary couples, and so
on, until the object of analysis is those infinitesimal oppositions, beloved of
ritual. The other axis, which is specifically that of myth, is related rather to
the category of metaphor; it subsumes individualities under the heading of
the paradigm, and simultaneously broadens and thins out the concrete data
by obliging them to cross the successive, discontinuous thresholds separating the empirical order from the symbolic order, then from the order of the
imagination, and lastly from schematism.

The fact that ritual constantly has recourse to non-verbal means of
expression, such as gestures and material symbols, is to be explained by the
increasingly difficult struggle — as thought progresses along these perpendicular axes and so moves away from their common origin — to maintain
diagonal connections between them. Almost everywhere, the foundation
myths of ritual express the need to slow down, hold back and reunite these
divergent impulses. There are myths which say that, for ritual to be
invented, some human being must have abjured the sharp, clear distinctions existing in culture and society; living alongside the animals and
having become like them, he must have returned to the state of nature,
characterized by the mingling of the sexes and the confusion of degrees of
kinship; a status of chaos which — contrary to the evidence of practical
experience — is said immediately to cause the creation of rules for the benefit of a chosen individual and the edification of his kinsfolk (Boas 4,
pp. 40–43; Teit 5, p. 259), in other words, the reverse of the interminable
and fruitless road, at the entrance to which ritual itself struggles in vain.

Thus, while myth resolutely turns away from the continuous to segment
and break down the world by means of distinctions, contrasts and oppositions, ritual moves in the opposite direction: starting from the discrete
units that are imposed upon it by this preliminary conceptualization of
reality, it strives to get back to the continuous, although the initial break
with lived experience effected by mythic thought makes the task forever
impossible. Hence the characteristic mixture of stubbornness and ineffectiveness which explains the desperate, maniacal aspect of ritual. Hence,
too, on the other hand (and this may be why, in spite of what has just been
said, men have never given it up, although they ought to have been
enlightened by its failure or its vacuity), what might be called the 'senator-

ial' function of magic, a complicated and, unlike mythic thought, essentially irrational activity, but one which has proved indispensable, since it introduces into any moderately serious undertaking an element of deliberation and reflection, pauses and intermediary stages, and acts as a tempering factor even in war.

Contrary to the assertions of old-fashioned naturalism, ritual does not arise, then, from a spontaneous reaction to reality: it turns back towards reality, and the anxiety states which prompt it, or which it causes — and which therefore, it is said, accompany it in either case — do not express (supposing they exist) an immediate relationship between man and the world, but the reverse: in other words, a lurking thought originating in the fear that the human mind, starting from a conceptualized and schematic vision of the world, that immediate datum of the unconscious mind,[9] will be unable to find its way back to reality. When Turner (1, p. 7) states that religious rites 'create or actualize the categories by means of which man apprehends reality, the axioms underlying social structure and the laws of the moral or natural order', he is not fundamentally wrong, since ritual does, of course, refer to these categories, laws or axioms. But ritual does not create them, and endeavours rather, if not to deny them, at least to obliterate, temporarily, the distinctions and oppositions they lay down, by bringing out all sorts of ambiguities, compromises and transitions between them. Thus, I was able to show in another context (L.-S. 9, pp. 294–302) how a rite such as sacrifice is in diametrical opposition to totemism as a system of thought, although both are concerned with the same empirical material: animals and vegetables, in the one case doomed simply to destruction or to be eaten, and in the other given an intellectual significance which may rule out their consumption as food, or limit it in various ways.

In the particular case of ritual as in the more general one considered on p. 658, the emotional aspect is not a primary datum. Man does not feel, indeed cannot feel, anxiety in the face of the circumstances of pure and immediate living, except when some internal and organic disorder is part of these circumstances. When this is not so, and certainly in the case of ritual, the accompanying anxiety is of quite a different order; it is not existential, but rather epistemological. It is connected with the fear that the segmentation effected on reality by discrete thought in order to conceptualize it will, as was pointed out earlier (p. 675), make it impossible to recover contact with the continuity of lived experience. It is, then, an anxiety which, far

---

[9] TRANSLATORS' NOTE: . . . *cette donnée immédiate de l'inconscience.* This is a play on the Bergsonian expression: *'les données immédiates de la conscience'.*

from moving from life to thought, as the functionalists believe, proceeds in exactly the reverse manner, and results from the fact that thought, merely by being thought, creates an ever-increasing gap between the intellect and life. Ritual is not a reaction to life; it is a reaction to what thought has made of life. It is not a direct response to the world, or even to experience of the world; it is a response to the way man thinks of the world. What, in the last resort, ritual seeks to overcome is not the resistance of the world to man, but the resistance of man's thought to man himself.

It has already been said (see above, p. 658) that laughter expresses an unhoped for gratification of the symbolic faculty, since a witticism or a comic anecdote spares it the trouble of making a long, roundabout effort to link up and unify two semantic fields. On the other hand, anguish – a persistent constriction of the internal organs, and thus morphologically in opposition to the external and spasmodic relaxation of the muscles in laughter – appears, we said, as the contrary emotional state, resulting from an unavoidable frustration of the symbolic faculty. But, in either case, the symbolic faculty, whether gratified or inhibited, inevitably comes between the world as it is thought and the world as lived experience.

I am not, then, ignoring emotional states in assigning them their true position – or, what amounts to the same thing, the only position in which they are comprehensible – a position which does not precede the apprehension of the world by thought, but on the contrary is posterior and subordinate to it, and which is seen to be theirs, once we have grasped the contradiction, inherent in the human condition, between two inevitable obligations: living and thinking.

It is true that states which may be comparable to anguish can be observed in animals, and that we can, from inner experience, recognize something animal-like in anguish, so much so indeed that it, more than anything else, can give us the experience of being reduced below the human level and put in touch again with our original animal nature. It will be agreed that the symbolic faculty is essentially human. It might be thought, then, that intellectualist interpretations are invalidated from without by animal ethology, and from within by subjective observation. But, on reflection, they can be seen, on the contrary, to be confirmed from both sources. If it is possible to imagine animals in contrasting states, so that they move, without any transition, from an unthinking enjoyment of existence, during which they are entirely relaxed, to sudden crises of anxiety caused by a noise, a scent or a shape, so that they can be seen, from one second to the next, tensing their nerves and their muscles for flight, this is surely because, in them, the disproportion is infinitely greater than it is in man between powerful and efficient physical resources and the symbolic faculty; they are not entirely lacking in this faculty, but it is rudimentary, and therefore exposed to frequent and more serious frustrations through the problems of life in the wild, so that these frustrations reach an intensity comparable to what we might feel, if a creaking noise in the night made us suspect that thieves had broken into a lonely house where we were asleep. But the same type of occurrence, which provokes a ready-made response in the animal, creates a global state of inhibition in man. In a fraction of a second, a thousand painful possibilities and anticipatory images of the various fates that may be in store for us and of the ways we might avoid them, invade the mind and fight for precedence in the consciousness, which is dominated by a sense of urgency and yet paralysed by the complexity of the problems facing it, and by the lack of time in which to synthesize all the elements effectively.

It follows, then, that the interpretation of anguish I proposed earlier is not wrong; what is wrong is the constant use made by zoologists – and too often, after them, anthropologists – of the concept of ritual to characterize the stereotyped behaviour patterns noticeable in numerous animal families on various occasions, such as the mating season and encounters between individuals of the same sex; because of their complexity and their detailed and hieratic character, the term 'ritualization' has been applied to them. In spite of appearances, these features make them the opposite of ritual, through proving that they consist of ready-prepared mechanisms, which remain inactive and latent until they are automatically set in motion by the occurrence of a particular type of stimulus.

It has been rightly emphasized that the effect of ritualization is 'to sharpen the messages and reduce them to a discontinuous code' (Bronowski, p. 377). Therefore, the term 'ritualization' is an inaccurate borrowing from human behaviour since, in man, ritual fulfils the opposite purpose of reconstituting the continuous by means of practical operations, on the basis of the speculative discontinuity which provides the starting-point. The difference between the discontinuous of the intelligence and that of instinctive behaviour patterns, lies in the richness of the former and the poverty of the latter, since the complexity of the intellectual operations involved in the one has as its counterpart in the other only patterns which, however complex, are pre-programmed in the organism, instead of being produced as ideas by the understanding.

It is no doubt legitimate to try to explain man in general to some extent by means of observations on mammals, insects and birds: the gap between the animals and man is so incommensurably greater than the differences between men that it makes the latter differences negligible. On the other hand, and for the same reason, it would be radically impossible to explain the differential gaps between human groups, such as the so-called primitives and civilized societies, or between several so-called primitive societies, by comparing the customs peculiar to any one of these groups with animal behaviour patterns, either generic or specific. To find an area in which it is plausible to make some comparison between what I may call the respective soul-states of humans and animals, one has to look elsewhere.

A man accustomed to driving a car controls this supplementary power by means of a nervous system adapted to the more modest function of controlling his body. We see here, then, the same disproportion as in the animal between a symbolic faculty whose capacity for synthesis is remarkably limited in relationship to the problems that it may have to solve, and the enormous physical resources available for the solution of the problems.

A man is driving at speed along an open road; there is nothing special to attract his attention; he falls into a state of blissful, dreamy absent-mindedness and trusts to his automatic reactions as an experienced driver for the carrying out of slight and precise movements that he no longer need control consciously, since they have become second nature to him. But if suddenly, some object that he has carelessly thrown on to the seat and forgotten about, falls out of place, producing an unexpected noise that cannot be confused with the hum of the engine or the familiar vibrations of the car body, his attention is immediately alerted, his muscles begin to tense, his whole being is seized with feverish anxiety through fear of some incomprehensible mishap that could in a fraction of a second, lead to disaster. In no less short a time, his mind reels off the list of possible explanations, his defence mechanisms spring into action and his memory is called upon to function: the effect is then linked with its cause, and the occurrence is understood as the insignificant matter it is. It was nothing of any importance, and yet, for a moment, the nervous system of an ordinary human body has had to cope with the risks inherent in the enormous surplus of power bestowed on it by the engine. One sometimes reads in the newspapers that drivers, at the wheel, behave like animals; as can be seen, there is another sense too, an intellectual not a moral one, in which the use of a machine produced by human inventiveness, paradoxically takes man back to the animal condition: his symbolic capacity, although incomparably greater than that of an animal, is, as it were, minimized by his being in charge of an artificial body whose physical power is far in excess of that of his natural body. It is in such a situation, which has nothing to do with ritual, that the messages become impoverished, schematic and discontinuous, and call for an all-or-nothing answer.

But the resemblance goes no further. At the same distance from ritual, the animal acts out its myths, and man thinks his; and the universality of the binary code is demonstrable only at the point of common origin of these divergent tendencies: in a code reduced to its simplest expression, i.e., in the elementary choice between a yes-answer and a no-answer. In the animal, the two possibilities, which are controlled from without, come into play to release or inhibit a chain of pre-programmed actions; in man, on the contrary, the all-or-nothing response marks the lower limit at which, through the effect of a paralysis felt throughout the organism, the resources of a combinatory system rooted in the understanding seize up and cancel each other out; this same combinatory system puts on, in the form of myths, a parade of ideas no less fantastic than the indescribably poetic performance that the genius of the species, during the mating season, imposes on bower-birds.

This conception of the understanding as the source of an autonomous activity, which is subject in the first place to its own constraints, is criticized by all those who imagine that a display of fine feelings can be a substitute for the search for truth, and who do not hesitate, in the defence of what they call the freedom, spontaneity and creativity of the subject, to enter into unnatural alliances, for instance with certain trends in contemporary linguistics, whose philosophical and methodological bias is nevertheless contrary to theirs; after the successful analysis of language in the preceding phase of linguistics, the present practitioners are tackling the complementary problem of the synthesis of utterance, and are moving still further in the direction of determinism. It would be irrelevant, in this context, to discuss the specifically linguistic controversies to which this change of approach has given rise; in any case, I feel they are hardly my concern since, as early as 1945 (L.-S. 5, Ch. II, XIII), I applied transformational rules to sociological data and artistic works, with the conviction that I was respecting the teachings of structural linguistics, the same form of linguistics as is now declared to be out of date by people who do not even realize that it has been given a natural and objective status through the discovery and the cracking of the genetic code: the universal language used by all forms of life, from micro-organisms to the higher mammals, as well as by plants, and which can be seen as the absolute prototype, the model of which is echoed, on a different level, by articulate language: the model itself consisting, at the outset, of a finite group of discrete units, chemical bases or phonemes, themselves devoid of meaning, but which, when variously combined into more complex units — the words of language or triplets of nucleotids — specify a definite meaning or a definite chemical substance. Similarly, the words of language or the triplets of the genetic code combine in turn to form 'sentences', that life composes in the molecular form of DNA, this form being the bearer of a differential meaning, the message of which specifies such and such a protein of a given type. As can be seen, when Nature, several thousand million years ago, was looking for a model, she borrowed in advance, and without hesitation, from the human sciences: this is the model which, for us, is associated with the names of Trubetskoy and Jakobson.

Technical discussions among linguists are one thing; it is quite a different matter when certain philosophers make illegitimate use of such discussions, through the naïve illusion that linguists, in shifting attention from the language code to the process of utterance, are re-erecting the statue of a free, creative subject which was overthrown by their sacrilegious predecessors: it is rather like imagining that the way in which people make love relieved them of the constraints of the genetic code. But if the genetic code did not exist, they would not 'make' anything at all, and only because it exists do they have the very limited possibility of bringing it into play, with small variations independent of their consciousness and their will. Language in its entirety is potentially pre-existent to any utterance that is selected from it, as all the genomes are potentially pre-existent to the particular individuals that other individuals, through the effect of chance or elective affinities, come together to create.

When linguists emphasize that language, even when reduced to a finite set of rules, can be used to generate an infinite number of statements, they are putting forward a thesis which, although approximate, is nevertheless legitimate from the strictly operational point of view, since the wealth of possible combinations is such that, in practice, it is as if the relative formula had absolute validity. The situation is not the same when philosophers try to draw metaphysical inferences from this methodological principle. Strictly speaking, a finite set of rules governing a finite vocabulary, used to produce sentences the length of which is not definitely limited but which, at least in the spoken language, rarely if ever exceeds a certain extent, can only generate a discourse which is itself finite, even if successive generations, each consisting of millions of speakers, do not exhaust the possible combinations.

The fact that a finite set of rules can generate a practically infinite series of operations is interesting, but no more so than the fact that individuals

endlessly different from each other are engendered through the operation of
a finite genetic code. By shifting the centre of interest from the finite nature
of the code to the infinite number of operations, the philosophers seem to
believe that, when it is a question of human thought, the code becomes
secondary in comparison with the relatively indeterminate nature of its
effects: as if, to study and understand the human make-up, it were less
important to know that each individual has a heart, lungs, a digestive tract
and a nervous system, than to pay particular attention to certain statistical
fluctuations, such as the fact that one individual is five foot ten inches and
another six feet, or that one has a rather round, and another a rather long
face, etc. Such details, however interesting their explanation might be, are
not of prime importance, and biologists, quite rightly, do not pay much
attention to them, being content to conclude provisionally that every gene
does not determine a characteristic with strict accuracy, but only the
approximate boundaries between which the characteristic will vary according to external contingencies.

As in genetics, the practically unlimited number of possible utterances,
that is, of verbal combinations, is in the first place a consequence of the
fantastic range of elements and rules that can be brought into play. The
statisticians tell us that two pairs of chromosomes determine four possible
genomes, and that n pairs of chromosomes will give a corresponding
potential total of 2^n genomes which, in the case of man, is 2^{23}. All things
being supposed equal, the probability of two parents giving birth to two
identical children is, then, of the order of $(1/2^{23})^2$, or one chance in millions
of millions. The combinatory system of language is richer still than that of
life, so that even if it is admitted to be theoretically finite, there is no
possibility whatever, within observable limits, of the recurrence of two
identical statements of a certain length, even if we leave out of account the
diachronic changes which take place, independently of the conscious
awareness or intentions of the speakers concerned, through the effect of the
grammatical and phonological mutations involved in the evolution of
language, and of the biological mutations and other accidents, such as the
crossing, overlapping and translocation of chromosomes, involved in the
evolution of life, with the result that, after a certain lapse of time, the same
sentences and the same genomes cannot reappear, for the simple reason that
the range of genetic and linguistic possibilities has altered.

But we can also see the fundamental reasons for the epistemological
perversion resulting from the change of perspective advocated by the
philosophers; disregarding their primary duty as thinkers, which is to
explain what can be explained, and to reserve judgment for the time being

on the rest, they are chiefly concerned to construct a refuge for the pathetic treasure of personal identity. And, as the two possibilities are mutually exclusive, they prefer a subject without rationality to rationality without a subject. But although the myths, considered in themselves, appear to be absurd narratives, the interconnections between their absurdities are governed by a hidden logic: even a form of thought which seems to be highly irrational is thus contained within a kind of external framework of rationality; later, with the development of scientific knowledge, thought interiorizes this rationality so as to become rational in itself. What has been called 'the progress of consciousness' in philosophy and history corresponds to this process of interiorizing a pre-existent rationality which has two forms: one is immanent in the world and, were it not there, thought could never apprehend phenomena and science would be impossible; and, also included in the world, is objective thought, which operates in an autonomous and rational way, even before subjectivizing the surrounding rationality, and taming it into usefulness.

Through the acceptance of these postulates, structuralism offers the social sciences an epistemological model incomparably more powerful than those they previously had at their disposal. It reveals, behind phenomena, a unity and a coherence that could not be brought out by a simple description of the facts, 'laid out flat', so to speak, and presented in random order to the enquiring mind. By changing the level of observation and looking beyond the empirical facts to the relations between them, it reveals and confirms that these relations are simpler and more intelligible than the things they interconnect, and whose ultimate nature may remain unfathomable, without this provisional or definitive opacity being, as hitherto, an obstacle to their interpretation.

Secondly, structuralism reintegrates man into nature and, while making it possible to disregard the subject — that unbearably spoilt child who has occupied the philosophical scene for too long now, and prevented serious research through demanding exclusive attention — involves other consequences that have not been sufficiently noted, and the implications of which ought to have been understood and appreciated by those who criticize linguists and anthropologists from the point of view of religious faith. Structuralism is resolutely teleological (L.-S. 23, pp. 14–15); finality, after being long banned by a form of scientific thought still dominated by mechanism and empiricism, has been restored to its true place and again made respectable by structuralism. The believers who criticize us in the name of the sacred values of the human person, if they were consistent with themselves, would argue differently: they ought to be putting the question:

if the finality postulated by your intellectual method is neither in the consciousness nor in the subject, since you attempt to locate it on the hither side of both, where can it be, except outside them? And they would call upon us to draw the logical consequences . . . The fact that they do not do so, shows that these timorous spirits attach more importance to their own selves than to their god.

However, it should not be assumed that I am trailing my coat, since this would be inconceivable on the part of someone who has never felt the slightest twinge of religious anxiety. Structuralism is attentive, of course, to the purely logical arguments put forward by mathematicians to reveal the inadequacy and the contradictions of the Neo-Darwinism that is still accepted by most biologists (Moorhead-Kaplan). But even the clumsy, slow, obstinate, anonymous drive by which we might be tempted to explain the fact that, since its creation thousands of millions of years ago, the universe, and man with it, are, to quote the cautious terms used by Piaget (see above, p. 627), 'in a state of constant construction', would not provide any common ground with theology. Although structuralism does not herald any reconciliation of science with faith and argues still less in favour of any such reconciliation, it feels better able than the naturalism and empiricism of previous generations to explain and validate the place that religious feeling has held, and still holds, in the history of humanity: religious feeling senses confusedly that the hiatus between the world and the mind, and between causality and finality, does not correspond so much to things as they actually are as to the limit beyond which knowledge strains in vain to reach, since its intellectual and spiritual resources will never be commensurable with the dimensions of the essence of the objects it studies. We cannot overcome this contradiction, but it is not impossible that we shall more easily adjust to it, now that the astronomers have accustomed us to the idea of the expanding universe. If an explosion, a phenomenon that sensory experience allows us to perceive only during a fraction of a second, and without being able to distinguish any of its details because of the suddenness and rapidity with which it occurs, can be the same thing as cosmic expansion, which appears infinitely slowed down in comparison with the scale of the phenomena in which we live our daily lives, and which we cannot imagine but can only translate into the abstract formulae of mathematics, then it does not seem so incredible that a project conceived in a flash by a lucid consciousness, together with the appropriate means for its realization, might be of the same kind, on an infinitely reduced scale, as that obscure drive which, over millions of years and with the aid of tortuous and complicated devices, has ensured the pollinization of orchids, thanks to transparent windows allowing the light through to attract insects and guide them towards the pollen enclosed in a single capsule; or has intoxicated them with the secretions of the flower so that they wobble, lose their balance and slide down an artfully directed slope or fall into a little pool of water; or again sets a trap, the mechanism of which is touched off unwittingly by the insect so that it is held for the necessary length of time against the pollen; or deceives it by giving the flower a shape reminiscent of the female insect, so that the male attempts a sterile copulation which results in genuine fertilization for the plant; or places a tiny trigger so that the foraging bee inevitably bumps against it with its head, thus releasing a sticky capsule of pollen that, all unknowingly, it will carry off to another flower . . .

Nothing could seem more unacceptable, then, than the compromise suggested by Sartre (p. 89), when he says he is prepared to allow structure a place in the practico-inert, provided we recognize that 'this thing outside man is at the same time material worked upon by man, and bearing the trace of man'. He goes on to say further:

> You will not find, in nature, oppositions such as those described by the linguist. In nature there are only independent forces. The material elements are linked to each other and act upon each other. But this link is always external. It is not a matter of internal links, such as that which posits the masculine in relation to the feminine, or the plural in relation to the singular, that is, of a system in which the existence of each element conditions that of all the others.

These dogmatic assertions leave one bewildered. As if the opposition between, and complementarity of, male and female, positive and negative, right and left — which, as has been known since 1957, have an objective existence — were not written into biological and physical nature and did not bear witness to the interdependence of forces! Structuralism, unlike the kind of philosophy which restricts the dialectic to human history and bans it from the natural order, readily admits that the ideas it formulates in psychological terms may be no more than fumbling approximations to organic or even physical truths. One of the trends of contemporary science to which it is most sympathetic is that which, validating the intuitions of savage thought, already occasionally succeeds in reconciling the sensory with the intelligible and the qualitive with the geometrical, and gives us a glimpse of the natural order as a huge semantic field, 'in which the existence of each element conditions that of all the others'. It is not a type of reality irreducible to language but, as the poet says, 'a temple in which living pillars from time to time emit confused words';[10] except that, since the discovery of the genetic code, we know that the words are neither confused nor intermittent.

Binary distinctions do not exist solely in human language; they are also found in certain animal modes of communication: for instance, the chirring of crickets uses a simple reversion of rhythm $(x, y/y, x)$ to alter the nature of the message from a warning cry from male to male to a mating call from male to female (Alexander). And what better illustration of the interdependence of forces could one ask for from nature than the marvellously geometrical evolution of flower forms from the Triassic to the end of the Tertiary, which shows a development from amorphous structures at the beginning, first to two-dimensional radial symmetry then to four or five detector-units arranged on the same plane, then to three-dimensional structures and lastly to bilateral symmetry, all of which involved a complementary development of the pollinating insects, constantly adjusting to botanical evolution through a process one would have no hesitation in calling dialectical, were it taking place in the realm of thought.

In another area closer to man, communication usually appears to us to be at the opposite extreme from hostility and war. And yet it would seem that a hormone, whose function in mammals is to ensure communication between the cells during certain physiological processes, is identical with acrasin, which brings about the social aggregation of the amoebae; the basic cause of this phenomenon is, apparently, the attraction of the protozoa to bacteria on which they feed, and which secrete acrasin. This represents a remarkably dialectical transition from communication as a form of sociability to the conception of sociability itself as the lower limit of predatoriness (Bonner). In the lower organisms at least, social life is the result of a chemical threshold high enough to allow individuals to attract each other, but just below the level at which, through an excess of desire, they would begin eating each other. While awaiting further progress in biochemistry, we can leave it to the moralists to decide whether there are any other lessons to be drawn from these observations.

When, in La Pensée sauvage (pp. 270–72), I interpreted the names we give to birds as indicating that their various species, taken as a whole, appear to us as a sort of metaphorical counterpart of human society, I did not realize that an objective relation of the same type actually exists between

[10] TRANSLATORS' NOTE: La Nature est un temple, où de vivants piliers Laissent parfois sortir de confuses paroles . . . – the first two lines of a sonnet by Baudelaire, entitled Correspondances.

their brains and ours. It would seem that mammals and birds, in evolving from their common source, the reptiles, followed two divergent paths as regards the development of the brain and arrived at complementary solutions. In the higher mammals, intellectual operations take place in the cortex, which surrounds the extensive area occupied by various components of the striatum. In birds, on the contrary, as if through the effect of a topological transformation, the same operations (using a code simpler than, but of the same type as, the one programmed in the cortex) are carried out by the upper part of the striatum, which constitutes almost the whole mass of the brain, and which partly surrounds a rudimentary cortex lodged in a furrow at the top (Stettner-Matyniak). In so far as a metaphor always consists of referring to a total, implied semantic field by means of a complementary part of the whole, we can say, then, that in the field of possible cerebral organizations, the mammalian brain and the bird brain present a metaphorical image of each other.

The structuralist ambition to link up the sensory with the intelligible and to reject any explanation which sacrifices one aspect for the benefit of the other is also encouraged by the work of those who, like D'Arcy Wentworth Thompson following on from Dürer (see above, pp. 676–7), have been able to establish a term-by-term correspondence between abstract and intelligible relationships on the one hand, and, on the other, living forms – that one would have otherwise thought to be indistinguishable except through aesthetic intuition and long practical familiarity with forms of the same type – and chief among which is the human face, usually thought to be a visible expression of the personality, and its qualities of character and feeling. And what forester could say exactly how he identifies a tree from a distance? Yet only about a thousand instructions are needed to programme a computer to draw trees which, according to variations in the parameters, can be recognized by a botanist as firs, willows or oaks . . . Differences which might have been thought to be of a purely qualitative nature can be reduced, then, to the operation of a few simple mathematical properties (Eden, in Moorhead-Kaplan, p. 55).

Stereochemical theory reduces the range of smells – which one would have thought inexhaustible and indescribable – to seven 'primary odours' (camphoraceous, musky, floral, pepperminty, ethereal, pungent and putrid) which, when variously combined like the constituent elements of phonemes, produce sensations, both indefinable and immediately recognizable, such as the smells of roses, carnations, leeks or fish. According to the same theory, these sensory values can be related to the corresponding simple or complex geometrical forms of the odorous molecules, each of which fits into the olfactory receptor-site specialized to receive it through having a similar form (Amoore; Grive). The theory has not yet been generally accepted (Wright), but it may well be elaborated and refined through comparison with the chemistry of taste, which explains the sensation of sweetness by a change of form of one of the proteins of the body, through contact with certain molecules. Information about this geometrical change, when relayed to the brain, is expressed by the recognition of the appropriate sensation (Lambert). Bird-songs illustrate the opposite situation. Their inexpressible beauty eludes all attempts at description in acoustic terms, since the modulations are so rapid and complex that the human ear cannot perceive them, or does so only fragmentarily. But their hidden richness is directly seen in geometrical form in the oscillograms that have been made of them; expressed as graphs, the songs of the different species can be completely apprehended as incredibly delicate and refined shapes (Greenwalt), as if they were extraordinary masterpieces, in ivory or some other precious material, turned on a lathe.

In fact, structural analysis, which some critics dismiss as a gratuitous and decadent game, can only appear in the mind because its model is already present in the body. I have already mentioned (see above, p. 678) the exhaustive research that has been done on the mechanism of visual perception in various animals, from fish to cats and monkeys. It shows that each cell in the appropriate area of the cortex continues the processing already begun by several types of retinal or ganglion cells, each of which reacts to a particular stimulus: the direction of movement, the size of the moving object, or the relative rapidity of the movement of small objects, and so on. Consequently, in the first place the eye, and then the brain, do not react to objects which are independent of each other, and independent of the background against which they are seen. What we might call the raw material of immediate visual perception already consists of binary oppositions: simple and complex, light and dark, light on a dark background and dark on a light background, upward and downward, straight and slanting movement, etc. (Pfeiffer; Hubel; Michael). Structuralist thought, by following procedures that have been criticized as being too intellectual, rediscovers, then, and brings to the surface of the consciousness, profound organic truths. Only its practitioners can know, from inner experience, what a sensation of fulfilment it can bring, through making the mind feel itself to be truly in communion with the body.

The preceding remarks do not amount to a theory, and still less are they meant as the preliminary outline of a philosophy; I hope they will be taken for what they are: the free-ranging, intellectual musings, tinged with confusion and error, that the subject indulges in, during the short time when, having been released from one task, he does not yet know in what new one he will again dissolve his identity. As I cast a last look over the outcome of eight years' labour, which will soon be as foreign to me as if it had been the work of someone else, I think I can understand, and to some extent excuse, the mistrust with which it has been received in various quarters. The reaction is to be explained, I should say, by the doubly paradoxical nature of the undertaking. If any result emerges from it, it is, in the first place, that no myth or version of a myth is identical with the others and that each myth, when it appears to give gratuitous emphasis to an insignificant detail, and dwells on it without any stated reason, is in fact trying to say the opposite of what another myth said on the same subject: no myth is like any other. However, taken as a whole, they all come to the same thing and, as Goethe says about plants: 'their chorus points to a hidden law'.

The second paradox is that a work I know to be packed with meaning appears to some as the elaboration of a form without meaning. But this is because the meaning is included, and as it were compressed, within the system. Those who cannot enter into it through lack of knowledge of the immense anthropological storehouse represented by the native cultures of the New World are doomed to grasp nothing of its inner significance; seen from the outside, this significance cancels itself out. It is not surprising, then, that the philosophers do not feel themselves to be involved; they are not involved, in fact, because the scope of the undertaking is beyond their apprehension, whereas, being more directly concerned, semiologists may be interested in the form and anthropologists in the content.

I myself, in considering my work from within as I have lived it, or from without, which is my present relationship to it as it drifts away into my past, see more clearly that this tetralogy of mine, now that it has been composed, must, like Wagner's, end with a twilight of the gods; or, to be more accurate, that having been completed a century later and in harsher times, it foresees the twilight of man, after that of the gods which was supposed to ensure the advent of a happy and liberated humanity. At this late hour in my career, the final image the myths leave me with and – not only individual myths but, through them, the supreme myth recounted by the history of mankind, which is also the history of the universe in which human history unfolds – links up with that intuitive feeling which, in my early days and as I explained in *Tristes Tropiques*, led me to see in the phases of a sunset, watched from the point in time when the celestial spectacle was set in place until, after successive developments and complications, it finally collapsed and disappeared into the oblivion of night, the model of the phenomena I was to study later and of the problems of mythology that I would have to resolve: mythology, that huge and complex edifice which also glows with a thousand iridescent colours as it builds up before the analyst's gaze, slowly expands to its full extent, then crumbles and fades away in the distance, as if it had never existed.

Is this image not true of humanity itself and, beyond humanity, of all the manifestations of life: birds, butterflies, shell-fish and other animals, as well as plants and their flowers? Evolution develops and diversifies their forms, but always in view of their ultimate disappearance, so that, in the end nothing will remain of nature, life or man, or of his subtle and refined creations, such as languages, social institutions and customs, aesthetic masterpieces and myths, once their firework display is over. My analysis, by proving the rigorous patterning of the myths and thus conferring on them the status of objects, has thereby brought out the mythic character of those objective realities: the universe, nature and man which, over thousands, millions or billions of years, will, when all is said and done, have simply demonstrated the resources of their combinatory systems, in the manner of some great mythology, before collapsing in upon themselves and vanishing, though the self-evidence of their own decay.

The fundamental opposition, the source of the myriad others with which the myths abound and which have been tabulated in these four volumes, is precisely the one stated by Hamlet, although in the form of a still over-optimistic choice between two alternatives. Man is not free to choose whether to be or not to be. A mental effort, consubstantial with his history and which will cease only with his disappearance from the stage of the universe, compels him to accept the two self-evident and contradictory truths which, through their clash, set his thought in motion, and, to neutralize their opposition, generate an unlimited series of other binary distinctions which, while never resolving the primary contradiction, echo and perpetuate it on an ever smaller scale: one is the reality of being, which man senses at the deepest level as being alone capable of giving a reason and a meaning to his daily activities, his moral and emotional life, his political options, his involvement in the social and the natural worlds, his practical endeavours and his scientific achievements; the other is the reality of non-being, awareness of which inseparably accompanies the sense of being, since man has to live and struggle, think, believe and above all, preserve his courage, although he can never at any moment lose sight of the opposite certainty that he was not present on earth in former times, that he will not always be here in the future and that, with his inevitable disappearance from the surface of a planet which is itself doomed to die, his labours, his sorrows, his joys, his hopes and his works will be as if they had never existed, since no consciousness will survive to preserve even the memory of these ephemeral phenomena, only a few features of which, soon to be erased from the impassive face of the earth, will remain as already cancelled evidence that they once were, and were as nothing.

Paris, October 1967 — Lignerolles, September 1970

Bibliography

In the numbered entries, works already listed in the Bibliographies of the preceding volumes retain their original numbers; works appearing here for the first time are added at the end of the entry, regardless of date of publication.

ABBREVIATIONS:

AA   *American Anthropologist*
APAMNH   *Anthropological Papers of the American Museum of Natural History*, New York
ARBAE   *Annual Reports of the Bureau of American Ethnology*, Washington, D.C.
BAMNH   *Bulletins of the American Museum of Natural History*, New York
BBAE   *Bulletins of the Bureau of American Ethnology*, Washington, D.C.
CNAE   *Contributions to North American Ethnology*, Washington, D.C.
CUCA   *Columbia University Contributions to Anthropology*, New York
EB   *see* Albisetti, C. and Venturelli, A. J.
HA   Lévi-Strauss, C., *From Honey to Ashes*, London, 1973
HSAI   *Handbook of South American Indians, BBAE 143*, 7 vol., Washington, D.C., 1946–59
IJAL   *International Journal of American Linguistics*
JAFL   *Journal of American Folklore*
JRAI   *Journal of the Royal Anthropological Institute of Great Britain and Ireland*
JSA   *Journal de la Société des Américanistes*
L.-S.   Lévi-Strauss, C.
MAAA   *Memoirs of the American Anthropological Association*
MAFLS   *Memoirs of the American Folk-Lore Society*
MAMNH   *Memoirs of the American Museum of Natural History*, New York
Nim.   Nimuendaju, C.
OTM   Lévi-Strauss, C., *The Origin of Table Manners*, London, 1978
RBAAS   *Reports of the British Association for the Advancement of Science*
RC   Lévi-Strauss, C., *The Raw and the Cooked*, London, 1970
SWJA   *Southwestern Journal of Anthropology*
UCPAAE   *University of California Publications in American Archaeology and Ethnology*, Berkeley
UWPA   *University of Washington Publications in Anthropology*, Seattle

ABRAMS, L. *Illustrated Flora of the Pacific States*, 4 vol., Stanford, 3rd edn, 1955–60.
ABREU, J. Capistrano de. *Rã-txa hu-ni-ku-i. A lingua dos Caxinauas*, Rio de Janeiro, 1914.

ADAMSON, Th. 'Folk-Tales of the Coast Salish', *Memoirs of the American Folk-Lore Society*, XXVII, 1934.

AHLBRINCK, W. 'Encyclopaedie der Karaiben', *Verhandelingen der Koninklijke Akademie van Wetenschappen te Amsterdam, Afdeeling Letterkunde, Nieuwe Reeks, Deel 27, 1, 1931* (French trans. Doude van Herwinjen, miméogr. Paris, 1956).

ALBISETTI, C. and VENTURELLI, A. J. *Enciclopédia Bororo*, Vol. I, Campo Grande, 1962; Vol. II, *ibid.*, 1969.

ALEXANDER, R. D. 'The Evolution of Cricket Chirps', *Natural History*, 75, 9, 1966.

ALLISON, S. S. 'Account of the Similkameen Indians', *JRAI*, 21, 1892.

AMOORE, J. E., JOHNSTON Jr. and RUBIN, M. 'The Stereochemical Theory of Odor', *Scientific American*, 210, 2, 1964.

ANDERSON, D. D. 'A Stone Age Campsite at the Gateway of America', *Scientific American*, 218, 6, 1968.

ANDRADE, M. J. 'Quileute Texts', *CUCA*, 12, New York, 1931.

ANGULO, J. de and BECLARD d'HARCOURT, M. 'La musique des Indiens de la Californie du Nord', *JSA*, n.s., 23, 1931.

ANGULO, J. de and FREELAND, L. S. (1) 'The Lutuami Language', *JSA*, n.s., 23, 1931.

———. (2) 'Two Achumawi Tales', *JAFL*, 44, 1931.

———. (3) 'Miwok and Pomo Myths', *JAFL*, 41, 1928.

AOKI, H. 'On Sahaptin-Klamath Linguistic Affiliations', *IJAL*, 29, 1963.

AUDUBON, J. J. *Scènes de la nature dans les États-Unis et le nord de l'Amérique*, trans. Eugène Bazin, 2 vol., Paris, 1868.

AUFENANGER, H. (2) 'The Ayom Pygmies' Myth of Origin and their Method of Counting', *Anthropos*, 55, 1–2, 1960.

BAILEY, F. L. 'Navaho Foods and Cooking Methods', *AA*, 42, 2, 1940.

BALLARD, A. C. (1) 'Mythology of Southern Puget Sound', *UWPA*, 3, 2, 1929.

———. (2) 'Some Tales of the Southern Puget Sound Salish', *UWPA*, 2, 3, 1927.

———. (3) 'Calendric Terms of the Southern Puget Sound Salish', *SWJA*, 6, 1, 1950.

BANCROFT, H. H. *The Native Races of the Pacific States of North America*, 5 vol., London, 1875, 1876.

BANNER, H. (1) 'Mítos dos Índios Kayapó', *Revista de Antropologia*, 5, 1, São Paulo, 1957.

BARBEAU, C. M. (3) 'Contes populaires canadiens', *JAFL*, 29, 1916; 30, 1917; 32, 1919.

———. (4) 'Loucheux Myths collected by Ch. Camsell', *JAFL*, 28, 1915.

BARKER, M. A. R. (1) 'Klamath Texts', *UCPAAE*, 30, 1963.

———. (2) 'Klamath Dictionary', *UCPAAE*, 31, 1963.

———. (3) 'Klamath Grammar', *UCPAAE*, 32, 1964.

BARNETT, H. G. (1) 'Culture Element Distributions: VII. Oregon Coast', *Anthropological Records*, 1, Berkeley, 1937–9.

———. (2) 'Culture Element Distributions: IX. Gulf of Georgia Salish', *ibid.*

———. (3) 'The Coast Salish of British Columbia', *University of Oregon Monographs, Studies in Anthropology*, 4, 1955.

BARRETT, S. A. (2) 'Pomo Myths', *Bulletin of the Public Museum of the City of Milwaukee*, 15, 1933.

———. (3) 'The Material Culture of the Klamath Lake and Modoc Indians of Northwestern California and Southern Oregon', *UCPAAE*, 5, 4, 1910.

BAUDELAIRE, Ch. 'Richard Wagner et *Tannhäuser* à Paris', *Œuvres complètes*, éd. de la Pléiade, Paris, 1961.

BEAUCHAMP, W. M. 'Onondaga Tale of the Pleiades', *JAFL*, 13, 1900.

BECHER, H. (1) 'Algumas notas sôbre a religião e a mitologia dos Surára', *Revista do Museu Paulista*, 11, São Paulo, 1959.

BECKER, H. F. 'Flowers, Insects and Evolution', *Natural History*, 74, 2, 1965.

BECKWITH, M. W. (2) 'Mythology of the Oglala Dakota', *JAFL*, 43, 1930.

BEIDELMAN, T. O. 'Swazi Royal Ritual', *Africa*, 36, 4, 1966.

BENT, A. C. *Life Histories of North American Birds*, new edn, 20 vol., New York, 1963.

BENVENISTE, E. *Le Vocabulaire des institutions indo-européennes*, 2 vol., Paris, 1969.

BERREMAN, J. V. 'Tribal Distribution in Oregon', *MAAA*, 47, 1937.

BLOOMFIELD, L. (1) 'Sacred Stories of the Sweet Grass Cree', *Bulletin 60, Anthropological Series 11, National Museum of Canada*, Ottawa, 1930.

———. (3) 'Menomini Texts', *Publications of the American Ethnological Society*, 12, New York, 1928.

BOAS, F. (2) 'Tsimshian Mythology', *31st ARBAE* (1909–10), Washington, D.C., 1916.

———. (4) ed.: 'Folk-Tales of Salishan and Sahaptin Tribes', *MAFLS*, 11, 1917.

———. (5) 'Zur Mythologie der Indianer von Washington und Oregon', *Globus*, 63, 1893.

———. (7) 'Kathlamet Texts', *BBAE 26*, Washington, D.C., 1901.

———. (8) 'The Eskimo of Baffin Land and Hudson Bay', *BAMNH*, 15, New York, 1901–1907.

———. (9) 'Kutenai Tales', *BBAE 26*, Washington, D.C., 1901.

———. (10) 'Chinook Texts', *BBAE 20*, Washington, D.C., 1894.

———. (12) 'The Mythology of the Bella Coola', *MAMNH*, 2, 1900.

———. (13) 'Indianische Sagen von der Nord-Pacifischen Küste Amerikas', *Sonder-Abdruck aus den Verhandlungen der Berliner Gesellschaft für Anthropologie, Ethnologie und Urgeschichte*, 1891–5, 23–7, Berlin.

———. (14) 'Traditions of the Tillamook Indians', *JAFL*, 11, 1898.

———. (15) 'The Origin of Death', *JAFL*, 30, 1917.

———. (16) 'Second General Report on the Indians of British Columbia', *RBAAS*, 60, 1890.

———. (17) 'The Indian Tribes of the Lower Fraser River', *RBAAS*, 64, 1894.

———. (18) 'Twelfth and Final Report . . . [on] the North-Western Tribes of . . . Canada', *RBAAS*, 68, 1898.

———. (19) 'The Kwakiutl of Vancouver Island', *MAMNH*, 8, Part 2, 1909.

———. (20) 'Current Beliefs of the Kwakiutl Indians', *JAFL*, 45, 1932.

———. (21) 'Fifth Report on the Indians of British Columbia', *RBAAS*, 65, 1895.

———. (22) 'Kwakiutl Tales', *CUCA*, 2, New York, 1910.

———. (23) 'Tsimshian Texts (New Series)', *Publications of the American Ethnological Society*, 3, 1912.

———. (24) 'Bella Bella Tales', *MAFLS*, 25, 1932.

———. (25) 'Alexander Francis Chamberlain', *JAFL*, 27, 1914.

———. (26) *Primitive Art*, Oslo, 1927.

BOAS, F. and HUNT, G. (1) 'Kwakiutl Texts', *MAMNH*, 5, 1902–1905; 14, 1906.

———. (2) 'Ethnology of the Kwakiutl', *35th ARBAE*, Washington, D.C., 1921.

BONNER, J. T. 'Hormones in Social Amoebae and Mammals', *Scientific American*, 220, 6, 1969.

BORDEN, Ch. E. 'Radiocarbon and geological dating of the Lower Fraser Canyon archaeological sequence', *Proceedings of the Sixth International Conference on Radiocarbon and Tritium Dating*, Pullman, Washington, 1965.

BOWERS, A. W. (1) *Mandan Social and Ceremonial Organization*, Chicago, 1950.

BRASHER, R. *Birds and Trees of North America*, 4 vol., New York, 1961–2.

BREHM, A. E. (1) *Brehms Tierleben. Allgemeine Kunde des Tierreichs*, Leipzig und Wien, 10 vol., 1890–93.

———. (2) *La Vie des animaux*, 4 vol., Paris, s.d.

BRETZ, J. H., SMITH, H. T. U. and NEFF, G. E. 'Channeled Scabland of Washington: New Data and Interpretations', *Bulletin of the Geological Society of America*, 67, 8, August 1956.

BRIGHT, W. 'The Karok Language', *UCPAAE*, 13, 1957.

BRONOWSKI, J. 'Human and animal languages' *in*: *To Honor Roman Jakobson*, la Haye, 1967.

BROWMAN, D. L. and MUNSELL, D. A. 'Columbia Plateau Prehistory : Cultural Development and Impinging Influences', *American Antiquity*, 34, 3, 1969.

BRYAN, A. L. 'Early Man in America and the Late Pleistocene Chronology of Western Canada and Alaska', *Current Anthropology*, 10, 4, 1969.

BUCHLER, I. R. and SELBY, H. A. 'A Formal Study of Myth', *Center of Intellectual Studies in Folklore and Oral History, Monograph Series 1*, Austin, 1968.

BUECHNER, H. K. 'The Bighorn Sheep in the United States', *Wildlife Monograph* 4, The Wildlife Society, Washington, D.C., 1960.

CADOGAN, L. (4) 'Ayvu Rapita. Textos míticos de los Mbyá-Guaraní del Guairá', *Antropologia*, 5, *Boletim.* 227, Universidade de São Paulo, 1959.

CÂMARA CASCUDO, L. de. *Dicionário do Folclore Brasileiro*, 2nd edn, Rio de Janeiro, 1962.

CAMPANA, D. del. 'Contributo all'Etnografia dei Matacco', *Archivio per l'Antropologia e la Etnologia*, 43, 1–2, Firenze, 1913.

CHAMBERLAIN, A. F. 'Report on the Kootenay Indians of South-Eastern British Columbia', *RBAAS*, 62, 1892.

CLARK, E. E. *Indian Legends of the Pacific Northwest*, Berkeley, 1953.

CLINE, W. *et al.* 'The Sinkaietk or Southern Okanagon of Washington', *General Series in Anthropology*, 6, Menasha, 1938.

COLBACCHINI (3): *see below*.

COLBACCHINI, A. and ALBISETTI, C. *Os Boróros Orientais*, São Paulo-Rio de Janeiro, 1942.

COLLINS, J. M. 'Distribution of the Chemakum Language' *in*: M. W. Smith, ed. (4).

COOPER, J. M. (2) 'Scapulimancy', *Essays in Anthropology presented to A. L. Kroeber*, Berkeley, 1936.

COPLEY, J. S., ed. *Ancient Hunters of the Far West*, San Diego, Cal., 1966.

CORNPLANTER, J. *Legends of the Longhouse*, Philadelphia-New York, 1938.

CRABTREE, D. 'A Technological Description of Artifacts in Assemblage 1, Wilson Butte Cave. Idaho', *Current Anthropology*, 10, 4, 1969.

CRESSMAN, L. S. (1) 'Klamath Prehistory. The Prehistory of the Culture of the Klamath Lake Area, Oregon', *Transactions of the American Philosophical Society*, n.s., 46, 1956.

———. (2) 'Cultural Sequences at the Dalles, Oregon. A Contribution to Pacific

Northwest Prehistory', *Transactions of the American Philosophical Society*, n.s., 1960.

CURTIN, J. (1) *Myths of the Modocs*, Boston, 1912.

———. (3) *Creation Myths of Primitive America*, London, 1899.

CURTIS, E. S. *The North American Indian*, 20 vol., New York, 1907–30. New edn, New York, 1970.

DABLON, P. C. *Relation de ce qui s'est passé de plus remarquable aux missions des PP. de la Compagnie de Jésus en la Nouvelle France les années 1670 et 1671*, Paris, 1672.

DA MATTA, R. 'Mito e Autoridade Doméstica : Uma Tentativa de Analise de um Mito Timbira . . .', *Revista do Instituto de Ciências Sociais*, 4, 1, Rio de Janeiro, 1967.

DANGEL, R. 'Bears and Fawns', *JAFL*, 42, 1929.

DAVIDSON, G. 'Coast Pilot of California, Oregon, and Washington', *U.S. Coast and Geodetic Survey*, *Pacific Coast*, Washington, D.C., 1889.

DAWSON, G. M. 'Notes on the Shuswap People of British Columbia', *Proceedings and Transactions of the Royal Society of Canada*, 9 (1891), Montreal, 1892.

DELARUE, P. *Le Conte populaire français*, Vol. I, Paris, 1957.

DELARUE, P. and TENÈZE, M. L. *Le Conte populaire français*, Vol. II, Paris, 1964.

DEMETRACOPOULOU, D. 'The Loon Woman Myth : A Study in Synthesis', *JAFL*, 46, 1933.

DENSMORE, F. (2) 'Chippewa Customs', *BBAE 86*, Washington, D.C., 1929.

———. (3) 'Nootka and Quileute Music', *BBAE 124*, Washington, D.C., 1939.

DESBARATS, P., ed. *What they Used to Tell About. Indian Legends from Labrador*, Toronto, 1969.

DIXON, R. (1) 'Shasta Myths', *JAFL*, 23, 1910.

———. (2) 'Maidu Myths', *BAMNH*, 17, 1902–1907.

———. (4) 'Achomawi and Atsugewi Tales', *JAFL*, 21, 1908.

———. (5) 'The Mythology of the Shasta-Achomawi', *AA*, 7, 1905.

———. (6) 'The Northern Maidu', *BAMNH*, 17, 1902–1907.

———. (7) 'The Shasta', *BAMNH*, 17, 1902–1907.

DORSEY, G. A. (5) 'The Arapaho Sun Dance; the Ceremony of the Offerings Lodge', *Field Columbian Museum, Publ. 75, Anthropol. Series 4*, Chicago, 1903.

———. (8) *Traditions of the Caddo*, Washington, D.C., 1905.

———. (9) 'Traditions of the Osage', *Field Columbian Museum, Publ. 88, Anthropol. Series 7, 1*, Chicago, 1904.

———. (10) 'The Dwamish Indian Spirit Boat and its Use', *Bull. Free Museum of Science and Art*, University of Pennsylvania, 3, 1901.

DORSEY, G. A. and KROEBER, A. L. 'Traditions of the Arapaho', *Field Columbian Museum, Publ. 81, Anthropol. Series 5*, Chicago, 1903.

DORSEY, J. O. (1) 'The Cegiha Language', *CNAE*, 6, Washington, D.C., 1890.

———. (4) 'The Gentile System of the Siletz Tribes', *JAFL*, 3, 1890.

DORSEY, J. O. and SWANTON, J. R. 'A Dictionary of the Biloxi and Ofo Languages', *BBAE 47*, Washington, D.C., 1912.

DREYFUS, S. *Les Kayapo du Nord*, Paris-la Haye, 1963.

DRIVER, H. E. 'Culture Element Distributions : X. Northwest California', *Anthropological Records*, 1, 6, Berkeley, 1939.

DRUCKER, Ph. 'The Northern and Central Nootkan Tribes', *BBAE 144*, Washington, D.C., 1951.

DuBois, C. (1) 'Wintu Ethnography', *UCPAAE*, 36, 1, 1935.

DuBois, C. and Demetracopoulou, D. 'Wintu Myths', *UCPAAE*, 28, 1930–31.

DuBois, C. G. 'The Religion of the Luiseño and Diegueño Indians of Southern California', *UCPAAE*, 8, 1908.

Dumézil, G. (2) *La Saga de Hadingus. Du Mythe au roman*, Bibliothèque de l'École pratique des hautes études. Sciences religieuses, 66th volume, Paris, 1953.

——. (3) *La Religion romaine archaïque*, Paris, 1966.

——. (4) *Idées romaines*, Paris, 1969.

Dumond, D. E. 'Toward a Prehistory of the Na-Dene, with a General Comment on Population Movements among Nomadic Hunters', *AA*, 71, 5, 1969.

Eaton J. H. 'Description of the True State and Character of the New Mexican Tribes', *in*: Schoolcraft, H. R.: *Information Respecting the . . . Indian Tribes of the United States . . .*, Part 4, Philadelphia, 1854.

Edel, M. M. 'Stability in Tillamook Folklore', *JAFL*, 57, 1944.

Eells, M. (1) 'Traditions and History of the Puget Sound Indians', *The American Antiquarian and Oriental Journal*, 9, Chicago, 1887.

——. (2) 'Puget Sound Indians', *The American Antiquarian and Oriental Journal*, 10, Chicago, 1888.

——. (3) *The Twana, Chemakum and Klallam Indians, of Washington Territory*, Facsimile Reproduction, Seattle, 1964.

Ehrenreich, P. (2) 'Die Mythen und Legenden der Südamerikanischen Urvölker und ihre Beziehungen zu denen Nordamerikas und der alten Welt', *Zeitschrift für Ethnologie*, 37, 1905 (Supplement).

Elliott, W. C. 'Lake Lilloet Tales', *JAFL*, 44, 1931.

Elmendorf, W. W. (1) 'The Structure of Twana Culture [with] Comparative Notes on the Structure of Yurok Culture [by] A. L. Kroeber', *Research Studies, Monographic Supplement 2*, Pullman, 1960.

——. (2) 'Linguistic and Geographic Relations in the Northern Plateau Area', *SWJA*, 21, 1, 1965.

——. (3) 'Geographic ordering, subgroupings, and Olympic Salish', *IJAL*, 35, 3, 1969.

Elmendorf, W. W. and Suttles, W. 'Pattern and Change in Halkomelem Salish Dialects', *Anthropological Linguistics*, 2, 7, 1960.

Elmore, F. H. 'Ethnobotany of the Navaho', *The University of Mexico Bulletin, Monograph Series*, 1, 7, 1944.

Enciclopédia Bororo : *see* Albisetti and Venturelli.

Engels, F. *Anti-Dühring*, The Foreign Language Publishing House, Moscow, 1954.

Erikson, E. H. 'Observations on the Yurok: Childhood and World Image', *UCPAAE*, 35, 1943.

Farrand, L. (1) (Assisted by W. S. Kahnweiler) 'Traditions of the Quinault Indians', *MAMNH*, 4, New York, 1902.

——. (2) 'Traditions of the Chilcotin Indians', *MAMNH*, 4, New York, 1900.

——. (3) 'Kalapooian Family', *BBAE* 30, Washington, D.C., 1907.

Farrand, L. and Mayer, Th. 'Quileute Tales', *JAFL*, 32, 1919.

Felice, A. de. *Contes de Haute-Bretagne*, Paris, 1954.

Fenton, W. N. 'An Outline of Seneca Ceremonies at Cold Spring Longhouse', *Yale University Publ. in Anthropol.*, 9, New Haven, 1936.

Fletcher, A. C. and La Flesche, F., 'The Omaha Tribe', *27th ARBAE* (1905–1906), Washington, D.C., 1911.

FORTES, M. 'Totem and Taboo', *Proceedings of the Royal Anthropological Institute . . . for 1966*, London, 1967.

FOURNIER, P. *Les Quatre Flores de la France*, new edn, Paris, 1961.

FRACHTENBERG, L. J. (1) 'Coos Texts', *CUCA*, 1, New York-Leyden, 1913.

———.(2) 'Shasta and Athapascan Myths from Oregon (Collected by Livingston Farrand)', *JAFL*, 28, 1915.

———. (3) 'Lower Umpqua Texts', *CUCA*, 4, New York, 1914.

———. (4) 'Alsea Texts and Myths', *BBAE* 67, Washington, D.C., 1920.

———. (5) 'Coos' *in*: Boas, F., *Handbook of American Indian Languages*, Vol. 2, *BBAE* 40, Washington, D.C., 1922.

FRANCISCAN FATHERS. *An Ethnologic Dictionary of the Navaho Language*, Saint Michael, Arizona, 1910.

FRENCH, D. 'Wasco-Wishram' *in*: *Perspectives in American Indians Culture Change*, ed. E. H. Spicer, Chicago, 1961.

FRIKEL, P. (3) 'Os Xikrin', *Museu Paraense Emilio Goeldi, Publicações avulsas*, 7, Belém, 1968.

GARTH, Th. R. (1) 'Early Nineteenth Century Tribal Relations in the Columbia Plateau', *SWJA*, 20, 1, 1964.

———. (2) 'Atsugewi Ethnography', *University of California Publications. Anthropological Records*, 14, 2, 1953.

———. (3) 'Kinship Terminology, Marriage Practices, and Behavior toward Kin among the Atsugewi', *AA*, 46, 1944.

———. (4) 'Emphasis on Industriousness among the Atsugewi', *AA*, 47, 1945.

GATSCHET, A. S. (1) 'The Klamath Indians of South-Western Oregon', *CNAE*, 2, two parts, Washington, D.C., 1890.

———. (2) 'Der Tskan-Vogel', *Globus*, 52, 1887.

GAYTON, A. H. and NEWMAN, S. S. 'Yokuts and Western Mono Myths', *Anthropological Records*, 5, 1, Berkeley, 1940.

GEIST, V. 'A Consequence of Togetherness', *Natural History*, 76, 8, 1968.

GIBBS, G. (1) 'Tribes of Western Washington and Northwestern Oregon', *CNAE*, 1, Washington, D.C., 1877.

———. (2) 'Vocabulary of the Nitkuntemukh', *ibid.*

GIFFORD, E. W. (1) 'Western Mono Myths', *JAFL*, 36, 1923.

———. (2) 'Miwok Myths', *UCPAAE*, 12, 1917.

GIFFORD, E. W. and HARRIS, G. B. *Californian Indian Nights Entertainments*, Glendale, 1930.

GODDARD, P. E. (1) 'Hupa Texts', *UCPAAE*, 1, 2, 1904.

———. (2) 'Jicarilla Apache Texts', *APAMNH*, 8, 1911.

———. (3) 'Chilula Texts', *UCPAAE*, 10, 1914.

———. (4) 'Life and Culture of the Hupa', *UCPAAE*, 1, 1903.

———. (5) 'Lassik Tales', *JAFL*, 19, 1906.

———. (6) 'Kato Texts', *UCPAAE*, 5, 1909.

GODFREY, W. E. *Les Oiseaux du Canada*, Ottawa, 1967 (Musée National du Canada, Bull. 203, série biologique, 73).

GOETHE, J. W. de. *Essai sur la métamorphose des plantes*, traduit . . . par F. de Gingins Lassaraz, Genève, 1829.

GOLDER, F. A. 'Tales from Kodiak Islands', *JAFL*, 16, 1903.

GOLDSCHMIDT, W. 'Nomlaki Ethnography', *UCPAAE*, 42, 4, 1951.

GOULD, M. K. (1) 'Okanagon Tales', *MAFLS*, 11, 1917 (cf. BOAS 4).

———. (2) 'Sanpoil Tales', *MAFLS*, 11, 1917 (cf. BOAS 4).

GOULD, R. A. 'Seagoing Canoes Among the Indians of Northwestern California', *Ethnohistory*, 15, 1, 1968.

GRAVES, Ch. S. *Lore and Legends of the Klamath River Indians*, Yreka, Cal., 1929.

GREENWALT, C. H. 'How Birds Sing', *Scientific American*, 221, 5, 1969.

GRINNELL, G. B. (3) *Blackfoot Lodge Tales*, New York, 1892.

GRIVE, J. 'Les Molécules odorantes agiraient par leur forme et leur taille', *Science Progrès-La Nature*, 3343, 1963.

GROSSO, G. H. 'Cave Life on the Palouse', *Natural History*, 76, 2, 1962.

GUALLART, J. M. 'Mítos y leyendas de los Aguarunas del alto Marañón', *Peru Indigena*, 7, Lima, 1958.

GUIART, J. *L'Art autochtone de la Nouvelle Calédonie*, Noumea, 1953.

GUNTHER, E. (1) 'Klallam Ethnography', *UWPA*, 1, 5, 1927.

——. (2) 'Klallam Folktales', *UWPA*, 1, 1925.

——. (3) 'Ethnobotany of Western Washington', *UWPA*, 10, 1, 1945.

——. (4) 'An Analysis of the First Salmon Ceremony', *AA*, 28, 1926.

——. (5) 'A further analysis of the First Salmon Ceremony', *UPWA*, 2, 1928.

——. (6) 'A Preliminary Report on the Zoological Knowledge of the Makah', *Essays in Anthropology presented to A. L. Kroeber*, Berkeley, 1936.

HAAS, M. R. (2) 'Some Genetic Affiliations of Algonkin', *Culture in History. Essays in Honor of Paul Radin*, ed. S. Diamond, New York, 1960.

——. (3) 'Wiyot-Yurok-Algonkian and Problems of Comparative Algonkian', *IJAL*, 32, 1966.

HAEBERLIN, H. K. (1) 'Mythology of Puget Sound', *JAFL*, 37, 1924.

——. (2) 'Sbetedaq, A Shamanistic Performance of the Coast Salish', *AA*, 20, 1918.

HAEBERLIN, H. K. and GUNTHER, E. 'The Indians of Puget Sound', *UWPA*, 4, 1, 1930.

HAEBERLIN, H. K., TEIT, J. A. and ROBERTS, H. H. 'Coiled Basketry in British Columbia and Surrounding Region', *41st ARBAE* (1919–24), Washington, D.C., 1928.

HAILE, F. B. (1) 'Origin Legend of the Navaho Enemy Way', *Yale University Publ. in Anthropol.*, 17, 1938.

——. (2) *Origin Legend of the Navaho Flintway*, Chicago, 1943.

HAILE, F. B. and WHEELWRIGHT, M. C. *Emergence Myth According to the Hanelthayhe or Upward-Reaching Rite*, Santa Fé, New Mexico, 1949.

HAINES, F. *The Nez Percés. Tribesmen of the Columbia Plateau*, Norman, Oklahoma, 1955.

HALLOWELL, A. I. 'Bear Ceremonialism in the Northern Hemisphere', *AA*, 28, 1926.

HARRINGTON, J. P. (2) 'A Yuma Account of Origins', *JAFL*, 21, 1908.

HASTINGS, J., ed. *Encyclopaedia of Religion and Ethics*, 13 vol., New York, 1928.

HEIZER, R. F. (1) 'Domestic Fuel in Primitive Society', *JRAI*, 93, 2, 1963.

——. (2) *Languages, Territories and Names of California Indian Tribes*, Berkeley and Los Angeles, 1966.

HENISCH, H. K. 'Amorphous-semiconductor Switching', *Scientific American*, 221, 5, 1969.

HESTER, J. A. *Early Man in the New World*, revised by K. McGowan, New York, 1962.

HEWITT, J. N. B. (3) 'White Dog Sacrifice', *BBAE 30*, Vol. 2, Washington, D.C., 1910.

HILGER, I. M. (2) 'Arapaho Child Life and its Cultural Background', *BBAE 148*, Washington, D.C., 1952.

HILL-TOUT, Ch. (1) 'Report on the Ethnology of the Síciatl of British Columbia', *JRAI*, 34, 1904.

———. (2) 'Ethnological Report on the Stseélis and Sk.aúlits tribes of the Halkōmēlem Division of the Salish of British Columbia', *JRAI*, 34, 1904.

———. (3) 'Report on the Ethnology of the Stlatlumh of British Columbia', *JRAI*, 35, 1905.

———. (4) 'Sqaktktquaclt, or the Benign-Faced', *Folk-Lore*, 10, 1899.

———. (5) 'Report on the Ethnology of the South-eastern Tribes of Vancouver Island', *JRAI*, 37, 1907.

———. (6) *The Natives of British North America*, London, 1907.

———. (7) 'Notes on the Sk.qómic of British Columbia', *RBAAS*, 70, 1900.

———. (8) 'Report on the Ethnology of the Okanak.ēn of British Columbia', *JRAI*, 41, 1911.

———. (9) 'Ethnological Studies of the Mainland Halkōm'ēlem, a Division of the Salish of British Columbia', *RBAAS*, 72, 1902.

———. (10) 'Notes on the N'tlakápamuQ of British Columbia, a Branch of the Great Salish Stock of North America', *RBAAS*, 69, 1899.

HISSINK, K. and HAHN, A. *Die Tacana, 1. Erzählungsgut*, Stuttgart, 1961.

HOFFMAN, W. J. (1) 'The Menomini Indians', *14th ARBAE*, Washington, D.C., 1896.

———. (2) 'Selish Myths', *Bulletin of the Essex Institute*, 15 (1883), Salem, Mass., 1884.

———. (3) 'Vocabulary of the Selish Language', *Proceedings of the American Philosophical Society*, 23, 1886.

HOLMER, N. M. and WASSÉN, S. H. 'Nia Ikala. Canto Mágico para curar la locura', *Etnologiska Studier*, 23 Göteborg, 1958.

HOLT, C. 'Shasta Ethnography', *Anthropological Records*, III, 4, Berkeley, 1946.

HOLTVED, E. (2) *The Polar Eskimo Language and Folklore*, 2 vol., Copenhagen, 1951.

HOPKINS, D. M., ed. *The Bering Land Bridge*, Stanford, 1967.

HOPKINS, N. A. 'Great Basin Prehistory and Uto-Aztecan', *American Antiquity*, 31, 1, 1965.

HOUGH, W. 'Fire Origin Myths of the New World', *Intern. Congress of Americanists*, 20, I, 1924.

HUBEL, D. H. 'The Visual Cortex of the Brain', *Scientific American*, 209, 5, 1963.

HUNT, Ch. B. *Physiography of the United States*, San Francisco, 1967.

HYMES, D. H. (1) 'Two Wasco Motifs', *JAFL*, 66. 1953.

———. (2) 'The Wife who goes out like a man' (mimeogr.).

———. (3) Personal communication, June 19th, 1968.

IHERING, R. von. *Diccionario dos Animaes do Brazil*, São Paulo, 1940.

JACOBS, E. D. *Nehalem Tillamook Tales*, Eugene, Oregon, 1959.

JACOBS, M. (1) 'Northwest Sahaptin Texts', *CUCA*, 19, 1–2, New York, 1934.

———. (2) 'Clackamas Chinook Texts', 25, Parts 1–2, *IJAL*, 1959.

———. (3) 'Northwest Sahaptin Texts', 1, *UWPA*, 2, 6, 1929.

———. (4) 'Kalapuya Texts', *UWPA*, 11, 1945.

———. (5) 'Coos Narrative and Ethnological Texts', *UWPA*, 8, 1, 1939.

———. (6) 'Coos Myth Texts', *UWPA*, 8, 2, 1940.

———. (7) 'Notes on the Structure of Chinook Jargon', *Language*, 8, 1932.

——. (8) 'Our Knowledge of Pacific Northwest Indian Folklore', *Northwest Folklore*, II, 2, University of Oregon, 1967.

JENNESS, D. (2) 'Myths of the Carrier Indians', *JAFL*, 47, 1934.

JENNINGS, J. D. *Prehistory of North America*, New York, 1968.

JENNINGS, J. D. and NORBECK, E., ed. *Prehistoric Man in the New World*, Chicago, 1964.

JETTÉ, J. 'On Ten'a Folk-lore', *JRAI*, 38, 1908; 39, 1909.

JEWETT, S. A., TAYLOR, W. P., SHAW, W. T. and ALDRICH, J. W. *Birds of Washington State*, Seattle, 1953.

JOCHELSON, W. 'The Koryak, Religion and Myths', *MAMNH, The Jesup North Pacific Expedition*, 6, 1, 1908.

JONES, W. (2) 'Ojibwa Texts', *Publications of the American Ethnological Society*, 7, 2 vol., 1917–19.

——. (3) 'Kickapoo Tales', *ibid.*, 9, 1915.

JOSSELIN de JONG, J. P. B. de. (1) 'Original Odzibwe Texts, *Baessler Archiv*, 5, Leipzig-Berlin, 1913.

——. (2) 'Blackfoot Texts', *Verhandelingen der Koninklijke Akademie van Wetenschappen te Amsterdam, Afdeeling Letterkunde, Nieuwe Reeks*, Deel 14, 4, 1914.

KAHNWEILER, W. S.: *see* FARRAND (1).

KIRK, R. 'The Discovery of Marmes Man', *Natural History*, 77, 10, 1968.

KNIFFEN, F. B. 'Achomawi Geography', *UCPAAE*, 23, 1928.

KOCH-GRÜNBERG, Th. (1) *Von Roroima zum Orinoco. Zweites Band. Mythen und Legenden der Taulipang und Arekuna Indianer*, Berlin, 1916.

KOESTLER, A. *Inside and Outlook*, New York, 1949.

KOHL, J.-G. *Kitchi Gami. Wanderings Round Lake Superior*, new edn, Minneapolis, 1956.

KRAUSE, A. *The Tlingit Indians*, trans. E. Gunther, Seattle, 1956.

KROEBER, A. L. (1) 'Handbook of the Indians of California', *BBAE 78*, Washington, D.C., 1925.

——. (3) 'The Arapaho', *BAMNH*, 18, New York, 1902–1907.

——. (6) 'Gros Ventre Myths and Tales', *APAMNH*, 1, 2, New York, 1907.

——. (7) 'Wishosk Myths', *JAFL*, 18, 1905.

——. (8) 'Wiyot Folk-lore', *JAFL*, 21, 1908.

——. (9) 'Yurok Speech Usages', *Culture and History. Essays in Honor of Paul Radin*, New York, 1960.

——. (10) 'Linguistic Time Depth. Results so far and their Meaning', *IJAL*, 21, 1955.

——. (11) 'Tales of the Smith Sound Eskimo', *JAFL*, 12, 1899.

——. (12) 'Sinkyone Tales', *JAFL*, 32, 1919.

——. (13) 'Indian Myths of South Central California', *UCPAAE*, 4, 1907.

KROEBER, Th. *The Inland Whale*, Bloomington, 1959.

KRUEBER, J. R. 'Miscellanea Selica III: Flathead Animal Names and Anatomical Terms', *Anthropological Linguistics*, 3, 9, 1961.

KUIPERS, A. H. 'The Squamish Language', *Janua Linguarum, Series Practica* 73, la Haye-Paris, 1967.

LAMBERT, J. B. 'The Shape of Organic Molecules', *Scientific American*, 222, 1, 1970.

LANDES, R. *Ojibwa Religion and the Midéwiwin*, Madison, 1968.

LEACH, E. R. (2) ed. 'The Structural Study of Myth and Totemism', *A.S.A. Monographs*, 5, London, 1967.

——. (3) 'Ritualization in Man', *Philosophical Transactions of the Royal Society*, series B, 251, 1966.

——. (4) 'Brain-Twister', *The New York Review of Books*, Vol. IX, 6, October 12th, 1967.

——. (5) *Lévi-Strauss*, London, 1970.

LEENHARDT, M. *Gens de la Grande Terre*, Paris, 1937.

LEIGHTON, A. H. and D. C. 'Gregorio, the Hand-Trembler', *Papers of the Peabody Museum of Archaeology and Ethnology*, 40, 1, Cambridge, Mass., 1949.

LELAND, Ch. G. *The Algonquin Legends of New England*, London, 1884.

LÉVI-STRAUSS, C. (2) *Les Structures élémentaires de la parenté*, Paris, 1949, new edn, Paris-la Haye, 1967.

——. (5) *Anthropologie structurale*, Paris, 1958.

——. (6) 'La Geste d'Asdiwal', *École pratique des hautes études, Section des Sciences religieuses*, Annuaire (1958–9), Paris, 1958.

——. (8) *Le Totémisme aujourd'hui*, Paris, 1962.

——. (9) *La Pensée sauvage*, Paris, 1962.

——. (10) *The Raw and the Cooked*, London, 1970.

——. (14) 'The Deduction of the Crane', *AA* (forthcoming).

——. (15) *From Honey to Ashes*, London, 1973.

——. (19) 'Rapports de symétrie entre rites et mythes de peuples voisins' *in*: *The Translation of Culture*, London, 1971.

——. (20) 'Comment meurent les mythes' *in*: *Science et Conscience de la Société, Mélanges en l'honneur de Raymond Aron*, Paris, 1971.

——. (21) 'Religions comparées des peuples sans écriture' *in*: *Problèmes et méthodes d'histoire des religions, Mélanges publiés par la Section des sciences religieuses de l'École pratique des hautes études*, Paris, 1968.

——. (22) 'Les Mathématiques de l'homme', *Bulletin international des sciences sociales*, 4, 1955.

——. (23) 'The Future of Kinship Studies (Huxley Memorial Lecture 1965)', *Proceedings of the Royal Anthropological Institute for 1965*, London, 1966.

——. (24) *The Origin of Table Manners*, London, 1978.

LOEB, E. M. 'The Eastern Kuksu Cult', *UCPAAE*, 33, 2, 1933.

LORRAIN, F. (1) *Quelques Aspects de l'interdépendance entre l'organization réticulaire interne des systèmes sociaux et les modes culturels de classification*, Department of Social Relations, Harvard University, 1969 (MS.).

——. (2) *Tools for the Formal Study of Networks II*, Department of Social Relations, Harvard University, 1969 (MS.).

LOWIE, R. H. (2) 'The Assiniboine', *APAMNH*, 4, 1, New York, 1909.

——. (4) 'Shoshonean Tales', *JAFL*, 37, 1924.

——. (12) 'The Northern Shoshone', *APAMNH*, 2, New York, 1908.

——. (13) 'Eastern Brazil: an Introduction', *HSAI*, Vol. 1, *BBAE 143*, Washington, D.C., 1946.

McCLINTOCK, W. *The Old North Trail*, London, 1910.

McDERMOTT, L. 'Folk-Lore of the Flathead Indians of Idaho', *JAFL*, 14, 1901.

McILWRAITH, T. F. *The Bella Coola Indians*, 2 vol., Toronto, 1948.

MASON, J. Alden. 'Myths of the Uintah Utes', *JAFL*, 23, 1910.

MATTHEWS, W. (2) 'Navaho Legends', *MAFLS*, 5, 1897.

MAXIMILIAN, Prince of Wied. *Travels in the Interior of North America*, trans. H. E. Lloyd, London, 1843.

MAYBURY-LEWIS, D. *Akwè-Shavante Society*, Oxford, 1967.

MENDENHALL, W. C., Director. 'Geologic Map of the United States', *United States Geological Survey*, 1932.

MERRIAM, A. P. 'Ethnomusicology of the Flathead Indians', *Viking Fund Publications in Anthropology*, 44, New York, 1967.

MERRIAM, C. Hart. *The Dawn of the World: Myths and Weird Tales Told by the Mewan Indians of California*, Cleveland, 1910.

MÉTRAUX, A. (3) 'Myths and Tales of the Matako Indians', *Ethnological Studies*, 9, Göteborg, 1939.

———. (15) 'Tribes of the Middle and Upper Amazon River', *HSAI*, 3, *BBAE 143*, Washington, D.C., 1948.

MICHAEL, Ch. R. 'Retinal Processing of Visual Images', *Scientific American*, 220, 5, 1969.

MICHELSON, T. (5) 'The Mythical Origin of the White Buffalo Dance of the Fox Indians', *40th ARBAE*, Washington, D.C., 1928.

———. (8) 'Notes on the Fox Wâpanōwiweni', *BBAE 105*, Washington, D.C., 1932.

MILLER, J. *Life Amongst the Modocs. Unwritten History*, London, 1873.

MILNER, G. B. 'Siamese twins, birds and the double helix', *Man*, n.s., 4, 1, 1969.

MONOD, A. *Mythes trumaï* (MS.).

MOONEY, J. (1) 'Myths of the Cherokee', *19th ARBAE* (1897–8), Washington, D.C., 1900.

MOORHEAD, P. S. and KAPLAN, M. M., ed. *Mathematical Challenges to the Neo-Darwinian Interpretation of Evolution*, Philadelphia, 1967.

MORICE, A. G. 'The Great Déné Race', *Anthropos*, 1–5, 1906–10.

MÜLLER-BECK, H. 'On Migrations of Hunters Across the Bering Land Bridge in the Upper Pleistocene' *in*: Hopkins, D. M., ed.: *The Bering Land Bridge*, Stanford, 1967.

MUÑOZ-BERNAND, C. *Les Ayoré du Chaco septentrional. Étude critique à partir des notes de Lucien Sebag*, Paris, 1970 (MS.).

MURDOCK, G. P. (1) 'Social Organization of the Tenino', *Miscellanea Paul Rivet*, 2 vol., Mexico, 1958.

———. (2) 'Tenino Shamanism', *Ethnology*, 4, 2, 1965.

MURPHY, R. (1) 'Mundurucú Religion', *UCPAAE*, 49, 1, 1958.

NELSON, E. W. 'The Eskimo about Bering Strait', *18th ARBAE*, Washington, D.C., 1899.

NETBOY, A. 'Round Trip with the Salmon', *Natural History*, 78, 6, 1969.

NIMUENDAJU, C. (1) 'Die Sagen von der Erschaffung und Vernichtung der Welt als Grundlagen der Religion der Apapocúva-Guarani', *Zeitschrift für Ethnologie*, 46, 1914.

———. (5) 'The Apinayé', *The Catholic University of America, Anthropological Series*, 8, Washington, D.C., 1939.

———. (6) 'The Serenté', *Publ. of the Frederick Webb Hodge Anniversary Publication Fund*, 4, Los Angeles, 1942.

———. (8) 'The Eastern Timbira', *UCPAAE*, 41, 1946.

———. (13) 'The Tukuna', *UCPAAE*, 45, 1952.

OBERG, K. 'Indian Tribes of Northern Matto Grosso, Brazil', *Smithsonian Institution, Institute of Social Anthropology*, 15, Washington, D.C., 1953.

O'BRYAN, A. 'The Dîné: Origin Myths of the Navaho Indians', *BBAE 163*, Washington, D.C., 1956.

OLIVEIRA, C. E. de. 'Os Apinayé do Alto Tocantins', *Boletim do Museu Nacional*, 6, 2, Rio de Janeiro, 1930.

OLSON, R. L. (2) *The Quinault Indians*, new edn, Seattle-London, 1967.

OPLER, M. E. 'Myths and Legends of the Lipan Apache Indians', *MAFLS*, 36, 1940.

OSBORNE, D. 'Archaeological Tests in the Lower Grand Coulee, Washington', *Occasional Papers of the Idaho State University Museum*, 20, 1967.

OSGOOD, C. (2) 'Ingalik Mental Culture', *Yale University Publications in Anthropology*, 56, 1959.

———. (3) 'The Ethnography of the Tanaina', *Yale University Publications in Anthropology*, 16, 1937.

PACKARD, R. L. 'Notes on the Mythology and Religion of the Nez Percé', *JAFL*, 4, 1891.

PARSONS, E. C. (4) 'Micmac Folklore', *JAFL*, 38, 1925.

———. (5) 'Folk-Lore of the Antilles, French and English', 2 vol., *MAFLS*, 26, 1933–6.

PEARSON, T. G., ed. *Birds of America*, New York, 1936.

PEPPER, G. H. 'Ah-jin-lec-hah-neh, a Navajo Legend', *JAFL*, 21, 1908.

PERROT, N. *Mémoire sur les mœurs, coustumes et relligion des sauvages de l'Amérique septentrionale*, Leipzig and Paris, 1864. New impression, 1968.

PETITOT, E. (1) *Traditions indiennes du Canada nord-ouest*, Paris, 1886.

PFEIFFER, J. 'Vision in Frogs', *Natural History*, 71, 9, 1962.

PHINNEY, A. 'Nez Percé Texts', *CUCA*, 25, New York, 1934.

PIAGET, J. *Le Structuralisme*, Paris, 1968.

PITTS, Ferris N., Jr. 'The Biochemistry of Anxiety', *Scientific American*, 220, 2, 1969.

PLINE L'ANCIEN. *L'Histoire du monde*, trad. A. du Pinet, 2 vol., Lyon, 1584.

PLUTARCH. *Moralia*, Vol. V, Heinemann, London, and Harvard University Press, 1936.

POCKLINGTON, R. Letter to *Science*, 167, 3926, 1970, p. 1670.

POUSSEUR, H. *Fragments théoriques I sur la musique expérimentale*, Brussels, 1970.

POWERS, S. 'Tribes of California', *CNAE*, 3, Washington, D.C., 1877.

PREUSS, K. Th. (1) *Religion und Mythologie der Uitoto*, 2 vol., Göttingen, 1921–3.

PRINCE, J. D. 'Passamaquoddy Texts', *Publications of the American Ethnological Society*, 10, New York, 1921.

PROUST, M. *A Recherche du Temps Perdu*, Editions de la Pléiade, 3 vols, Paris, 1949.

RADIN, P. (4) 'Some Myths and Tales of the Ojibwa of Southeastern Ontario', *Canada Dept. of Mines, Geological Survey*, 2, *Anthropol. Series*, Ottawa, 1914.

———. (5) 'Wappo Texts', *UCPAAE*, 19, 1924.

RAND, S. T. *Legends of the Micmacs*, New York-London, 1894.

RAY, V. F. (1) 'The Sanpoil and Nespelem', reprinted by *Human Relations Area Files*, New Haven, 1954.

———. (2) 'Sanpoil Folk Tales', *JAFL*, 46, 1933.

———. (3) *Primitive Pragmatists. The Modoc Indians of Northern California*, Seattle, 1963.

———. (4) 'Lower Chinook Ethnograhic Notes', *UWPA*, 7, 2, 1938.

———. (5) 'Cultural Relations in the Plateau of Northwestern America', *Publ. of the F. W. Hodge Anniversary Publication Fund*, Vol. 3, Los Angeles, 1939.

———. (6) 'Pottery on the Middle Columbia', *AA*, 34, 1932.

REAGAN, A. B. 'Some Myths of the Hoh and Quillayote Indians', *Transactions of the Kansas Academy of Science*, 38, Topeka, 1935.

REAGAN, A. B. and WALTERS, L. V. W. 'Tales from the Hoh and Quileute', *JAFL*, 46, 1933.

REICHARD, G. A. (1) 'Wiyot Grammar and Texts', *UCPAAE*, 22, 1, 1925.

——. (3) 'An analysis of Cœur d'Alene Indian Myths', *MAFLS*, 41, 1947.

REICHEL-DOLMATOFF, G. (4) *Desana, Simbolismo de los Indios Tukano del Vaupès*, Bogotá, 1968.

RIBEIRO, D. (2) 'Noticia dos Ofaié-Chavante', *Revista do Museu Paulista*, 5, São Paulo, 1951.

RIGGS, S. R. (1) 'A Dakota-English Dictionary', *CNAE*, 7, Washington, D.C., 1890.

——. (2) 'Dakota Grammar, Texts and Ethnography', *CNAE*, 9, Washington, D.C., 1893.

RIGSBY, B. J. (1) 'Continuity and Change in Sahaptian Vowel System', *IJAL*, 31, 1965.

——. (2) 'On Cayuse-Molala Relatability', *IJAL*, 32, 1966.

——. (3) Personal communication, November 7th, 1968.

RINK, H. *Tales and Traditions of the Eskimo*, Edinburgh-London, 1875.

ROCHEREAU, H. J. (RIVET, P. and). 'Nociones sobre creencias, usos y costumbres de los Catios del Occidente de Antioquia', *JSA*, 21, Paris, 1929.

RODRIGUES, J. Barbosa. (1) 'Poranduba Amazonense', *Anais da Biblioteca Nacional de Rio de Janeiro*, 14 (1886–7), 1890.

ROUSE, I. 'The Carib', *HSAI*, Vol. 4, *BBAE 143*, Washington, D.C., 1948.

ROUSSEAU, J. (1) 'Ethnobotanique abénakise', *Les Archives de Folklore. Publications de l'Université Laval*, 2, Montreal, 1947.

——. (2) 'Caravane vers l'Orégon. Journal . . . du missionnaire Godfroi Rousseau', *Cahier des Dix*, 30, Montreal, 1965.

RUSSELL, F. (1) 'The Pima Indians', *26th ARBAE* (1904–1905), Washington, D.C., 1908.

——. (2) 'Myths of the Jicarilla Apache', *JAFL*, 11, 1898.

RYDBERG, P. A. *Flora of the Rocky Mountains and Adjacent Plains*, New York, 1954.

SAINT CLAIR, H. H. and FRACHTENBERG, L. J. 'Traditions of the Coos Indians of Oregon', *JAFL*, 22, 1909.

SANGER, D. 'Prehistory of the Pacific Northwest Plateau as seen from the interior of British Columbia', *American Antiquity*, 32, 1967.

SAPIR, E. (1) 'Wishram Texts', *Publications of the American Ethnological Society*, 2, Leyden, 1909.

——. (3) 'Yana Texts', *UCPAAE*, 9, 1, 1910.

——. (4) 'Yana Terms of Relationship', *UCPAAE*, 13, 4, 1918.

——. (5) 'Takelma Texts', *University of Pennsylvania, The Museum Anthropological Publications*, 2, 1, 1909.

——. (6) 'The Social Organization of the West Coast Tribes', *Proceedings and Transactions of the Royal Society of Canada*, Ser. 3, Vol. 9, Part 2, 1915.

——. (7) 'Vancouver Island Indians' *in: Hastings' Encyclopaedia of Religion and Ethics*, Vol. 12 (cf. HASTINGS, J.).

——. (8) 'Notes on the Takelma Indians', *AA*, 9, 1907.

SAPIR, E. and SPIER, L. (1) 'Notes on the Culture of the Yana', *University of California Anthropological Records*, 3, 1943.

——. (2) 'Wishram Ethnography', *UWPA*, 3, 3, 1930.

SAPIR, E. and SWADESH, M. (1) 'Yana Dictionary', *University of California Publ. in Linguistics*, 22, 1960.
——. (2) 'Nootka Texts', Philadelphia, 1939.
SAPIR, J. 'Yurok Tales', *JAFL*, 41, 1928.
SARTRE, J. P. 'Jean-Paul Sartre répond', *L'Arc*, 30, Aix-en-Provence, 1966.
SAVARD, R. 'Mythologie esquimaude. Analyse de textes nord-groenlandais', *Centre d'études nordiques, Travaux divers*, 14, Université Laval, Quebec, 1966.
SCHAEFFER, C. E. (1) 'The Bear Foster Parent Tale: A Kutenai Version', *JAFL*, 60, 1947.
——. (2) 'Bird Nomenclature and Principles of Avian Taxonomy of the Blackfeet Indians', *Journal of the Washington Academy of Sciences*, 40, 1950.
SCHENCK, S. M. and GIFFORD, E. W. 'Karok Ethnobotany', *University of California Anthropological Records*, 13, 6, 1952.
SCHMERLER, H. 'Trickster marries his Daughter', *JAFL*, 44, 1931.
SCHULTZ, H. (2) 'Informações etnográficas sôbre os Umutina (1943, 1944 e 1945)', *Revista do Museu Paulista*, 13, São Paulo, 1961–2.
SETON, E. Th. *The Arctic Prairies*, New York, 1911.
SHIMONY, A. A. 'Conservatism among the Iroquois at the Six Nations Reserve', *Yale University Publications in Anthropology*, 65, New Haven, 1961.
SHIPLEY, W. (1) 'Maidu Texts and Dictionary', *UCPAAE*, 33, 1963.
——. (2) 'Proto-Takelman', *IJAL*, 35, 3, 1969.
SIEBERT, F. T., Jr. 'The Original Home of the Proto Algonquian People', *Contributions to Anthropology, Linguistics 1 (Algonquian). National Museum of Canada, Bulletin 214*, Anthropological Series 78, Ottawa, 1967.
SIMMS, S. C. 'Traditions of the Crow', *Field Museum of Natural History, Anthropological Series*, 2, Chicago, 1903.
SKEELS, D. 'A Classification of Humor in Nez Percé Mythology', *JAFL*, 67, 1954.
SKINNER, A. (1) 'Notes on the Eastern Cree and Northern Saulteaux', *APAMNH*, 9, New York, 1911.
——. (10) 'The Mascoutens or Prairie Potawatomi Indians', *Bulletin of the Public Museum of the City of Milwaukee*, 6, 1–3, 1924–7.
——. (12) 'Societies of the Iowa, Kansa, and Ponca Indians', *APAMNH*, 11, 9, 1915.
SKINNER, A. and SATTERLEE, J. V. 'Folklore of the Menomini Indians', *APAMNH*, 13, 3, New York, 1915.
SMET, R. P. de. *Voyages aux Montagnes rocheuses et séjour chez les tribus indiennes de l'Orégon*, new edn, Brussels-Paris, 1873.
SMITH, E. 'Myths of the Iroquois', *2nd ARBAE* (1880–81), Washington, D.C., 1883.
SMITH, M. W. (1) 'The Puyallup of Washington' *in*: R. Linton, ed., *Acculturation in Seven American Indian Tribes*, New York, 1940.
——. (2) 'The Puyallup Nisqually', *CUCA*, 32, New York, 1940.
——. (3) 'The Coast Salish of Puget Sound', *AA*, 43, 1941.
——. (4) ed. *Indians of the Urban Northwest*, New York, 1949.
——. (5) 'Petroglyph Complexes in the History of the Columbia-Fraser Region', *SWJA*, 2, 1946.
SNYDER, L. L. *Arctic Birds of Canada*, Toronto, 1957.
SPECK, F. G. (3) 'Penobscot Tales and Religious Beliefs', *JAFL*, 48, 1935.
——. (4) 'Montagnais and Naskapi Tales from the Labrador Peninsula', *JAFL*, 38, 1925.

——. (5) 'Bird-Lore of the Northern Indians', *Public Lectures of the University of Pennysylvania*, 7, 1921.

——. (6) *Naskapi. The Savage Hunters of the Labrador Peninsula*, Norman, 1935.

——. (7) 'Myths and Folk-Lore of the Timiskaming Algonquin and Timagami Ojibwa', *Canadian Department of Mines, Geological Survey, Memoir, 71, 9 Anthropological Series*, Ottawa, 1915.

——. (10) *Penobscot Man*, Philadelphia, 1940.

——. (11) 'Some Naskapi Myths from Little Whale River', *JAFL*, 28, 1915.

SPENCER, R. F. 'The North Alaskan Eskimo' *BBAE 171*, Washington, D.C., 1959.

SPENCER, R. F. and CARTER, W. K. 'The Blind Man and the Loon: Barrow Eskimo Variants', *JAFL*, 67, 1954.

SPIER, L. (2) 'Klamath Ethnography', *UCPAAE*, 30, 1930.

——. (6) 'Tribal Distribution in Washington', *General Series in Anthropology*, 3, 1936.

SPINDEN, H. J. (1) 'Myths of the Nez Percé Indians', *JAFL*, 21, 1908.

——. (3) 'The Nez Percé Indians', *MAAA*, 2, 1908.

——. (4) 'Nez Percé Tales', cf. BOAS (4).

SPOTT, R. and KROEBER, A. L. 'Yurok Narratives', *UCPAAE*, 35, 9, 1942.

SPROAT, G. M. *Scenes and Studies of Savage Life*, London, 1868.

STEEDMAN, E. V. Cf. TEIT (9).

STEINEN, K. von den. (2) *Entre os aborigenes do Brasil central*, São Paulo, 1940.

STERN, B. J. 'The Lummi Indians of Western Washington', *CUCA*, 17, New York, 1934.

STERN, Th. (1) 'Klamath Myth Abstracts', *JAFL*, 76, 1963.

——. (2) *The Klamath People*, Seattle, 1965.

——. (3) 'Klamath Myths' (photocopies of unedited texts kindly provided by the author).

STETTNER, L. J. and MATYNIAK, K. A. 'The Brain of Birds', *Scientific American*, 218, 6, 1968.

STEVENSON, M. C. 'The Sia', *11th ARBAE*, Washington, D.C., 1894.

STEWARD, J. H. 'Myths of the Owens Valley Paiute', *UCPAAE*, 34, 1936.

STRADELLI, E. (1) 'Vocabulario da lingua geral portuguez-nheêngatu e nheêngatu-portuguez', *Revista do Instituto Historico e Geografico Brasileiro*, t. 104, Vol. 158, Rio de Janeiro, 1929.

STRONG, E. *Stone Age on the Columbia River*, Portland, 1959.

STRONG, W. D. and SCHENCK, W. E. 'Petroglyphs near the Dalles on the Columbia River', *AA*, 27, 1925.

SUTTLES, W. (1) 'Private Knowledge, Morality and Social Classes among the Coast Salish', *AA*, 60, 1958.

——. (2) 'Affinal Ties, Subsistence and Prestige among the Coast Salish', *AA*, 62, 1960.

SUTTLES, W. and ELMENDORF, W. W. 'Linguistic Evidence for Salish Prehistory' *in*: Garfield, V. E. and Chafe, W. L., ed., *Symposium on Language and Culture*, American Ethnol. Soc. Proc. of the 1962 Annual Spring Meeting, 1963.

SWADESH, M. (1) 'The Linguistic Approach to Salish Prehistory' *in*: Smith, M. W. (4).

——. (2) 'Salish Internal Relationships', *IJAL*, 16, 1950.

——. (3) 'Salish Phonologic Geography', *Language*, 28, 1952.

——. (4) 'Time Depths of American Linguistic Grouping', *AA*, 56, 3, 1954.

——. (5) 'Linguistics as an Instrument of Prehistory', *SWJA*, 15, 1, 1959.
——. (6) 'Kalapuya and Takelma', *IJAL*, 31, 1965.
SWAN, J. G. (1) *The Northwest Coast; on Three Years Residence in Washington Territory*, New York, 1857.
——. (2) *The Indians of Cape Flattery* (1868), Facsimile Reproduction, 1964.
SWANTON, J. R. (2) 'Tlingit Myths and Texts', *BBAE 39*, Washington, D.C., 1909.
——. (6) 'Social Condition, Beliefs and Linguistic Relationship of the Tlingit Indians', *26th ARBAE*, Washington, D.C., 1908.
——. (7) 'Haida Texts', *MAMNH*, 14, New York, 1908.
——. (8) 'The Indian Tribes of North America', *BBAE 145*, Washington, D.C., 1952.
——. (9) 'Haida Texts, and Myths', *BBAE 29*, Washington, D.C., 1905.
TAVERNER, P. A. 'Birds of Canada', *Nat. Museum of Canada, Dept. of Mines, Bulletin 72, Biol. Ser. 19*, Ottawa, 1934.
TEIT, J. A. (1) 'The Shuswap', *MAMNH*, 4, Leyden-New York, 1909.
——. (2) 'Traditions of the Lilloet Indians of British Columbia', *JAFL*, 25, 1912.
——. (4) 'Traditions of the Thompson Indians', *MAFLS*, 6, 1898.
——. (5) 'Mythology of the Thompson Indians', *MAMNH*, 12, Leyden-New York, 1912.
——. (6) 'The Salishan Tribes of the Western Plateaus', *45th ARBAE* (1927–8), Washington, D.C., 1930.
——. (7) 'Tahltan Tales', *JAFL*, 34, 1921.
——. (8) 'Kaska Tales', *JAFL*, 30, 1917.
——. (9) 'Ethnobotany of the Thompson Indians of British Columbia, edited by E. V. Steedman', *45th ARBAE* (1927–8), Washington, D.C., 1930.
——. (10) 'The Thompson Indians of British Columbia', *MAMNH*, Vol. 2, 1900.
——. (11) 'The Lilloet Indians', *MAMNH*, 4, New York, 1906.
——. (12) 'European Tales from the Upper Thompson Indians', *JAFL*, 29, 1916.
——. (13) 'The Middle Columbia Salish', *UWPA*, 2, 1928.
THEVET, A. *La Cosmographie universelle*, 2 vol., Paris, 1575.
THOMPSON, D'ARCY WENTWORTH. *On Growth and Form*, 2nd edn, 2 vol., Cambridge, 1952.
THOMPSON, S. (2) 'European Tales among the North American Indians', *Colorado College Publications, Language Series*, 2, 34, 1919.
——. (3) *Tales of the North American Indians*, Cambridge, Mass., 1929.
THOMSON, A. Landsborough, ed. *A New Dictionary of Birds*, London-Edinburgh, 1964.
TURNER, L. M. 'Ethnology of the Ungava District', *11th ARBAE* (1889–90), Washington, D.C., 1894.
TURNER, V. W. (1) *The Drums of Affliction : A Study of Religious Processes among the Ndembu of Zambia*, Oxford, 1968.
——. (2) *The Forest of Symbols. Aspects of Ndembu Ritual*, New York, 1967.
——. (3) *The Ritual Process. Structure and Anti-Structure*, Chicago, 1969.
TURNEY-HIGH, H. H. (1) 'Ethnography of the Kutenai', *RBAAS*, 62, 1892.
——. (2) 'The Flathead Indians of Montana', *MAAA*, 48, 1937.
UHLENBECK, C. C. 'Original Blackfoot Texts. A New Series of Blackfoot Texts', *Verhandelingen der Koninklijke Akademie van Wetenschappen te Amsterdam, Afdeeling Letterkunde*, Nieuwe Reeks, Deel 12, 1–13, 1, 1911–12.

VAN DER PIJL, L. and DODSON, C. H. *Orchids Flowers : their Pollination and Evolution*, Fairchild Tropical Garden and University of Miami Press, Coral Gables, Florida, 1966.

VESTAL, P. A. 'Ethnobotany of the Ramah Navaho', *Papers of the Peabody Museum of American Archaeology and Ethnology*, 40, 4, Cambridge, Mass., 1952.

VOEGELIN, C. F. and F. M. 'Languages of the World : Native America, Fascicle One', *Anthropological Linguistics*, 6, 6–9, 1964.

VOEGELIN, E. W. (2) 'Culture Element Distributions : XX. Northeast California', *University of California Anthropological Records*, 7, 2, 1942.

VOTH, H. R. 'Arapaho Tales', *JAFL*, 25, 1912.

WAGLEY, Ch. and GALVÃO, E. 'The Tenetehara Indians of Brazil', *CUCA*, 35, New York, 1949.

WALLIS, W. D. (1) 'Beliefs and Tales of the Canadian Dakota', *JAFL*, 36, 1923.

WASSÉN, S. H. (1) 'Cuentos de los Indios Chocós', *JSA*, 25, 1933.

——. (5) 'Estudios chocoes', *Etnologiska Studier*, 26, Göteborg, 1963.

WATERMAN, T. T. (3) 'The Swing Trick', *JAFL*, 27, 1914.

——. (4) 'Yurok Geography', *UCPAAE*, 16, 5, 1920.

——. (5) 'Paraphernalia of the Duwamish "Spirit-Canoe" Ceremony', *Indian Notes*, 7, New York, 1930.

WEISEL, G. F. 'Animal names, anatomical terms, and some ethnozoology of the Flathead Indians', *Journal of the Washington Academy of Sciences*, 42, 11, 1952.

WHEELWRIGHT, M. C. *Navajo Creation Myth. The Story of Emergence by Hasteen Klah*, Santa Fé, 1942.

WILLIAMS, M. I., ed. *Schoolcraft's Indian Legends*, East Lansing, Mich., 1956.

WISSLER, C. (1) 'Some (Oglala) Dakota Myths' I, II, *JAFL*, 20, 1907.

WISSLER, C. and DUVALL, D. C., 'Mythology of the Blackfoot Indians', *APAMNH*, 2, New York, 1908.

WORTH, S. and ADAIR, J. 'Navajo Filmmakers', *AA*, 72, 1, 1970.

WRIGHT, R. H. 'Why is an Odour?', *Nature*, 5023, 1966.

YOUNG, E. R. *Algonkin Indian Tales*, New York, 1903.

ZERRIES, O. (4) *Waika. Die Kulturgeschichtliche Stellung der Waika-Indianer des Oberen Orinoco im Rahmen der Völkerkunde Südamerikas*, München, 1964.

Index

Index of Myths

Numbers in boldface indicate complete myth

I. Myths listed in numerical order and according to subject-matter

a. New Myths

M_{529} Klamath–Modoc. 'The birth of the hero', **29–30**, 41, 48, 51, 60, 63, 78, 276

M_{530a} Klamath. 'The bird-nester' (1), **31–2**, 33, 34, 36, 37, 46, 48, 80, 82, 100, 114, 124, 165, 223, 276

M_{530b} Klamath. 'The bird-nester' (2), **32**, 33, 34, 35, 36, 37, 46, 48, 80, 82, 100, 114, 124, 165, 223, 276

M_{531a} Klamath. 'The bird-nester' (3), **33–7**, 33, 34, 35, 36, 37, 48, 76 n.7, 80, 82, 111, 114, 124, 267, 276

M_{531b} Klamath. 'The bird-nester' (4), 35, 36, 37, 48, 53, 76 n.7, 80, 82, 108, 109, 111, 114, 124, 165, 198, 267, 276

M_{532} Matako. 'The pregnant man', 39, **40**, 382, 388

M_{533} Nez Percé. 'The pregnant man', 39, **40**, 42, 388

M_{534} Wintu. 'The hidden child', **41**

M_{535} Lilloet. 'The hidden child', **42**

M_{536a} Klamath. 'The one-eyed women', **44**, 45

M_{536b} Klamath. 'The one-eyed women', **44**

M_{536c} Modoc. 'The two demiurges', **45**, 111

M_{537} Klamath. 'The visit to the underworld', **45**

M_{538} Klamath. 'The story of Aishísh', 33, 36, 42 n.3, **49–52**, 54, 56, 64, 65, 76, 77, 79, 82, 91, 98, 100, 108, 109, 111, 112, 113 n.9, 114, 124, 163, 164, 165, 198, 216, 217, 218, 219, 220, 222, 223, 225, 233, 234, 240, 241, 242, 267, 270, 271, 621

M_{539} Modoc. 'The star-brothers', **56–9**, 64, 65, 70, 71, 72, 76, 77, 78, 79, 81, 83, 95, 101, 111, 113, 116, 143, 147, 156, 163, 164, 198, 203, 216, 217, 233, 234, 240, 241, 271, 318, 389

M_{540} Modoc. 'The loon woman', **63–4**, 65, 77, 78, 95, 108 n.8, 109, 111, 112, 115, 198

M_{541} Modoc. 'The story of Aishísh', 33, 46, 60 n.3, **65–70**, 71, 72, 76, 77, 78, 81, 82, 83, 109, 110, 116, 163, 164, 165, 198, 232, 267, 273, 281

$M_{542a, b}$ Nez Percé. 'The butterfly woman', 40, **80**, 557

M_{543} Modoc. 'One of Aishísh's marriages', 74, **81–3**, 89, 90, 91, 95, 99, 390, 427

b. Myths Covered in Volumes I, II and III

c. References to Other Myths from Volumes I, II and III

2. Myths listed by tribe

Index